ᏅᎢᎧ

ENGLISH RECUSANT LITERATURE
1558–1640

Selected and Edited by
D. M. ROGERS

Volume 304

ROBERT PERSONS
A Treatise of Three Conversions
(VOLUME ONE)
1603

ROBERT PERSONS

A Treatise of Three Conversions

(VOLUME ONE)

1603

The Scolar Press

1976

ISBN 0 85967 316 2

Published and printed in Great Britain by
The Scolar Press Limited, 59-61 East Parade,
Ilkley, Yorkshire and
39 Great Russell Street,
London WC1

1918733

NOTE

Reproduced (original size) from a copy in the library of Stonyhurst College, by permission of the Rector. The second and third volumes of this work are reproduced in English Recusant Literature volumes 305 and 306.

References : Allison and Rogers 640; STC 19416.

A TREATISE

OF THREE

CONVERSIONS

OF ENGLAND

from Paganisme to Christian
Religion.

A TREATISE
OF THREE
CONVERSIONS
OF ENGLAND
from Paganisme to Christian Religion.

THE FIRST *vnder the Apostles, in the first age after* Christ: THE SECOND *vnder* Pope Eleutherius *and* K. Lucius, *in the second age.* THE THIRD, *vnder* Pope Gregory *the* Great, *and* K. Ethelbert *in the sixth age;* *vvith diuers other matters thereunto apperteyning.*

DIVIDED

Into three partes, as appeareth in the next page. The former two whereof are handled in this booke, and dedicated to the Catholikes of England.

VVith a nevv addition to the said Catholikes, vpon the nevvs of the late Q. death. and succession of his MAIESTIE *of Scotland, to the crovvne of England.*

By N. D. author of the VVard-vvord.

DEVT. 4. & 32.

Inquire of auncient tymes before yovv; remember th'old dayes of your forefathers; consider of euery age, as they haue passed: aske your father and he vvill tell yovv: demaund of your ancestors, and they vvil declare vnto yovv.

Imprinted vvith licence, anno. 1603.

The generall contents of the partes of this Treatise.

THE first parte handleth three conuersions of England to Christian faith, and sheweth all three to haue byn from Rome, and to the Romane Catholique faith, and that the same faith hath continued in England euer since throughout all ages to this day: and this parte was begun against Syr Francis Hastings in answere to his 7. Encounter, but continued, and enlarged against Iohn Fox his false Acts and Monuments.

The second parte searcheth out the beginning, state and progresse of protestant Religion from age to age, and is against the whole course of Iohn Fox his said Acts and Monuments from Christs tyme to this, especially against the former parte therof, from the primitiue Church downward to the tyme of K. Henry the eyght.

The third parte examineth more particularly the second volume of Fox his Acts & Monuments wherin he treateth of new martyrs, and Confessors of his Church, placed by him in an Ecclesiasticall Calendar in the beginning therof; which Calendar is discussed, and compared with the Catholique Calendar: And this parte growing to be longer then the rest, goeth printed a parte.

THE

THE
EPISTLE
DEDICATORIE
TO THE
CATHOLIQVES
OF
ENGLAND.

THOVGH vvhen I vvrote the Preface that doth en-sue; I had no purpose to adde any epistle dedicatory (most dearly beloued and vvorthy Catholiques) yet aftervvards thinking of some other circumstances both of matter & time, I deemed it not amisse to say somvvhat also in this kind of dedication, both for presentinge this vvoorke to

† 3   vvhome

vvhome principally it is due, as
alſo for aduertiſmēt in ſome fevv
points vvhich the preſent ſtate of
yovr affaires doth ſeeme to require.

2.   And for the firſt, vvho doth
not ſee and conſider, that this
treatiſe of the firſt plantinge of
Chriſtian Catholique faith in England, vvith the continuance and
preſeruation therof from age to
age vnto our times, doth chiefly
and principally belong to yovv
that are Catholiques, at this day,
moſt vvoorthy children of ſo re-
novvned parēts, moſt honorable
offſpring of ſo excellent anceſtors,
moſt glorious poſterity of ſo famous antiquity, vvhome future
ages vvill both eſteeme & extoll
aboue many of your predeceſſors,
for

Cauſe of
dedica-
tion.

for retayninge that in times of
vvarre, vvhich they lefte vnto
you in poſſeſſion of peace, & for
defendinge that by ſo ſingular
conſtancy of ſufferings, vvhich
they both receaued & bequea-
thed vnto you by quiet tradition.
3. VVhich tradition being ſett
dovvne, prooued and declared
moſt cleerlie in this enſuinge
vvoork, I do by offering the ſame
vnto you, but preſent you vvith
your ovvne, to vvit, the hiſtory of
your ovvne houſe, the records &
chronicles of your ovvne family,
the pedigree and genealogie of
your ovvne forefathers, the antiquity and nobility of your ovvne
progenitors, together vvith your
iuſt title & clayme to their inheritance, producinge iointlie for

the

the same, your vndoubted char-
tres, enrollements, euidences,
vvritings and vvitnesses, vvhich
no man vvith reason can deny or
call in doubt.

The sub-
stance
of the
booke.

4.　　And furthermore I do adde
in the end for more full comple-
ment of this vvhole cause, all such
former false & vvrong suits, pre-
tences, pleas, intrusions, sur-
reptions, or other like shifts or
vvranglings, vvhich any heretiques to this day (but specially
these of our times) haue made hitherto about the same, for shevve
of some title or right on their part
to this inheritance and succession
of yours. And lastly I do produce
also the iudgements, censures, sentences, & arrestes of all Christian
parlaments of the vvorld to vv itt,
the de-

the determination of all the higheſt Eccleſiaſticall tribunalls in
your fauour. By all vvhich I doubt
not, but that your right and title
remaineth moſt euident & cleere
to all men of iudgement, euen to
the enemies or aduerſaries themſelues. VVherfore moſt iuſtly I do
dedicate this treatiſe vnto you,
vvhich ſo many vvaies and for ſo
many reaſons, is your ovvne. And
ſo much for the firſt point.

5.   The ſecond alſo about the
circumſtances of the preſent time
is allready ſomevvhat touched in
that vvee haue ſaid, hovv by Gods
holie prouidence you are borne
in this time of vvarre, tribulation,
& contradiction, in ſteede of that
large and longe peace and tranquillitie, vvhich your aunceſtors

enioyed in the vſe of that Catholique religion for vvhich you
ſtriue and ſuffer novv, vvhich
thinge though for the preſent it
ſeeme vnpleaſant and diſtaſtfull
to fleſh and blood, yet vvill the
houre come vvhen it ſhal prooue
Time of a moſt ſingular benefit and priui-
tryall. lege to ſuch, as haue receaued
grace to manifeſt themſelues by
this occaſion, ſeeing that, accordinge to the Apoſtle, this is one
principall end in Gods euerlaſtinge vviſedome for permiſſion
of hereſies, *vt qui probati ſunt ma-*
1.Cor. 11. *feſti fiant*, that thoſe that be of
proofe be made manifeſt by this
occaſion.

6. VVherfore ſeeing as the ſame
Apoſtle ſaith in another place, it
is giuen to you (deare Catholiks
that

that liue in England at this day)
not only to beleeue in him, but also to Philip. 1.
suffer for him (a singular priuilege
by his accompt, yea and that vvee
may say of you, as he said, & glo-
ried of himselfe and his fellovves.
Vincula vestra manifesta fiunt in Ibidem.
Christo in omni prætorio. Your
bandes for Christ are made notorious throughout all the tribunalls, and iudgement seats of our
countrey. And yet further as he
vvrote to his deare Thessalonias,
in their highest praise and commendation. *You are become such* 1. Thess
followers of Christ and his Apostles, as sal. 1.
receauing the woord of God with ioye
of the holy Ghost in great tribulation,
you are made an example or spectacle
to all other faithfull people in Mace-
donia and Achaia, for that from you
                                    is di-

is diuulged the woord of God, not only in Macedonia and Achaia, but alſo in all other places, by reaſon of your faith which is published euery where throughout the worlde.

7. Seeing (I ſay) all this may be trulie vvritten of you, & that our countrey hath gotten more honorable renovvne in forraine Catholike nations, and the Church of God more glorie and comfort by this your patience and ſufferings in theſe fevve latter yeares, then by the peaceable calme of many former ages of your aunceſtors, I knovve no true ſeruant of God, that together vvith the commiſeration of your preſent hard afflicted eſtate, receaueth not alſo particular conſolation by your integritie and conſtancy,

praying

praying for your perſeuerance
in that moſt honorable courſe,
vvhich hitherto you haue helde
of true obedience to allmightie
God in matters of your ſoule, and
loyall behauiour of duty tovvards
your téporall Prince in all vvorld-
lie affaires, vvhich courſe though
it haue not eſcaped the calumnious tongues & pennes of ſome
carpinge aduerſaries,yet is it iuſti-
fiable and glorious both before
God and man, vvhere reaſon ru-
leth and not paſſion. And I doubt
not but that the vviſedome and
moderation both of her Maieſtie
and her ſage counſell, vvill rather in this point ponder your
ovvne factes, then your aduerſaries vvords, as alſo conſider hovv
rare ſuch examples of patience are

in

The ho-
norable
courſe
of Ing-
lish Ca-
tholiks.

in thefe our daies, vvhere fo great a multitude, for fo manie yeares, hath paſſed vnder the rodde of fo ſharpe afflictions, vvhich is your ſingular commendation vvith all vviſe & godlie men, let Cauillers and Calumniators ſay vvhat they vvill to the contrary.

Internal tribula-tions. 8. But Gods holie hand hath not ſtayed heere, in proouing you by theſe externall conflictations on-ly, but hath paſſed to the internall alfo; that he might ſaie of you as he did of his deareſt people vvhen he ment to doe them moſt good.

Eſai. 1. Conuertam manum meam ad te, & excoquam ad purum ſcoriam tuam: & auferam omne ſtannum tuum. I vvill turne my hand vpon thee, and vvill boyle out by fire all thy ruſt euen to the quick, and vvill
take

take from thee all thy pevvter,
therby to leaue thee pure ſiluer;
hevvould equall you in this point
vvith the priuilege of his Apoſtles,
that you might ſay vvith them
trulie. *Foris pugnæ, intus timores.* 1. Cor. 7.
VVee haue fights abroade, and
frights at home; you knovv vvhat
I meane, and others vvill eaſelie
gheſſe that haue hard of the late
ſtormes paſt. Onlie I vvill ſaie to
your high commendation, that
your moderate and ſage deporte-
ment, hath byn ſuch alſo in this
point of not admittinge the ſcan-
dall offred, as all men haue byn
edified by your vviſedome, and
pietie therin : ſeeing fulfilled, on
your behalfe, that vvhich the holie Ghoſt prophecied of holie,
vviſe, and peaceable men, trulie
fearing

Psal.118. fearing God. *Pax multa diligentibus legem tuam & non est illis scandalum*. Thofe that loue thy lavve (O lord) do enioy their invvard peace, and are not scandalized vvith vvhat externall tempefts foeuer do arife.

9.　In refpect of vvhich pietie of yours, it is to be prefumed that, Chrift our Sauiour hath vvrought againe by his Subftitute (and this vpon the fuddaine) that famous miracle recorded by S. Mathevve, S. Marke and S. Luke, of calminge the tempeft that put his difciples Math.8. in feare and ieopardy; *Exurgens* Marc.4. *imperauit ventis & mari, & facta* Luc.8. *est tranquillitas magna*. He rifinge vp, commaunded the vvinds and feas to ceafe, and thervpon enfued a great calme and tranquillitie, vvhich

vvhich kind of miracle is not lightly made among proteftants, for that they vvant the meanes therof. And therefore as a thing peculiar to the fubordination of Chrifts orderly Church, and vvrought by his diuine povver and vertue, I do the more admire and reuerence the fame, affuringe my felfe, that no good Catholique vvill euer heereafter foe much as mooue his finger againft it, but cooperate rather to the firme eftablishment and continuance therof as is moft behoofull; to the end, that as vvee are all one in faith and beleefe, fo vvee be alfo in life, fpeeche and actions, efpecially in this tyme of triall. VVhich God of his infinit goodnes graunt: to
*   vvhofe

vvhose holy protection I commend hartily both yovv and my selfe this first of March. 1603.

AN ADDITION OF THE
author to the aforesaid Catholiques, vpon the newes of the Queens death; and succession of the King of Scotland, to the crowne of England.

YNCE the wrytinge of the precedent epistle, aduertisment is come, that almighty God of his infinite mercy hath deliuered yow at length (deare Catholiques) from your olde persecutor, and as wee hope will also shortely from your persecution, his diuine Maiestie be thancked euerlastingly for the same. Heere generally the applause is no otherwise, then it was in old tyme among the Christians, vpon the entrance of *Constantine*, into the Empire after *Diocletian*; or of *Iouinian* after *Iulian*. But the former example seemeth more like, for that good *Constantine* was of a different Religion, when he entred, yet of singular hope to become such as afterward

afterward he did; both in respect of his exellent parts and of his pious mother *S. Helena*. The difference of the two Mothers, is, that the Empresse *Helena* did asist her sonne heer vpon earth, as *S. Paulinus* wryteth, towards the trueth and piety of religion, but *Queene Marie of Scotland and France*, being violently depriued of this life, will do yt (we trust) by her prayers in heauen. The comparison also is not vnproper in this, for that perhaps this our new King is the first that hath bene absolutely Lord of the whole *Ilande of Britany* (with the parts annexed therynto) since *Constantine*.

S. Paulin.ep.11. ad Seuerum.

2. Wee knowe, what commendation a heathen author gaue to Constantine while he was yet no Christian; and this in publike audience, at the day of marriage with the daughter of *Maximianus Herculeus*, both the Emperors beinge present and heeringe him. *Neque enim* (saith he) *forma tantum in te patris, sed etiam continentia, fortitudo, iustitia, prudentia, sese votis gentium praesentant.* Not only the forme and beauty of your father (Constantius) doth appeare in yow; but also his continency, his fortitude, his iustice, his wisedome do represent themselues in yow, according to the full desire and wish of all nations. Thus said hee of that Constantine. Wheryvpon *Eusebius* sheweth that the Christians of that tyme conceaued so great loue

Gallican. orator in Panegyric. 1. Constantini. The moral vertues of Constantine before he vvas a Christian. Euseb. lib. 8, Hist. cap. 26.

* 2   towards

towards him (though he were not yet a Chriftian) as his aduerfary *Maxentius* hearing of his comminge towards Rome, was glad to feigne that him felfe would be a Chriftian alfo, to retaine fomewhat therby their affections from Conftantine.

3. Wee reade of diuers exellent men in Chriftian religion, who were prefumed & foretoulde, that they would be fuch, before they were Chriftians indeed. And this only vpon the forefighte of their good natures and vertous inclinations, as *S. Martyn*, afterwards *B.* of *Tovvars*, *S. Nectarius.* Archb. of *Conftantinople*, *S. Ambrofe*, *B.* of *Milane* and *S. Auguftine*, *B.* of *Hippo*, albeit of *S. Auguftines* conuerfion from the herefie of *Manychees*, to Catholike Religion, *S. Ambrofe* added an other coniecture alfo or rather prophefie, to wit, that the prayers and teares of his good mother *S. Monica*, could not fuffer fuch a fonne to perifhe. All which yow fee how far yt maketh for vs., and for our hope, of this fecond Conftantine, who wanted not alfo a holy mother to pray and fhead teares aboundantly for him, whilft fhe liued, that he might be fuch, as wee moft defire now. Wherof my felfe amongft others can be a true witneffe, and this from her owne teftimony.

4. And for that I cannot perfuade my felf that fo holy endeauours of fuch a mother
in fuch

in such a cause can be frustrate with almighty God; I do not only hope well, but do attribute heervnto in great parte, the many blessings that haue fallen vpon this King euer since, but principally his Maiesties preseruation and straung deliuery from infinite dangers and most imminent perills as all men know; so as neyther *Cyrus*, nor *Romulus*, nor *Moyses* himselfe was more strangely preserued, than this King hath been since his infancy. And for that God doth neuer comonly worke those great effects, but to great ends: yow Catholiques of England, may with reason hope well therof, especially yf any thing came by his said good mothers intercession, who loued you all so dearly, as whatsoeuer shee asked at Gods hands for the life & prosperity of her deare sonne in this world, a great parte therof was meant (no dowte) for yow, and your good, yf euer yow came to be vnder his gouernment, as now God hath brought yow.

5. An other effect of this holy Queenes prayers for her only sonne, I holde to be that other blessinge before mencioned of so many rare parts discouered in his Maiesties person, which truly though I haue had euer in great conceyte vpon the reports of other men: yet hath the same bene exceedingly increased, vpon the late reading of a booke, written I suppose some yeares gone, by his

The strange deliuerances of his Maiestie from many perills.

* 3   by his

by his highnes , but printed in Londen this
very yeer 1 6 0 3. This booke is intituled in
the Greeke tongue *Basilicon Doron*, to witt a
kingly gyfte,fente by his Maieftie, vnto the
Prince his eldeft fonne (now alfo our Lord)
being in truth a golden gyfte in refpecte of
the exellent matter conteyned therin . And
it difcouereth fo many rare partes in the
writer , as may iuftely giue all Catholiks
good hope to fee one day that fulfilled in his
Maieftie, which moft they defire, & would
God this fingular Treatife had appeared rather to the world.

The
Kings
excel-
lente
booke
entitu-
led *Ba-
filicon
Doron.*

6. For fetting a fide one pointe only therin
handled , which is religion (wherin his
Maieftie muft needs fpeake , accordinge to
his perfuafion & education in that behalfe:)
all other matters are fuch, & fo fett downe,
as yow will exceedingly delite therin and
profitt alfo therby, if yow read with attention & ponder all well, but efpecially three
points aboue other, I noted, with no fmall
admiration to my felfe , which I fpeake in
all fincerity of truth as in the fight of allmighty God. The firft is the great variety of
felecte learninge in fuch a perfon and fo occupied otherwife as his Maieftie is. Secondly the greate maturity of iudgement in ap-
plyinge the fame fo fitly to the peculiar affaires of Scotland. The third is the feruent
& extraordinary affection of piety towards
God

Three
rare
points
of his
Maie-
fties
booke.

God and godlynes, vttered in so effectuall words, & vpon so good occasions through-out the whole booke, as a man may easily see it commeth from the hart. And how highly this one pointe of piety is to be estee-med in so high & mighty a prince, especially in these our dayes, when contentions in religion haue wrought so great coldnes of religious piety in many great mens harts, euery wise & pious man will easily cōsider.

7. But I will goe no further in this matter, least I may seeme to flatter, which I hate with my hart, & his Maiestie detesteth the vice most prudently and Christianly in this his booke: only I will add for our common comfort, that it seemeth impossible vnto mee, that such a witt, and so godly affected a mynd, as God hath bestowed vpon his Maiestie, can long bee deteyned with the vanity & inanity of sects & heresies, where no grownd, no head, no certaine principle, no sure rule or method to try the truth, no one reason at all can be found, why a man should rather be of one sect, than another. But only euery ones own will and particu-lar iudgment, grounded as each one will pretend vpon the scriptures, whereof yet himselfe only wilbe the Iudge and inter-preter. Which things being of themselues most absurd in so weighty a cause, as reli-gion is, that concerneth the eternall saluation

No rea-son to beyeel-dedvvhy a man should be rather of one sect than another.

* 4   tion

tion of our foules; yt is to be hoped, that his
Maieftie hauing the former two parts of
Iudgment and pious affection in that exel-
lency as hath byn faid, will eafily come in
tyme, to difcouer the fame, and therwithall
the contrary fubftantiall grounds and cleer
demonftratiõs for the Catholike Religion,
whervnto this Treatife alfo of the firft
planting of Chriftian Religion in our countrey, may (in my opinion) giue no fmall help
& light, yf it might pleas his Maieftie to be-
ftowe the cafting of his eye vpon the fame.

8.   Wherfore to conclude this addition to
my former letter, God hauing wrought fo
ftraungly this change, as heer is reported,
with fo generall peace and applaufe of the
whole Realme : Yow are to expecte at his
diuine Maiefties handes, the effects that are
conforme to his fatherly loue and care, euer
fhewed hitherto towards yow. And as for
the perfon now aduaunced, I know moft
certainly, that there was neuer any doubt or
difference among yow, but that euer yow
defired his aduauncement aboue all others,
as the only heyre of that renowned mother,
for whome your feruent zeale is knowne to
the world, and how much yow haue fuffred
by her aduerfaryes, for the fame. Yet do
I confeffe, that touching the difpofition of
the perfon for the place and manner of his
aduauncement, all zealous Catholiques
haue

haue both wifhed & prayed, that he mighte firft be a Catholike and then our King, this being our bounded duty to wifh, and his greateft good to be obtayned for him. And to this end and no other I affure my felfe hath byn directed, whatfoeuer may haue been faid, written, or done by any Catholike, which with fome others might breed difgufte.

9. Now it hath not pleafed allmighty God to giue vs our defires in the order of our wifhes, but firft to make him our King, and then to leaue vs in hope of the other at his due time. What fhall we fay in this & all the reft, but as Heli did: *Dominus eft, quod bo-* 1,*Reg.*3. *num eft in oculis fuis, faciat.* He is Lord, lett him do as he thinketh beft? And with patience, humility, longanimity, and obedience feeke by continuall prayer to haften that tyme of our full ioye by his Maiefties cc..iuerfion, which wee truft in his euerlafting wifdome and infallible prouidence is allready determined to be, *fuo tempore.* And in the meane fpace feing it is heere reported, that Catholiques, accordinge to their habilities, haue fhewed themfelues in euery country both ready & forward to aduaunce his Maiefties prefent admiffion to the crowne, I do not doubt, but they fhall find the effectes of his clemency for their deliuery out of fuch afflictions, calamityes and oppreffions, as

* 5   lately

latley they haue luffred by the inftigation
principally of fuch people, whoes manners
are moft excellently & prudently defcribed
by his Maieftie in the fecond booke of his
worthy treatife as to himfelfe well expe-
rienced:

10. And it is no fmall comforte in this
behalfe to haue a King of whome wee
may truly vfe the words of *Saint Paule,*
Hab. 5. which he fpoke of Chrift, *didicit ex eü quæ*
paffus eft, &c. He hath learned by that himfelfe hath fuffred by the fame kind of men.
And truly though in his own perfon (he
cannot be faid,nor would perhaps) to haue
fuffered properly for Cath. Religion, as
yow haue done: yet yf wee refpect his nea-
reft, eather in nature, bloud, or affection,
and their number, rank and quality, that
among them haue fuffered for the fame
caufe, he may be faid to haue fuffered per-
chaunce farre more, than yow. For that
more of his princely bloud hath bene fhed
in England, Fraunce, and Scotland, about
the quarrell of Cath. Religion, than of all
other Chriftian Princes ioyned togeather.

11. And for fo much as his Maieftie doth
vouchfafe of his princely gratitude to profeffe in one parte of his *inftructions to his fonne*
the Prince, that in all his troubles, ftraytes &
daungers, he hath found none fo fure and
confident vnto him,as thofe that remayned
loyall

loyall and faithfull to his good Mother the Queene (who all for the moſt parte were knowne to haue byn good Catholique) it is to be hoped, that he will make the ſame accompt alſo of yow that remayned conſtant and dutyfull, not only to her Maieſtie while ſhee liued, but to Gods diuine Maieſtie alſo in ſtanding & ſuffering for your conſcience in Religion. Which was the marke & badg (yf yow remember) wherby the foreſaid famous gouernor *Conſtantius*, father to our *Conſtantine*, did try his Chriſtian courtiers, though he were a pagan himſelfe; reiecting thoſe, who vpon his commaundement and inuitation had yelded, & done againſt their owne religion; and retayning and honoring others , that had byn conſtant euen againſt himſelfe. Which facte *Euſebius* recompteth with exceedinge praiſe of the mans iudgment, iuſtice and piety therin : Whoes example I hope our now King will imitate, and yow follow the example of the better ſorte of thoſe Chriſtians, whome *Conſtantius* for their conſtancy ſo much eſteemed and aduaunced.

Euſeb. lib. 1. de vita Cōſtant. cap. 11.

A TABLE

A TABLE OF THE
PARTICVLAR CONTENTS
and chapters of this
ensuing treatise.

The *Preface* vvherein *diuers principall points ar handled about iudgment in matters of faith, and vvith hovv great care and sollicitude the same ought to be considered of.*

The FIRST PART of this treatise concerninge plantinge and continuance of Catholike religion in England.

Of the

That

SECOND

SECOND PART.

For Searching of the Protestant Church and Religion.

The

The

The search of Iohn Fox *his Church is continued* 11.
vnder the gouernment, and raigne of K. Henry
the 8. and his children; and it is discussed vvhat man-
ner of Church Iohn Fox *then had, or may be ima-*
gined to haue had. CHAP. XI

VVhether Fox *his Church hath had any place* 12.
vnder K. Edward, Q. Marie, *and* her Maiestie
that novv raigneth : and hovv farre it hath byn ad-
mitted, or is admitted at this day. CHAP. XII.

The conclusion of both these former parts, toge- 13.
ther vvith a particular discourse of the notorious dif-
ferent proceeding of Catholiks and Protestants, in
searching out the truth of matters in controuersie.
CHAP. XIII.

THE THIRD PART,

About Iohn Fox his Calendar and Protestant martyrs therin conteyned.

1.

F OR *so much as this third part is to be printed*
seuerally, it seemeth not necessary to sett dovvne
the Titles of all the Chapters in particular : but yet
to th'end yovv may vnderstand vvhat in substance it
conteyneth, vve shall heere touch the summe therof.

The first tvvo Chapters do handle the Institution 2.
of Calendars and martyrologes, vvhat is meant by
them, to vvhat end and vses they vvere ordayned and
do serue in the Catholike Church, and hovv imper-
tinently and absurdly Iohn Fox *hath sought to dravv*
and apply the same to his martyrs.

          * *   The

3. The second tvvo Chapters, to vvitt the third and fourth, do difcuffe other points belonging to this matter, to vvitt, vvhat are the particular fects vvhervnto all the diuerfity of opinions found among Fox his martyrs may be reduced. And then, vvhat is to be thought of their vviilfull dying for the fame, vvhether yt mav be accompted conftancy, or rather obftinacy.

4. After this do enfue 12. other Chapters accoiding to the number of the monethes of the yeare, vvherin are examined the martyrs and confeffors vvhich Iohn Fox hath fet dovvne in euery moneto for faincts of his Church, vvho are compared afvvell among themfelues for their different fects and opinions in Religion, as alfo vvith the Cath. Saincts, vvhome he hath put out of the Calendar, to make roome for them.

5. Next vnto this is examined the different manner of Canonizing Saints vfed by the Cath. Church, from that of proteftant vvryters, among vvhome euery particular man maketh and vnmaketh vvhat Saincts he lifteth; and yt is further fhevved, that fcarfe any proteftant liuing at this day in England, vvill ioyne in faith fully and vvholy, vvith any of thefe martyrs and confeffors fett dovvne by Fox, and that for the moft of them, they do & muft difclayme from their beleefe.

6. Hervpon there is a Cenfure giuen in a feuerall Chapter, of Fox° and his vvrytings, and tvvo other books are fhevved to be in hand againft his Acts and Monuments, the one in Latyn intituled Certamen Ecclefiæ Anglicanæ pro fide Catholica, vvhich vvill conteyne diuers volumes: the other in Englifh, called the Hunt of an Englifh Fox, vvhich vvill

rvill difcouer the notorious falshood, fhifts & fleights vfed by Iohn Fox in his Acts and Monuments.

And for a taft of this there are layd forth breefly in another Chapter thofe 60. lyes or more, vvhich vvere promifed by a former pamphlet intituled, A relation of the conference had in France betweene the B. of Eureux and Plefsis Mornay, in the yeare 1600. vvhich multitude of lyes and falfifications, vvere promifed to be found vvithin the compaffe of tvvo leaues only of Iohn Fox his huge volume, to the end that therby a gheffe may be made of the whole.

7.

And laftly (yf the author for breuityes fake do not change his mynd) there is to enfue an examinatiō of a certayne ridiculous definition of a Catholike man, de- uifed and fett dovvne by Fox : and thervpon the true defcription both of a proteftant and Catholike man, and their difference afvvell in faith and doctrine, as vvorks and actions, is particularly declared.

8.

* * 2   *A note,*

A note, for direction of the Reader in perusing this booke.

I HAD once purposed (good reader) to haue sett dovvne tvvo other tables in the beginninge of this booke, as I did in that of the *vvarn vvord* the one of the speciall controuersies treated therin; the other of the cheefest lyes & falsifications of those vvryters vvith vvhome I deale: but being shortened in tyme for taking them out, I haue thought good to remitt all to the last table, vvhich goeth in the end of the booke, vvhere yovv shall find all particulars mentioned togeather, vvith the false and deceytfull behauiour of *Fox*, *Bale*, and the *Magdeburgians* (the principall aduersaryes vvith vvhome vve deale in this treatise) sett dovvne and specified vnder their seuerall names in the said Index. VVherfore the Reader that hath not leasure to peruse the vvhole, may haue recourse to this table, and therby make choyse of vvhat he desireth first to be informed of.

THE

THE PREFACE

To the Chriſtian ſtudious Reader
concerning the edition and argument of this treatiſe, and of
the methode held therin, and
principall points to be treated.

Sap. 9.

MAN *to be mutable or (as the ſcripture
ſpeaketh)* vncertaine in his forſight
*and prouidence, if no other argu-
mentes were to proue it (as there be infinite) yet my owne experience (gentle Reader) of the
ſucceſſe of this treatiſe were ſufficient: hauinge altered ſo often my firſt intention about the ſame, as it
beinge ready now to come forth, it ſeemeth nothing
leſſe, then that, which at the beginninge I had purpoſed.*

2. *My firſt deſignement was to haue written only
ſome fewe leaues or ſheetes of paper in anſwere to*
Syr Francis Haſtings, *who in his reply to the ſeauenth encounter of the warder, (which encounter
concerneth principally the Biſhop & Sea of Rome)
would ſeeme to diminiſh that obligation of gratitude,
which the warder ſaid, that England had aboue many other nations to that See, for two conuerſions of our
people to Chriſtian Religion receiued from thence.
The knight (I ſay) endeuored to ſtrike out or diminiſh
that obligation, by calling in doubt the ſaid conuer-*

Syr. Fr.
Haſtings
in his re-
ply pag.
192.

** 3   ſions,

The Preface to the Reader

*sions, or cauillinge at least at some particulars therof.
VVhervpon I thought it needefull, not only to confirme that which had bene written before of the two
foresaid conuersions vnder* Pope Eleutherius *&*
Pope Gregory *the first: but also to adde a third
more ancient then these two, to wit vnder* S. Peter
*himselfe and some other Apostles. And albeit all this
was ment so briefly, as I haue said, in the first designe-
ment: yet when I came to the woorke it selfe it grewe
more longe, & coulde hardly be dispatched in so many chapters, as I had purposed leaues or sheetes at the
beginninge.*

3. *The reason of this encrease was, for that comming to the examination of the matter, I found* Syr
Francis *to haue taken all that he had said concerninge that point out of* Iohn Fox; *though he cited
him not: and* Fox *againe the most part of his cauills
out of the* Magdeburgians. *So as of necessity
I was forced to encounter with all these three aduersaries together to examin their argumentes, dis-*

Hovv
the first
part of
this trea-
tise vvas
encrea-
sed.

*couer their fraudes, and refell their follies. VVhich
to do with any sufficiency (as also with the clearnes
and perspicuity, which I desired) drewe the matter
on to a bigger bulke, then well could be sette forth
as a part only of that encounter, whervnto it belonged. VVhervpon at the persuasion of some friendes,
resolution was taken to haue it diuulged in a seuerall treatise, as before hath byn shewed in the end
of the second encounter already printed.*

4. *But now, when it was taken in hand to be
reuievved for the edition, diuerse thinges occur-*
                                                    red

*rd to be added for the more fullneſſe of the trea-
tiſe. And namely, that not only the plantinge of
Chriſtian faith in England ſhould be auerred by
theſe three ſeuerall conuerſions : but that the continuation alſo therof (I meane of one ſelfe ſame
faith and beleefe) ſhould be ſhewed and de-
monſtrated from the firſt to the ſeconde conuerſion, and from the ſecond to the thirde vnto our
dayes. And with this came the diſcours to occu-
pie a dozen whole Chapters : VVhich was more
then twiſe ſo much, as in the firſt deſignement
was purpoſed.*

5. *But being arriued hither, there offred it ſelfe
a new cogitation of adding a ſecond part, no leſſe
important, then the firſt, for ſearching out our aduerſaryes religion in all this tyme. Accordinge to the
aduertiſement both of the philoſopher and Orator,
that it is not ſufficiēt only to confirme our owne cauſe,
except wee infringe and refute the contrary. VVhervpon it ſeemed neceſſary not only to ſhew the firſt,
ſecond and third plantinge of our Religion in England, together with the manifeſt and viſible continuance therof vnto our age : but alſo to demonſtrate the contrary in the religion of the proteſtants : to wit, that it vvas neuer planted in
England (I meane in ſuch points of doctrine,
vvherin they differ from the Catholique) nor
euer vvas receaued, nor had eſſence or being vnder the name of Chriſtian Religion from Chriſts
tyme to ours . And for that Iohn Fox aboue
all other Engliſh proteſtant vvriters taketh vpon
him*

Ariſt. in
Topicis.
Cicer.1.ad
Heren. &
de Orator.

VVhy
the ſecōd
part of
the ſe-
arch of
I. Fox his
Church
vvas ad-
ded.

him of purpose & by promise to prooue the contrary in his huge volume of Acts & Monuments; to wit to Fox in the title of his acts and monuments & in his protestation to the English Church. *shew the course and race of his Church (for so are his words) from the beginning of these latter ages: I was forced to ioyne issue with him in particular vpon both these parts. I meane in shewinge the beginning & continuance of our Church & religion: and the not beinge or continuance of his. For performance wherof I haue had occasion (as you see) to peruse ouer the first part of the said volume from the beginning of Christian religion to* Kinge Henry *the* 8. *conteyning aboue* 500. *leaues.*

6. *But for that the second part of that volume from* K. Henry *downward (being of no lesse bulke then the former) treateth of the principall pillars of his religion since that tyme, wherof some he maketh Confessors & other Martyrs, & distributeth them into a certaine Ecclesiasticall Calendar accordinge to the* VVhy the third part of this treatise was added about the examinatiō of Fox his calendar. *dayes of euery moneth, wherin their festiuall memoryes are to be kept; and placeth the said Calendar in the forfront of his Acts & Monuments, it seemed conuenient also, to the end that nothing should remayne wholly vnsearched or vnexamined in that woork of his, to adde a third part to the former two for the discussion of this Calendar, and some other necessary points belōging thervnto. VVhich third part growing more large in the prosecution then was expected at the beginning, & coming as it were to equall the other two: I was induced to print it in a seuerall volume apart. Partly that it may be more portable & comodious for the Reader; and then for that it treateth*
somwhat

somwhat a diſtinct matter, and finally for that the two former parts do conteyne a ſufficient full argument of themſelues beſides this third part.

7.   *Lo heere good Chriſtian Reader a breeſe ſumme of all my cogitations about that matter. VVhich if they may ſerue thee for thy ſpirituall vtility, either for confirming or eſtabliſhing the in Cath. Religion (if thou haue it alredie) or for thy reducing vnto it if hitherto thou be not partaker of ſo high & heauenly a bleſsing, I ſhal be gladde & think my labors happily beſtowed therin, well knowing of what importance this matter is for thy eternall ſaluation.*

8.   *In reſpect wherof, thou oughteſt alſo, if thou be in any doubt, not only to take vpon thee the labour of reading this, or any ſuch treatiſe that may help the therin: but alſo to trauaile both by Sea & land, countreis & kingdomes (yf wee beleeue S. Auſten, that both ſaid & practized the ſame) to ſeeke out the truth & certainty of Cath. Religion. VVherby only, & by no other wayes & meanes vnder heauen, may a man be ſaued or eſcape euerlaſting damnation, as holy Athanaſius proteſteth in his creede. VVherfore this ought to be vnto vs (as the ſame father ſaith) that riche Iewell found in the field, for buyeng wherof wee ſhould not ſtick to ſell or looſe all other temporall goods or riches, that wee haue: ſeeing Chriſt our Sauiour doth ſo much commend them, that did ſo, and therby inciteth vs alſo to do the like.*

9.   *And the ſame Doctor S. Auſten together with S. Chryſoſtome & other fathers, do reprehend greatly the ſluggiſhnes of diuerſe men in their dayes, that*

The diligence which men ought to vſe for in forming theſelues of the truth of Cath. religion in tyme of hereſies. Poſsidon. in vita Aug. & Aug. l 4. & 5 conſeſs. Athanaſ. in Simbol. verſ. 2. Matth.13. Aug. l. de morib. eccl. c 17. Chriſoſt. hom. 14. in cap 24. Matth.

sects & heresies to arise & diuersities of religion in almost euery countrey, did not bestirre themselues to try out the truth ; but were content either to accept of euery nouelty thrust vpon them, or to remayne doubtfull or indifferēt, vvhich in some sort is a woorse state then the other. For as the prophecy & prediction of our Sauiour is cleere, that such tymes of heresie & contradiction should come, vvhen one sect would say here is Christ, and another there is Christ ; one heretique would cry, here is the Church, here is the true doctrine, here is reformatiō, & another deny it, so the Apostle expoundeth the hidden prouidēce of allmighty God in this permission of his, to wit, vt qui probati sunt, manifesti fiant, that those who are men of proofe, should be made manifest among vs. And how then in a tyme of proofe & of so special triall, when so great a crowne is to be gayned, are men so negligent, slouthfull & fearfull in shewing & declaring themselues? S. Chrysost. yeldeth this reason, which is seuere. Quia neq; promissio beatitudinis eius (saith he) desideratur, neque iudicium comminationis eimetur, &c. It is, for that neither Gods promise of eternall felicity in the next life is desired by these slouthfull people, nor his threat of iudgment feared. And yet saith the same father. Si veltimenta empturus gyras vnū negociatorem & alterum, &c. If yow were to buy a garment yow go about from one seller or marchant to another, to see & examine, where the best is to be found. And how much more ought this to be donne to try out true religion?

10.   If a pretension were made (saith one) to take

away

Matt. 24.
Mar. 13.
Ioann. 7.

1. Cor. 11.

Chrysost.
opere im-
perfect. in
Matth. ca.
23 pag.
562.

Chrysost.
ibid.

away your temporall lands and liuings, or that any new doubts should be put in the titles of your inheritance,or that it should be called in queſtiõ by any promotors or buſie people, whether you were true owners of ſuch and ſuch landes and liuings, or no: you would quickly ſtart & beſtirre yourſelues, looking out recordes & writings for confirmation of your right & title, & would ſeeke after lawiers to pleade & defend the ſame, & you would make accompt of anciēt witneſſes for proofe therof. All which you neglecting in this caſe of trvall about Cath. Religion againſt hereſies (vvhich is more cleere in it ſelfe, if men vvould attend vnto it,then any other proofe of poſſeſſiõ,right, intereſt, title, or inheritance vvhatſoeuer) this negligence(I ſay)doth cleerly declare,that men haue more care and cogitation of temporalities,then of eternity: of earth, then of heauen: and of this miſerable ſhort & vaniſhing life,then of Gods euerlaſting kingdome and their immortall raigning with him.

11. *And thuſmuch be ſpoken by the way concerning the iudgement, ſenſe & feeling of ancient holy fathers, about the care and ſollicitude, that euery true Chriſtiã ought to haue for informing himſelf ſoundly and ſubſtancially(but eſpecially in time of hereſies) what the truth and certainty of Cath. Religion is. Leaſt being negligent in this ſearch & ſollicitude,and yeelding ouermuch to the cogitation of worldly affaires, he be deceaued before he be aware, and caried away to perdition by the preſent ſurge and ſway of innouations, vnder the colour,and name of nevv reformations : perſuading himſelfe, that he*

goeth

A repreſentation of ſuch as are negligent in examininge the truth of Cath. religion.

goeth right and hath no neede of further aduise or information therin.

12. *For preuention of which most perillous course held (alas) by to many of our countrey at this day (who perswade themselues, that either matters of religion appertaine not greatly vnto them, or that* they goe well as they are, or that they may remaine indifferent or attend to worldly affaires and let the other alone, or at leastwayes do imagine by the multitude of contradictions, which they see and heare euery where, that it is a hard matter to discerne, which party hath the truth, or where that certainty lyeth:) for helpe (I say) in all theise points (but specially in the last) I haue thought best to publish this treatise, which I trust shalbe a sufficient light for discerning truth to them that will vouchsafe to peruse the same. For that it doth briefly, cleerly, and in one whole summe or vewe, lay before them the verity of Cath. Religion, the offspring increase and continuance therof, together with the fraude & falshood of all sectes whatsoeuer, but specially those of our tymes.*

Dange-rous co-gitatios.

13. *And it is here to be noted, that, as in suites & controuersies about temporall landes and liuinges belonging to any state or lordship, a man may take two wayes of proofe and triall against quarrellers, that craftily and falsly would intrude or make pretension thervnto. The first by alleging particular euidences for euery part and parcell therof seuerally, as for this close, this medowe, this park, that pasture, those woods, that glebe-land, and the like. VVhich way*

(as you

About the argument of this booke.

(as yow see) is more prolix and troublesome: There is therefore a second more short & generall, wherby a man proouing one point prooueth all. As if wee would take vpon vs to shew, that the chiefe mansion house of the said lordship in controuersie (wheruuto all the rest belongeth) is ours, and hath byn euer holden by our ancesters, and that wee are true successors, heires and inheritors vnto them. This issue (I say) were more short and sure. And this is that, in which I do now ioyne plea with our aduersaries especially with Iohn Fox in name of all his brother protestants, To wit, that wheras other men hitherto haue taken vpon them to defend and prooue particular points of controuersies seuerally, as for example the reall presence, purgatory, prayer to Sainōts, seauen sacraments & the like, which are but branches of our whole cause, my purpose is to prooue alltogether, by ioyning the foresaid issue about the chiefe mansion house & true owners therof, that is to say the true Catholike-Church and lawfull family ther-vnto belonging, descending from Christ himselfe. For that wee proouing this only wee prooue the whole, no man being able to deny, but that where this house & family is found, there is all the right and interest, that may be pretended to the state and dignity aforesaid.

14. But now againe for proouing of this point, diuerse wayes are or may be held by different men, myne shalbe at this tyme after the fashion of two that striue & contend about the mansion house before mentioned, and therby pretend to the true title, and lawfull

The contention about the house & mannerplace.

lawfull inheritance of the foresaid state and lordship. The one part pretending only in generall termes that there is such a noble house, well and strongly built, with great and excellent qualityes and comodityes, and richly furnished, vvhervnto belongeth the said state and lordship, and that the owners and inhabitants therof haue greate priuileges and preferments before all other people, and that there are certayne ancient records extant, alfo of this matter, out of vvhich records, according to their owne expofition, they gather thefe propertyes of the said house and family, and doth apply both the one and the other to themselues.

15. But the other partie denyeng their pretence and expofition of old records saith that all this is false, and that according to the true expofition of the said vvritings and the markes and tokens therby giuen, the said house and manner place appartaineth vnto them only, and thervvith confequently the vvhole state and lordship vvithout controuerfie. VVhich they offer to try by coming to particulars, shevving vvhen, and vvhere, and by vvhat occafion, the said house vvas first builded, vvhat vvere the stones and timber that vvent thervnto, hovv the title of the vvhole state and lordship vvas tyed or annexed to this house, together vvith the dignityes and priuileges therof. And then to vvhat family this house vvas affigned at the beginning, vvho were the first inhabitants, dvvellers, guiders, and gouernors therof, and hovv it hath continued euer since from hand to hand, and from tyme to tyme, alvvays

rnder

The Catholike part his plea for the houfe.

vnder the same family by lawfull succession, and hath defended it selffrom al sorts of assaults made against it, aswell of secret domesticall theeues, as open enemyes, and that at this day the same family is in possession thereof, &c.

16.   And as for the other pretenders these men offer to shew further against them that they haue bene allways contemptible and vageant persons, dispersed here and there in seuerall cottages of their owne new building or patching, nor euer dwelt together in any one house vvorth the naming, and much lesse in so excellent a house as this is, and that if any of them haue at any tyme heretofore byn perhaps of this house or family, they vvere either dimissed and cast out for their disorders, or haue runne away as fugitiues for guiltines of their owne consciences.

17.   Now then this being so, vvho doth not see to vvhich party the said house and mansion place before mentioned is like to be iudged? And this is the true figure or representation (good Christian Reader) of our present controuersie vvith Ioнn Fox and his fellowes throughout all this treatise, for that he and his do pretend a certaine title to the true Church and religion of Christ from all antiquity, but bring forth as good proofes to challenge the same, as do other pretenders before mentioned for the said house and manner place, if not somewhat viorse as shalbe declared.

18.   But wee on the contrary side do follow the course of the other party in coming to particulars, setting downe first how Christs Church and religion began,

began, by whome, and vnder whome; who were the first beginners, promotors and professors therof, what they taught, what they did, whome they left their successors, with what promise and assurance of continuation, and finally how they haue endured vnto this day. And all this is handled in the first part of this treatise. And then in the second is declared the other point before mentioned; to wit, that the aduerse hereticall part, had neuer yet any house at all, & much lesse any such as hath bene spoken of; that is to say, they had neuer any Church or certaine family agreeing with it selfe, nor euer any certaine profession of any one faith or religion like in all points to it self, or to that of any others, were it good or bad, false or true, hereticall or Catholique. And this is obserued from the beginning of the world to our tyme, as yow shall see manifestly prooued afterwards in the prosecution of this woork; desiring thee (gentle reader) to take the paines, as to reade it ouer with some attention for thyne owne vtility. Though I presume that thy contentmēt also in reading therof, will easely equall thy paines, the argument being historicall, & not denoyd of gratefull variety both of tymes, men, and affaires.

19. But now, for that my end & scope in writing this treatise, and in handling this important argument of discerning betweene religion and religion, is not indeed so much (if I shall confesse the truth) to delight, as to mooue and proffit thee (good reader:) I haue thought conuenient for the second part of this my preface, to adioyne 3. or 4. points of principall conside-

(marginal notes:)

The Application of the two former examples.

Foure points of consideration about matters of faith.

*consideration about this subiect of faith and beleefe,
and therof deduce as many inferences of no lesse
importance, for thy good disposition in this behalfe,
and therwith leaue the for the rest to thine owne
iudgement, and more mature deliberation.*

20.   *The first of which points is, that almighty
God for mans greater humilitie and merit in beleeuing, hath placed the greater part of the obiect of
our faith and beleefe (that is to say, the things which
are to be beleeued) aboue the ordinary reach of mans
reason, and inuironed them with such difficultie and
obscuritie, in respect of our frailtie, as without the
light of his grace, & the concurse and free motion of
our owne, will, & good endeuor they are not to be at-
tained vnto. And this (as I said) aswel for mans hu-
miliation, in respect of the height of gods mysteries
reuealed by faith; as also that man may merit by his
free and willing concurse to beleefe: which he would
not do, if the articles or obiect of our faith were so
cleere as there were no obscurity or darknes in them:
for then according to the grounds of philosophy, mans
vnderstanding perforce must yeeld therunto; and
consequently our will also, wherof would ensue the
losse of all merit and reward, according to that
saying of saint Gregory:* Non habet fides meritum, vbi humana ratio præbet experimen-
tum, *saith hath no merit where mans reason doth
make the thing euidēt. And long before him S. Athanasius* : Fides de re euidenti concepta, Fides
dici non potest, *faith conceaued of an euident
matter, can not be called faith. And briefly, but pi-*

The first
point
hovv our
articles
of faith
are abo-
ue mans
reason.

Gregor.
hom. 26.
in euang.
Athan.
tract. de
aduent. 1.
cont.
Apollin.

* * *

thily

The Preface to the Reader

August.
tract. 79.
in Ioann.
& serm.1.
de festo.3.
Trinit.

thily S. *Austen*: Laus fidei est; si, quod credi-tur, non videtur. *The praise or merit of faith stands in this, that the thing be not seene which is be-leeued. And in another place*: Credo, quod ne-scio: & propterea scio, quia scio, me nescire quod nescio. *I do beleeue that which I know not: and therby I come to know, for that I know my selfe to haue byn ignorant in that which indeed I knew not. And finally S. Paule to the Hebrues maketh this plaine, vvhen giuinge a definition of faith, he vvri-*

Hebr. 11.

teth thus: Est autem fides substantia speran-darum rerum, argumentum non apparen-tium. *Faith is the substance or ground of things hoped for (in the next life) and an argument of such things, as be not apparent or manifest to humaine sense or reason. Thus teach they. And the matter is cleere in it selfe, & confoundeth the politique vayne heads of our daies, who will beleeue no more, then they see, or feele, or can comprehend by their owne vnderstanding.*

21.   *But now concerning the causes of this difficulty or obscurity in matters of beleefe, the same fathers do*

First
cause of
obscurity
in faith.

assigne two or three for principall. The first is, the heigth & sublimity of the articles & mysteries them-selues, that are to be beleeued, which being of Gods secrets, do surpasse the base capacity and reason of man. As are (for example) the creation of the world of nothing, the trinity of persons in one nature of diuinity, the incarnation of the sonne of God, and his birth without violating his mothers virginity, the re-surrection of our bodies, the being of Christ in the Sa-crament, & the like. VVhich humaine reason can not

reach

reach vnto ; though they be not contrary to it, but above it. Another cause is (as Saint Ambrose no- Second *teth) the Maiestie of almighty God, vvho vvill be* cause. *beleeued at his vvoord, vvithout being asked for proofe or reason for the same. For yf (saith he) a* Ambr.l.1, *graue honorable personage in this life) especially* de Abra- *yf he be of high authority and our superior) vvill* ham cap.3. *take it in disdaine to be asked a proofe, for that he* » *affirmeth: hovv much more ought God to be credi-* » *ted vvithout proofe of humaine reason,when he pro-* » *poseth vnto vs a matter above our reach or capacity?* »

22. The third cause is that which before I touched, The third *that man might merit more by beleeuinge that* cause. *which he seeth not euident, according to the saying of Chrift vnto Saint Thomas,* Quia vidisti (Thoma) credidisti. Beati qui non viderunt & Ioan. 2. crediderunt. *Because thou hast seene, Thomas, thou hast beleeued; but happy are they that haue not seene & yet haue beleeued. And for all theise causes if vvee consider the matter well, we shall find, that God hath proceeded strangely to mans eye from the beginning of the world, in reuealing the misteries of our faith vnto vs: discouering his will on the one side with infinite testification of his loue and desire* Hovv *that wee should knowe them : and yet on the other* God pro- *side with such reseruation in those reuelations, as* ceedeth *the matter might still be difficult, hard, or obscure,* in reuea- *in some respect. And this for the greater me-* linge his *rit (as hath byn said) of the beleeuer. As for ex-* miste- *ample, before the flood he appeared to diuerses* Pa- ries. *triarches from time to time, causing them to preach* Gen. 2. 6, 7. 8;

and open to others his vvill & the truth of that faith, which they were bound to beleeue: but yet he appeared not to all in those dayes, which he might haue donne, yf he would, & therby haue made the matter more cleere & out of doubt. But he would haue them beleeue others by words and tradition. And the like manner of proceeding he vsed after the flood with Abraham, Isaac, & Iacob for instruction of their posterity. And then againe foure or fiue hundreth yeares after that, vvhen he determined to bring the Hebrew people out of Egypt, and to giue them a written lawe, he appeared not euidently to all the people, but chose Moises to send vnto them in his name: and spake to him out of a firy bush at the beginning, and at other times out of a clowd on the top of a hill. All which things had still their doubts & difficulties for him, that would wrangle or had not good will to beleeue and credit them.

*Gene.20.
22.23.
Exod.1.2.
3.
Deut. 33.
Act. 7.
Ios. 15.*

Hovv Christ our sauiour proceeded in reuealinge his misteries aud vvhy he appeared not to all.

23. And finally when the sonne of God came himselfe in flesh to preach, thouge he vsed many and sufficient arguments to drawe men vnto him, and beleeue the mysteries reuealed by him, as in the next point shalbe shewed, Yet vsed he the same course notwithstanding, that had byn vsed before: for neither appeared he to the whole world (as he might haue donne by his diuinity and omnipotency) but to those of Iury only; nor there to all, nor did he woork miracles in euery place, but where he thought expedient. Nor when he rose againe from death (which is a point principally in this matter to be considered) did he appeare to all men, or publickely in the streats of Ie-

of Ierusalem, as he might haue donne, and therby haue made his resurrection cleere and out of cōtrouersy, but he appeared only to his Apostles and disciples. VVhich he expresseth in these words. Hunc Deus susci- **Act. 10.**
tauit tertia die, & dedit eum manifestū fieri, non omni populo, sed testibus præordinatis à Deo: nobis, qui manducauimus & bibimus cū illo, postquam resurrexit à mortuis. Et præcepit nobis prædicare populo & testificari, &c. *God hath raised vp this his Sonne from death the third day : and gaue him to be made manifest not to all the people, but vnto such as were preordayned before hand by him to be witnesses therof; that is to say, vs that did both eate and drink with him after his resurrection, and to vs he gaue commaundment to preach and testify to the people, &c.* 24. *Behold here the reason, why Christ after his resurrection dit not appeare to the whole people in Iury, but to his Apostles and disciples only who were his appointed witnesses to testifie and preach the same to others, to the end their faith might be of more merit according to his former speeche to S. Thomas:* Happy are they, who haue not seene and **Iohn. 20.** yet do beleeue. *And for the selfe same causes wee may not doubt, but that theise his apparitions and manifestations, which are recounted in scriptures to haue bene made by him at diuerse tymes, in sundrie places, and vpon different occasions, during his aboade on earth, for the space of forty dayes after his resurrection, (VVhich apparitions arrive to the number of 13. or 14.) were made in such particular man-*

Christs resurrection hovv & tovvhom it vvas made manifest.

net

Math. 28. *ner by him, as the scripture recounteth them. First to*
Iobn. 30. *those godly women, then to the Apostles, then to the*
Act. 2. 10. *disciples going to* Emaus, *and after that to others.*
1, 17.
Rom. 4. 8. *All (I say) vvere so made, as still remayned place for*
14. *our free vvill to merits in beleeuinge them, and di-*
1, Cor. 15. *uerse did doubt at the beginninge (as the scripture*
2. Cor. 5. *saith. And Christ vvas often forced to reprehend their*
2. Tim. 2. *coldnesse & backwardnesse in beleefe, as when he said*
Luc. 24. O stulti & tardi corde ad credendum! *O your*
foolish and slow of hart to beleeue! And at his last de-
Marc. 16. *parture from them* Exprobrauit illis *(saith Saint*
Marck*)* incredulitatem eorum & duritiem
cordis; quia ijs, qui viderat eum resurrexisse,
non crediderunt. *He did exprobrate vnto them*
,, *their incredulity and hardnes of hart, for that they*
,, *had not beleeued those, who had seene him risen from*
,, *death agayne: vvhich doubt and hardnesse of hart in*
beleeuinge, he cured vvholly afterwards by sendinge
the holy Ghost.

25. *But yet heerby vvee may euidently see that*
Christ required humility and obedience of beleefe,
euen in things vvhere our reason or sense resisted, re-
1. Cor. 10. *quiring vs to captiuate our vnderstanding (to vse S.*
Paules owne vvoords) vnto his obedience in matters
of faith. And not only to himselfe immediatly, but to
those also, that teach and preach vnto vs, by lawfull
ordination and authority from him; albeit they de-
liuer vs matters aboue our capacity, reach and vnder-
standing. And this vnder payne of eternall damna-
tion. For that our Sauiour himselfe hauing geuen
the commission of preaching in Saint Marks Ghospell
afore-

spel aforefaid; Ite & prædicate, *go and preache;*
he addeth prefently , qui non credid*e*rit, con- Marc. 16.
demnabitur: *he that vvill not beleeue , fhall*
be damned. And this is fufficient for the firft point
about the obfcurity of the obiect of faith and caufes
therof.

22. *The fecond point of this confideration , is,*   The fe-
that albeit allmighty God vvill haue vs to yeeld cond
his obedience of faith vnto him , afvvell for his due point of
honour, as for our ovvne vtility : Yet doth he not fideratiõ
leaue vs vvithout fufficient teftimony of the truth, nor that not-
requireth at our hands this obedience , but as ratio- ſtanding
nabile obſequium, *(to vfe Saint Paules vvoords)* the arti-
a reafonable obedience , or an obedience founded in cles of
all reafon of probability, inducement and credibili- our faith
ty. For proofe vverof vvee muſt vnderftand, that can not
albeit the moſt parts of Chriſtian beleefe do fo fur- monſtra-
mount (as in the former point hath bene fhevved) ted by
the reach and capacity of humaine reafon, as they can reafon,
not be comprehended therby (though of fome other they fuf-
there may be alfo demonſtration made , as fhalbe ficient
fhevved in the fourth point of this confideration:) yet argu-
for fatisfaction of our vnderftandings, his diuine piety credibi-
& prouidence hath left vnto vs fo many other proofes lity.
and arguments of perfuafion, and inducemens, called Rom. 1.
by fchoolemen argumenta credibilitatis, *argu-*
ments of credibility) as they being layd together
and vvell pondered may iuftly moue any indiffe-
rent , prudent , and difcreete man, to yeeld his
affent thervnto , and to reft fully fatisfied of the
truth . As lernedly yovv haue feene prooved
                    ** 4   theife

theise dayes paſt by a treatiſe ſet furth in Engliſh for answer of the new challanges of the miniſter O. I. this matter is handled more largely. But for my preſent purpoſe it is ſufficiēt to record vnto yow, that of theiſe argumēts of credibility are full fraught all the bookes & volumes of the ancient fathers: Therby to prooue the credibility, probability, and conueniency of Chriſtian religion, & of euery part & article thereof: therby to make them inexcuſable that will not beleeue the ſame. VVherof it ſhalbe ſufficiēt, that I alleage in this place the exāple only of S. Peter. VVho going about to perſuade his audience, vſeth theſe

2. Pet. 1. vvoords: Non indoctas fabulas ſequuti, &c.
» *Not induced by vaine fables(as the gētils were)haue*
» *wee beleeued & made knowne to yow the power &*
» *preſcience of our Lord Ieſus Chriſt; but for that wee*
» *haue byn made eye vvitneſſes of his greatneſſe, &c.*

Arguments of credibility vſed by Saint Peter.

27. *Thus began S. Peter to perſuade his hearers alleaging 2.or 3. ſtrong inducemēts of credibility for the ſame. Firſt that he & the reſt of his Apoſtles had conuerſed with Chriſt himſelfe vpon earth, and had byn eye witneſſes of all his doings. And ſecōdly he alleageth that famous miracle vpon the mount* Thabor, *vvhen he with S. Iames & S. Iohn were preſent*

Math. 17. *at his transfiguratiō & heard the voice from heauen;* This is my belooued ſonne, heare him. *And thirdly he alleageth the predictions of the old prophets concerning Chriſts comming, life, actions, death & reſurrection. VVhich S. Peter doth preferre before his ſight, knowledge, & experience, had vvith Chriſt, & vvorthily. For that the predictions of the ſcriptures & pro-*

About the argument of this booke.

& Prophets being writtē by Gods ſpirit ſo many ages before Chriſt vvas borne, and novv fulfilled ſo euidently in his perſon, the Apoſtles ſight and experience therof, vvas but a teſtimony to the others verity, and nothing ſo certaine in it ſelfe as the fortellings of the ſaid prophets ſo euidētly verified in their ſights.

28. And yet vvere all theſe things, but inducements and arguments of credibility (as I haue ſaid) and not demonſtrations. For albeit the truth of ſcriptures be moſt certaine and infallible in it ſelfe; yet to me, that muſt take them vpon credit of others, either concerning the books themſelues, traductions, or interpretations, or ſome other ſuch circumſtances, they can not haue the cleerneſſe and euidency to convince our vnderſtandings, vvhich philoſophicall demonſtrations haue: albeit the aſſent of our faith induced by theſe arguments of credibility (together vvith the help of our pious affection, and aſſiſtance of Gods grâce) be much more ſure firme and immoueable, then that, vvhich is gotten by humaine knovvlege. VVhich is partly ſeene, in that a ſtronger reaſon cōming againſt my knovvlege, I do change my iudgement. But not ſo in faith, if it be ſounde. The cauſe vvherof is, for that faith is grounded vpon a more certaine foundation, then is humaine ſcience, to vvit vpon the credit and authority of God himſelfe. VVherin alſo is to be noted, that theiſe inductions and arguments of credibility, may be much more euident to ſome, then to others. As for example, the miracles donne by God in bringing home of the Iewes from Egypt, vvere much more euident to thoſe

Iewes,

Arguments of credibility are not ſo euidēt as are philoſophicall demonſtrations.

Ievves, that then liued, and vvere present and savve them, then to others, that came afterwards. Albeit the faith & beleefe of some of the latter, might be as firme & constant, as of the former. And so the miracles of Christ & his Apostles were more euident to those, that savv them, then vnto vs, that heare them only by relation. Though yet our faith may be as good & firme, yea more commendable & meritorious then theirs, in that vvee beleeue them vvithout seeing, according to the foresaid saying of our Sauiour to Saint Thomas. And this is the great piety and mercy of almighty God, that vvee, that come after in the end of the vvorld, shall leese nothing (if vvee vvill) by our so late comming: but may be equall in merit to the first.

29. VVell then, this is the second point, vvhat arguments of credibility Christ hath left vnto vs for proofe of Christian faith. VVherof (as I said) all the ancient fathers books are full. And yovv may see many in Eusebius his lerned books, de preparatione, & demonstratione euangelica. But especially in those, that before him vvrote Apologies for Christians in tymes of persequution, as Iustinus Martyr, Tertullian, and others. S. Austen also in 22. excellent books, that he vvrote De ciuitate Dei, gathered many. And yovv may see good store laid together in our English tongue in the first booke of resolution cap. 4. intituled Proofes of Christianity. VVhich arguments being indifferently vveighed together, vvith the absurdityes of all other religions besids the Christian, do make our faith most credible, and sufficient to moue

Argumēts for proofe of Christian Religion.

any

any vvife confiderat man to beleeue the fame, though they do not inforce him,

30. *And the like may be faid and fhewed concerning the arguments for Catholique Religion againft all fects and herefies vvhatfoeuer. VVhich are fo many and pregnant in themfelues to him that vvill confider them duly, as there can be no probable doubt in the vvorld, vvhich is the truth, and vvhich is falshood. Though oftentimes for vvant eyther of diligence to know them, or pious affection to confider indifferently of them, (vvhich is the third point here to be mentioned) many mens iudgements are fo obfcured or peruerted, as they can not, or vvill not fee the truth. Of theife arguments of credibility for proofe of Catholique faith in generall againft herefies, you may fee many put together by* Tertullian *his excellent booke* De præfcriptionibus aduerfus Herefes, *and in Saint Auftens books* de vtilitate credendi, & de moribus Ecclefiæ, *and other fuch treatifes. And in all his other books againft the* Donatifts, Manichees, *and* Pelagians. *And in that golden treatife of* Vincentius Lirinenfis contra Prophanas hærefum omnium nouitates. *VVho vvrote foone after* S. Auguftine. *And in our tymes* Bofius de fignis Ecclefiæ, & diuerfe other *haue handled the fame argumēt. And more then this, there vvant not alfo ftore in our Englifh tongue of like matter, as* D. Briftow *his motiues & others. And you fhall find no fm all number of theife arguments in this treatife, yf you read it ouer. So as this*

point

point maketh any man inexcufable, that vvill pretend ignorance herin.

The
third
point of
confide-
ration
about
pious af-
fection.
Marc. 6.
Act. 24.

31. *But now there refteth the third point, vvhich (as I faid) is the key of all the reft to open the gate to true faith and beleefe. VVhich is a pious and purged affection, vvithout vvhich all the arguments of credibility in the vvorld, vvill do no good to moouea man to true religion; no more then the perfuafion of Saint Iohn Baptift did vvith Herode, nor the often fpeeches and conferences of Saint Paul preuailed vvith the Proconful Fœlix. The reafon vvherof is, that albeit naturally our iudgement and vnderftandinge fhould yeld to that vvhich appeareth trueft, & that our will and affection by the fame naturall courfe ought to folow our faid iudgemēt & vnderftanding: yet through the corruption of mankind vvee find daily by experience, that our vvill draweth after it our iudgemēt; & as fhe is affected or diffaffected, fo goeth our iudgment and vnderftanding alfo.*

Euill af-
fection
peruer-
teth the
vnder-
ftanding.
Ioann. 5.

32. *This point touched Chrift our Sauiour, vvhen he faid in Saint Iohns Ghofpell to certayne ambitious Iewes :* Quomodo vos poteftis credere, qui gloriam ab inuicem accipitis: & gloriam quæ a Solo Deo eft, non queritis ? *How can yow beleeue in me, vvhich do take and feeke glory one of another, & do not feeke that true glory which is only to be had from God? Here yow fee, that an ambitious affection did impoßibilitate their vnderftanding to beleeue; notvvithftanding vvhat argumentes, reafons, or motiues foeuer to the contrary. S. Paul alfo giuing the reafon, vvhy certayne infi-*

dels

About the argument of this booke.

dels did not beleeue the Ghospell preached by him vvith many signes & miracles, & other arguments to mooue them, he noteth the whole impediment to be in their affections, saying: In quibus Deus huius sę- 2. Cor. 4. culi excæcauit mentes, vt non fulgeat illu- minatio Euangelij gloriæ Christi, qui est imago Dei. *In vvhome the God of this vvorld hath blinded their minds and vnderstandinge, so that the light or illumination of the glory of Christs Ghospell cannot shyne in them, vvho is notwithstandinge the very image of God, &c.*

33. Here yow see, that there vvanted not externall light on the behalfe of Christ and his ghospell (vvhose glory shyned by so many miracles) in those dayes of Saint Paul; but that the loue of this vvorld and disor- derly affection to honor, ambition, riches, and other sensualityes therof (vvhich here by the Apostle are called the God of this vvorld, for that vvorldly men do adore them) this God, I say (or diuell rather) of corrupt affections, had so blinded their iudgements & vnderstandinge inwardly, as they could not see this shyning light of truth. So that vvhere this pious affe- Hovv ne- ction is nat; or at least vvise, vvhere it is not so purged cessary from sinister humors, as it remaineth vvith some in- pious af- differency of desire to knowe and follow the truth, if fectiō is. it be discouered: no good can be hoped for. In regard Luc. 23. vvherof Christ refused to do miracles before Herod or in his owne countrey. For that he knew them so Math. 13. obstinatly auersed in mind, as they vvould not profit by them. And for the same cause he refused to reason Ioan. 24. or argue vvith Pilate about his owne cause, vvhen he Ioan. 18.

gaue

gaue him occasion. For that he knew his affections to be so tied to the vvorld, and himselfe so addicted to please the people and to gayne the good will of Tiberius the Emperour, as his labor vvould be but lost in seeking to persuade him, being so obstinatly disposed otherwise. And thus much of this third point of pious affection; and the necessity therof to a mans saluation, seeing that, vvithout this all other trauaile and endeuor is desperat.

The fourth point of this consideratiō vvhether some articles of our faith may be demonstrated & hovv.

34. The fourth and last point of this consideration is, that though it be true vvhich is sett downe in the first point of these foure, to vvit, that ordinarily and for the most part the obiecte or articles of our faith are aboue reach of mans reason, and vvere first reuealed to man from God himselfe: yet some points therof there be also, vvhich by force of humayne reason may be knowne and demonstrated. As for example that there is a God, and that he is but one, and can not be many, and that the vvorld vvas made by him, and that he hath prouidence ouer the same, and other such like points. VVhich points and articles notvvithstandinge, for that on the other side, they are proposed also in the scriptures, and in the Nicene Creede, as articles of our faith, that must be beleeued by Christians, as reuealed from God: hence riseth no small question among schoole diuines, vvhether these points heere sett downe, may be knowne by two distinct vvayes or no, to vvit, euidently, by force of humayne reason or demonstration, and ineuidently, by light of faith, and reuelation from God. And the more common and probable opinion

Exod. 20.
Heb 11.
Simbol.
Nicæn.

About the argument of this booke.

opinion of schoolemen and more conformable to the scriptures and ancient fathers is, that they may. For that our vnderstandinge may haue tvvo lights to know one and the selfe same thing. The first by reuelation from God, vvhich allvvayes is vvith some darknes and obscurity to our reason (as before hath byn declared) and consequently our iudgment being not forced to yeld thervnto by the cleernesse of euidency, it followeth that our assent by faith is more free, and greater place is giuen to pious affection of our vvill, and therby also more merit to assent, as before hath byn shewed.

35.   The second light may be by force of mans reason and euidency of demonstration, which sometymes is so cleere in it selfe, as it admitteth no doubt at all. As vvhen vve shew this principle, that euery vvhole is greater then his part, or that man is a reasonable creature, or like euident things. And then is our vnderstanding forced to yeld thervnto, and consequently hath so much the lesse merit, by hovv much lesse freedome it leaueth to our vvill and affection to giue our assent, or no. But yet this knovvlege gotten by humayne reason doth not so take away the merit of the other, that proceeded of free assent of faith, but that both may stand together in one & the selfe same man, about one & the selfe same thing, (to vvit faith, and demonstration) as distinct lights gotten by different and distinct meanes, the one by reuelation from God, the other by demonstration of reason. For that otherwise, this great inconuenience (say the authors that hold this opinion) vvould follovv

that

Alex. Halens. 3.
par. q. 79.
Alb. Mag.
in 3. p. d.
24. art. 9.
Altisidior.
3. P. tract.
3. cap. 1.
Bonau. in
3. p. d. 24.
art. 2.
Durand
in nu. 39.
& alij.

Hovv
science
may
stand
vvith
faith.

that learned men should be in farre vvoorse case for

A great inconuenience.

their merit in faith, then the ignorant. For that vvhensoeuer the said lerned men do come by meanes of their studie to see cleerly by reason the truth of any conclusion of diuinity or article of beleefe, vvhich simply before they did beleeue only, as reuealed from God, (vvhich thing may very vvell happen, and doth often to lerned men:) that then they should leese their former faith, or at least vvise the merit therof, if it be graunted that faith and science may in no case stand together.

36. *But to leaue this to be disputed in schooles, and to returne to our purpose; there is no doubt, but that some points belonging to Christian faith, may plainly and absolutely be demonstrated, and prooued most cleerly by humaine reason & science. As those which I haue here touched of one God, his omnipotency,*

Demonstration by supposition.

prouidence, and the like. Some other there be, which though they can not be altogether so absolutely conuinced by demonstrations; yet may they in part, by vvay of supposition; that is to say, by supposinge some one or two points belonging thervnto, vvhich the aduersary vvill either graunt or can not deny. As for example, supposing there is a God, and that he hath appointed any religion to mankind, and that the prophets, and prophesies of the old testament are to be beleeued: it is not hard to prooue and demonstrate the verity of Christian religion against either Iewe or gentile. And the like is it in this matter here treated by me in this booke against Iohn Fox & his fellowes, about the beginning, planting, growinge, and conti-

nuance

tinuance of Catholike Religion. For if yow suppose only that Chrift is God, and that he hath appointed any Religion at all, and that the firft Religion and Church inftituted by him, vvas true and truly ment by him, and that he vvas able to performe his promises made to thofe firft Chriftians, or the preferuation and perpetuity therof; This (I fay) being graunted and fuppofed, the reft that I do inferre in this treatife, followeth by neceffary confequence of morall demonftration. As by viewing it ouer yew vvill fee, vvhervnto I remitte me.

37. *Thefe foure points then, I thought good (gentle reader) to touch briefly in this preface, meaning to make 4. feuerall inferences out of the fame, not vnproffitable (in myne opinion) to the purpofe wee haue in hand. For out of the firft point concerning the height and fublimity of matters of our faith aboue the capacity of mans reafon, I make this inference: that euery one ought to come to treate and talke of fuch things, as belong to faith and beleefe, vvith great reuerence, refpeΔ, modefty and fubmiffion of mind, not condemning that, vvhich his fenfe, or reafon, reacheth not vnto; nor making the depth of his owne capacity the rule and meafure of his beleefe. A thing noted in the feΔ of Manichyes by Saint Auften. VVho vvriteth, that for this caufe principally he was 9. yeares of their company: for that they told him ftill (he being a young man defirous of knowlege) that Catholiques did fuperfticioufly require faith before reafon, and that they (the Manichyes forfooth) did teach nothing but that, vvhich fhould*

The inference of the firft point.

Aug. l. de vtil.cred. cap. 1.

✱ ✱ ✱ ✱   *cleerly*

cleerly be discussed by force of good argument and
reason, before it was beleeued, &c. Vpon which
occasion also the said father wrote that excellent
booke before mentioned de vtilitate credendi, of
the great vtility and infinit commodities which Catholike Christian people haue, in beleeuing simply by
tradition of their ancestors, that faith which is established in the vniuersall Church of Christ; though
their owne reason arriue not to penetrate the same.
For that whosoeuer openeth once his eares (especially the vnlerneder sort) to harken to humaine
reasons against the misteryes of their faith, he is in
danger presently either to leese his faith, or at least-
wise the merit therof, together with the peace, comfort, and tranquillity of his mynd: and therby openeth a wyde gappe to the diuell and all his instru-
ments, as well infidells as heretiks, to enter in and
trouble the house of his conscience.

38. And as for heretiques it hath byn an old practise, to trouble or draw men from Cath. Religion, or
make them stagger by this meanes of pretending
humaine reason against beleefe. As wee haue shewed
by example of the Manichees, who tooke this trick
from the old heathen philosophers, whome S. Hierome for this cause principally calleth the patriarks
of heretiques. The Arrians also deceaued many by
this triks of humaine reason, drawing out their nap-
kins (as Theodoretus saith) and asking the common people whether three corners therof could be
one or no? and then inferring deceitfully thervpon,
said, no more could three persons be one God. The
Saduces

Marginal notes:

S. Augu-
stins
booke
de vtili-
tate cre-
dendi
what it
treateth
and why
it was
written.

Hier. l. 2.
con. Ruf-
finum.

About the Argument of this booke.

Saduces founded their herefie against the refurre-
ction of the flesh vpon the contrariety it feemed to
haue vvith humaine reafon. VVhich preuailed after-
wards with diuerfe forts of heretiques, that had in-
finite followers, as Simon Magus, Bafilides,
Hymenæus, Philetus, Valentinus, Marcion,
Apelles, the Ophites, Cerdoniftes, Cainites,
Albigenfes, *and others. And now in our dayes*
with Zwinglians, Caluiniftes, Anabaptiftes, Trini-
tarians, Family of loue, Browniftes and diuerfe
other fects, who do nothing but raue and blafpheme
againft the reall prefence of Chrift in the bleffed Sa-
crament; vpon the fame ground, that it feemeth con-
trary to fenfe and humaine reafon. And finally this is
a way to all mifbeleefe, atheifme, and infidelity, &c.

Many herefies founded in reafon againft faith.

39. *Out of the fecond point concerning arguments*
of credibility for our beleefe, my inference is: that
(feeing God hath left vs fuch ftore and variety of
arguments for our comfort and confolation in that
wee beleeue) euery man ought to be diligent and
carefull to feeke out and vfe the fame, and not fuffer
himfelfe to be ouerborne by deceitfull quarrelling
people, in a fute of fo great importance, as this is,
without looking vpon his writings and euidences,
that he hath for the fame. For hovv greatly
vvould vve condemne the flouth and negligence of
fuch a man, as defcending for many ages, as lawfull
heire from a moft ancient and noble houfe of
great riches and poffeffions, and feeing falfe pre-
tenders to make clayme thervnto, and by fleight and
intrufion to put both him and his pofterity from the

The inference vpon the fecond point about arguments of credibility. Intollerable flouth & negligence in not vieuing our euidencies for Cath. religion.

* * * * 2 *fame,*

same, how much (I say) shoulde we condemne him, if (hauing vvhole chests full of vvritings for his defence) he should neuer so much as looke them ouer, or take suruewe of them ; but should suffer himselfe to be cast and ouerthrowne in the vvhole sute, vvithout pleading at all for himselfe or his interest? which is the very case of many negligent Christian men in our dayes, vvho seeing so many assaultes to be made by different sectaries against the old possession of Catholike Religion (vvhich vvas their ancesters inheritance to saluation, and must be theirs if euer they be saued) do yeeld notwithstanding so dastardly in this conflict and iniury offred them, as they neuer somuch as examine, vvhat proofes or euidences they haue or may haue for their defence! A necligence no doubt inexcusable, and vvorthy of infinite rebuke and confusion.

The inference vpon the third point about pious affection

40.　*Out of the third point concerning the necessity of pious affection in him, that must profit by theise arguments of credibility: I do inferre, how highly it doth import euery man, that meaneth seriously to treat of his saluation in this behalfe, to dispossesse himselfe of his passions and sinister affections against the truth (At least vvayes vvhile he treateth this great affaire) and that he place himselfe in such an indifferency, equanimity, and serenity of mynd, as he may be able to discerne and looke vpon the truth vvith an vnpassionat eye, if she chance to appeare vnto him.*

A dredfull threat of our Sauiour.

41.　*The saying of our Sauiour in the place before alleaged of S. Iohns ghospell, to such as were ambitious*

tious

tion and intangled vvith the vvelth and honor of this world, and therby letted to beleeue the truth, is terrible and dreadfull. For hauing demaunded, how it vvas poßible for them to beleeue, and therby come to saluation, that vvere so intangled and euill affected in mind: he addeth presently. Nolite putare, quia ego accusaturus sim vos apud Patrem : est qui accusat vos. *Do not yow thinke that I shall haue need to accuse yow to my father (for theise corrupt affections of yours rising of ambition). for there vvanteth not one to accuse yow.* VVherby Christ insinuateth amongs other things, that himselfe at the day of iudgement vvas not to be accuser, but iudge: and that the condemnation of theise men vvas to be most greeuous, vvho for ambition, honour, vvelth, dignityes, and promotions, had nether tyme nor vvill to attend to matters of faith and true religion, vvherby only eternall saluation may be atchieued. VVhich is a point greatly to be considered and borne in mynd; especially by such, vvho are in the same or like case vvith those men of Iewry, to whome Christ our Sauiour vsed that dreadfull speeche.

Ioan. 5.

42. Out of the fourth and last point is inferred, that considering all the premisses, and that this matter of true religion is of so great moment, as hath byn shewed, and that in this treatise so short and cleere a vvay is taken for discußion therof, as by only ioyning issue about the planting, continuance, succeßion, and descent of Christian religion in England from the Apostles tyme vnto ours; the vvhole controuersie betweene vs and the protestants may fully be

The inference vpon the 4. point about demonstration by reason.

* * * * 3   cleered,

The Preface to the Reader

cleered. And that vvith such euidency of reason and neceſſary consequence; as suppoſing only, that Chriſt vvas Chriſt, and his promiſes true: all the reſt doth fo low by moſt certaine ſequele of argument, and moral demonſtration. Al this (I ſay) being ſo, it may encourrage and animate the ſtudious reader to runne ouer this ſhort treatiſe. VVhich if he do vvith that indifferency and attention, vvhich in the ſecond and third point of this diſcourſe haue byn touched; I do not doubt, but that he ſhall not need to read many other bookes for reſoluing himſelfe either about the grounded certaine truth of Catholike Religion, or the variety, vanity, inconſtancy, lightneſſe, and folly, of all ſects and hereſies, that euer haue or ſhall ariſe vp againſt the ſame. And vvith this (good Reader) I leaue the to the holy protection and benediction of almighty God, and to his merciful direction of thee, in this ſo vvaighty affaire. This vigil of the natiuity of our Sauiour. 1602.

Faults

Faults escaped in the printing.

Vouchsafe gentell Reader of thie curtesie , where in manie places of this booke , after the page 555. thou shalt find printed Cramner, *to amend for it* Cranmer. *Other greater faults whe haue heere noted, to be corrected by thy selfe , before thou peruse this woorke.*

P*Reface num.* 26. O. E. *this matter,* Reade O. E. vvhere this.

Pag. 89. *num.* 15. *make* 102. R. make 202. *ibid. who did.* R vvho died.

Pag. 107. *num.* 12. *permised,* R. promised.

Pag. 179. *num.* 7. *Epifcopo,* R. Epifcopos.

Pag. 197. *num.* 11. *canonizized,* R. canonized.

Pag. 284. *num.* 9. *English story,* R. English hyre.

Pag. 413. *num.* 13. *and Heliodorus,* R. ad Heliodorum.

Pag. 535. *num.* 27 *Iohn Fas,* R. Iohn Fox.

Pag. 541. *nu.* 34. *from to that daie,* R. from Chrift to that.

Pag. 558. *num.* 15. *that farre,* R. that none.

Pag. 576 *num.* 32. *taken flew,* R. taken flesh.

Pag. 582. *num.* 3. *who ioyning,* R. vvho ioyned.

THE

THE
FIRST PART
OF THIS PRESENT
TREATISE,
CONCERNINGE
THREE CONVERSIONS
OF OVR LAND,
to Chriſtian Catholique, Romane
Religion.

THE ARGVMENT.

 *HE purpoſe of this firſt part (gentle
Reader) is to declare by euident de-
monſtration, both of hiſtories, reaſons,
antiquities, and ſucceſſion of tymes,
and by confeſſion and other teſtimo-
nies of the aduerſaries them ſelues, that this our Ile of
England & people therof, the* Britans, Saxons, *&*
English *haue at three ſeuerall tymes receiued Chriſtian faith from Rome, and by Romish preachers. Firſt,
vnder the* Apoſtles, *in the firſt age after Chriſt,
and then vnder* Pope Eleutherius *in the ſecond
age, and thirdly vnder* Pope Gregory *in the beginning of the ſixth age, and that this faith and religion vvas no other then the Roman Cath. Faith generally receiued ouer all Chriſtendome in thoſe dayes,
and that it vvas one and the ſelfe ſame faith, at all*

A *theſe*

*theſe three tymes and that the ſame vvas continued
and profeſſed aftervvard in England publikely for
almoſt* 1400. *yeares togeather, to vvit from the A-
poſtles dayes vnto the raigne of* K. Henry *the* 8. *vnder diuers nations ſtates gouernments and variety of
tymes by Brittans, Saxons, Danes, Normans and Engliſh, and that the ſelfe ſame faith continueth at this
day in the Curch of* Rome *and Chriſtian Catholique
vvorld abroad, vvithout change or alteration of any
one ſubſtantiall Article or point of beleeſe. And that
all cauills & calumniations of heretiks and ſectaryes
in this behalfe are vayne and fooliſh, and moſt manifeſtly heere confuted. And finally a moſt cleere, eaſy,
euident, and infallible deduction viſible to the eye and
vnderſtanding of euery meane intelligent* Reader, *is
ſet dovvne and brought from hand to hand vvithout interruption from the firſt conuerſions of our
Realme vnto this day, and this ſo perſpicuouſly, as no
man, that vvill not vvilfully ſhutt his eyes, can but
ſee and behould the ſame, as by the* Chapters *follovving (God vvilling)more particularly ſhall appeare.*

WHETHER ENGLAND AND
ENGLISHMEN HAVE PARTI-
cular obligations to the Sea of Rome, *aboue other
nations; and of the firſt conuerſion of* Brittans *to
Chriſtian Religion in tyme of the Apoſtles.*

CHAP. I.

Taken
out of
the 4.
chapter

AFTER a certaine narration made
by me in my anſwere to Syr Francis
Haſtings about the 7. Encounter betwene
him

him & N.D. wherin I declared what reuerend respect other nations and Kingdomes
of the Christian world haue euer borne
to the Sea Apostolike and Bishop therof, vntill this miserable age of hereticall
spirits, who ridiculously do hold the same
to be Antichrist: I do inferre the conclusion
and comparison following about the particular obligacion of Englishmē towards the
same Sea and Bishop, aboue many other
Kingdomes, saying in my wardward thus.

2.   And yf all Christian nations haue and
ought to beare such reuerence and respect
to the Sea of Rome, then much more our
little Iland of England (as this man calleth
it) for that it hath receyued more singular
benefits from thence, then any one nation
in the world besides, hauing byn twise conuerted from paganisme to Christian religion, by the especiall diligence, labour and
industry of the same Sea. Once in the tyme
of the Britannes, about a hundred and eighty yeares after Christ, at what tyme Eleutherius that holy Pope and martyr conuerted K. *Lucius* and his subiects by the preaching of *S. Damianus* and his fellowes sent
from Rome to that effect. And the second
tyme 400. yeares after that againe when
our predecessors the English Saxons were
conuerted by S. Augustine and his fellow
preacheres, sent by S. Gregory the great

A 2   then

of the 7.
encoun-
ter.

VVard.
*pag.*103.
,,
The par
ticular
obliga-
cion of
Englifh-
men to-
vvards
the B. of
Rome.
,,
,,
,,
,,
,,
Bed. lib.
1 *histor.*
Ang. ca.
17. 18.
etc.

Guiliel.
Malmef-
bur. lib.
1.hiftor.
Angl. &
Pont. An
glor. lib.
1.cap.1.
then Bishop of Rome to the fame end. And
if it be moft certaine & cannot be denyed,
that thefe two fo great and vniuerfall benefits rightly confidered, are the higheft vnder
heauen, that our land could receiue from
any mortall men, and that the obligation of
this double fpirituall byrth of ours is fo
>> much greater, then the band we owe to
>> our carnall parēts, by how much more wei-
>> ghty and importāt is our eternall faluation,
>> then our temporall lyfe and generation : let
>> all men confider the barbarous ingratitude
>> of this man, that barketh with fuch fpite
>> againft the Sea of Rome, the mother of our
>> Chriftianity, and againft her Bifhoppes the
>> workers, of fo high a blefsing to vs. And
>> with this confideration I leaue the modeft
>> and difcreet readers to iudg of the matter, as
>> reafon and religion fhall induce them, and
>> not as the rage of this and other fuch ra-
>> vinge people would incite them.

3.   Thus wrote I then, and to this declaration and conclufion of myne our Knight
taketh vpon him now to anfwere in thefe
VVaft.
pag. 192.
An im-
pertinēt
and ca-
villing
anfvver
of the
Knight.
words : *VVheras this Roman aduocate fayth, that
this land ought to beare more reuerence to the Sea
of Rome, then other nations, for that it hath receiued
more fingular benefits from thence, namely that itvvas
conuerted from paganifme to Chriftian religion by
the fpeciall diligence, labour and induftry of the fame
Sea, I anfvvere firft, that it is apparant by fundry te-
ftimo-*

ſtimonyes, that this land vvas conuerted to the faith long before that tyme by yovv ſpecified, and not by the Biſhopp of Rome. Gildas teſtifieth that Britanny receyued the ghoſpell in the tyme of Tiberius the Emperour, and that Ioſeph of Arimathia vvas ſent by Phillipp the Apoſtle from France hither, vvhere he remayned till his death. And Bede (our countryman likevviſe) doth teſtifie, that in his tyme this land kept Eaſter after the manner of the Eaſt Church`, by vvhich may be gathered, that the firſt preachers came hither from the eaſtparts of the vvorld and not from Rome. More proofes might be ſett dovvne, but I ſpare them.

4. Marke (good reader) what manner of anſwere this is to my former ſpeech, & how directly theſe people do go to the matter. I ſaid before, that the Ile of England wherin ſo many at this day do rayle againſt Rome, hath more obligation of loue towards the ſame for benefitts receiued, then diuers other countryes. For that the people of this Iland haue byn twiſe couerted by men ſent from thence, once vnder Pope *Eleutherius*, almoſt 200. yeares after Chriſt, and againe vnder Pope *Gregory* the great about the yeare of our lord 600. Now to this the Kᵗ. thinketh to haue anſwered well by affirming two or three things : firſt out of Gildas, *that Britany receyued the ghoſpell in the tyme of Tyberius the Emperour,* before any of theſe two conuerſions named by me. Which how likely it is,

A 3 (Tibe-

(Tiberius living but 5. yeares after Chriſts
Aſcenſion) ſhall after be examined. Secŏdly,
that *Ioſeph of Arimathia* was ſent by Philip the
Apoſtle out of France into Britany, which
yet the true Gyldas hath not; but by theſe
two examples the Kt. would ſhew, that in
Britany the faith of Chriſt was not firſt of
all planted from Rome nor by the Popes
therof, or by their induſtry. And to the ſame
effect he alleageth out of Bede, *the vſe of obſer-*
ving Eaſter after the manner of the Eaſt church re-
mayning amongſt the Brytans in his tyme. Wherof
he inferreth as yow ſee, *that it is moſt like, that*
our firſt preachers vvere from the eaſt, and not from
the vveſt Church.

5.   But ſuppoſe all theſe things were true,
do they ouerthrow that which I ſaid before
in my wardword, that the Britãs were conuerted vnder *Pope Eleutherius.* or the Saxons
vnder Pope Gregory, and by ſeuerall preachers ſent from Rome by them? They
proove ónly that before theſe two publike
conuerſions, which we owe to the Church,
and Popes of Rome, there might be ſome
ſparkles of chriſtian faith alſo in Britany by
other meanes; which I neuer denyed, but
only ſayde that I would haue Ingliſhmen
gratefull to Rome for theſe two: Which
conuerſions noe man can deny without
apparant impudency, as after more amply
ſhalbe ſhewed, where alſo theſe examples
alleaged

How
imperti-
nent the
anſvvere
of the
Knight
is.

alleaged out of Gildas and S. Bede fhalbe examined, how farre they are true, or doe make for the purpofe heere in hand.

6. So that this firſt part of Sʳ. Francis anſwere being nothing to the purpoſe, as yow ſee, though all were graunted, which he alleadgeth: let vs heare his ſecond part. *Secondly* (faith he) *though it be graunted that Eleutherius ſendinghither preachers from Rome in K. Lucius his tyme did firſt conuert this land to the Chriſtian faith,* ★ *I ſay that there is not novv the ſame faith in Rome, that vvas then: There vvas then no maſſes ſaid, no ſetting vp of Images in Churches, &c.* Here now, yf we willtake Sr. F. word, we haue a ſhure warrant by his *(I ſay)* that the faith in Rome is not the ſame now, that it was in *Pope Eleutherius* his tyme. And that in particular, *there vvere nether maſſes then, nor images.* Wherin yow may note firſt, that cunningly he holdeth his peace of the cōuerſion of Englishmen vnder S. Gregory (which moſt concerneth vs, that be of that nation) for that he dareth not deny, but that both maſſe and images were in vſe in his tyme, in the Roman Church and faith. And ſo brought into England by S. Auguſtine that conuerted vs. Which is euident in S. Bede in euery place of his ſtory and particularly, where he relateth the firſt entraunce of S. Auſten and his felowes into Canterburrye in proceſſion with a croſſe and image of our Sauiour in a

★ I ſay.

Bed. lib. 1. hiſt. Angl. c. 34.

A 4   banner,

banner, and that they saide then firſt maſſes
there in an old church of S. Martin builded,
as he ſayth, by the old Chriſtian Romanes
before their departure out of Britannye.

7.   And for the tyme of Eleutherius vnder whome the Brytanes were conuerted,
though it were not hard alſo to prouè the
ſame particulars: yet wil I not take that diſputation now in hand, but ſhall leaue it to
a better occaſion afterward in this treatiſe,
where without ſtanding vpon theſe particular two doctrines of maſſe, and images,
heere mentioned by the Kt. I ſhall ſhew

The faith of Rome one and the same vnder Pope Eleutherius, Pope Gregor. and Pope Clemét the 8.

more generall & firme arguments that the
faith of the Church of Rome vnder *Eleuthe-*
rius 200. yeares after Chriſt, was the very
ſame and no other then was that, vnder *S.*
Gregory 400. yeares after, that againe nor this
vnder *Gregory*, differét from that, which now
is in Rome vnder *Clement* the 8. a thouſand
yeares after *Gregory*, and ſhall indure to the
worldes end.

8.   This (I ſay) we ſhall demonſtrate afterward moſt cleerely. But yet to the end the
Reader may ſee in the meane ſpace how
much creditt is to be giuen to this Knights

Maſſe cófeſſed in the 2. age after Chriſt.

(*I ſay*) let him read but the 4. Chapter of
his good maiſters and cheefe hiſtoricall Doctors the Magdeburgians, touching the ſecond age of Chriſt, wherin Eleutherius liued towards the end: as alſo the beginning
                                    of the

of the third age immediately enfuinge : and
he fhal find, that in the fecond age, vnder
their ordinary title of *Inclinatio doctrina com-*
plectens ftipulas & errores doctorum, that is to
fay: The falling away of Chriftian doctrine
conteyning the ftubble and errors of doctors, they reprehend *Ignatius*, who was
S. Iohn Euangelifts fchoiler for vfing the
phrafe: *Offerre & facrificium immolare.* to offer
and make facrifice. As alfo the holy martyr
Irenaus for faying; *that Chrift had taught a nevv*
oblation in the nevv teftament, vvhich the Church re-
ceiving from the Apoftles, doth offer vp throughout
all the vvorld, &c. And in the third age they
accufe that bleffed bifhopp and martyr *S.*
Cyprian of fuperftition for fayinge: *Sacerdote*
vice Chrifti fungi, & Deo Patri facrificium offer-
re. That the prieft fupplying the place of
Chrift doth offer facrifice to God the father.
They reprehend alfo *Tertullian* for vfing the
phrafe, *Sacrificium offerre*, To offer facrifice.
They condemne alfo *Saint Martiall* fcholler
of the Apoftles them felues for faying: *Sacri-*
ficium Deo creatori offertur in ara: facrifice is offered to God our creator vpon the altar a-
mong Chriftians.

9.   So that, yf by our maffe Catholiks vnderftand no other thing, but the publike externall facrifice appointed by Chrift in his
Church, as we do not: then may we fee,
that by confeffion of the Magdeburgians

A 5   them

Magde-
burg. cët.
2. & 3.
cap. 4. de
doct.
Ignatius
epift. ad
Smyrnës.

Iren. lib.
4. ca. 32.

Cyprian.
lib. 2. ep.
3.

Tertul.
lib. de
cœna
Domini.
Martial.
in ep. ad
Burde-
gal.

them ſelues, this maſſe was as vvell in vſe in
Eleutherius his tyme , as in tyme of Gregory the firſt after him. And the like might we
ſhew about the vſe of images , but that it
were ouer long for this place: our intention
being to treate only of the conuerſion of
our Countrey to Chriſtian religion , and to
note by the way, which is moſt to be credited by a diſcreet man , eyther the, I *ſay*, of a
courtly Knight , affirming that maſſe was
not in the tyme of *Eleutherius* ; or the teſtimonyes of ſo many graue and Learned fathers to the contrary, that lived in the ſame
age,to witt *Ignatius* , *Martiall*, *Irenæus* , *Tertullian*, *Cyprian*, and others.

S. Fran-
ces *I ſay*
reuerted

10. And this being ſufficiēt for refutation
of both parts of Syr F. idle reply, I ſhall
go forwards to diſcuſſe a little the firſt entrance of Chriſtian faith into Englād, how,
and in what tyme,and by whom it is likely
that it might be donne before the dayes of
Eleutherius : & whether this firſt conuerſion of ſowing the faith in our Iland may
be aſcribed alſo to Rome , as well as the o-
ther more publicke conuerſions afterward.
Which if it fall out to be ſo , then hath the
Knight in ſteed of diminiſhing our obligation to Rome , not a little encreaſed the
ſame by mentioning alſo a third conuerſion
from that Sea, which I for breuities ſake
and for that it was leſſe notoriuſly knowen,
                                          then

then the other two, thought good to pre-
termittin my wardword : But now being
mooued thervnto by S^r. Francis, who figh-
teth mightely for the moſt part againſt him
ſelfe, alleadging matters that make for vs,
I ſhall now briefely diſcuſſe more in particular this affaire.

11.   Firſt then, no man can deny, but that
the death Reſurrection and Aſcenſion of
our Sauiour, the comming of the holy ghoſt
vpon the Apoſtles, and ther beginning of
preaching preſently vpon the ſame, was in
the 18. yeare of *Tiberius* the third Emperour
of Rome. Who liuing fiue yeares after and
Caius Caligula other foure, there entred *Clau-*
dius, who raigned fourteene yeares, and *Ne-*
ro after him as many, who in the laſt yeare
of his raigne put to death *S. Peter* & *S.Paul,*
S.Peter hauing commen to Rome according
to *Euſebius* in the ſecond yeare of *Claudius,*
which was eleuen yeares after the reſurrection of Chriſt, though ſome other authors
differ in that accompt. *Euſebius* his words
tranſlated out of Greeke by S. Hierome are
theſe: *Petrus Apoſtolus natione Galilæus, Chriſtia-*
norum Pontifex primus, &c. Peter the Apoſtle
of the contrey of Galeley, the firſt chief bi-
ſhoppof Chriſtians, after he had founded
the Church of *Antioche* went to *Rome,* & hauing preached there the goſpell remained
biſhopp of the ſame Citty for 25. yeares togeather,

The be-
ginning
of prea-
cuing
the Chri
ſtiā faith
and pro-
greſſe
therof.

Euſeb. in
Chron.
an.Chri-
ſti 44.
,,
,,
,,
,,
,,
,,

geather,&c. S. Paul was sent thither prisoner by *Festus* , gouernour of *Iudæa,* in the 2. yeare of *Nero* his raine, that is 14. yeares after

Euseb. in Chron. Bedalib. 1. histor. Ang.c.3.

S. Peter, according to the same Eusebius.

12.   The next yeare after S. Peter came to Rome, which was the 3. yeare of *Claudius* his raigne , there began to be such warre in Britany, as the Emperour him selfe resolued in person to goe thither , and so he did whith admiration of the whole world. And

The first entrance of Christiã faith into Britany.

if there were any Christians in Rome at that tyme, as yt is likely there were , (the Christian faith , hauing byn now preached in the world some dozen yeares after Christes ascension,) it is very probable that some went with him into Britany : and that this was the first sparkle of planting Christian faith and religion in those contreyes , but much more afterward as their number increased, being that this warre continued for forty yeares togeather , that is to say to the fourth yeare of *Domitian* , when as well externe histories as our William of Malmesbury (to omitt other heathen wryters) doth teach, *that Britany was wholy subdued & brought into a perfect forme of Prouince.* And in this tyme there being continuall going and comming from Rome to Britany, and Christian religion euery day encreasing in Rome : the same could not chuse but be kindled also in Britany, especially for two or three considera-

Malm. in Fastis. anno ab vrbe cõdita 838. Christi 86.

derations. Firſt, for that there were many
Brittans inhabiting in Rome at that day,
ſome for hoſtages, ſome for their owne
pleaſures, therby to fly the warres & vnquiet
ſtate of their ovvne countrey, others taken
and carried by force as ＊ *Caractacus Sylurum*
Rex, Caractacus King of the Sylures, vvho
inhabited that part of Britany, which at
this day we call South-wales, vvho being
taken was ſent to Rome by *Oſtorius* gouernour of that countrey for *Claudius* the Emperour, in the 11. yeare of his Empire, and
much nobility with him, as *Tacitus* in his
ſtory doth relate.

Reaſons of the repaire of Chriſtians to Britany vnder Claudius.

＊ Corn. Tacit. li. 12. Ann.

13. Some alſo both Romans and of other
nations being Chriſtened and flying the
perſecution, which was in Rome againſt ſuch
men, eſpecially vnder *Nero,* gott themſelues
into Britany, as a place of more liberty and
leſſe ſubiect to examinations in ſuch matters, by reaſon of the warres and tumults
there. And this is conforme to that which
Gildas the ancient Britane writeth in his
complaint of the ouerthrovv of Britany.
Where hauing declared the extreme calamity come vpon his contreymen by that
warre and victory of the Romans againſt
them vnder *Claudius,* addeth preſently theſe
words: *Interea glaciali frigore rigenti inſulæ, &c.*
In the meane ſpace, while theſe vvarres laſted, there appeared and imparted it ſelfe to
　　　　　　　　　　　　　　　　　　　this

Gild. de excidio Britan. cap. 6.

,,
,,

" this cold Iland (remoued further of from
" the vifible funne, then other contreyes) that
" true and inuifible funne, which in the tyme
" of *Tiberius Cæfar* had fhewed it felfe to the
" whole world, I meane Chrift vouchfafed
" to impart his precepts, &c.

14.   This is the fomme and true fenfe of
his fentence, though the words be fomwhat
intricate, and his ftile obfcure. Which Syr
Francis vnderftanding not, citeth this place

Gildas   of *Gildas* (as before you haue heard) to
mifun-   proue that Britany receiued the ghofpell
derftoode vnder *Tyberius Cæfar*.which he faith not, nor
by Syr   is not likely (as before hath byn declared)
Francis.   both in refpect of the fmall tyme, which
Tyberius liued after the Apoftles began to
preach, as alfo for that in thofe dayes there
was noe warre in Britany, wherof Gildas
fpeaketh immediatly before.

15.   And thus much of the tyme and occafion, wherby Chriftian religion beganne
firft in Britany, within the firft 50. yeares

Niceph.   after Chriftes afcénfion, wherto alfo we
l. 3. hift. may adde the teftimony of *Nicephorus*, and
cap. 1.   before him of Theodoretus and Sophro-
Theod.   nius, ancient wryters, who do teftifie that
lib. 9. de *Britanniæ infula, &c.* the *Britan Ilands fell in di-*
curandis   *uifion among the Apoftles in their firft partition,*
Græc.af-   *vvhich they made of the vvorld*. And it is moft
fectib.   like that S. Peter being come to Rome to
Sophron.   teache and conuert the wefternparts of
in Cata-
log.   the

the worlde as Italy, Spaine and France by
name, thefe Ilands allfo receiued the fame
benefitt from him. And fo fay oure authors
whome afterwards I fhall alleadg for his
being in Britany.

16.   And this is another point of obligation betwixt England and Rome, (if Sr. F.
can be content to heare it) to wytt that the
firft B. of Rome went in perfon to conuert
our Countrey, as afterward wee fhall heare
graue authors affirme, to whome I remitt
me. Though who indeed were the very firft
teachers in Britany and preachers in particular or helpers thervnto is not fo certayne:
our auncient hiftoriographers by reafon of
the variety of tymes and our countreyes
calamityes hauing left noe cleere teftimony therof. True it is, that our later
wryters of the Englifh nation, namely *Ho-* *Holinſh.*
linshed and *Cambden*, do affirme, that one *in de-*
Claudia Ruffina à noble Brittish lady liuing *ſcript.*
then in Rome and being the wife as they *Britan.*
tom. I.
fay of one *Pudens* a Roman Senatour and *cap.* 9,
mother of the two famous Chriftian vir- *Cambd.*
gins *Praxedes*, and *Pudentiana*, did fend diuers *in ſua*
bookes and meffages vnto her friends in *Brit. p.*
Britany, and therby helped much to their *162.*
conuerfion. And this may appeare (fay they)
as well by the falutation fent from her by
S. Paules penne to *Timothe*, when he faid, *2. Tim. 4.*
Eubulus, Pudens, Linus, Claudia, and all the bre-
thren

The ſtо-
ry of
Claudia
Ruſſina
a Brit-
tiſh la-
dy.

thren do ſalute yovr. as alſo for that ſhe was
the firſt hoſteſſe or harberour both of S.Pe-
ter and ſaint Paul,at their coming to Rome;
it may be coniectured that ſhe was one of
the firſt Chriſtians of that citty. Wherof it
may be inferred, that if it be true that ſhe
ſent thoſe firſt meſſages, books or meſſen-
gers of Chriſtian knowledg into her countrey, ſhe was alſo the firſt, or one of the
firſt helpers to that conuerſion.

17.   But now the proofes of this matter
are not ſo ſtrong, as I could wiſh or deſire
for the honour of our countrey : but let vs
heare them,as they bee. Firſt the proofe that
ſhe was a Brittane, is by certaine verſes of
Martiall the Poet vvryten vnto her in his
epigrammes,thus:

Mart.li.
11.Epig.
35.

Claudia cæruleis cùm ſit Ruffina Britannis
     Edita,cur Latiæ pectora plebis habet?

Wheras Claudia Ruffina is borne of the
Britanes(that paint themſelues)how commeth it to paſſe, that ſhe hath gained ſo
much the good wills of the Italian people? And then he goeth forward to praiſe
her alſo for her beauty exceeding the beauty eyther of Italians or Grecians. He commendeth her beſides for three children
which ſhe had borne to her husband and
theſe children our men would interpret to
be the forſaid two virgins Praxedes and
Pudentiana togeather with *Nouatus* their
                                                    brother,

brother, all children of *Pudens* the Senatour
aboue named.

18.   But although I could wish much (as
I said) for the honour of our nation, that
this thing were true, especially her being
the wife to Pudens and mother of the for- *Argu-*
said children, that were all Saints: yet haue *ments*
I great arguments to the contrary. Wher- *the sto-*
of the first is the silence of all antiquity in *ry of*
this behalfe. *Martiall* also being a heathen,& *Claudia*
enemy to Christians; would hardly haue *Ruffina.*
commended her so much, and wrytten epigrammes to her of her rare beauty, if she
had bene a Christian, which was the most
odious thing that might be in those daies.
nor could she be so beautifull in his tyme,
liuing vnder *Vespasian* & *Titus* & dying vnder
Traian, duringe whose raigne, it appeareth
in *Martiall* that these verses were writen.
For so much as she must needs be very old
in those daies, seing that *Pudens* his house
placed *in decliuo montis Scauri*, in the side of *Baron.*
the hill called Scaurus, was the first by tra- *in mar-*
dition of all antiquitye that receyued Saint *tyr. ad*
Peter and afterward Saint Paul in Rome: *Maij.*
and is at this day a church dedicated to his
daughter *Saint Pudentiana*. And from the ar-
riuail of Saint Peter to Rome, vntill the
tyme of *Traian*, were almost 60. yeares. so
as if she were wife of *Pudens*, and mother of
those children, when Saint Peter came to

Rome, ſhe muſt needs be very aged, when Martiall wrote thoſe verſes of her beauty. Beſides this, our owne *Bede*, *Ado* Archbiſhopp of *Treuers*, *Vſuardus*, and other ancient authors in their martyrologes do aſſigne a nother wife vnto Pudens the Senatour, as mother to the forſaid 3. children, whoſe name was *Sabinella*; ſo that, though it be true, that there was ſuch a Brittiſh lady named *Claudia Ruffina* in Rome commended by Martiall for her beauty vnder *Traian*, and that S. Paul did commend a nother *Claudia* and *Pudens* for Chriſtian religion in his ſecond Epiſtle to *Timothe* (all which is ſufficiently proued:) yet, that this *Claudia Ruffina*, was the *Claudia* mentioned by Saint Paul, or that the ſame *Ruffina* was a Chriſtian, or wife to *Pudens*, or mother of *Praxedis* and *Pudentiana* (which are the principall points wherof the matter dependeth) this, I ſay, is not prooued nor any part therof, but only hudled vp by our later hereticall wryters vnder a ſhew of other profes, to witt, that there was ſuch a Claudia, that was of Britany, and another by S. Paul named; which are impertinent points to the principall, that ſhould haue byn prooued. And hereby we ſee that heretiks are but ſleight prouers and very deceytfull in all matters, as well hiſtoricall, as doctrinall.

Bed. Ado Vſuard. in martyr. ad 14. Cal. Iunij.

Points not proued in the ſtory of *Claudia Ruffina.*

19. Wherfore to lett this paſſe, & to ſpeake
of

of the firſt ecclefiaſticall teachers of Chriſtian religion in England, who through the
great perturbacion of warres (as hath byn
ſaid) were not ſo well knowne, nor diſtinctly obſerued, nor deliuered to writing in
thoſe dayes, as otherwiſe they might haue
byn: yet find I ſome mention (though diſperſed) of three ſeuerall Apoſtles of Chriſt
to haue preached there, to wit ſaint Peter,
ſaint Paul, and ſaint Symon of *Chananey* ſurnamed the Zealous. Two Apoſtolicall men
alſo in theſe firſt troubled times to haue byn
ſent thither : *Ariſtobolus* a Roman whome
S. Paul named in his Epiſtle to the Romans,
and Ioſeph of *Arimathia* a noble man of Iury that buryed Chriſt. Of all which fiue we
ſhall ſpeake ſomwhat in order.

The firſt preachers of Chriſtiã faith in Englãd.

20.   And firſt of Saint Peter him ſelfe to
haue byn in England (or Britany) & preached, founded churches, & ordained Prieſts
& Deacõs therin, is recorded out of Greeke
antiquities by *Symeon Metaphraſtes* a Grecian.
And it ſeemeth to be ſomewhat confirmed
by that which *Innocentius* I. Bishopp of
Rome hath left written aboue a thouſand
and two hundred yeares gone ſaying. *That*
the firſt churches of Italy, France, Spaine , Africa,
Sicilia, and the Ilands that ly betvvixt them, vvere
founded by ſaint Peter, or his ſchollers, or ſucceſſors.
For which cauſe *Gulielmus Eyſengrenius* in his
firſt Centuria or hundred yeares, doth write

Metaph. apud Su-riũ, die 23. Iunÿ pa. 862.

Innocẽt. epiſt. ad Decent.

B 2   alſo

Eyſeng.
cent. 1.
part. 7.
diſt. 8.
alſo; *That the firſt Chriſtian churches of Eng'and*
vvere founded by S. Peter vnder Nero. Whervnto it may be thought that the torſaid
Gildas had relation, when expoſtulating
with the Brytan Prieſts of his tyme for
their wickedneſſe (for which the wrath
of God had brought in the *Engliſh Saxons*
vpon them) he obiecteth among other

Gild. p.
1. ep. de
excid.
Brit.
things; *Quod ſedem Petri Apoſtoli inuerecundis*
pedibus vſurpaſſent. That they had vſurped the
ſeat of Saint Peter with vnshamfaſt feet:
meaning therby eyther the wholle church
of Britany firſt founded by him, or ſome particular place of deuotion or church which

Alred.
apud
Sur. 5.
Ian. pag.
131.
he had erected. And finally, *Alredus Rienuallus*
an Engliſh Abbot of the order of Cinterce
left wrytten about 500. yeares gone a certaine reuelation or apparition of S. Peter
to an holy man in the tyme of K. Edward
the confeſſor, ſhewing him how he had
preached him ſelfe in England, and conſequently the particular care he had of that
church and nation. &c.

21.   Yf any man aske, what tyme yt might

About
the time
that S.
Peter
vvęt in-
to Bri-
tany.
Act. 18.
be, that ſaint Peter left Rome and went
into Britany, and other contreyes round
about: Cardinall Baronius a famous learned hiſtoriogapher of our tyme, thinketh
that it was then, when Claudius the Emperour baniſhed all the Iewes out of Rome
(as in the acts of the Apoſtles it is recorded)
among

among whome it is like, that saint Peter *Baron.*
alfo, being by nation a Iew, retyred him- *to.1.An-*
felfe, and tooke that occafion to goe into *nal.pag.*
diuers pagan countreyes to preach the faith *512. an.*
of Chrift, that thing belonging efpecially to *Chrifti*
his charge as head of the Apoftles, accor- *58.*
ding to his owne words of himfelfe, *elegit* *Act.15.*
Deus per os meum, audire gentes verbum Euangelij
& credere. God hath chofen and appointed ,,
that gentiles fhall heare and beleeue the ,,
word of the ghofpel by my mouth. This ,,
then was the caufe why he was fo diligent
and carefull to goe & preach euery wheare
Chriftian religion, to the end he might ful-
fill and accomplish this will and ordination
of his maifter. And this was one caufe alfo
(to wit his abfence from Rome) why, according to *Baronius* and other learned men,
Saint Paul wryting to the Romans, did not
name or falute him in his epiftle, wherof
our heretiks doe brabble much. And thus
much of Saint Peter.

22. Of faint Paules being in Britany, there Of faint
are not fo many particular teftimonies. yet Paules
the forfaid *Theodoretus* doth affirme, that going into Bri-
from Rome he made certaine excurfions, tany.
in Hiſpanias & in Inſulas, quæ in mari iacent. Into *Theod.e-*
piſt.ad
Spaine & the Ilands lying in the fea neere *Tim. &*
about: & in an other place (as the ✶ Magde- *in pſ.116.*
burgians do cite him) he wryteth exprefly *lib. 9. de*
that Saint Paul preached to the Britans. *curand.*
græc. af.

B 3   And

Sophron.
ſerm. de
natal.
Apoſtol.

And the like hath *Sophronius* Bishop of Ieruſalem in his ſermon of the natiuitie of
the Apoſtles. *Venantius* alſo *Fortunatus* a moſt
learned & holy man, writing aboue 1000.
yeares agone of S. Paules peregrination,
ſaith thus.

Tranſit & Oceanum, vel qua ſacit inſula portum,
Quaſ̃q̃ Britannus habet terras, atq̃; vltima Thyle.

He paſt ouer the Ocean ſea to the ſland
that maketh a hauen on the other ſide, euen
to the lands which the Britans do poſſeſſe

Arnold.
Mirm.
in thea-
tro.

&c. For which reſpeȼt *Arnoldus Mirmannus* in
his Theater of the co̅uerſion of all nations,
affirmeth S. Paul to haue paſt to Britany
in the 4. yeare of *Nero* anno Domini 59. and
thére to haue preached, and afterward to
haue returned againe into Italy. And ſo
much of ſaint Paul. Whoe hauing 12. or 13.
yeares permitted him by Chriſt after his
comming to Rome, before his death, for
helping S. Peter and for aſſiſting the weſt
parts of the world, & Saint Peter him ſelfe
almoſt twiſe as much: it is not vnlike (their
zeale being conſidered & the ſtate of tymes
wayghed) but that they made many ex-
curſions, as the former authors do vvryte.
And thus much of them.

Of Sy-
mon the
zealous.
Nicep. li.
2. hiſtor.
cap. 40.

23.   For the preaching of the third Apoſtle
Symon Chananæus, ſurnamed the Zealous, vve
haue the teſtimony of *Nicephorus* out of
Greeke monuments, to vvhome agreeth

Doro-

Dorotheus a very auncient-vvryter, as alſo the
Greeke martyrologe, as teſtifieth *Baronius* in
his annotations vpon the Roman Martyrologe. And by this alſo vve ſee, that albeit
ſaint Peter had vndertaken to preache to
the vveſt part of the vvorld: yet did other
Apoſtles alſo help him therin, as ſaint Paul
in Italy and Spaine, and this *Symon* in Britany and other places, and *ſaint Philipp* in
France, &c.

*Dorot. in
Synopſ.
Baron.
ad diem
28. Octo-
bris,
Magdeb.
cent. 1.
lib. 2. c.
2.*

24. Of *Ariſtobolus* alſo ſaint Peters ſcholler do teſtifie in like manner the forſaid authors, *Mirmannus, Dorotheus, Baronius* out of the
Greeke Martyloge, that he was ſent by S.
Peter into Britany, and there made a Biſhopp. And that *Ariſtobolus* was a principall
knowne Chriſtian in Rome before ſaint
Paules arriuall there, it appeareth by the
epiſtle of the ſaid Apoſtle to the Romans,
where he ſaluteth him in theſe words. *Sa-
lute thoſe that be of the houſe of Ariſtobolus.* nor is
it read that euer this *Ariſtobolus* came baeke
from Britany to Italy againe. And this
of him.

Of Ari-
ſtobolus
his
being in
Britany.
*Mir. in
theatro
de couer.
gentium
pag. 43.
Dorot. in
Synopſ.
Baron.
ad diem
25. Mar-
tij.
Rom. 6.*

25. Of Ioſeph of *Arimathia* his comming
into France, and his ſending thence into
great Britany, eyther by ſaint Phillip (as
ſome ſay) who preached then in Gaule, or
(as others hold) by ſaint Peter himſelſe, as
he paſſed that way to and from Britany, &
how he obtained a place to exerciſe an ere-

Of Io-
ſeph of
Arima-
thia his
cōming
inro Bri
tany.

miticall life for him and his ten compagnions in the Iland called *Auallonia*, where *Glaſtenbury* after was builded : albeit I find no very certaine or auncient writer to affirme it, yet becauſe our later hiſtoriographers for two hundred yeares paſt or more do hold it to haue comen downe by tradition (and namely *Ioannes Capgrauius* a learned man of the order of ſaint Dominicke, and others after him) I do not meane to diſpute the matter heere, but rather to admire and prayſe the heauenly prouidence and goodneſſe of almighty God, who in theſe very firſt daies of his ghoſpell procured for ſo remote an Iland, ſo excellēt ſpirituall fathers, founders, and patrons, both of contemplatiue and actiue life in Chriſtian religion; the firſt foure, which I haue named, being all preachers : and this fifth hauing come out of Iury vnto *Marſilia* in France with *S. Mary Magdalen* and her company, and ſeene her extraordinary auſteritie of contemplatiue life and zeale of ſolitude, and doing pennance therin, he began that kind of life alſo in Britany, as our wryters do teſtifie, and namely Cambden among others doth obſerue. *Solitariam vitam amplexi ſunt, &c. vt ſeuero vita genere ad crucem perferendam ſe exercerent.* Ioſeph and his company did take vpon them a ſolitary life, that with more
,, tranquillity they might attēd to holy learning,

*Io. Capg.
in SS.
Britan.
Catalog.
Polidor.
Virg. in
hiſt. Anglic. li.1.
Cambd.
in deſcr.
Brit.pa.
162.
Harpesf.
in hiſt.
Eccl. fol.
3.*

*Cambd.
in deſcr-
Prouin.
Belg. Britan.*

ning, and with a feuere kind of conuerfa- „
cion excercife them felues to the bearing of „
Chriits croffe. „

26.   And albeit Iohn Fox (out of whome
Syr Francis hath ftollen all that he faith
in this matter, and moft of the reft that be
hiftoricall, though fupprefsing his name)
doth cavill vpon this mans going into England, making him firft a preacher and not
an ermite, and then faying, that he came not
from Rome, but out of Iury & France, and
confequently that the Church of Britany is
not the daughter of the Church of Rome,
nor had not her firft byrth or inftitution
from thence (and yet *S. Cyprian* glorieth in
that his church of Carthage in Africa, and
all the other Churches vnder her in *Mauri-*
tania and *Numidia* had receyved their firft inftitution of Chriftian faith from Rome as
from their mother:) all the world may fee,
that this is but a foolish and abfurd cauill of
Fox. For that albeit Saint Iofeph came not
immediately from Rome, nor was a Roman by birth (as none of the Apoftles
were) yet he taught in England the Roman
faith, that is to fay the fame faith that faint
Peter and faint Paul and *Ariftobolus*, that came immediatly from Rome, had taught before him, or did teach iointly with him in
Brytany. Of which Roman faith faint Paul
had written to the Romans themfelues be-

Foxes cauilla-
tion .re-
futed.

Cypr.ep.
45.

fore the going of S. Ioſeph into Britany:

Rom. 1. *Fides veſtra annuntiatur in vniuerſo mundo*: Your faith is preached and diuvlged throughout the vvhole world; ſignifying, that the Chriſtian faith planted in Rome by S. Peter, was deriued already for a platforme into all other parts of the world round about. For which cauſe *Tertullian* writing in Africa ſaid, that the authority of his church came from Rome. *Vnde nobis quoque authoritas praſto eſt*, ſayth he. And *S. Cyprian* (as before hath byn noted) called the Roman Church *matricem cæterarum omnium*, the mother and original Church of all other Churches. And *S. Innocentius* alſo, whoſe holyneſſe Saint Auguſtine ſo much admired, doth affirme, that all Churches generally of the weſtparts of the world were founded by S. Peter and his diſciples. And S. Auguſtine him ſelfe had no better way to defend his Church of *Hippo* and other of thoſe countreyes to be truly Catholike againſt the Donatiſts, then to ſay, that *they vvere daughters and children of the Church of Rome*: though ſome of them were very neare as farre of in diſtance of place, as England at this day.

Tert. l. de preſcrip. cap. 36.

Cypr. in ep. 45.

Aug. in pſal. contra part. Donat.

27.   Wel then, by this we ſee that the ſhift inuented to deliuer vs from all obligation to the Sea of Rome for our two côuerſions vnder *Eleutherius*, and *Gregory* the firſt, by ſaying that ſome had preached Chriſtian religion

religion firſt in Britany, before theſe two
publike conuerſions fell out, is a fooliſh
ſhift, and diminiſheth not our ſaid obligation but encreaſeth rather the ſame. For yf
this firſt preaching, and firſt faith taught in
England by our firſt preachers, was the
Roman faith, & deriued principally from
the citty and church of Rome, by the preaching of Saint Peter and Saint Paul, Ariſtobolus and others, as hath byn declared; and
yf the very firſt beames or ſparcles therof
before any preachers parhaps were ſent,
came by the acceſſe of ſome Roman Chriſtians vpon the warres and other occaſions,
which before hath byn declared: then all
this rather multiplieth our bounds to
Rome, then diminiſheth the ſame. And ſo
in ſteed of two conuerſions from Rome
(wherof I ſpake in my *VVardvvord*) now
we frind three. And conſequently a triple
obligation is come vpon vs for a double.

Hereti-
callvvrā
gling
turning
to theiſ
ovvne
confu-
ſion.

28. And this ſhall ſuffice to the firſt anſwere of Syr Francis or rather ſimple ſhift,
by which he would auoyd our obligation
to Rome, perſuading vs that our firſt preachers came not from thence, but from Aſia
and the eaſt Church. Of which argument
though I haue ſaid more heere, then I meāt
to haue donne: yet for that Syr Francis
and all other heretiks of our tyme, for ha-
tr3d to Rome do ſeeke certayne reaſons

or rather folihe coniectures to proue the
ſame, I ſhalbe forced to ſay ſomwhat more
therof in the Chapter following.

AN ANSWERE TO CERTAINE
CAVILLATIONS, LIES, AND
*falſifications of Syr Francis and his maiſtres, Fox,
and the Magdeburgians about the firſt preaching
o, Chriſtian religion in Britanye.*

CHAP. II.

ALBEIT the fond hereticall wrangling
before rehearſed againſt Rome, deſer-
ueth not ſo large a confutation, as I haue
already beſtowed theron, eſpecially in ſo
cleere a matter, as are the manifold benefits
which our Iland hath receyued from the
Sea of Rome : yet for that it is ſeene to be a
generall conſpiracy of all heretiks of our
tyme, as well Lutherans, as Swinglians,
Caluiniſts and Puritans to take from Rome
(yf they could) all the merite of bringing
Chriſtian faith into our countrey; I am forced in this place to ſtand longer vpon the
matter, then otherwiſe I would; for that
there followeth alſo another conſequence
hereof, of no ſmall moment which *S. Irenæus, Tertullian, Saint Cyprian, Saint Auguſtine*
and others are wont to vrge greatly againſt
heretiks: to witt, that yf our church be
the daughter and diſciple of the *Church of
Rome*, *then ought it to runne vnto her in all doubts
and*

*Iren. cõ-
tra hæ-
reſes.
Tert. de
præſcrip,
Cyp. l. 4.
s. 8. de
vnit. ec-
cleſ.*

and difficulties of matters of faith. Wherefore
we shall breefly discusse the truth of this
affaire.

A cóse-
quence
of the an
cient fa-
theis to
be noted

2. Besides the profes sett downe in the
former chapter how the cheefe of our firſt
preachers came from Rome immediately, as
Saint Peter, Saint Paule and Saint *Aristobo-
lus*; and that the other , as Saint Symon of
Chananey and Saint Ioseph of Arimathia,
yf they did not come from Rome, yet preached they the Roman faith conforme to
the preachings of Saint Peter & Saint Paul:
there remaine two other coniectures also
very probable to the same effect , to proue
that S. Ioseph was specially directed into Britany by the same Apoſtles. The firſt
is, for that King *Inas* aboue 900 yeares paſt,
when he laid the foundation of *Glastenbury*
abbey in memory of Saint Ioseph and his
fellowes, that had lived a solitary life there,
he caused these verses to be wrytten in the
Church, as Cambden and others teſtifie.

*Guiliel.
Cambd.
in descr.
Brit. de
prouin.
Belg. an,
Domini
690.*

Anglia plaude lubens, mittit tibi Roma salutem:
Fulgor Apostolicus Glasconiam irradiat.

Be glad (England) for that Rome sendeth
health to the, and Apoſticall brightnes doth
lighten Glaſtenbury . Which could not
well be spoken, yf the comming of these
Saints and firſt inhabitors there , had not
had some relation to Rome, and to the
Apoſtles that sent them.

3. More-

Beatus
Rhen.li.
3. rerum
German.
ſub Hello.
Pantal.
de viris
Germ.
part.3.
Stumpf.
ekronic.
Heluet.
lib. 7. c.
22.
Eyſengr.
cent. 2.
part. 5.
diſtin. 2.
The ſto-
rie of S.
Beatus a
Britan,
ſcholler
to S. Pe-
ter.
Anno
Domini,
116.

3.   Moreouer I fynd in the ancient Chronicles of the *Heluetians* , and ſundry authors (as B. *Rhenanus* in his ſtorie of *Ger-*
manie , yea and *Pantaleon* an hereticke ,
and others) do teſtifie , that one *Suetonius* a
noble mans ſone of *Britanie* being conuerted in *Britanie* by ſuch Chriſtians as firſt
planted the faith there, and called (after his
baptiſme) *Beatus* , was ſent by them to
Rome to *Saint Peter Apoſtolorum Corypheo* , (as
the ſtorie ſaith) that is to the chief head
of the Apoſtles, to be better inſtructed , and
confirmed who returning backward againe
from Rome towards Britanie through
Switzerland, found ſuch flocking of people
vnto him and ſuch propenſion to Chriſtian
religion , as he ſtaied continually among
them , and built himſelfe an oratorie to exerciſe a monaſticall lyfe therin, neare vnto a
towne called in their language *Vnder ſevven.*
not farre from the lake of *Thun* , where he
dyed about the yeare of Chriſt 110. And for
that this man applyed himſelfe to a monaſticall lyfe , and brought the ſame purpoſe
with him out of Britanie (as it ſeemeth:)
the coniecture is not improbable , but that
he was conuerted and ſent to Rome to Saint
Peter by Saint Ioſeph, and his fellowes that
followed the ſame lyfe in Britanie, and that
they had particular correſpondence with
the ſaid Apoſtle in that behalfe.

4. And

4. And thus much being added for confirmation of that which was said and discussed in the former chapter, about the first
preaching and receyuing of the faith in *Bri-*
tanie: there remayneth now, that we see
the obiections, which Syr Francis and his
men, and maisters do bring against this, to
proue that the first teachers of Christian
faith in *Britanie* were rather *Grecians*, and
of the east Church in *Asia*, then of the west
Roman Church; for which assertion hauing
no author at all, that euer wrote worde
therof nor any man liuing or dead that hitherto, affyrmed it, besyde them selues, or
before Luthers dayes: they are forced to
build their whole imagination (I meane
Syr F. & his maistet Syr Ihon Fox, & Fox
his maisters againe *Illyricus*, *Vigandus Iudex*,
and *Faber*, that make the *Quadrillio* or round
table of the Magdeburgeans in Saxonie)
vpon this bare coniecture, and fond inference. That for so much as in Bedes tyme
some in Britanie obserued the day of Easter
after the fashion of some east Churches,
(for all did not so vse it:) therfore it was
like, that the first preachers of that Iland
came not from Rome (which these men
cannot abyde to heare) but from the east.
As though (forsooth) this abuse might not
haue entred after those first preachers,
though they had come from Rome. But lett

VVhe-
ther the
first prea
chets in
Britanie
vvere of
the East
church,
or vvest.

The foe
lish in.
ference
of here.
ticall ca.
uillers.

V5

vs heare their words about this matter.

VV afvv.
pag. 192.

5.   Firſt Syr Francis writeth thus; *Beede our countryman doth teſt.fie that in his tyme this land kept Eaſter after the manner of the Eaſt Church by vvhich may be gathered, that the firſt preachers came hither from the eaſt partes oƒ the vvorld, and not from Rome :* Marke, I pray you, the knights good gathering ; might not a man as well argue thus, that diuers reliques of the Pelagian, or other ancient hereſies, were found in ſome partes of Britanie in Bedes tyme, *ergo* the firſt preachers in Britanie were Pelagians, or other heretiques? But let vs heare Iohn Fox who taught Syr Francis this argumét, though the other were not ſo gratefull a

Fox pa.
9 5.
col. 2.
nu. 78.

ſcholler as to name him. *I take (ſayth he) the teſtimonie of Bede , vvhere he affirmeth , that in his tyme, and almoſt* 1000. *yeares aƒter Chriſt, heere in Britanie Eaſter vvas kept aƒter the manner of the Eaſt Church in the full oƒ the moone, vvhat day in the vveeke ſoeuer it fell on and not on the Sunday, as vve do novv, vvherby it is to be collected, that the firſt preachers in this land haue come out from the eaſt parte of the vvorld , vvhere it vvas ſo vſed : rather then from Rome.*

6.   Heere youe ſee the Argument more fully ſett downe, and the ſame foliſh colle-ction made that was before. For except it could be proued, that this errour of keeping Eaſter day with the Iewes had begonne and indured in Britanie from the Apoſtles
tyme

tyme downward (which cannot be fhewed but rather the contrarie is certaine, as
after you fhall heare) this collection is not
worth a rush; And it is to be noted by the
way, that as Fox cannot tell any tale lightlie with out fome notorious lye: fo heere
be two very manifeft. The firft, that Saint
Bede affirmeth this cuftome of keeping
Eafter with the Iewes to haue byn heere
in Britanie in his time, as though all Britanie
had vfed it. Wheras in diuers places he doth
expreslie attribute the fame to the Scotts,
that dwelled in the Iland of Ireland principally, as alfo to fome of them that dwelt in
Britanie, and to fome Britans themfelues;
but all the English Church was free from
it. So as Ihon Fox his fpeach of Britanie in
generall is both falfe and fraudulent. But
the other Claufe that Saint Bede teftifyeth
this, for almoft 1000. yeares after Chrift, is
foolish and impudent, feeing it is notorious
that S. Bede dyed in the yeare 735. which
is almoft 300. yeares fhort of Fox his accoumpte & confequently could not teftifie
a thinge fo long after his death. But this the
raynard iugleth to make Saint Bede feeme
to be a late writer. Whome they cannot
abyde, for that he fetteth downe the beginning and progreffe of our Church farre different from theirs.

7. But I thinke good to put downe alfo

*Bed. lib.
2. Eccl.
hiſt. cap.
4.19. &
lib. 3.
cap. 25.*

Tvvo
lies of
Fox.

the words of the *Magdeburgians* about this
matter (out of whome Fox tooke his argument, and the Kt. of the Fox) to the end it

The
Magde.
burgiás
ſentence
about
the con-
uerſion
of Bri-
tany.
Magd.
cent. 2.
c. 2 p.9.

may appeare how one hereticke teacheth
another (though of different ſects) to cavill
lye, and cogg, and do agree all in one ſpirit
of malignity: though they differ in opiniõs.
Thus then theſe Captaine Lutherans do
write of this matter iu their famous lying
and deceiptfull Centuriall Story. *Quis fuerit,*
qui primùm in Britannia Euangelium docuerit, &c.
VVho vvas the firſt that taugʰt the ghoſpeil in Bri-
tany is not cleare, the thing that ſeemeth neereſt to the
truth is; that the British church vvas planted at the
beginning by Grecian teachers and ſuch as came
from the Eaſt, and not by Romans or other of the
VVeſtchurch. And to this vve are moved by tvvo con-
iectures. Firſt, that Peter Abbot of Claniacke vvri-
*ting to Saint Bernard ſaith: That the *Schotts in his*
tyme vvere vvont in old tyme to celebrate Eaſter
day after the manner of the Grecians and not of the
Romans: And ſecondly, for that Geſſrey the Cardi-
nall vvho lived about the yeare of Chriſt 700. doth
teſtifie in his Story of Britany lib. 8. cap. 4. that
the Britans vvould in no vviſe admit the younger Au-
guſtine legate of Gregory the great neyther acknovv-
ledg any primacy of the B. of Rome ouer them; vvhich
is another cleere ſigne, that religion vvas not planted
there by Romans. And Albeit Pope Innocentius the
firſt, in his Epiſtle diſtinctione 12. do affirme on the
contrary ſide that all the Occidentall Churches, and
  thoſe

*Scotos
græco
more
ſuo tem-
pore ſo-
litos o-
lim pa-
ſcha ce-
lebrare,
non Ro-
mano.

those of Africa vvere founded by Peter, or by his di-
sciples or succeßors:yet vve iudge that to haue byn spo-
ken by him rather of desyre of a little vayne glory or
of temporal povver, then for that the truth is so, or
may be proued out of storyes. 1918733

8. Thus our Magdeburgeses, whose words
I haue caused to be noted more at length
by that they require some consideration:
and that by these few the Reader may
iudge of the quality of that whole huge
lying story of theirs, which our Fox hath
followed in his actes & monuments, with
aboue ten thousand false additions of his
owne, and I speake farre within number
when I say ten thonsand : but lett vs returne to our present story.

9. First wheras they say, *that to them it see-*
meth neerest to the truth,that Grecians and other of
the East Church, and not of the VVest Church,vvere
*the firstpreachers in Britany,*must eyther be very impudently spoken against their owne
conscience, yf they haue read that, which
I before haue set downe out of diuers authors, (they hauing noe one author in the
world of their side, that euer wrote so, or
signified so before them selues :) or yf they
haue not read these authors alleadged,then
is it great presumptió in them to take vpon
them to wryte so vniuersall an history of all
matters,tymes, & nations, as they profeße,
with out procuring first to read the an-

The exa-
minatió
of the
Magde-
burgiás
false
dealing
about
the con-
uersió of
Britany.

C 2   cient

cient authors & writers therof, about common and vulgar thinges at leaſt. But hatred and malice to Rome doth make them
blynd, and ſo rather to runne into all kind
of abſurdityes, then to yeld any praiſe or
commendable thing to Rome, or to the Biſhopps therof. But let vs go forward to examine more particulars, for there ar ſtore in
this little Story or relacion about Britany.

10.   Their firſt coniecture or argument,
why Britany was conuerted by Grecians
and not by Romanes is, as you haue heard,
for that *Petrus Cluniacenſis* writeth: *Scotos Græ-*
co more ſuo tempore, ſolitos olim paſcha celebrare:
That the Scotts in his tyme, were accuſtomed in old tyme to celebrate Eaſter day
after the máner of the Grecians. What ſenſe
hath this? *The Scotts in his tyme, did celebrate in*
old tyme. What ſenſe, I ſay, or conſtruction
can this haue? I confeſſe that ſome Scotts
of old tyme (eſpecially in Ireland and Or-
chades, as diuers Britanes alſo) did hold
the Aſian cuſtome of celebrating the Eaſter togeather with the Iewes. And this
needed not to be prooued by ſo late an
Author as is *Cluniacenſis,* for that S. Bede 300.
yeares before *Petrus Cluniacenſis* doth teſtifie
the ſame in diuers places of his works. Albeit how the Scotts in *Cluniacenſis* his tyme
did (as theſe men ſay) *celebrate in old time Eaſter*
vvith the Grecians (the Greeke Church at
that

Bed. hiſt.
Angl. li.
1. c. 4. 19.
& lib. 3.
c. 2. 25.

that tyme being not different in this point
from the Roman, though some in *Aſia mi-
nori* were) this cannot be vnderſtood by
any reaſonable man. And it may be, it was
wrytten after dinner by theſe good Germans, when they had dronke hard. And ſo
I leaue it to their owne explication: though
in what ſenſe ſoeuer they ſpeake yt, or it
may be vnderſtood: a moſt fond coniecture
it is for that which they pretend, (as we
haue ſhewed) to wit, that the firſt preachers of Britanie came from the eaſt.

11.   About the ſecond coniecture vpon the
words of *Geffrey of Monmouth*, whome they
call *Geffrey the Cardinall* there ar as many
more vnlearned and malitious eſcapes to be
noted. For firſt he was neuer Cardinal in
his lyfe, as all our hiſtoryes do make it
plaine: but firſt a monke, then Archdeacon
of *Monmouth*, then preferred by K. Stephen
to the Biſhopricke of S. Aſſaph in North-
wales in the yeare of Chriſt 1152. as both
Mathevv Paris and *Mathevv of VVeſtminſter* do
affirme in their ſeuerall hiſtoryes handling
that yeare. Neyther did any man to our
knowledge ever call him Cardinall, but
only a certaine Venetian ſchoolemaiſter named *Ponticus Viruunius*. Who lyuing almoſt
a hundred yeares gone, tranſlated ſome part
of this *Geffreyes* Brittiſh ſtory, or rather
contracted the ſame into an Epitome for the

About
Geffrey
of Mon-
mouth
made Bi-
ſhopp
an. 1152.

C 3   pleaſure

vide
Præf. in
librum
rerum
Brit.
Gaufredi
&c. Hei-
delberg.
impreſſ.
1587.

pleaſure of a certayne noble family in *Venice*,
who in old tyme had come out of Britany.
And this man eyther of error or flattery to
that family, or both, calleth him Cardinall
forſooch againſt the cleere teſtimony of all
others that lived with him; as ſoone after
his death, did the forſaid *Matheww Paris* and
Gul. Neobrigenſis, long before this other late
Venetian ſchoolemaiſter.

12.   And of this could not be ignorant our
Magdeburgians, though they would needs
make Geffrey of *Monmouth* a Cardinall alſo:
for that in ſome things he ſheweth himſelfe to fauour the old Britans againſt S.
Auguſtine that came from Rome. Neyther
could they be ignorant alſo of the tyme
wherin *Geffrey* lived (except they will confeſſe themſelues to be very vnskilfull and
groſſe companions in deed) ſeeing ſo many
authors do teſtifie the ſame, to witt, in the
yeare of Chriſt 1152. in which yeare he was
made Biſhopp of S. Aſſaph and lived diuers
yeares after. So as our German heretiks appointing him for his more creditt to haue
lived in the yeare of Chriſt 700. doe ad of
their owne beneuolence to his antiquity,
foure hundred and fifty yeares, which is
ſomwhat more then Fox tooke from *S. Bede*
a little before, to diſcreditt him, and make
him ſeeme a young author. And theſe con-
federats do proceed ſo ridiculouſly, in this
                                    kind

kind of cosenage, as the one affirming, *Saint Bede* to haue liued a thousand yeares after Christ, and the other, that *Geffrey* of *Monmouth* lived seaven hundred, they come betwene them both to make the said *Geffrey* to be three hundred yeares elder then *Saint Bede*, wheras he was indeed 450. yeares younger, the difference is in all 750. yeares. And this not of error, as hath byn shewed, and is most playne: but of envy; desyring to preferre Geffrey, that seemeth to fauour them some tymes in his narracions about Saint Augustine, and to putt backe S. Bede, that is euery where and wholy against them. And yf you find this iugling in so small and short a matter, as this is: imagine what passeth in their whole volumes, I meane both of Fox and Magdeburgians, as before I haue noted. And thus much of the title and tyme of Geffrey of Monmouth. Now lett vs come to his words & assertiōs.

13. First in his sixt booke and 4. Chapter quoted by our Magdeburgians there is noe such matter handled at all as they mention, concerning the strife betweene the Britans and Saint Augustine. Nor in the next two books following, nor in all the 4. Chapters of any of the rest: But in the eleventh booke and 7. Chapter talking of the comming of the forsaid Augustine into England, he wryteth thus:

Notable falsification of Fox and Magdeburgiās in corruptinge of tymes.

C 4   *Interea*

Galfr.
Monu-
metens.
lib. 11.
cap. 7.

Intereà miſſus eſt Auguſtinus a Beato Gregorio &c.
In the meane ſpace vvas ſent into Brittany Auguſtine
by Bleſſed Gregory to preach to Engliſhmen the vvord
of God, vvho vvere yet blind in pagan ſuperſtitiō &c.
Though among the Britanes that Chriſtianity vvaſ
yet in force, vvhich being receyued from the tyme of
Eleutherius the Pope, had neuer fayled vntill that
day &c. Among vvhome there vvas an Abbot of Bangor named Dinoot, that had aboue tvvo thouſand
monks vnder his charge, vvho anſvvered to Auguſtine,
vvhen he required ſubiection of the Brittiſh Biſhopps
and that they vvould ioyne vvith him to conuert the
Engliſh nation: that the Britans ovved no ſubiection
vnto him, nor vvould beſtovv the labour of preaching
vpon their enemyes, ſeeing the Britans had an Archbiſhopp of their ovvne, and that the Saxons tooke from
them their countrey. For vvhich cauſe they hated
them extreemely, nor did not eſteeme their religion,
nor vvould communicate vvith them more then
vvith dogges.

14. Lo heere all that is to be found in Geffrey of Monmouth to this purpoſe. Which
is nothing els, as you ſee, but a paſsionate
and cholericke anſwere of the Britanes as of
men afflicted and exaſperated. Heere is noe
one word of their *not acknovvledging the popes
ſupremacy.* (as the Magdeburgians wryte)
but only that they acknowledged not the
Superiority of Auguſtine ouer the Britans,
ſeeing he was ſent only to the Engliſh. And
that the authority of their owne Archbiſhopp

ſhopp was not taken away by his comming
for any thing they yet knew, but remayned
as before. Which queſtion of iuriſdiction
betwene two Archbiſhops falleth out daylie, even where the Popes authority is moſt
acknowledged: & ſo we ſee that it is a manifeſt ly, which the *Magdeburgians* affirme ſo
reſolutely, *that the Britãs vvould not acknovvledge
any primacy of the B. of Rome ouer them.* Forthey
ſpeake (as you ſee) of Auguſtines authority
and not of the B. of Rome, from whome
we read not, that he had yet ſhewed to
them any authority to place him ouer their
Archbiſhopp. And conſequently it is a vaine
and malitious inference which the Magdeburgiãs heere doe make out of this anſwere
of the Britans (yf it had byn true) that forſo
much as they admitted not Saint Auſtins
authoritie they acknouledged not the primacie of Rome; and that this againe, *vvas a
cleere ſigne that religion vvas not planted in Britany
by the Romans.*

An ab-
ſurd
kind of
reaſo-
ning of
the Mag
deburg.

15. For how cleere is this, I pray yow?
or how hangeth this togeather? might not
this error of not acknowledging the power
of the Roman Sea (yf it had byn among
them) haue crept in after the firſt planting
of Chriſtian faith? will theſe Germans or
Syr Francis or Fox their ſchollers deny
that *Rauenna* in Italy (for example) was conuerted by *Saint Apollonaris* ſent thither from

C 5   Saint

Petrus Chryſ. ſerm. de S. Apollinari. Et Petrus Damianus de eodem, Membr. tom. 2. Vide Sur. 23. Iulij.

Saint Peter, for that afterwards the **Bishops** of that place for many yeares waxing proud and preſumptuous vpon the preſence and court of the *Exarches* and Viceroyes of the Emperours reſiding amongſt them, did refuſe to yeld to the Biſhopps of Rome? Or for that England at this day by error of proteſtant religion refuſeth to acknowledg any ſubiectiõ in ſpirituall affaires to Rome, will our men deny, that the Engliſh nation was euer conuerted to Chriſtian faith from Rome? who ſeeth not the impertinency of this kind of argument? And yet with ſuch like kinde of argumẽts and inferences, theſe abſurd people do deceiue the world.

16.   But the laſt point of theſe Germans aſſertion about Pope *Innocentius* the firſt, is a moſt egregious impudency, to ſay of ſo holy a father, ſo highly commended by Saint Auguſtine & other Fathers, that liued with him and after him, *that he ſpake of vaine glory*

Centuriatores Magdburg. Flacus Illyricus. Ioan. Vigandus. Matheus Iudex. Baſilius Faber.

and deſire of temporall-povver, when he wrote aboue twelue hundred yeares gone, *that all the vveſt Churches* (and the Brittiſh amongſt the reſt) *vvere founded by Saint Peter or his diſciples and ſucceſſors.* And let any indifferent or prudent reader in the world conſider of what waight theſe words of the Germanes may be, when hauing ſaid, that albeit *Innocentius* the firſt wrote ſo, *yet vve iudg that to haue byn ſpoken of vaine glory, &c.* A proud
censure

cenſure of ſo great a man by three or foure
poore compagnions, that wrote books for
their bread and begged the ſame commonly of euery prince, to whome they dedicated their ſeuerall Centuries: that ſo contemptible people (I ſay) ſhould preſume to
touch the honour and truth of ſo great and
worthie a Saint and father, as was holy *In-*
nocentius, ſo called commonly by *S. Auguſtine,*
S. Hierome, S. Baſil, Oroſius and others: and
whome all the reſt of the world togeather
with theſe men admired and reſpected in
his life for ſuch. *Sancti Innocentij* (ſaith Saint
Hierome to the virgin *Demetriades*) *qui Apo-*
ſtolicæ Cathedra, & B. memoriæ Anaſtaſij ſucceſſor
& filius eſt teneas fidem, nec peregrinam, quamuis
prudens callidáque vedearis, doctrinam recipias.
Hold the faith of holy *Innocentius* which is
the ſucceſſor & ſonne (in the ſeat of S. Peters
chaire) of Anaſtaſius of bleſſed memory that
went before him, & do not admitt any new
or forraine doctrine though thou maiſt
ſeeme perhaps wiſe & ſubtile to they ſelfe.
17. Thus wrote S. Hierome which is another manner of iudgemēt of *Innocentius,* both
for his holines of life & authority of place
to direct men in religion, then the Magdeburgians giue, who would make him
vaine glorious. But thus they vſe all ancient
fathers that ar againſt them. And ſo much
for this chapter.

Auguſt.
tom. 1.
pag. 36.
& ep.91.
ad Conc.
Carth.
Hier. ep.
ad De-
met. Ba-
ſil. ep. ad
Innocēt.
Oroſius
in hiſt.
lib. 2.

THE

THE FORMER CONTRO-
VERSY IS HANDLED MORE PAR-
*ticularly , hovv the Grecian cuſtome of celebrating
Eaſter day after the faſhion of the Ievves, came firſt
into the Britiſh and Scottiſh Church: & hovv vntruly
and vvickedly Iohn Fox and Iohn Bale do behaue
themſelues about this matter.*

CAP. III.

That the
cuſtome
of cele-
brating
Eaſter
vvith
the
Ievves
came
not in
vvith
the firſt
prea-
chers.

★*Sup.c.*1

BVT now lett vs returne (yf you pleaſe)
to ſpeake a word or two more of the
entrance of the forſaid cuſtome of celebrating Eaſter with the Iewes into Britany:
to witt, how and about what tyme or vpon
what occaſion it is probable , that it entred.
Wherin firſt it ſeemeth moſt certayne, that
it could not be brought in by the firſt preachers of Chriſtian religion, as Iohn Fox and
Syr Francis and the *Magdeburgians* , would
haue men beleeue . And this is proued , as
well by the reaſons & authorityes alleaged
★ before, to ſhew that the firſt preachers in
Britany eyther came from Rome or preached Roman doctrine : as alſo by the reaſons following.

The firſt
reaſon.

2.   Firſt, for that, yf *Damianus* and other
preachers ſent into Britany by Pope Eleutherius to inſtruct K. Lucius and the reſt in
Chriſtian faith about the yeare 180. had
found any ſuch cuſtome there contrary to
the Roman vſe from whence they were
ſent:

fent: they would haue remoued the fame, or at leaftwayes haue made fome mention therof. For fo much as at that tyme the contrary cuftome of celebrating Eafter vpon the Sunday was publike in the vfe of the Roman Church. And pope Pius the firft had made a decree for confirming the fame againft the Afian vfe aboue 40. yeare before their going into Britanie: to witt, in the yeare 144. as *Eufebius* teftifieth.

Eufeb. in Chron. an. 144.

3. Secondly Saint Bede declaring in many places of his works, the contention, that was in Britany about this point, as wel betwene Saint Auguftine, & the Brittifh Bifhopps, as betwene *S. Laurentius* and others his fucceffors with the Irifh and Scottish nation: he fheweth in his 2. booke, what lettres *Honorius* the pope, about the yeare of Chrift 635. as alfo Pope *Iohn* the 4 fome few yeares after, wrote to the faid nations about this error, *pro eodem errore corrigendo* (faith Saint Bede) *literas eis magna auctoritate atque eruditione plenas direxit.* The pope wrote them lettres ful of authority and learning for correcting this error. And then Beda addeth further, that pope *Iohn* in the beginning of his epiftle declared manifeftly, that this herefy was fprong vp among them very lately, *nupperrimè temporibus iftis exortam effe harefim hanc,* that this herefy was fprong vp very lately in thofe dayes. And that not the
whole

Bed. lib. 2. c. 2. 4. & 19. Item lib. 3. c. 25. The 2. reafon.

Bed. lib. 2. hift. cap. 19.

whole Irish and Scottish nations, but some
of them only were infected therwith, so as
this was neuer vniuersally receyued among
them, nor begonne by antiquitie.

4.   The 3. reason is for that Saint German
ad his fellowes goyng twise into Britany
almost 200. yeares before this tyme mencioned to resist the Pelagian heresy, neuer
made mention of this other heresy of *Quar-*
tadecimani, or of *Paschatitæ* (for so they were
called as after shall be shewed.) Which yet
was condemned for an heresy more then
200. yeares before that againe, to witt vnder Pope *Victor* as hath byn said, and so held
in all ages after, especially after the Councell
of Nice had reprooved the same, and allowed of the Roman Cath: vse. As not only

Saint Bede in the place before alleaged out
of the words of *S. VVilfrid* doth testifie: but
the same also appeareth by the Emperour

Euseb.
l. 3. *de*
vit.Con-
stant.
cap. 17.
& 18.

Constantine his owne letters registred by *Eu-*
sebius in his life. All which being so, it is
more then probable, that Saint German
wold haue said or written somwhat of so
great a controuersy, yf he had found the
contrary vse in practise among the Britans

in his daies.

5.   A fourth reason may be the testimony

of *Florentius Vigorniensis,* who writeth in the
yeare 628. of his chronicle: *Eo tempore errorem*
Quartadecimanorum in obseruatione Paschatis apud
                                        Scotos

Scotos exortum , Honorius Papa redarguit , &c.

At that time, *Honorius* the pope did reproue the error of the Quartadecimans in celebrating Ea ter, sprong vp amongst the Scotishmen. Thus wrote he vpon the point of 500. yeares past wherby is euident tha the held not this custome to haue come into Britany with the first preachers of Christianity.

6. Finally it appeareth by S. Bede that a Sinod or Councell was gathered of purpose in *Northumberland* about this matter in time of our English primitiue Church in the yeare of Christ 664. & the 22. of the raigne of *K. Ofvvyn*, who was there present with. *K. Egfride* his sonne. The cheefe disputers in this councell on the Scots behalfe for the Eastren custome was one Colmã an Abbot first, & after B. of *Lindisferne*, togeather with B. *Cedda* and some others. But in defence of the Roman vse were *Agilbertus* B. of the *VVest-Saxons* and *VVilfride* an Abbot of *Northumberland* afterward Archbishopp of all the kingdome of Northumbers , *vir doct ßimus, &c.* a most learned man (as S. Bede calleth him) whoe had studied both in Italy and France, &c.

The 5. reason. A councell in England about celebra-ting of Easter daie. Bed. l.3. hist.c.25.

7, The question was handled about the antiquitie (as hathe byn saied) of both vses and customes , but especially of that of the East among the Scottes and British. And albeit that B. Colman did alleadge the tradi-

A Synod and disputation about the controuersie

tradition of Aſia from S. Iohn the Euangeliſt downeward, as alſo the writing of one
Anatolius a learned Aſian Biſhop, that had
written therof allmoſt 200. yeares before.
Yet for the antiquitie therof among the
Scotts and Brittiſh nation, he alleaged noe
greater continuance, then from the Abbot
Columba, who liued not full 70. yeares before that daie. For that he died (as Iohn Bale
teſtifieth) in the yeare of Chriſt 598. *Nun-*

quid Reuerendiſſimum Patrem noſtrum Columbam
(ſaith B. Colman) *& ſucceſſores eius viros Deo*
dilectos, qui eodem modo Paſcha fecerunt, diuinis pa-
ginis contraria ſapuiſſe vel egiſſe credendum eſt?
Shall we thinke that our moſt reuerend Father Columba and his ſucceſſors being men
ſo beloued of God as they were, did vnderſtand or doe contrarie to holie Scriptures in
celebrating Eaſter as we doe now? &c.

The an-
ſvvere of
S. Vvil-
fride for
the Ro-
ma ne
vſe.

8.   Whervnto S. Wilfrid anſwered both
learnedlie & piouſlie, that this errour might
be tollerable in them that liued ſo diſtant
from the Sea Apoſtolike in a corner of the
worlde, ſo long as it was held without obſtinacie, they being perhaps pious men, that
at the beginning brought it in from the
Eaſt partes, and continued the ſame vpon
ſimplicitie delighted with the facility therof, & not vnderſtanding ſo eaſilie the Cath.
Roman Calculation which had many great
difficulties, as after ſhall appeare. *Simplicitate*
ruſtica,

rustica, faith he, *fed intentione pia, &c.* ad quos
Catholicus Calculator non aduenerat, By a rude „
kind of simplicitie, but godlie intentiō they „
erred &c. noe learned Catholike Calcula- „
tour of tymes and dayes hauing yet come „
to them. Of which point of Calculation we „
fhall fpeake fomewhat more presētly after.

9. But yet here now we fee by this difputation and conference of that Sinod, that
B. Colman himfelf did not afcribe the beginning of this euftome vnto the firft preachers of Ireland and Scotland, nor yet vn- *Marian-*
to *Saint Palladius* nor *Patritius* their knowen *Scot. in*
Apoftles, that 200. yeares before that tyme *Chron.*
were fent by Popé *Celeftinus* to conuert *an. 430.*
both nations in the yeare 430. & 432. as all *Profper.*
Authors do agree. And confequently it is *in chron.*
moft probable to be true, that which Pope *eod. ann.*
Iohn the 4. before named writeth vnto *Bed.l. 2.*
Thomianus, Chromanus, and other Scottishe *cap. 19.*
Bishopps, and to their whole Cleargie, that
this euftome of celebrating Eafter vpon the
full moone of Marche was begonne but of
late among them (I meane among the Scots
dwelling in Ireland, and in the Ilands neere
abowt, for that of them principallye Saint
Bede profeffeth him felf to fpeake.) And
thereby infinuateth, that by them alfo the
fame was imparted with the Pictes and
Britanes and other Scotts that lived in the
Ile of Britanie. And by this the Reader

maye fee , how good an argument-it is,
which the Magdeburgians and Iohn Foxe
doe vfe and vrge fo muche:to witt.That for
fo muche , as this Greeke or Afian cuftome
of celebrating Eafter with the Iewes, was
fownde among the Scotts & fome Britans
in Saint Bedes tyme and afterward : *Ergo* it
is likelie , that the firft preachers of Britanie
came not from Rome , nor were not of the
Romane Religion , but rather of the Eafte
partes: of which fequele I haue fnewed the
abfurditie before in the precedent Chapter.

VVhen   10.   But now perhaps yow will aske me,
& hovv   how and when it is probable , that this cu-
the Ea- ftome came in among the Britans? Where-
fterne   vnto I anfwere, firft for the Britanes , that
cuftome fome are of opinion it was brought into
came in Britannie it felf by Pelagius the heretike,or
among   fome of his followers, abowt the yeare of
the Bri- Chrift 420. who being a Britane borne and
tans.   a Monke (as fome thinke) of the famous
         Monafterie of Bangor, travayled into Italie
         firft, and then into Sicilia, Aegipt and other
         Eaft partes of the worlde to learne and ftu-
         die, as he profeffed . And by that profeffion
         of hipocrifie he crept into manie learned &
Auguft. godlie mens fpeciall loue and frendshipp.
ep. 105. And aboue others he entred with S. Pau-
Et de do- linus B. of Nola , and by him with S. Au-
no perfe- guftine. But afterward being difcouered by
uer. l. 2.
cap. 20. S. Hierom to haue taught herefies in fecrett
                                          together

together with his fellowe and difciple
Celeftius (who by the defcription made of
hym by S. Hierome maye feeme to haue *Hierom.*
byn a Scottifhe man, for he faieth, *habet enim praf. in*
progeniem Scotica gentis de Britannorũ vicinia, for *lib. in*
he hath his offpring from the Scottish na- *Ezech.*
tion neere to the Britans) wherfore thefe
two men being now difcouered to be heretikes, and condemned by Innocentius the
firft, and by diuers Sinods, are fayd for very
fhame to haue retyred into Britanie, and
being deadly enemies to the Pope and
church of Rome, that had cõdemned them,
& confidering that the Eafterne cuftome of
celebrating Eafter was oppofit to the fame
Churche, and yet defended by manie : it is
thought probable enoughe,that they might
bring in the fame. Wherewith doth feeme
to concurre fomewhat the woords of Her- *Herm.*
mánus Contractus a Chronicler,that wrote *Contr.*
aboue 500. yeares agoe. Who wryting of *an. 430*
the yere of Chrift 630. faieth : *His temporibus chron.*
hærefis de Pafcha & Pelagiana Britanniam turbat
In thefe daies the herefie about the celebra- „
ting of Eafter, and the Pelagian did muche „
trouble Britanie. By which words it feemeth that he would fignifie, that thefe two
herefies grew to be all one in Ingland, and
confequently like to be brought in by the
felf fame men.

11.   But yet all this notwithftanding it

feemeth

ſeemeth muche more probable according
to S. Bedes hiſtorie and the reaſons before
alleaged, that this vſe of Eaſter came not in
with Pelagius but longe after. For that
Saint German, and *Saint Lupus*, and others
made noe mention therof. But eſpecially
for that the wrytings of the Popes *Hono-*
rius and *Iohn* the fowrthe to the Scottish
nation and Bishops before mencioned, ſaye,
that this cuſtome of Eaſter was newly
ſprong vp in their dayes: it ſeemeth more
probable (I ſaye) that this cuſtome was
imparted to the Britanes by the ſaid Scottish nation, and namely by thoſe that dwelt
(as hath byn ſaied) in Irelad or in the Ilands
of Hebredes. But how they themſelues gate
it, is not ſo certaine; yet the moſt probable
ſeemeth that either ſome of them trauailing
into the eaſt cowntries, or others of thoſe
eaſt cowntries comming to them brought
the obſeruation therof. For albeit euer after
that the ſame was condemned by Pope
Victor, and the truth eſtabliſhed by the
Councell of Nice, the whole weſterne
Churche, yea, alſo (as Conſtantine ſaith) the
Conſtat: farr greater part of all the eaſt held the Ro-
epiſt. ad mane vſe : yet was not the contrarie ſo ex-
Ypiſcopos tinguiſhed, but that diuers Churches of *Aſia*
apud Eu-
ſeb.lib.3. *minor*, did hold and practiſe the ſame for a
cap. 18. long tyme. Eſpecially certaine heretiks as
de vita the *Nouatians*, *Montaniſts*, *Priſcillianiſts, Sab-*
eius.   *batians*

batians and others that seemed of the de-
uowter sort, and there with deceiued
many simple people, pretending that th s
vse was more pious then the other, as being
fownded in the expresse woordes of scriptures of the old testament and confirmed by
the example of Christ himself, who made
his Easter together with the Iewes vpon
the 14. daye of the Moone of Marche, as appeareth by the Euangelists.

12. For these (I say) and other like reasons,
it semeth (according to Saint Bede) that the
simple and rude Irish & Scottish Christians
(as there he called them) falling vpon the
vse of this custome, did like better of it, then
of the Romane, which required more exact
calculation and obseruation of times and
daies, as before hath byn touched, and as
appeareth by that, which *Nicephorus* writeth, that the old calculation of Easter according to the Romane vse (to wytt that it
should be vpon the first Sunday after the ful
Moone of March) was so hard to be obserued often times, as some certaine learned
men of Aegipt were appointed in *Alexandria*
to calculate euerie yeare the same before
hand, & that the Patriarch of that Churche
had care to send it abroad to other parts of
the world for their instruction & direction
therin, which office of calculating Easter
day was exercised for diuers yeares in
*Exod.*12.
*Leuit.*23
verf. 5.
Num. 9.
verf. 11.
& c. 28.
*Deut.*16.
5.
*Mat.*26.
*Marc.*14
Luc. 22.

*Niceph.
hist.Eccl.
l.4.c.*36.
*& lib.*5.
cap. 20.

Alexan-

Alexandria by one *Theophilus* a Prieſt of that
Church. Who afterward comming to be Patriarke wrote diuers paſchall epiſtles in
greeke for direction of finding out the true
day of Eaſter. Which epiſtles were tranſla-

Hier.in
ep.31.ad
Theoph.

ted by *S. Hierome* in the yeare of Chriſt 404.
And after the ſaid *Theophilus* made a *Cyclus*
or calculation to ſerue for 100.yeares together, as appeareth by *S. Leo* the Pope in his

Epiſt. 64
ad Mar-
tian.

epiſtle to the Emperour *Martian.* All which
obſeruacions and directions being hard for
men ſo farre diſtant (as Ireland and Scotland
was from Alexandria) to know & keepe: it
is like that they followed rather the other,
which was more plaine and eaſy.

13.   And this is inſinuated before by Saint

lib. 3.
*cap.*25.

Bede when he ſaith that *S. Wilfrid* obiected
to B. Colman that his anceſtors obſerued
this *ruſtica ſimplicitate,* by a kind of rude ſim-

Reaſons
of diffi-
culties
in the
Roman
accompt.

plicity, and added further that *no learned cal-*
culator of tymes had euer arryued vnto them, and
if any man will know the reaſons of the
difficultyes that were in this Eccleſiaſticall Roman accoumpt or computation for
celebrating Eaſter vpon the firſt ſunday
after the 14. day of the moone of March,let
him read the forſaid paſchall epiſtles of *Theo-*
philus, as alſo the learned diſcourſe of *Anatolius*

Euſeb. l.
7. hiſt.
cap. 29.

B. of *Laodicea* wrytten about 40. yeares before the Councell of Nice, part wherof is
ſett downe by *Euſebius* in his Eccleſiaſticall
hiſtory.

hiſtory. *S. Auguſtine* alſo in his anſweres to *Aug.l.*2.
the queſtions of *Ianuarius* ſhewing the Rea- *ad quaſt.*
ſons why the Church of Chriſt would not *Ian.cap.*
haue the feaſt of Eaſter to be ſtable & firme, 1.*& 2.*
as that of his Natiuity, Circunciſiō, & ſome
other feaſts are, but rather to follow the
motion of the ſunne and moone, for diuers
miſteryes therin conteyned : doth touch diuers points of the forſaid difficultyes. But
the principall grounds that make the matter hard to the common ſort, are: firſt
the inequality betwene *annus Solaris* & *annus
Lunaris,* that is to ſay, the yeare according to
the courſe of the ſunne, and according to
the courſe of the moone, the Church vſing
the ſecond and not the firſt. And the difference betwene them ſtanding in the odds
of eleuen dayes, for equalling wherof ſer-
ueth the rule of the epact anſwerable to the
Cycle of the golden number conſiſting of The vſe
19. yeares reuolution, for obſeruing the be- of epact,
ginnings and full moones that fall out in golden nūber,
euery yeare, ſeeing that Eaſter day muſt be & cycle
kept vpon the firſt Sunday after the firſt full of Do-
moone of March, as hath byn ſaid. And fur- minical
thermore for ſo much as this 14. day of the lettres
moone muſt be that, which falleth vpon for ob-ſerving
the very day of the ſpring equinoctiall or Eaſter
immediatly followeth the ſame (which daie.
equinoctium was obſerued by the Councell
of *Nice* to be in thoſe dayes vpon the 21. of

Marche, though fince that time it fell backe
by little and litrle to the eleuenth day, for
correction wherof *Pope Gregory* the 13. was
forced to make his reformation from the
yeare 1582. by detracting ten dayes as all
men know) for this (I fay) and for that yf
the 14. day of the moone of march fhould
happen to be funday, the celebration of Eafter, muft, by the fame ancient *fathers pre-
fcription, be transferred to the next funday:
For obferuing of thefe points the Cycle alfo
of the funne or circle of dominicall letters
conteyning the reuolution of 28. yeares,
was inuented as neceffary for this obferuation. I might add much more to this effect.
but this is fufficient to fhew the grounds of
many difficultyes, as alfo (returning home
to our affayre in hand) to fhew the beginning of the Eaftearn Cuftome among the
Scotts Picts, and Brittans, not to be of that
Antiquity which *Iohn Fox and his fellovves*
would pretend.

14.   But now befides this, we may not
omitt another point of more confideration
for the Readers vtility, which is the fmall
piety or religion of thefe fectaries of our
dayes. Who care not what they graunt, deny, or fay, foe they fay fomwhat againft
Rome, her Bifhops or religion, euen in the
firft ages or primitiue Church. For to this
end, and with this good mynd, you fhall
                                              fee

*See Eu-
feb.lib. 5.
Ecc. Hi-
ftor. cap.
23. and
S. Amb.
epift. ad
epifcopos
per Ae-
miliam
conftitu-
tos. and
S. Bede
l. de ra-
tione
temp. c.
57.
Vvhere
alfo they
do yeld
the rea-
fons of
this or-
dinatio.

see them heere preferre in effect the forsaid
Easterne custome of celebrating Easter vsed
by the Britans and Scotts, before the Cath:
custome of Rome . Albeit they well know
how many ages gone it hath byn condemned not only for error , but also for heresy.
Yea though themselues do practise the contrary custome at this day in England and
Germany. For that this is also a knacke of
these good men, to speake one thing for
aduantage & practise another: as for example when the question is about all those
books of the old and new testament, which
by Luther & Lutherans are reiected from
the Canon of canonicale scriptures as *Eccle-*
siasticus, Iudith, Hester, Machabies, S. Iames epistle,
the *Apocalips,* and other like: when we reprehend the Lutherans for this point, our protestants of England take their parts and defend them stoutly , as we see by the wrytings of *Fulke, Charke, VVhitakers* and others
against *F. Campian* , that obiected the same
to Luther and his followers. And yet on the
other side, they sett the same books forth in
their English Bibles , as books of the scriptures; what dealing I pray you is this ? For
eyther they be scriptures & consequently of
infallible truth, or noe. Yf the first, then why
do you defend the Lutherans, that call them
in doubt ? yf the second , why do yow sett
them forth to the people among scriptures?

The se-
ctaries
of our
time al-
lovv of
the cele-
brating
Easter
vvith
the Ie-
vves.

Camp.in
ration.
reddit.
cap. 1.

D 5   15. The

15.   The like example may be taken from

Luther
his opi-
nion of
Easter,
libr. de
Cócilijs.
Martyn Luther, who in his booke *de Concilijs* doth perfuade the German Princes to obferue Easter day, as an immoueable feaſt whenfoeuer it falleth out, without expe-cting funday, as the Roman Church doth. Which point he faith is contrary to the

Gal. 4.
Apostle, forbidding vs to obferue dayes, moneths, and yeares. And yet I do not heare, but that he and other Lutherans to this day do obferue the Roman vfe in pra-ctife of their Church cócerninge this point.

And the very fame may be noted heere of our English Caluinifts. Who though in practife of the English Church do obferue the fame Roman cuftome, as all men do know : yet in their wrytings they are con-tent to impugne the fame, as a matter com-ming from Rome. Which you may fe noto-rioufly performed by Iohn Bale a cheefe

Iohn
Bale de-
fendeth
the Ievv
ish kee-
ping of
Easter.
libr. 3.
c. 25.
ghofpeller in K. Henry the 8. and K. Ed-wards daies, who treating of the former difputation betwene *Colman* the Scottish Bishopp, and *S. VVilfrid* the English Abbott in the forfaid Councell of Northumberland related by Saint Bede, prayfeth highely the firſt, to witt *Colman* togeather with his lear-ning and piety in defending the Iewish cu-ftome, but fcoffeth very contemptuoufly and fpitefully at the fecond, that propugned the Cath. Roman vfe. Not withstanding
that

that Saint Bede, (as before yow haue heard)
calleth *Saint VVilfrid virum doctißimum,* a moſt
learned man, and other wayes alſo for his
holynes extolleth him exceedingly, affirming among other points, that for his rare
learning and great vertue, he was made
Archbishop of al the kingdome of *Northum-*
berland, deuided after him into two bisho-
pricks, *Yorke* and *Lindiſferne.* And when
afterward (as to the beſt men happeneth)
he was perſecuted and driuen out by violence of *K. Egfride* from his ſaid Archbishopricke, he went and preached to the South-
Saxons and conuerted all that kingdome
togeather with the Ile of *VVight,* working
many miracles in like manner among them.
Wherby he is trulie called the Apoſtle of
Suſſex.

*Bed. lib.
3. c. 25.
& lib. 4.
c. 3. &
14.
Anno
Domini
677. &
678.*

16. Thus wryteth Bede of *Saint VVi'frid*
Apoſtle of the *South-ſaxons,* who vanquished
alſo in the former diſputations *B. Colman* &
conuerted therby *K. Oſwyne* from his former
rite of obſeruing Eaſter with the Iewes
(which he had learned during his education in Scotland) to follow the Roman
vſe. But what (thinke you) ſaith *Iohn Bale*
therof? Yow ſhall heare in his owne words:
Stulté reſpondit VVilfridus (ſaith he) &c. Wilfrid anſwered like a foole ſaying that the
Apoſtle *Saint Iohn* did play the Iew in many
things, &c. ſo ſaith Bale which words beſides

*Bal. cen-
tur. 1.
ſcript.
Brit.*

ſides the contumely conteyne a moſt falſe
ly, and ſlaunder alſo: for that *VVilſrid* ſaid

Bed. l. 3.
cap. 25.

not ſo, as in Saint Bede may be ſeene: but
only that S. Iohn might tolerate perhapps
for a tyme certayne rites of the old law as
ſome of the other Apoſtles alſo had done

Act. 20.

(and namely S. Paul in circumciſing Timothy) *to bury the Synagog vvith honour, &c.*

17.　But harken yet further how this new
ghoſpeler, and old Apoſtata friar goeth for-

Bal. cent.
1. ſcript.
Britan.
in Col-
man.

ward againſt this holy man. *Temporum* (ſaith
he) *calculatores Euangeliſtis opponit.* *VVilſrid* did
oppoſe the Roman Computiſts or calcula-
tors of tymes againſt the authority of the
Euangeliſts. This is an open ly, as the place
in Bede will teſtifie, for he ſaith only, that
perhapps one cauſe, why the rude ſimplicity

Abſurd
calum-
niations
of Iohn
Bale.

of the auncienter ſort of Scottish Chriſtians
imbraced the Iewish cuſtome at the beginning, amõgſt other things might be, for *that
no learned calculator of the Roman vſe had in thoſe
dayes arriued vnto them.* He ſaith not one word
or oppoſing this to the Euãgeliſts: & yet by
the way do yow note, that this falſe Apoſtata would haue his reader thinke, that
this Iewish heretical cuſtome is conforme
to the Euangeliſts, then which nothing can
be ſpoken more wickedly.

18.　But let vs go forward and ſee what en-

Bal. ibid.

ſueth: *in fine* (ſaith he) *ſuis præualuit impoſturis,
demẽtatis qui aderãt Regibus, &c.* In the end *VVil-
ſride*

fride in his difputation preuailed by his im-
poftures hauing bewiched the two Kings
that were prefent, *K. Ofvvyne* and *K. Egfride.*
Did you euer heare a more fhamelefle con-
gue? But this he wrote of Saint Wilfrid
(*Obiter,* and by the way) in the narration he
maketh of B. Colman. But when he commeth to talke of him in particular and feue-
rally, he is farre more bitter and impudent
againft him. Telling vs firft, how that after
VVilfrid had byn in *Frauce, Italy* and *Rome* to
ftudy, and there learned the mathematicall
calculations of times out of the ghofpells,
reuerfus in patriam, Romanas confuetudines, contra
quartadecimanos (fic enim pios homines tunc deriforie
vocabāt) difceptationibus in Synodo publicis defende-
bat, gerebátque circa collum reliquiarum quas Roma
tulerat, capfulā quandam, &c. Et Archiepifcopus de-
niá, ob hæc & his fimilia conftitutus, bis nfra fpatium
45. annorum, non ob Regum infolentiam, vt Polido-
rus immodefté fcribit, fed ob fuam temeritatem, imò
malitiam atque nequitias plures, Archiepifccpatu
pulfus eft, & longo tandem confectus fenio, perijt anno
Chrifti 710. He returning from Rome
to his contrey did defend by publike di-
fputations in a Synod the Roman cuftoms
againft thefe men (whoe being pious and
godly were called fcoffingly in thofe dayes
Quartadecimans) he carried about his necke a
certaine box of faints reliques, which he „
brought with him from Rome. And being „

Bal.cent.
1. in
VVilfrid.

most ma
licious
speech of
Bale a-
gainft S.
vvilfrid.

for

,, for theſe and other like things made Arch-
,, biſhop, he was driuen out twiſe within 45.
,, yeares from his Archbiſhopricke. And this
,, not by the inſolency of the kings, that draue
,, him out (as Polidor doth immodeſtlywryte)
,, but rather for his owne raſhnes, yea malice,
,, and many wickedneſſes, &c. And ſo at
,, length being conſumed with old age he pe-
,, riſhed in the yeare of Chriſt 710.

19. Behould heere a narration worthy the
ſpiritt of a new ghoſpeller and old Apoſtatá
againſt ſo venerable and worthy a pillar of
our primitiue Engliſh Church, as was Saint
Wilfrid. Marke how he is taxed for traue-
ling and ſtudying at Rome, for defending
by publike diſputations, the Roman cuſtome of celebrating Eaſter, which yet was
defended and decreed openly by the generall Councell of Nice, as before yow haue
heard and after ſhalbe proued. For bearing
a box of reliques about his necke brought
from Rome, which no doubt is one of the
things that moſt troubleth the ſpiritt of *Iohn
Bale* as it did the diuells and wicked ſpiritts
in England, who cryed and were caſt out
by the ſame, as you may read in them that
wryte his life.

Crimes obiected by Bale to Saint vvilfrid.

20. Moreouer he ſaith that for his owne
wickednes he was driuen out of his Archbiſhopricke, and ſo finally periſhed in the
yeare 710. As for his periſhing, yf he periſhed,

fhed, that liued fo auftere a religious life,
conuerted fo many thoufand English Heathens to Chriftian faith, wrought fo many
Miracles, as are recorded of him: then woe
to vs, that cannot imitate fo great holynes,
and woe to Iohn Bale that ran out of religion, & being a friar tooke a wench named
faithfull Dorothie. And that, as himfelfe
braggeth, *neque ab homine, neque per hominem fed* *Bal.*
ex fpeciali Chrifti dono, neyther from man nor *cent. 5.*
by man but by the fpeciall gift of Chrift, as *de fcript.*
though Chrift did vfe to deuide fuch gifts *Britan.*
to friars, that had vowed chaftity. And how *fol.* 244.
good a fellow he became afterward, and
how pleafant a companion, yow may vnderftand by his owne words, when wry-
ting of his works he faith: *Facetias & iocos fine* *Cent.*
certo numero feci, I haue wrytten iefts and pa- *ibid.*
ftimes without any certayne number (a fit
argument for a new ghofpeling friar.) But
yet how farre this exercife of iefting was
from the grauity & holynes of S. Wilfrid,
no man can doubt. And fo himfelfe (mife-
rable man) may be thought to haue perifhed, while the other raygneth eternally in
heauen.

21. And as for refutation of the horrible
flaunder that for his wickednes *S. VVilfride*
vvas driuen out of his Archbishopricke, I haue no
better meanes prefent, then to oppofe
againft this one lying Apoftata the vniuerfall

fall confent of all antiquity, especially thofe
that wrote his life, as *S. Bede*, and after him
Hedius, *Odo*, *Fridegenus*, *Petrus Blefenfis*; and
others. Who haue wrytten both his life and
death, as of a great Saint. And his memory
and feftiuall celebration is held throughout
the vniuerfall Church vpon the 12. day of
October, as all Martyrologes do teftifie.
And thus much of the infolency of Iohn
Bale againft the parfon of *Saint VVilfrid*.

* Se the
martiro-
loge of
Vfuard
and the
annot. of
*Molan.
die*. 12.
Octob.
and *Ba-
ronius*
vpon
the *Rom.
Marty-
rolog eo-
dem die*.

22. But now wheras further he is not ashamed to defend the Iewish cuftome, and the
quartadecimans condemned for it, faying that
they were pious men and were called by
the nickname of *Quartadecimans* for a fcoff
only, I am forced to deale further therin, &
to fhew him firft to be an hereticall and
moft fhamelefse calumniator, for that the
name of *Quartadecimani* or *Quatuordecimani*
(fignifying thofe that obferue the 14. day of
the moone of March to celebrate Eafter) is
an old name appointed to thofe that held
that hereticall vfe for many ages gone, as
may appeare by *Saint Epiphanius* that wrote
1200. yeares gone whofe words are thefe:

*Epiph.
hæres* 50.

*Emerfit rurfus mundo alia hærefis Tefferadecatita-
rum appellata, quos quartadecimanos quidam appel-
lant*. There is another herefie fprong vp in
the world, of fome that are called in greeke
Tefferadecatites which other in latin do call
Quartadecimãs, &c. The explication of which
words

words Saint *Augustine*, after him, in his booke of heresies written to *Quod-vult-deus*, doth sett downe thus: *Hinc appellati sunt, quòd* *August.* *non nisi quartadecima luna mense Martio pascha ce-* *har. 29.* *lebrāt.* These people are called by the Greeke words *Tesseradecatites* and by the Latin *Quartadecimans* for that they do celebrate Easter vpon the 14. day of the moone of march. *Vnde etiam Quartadecimani cognominati sunt,* saith *Nicephorus lib.4. histor. cap. 36.* for which cause they are called also *Quartadecimans.*

23. And yet further the same men were called also by a third name of *Paschatites*, as appeareth both by *S. Philastrius* Bishopp of *Philast.* *Brixia* somwhat before *S. Epiphanius.* Who in *in catal.* his catalogue of heresies numbring vp these *hæres.* *Paschatites*, yeldeth the reason of theire name in these words : *qui asserunt quartadeci-* *ma luna celebrandum esse Pascha, non autem sicuti* *Ecclesia Catholica celebrat*, who affirme that ,, Easter day is to be celebrated vpon the 14. ,, of the moneth of March (vpon whatsoeuer ,, day it shal fall out) and not as the Cath. ,, church doth accustome to expect the ,, sunday.

24. Well then, we see, that *Saint VVilfride* and other Roman Catholiks of his time did not inuent the name of *Quartadecimani* for a schoffe to disgrace godly men therby, as vngodly Iohn Bale blusseth not to auouch: but that it is an old name inuented and ap-

E   pointed

pointed by the vniuerfall primitiue Church
to them, that defended obftinately the
Iewifh cuftome of celebrating Eafter day
ftrictly vpon the 14. day of the moone of
March, according to the prefcript of the
Moyfaicall law. Which cuftome hath byn
accoumpted naught, Iewifh and hereticall
for the fpace of 1400. yeares, to witt euer
fince the decree of *S. Victor*, Pope of Rome
againft the fame, fince which time all authors that haue wrytten of herefies, haue
held for heretikes thofe that defended this

Tert. de prafcrip. aduerf. heref.

cuftome: as may appeare firft by *Tertullian*,
that liued in that very time of *Pope Victor*, or
prefently after. As alfo by the firft Councell
of Nice, which was held fome 100. yeares
after *Victor* againe, and *Victors* decree therin
confirmed. As after againe, in the Councell

Concil. Antioch. cap. 1. Concil. Laod. cap. 7. Theod. l. 3. c. vlt. de fab. haret. Niceph. lib. 4. hiftor. c. 36 Damafc. haref. 50

of *Antioch* gathered togeather almoft 50.
years after that of *Nice*, and fomwhat after
that againe by the Councell of *Laodicea*. And
then by *Philaftrius* and *Epiphanius* before cited,
and finally by *Saint Auguftine, Theodoretus, Nice-*
phorus, *Damafcenus* and others that enfued.
And the defenders of this herefie (howfoeuer Iohn Bale & his fellowes will fanctifie
them now againe for pious men, for that
they holde againft the Roman Church)
were fo odious to the Cath. Fathers, euen
of the Greeke & Eaftern Church, efpecially after the determination of the Councell
of Nice

ofNice (which determination though it be
not extant now in the said Councels Decrees, yet is it testified sufficiently both by
Theodoretus and the letters of Constantine
himselfe recorded by *Eusebius*) that *Socrates*
in his story writeth of *Saint Iohn Chrisostome*
Archbishopp of *Constantinople* these words:
sis, qui in Asia festum Paschatis 14. *die mensis
primi celebrabrant, Ecclesias, non secus quam No-
uatianis, ademit.* Saint Chrisostome did take
away churches throughout his iurisdiction
from those that in Asia did celebrate the
feast of Easter vpon the 14. of March no
lesse then from the Nouatian heretiks them
selues. And no lesse doth the same author
report of *Leontius* B. of *Ancyra* in Asia, and
other Eastearn Bishopps.

*Theod.l.
6.cap. 9.
Euseb.li.
3.de vi-
ta Con-
stant.c.
17.&18.
Socrat.
lib.6.hi-
stor.cap.
10.& 20
,,
,,
"*

25. And the reason heerof was not only
for that by this different custome of celebrating Easter there grew great schismes
amongst Christians, but for that indeed the
true formality of this heresie (consisting in
that they would make it of necessity, to
keep the old law in this behalfe) was begon first by an heretike called *Blastus*, as appeareth by Tertullian, who (to vse his owne
words) saith thus; *Latenter Iudaismum introdu-
cere voluit, dicens, Pascha non aliter custodiendum
esse, nisi secundum legem Moysis* 14. *mensis.* He
meant couertly to bring in Iudaisme affirming that Easter was not to be kept, but ,,

*Tert.lib.
de præsc.
contra
hæres.*

E 2   accor-

VVhie the Aſiā cuſtome of cele-brating Eaſter vvas cō-demned.

according to the law of Moyſes vpon the 14. day of the firſt moneth. For refutation of which hereſie *Tertullian* ſaith : *Quis autem ne-ſciat, quoniam Euangelica gratia euacuatur, ſi ad le-gem Chriſtus redigitur?* Who doth not know but that the grace of Chriſtes ghoſpell is made voyd, yf Chriſt be reduced againe to the obſeruation of the Moſaicall law?

26. This then was the very eſſentiall point of this hereſie, & of them that defended the ſame : to witt that they would bynd Chri-ſtians to the obſeruation of this point accor-ding to the Moſaicall law. Againſt which point of obligation Saint Paul is ſo earneſt in many places of his epiſtles, as he reſiſted Saint Peter openly, for that by his conuer-ſation only, he did ſeeme to force or bynd men to Iudaicall obſeruations, *Gentes cogis iu-daizare,* you do force gentills to follow the Iewes. And for this cauſe he wrote ſo ear-neſtly to the Galathians : *Ecce ego Paulus dico vobis, ſi circumcidamini, Chriſtus nihil vobis proderit.* Behould I Paull do teſtiſie vnto you, that yf you do circumcide you ſelues (or vſe this *Moſaicall* ceremony) Chriſt ſhall profit you nothing.

27. And againe, he telleth them in the ſame place, that whoſoeuer vſeth but this one ceremony of circumciſion, byndeth himſelfe therby to the obſeruation of all the old law: and conſequently doth depriue himſelfe

Gal. 2.

Gal. 5.

himſelfe of the whole grace of Chriſt.
which yet is to be vnderſtood (as Auncient
Fathers do expound) after the ghoſpell of
Chriſt was fully diuulged, and in them that
did vſe any of theſe ceremonies as of neceſſitie. For that otherwiſe we read of the
Apoſtles themſelues gathered togeather n
Councell, that they gaue leaue to Chriſtians
for a time at the beginning, *abſtinere à ſanguine
& ſuffocato*, to abſteyne from bloud. and that
which is ſtrangled, or rather did ordeyne
the ſame. Which yet afterwards was taken
away againe by authoritie of the church, ſo
as it is euident, that the toleration was for a
time only, & as a thing indifferent without
obligation. And for like reſpect we read of
Saint Paul himſelfe, that albeit afterward
he did forbidd to the *Galathias* the vſe of circumciſion, with ſuch ſeueritie, as you haue
heard, yet at the beginning he circumciſed
Timothe for reſpect of the Iewes, as S. Luke
teſtifieth, for that the ghoſpell was not yet
ſo farre preached, as it made the obſeruations of the Moſaicall law to be wholie vnlawfull: eſpeciallie if they were vſed as
things indifferent, and not of neceſſitie. As
it is probable, that both *Saint Iohn Euangeliſt,
Polycarp* and others of the Eaſt Church did,
when for a time they vſed the feſtiuall day
of celebratinge Eaſter, as an indifferent
thing, obliging no man to follow the one or

*Hovv
the cele-
brating
of ſome
ceremo-
nies or
cuſto-
mes for
a time
might
be lavv-
full.
Act.* 15.
verſ. 29.

Act. 16.
verſ. 3.

H ovv
the Ro-
man vſe
beganne
of cele-
brating
Eaſter
vpon a
ſundaie.
Bed. lib.
de ratio.
tēp.c.42.
Ignat.
ep.6.ad
Magnes.
& 8. ad
Philip.
*Apoc.*1.
*ver.*10.

the other vſe, to witt, eyther this of the 14.
day commaunded by the old law, or the
other of the ſunday brought in by tradition
from Saint Peter and Saint Paul in the Roman Church. As among others *S. Protherius*
Patriarch of *Alexandria* (by the teſtimonie of
Saint Bede) doth write to Pope Leo. And
long before them both *Saint Ignatius* B. of
Antioch (which Church was founded by
Saint Peter) doth teſtifie in diuers epiſtles
that Eaſter daie was to be celebrated vpon
a Sundaie. Yea Saint Iohn himſelfe making
mention of *dies dominicus*, the Lords daie, in
the beginning of his Apocalips, as of a ſolemne daie aboue the reſt (which no man
will denie to be ſundaie:) there is no other
reaſon, why this daie ſhould be called our
Lords daie with ſo ſpeciall title of feſtiuitie,
but onlie for that it was dedicated in the
Apoſtles time to the reſurrection of Chriſt.
And yf in euerie weeke it be kept feſtiuall
for that reſpect, & that the whole Sabboth
be turned into it: then much more iuſt is it,
that the great Sabboth of Chriſts reſurrection ſhould be once a yeare celebrated
vpon this daie. Yet was the matter, as you
haue heard, left for arbitrarie & indifferent
for diuers yeares in Aſia, without conſtraint on eyther ſide.

28.　But when in proceſſe of time the
Bishops of Rome, eſpeciallie *Pope Pius* the
firſt

firſt and *Victor* had perceyued that by this
toleration and difference of obſeruation not
onlie ſchiſmes & diſſentiõ grew, but hereſie
alſo and Iudaiſme was meant to be brought
in: then the ſaid *Pius* the firſt in the yeare
of Chriſt 148. (as *Euſebius* teſtifieth) made a
decree againſt the Aſian Iewiſh obſeruation, and after him againe in the next age
following *Pope Victor* ſeing the ſame incon-
ueniences greatlie to encreaſe, wrote a letter to *Policrates B.* of *Epheſus* to gather a Synod againſt it about the yeare of Chriſt 249.
as Euſebius teſtifieth. And when he percei-
ued, that both he and diuers Aſian Biſhops
did ſtand more ſtiffelie in defence therof,
then he expected; yea that they began, not
onlie to ſhew obſtinacie therin againſt the
former decree of *Pope Pius* and the ſea of
Rome, but to draw neere alſo to the verie
formalitie of hereſie before mentioned, to
witt that it was neceſſarie to obſerue the 14.
daie; naie further that it was *ex Euangelij pra-
ſcripto, & ſecundum regulam & normam fidei*, by
the preſcription of the ghoſpell, and according to the rule and norme of faith, as the
ſaid *Polycrates* in his epiſtle to *Pope Victor* writeth; when *Victor* (I ſay) ſaw this, he reſolued after counſell taken by conference
with diuers Synods both of the Weſt and
Eaſt Churches to excommunicate thoſe
Aſian Biſhops that reſiſted, yf they would

*Euſeb. in
Chron.
an.* 148.
*De cõſe-
crat. diſ.*
3. *cap.*
Noſte.
*& ibid.
diſ.* 4. *ca.*
Celebri-
tatem.
Euſeb. l.
5. *hiſt. c.*
23. *& 24*

*Ibidem
cap.* 22.

The de- not agree. Which determination albeit *Ire-*
cree of *næus* & fome others at that time did miflike
popeVi- and dehort *Pope Victor* from it, as a thing pe-
&or a- rilous, and fcandalous, and fubiect to manie
bout troubles (as Eufebius reporteth:) yet did ne-
keeping uer anie of them fai that he could not doe it;
Eafter. but rather, when he had done it in deed,
they did accommodate themfelues thervnto both in Weft and Eaft, ratifying and confirming the fame by diuers particular Sy-
Niceph. nods as *Nicephorus* recounteth, to witt, in
l.4.c.36. *Ierufalem*, *Cæfarea*, *Tyrus*, *Ptolomais*, *Corinth*,
Lions of France, where *Saint Irenæus* himfelf
was Bishopp and other places, &c.

29. And finallie the Councell of Nice confirmed the fame; as the fathers therof do teftifie by their particular letters to the Clergy of Alexandria, whofe words ar thefe, as
Theod. *Theodoretus* relateth them: *Scitote controuerfiam*
l. 6. c.9. *de pafchate fufceptam, prudenter fedatam effe. Ita vt*
omnes fratres, qui orientem incolunt, iam Romanos,
nos, & omnes vos, fint confentientibus animis in eodem
celebrando deinceps fequuturi. Yow muft vn-
„ derftand, that the controuerfie about cele-
„ brating Eafter taken in hand by vs, is pru-
„ dentlie pacified: fo as all our brethré that in-
„ habit the Eaft parts will follow for the time
„ to come the Romás (or the Roman church)
„ vs (and the authoritie of the Councell) and
„ all yow (of the Egiptian Church) with full
„ confent of mind in celebrating the fame
feaft.

feaſt. Note heere that the Councell doth put the authoritie of the Church of Rome in the firſt place euen before themſelues, and then themſelues and the authoritie of the Councell in the ſecond place, and thoſe of *Alexandria* in the third. Which is another reconning, then our heretiks are wont to make of the Roman Church.

30. Conſtantine alſo the Emperor writing his letters to all Biſhops of the Chriſtian world, that had not byn preſent at the Councell of *Nice*, nor could come, yeldeth accoumpt vnto them with great Chriſtian modeſtie and zeale of the cheefe matters handled in that Councell. Where comming to ſpeake of the decree of celebrating Eaſter, he ſaith thus: *Cùm de ſanctiſſimo feſto Paſchatis diſceptaretur, communi omnium ſententia videbatur rectum eſſe, vt omnes vbique vno, eodemá, die illud celebrarent.* when the queſtion was propoſed about celebrating the holie feaſt of Eaſter: it ſeemed good by the common conſent of all that were preſent in this Councell, that all Chriſtians ſhould celebrate the ſame in one and the ſelfe ſame daie. Which day he ſheweth to be Sunday, and refuteth at large the cuſtome of celebrating the ſame with the Iewes vpon the 14. daie of the moone, though it were a *Feria* concluding thus: *Quæ cum ita ſe habent, &c.* Which things being ſo, do you willinglie

E 5   imbrace

,, imbrace this decree of the Councell as a
,, great gift of God & a commaundment sent
,, from heauen : For so much as what soeuer
,, is decreed by holie Councell of Bishops,
,, that must be ascribed to Gods holie will.
,, Wherfore do you declare and denounce
,, vnto all our deare brethren liuing among
,, you, the decrees of this Councell, and
,, namelie the decree of celebrating this holie
,, feast, &c.

31. Thus wrote our good British Emperor *Constantine* with a farre different spiritt
from those Christian inhabitans of Britanie, which afterward defended the contrarie custome without respect of holie decree
of the Nicen Councell : but farre more opposite and contrarie is the wicked spiritt of
Iohn Bale, Iohn Fox, and other such later bru-
tish rather then British sectaries, that euen
in our dayes, after that the Roman Cath.
vse hath byn receiued for 13.hundred yeares
since the said Councell, they ar content
for hatred of the name of Rome, to bring
it into controuersie againe, and to allow rather the Iewish vse, and to praise them that
defend it in our Countrey (as you haue
heard) reiecting and defacing others that
stood for the Cath. partie, though neuer
other wise so famous, and illustrious for
their learning and vertue, as *Beda, Agilbert*
VVilfride and others the cheefest pillars of
our

The
vvicked
spiritt of
our se-
ctaries.

our primitiue English Church were. But this is their fhamelefſe ſpiritt, to dishonour wherin poſsiblie they can their forefathers. 32. And thus much of this matter, about the firſt conuerſion or preaching of Chriſtian faith in Britanie vnder the Apoſtles. Now will we paſſe to the more publike conuerſiõ of our land vnder *K. Lucius*, which as in my *VVard-vvord* I called the firſt in reſpect of our two publike conuerſions from paganiſme: ſo do I heere name it the ſecond in regard of the former preaching in the Apoſtles tyme. About which conuerſion, though in effect our moderne heretiks dare not deny the ſame: yet ſhall you heare no leſſe wrangling of them about this, then the former, for the great greefe they receaue, in that it ſhould be ſaid, or thought to come from Rome.

OF THE SECOND CON-
VERSION OF BRITANY VN-
der K. Lucius, *by* Pope Eleutherius, *and teachers ſent from him, about the yeare of Chriſt* 180. *and of the notorious abſurd cauillations of heretiks about the ſame alſo.*

CHAP. IIII.

A**LL** that hitherto hath byn ſpoken, is about the firſt preaching of Chriſtian religion in Britanie by particular men within the firſt age or hundred yeares

yeares after Chriſt. Which our Roman
enemies only vpon enuy and animoſitye
without any one teſtimony of antiquity,
will needs take from Rome and the Roman Church, and giue it to the Grecians of
Aſia , and to the Eaſt-parts, as you haue
heard. Now doe follow two other more famous and publike conuerſions of the ſaid
Iland vnder the two renowned Popes of
Rome, & by their ſpeciall induſtry. Which
are acknowledged , and regiſtred by the
whole Chriſtian world, & do ſo much preſſe
the ſplene & mooue the galle of our Rome-
biters, as they leaue no corner of their wits
vnſifted to diſcredit or reiect the ſame.

2. The firſt conuerſion was (as the warder
ſaith) vnder *Pope Eleutherius* towards the end
of the ſecond age after Chriſt. When K. *Lu-*
cius of Britanie hearing of the great and horrible perſecutions of Chriſtians in Rome, &
of their often martyrings, and that they remayned conſtant notwithſtanding in their
Chriſtian faith, to all mens admiration, and
that their number did encreaſe daylie euen
of the cheefeſt nobilitie, and that two worthie Senators in particular *Pertinax* and *Tre-*
tellius had byn latelie conuerted from Paganiſme to profeſſe Chriſt, yea that the Emperor himſelfe *Marcus Aurelius* then liuing, began to be a frend to Chriſtians in reſpect of
a famous victorie obteyned by their prayers
                                                        (all

Reaſons
mouing
K. Lu-
cius to
inquire
of Chri-
ſtian re-
ligion.

(all which things *Baronius* sheweth the Emperors legate in England to haue told *Lucius:*) for these causes (I say) and for that he hated the Romans and their old religion, to whome he vnderstood the Christians to be contrary, he resolued to be instructed in that religion. And vnderstanding the cheefe fountaine therof to be at Rome, contented not himselfe eyther with instructions he might haue at home by Christians there, nor yet from the Christian Bishopps florishing then in France, as *S. Irenæus, Photinus,* and others: but sent men to Rome to demaund preachers of Eleutherius the Pope. Who directed to him two Romans, named *Fugatius*, and *Damianus*, by whome the said K. and his countrey were conuerted about the yeare of Christ 180. (as Iohn Fox holdeth) but as *Baronius* thinketh 183. from whome *Pamelius*, *Genebrard*, *Nauclerus* and other chronographers do little dissent, though *Marianus Scotus* doth put it in the yeare 177. And this conuersion of Britanie vnder K. *Lucius* is testified both by the auncient books of the liues of the Roman Bishopps attributed by some to *Damasus*: as also by the auncient Ecclesiasticall tables & martirologes yet extant, as *Baronius* proveth, & by ✶ *S. Bede* in his historie of England, and after him by *Ado* Archbishopp of *Treuers*, & *Marianus Scotus* anno 177. & all authors since.

Baron. in Annal. Ecc. an. Christi 183. *Tom.* 2.

Vvhen K. Lucius vvas conuerted. ✶*Beda de gestis Angl. l.* 1. *c.* 4. *& de sex. ætat. sub. Ant. Vero. Ado in chron. sub. Commodo Imp. Mar. Scot. in* 6. *ætat. Pol. virg. lib.* 1.

3. This

3.   This then being ſo, and Iohn Fox the
father or lyes not daring openly to impugne
the ſame : yet graunteth he the thing with
ſuch difficultie, and ſtrainings and telleth
the ſtorie with ſo manie *hems* and *havvs*, *ifs*
and *ands,* interpretations and reſtrictions, as
a man may ſee how greatlie it greeueth him
to confeſſe the ſubſtance therof, I meane of
this ſecond conuerſion by *Pope Eleutherius.*
And therfore he turneth himſelfe hither &
thither, now graunting, now denying;
now doubting, now equiuocating, as is
both ridiculous and ſhamefull to behould.
For as on the one ſide, he would gladly deny the truth of this ſtorie : ſoe on the other
ſide being preſſed with the authorityes before alleadged, and generall conſent of all
writers, he dareth not to vtter himſelfe
playnelie, but endeauoreth to leaue the reader in ſuſpence, and doubtfull whether it
were true or noe. Which is the effect moſt
deſired commonlie of hereticall writers, to
bring all things in doubt, and queſtion, and
there to leaue the reader. And to this purpoſe doth the *Fox* tell vs firſt, that diuers authors of later times, *do not agree about the cer-*
tayne yeare vvherin this conuerſion of K. *Lucius did*
happen, ſome ſaying more, and ſome ſaying leſſe. But
what is this to the ouerthrow of the thing
it ſelfe, for that about the particular times,
wherin things were done, there is often
found

Iohn
Fox his
Tergi-
uerſatiõ.

Fox act.
and mon.
pag. 96.
col. 2.

found no small varietie among principall writers, and about principall points and misteries of our faith; as about the comming of the *Magi*, and martyrdome of the infants, about the time of Christ his baptisme, yea also of his passion, what yeare and daie eache of these things happened: which yet doth not derogate from the certainty of the things themselues.

4. And this is his first cauill, or rather light skyrmish, wherby he would somwhat batter or weake the creditt of the storie, before he commeth to lay the full assault, which insueth immediatly with seaven double canons plated by him, which he calleth *seauen good coniecturall reasons*, against the tradition of antiquity about this conuersion of Britany from *Pope Eleutherius.* Wherin not withstanding yow must note, that he proposeth the controuersie, as though his purpose were onlie to prooue that *Pope Eleutherius* was not the first, that couerted Englād: which thing, as it might be graunted in the sense before often touched, yf he spake or meant plainely: so finding him to deale guilfully, and to go about to prooue in the end (as appeareth by his conclusion) that *Eleutherius* couerted not *King Lucius* at all: but onlie holp perhaps to conuert him, or to instruct him better in religion (being a Christian before) I am constrayned to examine briefly the

First cauill.

The effecte of seauen cannons planted by Iohn Fox to batter the storie of K. Lucius conuersiō from Rome.

force

force (or rather fraud and follie) of thefe his
feauen arguments , to the end yow may
iudge therby, how he behaueth himfelfe in
fo mayne a volume , as his acts and monuments do conteyne; feing that in this one
matter he beareth himfelfe fo fondlie and
malitioufly. And for breuities fake I will reduce the faid feauen arguments to three generall heads or kinds , fhewing firft that all
ar *impertinent*. Secondlie that fome befides
impertinency haue alfo *groffe ignorāce*. Thirdlie that others befides thefe two commen-
dations, haue *fraud & plaine impofture* in them.
5.   To the firft kind of *impertinent*, do ap-
partaine his 4. 5. and fixt arguments handled by me before againft the Magdeburg-
gians , to witt , that Saint Bede faid , in his
time , *that the Britans celebrated Eafter after the*
fashion of the Eaft Church: that Petrus Cluniacenfis
teftifeth the fame in his dayes of fome Scotts: and
that Nicephorus faith that Simon Zelotes , preached
the ghofpell in England. All which three arguments,as they do ferue to no purpofe heere,
but to fhew that Fox ftealeth all out of the
Magdeburgians : fo no other anfwere is
needfull to be made vnto them , then that
which before hath byn written; feing that,
all being graunted , that heere is faid : yet
proueth it nothing,that *the faith of Britany ca-*
me not from Rome,and confequently all is impertinent.

Fox his
firft kind
of argu-
ments.
Imperti-
nent.

6. Of

6.   Of the second sort both impertinent
and ignorant arguments, are his second and
third probations. *My second reason is* (faith he)
out of Tertullian, vvho liuing neere about or rather
somvvhat before this Eleutherius, teſtifieth in his booke
contra Iudæos, that the ghoſpell vvas diſperſed abroad
by the ſound of Apoſtles in diuers contreyes : *and then*
among other kingdoms he reciteth alſo the parts of
Britany, &c. This you ſee how impertinent it
is to the purpoſe we haue in hand. For that
it concludeth not , but that *Pope Eleutherius*
after the Apoſtles time might conuert K.
Lucius and his people publikely by *Fugatius*
and *Damianus* , as we affirme . And then ſecondlie it includeth notorious error and
ignorance, in that he ſaith: *Tertullian liued be-*
fore Eleutherius. For that it is proued out of
Tertullian his owne works and words, eſpeciallie in his booke *de Pallio* (wherin he yeldeth the reaſon , wherfore he chaunged his
habite from a gowne to a cloake , as Chriſtians were wont to doe in thoſe daies) that
he was conuerted to the Chriſtian faith in
the tenth yeare of *Pope Victor* , that was ſucceſſor to *Eleutherius.* Which was anno Domini 196. And moreouer he wrote his booke
contra Iudæos cited by Fox diuers yeares after
that againe, as *Pamelius* & others do demonſtrate in his life. So as *Eleutherius* raigning 15.
yeares before *Victor* (as all authors doe agree)
it followeth , that he was Pope 25. yeares

F   before

before *Tertullian* was a Chriftian. And for fo
much as the conuerfion of England is afsi-
gned to haue ben in the fifth yeare of *Eleutherius*, it followeth, that *Tertullian* was not a
Chriftian in 20. yeares after that time. And
thus much for his fecond reafon. Now lett
vs heare his third.

Fox. ibi.
col. 2.
n. 73.

7.   *My third probation* (faith he) *I deduct out of
Origen, whofe words are thefe: Britanniam in Chri-
ftianā confentire religionē. That Britany did confent
in Chriftian religion. VVherby it appeareth, the faith
of Chrift was fparfed heere in England before the
dayes of Eleutherius.* Marke his owne contradiction, marke his inference, and note his
impofture. He affirmeth out of *Origen*,
That Britany did confent in Chriftian religion: And
yet he faieth in his inference, *vvherby it appeareth it vvas fparfed in England. Sparfing* importeth, that particular men heere and there
were conuerted : *confent* importeth a generall conuerfion, fo that by *Origens* words of
confent it may feeme, that he meant the publike conuerfion made by *Eleutherius*. And
by Fox his owne falfe interpretation and
foolish inference he is made to fay, that
there were onlie certaine fparkles of Chriftian religion in his daies in Britanie. But

Orig. ho.
4. in E-
zechiel.
circa me-
dium.

the true words of *Origen* corrupted by *Fox*
do make the matter more cleere . Who di-
fputing againft the Iewes , vrgeth them
with this queftion. *Quando enim terra Britannia*

nia ante aduentum Chrifti in vnius Dei confenfit re-
ligionem? For when did the land of Britanie
agree in the religion of one God before the
comming of Chrift?

8. Heere you fee the words of *Origen*, firft
not trulie but corruptlie alleadged before
by *Iohn Fox*. And fecondlie, that *Origen* doth
fpeake them of a confent in religion throughout all the land of Britanie. And therby
feemeth to fignifie, not the particular conuerfion of feuerall men before *Eleutherius* his
time (as *Fox* would enforce it:) but rather
the publike conuerfion (as I haue faid) vnder *K. Lucius* and *Eleutherius*. Which conuerfion according to the former accoumpt of
Fox himfelfe (who faith it was in the year
of Chrift 186.) was about 76, yeares before
the death of *Origen*. For that (as *Eufebius* teftifieth) *Origen* died in the yeare of Chrift
256. and was of age 69. when he died, fo as
he was borne 7. yeares after our faid conuerfion vnder *Lucius*. And confequently he
might meane of this conuerfion in his former homilie. And it is not onlie ignorance,
but willfull malice and impofture alfo in
Iohn Fox, to make his reader beleeue, (as before in *Tertullian* fo in this man) that he was
eyther equal or elder then *Pope Eleutherius*.
And for this caufe, that *Origen* in his forfaid
homilie muft needs meane of a former conuerfion of Britanie, that came not from

The age
of Ori-
gen pet-
uerted.
Eufeb.li.
7. hift.c.
1.

Rome. Conſider the mans honeſtie & witt in theiſe ſhiftes.

9.   And albeit this may be ſufficient, and more than inoughe, to ſhew his falſe dealing, and lacke of fidelity in euery thing he handleth: yet will I add his two laſt arguments, which he calleth his firſt & ſeaueth. And in which (as I ſaid before) that not only the former two qualities of impertinency and error are to be found: but manifeſt fraud alſo and wiſull deceypt, Let vs heare his words. But firſt I muſt both pray, and preuent the Reader to take in patience the hearing of one and the ſelfe ſame thing many tymes repeated, for that we hauing to deale with three ſeuerall partyes, that do tell vs tales by retaile one to another of them (to witt, *Syr Francis, Syr Fox*, and *Meſſiers the Magdeburgians*) we cannot well ſee or ſett downe, what each of them ſaith, and borroweth one of another, but by repeating the ſame things. Yet ſhall it be very breefly. Thus then writeth Fox in that, which he calleth his firſt probation againſt the firſt cõuerſion of England by *Eleutherius.*

A re-queſt & preuen-tion to the rea-der,

Fox pag. 96.

10.   *My firſt probation* (ſaith he) *I take out of the teſtimony of Gildas, vvho in his ſtory affirmeth plainely, that Britany receyued the ghoſpell in the time of Tiberius the Emperour: and that Ioſeph of Arimathia vvas ſent by Philipp the Apoſtle from France to Britanie. Gild. lib. de victoria Aurel. Ambroſy.* Heere

you

you fee firft not only *crambe recocta* according to the prouerbe, that is to fay cole-
warts and other trash twice fodden: but
many tymes alfo both fodde and fett before
vs. For all this yow heard before more then
once, both out of Syr Francis & the Magdeburgians. And when all is graunted, yet is
the whole argument but a vaine and chil-
dish cauill: fot it proueth only, that *Damianus* and *Fugatius*, fent by *Eleutherius*, were not
the very firit of all, that preached Chriftian
faith in Britany, which we neuer affirmed:
but only that Britanie was conuerted publikely vnder *Eleutherius*, which this impugneth not. And fecondly for the receauing
of Chrifts faith vnder *Tiberius* the Emperour, I haue fhewed before that it is vnlikely feeing *Tiberius* liued but 5. yeares after
the afcenfion of our Sauiour, and that the
place alleadged for yt out of Gildas (if he
meane the trew Gildas now extant) proueth it not: but only that Chrift himfelfe
appeared to the world in the tyme of *Tiberius*, and that the faith of Chrift entred Britanie afterward vnder *Claudius*, as may appeare euidently to him that will reade and
examine the place with attention. Which
the *Fox* perceauing, thought it not beft to
alleadg vs the faid true Gildas publifhed by
Polydor Virgill, and allowed by all learned
men of Chriftendome, wofe title is, *De exci-*

A forged Gildas brought in by Fox.

F 3   *dio*

dio Britanniæ : but runneth to a forged Gildas,
De victoria Aurelij Ambrosij, to confirme his al-
legacion withall, of which Gildas the said
Polydor after due examination of the matter
had, writeth as followeth.

Pol.Vir.
lib.1.hi-
ftor.pag.
16.

11. Extat item alter libellus (vt tempestiue lectorem
nefariæ fraudu admoneamus) qui falsissimè inscri-
bitur Gildæ commentarium, haud dubiè à quodam
pessimo impostore compositum, &c. Sanè is nebulo longe post homines natos impudentissimus, &c. There
is extant besides, another booke also (that
I may by this occasion aduertise the Reader
in time of a wicked imposture) which is
most falsely intituled, the Commentary of
Gildas, deuised no doubt by some naughtie
deceiuer,&c.Truly he was the most impu-
dentst knaue that euer lived, &c. Thus said
Polydor of the inuentor of this booke: and as
much would he haue said of Syr Iohn Fox,
that obtrudeth the same for a true author,
yf he had liued in our daies, And seeing that
the Caluinists themselues of Heidelberge in
Germany, taking vpon them to sett forth
all the British writers anno 1587. (as Gildas,
Geffrey of Monmouth , Ponticus Virunnius, and
others) durst not sett forth this fained Gildas
alleadged by Fox, but onlie the former true
Gildas printed before by Polydor:it is a token,
that Fox is more impudent and more greedy
to deceiue , then they . As you shall much
more preceyue by his last argumét ensuing.

12. For

11. For my *seauenth argument* (faith he) *I may make my probation by the plaine vvords of Eleuthe- rius by vvhofe epiftle vvrytten to K. Lucius vve may vnderftad that Lucius had receyued the faith ofChrift in this land before he fent to Eleutherius for the Romā lavves. For fo the expreffe vvords of the letter do ma- nifeftl' purport, as heereafter follovveth to be feene.* Fox pag. 96. Fox his laft and falfeft argu- ment.

Thus faith he, and citeth for his proofe in the margent *ex epiftola Eleutherij ad Lucium.* And by this laft and ftrongeft argument of his, the fillie fellow thinketh to ftrike the nayle dead, and to proue, that *K. Lucius* was a Chriftian before he receaued preachers from *Pope Eleutherius.* Ahd confequentlie that all is falfe, which antiquitie hath held attri- buting the conuerfion of that kingdome and of the Kinge him felf to the Bifhopp of Rome, For which caufe *Fox* addeth prefen- tlie ; *peraduenture Eleutherius might help fomthing eyther to conuert the King or els to encreafe the faith nevvly fprong vp then among the people.*

13. So defin'th he the matter, and & con- fider, I pray you, what he attributeth to *Eleutherius* in this conuerfion : *Peraduenture* (faith he) *he might help fomthing to K. Lucius his couerfion.* And is not this a great matter, efpe- cially being qualified (as it is) with the re- ftriction *Peraduenture* ? Yf a man fhould fay of Efops fables, *that peraduenture fome of thcm, in fome points might be true:* vvere it not as much as *Iohn Fox* doth attribute to all this con-

F 4 fent

ſent of authors for this conuerſion vnder *Pope Eleutherius*? ſeeing he ſaith not abſolute-ly, *Eleutherius* did conuert *K. Lucius* or help in-deed thervnto: but, that *peraduenture he might help ſomthing &c.* Yow may marke the dimi-nutiues vſed by Fox to leſſen the benefitt, to witt, *Peraduenture, might ſomthing, &c.* And thereby conſider what a holy itomake he hath to Rome, and what little accoumpt he maketh of the authority or conſent of all antiquity, when they make againſt him.

Contēpt of the teſtimo-ny of an tiquitie.

14. But now let vs weigh further his proo-fes & by them alſo his frauds & impoſtures. Firſt of all for proofes, that *K. Lucius* was a Chriſtian before he dealt with *Eleutherius,* he alleadgeth the epiſtle it ſelfe of *Eleuthe-rius.* Which he ſetteth downe as authenti-call citing only in the margent *ex vetuſto co-dice Regum antiquorum,* taken out of an old booke of old Kings: but telleth not where we ſhall find this old booke. And it may be (perhaps) of as good creditt (if it were found) as the booke of *Gildas* before allead-

About the epi-ſtle of P. Eleuthe-rius to K. Lu-cius ci-ted by Fox.

ged, *De Victoria Aurelij Ambroſij,* or as many other fabulous things be in the Storie of *Geffrey of Monmouth,* and *Iohn Fox* after him.

15. And in deed yf we conſider the begin-ning of the firſt words of the epiſtle it ſelfe, we ſhall find certaine doubts, which ney-ther Fox nor his fellowes will euer be able to ſolue, as firſt of all, that it was written

after

after *Eleutherius* was dead. For so it appeareth by the accoumpt of time noted in the title, which is this in Latin, as Fox relateth: *Anno Domini* 169. *à passione Christi scripsit D. Eleutherius Papa, Lucio Regi Britaniæ ad correctionem Regis & Procerum regni, &c.* which words Fox omitteth to tranſlate into English, for that they make againſt him, and therfore would not haue his vnlearned reader to vnderſtand the abſurditie therof: for they ſay, *that Pope Eleutherius vvrote this epiſtle to Lucius K. of Britanie to correct both him and the nobility of his Kingdome in the yeare* 169. *after the paſsion of Chriſt.* To which 169. yeares yf we add other 33. which Chriſt liued before his paſsion they make 202. which is 19. yeares after *Eleutherius* death who did in the yeare of Chriſt 184. as all authors agree. For which cauſe Fox him ſelfe in this verie place, & els where often, doth appoint the conuerſion of *K. Lucius* to haue byn in the yeare of Chriſt 180. and the tenth of *Eleutherius* reigne, but this epiſtle appointeth it 22. yeares after, to witt *anno Domini* 202. ſo wiſe a man is Fox in bringing it in.

16. Secondly this epiſtle was written in latin: and ſo ſhould Fox haue deliuered the ſame vnto vs wholie, yf he had dealt plainelie. But he hath not ſo done, but onlie giueth vs the title in latin without any interpretation, as now hath byn ſaid: & the remnant (or at leaſtwiſe ſo much as he thought con-

Fox pag. 96. col. 2. n. 40.

Fox his subtilty in concealing the original in Latin.

uenient) in English onlie, and this of his
owne tranflation without letting vs fee the
Originall. And fo he plaieth the Fox in
euery thing. But, to returne againe to this latin title of the epiftle, there is another caufe,
why Iohn Fox would not traflate it into
Engiish. And this is, for that it is faid
therin that it was written by the Pope *ad
correctionem Regis & Procerum regni, &c.* to correct the King, and nobility of the realme.
Which proueth that the Pope tooke him
feif to be their Superiour alfo in thofe daies,
and they to be fubiect to his correction. For
which caufes Fox his fchollers, *Holinshed,*
Hooker, and *Harifon* do leaue out this title altogeather in their chronicles. For that the
word *correction* vpon the King and nobilitie
is an odious thing in thefe daies, efpeciallie from Popes.

17.   And thus much of the title and fraud
vfed therin. Now lett vs paffe to the bodie
of the epiftle. Thus it beginneth in Iohn
Fox.pag. Fox his tranflation. *Ye require of vs the Roman*
96. *lavves and the Emperors to be fent ouer vnto yovv,*
vvhich yovv may practife and put in vre vvithin your
Realme. The Roman lavves and the Emperors vve
may euer reprooue: but the lavv of God vve may not.
Yovv haue receyued of late through gods mercy in the
Realme of Britany the lavv of Chrift, &c. Thus
faith the epiftle, and out of thefe laft words,
I. Fox doth frame his former feauenth argument,

ment, that K. *Lucius* had receiued the faith of
Christ, *before he sent to Eleutherius for the Roman
lavves.* Well suppose it was so, and that this
sending was a secod Embassage some yeares
after his conuersion, how doth this inferre,
that K. *Lucius* was a Christian before he dealt
with *Eleutherius*, or before he sent the first
time vnto him? and so that he was rather
conuerted by Grecians, then by Romans, as
the next immediate words of Fox are? *And
that hence it may be inferred that Eleutherius did rather help perhaps to his conuersion, or to encrease the
faith novvly sprong vp, then conuert him?* Are not
these notorious shifts and shamelesse win-
dings of our Fox, to delude his Reader?

18. But you will aske me perhaps, how
I do proue that this was a second Embassage sent by K. *Lucius to Eleutherius*, *and the
Popes ansvvere to the same?* Wherto I say, that
this is confessed & proued by Fox himselfe,
who writing of K. *Lucius,* saith, that some
yeares after his conuersion, when he had put
his realme in order, for matters of religiō, he
wrote againe to haue the ciuill & imperiall
lawes sent ouer to him, wherby to gouerne
his kingdome according to Christiā religiō.

19. All this I say dothe Fox sett downe
afterward verie particularlie, shewing that
after K. *Lucius* and his realme had receyued
the baptisme of Christ, were made Christians, & had turned 28. heathen flaminies,

Fox act
and mo-
nument
*pag.*96.
*col.*2.*n.*
30.

and

and three Archflaminies, that were before
of Gentiles, into fo manie Chriftian Bifhopps & Archbifnopps, all this being done

Act. and
monn.
ibid.

and well fettled: *the forfaid K. Lucius* (faith he)
fent againe to the faid Eleutherius for the Roman
lavves, therby likevvife to be gouerned, as in religion
novv they vvere framed accordingly. Vnto vvhome
Eleutherius againe vvryteth after the tenour of thefe
vvords follovving : Ye require of vs the Roman
lavves, &c.

20.   Wherby it is euident, that this letter
of Eleutherius (yf it be true, & not raigned
by Fox) was written to *King Lucius* fome
number of yeares after his couerfion, feeing
he could not fettle his realme, as heere Fox
defcribeth, but in fome good fpace of time.
Holinfhed, Hooker, and *Harifon* (difciples alfo
of this Fox) in this do take vpon them to
determine the tyme (though I know not
by what authoritie) faying, that it was
three yeares after K. Lucius his conuerfion

Holinfh.
pag. 14.
difcript.
Angl.col.
2. n. 40.

and baptifme. *The faith of Chrift* (fay they)
being thus planted in the Iland an. 177. *it came to*
paffe the third yeare of the ghofpell receaued, that Lu-
cius did fend againe to Eleutherius the Bishopp, requi-
ring that he might haue fome breefe epitome of the

The có-
trariety
betvven
Fox and
his fchol
lers.

order of difcipline then vfed in the Church, &c.
21.   Thus hold they, and that vpon this fecond Embaffage followed the forefaid letter of *Eleutherius* to K. *Lucius.* Which yf it be
true, then let them giue fentence of their
good

good father what an egregious hypocrite and deceauer he·was, to argue out of this letter, that, for so much as it apeareth by the same, that K. *Lucius* was a Christian, when this letter was written : ergo K. *Lucius vvas not conuerted by Eleutherius, but by some other before him; though perhappes he might help somvvhat to his confirmation in religion, &c.*

22.   But now to the substance of the letter it selfe or rather of the peece or parcell that it hath pleased Fox and these his schollers to impart with vs. You must note first, that these good schollers seeing their maister to haue left vs this English epistle of *Eleutherius* so imperfect and cutted, as it seemeth to haue neyther end or iust beginning, do say that the rest was lost, which yet Fox telleth vs not. Secondly, they seeing the title to make much against them, left it out, as before hath byn said. Thirdly touching the very corpes it selfe of the epistle sett downe by him, they put it downe so different both in words, sentences, authorities and textes of scriptures, from that which Fox hath: as it sheweth, eyther the thing to be wholy faigned by them, or their maister; or that they haue a great liberty and priuiledg to alter the same at their pleasures.

About the substance of Eleutherius epistle to kinge Lucius 183.

23.   And this would be sufficient for this matter: but further perchance yow might demaund, why this Epistle of Eleutherius is al-

is alleadged & vrged ſo earneſtly by them?
ſeeing it ſeemeth to make ſo little for them?
Whervnto I anſwere , that the cheefeſt
causes ſeeme to be two or three. The firſt,
that Fox might frame thervpon his former
fooliſh argumēt: that for ſo much as by this
epiſtle it appeareth , that K. *Lucius* was a
Chriſtian when this epiſtle was written by
Eleutheſius: yt may ſeeme that *Eleutherius* conuerted him not , nor any other ſent from
Rome: the falſhood and childiſhnes of
which argument hath byn ſufficiently layd
open before.

Firſt cauſe.

24. The ſecond cauſe is, to found two
points of doctrine theron. The one, that
ſcriptures onlie ar ſufficient to gouerne any
kingdome without other Eccleſiaſticall, ciuill, or temporall lawes . Which yèt themſelues do not practiſe, where they haue dominion , as experience teacheth vs . The
other point is , that euerie king is Gods vicar, that is to ſay, abſolute & ſupreme head
in all cauſes as well ſpirituall as temporall
within his realme: & to this end is brought
in the teſtimonie of this letter of *Eleutherius*,
not onlie by *Fox, Holinſhed, Hooker, Hariſon, Ha-*
ſtings and other of that crew , taking one
from another that argument: but euen their
great Champion *Ieuvell*, as *Holinſhed* relateth in the firſt volume of his ſtories.

2. cauſe.

Hol. l. 4.
hiſt.
Angl.
cap. 19
pag. 52.

25. The Reuerend Father *Iohn Ieuell* (ſaith he)
                                             ſome

fometyme Bishopp of Salsbury vvryteth in his reply vnto Hardings anfvvere, that the faid Eleutherius for generall orderto be taken in the realme and churches Ievvell. heere, vvrote his aduife to Lucius in manner and fox. 119. forme follovving. Yee haue receyued in the kingdome of Britany by Gods mercy both the lavv and faith of Chrift, yee haue both the nevv and the old teftament. Out of the fame through Gods grace by the aduife of yovv realme make a lavv, and by the fame through Gods fufferance rule your kingdome of Britanie. For in that kingdome yovv are Gods Vicar, &c.

26. Thefe are the words alleadged by May-fter Ievvell out of this epiftle. Which differ not much from that, which is in Fox and Holinfhed. But both of them do ad a third claufe out of the faid epiftle, which is this: *A King hath his name of ruling, and not of hauinge a realme. Yovv fhalbe a King, vvhile yovv rule vvell, but yf yovv do othervvife, the name of a King fhall not remayne vvith yovv, but yovv fhall vtterly lofe, and forgoe yt, vvhich God forbidd.* And then ma-keth Holinfhed this annotation in thefe words: *Hitherto out of the epiftle that Eleutherius fent vnto Lucius. VVherin many prety obferuations are to be collected, yf tyme and place vvould ferue to ftand vpon them.*

27. So he faith: but what annotations thefe ar, he declareth not, though it be eafy to gheffe by others which he maketh in other places. For that in the very next page be-fore, he maketh vs a very graue difcourfe

Fox acts and mon. pag 96. Hol. de-fcript. Brit. pag. 25.

hovv

howv that *Lucius* fent to Rome the fecond tyme for a
copy of fuch politike orders, as vvere then vfed in the
regiment of the Church. But that *Eleutherius* for diuers reafons thought it beft , not to lay any more vpon
the necks of the nevv conuertites of Britany, then
Chrift and his Apoftles had already fett dovvne to all
men in the fcriptures. And is not this a wife difcourfe? as though no temporall lawes were
to be made in a Chriftian comon welth, but
onlie thofe , that are fett downe in fcriptures. Who feeth not the madneffe of thefe
conclufions or illations? nay, who doth not
confider, how greatlie this matter is againft
themfelues? that K. *Lucius* dwelling fo farre
of from Rome, (as he did) yea, being otherwife an enemy to the Roman nation, as
thefe men confeffe that he was : did not
withftanding foe highlye refpect , euen in
thofe auncient 'daies, the Sea & Bifhopp of
Rome, that he fubmitted himfelfe therto,&
demaunded from thence direction, not only
in matters of Religiõ & Ecclefiaftical lawes;
but in temporall and ciuill alfo. And *Eleutherius* knowing his owne authority ouer him
and his, doubted not to appoint them, what
was to be done. And albeit M. Iewell doth
call it an aduife, as yow haue heard ; yet the
title of the epiftle imployeth more , faying
that it was *ad correctionem Regis & Procerum regni*, as aboue we haue declared. And this for
the firft point contayned in this epiftle.

28. And

28. And for the second, wherin *Eleutherius* saith that *K. Lucius* was Gods vicar or vice-gerent (as Holinshed translateth it) within his owne realme: what Catholike euer denyed this , or that any lawful temporall prince is not Gods vicar and substitute in gouerning his people vnder hym? Sure we are, Saint Paul speaking euen of a heathen prince or magistrate, saith : *Dei enim minister tibi est in bonum* : for he is Gods substitute to thee for thy good. And in another place teaching seruants how they should obey their heathen lords and maisters, he saith: *Serui obedite Dominis carnalibus, cum timore & tremore, sicut Christo.* Seruants obey your carnall or temporall lords, as to Christ himselfe. And againe in the same place *Sicut Domino, & non hominibus*, as vnto our lord Iesus and not as vnto men . And doth not heere the Apostle confesse expressely, that temporall lords & princes, yea though they were pagans, are Christs vicars and substitutes in their gouernement of temporall affaires? But yet I do not thinke, that eyther *Fox* or *Holinshed* will say, that they were Christs vicars also in spirituall affaires or heads of the Church within their Realmes: as by this epistle of *Eleutherius* they would make *K. Lucius* seeme to be.

29. And so finallie whether this epistle of *Eleutherius* be true our feigned, it maketh

little

Reaſons vvhich make the epiſtle of Eleutherius ſuſpected.

little for them, but much rather againſt them. And there be diuers things in it, which do make it probable, that it is a feigned matter. Firſt, for the time ſett downe in the title, ſhewing it to be written after *Eleutherius* was dead. Secondlie, for that neyther *Fox* nor *Holinshed* would deliuer it vnto vs in latin as it was written. Thirdly, for that the copie ſett downe by *Holinshed* hath manie texts of ſcriptures full little to the purpoſe, and fondlie applied, & vnworthie the great learning of *Pope Eleutherius.* Which

Iohn Fox plaieth Reinold the Fox.

Iohn Fox perceiuing, like a wylie Fox indeed, left them quite out of his copie. Profeſſing notwithſtanding to put downe the epiſtle wholie, as he found it.

30.   Fourthlie, the laſt point of doctrine therin taught, *that Kings are no longer Kings then they rule vvell: and do looſe and vtterlie forgoe the ſame, vvhen they do othervvayes*, is a doctrine not fitt for *Eleutherius* : but agreeing rather with

Encoūt. 2. c. 4.

that of *Huſſe* & *VVickliffe* mētioned before in the 2. Encounter, as condemned by the generall Councel of *Conſtance.* And this ſhalbe inough about this firſt hereticall cauillation concerning the couerſion of Britanie vnder *Pope Eleutherius,* which our Engliſh Sectaries for hate to Rome will needs call in doubt. But not being able to ſtand in this quarrel, they fly to another of more moment, which ſhalbe handled in the enſuing Chapter.

O F

OF ANOTHER HERETI-

CALL SHIFT, ABOVT THE FORMER
Conuersion of Britany, *vnder* Pope Eleutherius, *and* K. Lucius, *as though the faith of*
Rome, *that vvas then*, *did not remaine novv*;
vvhich is reprooued by tvvo euident demonstra-
tions, the first negatiue, the other affirmatiue.

CHAP. V.

WHEN all the former Foxly shifts and
deuises will not serue to shake of the
praise of our Britans conuersion from
Rome by meanes of *Eleutherius*, our Fox
diggeth to him selfe another starting hole
whervnto, when he is pressed, to runne: &
his good cubbe Syr Francis followeth him
diligently at the heeles. The Fox his words
are these : *But graunt vve heere, that it be, as they*
vvould haue yt (and indeed the most part of our En-
glish storyes do confesse yt) neyther vvill I *greatly*
sticke vvith them therin . Yet vvhat haue they got
therby, vvhen they haue cast all their gaine? In fevv
vvords to conclude this matter: yf so be, that the Chri-
stian faith and Religion vvas first deriued from Rome
by Eleutherius; *lett them but graunt to vs the same*
faith and religion, that vvas taught in Rome, and
from thence deriued hither by Eleutherius, and vve
vvill desire no more. For then vvas there not any vni-
uersall Pope, neyther any name or vse of the masse, nor
any sacrifice propitiato:y, nor any transsubstantiation,

Fox his
confes-
sion act.
and mon.
pag. 96.

1.
2. 3.

4.

G 2   *neyther*

neyther any images of Saints departed ſett vp in the Churches, &c.

Compa-
riſon be-
tvvene
the Fox
and the
Cubbe.
VVaſt.
pag.192.

2.   Thus ſaith the Fox, graunting by teſtimonie of moſt writers, that which before
he laboured ſo much to impugne. Now lett
vs heare the cubbe how well he hath learned to barke after his ſire. *Though it be grauted*
(ſaith he) *that Eleutherius ſending hither preachers*
from Rome in K. Lucius his time, did firſt conuert this
land to the Chriſtian faith, I ſay there is not novv the
ſame faith in Rome that vvas then: there vvas then no
maſſes ſaid, no tranſſubſtantiation knovvne, no ſetting
vp of Images in Churches, noe vniuerſall Pope, &c.

3.   Heere you ſee the ſelfe ſame ſpeech, with
the ſelfe ſame ſpiritt, betwixt the cubbe, &
the Fox, the ſcholler, and the maiſter: But
that the ſcholler altereth ſomwhat the order, to couer therby his borrowing from
the other. Nay we may note another thing
alſo which is vſuall in ſuch people; the
ſcholler is more earneſt and eager then his
maiſter of whome he tooke it, & more ouer-
laſhing. So as what the one ſpeaketh but
doubtfullie, the other affirmeth moſt reſolutelie; what the one ſaieth, the other ſwea-
reth. *Let them graunt vs* (ſaith Fox) *the ſame*
faith vvhich vvas then at Rome, and vve deſire no
more. This was ſomwhat modeſt, though
falſe and hipocriticall. For he meaneth it
not, whatſoeuer yow graunt him or proue
againſt him. But what ſaith his ſcholler?

I ſ.iy

I say (quoth he) *there is not novv the same faith in Rome that vvas then.* This is more resolute and peremptorie as yow see. For who saith it I pray yow? *I say it* (quoth he.) as though he would chaleng the held of him that will dare to deny it or proue the contrarie. But who are yow (Sir) that we should yeld vnto yow this Pythagoricall authoritie of *ipse dixit?* graunting all things vpon your owne assertion without further proofe? yf you be the man that so often before haue byn made a mouse, and your creditt so manie times shaken by shewing your false dealing; then may it be now an argument rather to the contrarie: to witt, Syr Francis saith this or that without alleadging any proofe, *Ergo* it is probable that the matter is eyther feigned or fallified: and this consequence you shall see much confirmed both in him & his father Fox, by this that heere we are to examine.

4. For first both of them do affirme (as you haue heard) and that with great asseueration, that in the time of *Eleutherius* the Pope, that is to say, in the second age after Christ, *there vvas not the faith in Rome that novv is*; For that there was no mentio or knowledg then, *eyther of any vniuersall Authority of the Church or B. of Rome, or of the name or vse of masses, or sacrifice propitiatory, or of transubstan:iation, or of images vsed in Churches and the like.*

5. To which vayne arguments of both

G 3   these

theſe poore men, I might anſwere ſufficien-
tlie, by telling them (yf they will learne)
that albeit it were true in ſome ſenſe, that
theſe doctrines, which here they alleadg &
ſome other in controuerſie betweene vs,
were not found in the ſecond age, when
Pope Eleutherius liued, ſo expreſſely ſett forth,
as in other ages afterward, when better occaſion was offered, and the times did more
permitt the ſame: yet is this no good argument to proue, that they were not beleeued
then alſo in the Cath. Church. For if this
conſequence ſhould be admitted, then as
well might it be admitted alſo againſt many
other principall points and articles of our
faith, which are acknowledged & beleeued
by Proteſtants alſo at this daie, though not
expreſſely handled, diſcuſſed or determined
in thoſe firſt two hundred yeares after
Chriſt: as for example, the name & doctrine
of the *Bleſſed Trinity, the tvvo diſtinct natures, and*
one parſon in Chriſt, his tvvo diſtinct vvills, the virgi-
nity of our B. lady both before & after her childbirth,
the proceeding of the holy ghoſt, as vvell from the
ſonne, as from the father, &c.

6. All which points and ſome others are
not found to be handled ſo clearly and diſtinctly by authors of the firſt two hundred
yeares, as afterward, partly for that they
were occupied in other matters againſt
Gentiles and heretiks that touched not
theſe

Points
of reli-
gion
not ex-
preſſelie
handled
or deter-
mined
by the
Church
vvithin
the firſt
tvvo
hundred
yeares.

these points, and partly for that generall
Councells could not yet be gathered togeather to discusse and declare them distinctly,
though no good Christians will or may
doubt, but that they were beleeued in the
Church before, from Christ downeward,
and that the generall Councells that determined them afterward for articles of true
beleefe against heretiks, that had called
them in question, did not so determine
them, as yf they had made them articles
which were not before (for this the church
could not do, as is held by all Catholiques)
but onlie that they being articles of true &
Cath. beleefe before, the Church did now
declare them to be such.

Wherfore this being so, I might answere
(and I see not how they could reply) that
Iohn Fox and his scholler may as well deny and call in question all or any of these
forsaid articles, as the other, which they recite. For that they were as little, or perhaps
lesse specified in the first two hundred yeares,
then these, which they obiect.

7. But I will deale more liberallie with
our minister & Knight, & will seeke to satis-
fie them with reason, who do brabble and
argue against vs without reason. I shall endeauour to do the same by two wayes; ho-
ping to make their follie appeare to euery
indifferent man by them both. The first
Tvvo
vvaies of
proofe
the one
negatiue
the other
affirma-
tiue.

shalbe

ſhalbe *via negatiua,*the negatiue way, by putting them to ſome proofe . And the ſecond
ſhalbe affirmatiue , ſhewing them what
proofes may be brought for our ſide . No
thing doubling, but that each ſhalbe ſufficient to ſatisfie the equall Reader : Let the
firſt kind of argument then , by the way of
negatiue be this.

8.   We deny that the faith now heid in
Rome, and namely the articles heere mentioned, of the *Pope, maſſe, tranſſubſtantiation,* &
vſe of images, were not beleeued in *Pope Eleu-*
therius daies, as now for the ſubſtance or the
doctrine. And lett them proue it if they can,
and yf they ſay, that it is hard to proue a negatiue, we are content that they proue only
an affirmatiue , whereby the ſaid negatiue
may be inferred, to witt , that any one of
theſe doctrines did begin to enter into the
Church after *Eleutherius.* And to this proofe
they are bound in all equity and reaſon , as
we ſhall ſhew by our ſequent diſcourſe. For
if it be true, that the articles and points of
doctrine heere mentioned by Fox and Syr
Francis wherin they differ from vs, be indeed not things heard of, or beleeued at
Rome in the time of *Pope Eleutherius* (which
yet they deny not, but that in other ages
after they were generallie receyued) then
followeth it, that Fox & his fellowes muſt
ſhew the time, place, men and occaſion of
their

The firſt
vvay of
argumét
negatiue
againſt
Prote-
ſtants.

their beginning, to witt, when, where, and
by what men, and vpon what caufes, and
with what authoritie, or induction, or violence, or by what deceipt, or with what
contradiction of others thefe doctrines entred firft, & were continued in the Church.
All which points we can fhew of euery
other error or herefie, that hath rifen and
was held for fuch, from Chrifts time to ours.

9. And yf eyther Fox or his cubbe, or any
of that kennell can or will fhew this, and
ioyne iffue with vs vpon this one point, we
do accept therof, and the matter may be
quickiie difpatched. But yf this cannot be
done, then muft we follow the rule of *Saint* **The firft**
Auguftine held by him for infallible in fuch **ground**
affaires: to witt, that when any doctrine is **of Saint**
found generallie receyued in the knowen **Augu-**
vifible Church, at any time, or in any age, **ftines**
wherof there is no certaine author, time, **rule.**
or beginning found: then is iffure, that all "
fuch doctrine hath come downe from "
Chrift and his Apoftles. "

10. This doth that holie Doctor and great
pillar of Gods Church *Saint Auguftine* affirme
and reiterate in euery place of his works
againft Heretiks of his time, which argued,
as our men do, by denying onlie, & putking
Catholiks to proofe. As for example, againft
the Donatifts denying the cuftome of baptizing infants, for that it was not in fcripture

G 5 nor

nor recorded by Fathers of the firſt ages,

Ang. l. 4. de Bapt. cont. Donat. c. 6.

Saint Auguſtine anſwereth thus. *Illa conſuetudo, quam & tunc homines ſurſum verſum aſpicientes non videbant à poſterioribus inſtitutam, recte ab Apoſtolis tradita creditur.* That cuſtome of baptizing of
,, infants, which men before vs in the Church
,, looking vpward to antiquitie, did not find
,, to haue byn ordained by them that came
,, after the firſt ages, is rightlie beleeued to
,, haue byn deliuered by the Apoſtles.

11.   And againe in another place ſpeaking

lib. 4. de bapt. c. 24.

of Eccleſiaſticall cuſtomes, he ſaith: *Quod vniuerſa tenet Eccleſia, nec Concilijs inſtitutum ſed ſemper retentum eſt, non niſi authoritate Apoſtolica traditum rect ſsimè creditur.* That, which the
,, the vniuerſall Church doth hold, and was
,, not inſtituted by any Councell, but hath
,, byn ſtill retayned in the Church, this we
,, may moſt iuſtlie beleeue to haue come
,, from no other authoritie, then from the
,, Apoſtles.

And the like ſpeeches vnto this hath *S. Auguſtine* in diuers other places both of this booke againſt the Donatiſts, as *l. 2. c. 7. & l. 5. c. 23.* as alſo *lib. de vnitat. Eccleſiæ. c. 19. & epiſtola 118. &c.* And as for that he ſpeaketh of inſtitution by Councells, he meaneth of cuſtomes and ceremonies, & not of articles of beleefe. Which no Councell can appoint, but onlie declare and expound, as before we haue ſhewed.

12. This

12.   This position then of *Saint Augustine* is
most true and consonant to the doctrine of
all other Fathers in that behalfe, that when
any thing is found generallie receyued in
the Church, & no author, institutor, or beginning can be found therof, this without
all doubt cometh downe from the Apostles.
And of this position may be alleadged two
infallible grounds. The one of faith, the
other of euident reasons. For in faith who
can thinke so baselie of Chrifts power or
will in performing his promises made vnto
his Church, to conserue her in all truth vnto the worlds end, as that he should permit
her notwithstanding to admitt or teach generallie any one false article of doctrine, &
much lesse, so manie as these men obiect
against vs? For wheras he permised his holie Spiritt to be with her vnto the worlds
end, and that she should be the *pillar* and *fir-*
mament of truth to direct others, and finallie
that *hell gaets should neuer preuaile against her*:
How should all this be performed, if she
fell into these errors, of which proteftants
accuse her? or what greater victorie could
the gates of hell haue against her, then that
from an Apostolicall Church, of whome
Chrift spake, she should become an Aposta-
ticall Church, as these men do call her?
which is the greateft Blafphemy against
Chrift, and his diuinitie, that possible can
be ima-

Tvvo
reasons
vvhy
that
vvhich
is gene-
rallie re-
ceaued
in the
Church
and hath
no kno-
vvne be-
ginning,
may be
presu-
med to
come
from the
Apost-
les.
Ioa. 14.
15. 16.
Mat. 16.

be imagined, ſeing it doth euacuate his whole incarnation, life, death, doctrine, reſurrection and other benefitts of his comming, which were all imployed to this end, to make vnto himſelfe a Church and kingdome in this world, that ſhould direct men in all truth to their ſaluation. And this being taken away, & the other graunted, that the Church her ſelfe may fall into error & falſe doctrine; then is there no certaintie in anie thing. And conſequentlie it cannot be, that any erroneous doctrine ſhould be taught or receiued generallie by the Church. And this is the firſt ground of *S. Auguſtines* aſſertion.

The 2. ground of Saint Auguſt. rule.

13. But beſides this, there is another founded in Reaſon and experience, which cannot be denied. And for that it is a conſideration of great importance and may ſerue the Reader to manie purpoſes of moment, for decerning of doubts and controuerſies; I ſhall deſire him to be attent in peruſing the ſame. We do find by experience, & that not onlie in Eccleſiaſticall, but temporall affaires alſo: that when orders, lawes and cuſtomes are once ſetled in anie common welth, it is hard to alter or take them away, or to bring in things oppoſite or different to them without ſome reſiſtance, diſpute, contradiction, or at leaſt ſome memorie therof, how, whie, and by whome it was done. As for example, yf a man would go about to
bring

bring in anie innouation in the particular
lawes of London, and much more in the
generall lawes of all the land: no doubt, but
he should find some resistance therin, some
that would dispute about the matter, al-
leadginge reasons to the contrarie: others
would resist and oppose themselues. And
when all did faile, at least wise, some record,
storie or memorie would be left of this
chaunge.

14. But much more yf this matter did concerne religion, which is most esteemed
aboue other points. As for example, yf a
man would beginne to teach anie points of
doctrine at this day in England contrarie or
different from that which is there receiued,
and established by publike authoritie; he
should presentlie be noted & contradicted
by some no doubt: as vve see the *Puritans,*
Brovvnists, Family of loue, and other such newer
teachers haue byn, and the historie therof is
notorious, and will remaine to postetitie.

15. And this is the verie reason also, why
all heretiks and heresies from the beginning
did no sooner peepe vp in the visible Cath.
Church, but that they were noted, impugned, confuted, and finallie cast out from
that bodie, to the deuils dung-hill. And the
Records therof do remaine, who were the
authors, and beginners, who the fauourers
and setters forward, at what time, vpon
vvhat

what occafion, vnder what Popes & Kings, and other fuch like circumftances. And this will endure to the end of the world.

The pro-
per ftate
of the
queftion 16.   This then being fo; we now come to the ftate of our queftion, and to ioyne with the Proteftants vpon this iffue. That feeing the doctrines before mentioned, of the *Popes authority, Sacrifice of the Maffe, Tranffubftantiation, Vfe of Images,* and the like, were found to be generallie receyued and beleeued in the viïible and vniuerfall Cath. Church of Chriftendomme, when Martyn Luther firft began to breake from the fame, Yea and manie ages before by their owne confefsion: they muft fhew vs, when the faid doctrines were brought in afterwards to the Church, not being there, nor beleeued therin before. To witt by what man or men, with what authoritie, conftraint or perfuafion, with what repugnance of them, that mifliked the fame, and other like circumftances before mentioned. Which yf they be not able to do, moft certayne it is, that whatfoeuer they prattle againft thefe doctrines, faying they were not in *Eleutherius* his time, it is nothing, but cauills and hereticall fhifts.

17.   And now that they cannot fhew any fuch particularities for the entrance or admittáce of thefe doctrines into the Church, is moft euident. For whatfoeuer time they afsigne for their beginning, we can ftil fhew,

shew, that before that time, they were in
vse, yf they meane of the things themselues
and not onlie of words or phrases. As for
example, when they obiect, that in the
Councell of Lateran vnder *Pope Innocentius*
the third in the yeare of Christ 1215. the
vvord of *Transsubstantiation* vvas first vsed:
we answere, that albeit that vvord vvas
then added for better explication of the
matter, as these words *Homousion, consubstatial,*
Trinity & the like vvere, by the first generall
Councell of *Nice*; yet the substance of the
article was held before from the beginning,
vnder other equiualent words of *Change and*
immutation of natures, transformation of elements,
& thelike. As for example, that of *S. Ambrose,*
speaking of the words of Christ in the con-
secration, *Non valebit sermo Christi, vt species mu-*
tet elementorum? Shall not the vvords of
Christ be of power to chaung the natures
of elements? And againe, *Sermo Christi, qui po-*
tuit de nihilo facere, quod non erat, non potest ea, quæ
sunt in id mutare, quod non erat? The speech of
Christ that vvas able to create of nothing
that vvhich vvas not before: shall it not
be able to change things that are alreadie,
into that vvhich they vvere not before?
He meaneth the bread and vvine into the
bodie and bloud of Christ, as himselfe doth
expound.

18. So as heere vve see the change of the
natures

Tran-
substan-
tiation
euer in
the
Cath:
Church.

Amb. l.
4. 5. & 9.
de Sa-
cramen-
tis.

„
„
„
„
„

natures of elements, and of the ſubſtance of one body into another, auerred by *S. Ambroſe* longe time before the Councell of Lateran. Which is the ſame, that vve meane by Tranſſubſtantiation. And conforme to this do ſpeake alſo other ancient Fathers, as wel Greeke, as Latin, and one thing is ſpecialiie to be noted, that both the Greeke & Latin Church did agree therin in the ſaid councel, There being preſent two Patriarcks of the Greeke Church: to vvit, thoſe of *Conſtantinople* and *Hieruſalem*, and others bothe Archbiſhopps, Biſhopps, and Prelates. So as of bothe Churches, the Archbiſhopps vvere 70. the Biſhops 412. Abbates & Priors 800. and Prelats in all 1215. togeather vvith the Legats, Doctors and Embaſſadors of both Empires vveſt and eaſt, as alſo of the Kings of France, Spaine, England, Hieruſalem, and others. So as this point of doctrine, about Tranſſubſtantiation was not handled in corners, but publikely. And the Councell doth not deliuer the ſame, as any new doctrine: but onlie as an explication of that, vvhich euer had byn held before.

The councell of Lateran vnder Innocétius 3. anno 1215.

19.   And the ſame is anſwered to the other like hereticall cauills about other points heere obiected by Fox and Syr Francis of *an vniuerſall Pope, The vſe of the maſſe, and propitiatory ſacrifice, the ſetting vp of dead mens images,* and the like. For yf they vnderſtand by the firſt,

the

the primacie and supreme authoritie Ecclesiasticall of the Sea of *Rome*, and her Bishops;
and by the second, the Christian externall
sacrifice of the bodie and bloud of our Sauiour instituted by himselfe, as the comple-
ment of all other sacrifices that went before; and by the third, sacred memories and
images of Christ and his Saints, that are not
dead, but liuing and raigning euerlastinglie
in heaue: then are all these doctrines (howsoeuer disguised by heretiks with different
words, to make them more odious) most
true and Cath. Doctrines, and receaued in
the Church from the beginning, and continued from the Apostles downeward.

20.   And albeit these people to continue
cauilling, do alleadg diuers times, that the
first of these articles, about the *Popes supremacy*,
did begin first vnder *Pope Gregory* the great &
Phocas the Emperour, about the yeares of
Christ 600. and that the last about the *vse of
images* was decreed in the second generall
Councell of *Nice*, about the yeare 700. and
that the other of the *vse of Masse* began by
little and little they cannot tell when: yet is
this all most ridiculous, and themselues dare
not stand to anie certaine time by them as-
signed. For that presentlie we appoint another time before that, wherin these things
were also acknowledged. Which they cannot do in the heresies by vs obiected to
them.

A selie
shifte of
the here-
tiques.

H

them . For that we ſhew indeed the verie
true time, wherin they began, and had their
offspring, togeather with the proper authors, places, occaſions, and other like particularities, recorded not by our ſelues, but
by other authenticall writers before vs, ſo
as reaſonablie there can be no doubt therof.
And heerin ſtandeth the true difference betwene vs. We reallie and ſubſtantiallie ſhew
the beginning and authors of their hereſies,
for that they are hereſies indeed . But they
cannot ſhew the beginning or author of
anie of our articles of beleefe ſince Chriſt
and his Apoſtles, for that they are no hereſies, but Catholike doctrines, and haue euer
indured from Chriſt downeward. Though
in ſome ages more then other, they haue
byn expounded or declared by fathers and
councels according to the neceſsities of the
time . And this is one proper office of the
holie Ghoſt appointed for guider of the
church to explane matters, as douts do ariſe.

21.   Wherfore this is the firſt way of triall,
The in- whether the forſaid articles of the Roman
ference Religion taught at this daie about *Tranſſub-*
vpon all *ſtantiation, Maſſe,* and *the like,* be the ſame that
the for- *Pope Eleutherius* held and ſent into Britanie,
mer ne- or not. And I do call all this kind of argu-
gatiue ment negatiue: both in reſpect of our aduer-
argu- ſaries that deny them to haue byn then in
ment. vſe; and of vs that deny them to haue byn
brought

brought in afterward. And they ought to
proue the seconde, seeing they cannot deny
but that they were once generally in vse &
receaued ouer Christendome. Wherof we
do make the former most infallible inference with *Saint Augustine*: that for asmuch as
they were once in vie and generally receaued and no particular beginning can be shewed of them or of theire entrance, *ergo* they
came from the Apostles themselues.

22. To this inference the sectaries & heretikes of our time, haue one only shift more,
which is, that albeit these doctrines haue
for many ages byn receiued generally in the
Church of Christendome ; Yet that they
crept into the same by little and little, and
finding no resistance, began at last to be vniuersally beleeued. But this creeping instáce
can haue no place heere by any probability.
For to say nothing of the prouidence of
God in protecting his Church from such
creeping errors, nor yet of the promises of
Christ before mentioned to the same effect:
reason it selfe doth demonstrate also, that
this possiblie could not be. For if the Doctors and Fathers of the Church did note
and discouer from time to time euery least
heresie or error, that did peep vp in their
daies, and this not onlie in heretiks, but in
diuers principall fathers also, that held anie
particular opinions, as is manifest in *S. Cy-*

That het
resies
could
not
creepe
into the
Church
vvithout
beinge
espied.

prian,

prian, Lactantius, Arnobius, Caßianus, and others:
if this diligence (I fay) were vfed by them
in all other occafions, how could it happen, that fo manie, fo manifeft, and fo important doctrines, as are in controuerfie
betwene vs and Proteftants, fhould be lett
paffe without note or contradiction, if they
had byn eyther new or erroneous? how
fhould it come to paffe (I fay) that noe one
of thefe auncient fathers fhould euer impugne anie of thefe doctrines, if they were
new opinions and brought into the Church
contrarie to the doctrine that was before, as
thefe men do fay? yea, how fhould it fall
out, that noe one record in the world fhould
be left by our aunceftors, that at fuch a time
by fuch or fuch occafiós began the doctrine
*of Purgatory. of Praying to Saints, of the Reall pre-
fence, of the vfe of Images, of Maffe & facrifice, of 7.
Sacraments* and the like, that were not held
in the Church before?

An ex-
perimé-
tall de-
duction.

23.   And that this is impofsible, may be
fhewed by this experimentall deduction,
which now I will fett downe. Let vs imagine that none of thefe doctrines were in
the firft age vnder the Apoftles, and namely,
that then there were but *tvvo Sacraments, no
purgatory* at all, or anie *externall facrifice* held.
We aske them concerning the fecond age,
wherin *Iuftinus, Policarpus, Irenæus, Clemens
Alexandrinus,* and *Tertullian* were cheefe teachers,

chers, whether these doctrines were in this
age or noe? yf they denie it, though vve
might proue the contrarie out of their
works, yet not to passe from this first kind of
argument, we aske the like of the third age,
vnder *Origen, Cyprian, Dionysius Alexandrinus,
Pamphilus, Arnobius* and the rest. And yf they
denie of this age also, that these doctrines
were not held by them: we go to the 4. age
vnder *Athanasius, Hilarius, Optatus, Basill, Nazianzen, Ambrose, Hierome, Chrisostome, Epiphanius, Cy-
rillus.* In whose writings euery where there
is mention of all these doctrines, as afterward in our second argumét, we shall shew
out of the Protestáts themselues: & namelie
the Magdeburgians, that professe to note all.
24. Now then, I aske our aduersaries
touching this creeping instance; how could
these doctrines so creepe into the Catholike visible Church in this fourth age, for
example, and be receaued so generallie ouer
all nations, countries, & kingdoms by these
principall lights, captaines, watchmen, and
guiders of the same, as no note, detection,
resistance or memorie should be left of anie
doubt, dispute or opposition made against
them? Is this likelie? is this possible? Read
all the Fathers works ouer, and find if yow
can, but one place, wherin one Father did
euer hitherto note another for holding *Purgatory, Praying to Saints, beleeuing the Real presense,*

or

or the like : as they did *Cyprian* (though otherwise a moſt learned and holie man) for teaching rebaptization of heretiks, and ſome other Fathers, for other particular opinions different from the Catholike doctrine of that age. Wherof we may inferre, that they would haue done the like alſo in theſe other points, yf they had byn held for new or erroneous in thoſe daies. And hereof alſo may be inferred another ſequele or obſeruation of verie great moment againſt our heretiks, that whenſoeuer any doctrine is found in any of the ancient Fathers, which is not contradicted nor noted by any of the reſt as ſingular: that doctrine is to be preſumed to be no particular opinion of his, but rather the generall of all the Church in his daies. For that otherwiſe, it would moſt certainely haue byn noted and impugned by others. Wherby it followeth, that one Doctors opinion or ſaying in matters of controuerſie not contradicted or noted by others, may ſometimes giue a ſufficient teſtimonie of the whole Churches ſentence & doctrine in thoſe daies. Which is a point verie greatlie to be conſidered.

A conſideration of much importance.

25. But yet further to all this may be added another conſideration of no ſmall weight, which is the difficultie of bringing in certaine doctrines if any man would haue attempted it, as for example, the doctrine of

The difficultie of bringing in 5. newv Sacraments.

7. *Sa-*

7. *Sacraments*, if there had byn but two only before in the Apoſtles time: it had byn an extreme great noueltie to haue added fiue more, which neuer would haue byn admitted whithout much ſtrife and reſiſtance, ſeeing all Catholiks do hould, that Chriſt only could inſtitute Sacraments, for that he only could aſſure the promiſe of grace made thervnto, as excellently doth declare the Councell of ⋆ Trent; and long before that againe the *Maiſter of Sentences.* And ⁕ *S. Thomas* in name of all Catholiks did leaue that doctrine regiſtred: and there can be no doubt therof.

⋆ *Seſſ.7. cap. 1.*
⁕ *4. diſt. 5. q. 10. art. 1. & part. 3. q. 64. act. 4.*

26. Wherfore this truth being admitted, that the whole Church hath no authority to inſtitute any Sacrament or to alter any thing about the ſubſtantiall partes therof, to witt, the matter, forme, or number! (as the ſame Councell of *Trent* in another place declareth:) how was it poſsible, that fiue whole Sacraments ſhould be added or brought into Catholike doctrine, and receiued and beleeued throughout Chriſtendome without any reſiſtance or oppoſition at all, yf there had byn but two only inſtituted by Chriſt, and exerciſed by the Apoſtles in the firſt age? How I ſay, could fiue more ben brought in afterward? by whome? at what time? in what countrey? &c. For yf any one had begone to do it, others would

Seſſ. 21. cap. 7.

Impoſſi-bilities.

H 4   haue

haue refifted, it being a matter of ſo high
moment. And yf one countrey, prouince, or
church had admitted them, another would
haue refuſed, or at leaſt wayes there would
haue byn ſome doubt or diſputation, and
ſome generall meeting, and Synode, or
Councell gathered about that matter. And
ſome parts would haue admitted one number, and ſome another, as we ſee that the
ſectaries of our time haue done, ſynce the
matter hath bin called in queſtion by them,
ſome allowing fiue, ſome fower, ſome three
ſome two. But noe memorie of any of theſe
differences being to be found among Catholiks: moſt certaine it is, that this number
came downe from Chriſt, and his Apoſtles
themſelues.

The dif-
ficultie
of brin-
ging in
the vſe
of con-
feſſion.

27.   The like or greater difficulty would
alſo haue byn about the vſe of ſacramentall
confeſſion, if it had not byn appointed by
Chriſt, and putt in vre preſently, & ſo continued from time to time. For that it being
a thing in it ſelfe moſt repugnant to mans
ſenſuall nature, to be bound to open his
particular ſinnes to another, with that humility & ſubiection, which Cath. doctrine
doth preſcribe in the vſe of that Sacrament:
cleere it is, that if it had not byn in vre euen
from the Apoſtles time, and that as a matter of abſolute neceſſity, it could neuer haue
byn receaued afterward, nor yet brought in
by any

by any humane power, art, or deuise. For
who (I pray you) should or could bring in
such a thing of so great repugnance and difficultie vpon the whole Christian Church?
will they say any Pope ? let them name eyther him or them to geather with the time
and other particularities. Which they neuer
will be able to doe.

28. Besides this I aske them further, what
Pope would euer haue attempted this, if it
had not byn by obligation before him? seing
that Popes themselues the more great and
eminent they be aboue others, the more naturall repugnance must they needs find in
themselues, to goe and kneele downe at the
feete of an inferior Priest, and confesse vnto
him their most secrete sinnes. And the like
may be said of temporall Princes & Emperors. Who if any Pope or power Ecclesiasticall would haue laid such a burthen vpon
them not vsed , nor of obligation before,
how vvould they haue yelded vnto yt?
which of them would not haue answered,
that seing their fathers and ancestors were
saued without this subiection, & irkesome
obligation of reueyling their particular sinnes: they would hope to be so also. And finallie some great difficultie, doubt, or contention would haue byn about this matter,
before it could haue byn so brought in, and
established ouer all the Christian world, as

we

we ſee by experience it was. And at leaſt wiſe ſome memorie would haue remayned therof in hiſtories, which we find not. And conſequentlie we may conclude, that there was neuer any ſuch thing. And this is ſufficient for our firſt argument. Now lett vs paſſe to the ſecond.

IT IS PROVED BY THE SE- COND KIND OF AFFIRMATIVE *or poſitiue arguments, that the pointes of Catholike doctrine before denied by* Fox, *and* Syr Francis, *vvere in vſe in* Pope Eleutherius *his time, and in other ages immediatlie follovving; and this by teſtimony of Proteſtant vvriters themſelues.*

CHAP. VI.

ALBEIT the reaſons and conſiderations before alleadged, wherby our aduerſaries are vvilled to ſhew the beginning of ſuch articles and points of our Catholike doctrine, as they deny to haue come downe from the Apoſtles time, vvere ſufficient to put them to ſilence, being not able to performe any part therof; and conſequentlie alſo may open the eyes of any ſtudious reader to ſee the infirmitie of their cauſe, & the ſtrength and truth of ours: yet vvill vve for greater ſatisfaction of all ſorts, paſſe ouer to the other part alſo of poſitiue and affirmatiue prooſes, which are ſo abundant in

this

this behalfe, as if I would sett them downe all, this onlie point would require a particular treatise, wherfore I meane to abbreuiate the matter, as much as I may.

2.   For which respect, wheras there are two meanes to sett downe these proofes, one out of the authors themselues that liued in the same age with *Eleutherius*, and the next after; and the other to cite the same out of Protestant writers : I haue made choice of the second way in this place, both for that it is shorter, and seemeth also more sure and effectual. For if I should cite the places, as for example in the second age *Saint Irenæus lib.*5. *aduers.hæreses*, for the supremacy of the B. of Rome , & the same *lib.*4. *cap.*77. and with him *Iustinus Martyr* , q. 103. togeather with *Theophilus, Athenagoras, Clemens Alexandrinus,* for freewill , and the same *Clemens lib.*5.*stromatum,* and diuers other of that age, for the meritt of good works , for the manner of dooing penance, and the like : and if I should alleadg the said *Irenæus lib.* 4.*cap.*32. for the sacrifice of the masse ; and *Iustinus Martyr Apolog.*2. and *Clemens Alexandrinus lib.*7. *Stromatum* , about the rites and ceremonies of the said masse, and the same *Iustinus* q.136. & the same *Irenæus lib.*1. *c.*18. for the ceremonies of Baptisme and chrisme vsed in those daies: Yf (I say) I should alleadge these & other authors of that time for positiue proofes

Tvvo meanes of proofes by citinge authors.

proofes of Cath. articles againſt Proteſtants in *Eleutherius* daies, the matter would firſt grou to be very long. For that I muſt alleage the places at length; ſeeing that otherwiſe the quarrelling aduerſary would ſay, that I left out the antecedents and conſequents, as themſelues are wont to do, when they meane not to haue any text rightly vnderſtood. Secondly they would quarrell with vs (when they ſee them ſelues preſt) about the authors bookes, whether they be truly theirs or noe. And thirdly about the tranſlation, words and ſenſe. All which would bring a long diſpute.

3.   But now finding that certaine authors of their owne religion, (yf they be of their religion) I meane the *Magdeburgians*, called otherwiſe the *Centuriatores*, haue taken vpon them to ſett downe the whole ſtorie of the Church, and haue heere with all treated aſwell of the doctrine, as alſo the Doctors of euerie age : I haue thought beſt to take my proofes out of them, being Confeſſions as it were againſt themſelues, & their mates the Caluiniſts (though not very frendly mates in many matters of doctrine, as yow ſhall heare) and their ſtorie being the verie ground and fountaine of all Iohn Fox his volume of *Acts* and *monuments*, except onlie thoſe things vvhich concerne England in particular. Wherin vvether he or they behaue

Ordinarie cauillatiō of the aduerſaſie.

haue themſelfes with leſſe honeſtie or conſcience, is hard to ſaye. But in this treatiſe
you ſhall haue diuers taſtes óf them both.
And this being ſpoken as it were by the
way of preface, we ſhall now take in hand
the matter propoſed.

4. Theſe men being 4. Saxons, vvhome
before vve haue named, gathered togeather
in the Citty of *Magdeburge* to vvitt *Flaccus Il-*
lyricus, Ioannes Vigandus, Mathaus Iudex and *Ba-*
ſilius Faber, and in Religion ſtrict or riged
Lutherans; tooke vpon them (as hath byn
ſaid) to write the whole Eccleſiaſticall hiſtorie from Chriſt to their time by centuries or ages: allowing 100. yeares to euerie
age, vvherof they are called *Centuriatores.*
And in euery age they handle theſe and like
Chapters, of the Church, & increaſe therof,
or doctrine therin taught, of hereſies & heretiks, of Doctors and writers and the like.
But amongſt other points eſpeciallie to be
noted to our purpoſe, that preſentlie after
the Apoſtles in the ſecond Centurie, they
make this chapter, repeating the ſame in
euery age after : *Inclinatio doctrina, complectens*
peculiares & incommodas opiniones, ſtipulas, & erro-
res Doctorum qua palam quidem, hoc eſt ſcriptis tra-
dita ſunt? That is : The declyning of true
Chriſtian doctrine, conteyning the peculiar
and incommodious opinions of Doctors,
their errors, ſtraw, or ſtubble, which were

left

The ſto-
rie of
Magde-
burgiás.

A proud
title
againſt
the Fa-
thers
vvry-
tings.

„ left publikelie by them, that is to say, in
„ their writings.

5. This is the title of this chapter in euery
age, and those last words seeme to be added,
therby to insinuate to the Reader, that the
said Doctors inwardlie did hold perhaps
manie more errors and straw opinions, in
these mens iudgments, then they left openlie in writing. And by this arrogant title,
yow may see these 4. good fellowes meane
to iudg and censure all from the beginning
of Christian religion vnto their daies, and
among other they will censure *Iohn Fox* also
and his fellowes, as you way see in the preface of one of their Centuries dedicated vnto the Q. of England the third yeare of her
raigne 1560. where hauing told her Maiestie a long tale of the ghospell and pure
word of God, naming the same aboue halfe
a hundred times (yf I haue counted right) in
this one epistle, and shewing how Princes
must haue noe other rule of gouernment
then the said word (but yet vnderstood as
these men will interprete it) they tell her
also, that they now do bring her antiquitie
to looke vpon, yet complayning that few
in auncient times did write *luculenter, & cum
iudicio*, perspicouslie and with iudgment,
And then againe : *Sacrosanctæ antiquitatis titulo
plurimos quasi fascinari, vt citra omnem attentionem,
rectumáq; iudicium, quantumuis tetris erroribus ap-
plaudant.*

*Magdeb.
in præf.
Ep. dedi-
cat. ad
Elizab.
Angl.
Reginā
in cent.
4.*

plaudant. That verie manie are as it were fo
bewiched with the holie title of antiquitie,
that vvithout all attention and vpright
iudgment, they do giue willinglie confent
to neuer fo foule errors, if they be fet doune
by antiquitie.

6. Lo heere what an entrance this is of
them that profefle antiquitie, to difcredit by
their preface all antiquitie of Chriftian religion, & of the eldeft & primatiue Church,
whofe acts and gefts they promife to fett
downe, but the verie point indeed is, that
they themfelues wilbe iudges of all (as the
fafhion of proud heretiks is) and admitt
onlie fo much as maketh for their particular
fect, and difcreditt or reiect the reft. And in
this point our English Caluinifts are like to
find as little fauour at their hands, as we
that are Catholiks, and lefle too. For that by
the whole courfe of antiquitie, they do
fhew thefe men to be cleerlie heretiks, and
their opinions about the *Sacraments Inui-
fibilitie of the Church,* and *other like,* to be
hereticall. Wheras our doctrines, which
they find in auncient Fathers differing from
them, they call eyther incommodious opinions, blotts, ftubble, or errors of Doctors,
as before you haue heard: and not lightlie
herefies. As in this their preface to the Q.
they admonish her Maieftie more carefully
to beware of their doctrine, then of ours in
thefe

[marginal note: Magde-
bugians
againft
the Cal-
uinifts.*]*

The
Magde-
burg.
ſpeech
to her
Maie-
ſtie
againſt
Calui-
niſts.

theſe words: *Cùm iam varia graſſentur quaſi fa-*
ctiones opinionum , &c. Wheras euery where
now adayes diuers factions of opinions
,, grow vp among them , that profeſſe the
,, ghoſpell: there are ſome among others, who
,, by certaine philoſophicall reaſons go about
to euacuate, or make voyd the teſtament of
our lord, ſo as they would remooue the preſence of the true bodie and bloud of Chriſt
from the communion, and would by a certaine ſtraunge perplexitie of words deceiue
the people againſt the moſt cleere, the moſt
euident, the moſt true, and the moſt potent
words of our Sauiour himſelfe. Wherfore
,, your Maieſtie muſt principallie looke to this
,, point, and prouide , that the articles of our
,, faith be kept without ſuch phariſaicall le-
,, uen , and that the Sacraments inſtituted by
,, Chriſt , be reſtored without all corruption
,, and adulteration. Thus farre the Magdeburgians to her Maieſtie by which you may
perceaue, why I call them Fox his maiſters
in lying, but not his mates in beleeuing.

7. To come therfore now to our purpoſe, I
might as before hath byn ſaid if it were not
ouer long vſe two wayes for this poſitiue
proofe, that theſe articles denied by Fox &
his ſcholler, were heard of and acknowledged in *Eleutherius* time. The firſt by citing
the places themſelues out of the principall
Doctors that then liued; but this (as I haue
ſaid)

faid) would be ouerlong. Yet one place
I cannot omitt of *Irenæus* in the verie age we
fpeake of, and vvritten vvhile *Eleutherius* yet
liued. The vvords are thefe: *maxima & anti-*
quißima Ecclefia, &c. We fhewing the *Tradi-*
tion of the greateft,& moft auncient Church
of Rome known to all the vvorld , as founded by the two moft gloriousApoftles Peter
and Paul, (vvhich tradition & faith fhee re-
ceiuing from the Apoftles,hath preached &
deliuered vnto vs by fuccefsion of her Bifhopps from time to time vnto our daies)
do confound therby all thofe *(Heretiks)*
vvhich by any waies, eyther through delite
in themfelues,or vaine glorie,or blindnes of
vnderftanding do gather otherwife , then
they fhould . For that vnto this Church in
refpect of her more mighty principalitie, it
is neceffarie that all Churches muft agree,
and haue acceffe : that is to fay, all faithfull
people vvherfoeuer they liue . In vvhich
Church the tradition, that hath defcended
from the Apoftles, hath euer byn kept by
thofe that liue in any place of the world.

8. And againe a little after, hauing for
proofe of his faith, & confirmation of Apo-
ftolicall tradition,recounted all the Bishops
of Rome from S. Peter to his daies,he faith:
Nunc duodecimo loco, &c. Now in the twelth
place from the Apoftles hath *Eleutherius* that
Bifhopricke,& by this fuccefsiō *(of the forfaid*

I   *Roman*

Iren.lib.
3.cap.3.
aduerf.
hæref.
"
"
"
"
"
"
"
"
A nota-
ble fpech
of Ire-
næus,
that li-
ued
vvith *E-*
leuthe-
rius.
"
"
"
"

,, *Roman Bishops*) is the tradition of the Apoſtles
,, conſerued in the Church, & the preaching
,, of the truth hath come downe vnto vs; and
,, this is a moſt full demonſtration', that one
,, and the ſelfe ſame liuely faith, hath byn con-
,, ſerued in the Church from the Apoſtles
,, time, and deliuered vnto vs in truth, &c.

9. Lo heere tradition of the Apoſtles deliuered and conſerued by the ſucceſsion of
the Biſhops of Rome! Lo heere the Church
of Rome called ſo long agoe the greateſt &
moſt auncient of all other Churches, her
principality both named and confirmed!
Behould the obligation of all other Churches of the world, yea and of all faithfull
Chriſtians, to agree and haue acceſſe to her.
See heere all vaine glorious and ſelfe willed
heretiks confounded by *Irenæus*, with the onlie tradition and ſucceſsion of this Church
of Rome & her Biſhops, euen from *S. Peters*
time to *Eleutherius*, that liued with *Irenæus*.
What Catholike man could ſaie more at
this daie! and will anie iangling *Fox* or *Syr
Francis* avouch yet without ſhame, that
none of theſe points were euer knowne or
heard of in *Eleutherius* time?

10. Well then, this is one way to confound
them, if I would follow it. But being ouer
tedious, I meane to take another, and ſhew
out of their owne hiſtoriographers the *Ma-
gdeburgenſes*, that al theſe doctrines denied by

*A colle-
ction v-
pon Ire-
næus
vvords.*

Fox,

Fox, and his follower heere, were knowne
& in vſe among the cheefeſt writers in the
primitiue Church, & firſt ages after Chriſt.

And firſt of all to beginne with this very
matter firſt named by them *of the Primacie of
the Pope and Church of Rome* : The Magdeburgians haue an eſpeciall paragraph therof,
De primatu Ecclesiæ Romanæ vnder the forfaide title *of the incommodious opinions ſtubble,
ſtravve, and errors of the Doctors that liued vvithin
the firſt 200. yeares after Chriſt.* And in that paragraph they not onlie doe alleadge for
ſtubble, this laſt authoritie of *Irenæus* by me
cited, (though they alleadge it ſo miſera-
bly maimed, as of ſixe partes they leaue oute
more then fiue) but alſo an other place of
Saint Ignatius, that liued in the firſt age with
the Apoſtles themſelues, to the ſame purpoſe, which they cite in like manner *vnder the
ſame title of Stravve & ſtubble & incommodious o-
pinions.* And then paſſinge to the third cētury
or ſecond age after that of Chriſt, they cite
Tertullian for the ſame incommodious opinion, aboute the primacie of the Roman
Church and Biſhop, ſayinge of him. *Non ſine
errore ſentire videtur Tertullianus claues ſoli Petro
commiſſas, & Eccleſiam ſuper ipſum ſtructam, &c.*
Tertullian doth ſeeme not without error to
thinke that the keyes of the Church were
giuen onlie to S. Peter and that the Church
was built butt on him.

About
the pri-
macie of
the Pope
&church
of Ro-
me.

Cent. 1.
cap. 4.
pag. 63.

*Ignat.
epiſt. ad
Rom.*

*Tert.lib.
de præ-
ſcript.
Cent.*3.
cap. 4.
*pag.*84.

11.   They cite alſo fowre or ſiue places oute of *Saint Cyprian* where he holdeth the ſame with *Tertullian,* and ſoe they are bothe confuted for ſtubble Doctors togeather. Yet go they furthe with *Saint Cyprian* citing diuers other places out of him to the ſame effect, for the B. and Church of Rome, all which they take for ſtubble as where he ſaith *One God, one Chriſt, one Church, one Chayre builded vpon the arke by the vvord of oure Sauiour.* And three or foure like places more, which for breuitie I omitt, and finallie they ſay of him & three other Fathers of his time, *Cyprianus, Maximus, Vrbanus* and *Salonius,* doe thinke that one (Chief) B. muſt be in the Catholike Church, &c. Loe fowre olde Fathers that liued almoſt 14. hundred yeares agonne, and were the lightes of that primitiue church, reiected heere by fowre drinckinge *Germans,* gathred togeather in ſome warme ſtowe of *Magdeburge,* tipplinge ſtronglie, as a man may preſume, and iudginge all the worlde for ſtubble beſides themſelues: for which cauſe the third perſon in this quaternitie is called perhaps *Matheus Iudex.* But lett vs goe forward.

12.   They are not content with this reiection of *Saint Cyprian,* but they fall vppon him againe in theſe words. *Cyprian affirmeth expreſlie vvithoute all foundation of holy ſcripture that the Roman Church muſt be acknovvledged by all*
                                            Chriſtians

Cypr. li. 1. epiſt. 8.

Cyprian egregiouſly abuſed by the Mag deburgians.

Chriſtians *for the mother and roote of the Catholike*
Church. And further yet in an other treatiſe
That this Church is the Chayre of Peeter from vvhich
all the vnitie of Priſthoode proceedeth. And finallie
Cyprian ſay they, hath diuers other perilous opi-
nions about this matter, as for example, that he tyeth
the office of trevve Paſtorſhip to ordinarie ſucceſſion,
and that he denieth that Biſhops can be iudged, &c.
And Origene alſo in this age hath noe meane blotts
aboute the povver and office of the Church, &c.

13. Hitherto are the woords of the *Magde-*
burgians againſt the chief writers of theſe
two firſt ages after the Apoſtles, concerninge the pointe of principalitie and ſupremacie of the Church and Biſhop of Rome,
ſo clearly confeſſed by the ſaide Fathers (as
the *Magdeburgians* do graunte)& on the other
ſide ſo boldlie denied by the Fox, and the
K. his follower and Proſelite as a thinge not
ſo much heard or dreamed of in theſe firſt
ages. Wherof you haue heard theire ſeuerall
and reſolute aſſeuerations before. *Let them*
but graunte me (ſaith Fox) *and then I ſay* (quothe
the knight) *Their is no ſuch matter, &c.* And by
this one pointe onlie of the fiue articles before obiected by them, and denied flatlie to
haue ben knowne or beliued in *Eleutherius*
time, you may ſee howe they behaue themſelues,& what may be ſaide on oure part,&
howe greate a volume this booke woulde
growe vnto, if I ſhoulde proſecute all the
I 3 other

Cypr. ca.
4. epiſt.
8.
Tract. de
ſimplic.
Prælat.
Cypr. li.
1. epiſt. 6.
& lib. 4.
cap. 4.
epiſt. 9.
Origen.
tract. 1.
in Matt.
& hom.
15. in
Leuit.

other fowre articles alſo by them mentioned before, and ſhoulde paſſe through the
firſt three or foure or fiue hundred yeares
afrer Chriſt (for ſo much oure aduerſaries
ſometimes vppon a good moode of brag-
ginge will ſeeme to allow vs) to ſhewe
not oute of the bookes and writinges of the
auncient fathers themſelues, for that this
were ouerlonge, but what thes *Magdebur-*
gians doe note & gather againſt themſelues
oute of theire workes, for the antiquitie of
that doctrine which they impugne, reiectinge afterward all againe with this onlie
friuolus & fonde cauill, that thes opinions
of the Fathers were but *naui, ſtipula, & palia*
Doctorum, ſtaynes, ſtubble and ſtrawe of Doctors, *opiniones incommoda, &c.* and incommodious opinions.

Greg. de
Valent.
The ri-
diculous
manner
of pro-
ceedin-
ge of the
Magde-
burgians

14.   Wherin it is well noted by a lerned
man of our time, that thes fellowes do pro-
ceede, as if one beinge ſuſpected or accuſed
of thefte, hereſie, or anie other greeuous
crime, ſhoulde willingly preſent himſelf before the Magiſtrate, or Senate of the Cyttie:
& there firſt of all for his clearing, ſhoulde
bringe in for witneſſes againſt himſelf, the
beſt lerned, moſte graue, auncient and beſt
,, reputed honeſt men of all that citty, to te-
,, ſtifie that he is indeed ſuch a one, to witt a
,, falſe theefe, an heretike, or the like, but yeat
,, hauinge ſo donne, woulde endeuour to refute

fute all thes againe by one bare reiection „
fainge that they fpake rafhly and incom- „
modiouslie, and that they were ouerfeene „
& knewe not what they teftified, or were „
in a dreame when they fpake or teftified ,,
againft him, and finallie that all were de- „
ceaued, and he alone to be beliued againft „
them all: & woulde this fhifte (thinke you) „
counteruayle foe graue witneffes againft „
him ? or would anie indifferent iudge leaue „
to condemne him for this euafion ? or
woulde anie man thinke him much better
then madd, that woulde take fuch a courfe
of defence? And yeat this is the very courfe
of thefe *Magdeburgians*, who citinge firft the
graueft and moft auncient Fathers of Chriftendome againft themfelues, do reiect the
fame againe with this onlie ieft and contu-
melie, that they fpake incommodiouflie,
ignorantlie, and were ftubble Doctors.

15. Well then, for fo muche as concerneth
the firft article mencioned by Fox and Syr
Francis, as a thing not heard of in *Eleutherius*
time, (to witt the vniuerfalitie and *Primacie
of the Churche and Bishopp of Rome)* you fee, that
with going to the Authors themfelues of
that age, the *Magdeburgians* do make it cleare
againft themfelues. And for the fecond
pointe concerning the vfe of Maffe, and About
propitiatorie Sacrifice, we haue cited fuffi- Maffe &
cientlie before in the firft Chapter of this facrifice·

I 4 Treatife

Treatiſe out of the ſame *Magdeburgians*, who
condemne diuers of the moſt auncient Fathers for teſtifying this matter. And we
maye do the like in all the other Articles
ſpecified by Fox and his Knight, but that it
would be ouer tedious. And therfore I do
remitt the curious Reader to the volumes
of the *Magdeburgians* themſelues, if he haue ſo
muche time to leeſe, as the reading therof
doth require. Onlie in this place I am to
note vnto him, for his better inſtruction,
three or fowre kindes of ſhiftes and fraudes
vſed ordinarilie by theſe Proteſtant Germans, in ſetting downe theſe and other like
matters out of the Fathers, which I ſhall do
in the next enſuing Chapter.

THE SAME ARGVMENT IS
CONTINVED, AND IT IS SHEVVED
ovvt of the Magdeburgians, hovv they accuſe and
abuſe the Fathers of the 2. and 3. age for holding
vvith vs againſt them.

CHAP. VII.

Three
manner
of frau-
dulent
ſhiftes
in allea-
ging &
diſcredi-
ting the
Fathers.

1.

D IVERS are the ſhiftes and fraudes &
maniefold the abuſes which Prote-
ſtant writers, and namelie the *Magdeburgians*,
do offer to the auncient Fathers in examy-
ning their ſentences about Controuerſies in
Religion. Wherof one principall maye be
accoumpted, that of fowre, or fiue places, or
more

more that maye be alleaged out of them for
vs and our doctrine, in the queſtion propoſed, they will not cite two, leaſt the multitude of authorities (yf they alleage all that
in the Fathers are found) ſhould giue our
cauſe to muche creditt. Secondlie of foure **2.**
or fiue partes of the Fathers woordes, conteyned in the places by them alleaged, theſe
good fellowes doe cutt of ordinarilie three:
leaſt if they did ſett them doune at lengthe
with their reaſons, antecedents and conſequents, their opinions might appeare more
probable and plauſible , then theſe men
would haue them. And of this you haue
had an example in the firſt authoritie alleaged by me euen now, out of *Irenæus* about
the principalitie of the Churche of Rome.
Which being ſett downe ſomewhat at
leingthe, as it is in the author, maketh the
matter cleere. But ſhuffled vp in fowre or
fiue woordes after a moſt cutted ſort (as the
Magdeburgians do alleage them) do ſcarſe
make anie ſenſe at all. Which is the thing
the alleagers do deſire, therby to diſcreditt
the author.

2. Their third fraude is, that hauing allea- **3.**
ged the firſt authorities for vs, and againſt
themſelues, they deuiſe diuers prettie and
wittie ſleights to diſcreditt them againe. As
ſometimes ſaying, that in other places the
ſaid Father expoundeth or contradicteth

I 5 himſelf.

himſelf. Sometimes, that he ſpeaketh ra-
ſhlie, or incommodiouſlie, or without Scripture, and other ſuch contemptuous reie-
ctions. As for example, talking of *S. Cyprian*
that famous Biſſhopp, Doctor and Martyr,
and the Chriſtian Phenix of his age (as *Saint
Auguſtine* iudgeth of him) theſe men do
handle him this ſorte.

Cen.3.
c.4.

3. *Cyprianus ſine Scriptura loquitur*, Cyprian
ſpeaketh without ſcripture. *Cyprianus ſuper-
ſtitioſè fingit*, Cyprian doth faigne ſuperſti-
tiouſlie. *Cyprianus malè iudicat*, Cyprian doth
iudge naughtelie, and the like. Nay, they
endeuour to diſcreditt the whole multitude of Doctors and Fathers in euerie age.
As for example, in the beginning of the firſt
age next after the Apoſtles, they write thus.

Cent.2.
c.4.p.55.
The
iudgmét
of the
Magde-
burgiás
concer-
ning the
ſecond
age.

Tametſi hæc ætas Apoſtolis admodum vicina fuit, &c.
Albeit this age was neareſt to the Apoſtles:
yet the doctrine of Chriſt and his Apoſtles,
beganne to be not a litle darckned therein,
and manie monſtruous and incommodious
opinions are euerye where found to be
ſpread by the Doctors therof. Perhaps ſome
cauſe hereof might be, for that the gifte of
the holie Ghoſt in theſe Doctors, did be-
,, ginne to decaye, for the ingratitude of the
,, world towards the truthe.

4. Lo heere what a Preface this is to make
contemptible to the Reader all the Fathers
of the verie firſt age after the Apoſtles. But
what

what then do you thinke they will saye of the next following? you shall heare by their owne woords in the Preface of that age, which are these. *Quò longiùs ab Apostolorum ætate recessum est, eò plus stipularum doctrinæ puritati accessit.* The farther that we goe of from the Apostles age, the more stubble we shall find to haue byn added to the puritie of the Christian doctrine. Thus they saie of these two ages, and by this last sentence you may imagine what they will saie of all the ages following.

Cent. 3, cap. 4. p. 17.

5. And this is now spoken by them by way of preuention to discredit generallie the Fathers of these first ages, when they saie anie thing against them. But when they come to particulars, they haue notable quippes for them. Wherof, for example sake, we shall let you heare some few, whereby you maye as well learne their sharpe witts, as heretical spiritts. About the matter of *Mans Free-vvill*, whether it were wholie lost by originall sinne (as Protestants saie) or wounded onlie, as Catholiks holde, and strengthened againe by Gods grace, to do good in him that will; they write thus of the Doctors of the second age. *Nullus ferè doctrinæ locus est, qui tam citò obscurari cœpit, atque hic de libero arbitrio:* Noe one place or part of Christian doctrine beganne so soone to be darckned, as this of Free will. And then they goe on thus with the

Magdeburgians quippes against the Fathers.

About Free-vvill.

Cent. 2. cap. 4. pag. 53.

Iren.l.4. the chiefeſt Doctors of that age . *Irenæus di-*
cap.72. *ſputes not diſtinctly and vvreſteth the ſpeeches of*
Chriſt and of S. Paule in fauour of Free vvill ſaying.
That there is free vvill alſo in faith and belief,
Sed hæc ſatis craſſe dicuntur, & aliena ſunt à ſcriptu-
ris. But theſe things are ſpoken groſſe, by
Irenæus, and are farre from the ſenſe of ſcriptures . But whether theſe good-fellow-
Saxons may be accompted leſſe groſſe in
witt or grace, then *Irenæus*, is eaſy to gheſſe.
　　6.　From S. Irenæus they paſſe to *Clemens*
Clemens *Alexãdrinus* another piller of that age, ſaying:
Alexan. *Eodem modo Clemens Alexandrinus liberum arbi-*
trium vbique aſſerit, vt appareat in eiuſmodi tenebris
non tantùm fuiſſe omnes eius ſæculi authores : verum
etiam in poſterioribus eas ſubinde creuiſſe & auctas
eſſe. Clemens Alexandrinus doth in like
All Do- máner euery where affirme freewill, wher-
ctors in by it appeareth, that not only all the Do-
Eleuthe- ctors of this ſecond age were in the ſame
rius time darkeneſſe, but that the ſame did grow and
ſaid to was increaſed in the ages following. Be-
be in hold here their generall ſentence , both of
darknes this age, & the other enſuing. To what end
about then ſhould we alleadge more particulars in
freevvill this matter , ſeeing their reſolution to diſcredit all ? In the third age they do berate
ſhamefully *Tertullian, Origen, Cyprian* and *Me-*
thodius for the ſame doctrine of free will
Cent. 3. ſaying : *They do abuſe the ſcriptures intolerably for*
c. 4 p.77 *maintenance thereof.*

7. For

7. For the fourth age hauing giuen this ge-
nerall sentence; *Patres omnes fere huius ætatis de* **Cent. 4.**
libero arbitrio confuse loquuntur: All the Fathers **cap. 4.**
almost of this age do speake confusedly of **pag. 291.**
freewill, &c. they adde also, *contra manifesta*
scripturæ sanctæ testimonia, cõtrary to the manifest testimonyes of holie scripture. And then
they take in hand to course 7. cheefe Fathers
& Doctors in particular, *Lactantius, Athanasius,*
Basilius Nazianzenus, Epiphanius, and *Hierony-*
mus, saying *that they vvere all deceiued, all in dar-*
kenes, all misledd about this doctrine of mans free
vvill. So as it is noe marvaile, if Syr Francis
sharp sight discouer so many thicke clouds
and darknesse in the Cath. Church of our
daies; seeing his maisters the Magdeburg-
gians discouer so many in the primitiue
Church, as by this you may see.

8. About the point of Iustification they beginne the next age after the Apostles thus: The cõ-
Doctrina de Iustificatione negligentius & obscurius trouersie
ab nis doctoribus tradita est. The doctrine of Iu- of Iusti-
stification, was deliuered by the Doctors of **Cent. 2.**
this second age after Chrijt, more negligent- **pag. 59.**
ly and obscurely, then it ought to haue byn.
And the same they saie of the third age also: *Hunc summum articulum de iustificatione ob-*
scuratum esse, iustitiam enim coram Deo operibus **Cent. 3.**
tribuerunt. that this cheefe article of Iustifi- **pag. 79.**
cation hath byn obscured in this age, for
that the Doctors therof did attribute iustice
before

before God vnto workes, and not to only
faith. &c. And then againe in the fourth

Cent. 4.
pag. 191.

age, they reprehend greatly *Lactantius, Nilus,
Chromatius, Ephrem,* and *Saint Hierome* for the
ſame doctrine. The other lower Centuries
I haue not lying by me, but it is eaſy to
gheſſe, what theſe men will ſay of later
ages authors, ſeeing they doe exagitate ſo
greatly the more auncient.

About
the Sa-
crament
of Pe-
nance.
Cent. 2.
pag. 62.

9. About the Sacramēt of Penance, which is
another cōtrouerſy betwixt vs, they write
in the beginning of the 2. age thus: *Quòd iam
tum cœperit hæc pars doctrinæ de pœnitentia labefa-
ctari, ex Tertulliano, Cypriano, & hæreſi Nouatiana
infra patebit.* That this part of Chriſtian doctrine about Pennance, euen then *(in the firſt
age after the Apoſtles)* began to be weakened,
ſhall appeare afterward by *Tertullian, Cyprian*
and the *Nouatian* hereſie. Thus they write
boldlie and confidentlie as you ſee. And

Cent. 3.
pag. 81.

then in the age following: *Plerique huius ſæculi
Doctores, doctrinam de pœnitentia mirè deprauant.*
The moſt of the Doctors of this age, do
wonderfullie depraue the doctrine of pennance. And what is the reaſon thinke you?

Cent. ib.

They tell vs preſentlie. *Ad ipſum tantum opus
pœnitentis, ſeu contritionem, eam deducunt: de fide in
Chriſtum nihil dicunt.* They reduce pennance
onlie to the worke of the penitent, that is to
ſaye vnto contrition: & do ſpeake nothing
at all of faith in Chriſt. But who doth not
ſee

fee this to be a notorious flaunder? For how is it pofsible to haue contrition without faith? Confider then how little it is to be maruayled at, if thefe companions & others of their crew, do flaunder and calumniate vs, that liue in thefe daies: when they fhame not to do it, againft fo manie holie and learned auncient Fathers of the primitiue Church? But lett vs go forward.

10. About the perfection and meritt of good works, thefe Cenfurers affirme alfo; *that the true doctrine of* Chrift *in this behalfe, vvas obfcured in the fecond age, immediatly after the Apoftles.* And they do wounderfully by name fall out with *Clemens Alexandrinus* for that he faith; *Gratia faluamur, fed non abfque bonis operibus:* we are faued by Chrifts grace, but yet not without good works. Which is the verie expofition that Syr Francis himfelfe holdeth before in the fecond Encounter: but his maifters heere do denie it. And then in the next age they fay: *magis, quàm fuperioris fæculi, Doctores huius ætatis, à vera doctrina Chrifti & Apoftolorum de bonis operibus declinarunt.* The Doctors of this age are fallen away from the doctrine of Chrift, and of his Apoftles about good works, more then the Doctors of the former ages. And then in particular they cry out of *Origen,* that he writeth: *That God giueth glory to euery one in the life to come pro menfura meritorum, according to the meafure of his me-*

About good vvorkes. *Ibidem* pag. 59.

Clem. li. 5. ftrom.

Enc 2. cap. 16.

Ibidem pag. 80.

Orig. l. 2. in epift. ad Rom.

Cipr. lib.
epist. ep.
25.

his meritts. Et simili errore (say they) *Cyprianus
meritorum præcedentium defensione obuelari peccata
subsequentia.* And that Cyprian by like error
(to *Origen*) doth saye, that by the defence of
precedent meritts, sinnes that follow, may
be couered. Which they cannot abyde to
heare.

About
fasting,
virginity, obseruatió
of holy
daies.

11. Well, I might runne ouer manie other
things, as about *Lavves of fastings, Obseruation of
holy dayes, Virginitie, Continencie,* and the like:
wherin the auncient Fathers no lesse disagreed from these our new ghospellers, then
we do at this daie. And they complayne
therof euen at the verie first entrance of the
second age, saying : *Doctrina de libertate Christiana nonnihil cæpit obscurari, &c.* The doctrine
of Christian libertie began greatlie to be
obscured in these daies. Note I pray you,
that still their complaint is of *obscuritie* and
darknesse no lesse in those auncient first ages:
then now they complayne of oures, and
with the selfe same reason . For what is the
reason thinke you, why they complaine so
greatly here of *Christian liberty* abridged 1500.
yeares gone ? You shall heare the particulars, which they alleadg, complayning first
of these words of *Saint Ignatius* scholler to
the Apostles: *Do not dishonour* (saith he) *the holydayes; do not neglect the fast of the lent, for that it
conteyneth the imitation of God, vvhile he liued vpon
earth. Despise not the passion vveeke; but do yovv fast*
vvednes-

Cent. 2.
pag. 65.

Cent. 2.
pag. 65.

Ignat.
epist. ad
Phil.

vvednesdayes and fridayes, and giue the rest of your meat to the poore, &c.

12. Thus said he and it misliked greatlie the *Magdebnrgians* to heare so much talke of fasting. And from this complaint they passe to another against all the Fathers of that age saying: *De martyrio nimis magnifice sentire cœperunt.* The Doctors of this age did begin to haue to magnificent an opinion of martyrdome. And about the consecrating of virgins to Christ, they mislike greatly certayne speeches of *S. Ignatius.* As for example *epistol. ad Antiochen. Virgines videant, cui se consecrarint*. Les virginnes consider well, to whome they haue consecrated themselues. And againe *epistol. ad Tharsen. Eas, quæ in virginitate sunt, honorate, sicut sacras Christo.* Do you honour them, that liue in virginity, as consecrated vnto Christ. And yet further in this epistle *ad Heronem. Virgines custodi; tanquam Sacramenta Christi.* Haue care to keepe virgins, as sacraments of Christ. Which kind of speeches misliking our *Magdeburgians*, they say, that *they vvere an occasion and opened the vvay to those things, vvhich aftervvards vvere therupon founded, concerninge cloisters and vovves.*

13. In the next age after, to witt the third, they also complaine greatlie of the same things, and manie other the like. As namelie about chastitie and virginitie: *nimium prædicari & extolli continentiam,* That continency

Against martyrdome.

Sacred virginitie.

pag. 65.

Cent. 3.
pag. 86.

K   and

and chaſtitie was to much commended and extolled. And they are ſo earneſt againſt *Tertullian, Origen,* and *Cyprian,* for this matter, (eſpeciallie the later) as they do accuſe the holy man for hatred to womankind, ſaying:

S. Cyprian accuſed to hate vvomen.

ex profeſſo quaſi vbique　teſtatur muliebrem ſexum, he dothe euerie wh   e almoſt euen of purpoſe deteſt woman-   nd. But in what ſenſe I pray you? In noe other point (without doubt) but that hé had no deſire to haue a ſiſter for himſelfe, as each of our Germane miniſters may be preſumed to haue. But why is this falſe ſlaunder of deteſting women-kind laid vpon holie *Saint Cyprian* by theſe good fellowes? for ſooth for that he praiſed ſo much *Virginitie,* affirming as they

Cypr. li. de bono pudititia.

alleadge him; *That Virginity doth equall it ſelfe to Angells. Yea yf vve do examine vvell the matter, vve ſhall find it to exceed Angells. For that contrary to nature, it getteth a victory in fleſh, againſt fleſh, vvhich Angells do not.* And againe in another place:

Cyp. ſer. de natiu. Chriſti.

Albeit mariage be good & inſtituted by God; yet continency is better, & virginity exceedeth all. Behold the cauſe why theſe proteſtants affirme *S. Cyprian* to haue hated the feminyne ſexe.

Martyrdome.

14. They ſay alſo of *Martyrdome,* that the Fathers of this age ſpoke immoderately therof: *Martyrium immodicè extulerunt omnes huius ætatis doctores.* All the Doctors of this age, did praiſe immoderatlie martyrdome. And then againe of *Inuocation of Saints.*

Videas

Videas in doctorum huius saeculi scriptis non obscura pag.83.
vestigia inuocationis Sanctorum : You may see in
the writings of the Doctors of this second
age, cleere stepps of inuocation or prayer to
Saints. And then of *Purgatory, Semina pur-*
gatorij in aliquot locis apud Originem subinde sparsa
videas : You may see the seeds of purgatorye
dispersed in this age in the writings of *Ori-*
gen. And you must note, that thes good fellowes do speake by diminitiues of purpose,
calling it *signes or footsteppes of prayer to Saints, &*
seeds of purgatory, and the like. But presentlie
in the next age they accuse openlie and by
name, *Saint Athanasius, S. Basill, S. Gregory Na-* Cent. 4.
zianzen, S. Ambrose, Prudentius, Epiphanius and c.4 pag.
Ephrem, eight great Doctors and principall 295.
guides of the Christian Church, for this error of Praying to Saints. They accuse also Ibid. pa.
for expresse holding of Purgatory *Lactantius,* 304.
Prudentius, and *Saint Hierome* in the same age.
15. They accuse all the Doctors of this age, Tradi-
for attributing to much to *Traditions* and tions.
obseruations of the Church : especiallie
about *Monasticall life, virginitie', honoring the* Mona-
memorie and reliques of martyrs. And they are sticall life.
so earnest and impudent in thes fanta- Reliques
sies of theirs, as hauing cited the Fathers
sentences against them selues, they cannot lett them passe without intollerable
reprochfull words. So do they accuse holie
Athanasius of superstition, for comending virginitie.

ginitie. And hauing alleadged a long place *pag.300.* of S. *Baſill* in prayſe of monaſticall liſe , they add this cenſure: *Quæ quidem omnia & præter, & contra ſcripturam ſunt.* All which word; (of S. *Baſill*) are bothe beſides and contrarie to holie ſcripture . Then take they in hand *lib. 2. ad* Saint *Ambroſe* ſaying: *nimis inſolenter pronunciat Marcell. de virginum meritis Ambroſius.* Ambroſe doth pronounce to to inſolently of the meritts of virgins. And for that holie *Ephrem* had ſaid, *Ephr. l.* that all pious people *ſhall come merilye in the day of de lucta-* iudgment *before the face of Chriſt : but eſpeciallye min. ſpi-* monks, *and other ſuch as haue liued in deſerts in cha-* *ritus c. 2.* ſtity, labors, vvatchings, faſtings and the like. Theſe good fellowes , whoſe greateſt labours of pennance haue byn to drinke and be merie *pag.301.* in warme ſtowes, ſaie : *Quid poteſt monſtroſius dici contra meritum Chriſti?* what can be ſpoken more monſtrouſlie againſt the meritt of Chriſt? And then to a Godlie ſpeech of *Saint Ambroſe,* about the pious honouring of mar- *Ambroſ.* tyrs tombes , they giue this cenſure : *Cogitet ſerm. 6. pius lector, quàm tetra ſint iſta.* Let the Godlie *de marg.* reader conſider how horrible theſe things *tom.3.&* are, vtered by *Ambroſe.* *in orat. funeb. de* 16. And in another place vpon certayne *obitu* words of Saint *Ambroſe* about the holie croſſe *Theodo-* found ont by *Saint Helena,* they haue in their *ſy.* iniurious ſpeches : *Multa commemorat ſuperſti-tioſa, quæ vehementer contumelioſa ſunt in meritum Chriſti, & repugnantia fidei.* Ambroſe doth reckon

reckon vp many superstitious things, which
are greatlie contumelious against the meritt
of Christ, and are contrarie to faith. And
thus they goe forward against the rest of the
Doctors and Fathers, that agree not with
them in their fancies and heresies. And generally hauing sought to discredit about the
article of Iustification and good works this
fourth age after Christ, and the cheefe Doctors therof by name, as *Lactantius*, *Gregory*
Nissene, *Hilarius*, *Nazianzen*, *Ambrose*, and
Ephrem by name: they coclude with this con-
tumelie against them all. *Iam cogitet pius lector,* Cent. 4.
quàm procul hæc ætas in hoc articulo, de Apostolorum pap. 293.
doctrina desciuerit. Let the godly Reader now
consider, how farre this fourth age departed
from the doctrine of the Apostles in this article, *of good vvorks* and *Iustification.*

17. Well then in all these points of controuersie betwene vs and the protestants, to
witt; *the primacy and principality of the Church* The
and Bishopp of Rome, the Sacrament and sacrifice of summe
the altar, otherwise called the *masse,* *freevvill,* of this
iustification, pennance, meritt of good vvorks, tradi- chapter
tions, obseruing of fasts, holy daies, sacred virginity, me full
continency, monasticall life, prayer to Saints, purga- shifting
tiry, memory, and reliques of martyrs, and otherlike of here-
(which in effect are the principall points tiques.
wherin the protestants do disagree from vs)
we see by the testimonie and wittnesse of
their owne men, that the auncient Fathers

of

of *Eleutherius* daies,& the next two ages after him (for I goe no lower) did wholy agree with vs againſt them. And this, ſo farre forth, as the *Magdeburgians* do ſay,more then once,of all the Doctors of the ſecond age after Chriſt(wherin Eleutherius liued) *that they erred and liued in darkeneſſe*, for that they held with vs, as now you haue heard. And

Cap.5.
num.2.

Suprà
ibidem.

with what face then doth Iohn Fox ſay a little before: *let them but leaue vs the religion that vvas in Eleutherius tyme, & vve vvill aſke no more.* With what forhead alſo doth Syr Francis his ſcholler add, *I ſay there is not novv the ſame faith in Rome that vvas then, there vvas then no maſſes, no vniuerſall Pope, &c.* But with ſuch men vve deale,that care not vvhat they ſay or deny, ſo they may beare out the matter for the preſent, and ſeeme alwayes to haue ſomwhat to ſay.

18. But now will we leaue this, and paſſe to another conuerſion vnder *S. Gregory* the great, which concerneth vs Engliſhmen more particularly, then the former, wher-about you ſhall ſee no leſſe hereticall fraude and malignity vſed,then in the other before métioned,if not more.For that theſe people finding all antiquitie againſt them,and ha-uing no other authorities for proofe of their Religion, but onlie their owne inuentions, with ſome light ſhew of Scripture expoun-ded by themſelues : are forced to vſe moſt

ſhamefull

shamefull, and desperate shiftes, when their
cause is examined by the histories of former
ages. And somuch of this point.

OF THE THIRD CONVER-
SION OF OVR ILAND AND EN-
glish nation by Saint Augustine *& his fellovves
sent from* Pope Gregory *the first , anno* 596.
*And of diuers notorious hereticall shiftes & im-
pudences vsed to deface the said tvvo excellent
men, & the religion brought into Englād by them.*

Chap. IIX.

Yov have heard the two shifts before
vsed about the first publike couuersion
of Britanie by *Pope Eleutherius,* to witt, first of
all to discreditt this storie so much as in
them lay, & then being forced to graunt it,
their last refuge was to say, that the same
faith was not then in *Rome* that is now , nor
that the points of doctrine now beleeued
and taught, were knovvne and acknowle-
ged then. Both which shifts haue byn most
euidently refuted , and the same religion
shewed to haue byn in Rome vnder *Pope
Eleutherius,* which at this daie is there taught.
2. But novv there remaineth the other
publike couuersion of the English nation
from *Pope Gregory* vnder K. *Ethelbert* of *Kent*
some foure hundred yeares or more after
the other, in which neither of the two for-

mer

Bed.l.1.
hiſt.
Angl. c.
23. &
deinceps.
Malm.
de geſt.
Regum
Angl.l.1.
& de
Pont.
Angl.l.1.
Galf.
mon.hiſt.
Angl. l.
11.c.22.
Hütingt.
hiſt. l. 3.
cap. 1.

mer ſhifts can be vſed by our aduerſaries.
For neither can thy denie or bring in doubt
the hiſtorie it ſelfe, recorded by all writers
of that time & ſince (and namelie and moſt
abundantlie by our countreymen *Saint Bede,*
& his continuator *VVilliam of Malmesbury,* &
others) nor can they ſay, that the faith of
Rome then deriued into England, was any
other then that, which is now in Rome.
Which later point, he that will ſe proued
ſubſtantially, and examined article by article, and point by point, by conferring the
doctrine, rites and ceremonies brought into
England by our ſaid Apoſtle *Auguſtine,* with
that which at this daie is taught, and practiſed in the Roman Church: lett him read
the tranſlation of the ſaid Storie of *Bede,* put
into Engliſh by our famous learned countreyman M. Doctor *Stapleton,* with his notes
to the ſame; and the learned treatiſe, which
theron, and by that occaſion he made, intituled *the Forterreſſe of faith,* which ſheweth the
ſame to be coforme likewiſe to al antiquity

3.   Wherfore our wyly knight Syr Francis
ſeeing this, hath anſwered not one ſentence
or ſyllable in this his reply or Waſt-woord,
to this conuerſion of Engliſhmen vnder
Pope Gregory, though I vrged the ſame ſom-
vvhat earneſtly in my Ward-word. And
yet for that vpon other occaſions, he ſaith
once or tvvice in his booke, *that Auguſtine*
brought

brought in the Romish religion: as though the Romish religion had byn different at that daie from that of the Christian Britans; and for that his maister *Iohn Fox* (out of vvhome he hath stoine all this storie) runneth also to this shift vpon diuers occasions: I am forced to say somwhat thervnto in this place.

4. You must then vnderstand, that *Fox* & his fellowes being excluded from the former two shifts (as I haue said) and yet forced to seeke out somwhat, againft this euident deduction of our English faith from the Sea of Rome, they betake themselues to two other refuges, as absurd, or rather more, then the former. The first wherof is, to discredit by all meanes, they can deuise, the authors of this conuersion, to witt, *Saint Gregory* the Pope, and *S. Augustine* our Apostle. *About this tyme* (saith Fox) *departed Gregory B. of Rome, of vvhome it is said; that of the number of all the first Bishopps before him in the primitiue Church, he vvas the basest, and of all them that came after him, he vvas the best.*

Tvvo nevv vvicked deuised shifts.

Fox act. & Mon. p. 107. col. 2. n. 84.

5. Lo heere enuy and malice how blind they are; for as for basenes, if he meane in bloud or worldlie honour, it might perhappes with more probabilitie haue byn attributed to all, or anie of the Popes that were before him, then to *Gregory*, who was (as is knowne) the sonne of a most noble & riche Senatour *Gordianus*, as all authors do

The defence of S. Gregorie againft heretiks.

K 5 testifie.

Ioannes Diac. in vita Gregor. Magni.

teſtifie. Whoſe pallace on the hill *Scaurus* neere to that of the Emperours, is at this daie a faire church and monaſtery. And this man beinge his Fathers heire, built with his owne ſubſtance 7. monaſteries, and endewed them with rents before he entred into anie religious order himſelfe. Wherfore touching birth & wordlie wealth, this man was ſo farre of from the baſenes, wherwith *Fox* would diſgrace him, as he might perhaps with more probabilitie haue aſcribed this note (as before I ſaid) to anie other Pope from *Saint Peter* downeward, then to *Saint Gregory.* And as for rare and ſingular learning (which impugneth alſo baſenes) or for holines of life (that increaſeth much nobilitie) I thinke *Iohn Fox* dareth not to make *Saint Gregory* inferior to many Popes, that went before him, though he were noe martyr as manie of them were. So that hard it were to determine wherin this baſeneſſe doth conſiſt, but that the ſimple fellow would needs ſaie ſomwhat to ſo great a mans diſgrace. And as for terming him the beſt of all that followed, this is not ſpoken ſo much to praiſe him, as to diſpraiſe the reſt: or to make baſe and beſt to fall out in tune. And ſo we paſſe it ouer as impertinent ſpeech.

6.   But if we would ſtand vpon the teſtimonies of antiquitie in this behalfe, to oppoſe

poſe them againſt *Iohn Fox*, as namelie *Ioannes Diaconus* that ~~wrote~~ wrote his life, and manie other after him : we ſhould oppreſſe the poore fellow with multitude of wittneſſes. Yet cannot we let paſſe two that liued in Spayne at the ſame time, the one and the other ſoone after. The firſt is *Iſidorus* Archbiſhopp of *Syuill*, who writeth thus preſentlie vpon his death : *Gregorius Papa, Romanæ Sedis & Apoſtolicæ præſul, compunctione timoris Dei plenus & humilitate ſummus, tantóque per gratiam Spiritus ſancti ſcientiæ lumine præditus, vt non modò illi præſentium temporum quiſquam, ſed nec in præteritis quidem par fuit vnquam.* Pope Gregory Biſhopp of the Romane & Apoſtolike Sea, being full of compunction of the feare of God, and moſt highe in humilitie, was indued by the grace of the holy Ghoſt with ſo great light of knowledg, as not onlie anie man of the preſent time is equall vnto him, but nether of the ages paſt.

7. This is his iudgment, which holie *Saint Hildefonſus* Archbiſhop of *Tolett*, hauing cited in a booke of his of the ſame title not long after, yeldeth as it were the reaſon of this aſſeueration of *S. Iſidore* in theſe words : *Ita enim cunctorum meritorũ claruit perfectione ſublimis, vt (excluſis omnium illuſtrium virorum comparationibus) nihil illi ſimile demonſtret antiquitas. Vicit enim ſanctitate Antoniũm, eloquentia Cyprianum, ſapientia Auguſtinum, &c.* For *S. Gregory* did ſhine „ with

Iſid. de viris illuſt. ca. 27. The teſtimony of Iſidorus concerning S. Gregory.

Hildef. libel. de viris illuſtrib.

with ſo high a perfection, of ail kind of meritts , as (the compariſons of all other worthy men being excluded)antiquity hath nothing to ſhew like vnto him; ſeing that in
„ holines he ſurpaſſed *S. Anthony*, in eloquence
„ *Saint Cyprian*, in wiſdome *Saint Auguſtine, &c.*

Thus wrote theſe men in thoſe daies,and
albeit it may ſeeme ſome kind of exaggera-
tion:yet we may herby behold the iudgmēt
of thoſe ages, & the ſenſe of theſe two learned & holie prelats, how differēt they were
from *Iohn Fox* & his mates in our daies, that
ſeeke ſo fondlie to diſcredit ſo rare a man.
And this ſhal be ſufficient for *Saint Gregory.*

8.   Now as for our Apoſtle *Saint Auguſtine,*
though the malice of our heretiks be exceeding great, both againſt his perſon, and
actions: yet is *Fox* oftentimes forced to
ſpeake well of him and his companie. As in

theſe words; *At length vvhen the King* (Ethelbert) *had vvell conſidered the honeſt conuerſation of
their life , and mooued vvith the miracles vvrought
thorough Gods hād by them:he heard them more gladly ; & laſtly by their holſome exhortations & example
of godly life,he vvas by them conuerted & Chriſtened
in the yeare aboue ſaid* 596. *and the* 36. *of his raigne.*

9.   Thus writeth he there. And moreouer talking of a great and ſpeciall miracle
wrought by *Saint Auguſtine* in ſight of the
Britans, then his aduerſaries, for confirmation of the Roman doctrine in obſeruing
the

the Easter feaſt, as now it is vſed, (which
miracle was the reſtoring of a blind man to
his ſight, by only kneeling downe & praying to God for him in the preſence of the
multitude (whoſe prelates had attempted
the like before, but could not acheiue it:) he
ſaith, that the ſtories both of *Bede, Polychrony-*   Fox *act.*
con, Huntington, Iornalenſis, Fabian, and others   *p.* 107.
moe do agree in this matter. And yet in the   *col.* 1.
verie next page following. he goeth about
do diſcredit him by all meanes poſsible, and
to diminiſh the opinion of ſanctitie in him.
For talking of a certayne meeting of 7. Britan Biſhops with him, where they ſay *S. Au-*
ſtine being made now Archbiſhopp and primate of England, would not ariſe nor moue
his bodie at their comming in, Fox writeth
thus. *Much leſſe vvould his phariſaicall ſolemnitie*
haue girded himſelfe as Chriſt did, and vvaſh his bre-
threns feet after their iourney. but how knoweth
Iohn Fox this? heare his reaſon: *ſeeing his lordſhip*   Fox ſee-
vvas ſo highe, or rather ſo heauy, or rather ſo proud: keth to
that he could not find in his heart to giue them a little   diſcredit
moouing of his body, &c.   S. Au-
                                                            guſtine.
10. By this is his affection ſeene to the man,
and alſo by that he would gladly bring him
in ſome manner of ſuſpition, to haue byn
ſome part of the cauſe of the ſlaughter of
the Brittan monks of *Bangor*, ſlaine by *Ethel-*
fride a heathen K. of Northumberland, for
that they came to Cheſter to pray againſt
                                                            him.

him. Wheras *Fox* himſelfe not withſtanding
doth confeſſe, that both *Huntington* & other

Bed. lib.
1. hiſt. c.
35.

authors (and he might haue ſaid alſo Bede
himſelfe) do ſay, that *S. Auguſtine* was dead
when this ſlaughter happened, nor could
any way this matter appertaine vnto him,
or to any occaſion giuen by him. Yet doth
another companion of Iohn Fox go further, and more malitiouſly againſt this holy
man our Apoſtle: to witt, *Iohn Bale* the Apo-

Io. Bale
cent. 1.
ſcrip.
Britt.
fol. 35.

ſtate friar, who writeth thus: *Auguſtinus Ro-*
manus à Gregorio primo ad Angloſaxones papiſtica
fide intiandos Apoſtolus mittebatur. Auguſtine
the Romane was ſent as an Apoſtle from
Gregory the firſt, to couert the Engliſh-Sa-
xons to a popiſh faith. Behold heere, how
auncient papiſts the Catholiks of England
are, by this mans opinion.

Bales
ſcurri-
litie a-
gainſt
Saint
Augu-
ſtin.

11.   I paſſe ouer the reſt of *Bales* falſe and
contumelious ſpeech concerning *S. Augu-*
ſtine, as that *he being ignorāt of the ſcriptures, taught*
falſe doctrine, and that he made himſelfe Archbi-
ſhopp by violence; that he attended more to gett tithes
and oblations for maſſes, then to preach the goſpell, &
that he vvas cauſe of the ſlaughter of 1200. *monks*,
and other ſuch like reprochfull lies. Againſt
whome I could propoſe the whole ſtreame
of the beſt authors euer ſince his time, both
domeſticall and externe, yf it were worth
the ſtriuing with ſo contemptible an aduerſary. And if nothing would reſtraine the
libertie

libertie of fo reprochfull a tongue: yet at
leaſt waies the reſpeꞓt of our nation conuerted by hym, and fo many great miracles
wrought to that effeꞓt, as both *S. Bede* and
others do recount, and Fox dareth not deny, ought to haue byn fome bridle to this
fhameleſſe Apoſtata. For that not only *Saint
Bede, Malmesbury, Marianus Scotus, Sigebert*, and
others do recount them: but euen *Saint Gre-*
gory himſelfe wrote the fame by his owne
pen to *Eulogiu* Archbiſhopp of *Alexandria*,
who had written vnto him of fome like miracles wrought in Egypt alfo about that
time, in the conuerſion of new Chriſtians.
Saint Gregories words are thefe.

    12.   *Sed quoniam, &c.* But for that truly
the good, which they do there, is much increaſed by the ioy you take of other mens
good alfo: I will requite yow with the like
good newes, as yow haue vvritten to me.
Knovv then, that, vvheras the English nation placed in a corner of the vvorld haue
remained hitherto in their infidelity, vvor-
ſhiping ſtones and blocks, I did by the help
of your prayers thefe daies paſt (God, as I
hope, mouing me therunto) fend vnto that
nation a monke of my monaſtery to preach
vnto them. Who vpon my licence, afterward being made Biſhop in the countreyes
neere vnto them, arriued at laſt vnto that
end of the world. And now lettres are come,
                vnto

Of the
miracles
vvrougt
by Saint
Augu.
ſtiue.

Greg. li.
7. epiſt.
30. In-
dict. 1.
,,
,,
,,
,,
,,
,,
S. Gre-
gories
relacion
of En-
glish af-
faires.
,,
,,

,, vnto vs both of his health and of his worke,
,, that he hath in hand. And furelie eyther he
,, or they which were fent ouer with him, do
,, worke fo manie miracles in that nation, as
,, they may feeme therin to imitate the power
,, and miracles of the Apoftles themfelues.
,, And in this verie laft folemnitie of Chrifts
,, natiuitie paft, there were aboue tenn thow
,, fand Englifhmen baptized by the hands of
,, this our brother and fellow Bifhopp, &c.

13.   Thus farre *Saint Gregory.* Who is another manner of wittneffe then *Fox* or *Bale.*
though Fox doth confeffe, (as yow haue
heard before)both the vertuous life and miracles of *S. Auguftine* and his fellowes. And if
he do fo indeed, and do thinke them to haue
byn wrought by Gods power, and not by
the operation of Sathan: then is it great
blafphemie both in him and his fellowes, to
thinke, that God would concurre by miracles to the planting of falfe doctrine and error, which fcornfullie they call the papifti-
call faith. Wherof now we fhall treat more
in particular, hauing difputed thefe things
about *Saint Auguftines* perfon.

About
the do-
ctrine
brought
in by *S.*
Auguft.

14.   About which doctrine thefe good fellowes feeke to quarell much more, giuing
fimple people to beleeue, that he brought
from Rome a different Chriftian religion
from that, which was in Britanie before, as
out of Syr Francis owne words alleaged
may

may appeare. And albeit Iohn Fox in his hiſtorie treating of this matter, doth not dare
to affirme it plainelie, but rather ſeeketh
heere & there to picke out ſome differences
betwene the Roman Religion, that *S. Auguſtine* brought in, and that vvhich is novv,
as for example vvhere he ſaith: *Note by the
vvay, Chriſtian Reader, that vvheras it is ſaid that
Auguſtine* ＊ *baptized ten thouſand Engliſh Saxons
vpon a Chriſtmaſſe day in à Riuer, yt follovveth* (ſaith
he) *that then there vvas no vſe of fonts, &c.* Yet in
a certayne Preface of his, vvhich he calleth
his Proteſtation to the whole Church of
England, he hath theſe words: *All this vvhile
about the ſpace of 400. yeares* (*after the conuerſion
of Kinge Lucius*) *religion remayned in Britany vncorrupt, & the vvord of Chriſt truly preached; till about
the comming of Auguſtine and his companions from
Rome, many of the ſaid Britan preachers vvere ſlayne
by the Saxons. And after that began the Chriſtian
faith to enter and ſpring amongſt the Saxons after
a certayne Romiſh ſort: yet notvvithſtanding ſom-
vvhat more tollerable, then in other times, vvhich
after follovved, &c.*

15. Thus writeth Fox maliciouſlie ynough
(as you ſee) to bring in doubt and diſcredit
our firſt Chriſtian religion, planted by Saint
Auguſtine. But yet heerby it is euident, that,
if Engliſh men vvere euer true Chriſtians
eyther at their firſt conuerſion, or for more
then 900. yeares after, they vvere *Roman*

L *Chriſtians,*

Fox pag.
107. col.
2.

＊A vviſe
conſe-
quence!
for that
novv al-
ſo fonts
vvould
hardly
ſuffice
to ba-
ptize
10000.
in a day.
Fox in
Proteſt.
pag. 9.

VVhe-
ther S.
Augu-
ſtine
taught
the Sa-
xons
true re-
ligion.

Chriſtians. But vvhether they vvere euer
true Chriſtians in deed, or not: that point
Fox dareth not plainly to determine in
this place. But onlie, as the faſhion of hereticks is, to call matters in queſtion & leaue
them in doubt; ſo doth he: and (as one ſaid
vvell) To lay the eggs for an other to hach
the ſerpents. For that *Fox* his Schollers, *Holinſhed*, *Hooker*, and *Harriſon*, and other like
haue preſumed vpon this foundation, to determine reſolutlie the matter: that Engliſhmen vvere neuer true Chriſtians in deed
before Luther beganne his doctrine. Which
appeareth in theſe their vvords follovving,

*Holin. in
deſcript.
Britan.
c. 27. col.
1.*
ſpeaking of the inhabitans of *Britanie. VVhen
thes heepe of Gods paſture (ſay they) vvould receiue
no holſome fodder, it pleaſed his Maieſtie to let
them runne on headlong from one iniquitie to an
other. In ſo much that after the doctrine of Pelagius,
they receiued that of* Rome *alſo, brought in by Au-
ſtine and his Monks. VVherby it vvas to be ſeene, hovv
they fell from the truth into hereſie, and from one hereſie ſtill into an other, vntill at laſt they vvere drovv-
ned all together in the pitts of errour, digged vp by
Antichriſt, &c.*

16. Thus do vvrite theſe Compagnions
of the firſt conuerſion of Engliſh-men by
*Vvhe-
ther En-
gliſh mē
vvere e-
uer true*
Saint Auguſtine: but vvhether they meane of
the *Britans*, or of Engliſh-men, or both, that
fell into theſe pits: it is not ſo eaſie to iudge.
For they name both, and do determine or
distin-

distinguish neyther people . And vvhich
vvay ſoeuer you take it, it hath not only
falſhood & impiety: but open contradictiõs
alſo in it ſelfe. For if they meane of the Bri-
tons, then is it euidẽtly falſe, that they were
conuerted by S. Auguſtine and his monkes.
And if they meane of the English , it is
much more falſe , that they euer receiued
the doctrine of *Pelagius*, or fell from truth to
hereſie, as theſe phantaſticall men both
ignorantlie, & malitiouſlie do affirme. But
lett vs heare yet further their blaſphemous
and deſperate ſpeches of our firſt Apoſtle
Saint Auguſtine.

This Auguſtine (ſay they) after his arriuall con-
uerted the Saxons in deed from Paganiſme , but as
the prouerbe ſaith, bringing them out of Gods bleſsing
into the vvarme ſunne, he imbued them vvith no leſſe
hurtfull ſuperſtition, then they did knovv before. For
beſide the only name of Christ, and externall con-
tempt of their priſtinate Idolatrie , he taught them
nothing at all , but rather made an exchange from
groſſe to ſubtile treacherie , from open to ſecret Idola-
trie , and from the name of Pagans to the bare title
of Chriſtians, &c.

17.   Lo heere theſe mens cenſures of the
firſt conuerſion of our English nation to
Chriſtianitie. They compare Paganiſme to
Gods bleſsing, and our nevv Chriſtian religion to the warme ſunne, and all our forefathers faith and religion, for more then

900. yeares to geather, they define to be no-thing but fuperftition, treacherie & Idola-latrie, no leffe hurtfull then the Paganifme it felfe, which they profeffed before: & that they liued & dyed only with the bare name of Chriftians without the fubftance,&c. & confequently are moft certainly damned all eternally. Now if the worft diuell that is found in hell had a mouth, and fhould be lett foorth to preach, curfe, or fcold againft vs, as thefe men do ; could he fpeake worfe, or more blafphemouflie (thinke you) againft the firft Chriftianitie of our nation, or a-gainft Cod himfelfe, that teftified the truth and fanctitie therof by fo manie rare mi-racles, as before hath byn fhewed ? Could this diuell (I fay) in his owne fhape or lan-guage fpeake more opprobrioulie of our primitiue English Chriftian Church, then thefe new Ghofpellers doe ? efpecially if we ad that which Fryar Bale hath in thefe

Baleus de fcript. Britan. cent. 1 *fol.* 35.
words, *Carnalis illa Anglorum Synagoga, qua Roma venerat, illam perfequebatur Ecclefiam, qua fecundum Chrifti fpiritum, apud Britannos erat.* That Carnall Synagoge of English Chriftians, that came from Rome, did perfecute the Church that was in England, according to the fpirite of Chrift before Auguftine came.

18. Behold our firft Chriftian English Church not onlie called a fynagoge, but a carnall fynagoge : and the British Church, which

which a litle before Holinſhed condemned
(as you heard) of hereſie, is now called the
true Church, according to the ſpirite of
Chriſt. But what ſpirituall man, (thinke
you) was this, that ſo ſpeaketh of ſpirite and
condemneth our primitiue Engliſh Church
of carnalitie? You ſhall heare him deſcribed *Ibidem*
by his owne penn. And firſt of his vocation, *cent.* 5.
how he became a fryar. *Duodecim annorum* *fol.* 245.
puer, (ſaith he) *in Carmelitani Monachatus Bara-* Hovv
thrum, *Nordouici detrudebar.* When I was a Iohn
boy of twelue years old at Norwich, I was Bale be-
thruſt into the pitt of being a white Fryar. came a
So he ſayth, and out of theſe vvords two friar.
things may be noted of his ſpirite, which is
no doubt of lying, for that both of them are
ſlaunderous fiCtions of his owne. Firſt that
he vvas made a fryar at the age of tvvelue
yeares, for that no religious order can admit
men to the ſame, according to Eccleſiaſticall
Canons, but of conuenient yeares, & fitt to *De reg.*
make their choyſe for ſo great an attempt, as *iuris lib.*
is to renounce the world, and lead a reli- 6.*c.* Non
gious life, according to the vowes they *ſolum.*
make: which before the Councell of Trent *& Caët.*
was at 14. yeares, whervnto the ſaid Coun- *in Sum.*
ceil added two yeares more. It might be *Concl.*
then perhaps, that this boy was put into the *Trident.*
white Fryars monaſterie at Norwich at *ſeſſ.*28.
tweiue years old, to ſweepe the Church, or *cap.*15.
cleanſe Candleſticks, or other ſuch offices

L 3   fitt for

fitt for that age, and his perſon : but not to
be a fryar, or to be admitted into the order
it ſelfe, and much leſſe (which is the ſecond
lie) can it be probable, that he was forced
therunto, as heere he telleth his Readers:
for that it is well knowne, that ſuch profeſsion were not auaylable, for which cauſe
euerie order of Religion hath their nouice-
ſhips, or times of probatiõs appointed, wherin men are to be proued, and to proue alſo
themſelues, & to haue free libertie to make
their elections, without force or conſtraint
at al. And ſo do all true religious men know
and profeſſe, albeit this miſerable Apoſtata,
hauing loſt all ſpirite, and ſenſe of religion,
and become wholie carnall indeed, would
haue it thought, that he was put into Religion againſt his will.

19.   But hovv did he gett himſelfe out
againe (trow yow) from this ſeruitude into
libertie of the fleſh, world and diuell, and of
his nevv ghoſpell, you ſhall heere it alſo
from himſelfe, *Apparente Dei verbo* (ſaith he)
deformitatem meam vidi, &c. The vvord of the
Lord appearing, I ſawe myne owne defor-
mitie of being (to vvitt) a prieſt, & a fryar.
Well, & vvhat followed? *horribilis beſtiæ male-
dictum characterem deinceps eraſi.* I did preſently then ſcrape out the curſed marke or character of the horrible beaſt, ſo he calleth his
old character of prieſthood, his vowes of
pouertie

Hovv
Bale
vvas vn-
friared,
& made
an Apo-
ſtata.

pouerty, chaftitie, and obedience, and other obligations of Religion.

20. But vvhat vvas the meanes to fcrape out thefe characters? you fhall haue it from himfelfe in like manner, *Non enim* (faith he) *ab homine, neque per hominem, fed ex fpeciali Chrifti & verbo, & dono, vxorem fideliſsimam accepi Dorotheam.* For that I tooke vnto me (and you ,, muft marke the vvord *enim* that yealdeth ,, the caufe) a moft faithfull vvyfe Dorothie ,, (fome Nunne you may imagine, as faithfull ,, in keeping her vow of chaftitie as himfelfe) ,, & this not from any man, nor by any mans ,, helpe, but by the efpeciall gifte and vvord ,, of Chrift, &c. Lo heere Chrift made a woër ,, for this fryar to marry a Nunne againft both their vowes, and promifes made to him before. And is not this a fitt fpirituall Father to call the vvhole primitiue Church of England a carnall Synagoge, &c.

Bal. ibi.

21. But yet heare him out further, vvhat he vvriteth of our firft Chriftian *K. Ethelbert,* and of the Religion receyued by him from *Saint Auguftine :* and therby confider, vvhat manner of men this new Ghofpell bringeth foorth. *Ethelbertus Rex* (faith he) *Romaniſmum, cum adiunctis fuperſtitionibus, tandem fufcepit : hac nimirum adiecta conditione, vt omnino liber & non coactitius eſſet nouus ille Deorum cultus.* K. Ethelbert at length hauing heard the preaching, and confidered (as Fox faith) the Miracles

Fox pag. 105. col. 2. nu. 5.

L 4   and

,, and vertuous life of *Auguſtine*, and his fello-
,, wes, admitted the Roman Religion vvith
,, all the ſuperſtitions adioyned thervnto, but
,, yet with this condition, that this new wor-
,, ſhip of Gods (vvhich he now admitted)
,, ſhould be altogeather free, and no way ſub-
,, iect to coaction, &c. In which words the
Apoſtata (if yow marke him) doth not only
ſpeake blaſphemouſlie of our vvhole firſt
Chriſtianitie, calling it a new worſhipp of
many Gods: but ſeemeth alſo to inſinuate,
that it vvas ſo admitted by *King Ethelbert*,
at the beginning, as it might be free for men
to leaue it againe, vvhen they would. Then
which contumelious ſlaunder (if he meane
it ſo) nothing can be ſpoken or imagined
more abſurd or wicked. Let any man read
Saint Gregories letters to *K. Ethelbert* after his
conuerſion, and he ſhall ſee an other leſſon
there taught him : to witt, his great & per-

Bed. lib. petuall obligation to God for ſo ſingular a
1. hiſtor. benefitt, confirmed from heauen with ſo
cap. 33. manie miracles, and ſuch other points.

The vvic- 22.   But by this we may ſee, whither theſe
ked en- mens drifts do tend : which is to diſcredit
tents of all antiquitie and religion, and to bring in
our ſe- queſtion, whether Engliſhmen were euer
ctaries. true Chriſtians hitherto, or noe. And as for
the ſpace of 900. yeares togeather after *Saint
Auſtens* time vnto Luther, theſe men deny it
flatlie. For ſo much as they ſay, that our firſt
                                                        faith

faith receyued from Rome, was not the true
faith of Chrift, nor of Chriftendome: but a
particular Romish faith, full of errour, fuperftition, and Idolatrie, as you haue heard;
Yea vvorfe (if vve vvill beleeue *Holinshed,*
Hooker and *Harrison*)then was the Paganifme,
which Englishmen profeffed before their
conuerfion. And then followeth, that for fo
much as they hold alfo, that the longer religion endured in England, the vvorfe it
vvaxed : needs muft they conclude, that
when Luther began his ghofpell, our fathers & grand-fathers were no Chriftians
at all, and much leffe true Chriftians. And
this for them.

23.   But if vve vvill talke of our felues, that
now liue in England, vve muft needs alfo
conclude the fame : to vvitt, that after all
mutations made in England about Religion, fince Luther began, the proteftants
cannot be fure, vvith any reafon, that they
are true Chriftians, or haue yet receyued
the right faith or ghofpell vnto this daye.
Which I proue thus. Firft, for that the ghofpell preached by Luther, was neuer yet admitted wholie into England. For that at the
verie beginning therof vnder *K. Henrie,* it
was contradicted by him and the ftate, during his whole raigne, yea condemned for
hereticall, as by manie decrees as vvell of
Parlaméts ★ as otherwife by particular ordi-

*That
Prote-
ftâts can
not be
fure that
they are
Chrifti -
ans ac-
cording
to Fox
& Ho-
linshed .*

★ *See the*

L 5   nances

acts of
Parlam.
anno 31.
Henr. 8.
cap. 14.
& *anno*
32. *c.* 26.
& *anno*
34. *ca.* 1.
nances is manifeſt : his maieſtie alwayes
holding Luthers opinions for hereſies, and
according thervnto, burned the profeſſors
therof for heretiks vnto his dying day, as is
notorious: Though in one article about the
Popes Supremacy he concurred with them:but
not as taking the ſame from Luther or his
doctrine.So as Luthers ghoſpell (if it were a
ghoſpell, as Iohn Fox calleth it euerywhere
in his acts and monuments) was neuer yet
receyued in England. For that in K. *Edvvards*
dayes the doctrine of Zwinglius and not of
Luther was admitted. Which doctrine Luther alwayes held for oppoſite to his, & for
plaine hereſie, as before at large hath byn
declared.

24. And as for her Maieſties time that now
Enc. 1.
c. 3. 4. 5.
is, cleare it is that neyther of both the former doctrines or Ghoſpels haue formallie,
or fullie byn admitted : I meane neither the
Lutherans, or Zwinglians, but rather the
doctrine of a third,oppoſite in many points
to them both; to witt of Ihon Caluin. And
yet neither hath this ghoſpell byn ſo fran-
klie, or generallie receyued or practiſed, as
the cheefe profeſſors therof, & ſuch as take
themſelues to follow the ſame moſt exactlie (I meane the Puritans) do remayne
content, but rather complaine, that their
true doctrine in deed, and ghoſpell vvas
neuer hitherto trulye eſtablished in our
country,

country, as in the firſt Encounter againſt *Sup. ibi.*
Syr Francis we haue ſhewed abundantly.

25. So as if the firſt ghoſpell of *S. Auguſtine*
brought into England from Rome, vvher-
vvith our Anceſtors liued and profeſſed
Chriſtianitie for 900. yeares together, were
not the true Ghoſpell of Chriſt in deed, nor
the other Ghoſpell of Martyn Luther, that
appeared to the vvorld in the yeare 1517.
was euer admitted into England in K. *Hen-*
ries time, that died in the yeare 1547. and if
from thence forward vnder *K. Edvvard, Zuin-*
glius his doctrine and not Luthers was eſtabliſhed, for the Engliſh ghoſpell of that
time: And if vnder her maieſtie that now is,
neyther of theſe two, but Caluins doctrine
and ghoſpell hath byn admitted (though
yet with ſuch reſtrictions, and alterations,
as the pureſt patrones therof ſay it is not
their ghoſpell, but a patched thing, as ✱ be- ✱ *Enc.*
fore at large we haue declared) what follo- 1. *c*. 6.
weth then (I ſay) but that we Engliſhmen 10. & 12.
haue yet no true ghoſpell at all, nor euer
had, and conſequentlie we were neuer yet
true Chriſtians, nor are at this day. For that
the Chriſtianitie of the ancient Engliſh
from K. *Ethelbert* to K. *Henrie* the 8. was no
true Chriſtianitie, as theſe men ſay; and
much leſſe will they graunt of the Religion
eſtabliſhed by K. *Henrie* as oppoſite as well
to Proteſtants as to Catholiques. That alſo
of K.

of K. *Edvvards* dayes was different from all, and that which now is in England, is contradicted as well by *Lutherans*, *Zvvinglians*, and *Puritans*, as by *Catholiques*. Where then and among whom shall we find the true ghospell?

26.   One only shifte thefe people do pretend, which is to runne to the Britans Religion at that time, when Saint Augufline came into England. For this both Fox and Bale do acknowledge to haue byn the right Religion, and (to vfe their words) *the naked vnfpotted ghofpell*, *and farre different from the Romish religion*, *that Augufine brought in from Gregorie.* Wherfore that point refleth now to be examined. And albeit you haue heard a litle before, how Holinshed accufeth the Britans religion of *Pelagianifme* and *other herefies*; yet Bale writeth thus, *Priùs illic fuerat Chriflia-*

Bale us de ferip. Britan. cent. 1. fol. 35.
nifmus, &c. Chriftian religion was in Britanie before the comming of Augufine and his fellowes. But it was not to their commoditie, for that it was without Maffes, &
,,   without diftinction of meates or daies. And
,,   the Britans obferued the bare naked gho-
Fox in his proteftation to the church of England p. 9
,,   fpell without Iewish ceremonies, &c.

27.   So writeth he. And Fox as before (:as you haue heard) faid, that for 400. yeares after *Pope Eleutherius* and K. *Lucius*, religion remained in *Britanie* vncorrupt, & the word of Chrift truly preached, till about the comming
ming

ming of Augustine and his fellowes from
Rome,&c. And yet he cannot denie, but that
in this space both the *Pelagian*, and other heresies had entred also among them, and that
some reliques therof remained, euen when
Augustine arriued: & wheras they say, that
the British religion before the comming of
Augustine was vncorrupt, and free from
all Iewish ceremonies, it is ridiculous: for so
much as we haue shewed ✷ before, that the ✷ *Supr.*
Chiefest defference betwene these two re- *cap. 3.*
ligions at that day, was about a Iewish ce-
remonie obserued by the *Britans*, against the
order and faith of the Church of *Rome*; to
wit, the superstitious keeping of Easter day,
vpon the 14. of the first mone of March,
together with the Iewes.

28. But as for other substantiall points of
faith (especially such as be at this day in
controuersie betwene vs and Protestants, as
Masse, Sacrifice, Fasting, Obseruing of holy dayes, and
the like heere named) the old Britans religion did agree with that of *Rome*, brought in
by Saint Augustine, and so hath continued
vntill this daie, and this shall we shewe in
the chapter following. So as if the old British faith was the true faith, we haue it
among Catholiques at this day, and not
Protestants, as shalbe declared.

THAT

THAT THE ROMAN RELI-
GION BROVGHT INTO EN-
gland by Saint Auguſtine *vnder* Pope Gregorie, *vvas the verie ſame , that vvas brought in
before vnder* Pope Eleutherius *by* Fugatius
and Damianus, *& continued aftervvard among
the* Britans *vntill the comming of* Saint Auguſtine *to the English Nation.*

CHAP. IX.

W E haue ſheweed before how that
the Chriſtian faith, preached in England in the Apoſtles tyme, was the
Roman faith; and that the encreaſe, or publike
eſtabliſhment therof againe vnder *K. Lucius,*
was alſo from Rome : and finallie that the
third propagation was in like manner from
the ſame cittie, vnder *Pope Gregorie* by *S. Auguſtine.* Now remaineth it that we ſhew and
declare, how the *Britans* from *K. Lucius* time
vntill the comming of *Saint Auguſtine* (which
was foure hundred yeares & more) downward did not alter their faith , nor yet the
Sea of *Rome* hers: and conſequentlie, that the
faith remayning among the *Britans ,* when
Saint Auguſtine entred , and that which was
brought by him from *Rome,* and taught vnto
the Engliſh, was all one.

2. And firſt for the Church of *Rome,* if we
count the Biſhops therof that held that ſea:

from

*Sup. c. 1.
3. 5. 6.*

from *Eleutherius* the fourtenth *Pope* after *S. Peter*, who died *anno Domini* 196. vntill the beginning of *Pope Gregorie* the firſt, the 66. *Pope*, & was choſen *anno Domini* 590. in this ſpace (I ſay) of 400. yeares, there paſſed fiftie *Popes* all of one faith, nor ſhall it be found, that any one of them chaunged his religion; or was different in beliefe the one from the other. Which is a ſufficient proofe, that the *Roman* faith in *Gregories* time was the ſame, that it was in *Eleutherius* his time. *That Rome changed not her faith frō Eleutherius to S. Gregory.*

3. And as for the *Britans*, we read not, but that from the time of *K. Lucius* they continued the faith receyued vnder him, from *Pope Eleutherius*, vntill the riſing vp of the heretique *Pelagius:* which was ſomwhat more then two hundred yeares after. And for other two hundred yeares againe after that, to witt, from the time of *Pelagius* vntill the comming of *S. Auguſtine*, we find not in any hiſtorie, that the *Britans* (being once deliuered from the hereſie of *Pelagius*, by the helpe of *S. German* and *Lupus* Biſhops of the *Roman* faith) they euer chaunged their Religion in any one ſubſtantiall point, nor that they ſwarued from the generall faith of the reſt of Chriſtendome, except onlie ſome fewe of them infected vvith the forſaid hereſie vvhiles it laſted, and the cuſtome of keeping the *Eaſterday* vvith the *Iewes*. Which before we haue ſhewed to haue byn perhaps ſome *That the British Chriſtiā faith vvas the ſame vvith the Romans. Sup. c. 3.*

remain-

remainder of Pelagianiſme, or otherwiſe
brought in after. But how ſoeuet it gott in,
certaine it is, that in other ſubſtantial points
of doctrine & religion, there vvas no difference betweene the *Britans* & *Romans* at that
day, to witt, vnder *Pope Gregorie* that ſent
hither *Auguſtine,* Which I ſhall ſhew by the
reaſons following.

First
reaſon.

4. Firſt, that if *Saint Anguſtine* at his comming, had found anie other ſubſtantiall difference of beleefe in the *British faith*, from
that which he brought from *Rome*, he
would haue reprehended the ſame, as well
as he did their different cuſtome in celebrating Eaſter after the Iewiſh manner, and
ſome fewe other rites of leſſe moment: or
at leaſtwiſe, being afterward made Archbiſhopp and Primate of all the land, and conferring with the British Biſhops in Coun-

Fox pag.
117. *col.*
2.

cel (as Fox ſaith he did) he would haue com-
muned whith them about the ſame, or obiected it vnto them, or at leaſtwiſe, haue
made ſome mention therof, either in his
letters to *Pope Gregorie* (as he did of farre
leſſer matters) or to ſome other man. But
anie ſuch thing we do not read, and conſequently it may be concluded certainely,
that there was no ſuch difference in matter
of faith and doctrine.

2. rea-
ſon-

5. An other reaſon may be taken on the
other ſide, from the *Britans* towards *S. Auguſtine.*

ftine, who being in controuerfie with him about his preaching to the *Saxons*, whofe conuerfion for the prefent they feemed not to defire (in refpect of mannie iniuries receyued from them, as *Saint Bede* affirmeth) they did obferue all occafions, caufes, and reafons vvhich they might alleage by any probabilitie, why they would not ioyne with him in that worke, and if they could haue alleaged this caufe, that the doctrine vvhich he preached had byn different in any one point of faith from that, vvhich they had receyued and obferued before, it had byn a verie fufficient excufe and reafon for them. But we do find no fuch exception alleaged by them, & confequentlie we may conclude (as before) that there was none.

6. Our third argument or reafon may be deduced from the confideration of the vniuerfall ftate of Chriftian faith in thofe daies, to witt, vnder *Gregorie* the firft, who was chofen *Pope* about the yeare of Chrift 590. at what time there was vnitie and conformitie of one religion throughout all Chriftendome, except onlie in fome places of the world certain reliques of a *Pelagians*, b *Originifts*, c *Donatifts*, and d *Eutychians*, out of whom fprong alfo in thofe dayes the e *Armenian* errours, as appeareth by the hiftorie of thofe times, efpeciallie out of *S. Gregorie* his owne works. Neyther do we read, that the *Britans*

were

3. reafon.

a*Greg.l.* 5.*ep.*14.
b *Philaf. l.de har.*
c*Greg.l.* 3.*ep.*32.
d*Greg.l.* 10.*in Iob c.*29.
e*Niceph. l.*18.*c.*53

were noted with anie of theſe hereſies, but onlie with *Pelagianiſme* ſome yeares before. From which they had byn deliuered by the preaching of the French Biſhops *S. Germane* and *S. Lupus:* and by the diligence of their owne Metropolitans *S. Dubritius,* & *S. Dauid* afterward. Seing then *Saint Auguſtine* came from *Rome* by Italie and France, and was directed to the Biſhop of Arles, from whom he paſſed through France into Britanie: it is certaine he brought no other faith, then the vniuerſall faith of Chriſtendome receyued, and beleeued in thoſe daies. From which ſeing that *Britanie* was not held nor noted to be different, nor yet excommunicated (as certaine Biſhops of Ireland appeare to haue byn, by diuers letters of *S. Gregorie* himſelfe written to them in their reprehenſion, for participation with certaine ſchiſmatiks:) it followeth, that the faith, which *Saint Auguſtine* brought, and that which the *Britans* had before, muſt needs be one, and the ſelfe ſame in all materiall, & ſubſtantiall points.

7. To which effect alſo may be added, that in the verie next age among the *Britans* before the Engliſh entered, there were *British Biſhops* in diuers generall & nationall Councels, as in the time of *Conſtantine* and *Pope Syl-ueſter* vve read, that one ∗ *Reſtitutus* a famous Biſhop of London, was preſent at the Synode of Arles in France, in the yeare of Chriſt

Bed. lib. 1.c.25.

Greg.li. 2.ep.36. indict. 10.& li. 9.ep.61. indict.4.

4 Argument.
The preſence of British Biſhops in forain coũcels.
∗See Syn.

Chrift 325. & fubfcribed to the fame, as by
the Actes of the faid councell appeareth:
wherin among other points was ordeyned,
that no man hauing a wife fhould be made
prieft, but with his wiues confent, promi-
fing to forbeare her companie for the time
to come. It appeareth alfo by the Apologie
of *S. Athanafius* that diuers Bifhops of *Britanie*
were prefent at the councell of *Sardica* held
for *S. Athanafius*, againft the *Arrians*, about the
yeare of Chrift 350. As alfo at the councell
of *Ariminum*, wherin though the greater
parte of that councell were beguyled by the
Arrians: yet *S. Hilarie* doth praife diuers good
Bifhops for their conftancie, and among
other *Prouinciarum Britannicarum Epifcopo,*
certaine Bifhops of the *Britan Prouinces.* By
all which is fhewed, that the Chriftian
Religion of *Britanie* was catholique & vniuerfall, and concurring in all points with
the *Romane* in thofe dayes, as *Athanafius* and
S. Hilarie, who prayfed thefe Bifhops, are
knowne to haue done. And confequentlie
it cannot be prefumed that eyther the *Bri-*
tifh Religion fhould be different from the *Ro-*
man in the next ages after, when *S. Gregorie*
fent *Auguftine* to conuert the English, or that
the *Romane Religion* brought in by *S. Auguftine,*
fhould be different from the *Britifh,* except
onlie in certaine rites, or reliques of *Pelagia-*
nifme, which yet were not generallie recey-

ued

Side notes:

2. *Arela-*
ienf. to. 1
Concil.
and the
fubfcri-
ptions.
Cap. 2.
& 3.
Athan.
Apolog.
2. *cötra*
Arrian.

Hilar. de
Synod.
aduerfus
Arian.

ued of all, as before hath byn declared.

5. Argu-
ment.
Obfer-
uations
out of
hiftories

8. The fifth argument ftandeth vpon fome obferuations taken out of hiftories, & other monuments of antiquitie. Wherby it may be gathered more or leffe, what points of Religion among fuch, as now are called in controuerfie by Proteftants, were beleeued in thofe daies by the Auncient Britans. For albeit the ftorie of that Church before the comming of *S. Auguftine* be not fo left writ-ten by anie Authenticall Author, as were to be wifhed, and as other countryes haue (and namelie ours by *S. Bede)* and this in re-fpect of the manifold warres, great mife-ries, and continuall calamities fallen vpon the Britifh nation for 200. yeares togeather before the conuerfion of the Englifh (wher-by neyther the orderlie fuccefsion of their Bifhops, neither their meetings in Synods & Councels, neither the obferuation of Ec-clefiafticall difcipline, neither their commu-nication vvhich the Churches of other countries, and efpeciallie the *Sea* of *Rome,* could be fo well performed, or recorded) yet of the fmall fparkles, & reliques that do remaine, it is not harde to gheffe (befids the reafons, and confiderations before alleaged) what Religion the Britans were of, and whether their faith agreed more with the Proteftants of our daies, then with the Re-ligion of *S. Auguftine* brought in from *Rome,*
and

and continued by Catholiques vnto this present.

9. For firſt if we will heare externall Authors, *Saint Chryſoſtome* teſtifieth againſt the Gentils in his daies, that in *Britanie* there vvere *Altaria Chriſto dedicata*, Altars dedicated to Chriſt. Which Altars do inferre *Sacrifice*, and *Sacrifice*, *Prieſthood*, as in his books *de Sacerdotio* he proueth. So as in *S. Chryſoſtomes* age, vvhich vvas the verie ſame vvherin the *Saxons* entred into *Britani*, the *Britans* religion vvas Catholique, according to *Saint Chryſoſtome*, agreeing as vvell vvith the vveſterne, as Eaſterne Church, vvherof himſelfe vvas. For if they had byn different, or had followed anie other Religion, then the common, he would not ſo much haue bragged of them, as againſt the Gentils he did.

10. But let vs returne to Britiſh Authors themſelues. If we reade ouer with attention the little treatiſe or Epiſtle of Gildas, which he writeth of the deſtruction, & conqueſt of his Countrie (he being the only Author in deed of intire credit, which we find extant of thoſe auncient times)we ſhall find ſignes and footſteps ynough, of what Religion the Britás were of: though his purpoſe was not to write any Eccleſiaſticall hiſtory. He liued a good while before the comming of *Saint Auguſtine*, and in the ſecond parte of his ſaid treatiſe reprehendeth grievouſſie, the

M 3 moſt

Chryſ. orat. cõtra Gentes, quod vnus eſt Deus.

moſt horrible ſinnes of the *Britans*, for which
theſe calamities of the Picts, Scotts, and Saxons, came vpon them. And he beginneth
his complaint firſt of their Kings & Iudges,

Gild. de
excidio
Britan.
cap. 26.

ſaying, *Reges habet Britannia, ſed tyrannos; Iudices
habet, ſed impios; crebrò iurantes, ſed periurantes; vo-
uentes, ſed continuò propemodum mentientes.* Britanie hath Kings, but they are become ty-

"   rants: it hath Iudges, but they are impious:
"   ſwearing often, but forſwearing: making
"   vowes, but preſently almoſt breaking the
"   ſame, &c.

11.   Heere we ſee that breaking of vowes
was held for no ſmal ſynne in thoſe dayes.
But he goeth further talking of the ſaid
Princes: *Inter altaria iurando demorantes, & hæc
eadem ac ſi lutulenta paulò pòſt ſaxa deſpiciētes, cuius
tam nefandi piaculi non ignarus eſt Conſtantinus.*

The Bri-
taus vſe
of ta-
kinge
ſanctua-
rie, and
ſvvea-
ring
vpon al-
tars.

They runne to the Altar and ſweare (when
they are in necesſitie) and a litle after they
deſpiſe the ſaid Altars againe, as if they were
but durtie ſtones, of which wicked ſacrilege
K. *Conſtantine* is not ignorant, &c. Heere
you ſee Altars made of ſtone in thoſe daies,
and Princes accuſtomed to ſweare by Altars, and to ſeeke their refuge in perill or
necesſitie, by running to them, and ſtaying
by them in Sāctuarie, or when they would
do any act with religious ſolemnitie, and
that it was counted a heynous ſinne to
breake promiſes made vpon Altars in thoſe
daies.

daies. Which yet proteſtants make no
ſcruple of.

12. But now what this oth of K. Conſtantine was, (wherof Gildas ſpeaketh) and
in what forme it was made, it appeareth in
the next words after which amongs other
are theſe. *Hoc anno poſt horribile iuramenti ſa-*   Gildas
cramentum, quo ſe deuinxit, &c. Deo primum,   ibid.
Sanctorum demum choris, & genetrici comitanti-
bus, &c. Latera regiorum tenerrima puerorum vel
præcordia crudeliter inter ipſa! (vt dixi) ſacroſancta
altaria nefando enſe, haſtaq; prodentibus lacerauit.
Ita vt ſacrificij cæleſtis ſedem & purpurea pallia coa-
gulati cruoris attingerent, &c. Euen this yeare „
after a moſt dreadfull othe, wherby Con- „
ſtantine bound himſelfe, &c. firſt to God, & „
then to the whole quire of *Saincts*, and the „
mother of Chriſt accompagning the ſame, „
&c. He paſſed with his wicked ſword and „
ſpeare, the moſt tender ſides and hartes of „
two yong princely children. And this ſo „
neere to the holie Altars, as their purple „
cloakes all beſprincled with blood did touch „
the ſeate of the heauenly ſacrifice, &c. Behold heere an oth broken, which was made
to God vpon the holie Altars, in the ſight
of his mother, and of all the Saincts of heauen, for the preſeruacion of the ſaid two
princely children committed to Conſtantine, & moſt cruelly murdered by him, euen
at the ſyde of the ſaid Altars, ſo neere that

their

their purple cloakes did touch the feate of the heauenly facrifice. Which is the fame phrafe that other auncient fathers did vfe to defcribe holy altars; callinge them the *feate of the bleffed facrifice* or (which is all one) *the feate, of the body and blood of our Sauiour.*

Optat.
lib. 6.

Quid eſt enim altare (faith *Optatus*) *niſi ſedes corporis & ſanguinis Chriſti?* what is an altar but the feate of the body and blood of Chriſt?

13. And novv I vvould aske our men, whether thefe fpeeches of Gildas do agree better to Proteſtants religion, or to ours? would any Proteſtant fpeake or write thus? But lett vs heare hovv he goeth forvvard againſt another Britane Prince of that time called *Aurelius.* Among many other crimes

Againſt
K. Aure-
lius.
Gildas
ibidem.
pag.122.

he obiecteth this : *Propriâ vxore pulsâ, furcife-*
ram germanam eius, perpetuam Deo viduitatis caſti-
moniam promittentem, ſuſcipis. Thou hauing driuen away thine vowne wife, takeſt vnto the her wicked fiſter, vvhich had promifed to God perpetuall chaſtitie of vviddowhood. And then to another vvicked Prince *Maglocunus,* he obiecteth, that hauing made a vow to be a monke, he returned to the

Againſt
K. Ma-
glocunus
for lea-
ving to
be a
Monke.

vvorld againe, faying: *Coram omnipotente Deo.*
Angelicis vultibus, humaniſque, perpetuò monachum
vouiſti, &c. O quàm profuſus ſpei cæleſtis fomes
deſperatorum cordibus (te in bonis permanente) inar-
deſceret! ô qualia, quantáque animum tuum regni
Chriſti præmia in die iudicij manerent! &c. Thou

didſt

didst vow to be a perpetuall Monke before „
almightie God in the fight both of Angels „
and men. O how great a flame of heauenly „
hope would burne in the hartes of them, „
that now difpaire of the, if thou hadft re- „
mained in that good ftate! O how great „
rewards of Chrifts Kingdome would re- „
maine for the in the day of Iudgment, &c. „
14. Thus faith he. And vvould proteftants
(thinke you) fpeake thus alfo ? feing Iohn *Fox a&.*
Fox doth fo greatlie condemne our ancient *& mon.*
Kings, and Princes of the English nation, *pag.* 10$.
for that fo manie of them in the fervour of
the primitiue Church, made them felues
Monks. Yet Gildas (you fee) on the contrary fide, commendeth highly that fact in the
Prince *Maglocunus*, and greatlie condemneth
him for leauing that holie ftate. And hereby
alfo is refuted that folifh refuge of Fox and
his compagnions, who fay & affirme without fhame, that Monks had noe vowes in
thofe daies: But only that monafteries were
fchooles & places of learning without any
obligation to perfeuer therin, or to abftaine
from mariage, &c. But let him fhew, that
euer any of thofe 2000. Monks, that he faith
liued in the Monafterie of *Bangor* together,
did euer marrie, or pretend to haue libertie
fo to doe after they were profeffed Monks,
& then he faith fomwhat. And as for vow-
ing and publique profeffion made to God

M 5   in the

in the ſight of his Angels, and the whole
Church: the matter is euident ynough in
this place, what was then in vſe among the
Britans.

15. But lett vs paſſe from Princes to Prieſts.
what ſaith *Gildas* of them? Yovv ſhall heare
his words: *Sacerdotes habet Britannia, ſed inſi-*
pientes: &c. Eccleſiæ domus habentes, ſed turpis lucri
gratia eas adeuntes. &c. rarò ſacrificantes, & nun-
quam puro corde inter altaria ſtantes, &c. *Sedem*
Petri Apoſtoli, immundis pedibus vſurpantes, &c.
„ Britanie hath prieſts, but without wiſe-
„ dome, &c. they poſſeſſe the houſes of the
„ Church, but goe vnto them onlie for filthie
„ lucres ſake, &c. They do ſeldome ſacrifice,
„ but neuer goe to the altar with a pure harte,
„ &c. they do vſurp the Seat of *Peter* the
Apoſtle, with vncleene feete, &c.

16. Lo heere maſſing and ſacrificing prieſts
in thoſe daies, which are ſo hated, and perſecuted at this day in England, though, God
be thanked, free from theſe vices of impure
life, which heere is obiected to the Prieſts
of that time. But let vs heare yet Gildas further: *In Apoſtolicis ſanctionibus ob inſcitiam hebetes,*
they are dull in obſeruing Apoſtolicall ſan-
ctions, for that they are vnlearned, and vnderſtand them not. Lo heere Prieſts reprehended for lacke of ſkill in the Eccleſiaſticall Canons, and Apoſtolicall Decrees. And
yet he goeth further: *Deſperatiùs errant, quo non*
ab Apo-

Againſt
prieſts
that ſaid
Maſſe,
ſeldome
and yll.
Gil. ibid
pa.132.

Gildas
ibid.

Ibidem
pa. 133.

ab Apostolis, vel Apostolorum successoribus , sed a Ty-
rannis, & à patre eorum diabolo emunt sacerdotia.
These men do erre the more desperatlie, for
that they buy vnto themselues the office of
priesthood not of the Apostles or their successors (as * *Symon Magus* would haue done
the holie Ghost) but of tyrant Princes, and
of the diuell their father.

Buying
of priest-
hood.
Act. 2.

17.   Heere you see that priesthood in those
daies was not wont to be giuen by the Authoritie of lay princes , but by the Succes-
fors of the Apostles, to witt, Bishops. And
then further he goeth forward shewing
how these naughtie Priests, being once pos-
sessed of that dignitie, and made proud therby; presumed to saye Masse vnworthilie.
Manus non tam venerabilibus aris, quàm flammis
inferni vltricibus dignas, in tale schema positi sacro-
sanctis Christi sacrificiis extensuri . These Priests,,
being put once in this dignity or ornament, ,,
they presume to streech out their hands to ,,
the most holie Sacrifices of Christ, though ,,
their hands be more worthy of the burning ,,
flames of hell, then to touch the venerable ,,
Altars.

Gildas
ibid.

18.   Thus he wrote of *Altars* and *sacrifice*
among the Britans in those daies , & diuers
other points like vnto this, which, for breuities sake I omitt. Onlie I would aske our
men in generall, whether this be spoken, as
of protestants or noe? And then would I de
maund

Altars
and sa-
crifice
among
the Bri-
tans.

maund of Iohn Fox in particular, how that can be true, which he affirmeth; *that the Britans had no maſſe in thoſe daies*, ſeing *Gildas* talketh ſo much of Prieſts that did Sacrifice vpon Altars? And if he will ſaye that *Gildas* vſeth not the word Maſſe, it is a plaine cauill, ſeing nothing is ſignified by the Maſſe, but onlie the externall Sacrifice of Chriſtians heere mentioned. And that the word *Maſſe* vvas generallie vſed in the Latin Church for Sacrifice long before this time of *Gildas*, appeareth by manie Authors, but eſpeciallie by *Saint ＊ Auguſtine* the Doctor in diuers places of his works, wherof ſome in the margent we ſhall note.

19.　I would aske alſo of *Iohn Bale*, how the Religion of the *Britans vvas the pure and naked Ghoſpell in thoſe daies* (for ſo he ſaith) if it had in it not only that cuſtome of the Iewes before mentioned of the *Quartadecimani*, but all theſe other points alſo, vvhich his Church counteth for errors, to witt, of *profeſſed Monks* & *Conſecrated Nunnes*, of *Sacrificing vpon Altars*, and the like, how (I ſay) could this Britiſh Church be accoumpted by him and his, ſo pure & vnſpotted? But litle heed is there to be giuen to theſe mens ſaying, or vnſaying: but as the preſent occaſion of neceſsitie vrgeth them. And therfore we will go forward to ſhew ſome other obſeruations in this kind.

＊ *Aug. 10. 10. ſer.* 237. & 251. *de temp.* & *in cōcil. Milenit. c.* 12. & *Carthag.* 2. *c.* 3. & *Conēil. Cartha 4. c. 84. quibus inter ſuit Auguſtinus. Epiph. hareſ.* 50 *Euſeb. li.* 5. *hiſt. c* 23. & *in vita Conſtan. l.* 3. *c.* 17.

THE

THE CONTINVATION OF
THE SAME MATTER, VVHERIN IS
ſnevved by diuers proofes and examples , that the
Britans *before* S. Gregories *time, vvere of the*
ſame religion that he ſent into England by Saint
Auguſtine: *to vvitt , of the* Romane.

CHAP. X.

AND firſt of all to beginne with the firſt
entrance of our firſt Engliſh Apoſtles,
Saint Beed writing of the Cittie of *Canterburie*
at the comming of *Saint Auguſtine,* before K.
Ethelbert was conuerted, ſaith thus. *Erat au-* | *Bed. lib.*
tem prope ipſam ciuitatem ad orientem, Eccleſia in | *1.c.27.*
honorem S. Martini antiquitus facta, dum adhuc Ro-
mani Britanniam incolerent, &c. in hac ergo ipſi
primò conuenire, pſallere, orare, miſſas facere, prædi-
care & baptizare cœperunt. There was a church | Achurch
neere to the Cittie on the Eaſt ſide, built in | dedica-
old time in the honour of *S. Martyn* , while | ted to S.
yet the *Romans* did hold *Britanie, &c.* Wher- | Martin
fore in this Church , *Auguſtine* and his com- | among
panie did firſt vſe to meete together, to ſing | the aun-
pſalmes, to pray , to ſaye Maſſes, to preach, | cient
and to baptiſe the people, &c. | Chriſtiã
| Britans.

2.   Note heere , that ſeing the *Romanes* left
England preſently vpon the deſtruction of
Rome by the *Gothes* (to vvit about the yeare
of Chriſt 400. which was ſome 50. yeares
before the entraunce of the *Saxons*) then
was

was the vſe of building Churches in the honour of *Sainets* in practiſe among the *Britans*, and *Romane* Chriſtians of thoſe daies liuing in Britanie. And for aſ much as this Church of *Sainct Martins* was found fitt to ſay Maſſe, and baptize in, according to the vſe of *Rome*, and for thatthe Britane Chriſtians were neuer found to haue reprehended, or miſliked this manner of ſeruing God, vſed by *Sainct Augustine* & his fellowes: it is an euident argument, that the ſame was and had byn in vſe alſo among them, from all antiquitie: neither was it a noueltie brought in by *Sainct Augustine.*

An euident demonſtratió that the Britiſh religion agreed vvith that of S. Auguſtine.

3.   Moreouer about the ſame time of the *Romanes* going out of *Britanie*, or ſoone after (to witt, about the yeare of Chriſt 440.) it appeareth by *Bede*, that the two french Biſhops, *Saint German*, and *Sainct Lupus* the firſt tyme, and *Sainct German* and *Sainct Seuerus* the ſecond time, came into *Britanie* to reſiſt the *Pelagian* hereſie, and to reeſtabliſh the Catholike faith that was among them before. And ſo they did as wel by working many miracles, as by their preachings, which *Bede* recounteth at large throughout many chapters. But now that theſe three holy Biſhops, (the firſt of *Antiſiodor in France*, the ſecond of *Troy in Champanie*, the third of *Treuers in Germanie*) were all of the *Roman Religion*, and held in all points of controuerſie   againſt

S. German & S. Lupus

Bed. lib. 1. hist. c. 17. 18. 19 20. 21.

againſt the proteſtants of our time, both in
doctrine, and practiſe: is euident, not only
by that the *Roman* Church doth hold them
all three for canonized Saincts, and cele-
brateth their memories, the firſt vpon the
31. of Iulie, the ſecond vpon the 29. of the
ſame moneth, the third vpõ the 15. of October, which would neuer be permitted if
they had byn different in any one point of
faith: but alſo the ſame is cleare, as well by
their owne writings that are extant, and
by their liues written by others, as alſo by
diuers things recounted by S. Bede in his
ſtorie of their doings in England: as namely where he writeth of *Sainct German*, how
he cured the *Tribunes* daughter of blyndneſſe
by his prayer, and by applying the reliques
of certaine *Saincts* vnto her eyes in the ſight
of al the people. *Deinde* (ſaith he) *Germanus
plenus Spiritu ſancto*; *&c.* Then Sainct German full of the holie Ghoſt, did inuoke the
name of the bleſſed *Trinitie*, and preſently „
tooke from his ſyde a certaine box of *Saincts* „
reliques, that he vvas vvonte to carrie about „
his necke, and with his hands did putt „
them vpon the maids eyes, which out of „
hand receyued perfect ſight therwith. „
Wheratt the parents of the maide reioyced „
exceedinglie, and all the people did trem- „
ble at the ſight of the miracle, &c.

4.   Thus writeth Sainct Bede of that act.

And

That S.
German
S. Lupus
& S. Se-
uerus
vvere
Roman
Catho-
liques.

Reli-
ques of
Saincts.
Ibid. ca.
18.

And further that the ſaid Biſhop went to
the ſepulcher of *Sainct Alban* (which euen at
that tyme appeareth to haue byn kept with
great deuotion) prayed to the *Sainct* largly,
and there left in his ſepulcher parte of the
reliques of all the Apoſtles, and of diuers
other Saincts, which he had brought with
him out of France, And caried away with
him, in exchange therof, much of the earth,
that was died with the bloud of *Saint Alban.*
Which he would not haue done if he had
byn a proteſtant. And then yet further, talking of an other famous miracle and victorie acheeued by the ſaid *Saint German,* againſt
heretiques, with ſounding out the word *Alleluia, Saint Bede* ſaith : *Aderant Quadrageſimæ
venerabiles dies, quos religioſiores reddebat præſentia
ſacerdotum, &c.* The venerable daies of lent
were come, which the preſence of theſe
prieſts (of God) made more religious, &c.

Ibid. ca.
18.
The vſe
of lent
among
the Bri-
tans.

5.   Behold heere now almoſt 200. yeares
before *Saint Auguſtine* came into England,
*the vſe of Reliques of Sainčts, of praying to Martyrs,
and honoring their ſepulchers,* the *vſe of Alleluia,*
the *Religious obſeruation of the Lent,* and ſuch
other points recorded to be in practiſe
among the Chriſtian Britans. Is this proteſtant like, thinke yow? or can theſe men be
preſumed to haue byn of our new Religion? But lett vs proceed to talke of ſome
Britan teachers and paſtors themſelues.

6. Geffrey

6. Geffrey of *Monmouth* in his *British Storie,* much esteemed, and alleaged by our aduer-saries, vvriteth ; that at a certaine feast of Pentecost at Chester, about the yeare of Christ 522. (as Bale holdeth) K. *Arthure* being present, there was a great meeting of Princes, Lords, and Bishops for his corona-tion, and that of the three Archbishops of Britanie at that tyme, (which were *London, Torke,* and *Chester*) *Dubritius* Archbishop of Chester did the office of the Church that day, of whom he saith : *Hic Britanniæ Primas, & Apostolica Sedis Legatus, tantâ religione clare-bat, vt quemcunque languore grauatum, orationibus sanaret.* This man being Primate of Britanie and Legate of the Sea Apostolique, was so famous for his religion and sanctitie, as he did heale anie sicke man by his prayers.

S. Du-britius Primate of Brita-nie anno 522. Galf-hist. Brit.l.9. cap. 12. & 13.

7. Lo heere the Popes Legate among the *Britans* did also miracles before the cōming of *Saint Augustine.* And then further talking of the Church solemnitie that daie, he saith: *Postremò (peractâ processione) tot organa, tot cantus fiunt vtrisque templis, &c.* Lastlie the proces-sion being ended, there vvere so many or-gans did sound, & so great varietie of mu-sicke heard in both Churches, as was won-derfull, &c. Behold *Procession* & *Organs* in *Bri-tanie* before *S. Augustines* comming. This man afterwards lefte of his owne will the said Archbishoppricke, & became an Ermite, as

Ibidem pag. 70. *Processiõ & Or-gans.*

N   both

both Geffrey, & *Iohn Bale* do teftifie, which
proteftant Bifhops are not wont to doe.

8.   And further, Bale writeth of him that
he died the 18. day before the Calends of
December, anno Domini 522. and that his body
afterward in the yeare of our Lord 1120. the
6. of May was tranflated vnder *Vrbane* Bifhop of *Rome*, to the Church of *Landaffa* in
Southvvales. All which could neuer haue byn
done, nor permitted by the Bifhop of *Rome,*
if there had byn any fufpition, that he had
held any point of doctrine different from
the Church and faith of *Rome* at that time.
Which maketh alfo the matter euidét, that
the hereticall cuftome of celebrating Eafter
according to the Iewes, (which in *S. Gregories* time was found in Britanie) was a later cuftome not held by all, but by fome
fewe only.

9.   In this mans place was made Archbifhop the famous man *Dauid Meneuenfis, K.
Arthurs* oncle (as Geffrey and Bale do teftifie) who paffed the faid Archbifhopricke
from Chefter to *Saint Dauids,* and fo it is called at this day of his name. This Dauid
(faith Bale) was a goodly man of ftature,
aboue 4. cubitts high, learned and eloquent.
and after ten whole yeares ftudy in the
Scripture, expounded the fame as a trom-
pett, carrying alwayes the text of the ghofpell with him. He extinguished the re-
liquos

*Bal. de
fcript.
Eccl. fol.
30.*
S. Dauid
of VVa-
les *anno
Domini*
540.

liques of the Pelagian herefies in *Britanie*,
preached inceſſantlie, cured manie ſicke, &
built 12. *Monaſteries,* and was held for a verie
great *Sainct* in his dayes, and Canonized
afterward by *Calixtus* 2. Biſhop of *Rome*, &c.
Per Calixtum 2. (ſaith he) *Papiſticorum deorum
aſcribitur in Catalogum,* He was put in the catalogue of the *Papiſticall* Gods by *Calixtus* the
ſecond. Wherby appeareth, that the Britans
were not onlie *Papiſts* in thoſe dayes before
the comming of *S. Auguſtine:* But had Papiſt
Gods and Sainⸯts alſo there. Yet this man
might liue (according to Bale) to haue ſeene
the time of *S. Auguſtines* entrance. For that
he ſaith he floriſhed in the yeare 540. and
liued in all 146. yeares. Though *Gerard Cam-* *Camb.in*
brenſis, Polydor, and other do make him ſom- *Catal.*
what more auncient. *ſcript.*
Britan.
10. And for that we haue talked heere of *Poli d. li.*
Iohn Bale, and that the teſtimonies taken *hiſt.*
from enemies themſelues are of greateſt *Angl. in*
weight againſt themſelues: we ſhall in this *fine.*
place, touch certain points brieflie of the
chiefe preachers and paſtors among the *Bri-*
tans in thoſe dayes; to witt, for the next two
hundred yeares before the comming of *Fox in*
S. Auguſtine into England. Which preachers *his pro-*
are mentioned, and much praiſed both by *teſtati.*
Fox & Bale, as true teachers in thoſe daies, *Church*
wherof Fox writeth thus. In this age ('to *of Engl.*
witt after the peace reſtored to the Church *pag. 9.*

N 2   by

19. Britiſh Biſhops & Doctors pretended by Fox to haue bene proteſtants.

” by Conſtantine) followed heere in the land of Britanie *Faſtidius, Ninianus, Patricius, Bacchiarius, Dubritius, Congellus, Kentegernus, Helmotus, Dauid, Daniel, Sampſon, Elnodugus, Aſſaphus, Gildas, Henlanus, Elbodus, Dinothus, Samuel, Niuius,* and a great ſort more, which gouerned the Britane Church by Chriſtian doctrine a longe ſeaſon: Albeit the ciuill gouernors for the time were diſſolute and careieſſe, (as Gildas verie ſharplie doth lay to their
” charge) and ſo at length were ſubdued by
” the Saxons. And all this while about the
” ſpace of 400. yeares, (to witt from the time
” of *K. Lucius*) religion remayned in *Britanie*
” vncorrupt, and the word of Chriſt trulie
” preached, vntill about the comming of Au-
” guſtine & his compagnions from *Rome,* &c.

11.   Heere now you ſee the chiefe teachers of the *Britiſh* Church (19. in number) for the ſpace of 400. yeares (as Fox auoweth) ſett downe in order, & highlie praiſed by him.

Neither order nor Argument good in Fox.

But neyther his order or argument is worth a ruſh. For as for his order, he beginneth with *Faſtidius,* that liued not 200. yeares before *S. Auguſtines* comming, though he name 400. And then he putteth ſome before, that liued long after the reſt, & ſometimes ſkippeth ouer 100. yeares togeather from one to an other, as you ſhall ſee by the examine. And as for his argument, how manie lies & errors it conteyneth, ſhall eaſelie appeare by the

the sequele of this difcourfe. For firft concerning two of the chiefe in this catalogue
conteined, (to witt *Dubritius*, and *Dauid*,
Archbifhops of the *Britans*) yovv haue feene
before, that they were Roman Catholiques
and canonizized many ages after their deathes by Roman Bifhops, which they would
neuer haue done, if they had differed from
them in any one point of religion. But now
lett vs fee of the reft, for I fee not what reafon there is, why Fox fhould fo commend
thefe two.

12. The firft foure are *Faftidius*, *Ninianus*,
Patritius, and *Bacchiarius*. all which are found
to haue byn Catholique men, and held the
common faith of *Rome* in thofe daies, nor
any one of them euer fauoured any of thefe
new doctrines, brought in by our new ghofpellers. *Trithemius* maketh mention of *Fafti-*
dius whofe fyr-name was *Prifcus*, Bishop of
the *Britans*, a man of rare life, and great learning in the Scriptures, and a fingular preacher, and liued in the time of *Honorius* and
Theodofius the Emperours, about the yeare of
Chrift 420. The fame do write of him both
Honorius, *Gennadius*, and *Bergomas*. And Iohn
Bale concurreth with the reft, adding that
he was Archbishop of London, and that
amongft other his works he wrote one *de*
Viduitate feruanda, of keeping wydowhood,
without marrying againe. By which only

Faftidius
Prifcus.
Trit. de
feript.
Eccl.
Bal. fol.
23.

N 3 worke

worke yovv may knovv that he was not of
Iohn Bales religion. What we haue written alfo of the religion of *S. German* & his fe-
lowe Bifhops, that came into England, may
eafely declare what religion this man was
of, who being then Archb. of London, muft
needes be prefumed to haue had a great
part in their calling in, as alfo to haue ioined
with them againft the *Pelagians*, which he
wold not haue donne, if they had not bene
all of one religion. And thus much of him.

S. Ni-
nianus.
Bed. c.4.
Hector.
Boet.lib.
7. & 15.
Ioan.
Fordo-
nius lib.
3. cap.9.
Bal.ibid.

13.   Of *S. Ninianus*, who conuerted the *Picts*
to Chriftian religion, *Saint Bede* maketh moft
honorable mention in the 3. booke of his
Ecclefiafticall hiftorie, and the *Roman Marty-*
rologe doth cite him for a *Saint* vpon the 16.
daie of *September*. Which would neuer haue
byn permitted, if he had byn in any one
thing different from the *Roman* faith. Nay
Iohn Bale writeth of him thus. *Ninianus Ber-*
nitius ex Regio Britannorum fanguine procreatus,
Italiam adhuc adolefcens petijt, Romæ apud diuini
verbi miniftros myfteria veritatis edoctus ad plenum,
celer in patriam remigrabat, &c. *miraculis ac fan-*
ctitate clarißimus obijt anno 432. S. Ninian Ber-
„ nitius being defcended of the bloud of the
„ Kings of Britanie, went in his youth into
„ Italie, and being fully taught the myfteries
„ of truth by the minifters of Gods vvord in
„ Rome, he returned fwiftlie to his country
„ againe, where he florished exceedingly in
miracles

miracles and sanctitie of life, and after died „
in the yeare of Christ 432.   „

Marke heere, that princes children became preistes in those dayes, and went to
Rome to learne diuinitie, and that this man
hauing donne so, and brought backe into
Britanie the Christian doctrine of *Rome*,
wrought miracles thereby. *Ergo* he was noe
Protestant i, so that heere Bale testifieth
against himself.

14. There followeth of *Patricius* in Iohn
Fox. But indeede he should haue putt *Palla-*
dius before *Patricius*. For so doth *Bale*, and he
hath reason. For that he was a famous tea-
cher in Britanie, and sent from Rome by
Pope Calestinus before *Patricius*, as Bale doth
note, sayeing first of *Palladius*: *Hic à Calestino*
Romanorum Pontifice Antistes mittebatur, *&c.*

This man was sent Bishop from *Calestinus*
Pope of Rome, to driue out of Britanie the
Pellagian heresie, which at that time had
infected the greater part therof, and to reduce the Scotts to true pietie, &c. he florished about the yeare of Christ 431. &c.

So saith he. And the same is confirmed
by that which *Prosper* (a farre better author
than *Bale*) writeth in his chronicle, where he
saith that *Palladius* was sent by *Calestinus* Pope
in the yeare 432. into Britanie, but especiallie to the Scotts, as testifieth also *Saint Bede*
in his storie. So as in this time also the Popes

margin notes:
S. Patri-
cius.
S. Palla-
dius.

Bal. ibid.
fol. 23.
Marian.
Scotus. in
Chron.
eodē an.
430.

Prosper
in Chron.
an. 432.
& 434.
Bed. lib.
4. *histor.*
cap. 30.

of Rome

of *Rome* had fupreme care in fpirituall affaires both among the Britans & Scots, feeing he appointed them Bishoppes from Rome.

15.   And this is confirmed alfo by the other example of *Patricius*, vvho (as Iohn Bale faith) was furnamed *Magonius*, & was borne in Britanie of the familie of Senators, and thereby called *Patricius*, but yet of kindred, by his mother, to *S. Martine* Bishop of *Tovrres*, Studied diuinitie in Rome, and thence fent by *Cælestinus* the *Pope* to preache to the Irishe men. *Istum* (faith he) *ad Scotos & Hibernos post Palladium Græcum misit, vt eos à Pelagianorum tueretur erroribus*. This man did *Cælestinus* Bishop of Rome fend to the Scotts and Irishemen (efpecially thofe that liued in Britany) after *Palladius* the Grecian, to defend them from the errors of the Pelagians.

16.   Behold the care and authoritie of the Bishop of Rome in thofe dayes. But what followeth in Bale ? *This man* (faith he) *did preache the Ghofpell vnto the Irishemen, vvith incredible fervour of fpirite for* 40. *yeares together. And did conuert them to the fincere faith of Chrifte . He vvas most excellent both in learning and holyneffe, and among other miracles that he did, he continued in praying and fasting* 40. *dayes &* 40. *nightes, Founded manie Churches, healed manie ficke, deliuered manie poffeffed of deuilles, and rayfed to life* 60. *that vveare dead, &c.*

17.   Behold the effects of Preachers fent forth

S. Patricius.

Bal. de script. Britan. Cent. 1. fol. 25.

Ibid.

forth by the Bishoppes of Rome, recoump-
ted by the heretikes themselues. Lett Fox
or Bale shewe vs any such example of miracles, wrought by Preachers sent by them &
their sect. And that this man also was made
Bishop by *Cælestinus* the Pope, and sent thither
after *Palladius*, is testified by *S. Prosper*, that liued in that time, and after him by *Saint Bede*,
Marianus Scotus, *Sigebert*, and others. Who say
also, that he died in the yeare of Christe
491. being of the age of 122. yeares. And his
memorie is helde in the Romane callender
vpon the 17. day of Marche, &c. And nowe
our *Fox* and *Bale* being taken in these examples to speake against themselues, wee
might passe ouer the rest with silence, assu-
ring the reader that all is like vnto this. Yet
somme points more wee shall note.

Prosp. contr. lib. Collat. in fine. Bed. hist. Angl. l. 1. cap. 13. & in lib. de sex ætat. Marian. Scot. l. 2. sex ætat. an. 432.

18. The fourth before named *Bacchiarius*,
though he be not mentioned by Iohn Bale:
yet other authors doe report that he was
brought vp in Rome, and in good creditt
with *Pope Leo the first*, to whom he dedicated
a booke written in defence of his pilgri-
mage to Rome. He had ben the scholler of
S. Patricius. And by this yow may ghesse of
what Religion he was.

Bacchia-rius. Ioan. cap. in catal. SS. Brit. Polid. Virg. lib. 1. histor. Harpesf. sæc. 6. cap. 22. Gongel-lus.

19. *Congellus* is the sixt preacher of true Religion cited in Fox his catalogue (for of *Dubritius* which is the fifte we spoke of before.)
whom Bale saith to haue florished about

N 5　　the

the yeare of Chriſte 530. and that he was
the firſt Abbot of the Monaſterie of Bangor. But what more thinke yow? *Ab iſto Mo-*
nachiſmus à Pelagio introductus, &c. From this man
(ſaith he) *the Religion of Monkes brought in by Pe-*
lagius the hereticke, vvas not onlie ſpread ouer Brita-
nie vnder ſhevve of true Religion, but vvas dilated
also into other countries, &c. Behold how Fox

Bal. fol.
29.

& Bale agree. Fox ſaith he was a true Preacher of the word of God, and Bale ſaith he
was a Father of Pelagian monkes. And note
heere by the way, that Fox profeſſing to
ſhewe the continuall ſucceſſion of the Britane Church, leapeth from *Patricius* to *Du-*
britius, of whom wee ſpake before, and betweene whom there was aboue 100. yeares
diſtance, if wee beleeue *Bale* and other au-

Kente-
gernus.

thors. And then followeth *Kentegernus* and
Helmotus before *Dauid Meneuenſis,* who ſhould
haue comme after him in reſpecte of time.
Though of *Helmotus Bale* maketh noe mention. But of *Kentegernus* he ſaith *that he floriſhed*
in the yeare 560. *& liued in all* 185. *yeares.* which
if it be ſo, he muſt needes be aliue long after

Bal. fol.
32.

the entrance of *Saint Auguſtine.* He ſaith, *he*
vvas a monke and had 300. *ſchollers in one colledge,*
vvhich he ſent to preaching heere & there, &c. And
then he addeth further, *melote vtebatur, &c.*
he vſed a garment made of goate ſkinnes vvith a
ſtraite hoode, hauing a vvhite ſtole about his necke
after the faſhion of the primitiue Church. He conuerted

ted manie to the Faith of Chriſte, recalled manie Apo-
ſtataes, driued out Pelagians, builded Churches, mi-
niſtred to the ſicke & healed their ſickneſſe, and liued
in very great abſtinence, &c. Thus he deſcribeth
him, & whether this deſcription doth agree
to a Proteſtant miniſter, or to a Catholike
Abbott, lett the reader conſider.

20.   There do follow in Fox his catalogue, *Dauid, Daniel, Sampſon, Elnodugus, Aſſaphus,* and *Gildas.* But of *Saint Dauid,* the firſt
of this number, wee haue ſpoken before in
this chapter. And as for *Gildas* (which is the
laſt of this rancke) Bale ſaithe, he was a
moncke of *Bangor.* And further it may eaſilie
appeare by the ſpeaches themſelues, which
before we haue alleadged out of him in the
former chapter, of what religion he was.

Of *Daniel, Sampſon,* and *Elnodugus,* though   *Io.Capg.*
Iohn Bale ſpeake littell or nothinge : yet   *in catal.*
Capgraue, Leland, and others ſhewe, that   *Sanct.*
                                             Brit.
they were of the ſame religion with the
reſt: *Daniel* beinge the firſt Biſhop of Bangor : and *Sampſon* next after *Saint Dauid* vvas
Biſhop of that place.

21.   Of *Aſſaph* Bale ſaith, *he vvas ſcholler to*   S. Aſ-
the aforſaide famous Abbott Kentegerne, and vvas   ſaph re-
made Biſhop of Elgoa in VVales, vvhich of his name   ceaued
vvas called Aſſaph euer ſince. He florished in the yeare   his con-
590. *and ſavve the comminge in of Auguſtine & his*   ſecratiõ.
fellovves from Rome. And vvas the firſt of the Britans   from
(ſaith Bale) *Qui a Gregorij Romani diſcipulis in*   Rome.
                                                     Bal.ibid.
                                    Angliam   fol. 34.

Angliam aduentantibus auctoritatem & vnctionem accepit. That tooke his auctoritie & vnction (or conſecration) From the diſciples of *Gregory* Biſhop of *Rome*, that came into Engladͤ. So writeth *Bale*, and by this ſheweth, that *S. Aſſaph* helde nothinge againſt the Roman Religion, ſeeinge he accepted his authority and conſecration from the Biſhop of *Rome*. Beſides this, this Biſhop, *S. Aſſaph*, hath his memorie celebrated in the Roman martyrologe vpon the firſt day of may, which he ſhoulde not, if he had bene different in any one pointe from the Roman religion.

22. And ſo beinge come downe nowe to *S. Auguſtines* time, it is to noe purpoſe to goe any farther, or name the reſt that do enſue in Fox, to witt, thoſe fiue *Herlanus*, *Elbodus*, *Dinothus*, *Samuel* and *Niuius*, for that they liued after *Saint Auguſtines* entrance. Whereas Fox his promiſe was to cite only *Britiſh* teachers, that were before him and different from the Roman Religion, wherof he hath

Bal. ibid. fol. 35.
named hetherto noe one. Beſides that of three of theſe fiue, Bale writeth not. And as for *Dinothus* Abbot of Bangor, he was the chiefeſt of thoſe, who oppoſed themſelues againſt *Auguſtine*, and ſett other men againſt him alſo in *Synodo VViccionum*, and was ſeuerelie punniſhed afterward for the ſame by

Bed. lib. 2. hiſtor. cap. 2.
the prouidence of God, as *Saint Bede* noteth, to witt, by the ſword of *Ethelfredus* a heathen kinge

kinge of Northumberland longe after the
death of *Saint Augustine:* when the saide *Dino-*
thus and 12. hundred monckes were slaine
at *Chester* by the souldiours of the saide *Ethel-*
fride, Augustino iam multo ante tempore (saith *S.*
Bede) *ad cælestia regna sublato: Saint Augustine*
beinge taken to heaué longe before, though
Bale be not ashamed to say, that it was donn
by his suggestion : praisinge the forsaide
Dinothus, and his confederates, for that they
woulde not preach Baptisme and celebrate
Easter day, accordinge to the custome of
Rome and vniuersall Catholike Church.

23.   So as nowe wee see , that theise men
care not what they say or auouch , so they
say somwhat against Rome, and those that
anie way fauored the same. Wherin passion
doth so greatlie blinde them, as they cannot
discerne, when they alleadge matters plainlie against themselues : as yow haue sene in
the former enumeration of *British* teachers
Pastors and prelatts . Whome they woulde
haue vs thinke to haue ben of a different
religion from that of Rome : Where as
theire owne words, testimonies, condition
and'state of life do testifie the contrary. And
so I leaue theise men to theire follie and impudency in this behalf.

                    THE

THE DEDVCTION OF THE

AFORESAID CATHOLIQVE ROMAN *Religion planted in England by* S. Augustine *from his time to oure dayes. And that from* Kinge Ethelbert *vvho firft receaued the fame vnto* K. Henry *the* 8. *there vvas neuer any publike interruption of the faid Religion in oure land.*

Chap. XI.

HAVINGE fnewed before, how that the Roman Catholike faith was firft prea-ched in oure Iland vnder the Apoftles, and then againe in the next age vnder *Pope Eleu-therius*, and thirdlie fowre ages after that againe vnder *Pope Gregory*, and that all this was but one & the felf fame Religion con-tinued, renued and reuiued in diuers times vnder diuers ftates & people of the realme: there may feeme to remaine onlie nowe two other pointes confiderable in this af-faire. The firft, whether this religió brought in by *S. Auguftine* to England, were helde at that day for the onlie trewe Religion of Chriftendome, and fo accepted by all the worlde: The other, whether that religion then planted, hath com downe & ben con-tinued in England euer fince by continuall fuccefsion, vntill the firft publique altera-tion made therof in our dayes. For if this be fo, then is the demonftration eafie to be

made

made euen from the Apoſtles times to
oures.

2. And for the firſt, though we haue handled the ſame ſomwhat before: yet briefly
wee will add now, that theire can be no
doubt at all in this matter with men of reaſon and iudgment, but that *S. Auguſtine* and
his fellowes brought in with them the
whole corps of Religion, as well touching
articles of belief, as ceremonies, and Eccleſiaſticall cuſtomes, which were at that time
in vſe at Rome, whence they came; and in
other Catholique Countreyes by which
they paſſed, namely *Italy, France* & *Flaunders,*
from which Countreyes *Pope Gregorie* himſelf exhorteth them by his letters, to take
ſuch good Eccleſiaſticall vſes as they ſhould
ſee moſt agreable to piety, edification and
deuotion. Which is a ſigne, that all thoſe
countreyes agreed fully in faith and beleefe
with Rome at that day, and were perfectly
Catholike: though in ſome externall ceremonies, belonging to deuotiõ, there might
be difference. And for ſo much as the french
Biſhops *S. Germanus, S. Lupus* & *S. Seuerus* 150.
yeares (as hath byn ſaid) before the entrance
of *S. Auguſtine,* planted in Britanie the french
Cath. faith againſt the *Pelagians,* and theſe
men comming from Rome, found no fault
therwith: moſt certayne it is, that all was
one. And finallie if we do conſider the

That the
religion
brought
in by *S.
Augu-
ſtine*
vvas Ca-
tholike.

*Greg. in
epiſt. ad
Auguſt.*

*Bed. l. 1,
hiſt. c. 18.
19. &c.*

workes,

works, writings and actions of *Pope Gregory*, related by vs before partely out of *S. Iſiodore*, liuing at that time in Spaine, partely out of his owne epiſtles yet extant, writen to the cheefeſt Biſhops of the Chriſtian world, and their anſwers to him againe, together with their agreement in faith & religion. If we do conſider alſo the hereſies, condemned in his dayes by him & his authority, as the *Eutichians, Monothelites,* and others, which our proteſtants alſo do condemne for hereſies at this day: by all this (I ſay) and by infinite other arguments & demonſtratiōs, that may be made, it is moſt euident, that eyther Chriſt had no viſible Church or Catholike religion in thoſe dayes (which were moſt foolish or wicked to imagine) or that the religion of *S. Gregory* and his Church of Rome, and others of the ſame communion was in that age, the onlie true Cath. Church, and conſequentlie had in it the onlie true Cath. faith and religion of Chriſt, wherby Chriſtians might be ſaued. Which alſo is proued moſt euidetly by infinite miracles wrought in England and in diuers other countreyes, vpon manifold occaſiōs, during this time of our primitiue Church, as ſhall appeare more in particular in the deduction of our ſecond point. Which is the continuance of this ſame religion from *Saint Auguſtine* to *Thomas Cranmer,* the firſt and laſt Archbishopps of Can-

Either no trevv Church or religion vvas in S. Greries time, or els it vvas the Roman.

Canterbury, following by fuccefsion the
one the other, for the fpace of aboue 900.
yeares. The firft dying a Sainct, the laft ending in Apoftafy, as after fha be fhewed.

3. Wherfore to come to the fecond point
about the deduction of Catholike religion
in our nation from *S. Auguftin* downeward,
firft of all, *S. Bede* talking of the planting
therof, and of our firft primitiue Church,
(whofe progreffe & increafe he defcribeth
for the fpace of almoft 140. yeares after the
entrãce of *S. Auguftine*) hath thefe words: *Gre-*
gorius Pontifex diuino admonitus inftinctu , feruum
Dei Auguftinum, & alios plures cum eo monachos, ti-
mentes Dominum mifit, prædicare verbum Dei genti
Arglorum. &c. Gregorie the Pope, being ad-
monished by heauenlie inftinct did fend
Gods feruant *Auguftine*, and other monks
with him, that feared God, to preach his
word to the English nation, in the 14. yeare
of *Mauritius* the Emperour which vvas of
Chrift 596. and the fourth after that *S. Gre-*
gory was made Pope.

4. Thefe holie men landed in the Ile of
Thanet belonging to the kindgome of *Kent.*
For that the whole dominiõ of the Saxons
in thofe dayes (which was all the land, ex-
cept *Scotland*, and the other part now called
VVales, whither the reliques of the Britans
were retyred) was deuided into 7. feuerall
States and dominions, vvhich they called

The cõ-
tinuatiõ
of reli-
gion frõ
S. Aug.
dovvn-
vvard.

Bed. hift.
Angl. l. 1.
cap. 22.

S. Aug.
and his
compa-
nie lan-
ded in
the Ile
of Tha-
net.

O   kingdo-

The firſt
king-
dome
of Kent
conuer-
ted to
Chriſtiā
faith *an.
Domini
600.
Bed. l.1.
hiſtor.
Malm.
l.2. hiſt.
2. King-
dome
of Eaſt-
ſaxons
conuer-
ted 604.*

kingdomes. Tne firſt wherof (to ſpeake of
them according, as they receyued the faith)
was the kingdome of *Kent*, whoſe King
Ethelbert, (being the fourth in number from
Hengiſtus, that began the ſame about the
yeare of Chriſt 450.) afterward, firſt of all
other receyued the Chriſtian faith at the
preaching of *Saint Auguſtine*, about the yeare
of Chriſt 600. that is to ſay, a hundred and
fiftie yeares, after they had raigned as Pay-
nims there.

5.   The ſecond kingdome was of the *Eaſt-
ſaxons*, and conteyned the ſhires now called
Eſſex, *Middleſex*, and *Hartſordſhire*. The firſt
foūder of wnich kingdome was *Erchenvvine*,
about the yeare of our Lord 527. as *Storv* and
ſome others do hould. Though *Malmesbury*
do write differentlie. But both ao agree,
that vnder K.*Seebert* (or as ✶Bede calleth him
Sabered) thoſe prouinces were conuerted to
Chriſtian religion, by the preaching of *Saint
Mellitus* fellow to *Saint Auguſtine*, and firſt Biſhopp of there cheefe citty of *London*, whither he was ſent by S. *Auguſtine* from Canterburie, in the yeare of Chriſt 604.

3. King-
dome of
the Eaſt-
angles
conuer-
ted *anno*
609.

6.   The third Kingdome was of the *Eaſtangles*, which conteyned the ſhires of *Norfolke*
Suffolke, *Cambridge*, and the Ile of *Ely*. Which
kingdome was begone about the yeare of
Chriſt 492. by one *Vſſa*, but conuerted after
to Chriſtian religion vnder K.*Sigebert*, about
the

the yeare of Chrilt 609 . and that by the
preaching principally of their firlt Bishop
Felix, borne in *Burgundy* in France, being ordayned Bishop of a cittie there, called *Dun-*
vvich at that time, which now is more then
halfe confumed with the Sea.

Malm.
l. 1. hift.
cap. 6.

7.   The fourth kingdome was of the *Nor-*
thumbers, vvhich contayned manie fhires
towards the North : to witt, *Lancashire*,
Torkeshire Cumberland, VVeftmerland, Northum-
berland, Durham, and fome part of *Scotland.*
The firlt monarch of this kingdome is accoumpted *Ida.* And it receaued the faith of
Chriltian religion vnder their 13. King *Ed-*
vvyne in the yeare of Chrilt 626. by the preaching of *Saint Paulinus,* fent thither to preach
by *Iuftus* third Archbishopp of Canterbury.
By whome the faid *Paulinus* was tranflated
from the Sea of Rochelter, to be Archbifhop
of Yorke.

The 4.
King-
dome of
Nor-
thum-
bers cō-
uerted
an. 626.

8.   The fifth kingdome was of the *VVeft-*
faxons, which conteyned the countreyes of
Cornvvall , Deuonshire, Dorfetshire, Sommerfett-
fhire, VViltshire, Barkeshire and *Hampshire.* The
firlt founder therof was *Cerdicke*, about the
yeare of Chrift 509. And vnder *Kenegilfus*
their ffth king, they receaued the Chriltian
faith, by the preaching of *Saint Berinus* their
firlt Bishopp of *Dorchefter*, in the yeare of
Chrilt 635.

5. King-
dome of
Vveft-
faxons
conuer-
ted 635.

9.   The 6. kingdome was of the *Mercians*

6. King-

O 2   or

dome
of Mer-
cians
conuer-
ted 635.

or middle countrey being in that time the greateſt of all the reſt, and conteyning ſome 15. or 16. ſhires, as *Gloſter, Hereford, Cheſter, Stafford, VVorceſter, Shrovvesbury, Oxford, VVarvvicke, Darby, Leiceſter, Bucchingham, Northampton, Nottingam, Huntington* and *Rutland.* The firſt founder of this monarchy is ſaid to be one *Creda,* about the yeare of Chriſt 586. And the còuerſion therof to Chriſtian faith, was about the yeare of Chriſt 635. vnder prince *Peda,* ſonne and heyre vnto the notable perſecuting pagan *Penda.* Their firſt Apoſtle was *B. Finan,* who baptized *K. Peda* againſt his fathers will in the kingdome of the *Northumbers,* at a towne by *Barvvicke* called *Ad murum:* and this by the inſtance of the good Chriſtian *K. Oſvvyne, K.* of *Northumberland,* who gaue *K. Peda* his daughter in marriage on this condition, that he would become a Chriſtian.

7. King-
dome
of the
South-
ſaxons
conuer-
ted *anno*
662.

10. The 7. kingdome was of the *Southſaxons* conteyning the ſhires of *Suſſex* and *Surrey,* and beganne about the yeare of Chriſt 478. by one *Aelus* a Saxon, and was conuerted to Chriſtianity vnde *K. Ethelvvold,* (or *Ethelvvach,* as *Saint Bede* nameth him) about the yeare of Chriſt 662. by the preaching eſpecially of *S. VVilfride* their firſt Biſhop, who erected a monaſtery for the Epiſcopall Sea in a place called *Seolyce* or *Selcey.*

11. Well then, thus we ſee, that within the

the fpace of 40. yeares more or leffe, fix
kingdomes of England receyued the ghofpell, and the feauenth not long after, vnder
their firft preachers and Apoftles before
mentioned. And what great variety of miracles, God did worke by thefe his feruants,
and their helpers & afsiftants in this worke
of the conuerfion of our countrey, is euident
by all ftoryes of that time and after. And noe
man, but an infidell or mifcreant, can with
any probable reafon call them in doubt.

12.　And it feemeth that the promife of our
Sauiour made to his Apoftles at his laft far-
well, in *Saint Marks* Ghofpell, for miracles
to be vvrought in the conuerfion of nations (efpecially of Gentills, as *Saint Gregory*
obferueth) was as aboundantlie fulfilled in
the firft conuerfion of our English nation,
as of any other lightly in the world. *The fignes
and miracles* (faith Chrift) *vvhich fhall follovv
them, that fhall beleeue in me, or receyue my faith*
(efpeciallie in the beginning) *are thefe : that,
they fhall caft out diuells in my name ; they fhall
fpeake vvith nevv tongues ; they fhall remooue fer-
pents, and (yf they fhould drinke poifon) yt fhall
not hurt them; they fhall lay their hands vpon ficke
men, and thervvith heale them, &c.*

13.　All thefe things promifed Chrift our
Sauiour, and performed them moft aboundantlie in the firft conuerfion of nations,
while the faid miracles were neceffarie to

Marc.16

*Gregor.
hom. 29.
de fefto
Afcenf.
Domini.
Marc.16*

plant and confirme the faith. But when (as

„ *S. Gregory* in the place before alleadged faith)

„ the yong plants had no more need of fuch

daylie watering by miracles, then ceafed they. Though in our countrey and primitiue Church, they indured no fmall time, as were eafie to fhew, if I would ftand in this place to runne ouer the Ecclefiaticall ftories, of the leaft part of the aforefaid 7. kingdomes. Wherof yet many things wil be fpoken of afterward.

14.   For in the onlie kingdome of *Kent*, for the firft hundred yeares after the conuerfion of *K. Eihelbert*, there poffeffed the Sea of Canterbury from *S. Auguftine* vnto *Bertualdus*,

(who died in the yeare of Chrift 730. and with whome *Saint Bede* endeth)eight Archbishops, all moft godlie, and holie men, to witt; *Auguftine, Laurence, Melitus, Iuftus, Honorius, Deufdedit, Theodorus* and *Bertualdus.* Which Bishops were held for great Saints in our primitiue Church, as appeareth by the writing both of *Saint Bede*, that liued alfo himfelfe in that age, & by *VVilliam* of *Malmesbury*, that liued fome ages after. Who yet alleageth a more auncient author then him felfe,

Malmf.
l. 1. de
geftis
Pont.
Angl.
pa. 112. called *Goffelinus*, that wrote the liues and miracles of all thofe 8. Archbishops of Canterburie, & of fome other Saints of our countrey. *Horum* (faith he) *& non minùs fancti Letardi, &c.* Of thefe Archbishopps as alfo of

Saint

Saint Letard, that in auncient time came in „
with *Q. Berta*, the author before mentioned „
Gosselinus hath written their maruelous and „
admirable vertues, out of *Bede* and others. „
Adding also manie things, which he saw „
himselfe with his owne eyes, shewing the „
great miracles and signes, which they did, „
&c. He doth recount also the ranke of „
Kings, with their kinredd, that lay buryed „
in his dayes in the Church of *Saint Augustine* „
at Canterbury. Which he doth worthelie „
call the lights of England, and the Senators „
of the English heauenly court of Parlament. „
And to this quyre of Saints and crowne or „
diademe of our eternall King Christ, he „
addeth other pretious stones also of inesti- „
mable glory, to witt *Saint Adrian* the Abbot, „
and *Saint Mildred* the virgin, as conspicuous „
in glory of miracles as the rest, &c. „

15. Thus writeth *Malmesbury* of these seruants of God of the Church of Canterbury, for the first hundred yeares after Christs
faith receiued: but he that would recount
the like of all the other six kingdomes and
English churches, should haue greate store
of matter. Especially if he would enter into
the particular liues & actions of such eminent holy men, as that age by the force and
vertue of that primitiue Christian religion
brought forth. And then, if with all this he
remember in like manner that most cer-

An infallible principle.

taine principle before mentioned ; *that God vvould neuer haue concurred vvith ſuch abondance of piety, holines, and miracles to the ſetting vp of a faſe religion,* he will eaſily ſee, now plaine a demonſtration this is for the truth of that religion, which was thus planted amongeſt vs by S. Auguſtine, and maligned by theſe ſectaries of our time.

Catholike religion planted in England vvith greate povver of miracles.

Marc. vltimo.

16.   Well then, in this manner was religion firſt planted among vs, according to that which *Saint Marke* the Euangeliſt ſaith of the firſt preachers & preachinges among other nations and Gentiles in his time : to witt, *Domino cooperante & ſermonem confirmante ſequentibus ſignis,* Chriſt working with them, & confirming their preaching with ſignes and miracles, And this faith being once planted, did take ſuch deepe roote by the ſaid watering of Chriſt the author therof, as it continued and held out from time to time, through all difficulties & differences both of times, men, and ſtate, and by perill, diuiſions, enimities, and cruell warres, that fell out euery day betweene thoſe 7. kingdomes, vntil they were vnited all vnder one monarchie ſome 200. yeares after ; to vvit, vnder K. *Egbert*, King of the Weſt-Saxons. And from him againe the ſame indured other 200. yeares vnto K. *Edvvard* the Confeſſor before the Conqueſt.

17.   And that vvhich is worthy, alſo the noting

noting in this case, is, that during the time
of all this enimitie, emulation, suspitions,
iealousie of kingdomes and states, and bloudy battailes betvvene these kingdomes for
the space of the foresaid 200. yeares, from
their conuersion to Chritianity vntill they
came to be a monarchy: they all liued vnder
one Archbishopp and primate of Canterburie, holding their due subordinacion and
good correspondence with him, & by him
vvith the Sea of Rome, and other Cath.
countreies for matters of faith and Ecclesiasticall affaires, no othervvise than if they
had been all frends, yea subiectes and prouinces of one and the selfe same kingdome,
and this is the vertue & force of Catholike
vnion. Whereas amongst Sectaries, euery
little difference of temporall states, (yea of
townes, cities, and gouuernments) doeth
presently cause a diuersity also in faith and
religion. As vve see at this day, that Saxonie
(for example) where the name of the Protestants first began, being vnder a different
Prince hath a greate difference also in religion from other partes of Germanie, that
call themselues Protestants, and the kingdomes of Denmarke & Suerhland, though
they professe all Lutheranisme, yet is the
manner so different in these different states,
as not only the one vvill not depend of the
other in any sorte of subordination, or Ec-

One Ca-
tholike
religion
vnder
states
that
vvere
ene-
mies.

Diuer-
sitie of
states
vvor-
keth di-
uersitie.
of reli-
gion
amongst
sectaries.

clesia-

clefiafticall iurifdiction (as in England we
fee they did) but neither doe they agree in
any one forme of religion, or fubftance of
beliefe in all pointes, no nor in one ftate it
felfe, where all profeffe themfelues to be
Lutherans, as in Saxonie, where the higher
Saxons allow only rigide or ftreight Lutherans : but the lower Saxonie alloweth
only the fofter forte, and expelleth the rigide or feuere Lutherans ; as the other doe
them, where they gett dominion.

18.   *Geneua* and *Berna* are both citties and
ftates, of the Switzers, & both of them profeffe proteftancy, though not according to
Luthers doctrine.   But yet the temporall
ftate of the faid two townes beeing different, the magiftrates haue appointed a different and diftinct forme.   Which in England allfo we fee by experiece, how much
they differre from thofe of *Scotland*, *Holland*,
and *France*, who profeffe themfelues Proteftants of the fame Caluiuian fchoole : but
euery nation and Church after his owne
fashion.   And finallie what differences haue
rifen in England it felf, during her Maiefties
onlie gouernement, betwixt *Puritanes*, *Brovv-*
niftes, *Familie of loue* and *State Proteftants* (as
★ *Thomas Digges* calleth them) no man can
be ignorant.   But to what differences and
diuifions they would growe in two or three
hundred yeares (yf Sects could laft fo long,
and

★ In his
humble
motiues
an Do⸗
mini
1601.

and that the states vvhich professe them were enemies in temporall affaires as it was in England) is easie to gheffe.

But the reason hereof is manifest, to witt, that for so much as Sectaries making their owne iudgments and inuentions the rule of their beliefe and religion, and their tempo rale Princes their absolute guiders and im mediate heades in Ecclesiasticall matters : it must needes follow, that as these princes or states do chaunge or alter for any respect whatsoeuer (as they do for manie) religion also must needes alter and chaunge for con- tentement or interest of the said states or Princes.

VVhy sectaries doe chaunge so often their re ligion vnder different states.

19. But to returne to our deduction and continuation of Catholike religion among the English Saxons after they came to be a monarchy, (to wit, from the yeare of Christ 800.) it is first to be noted that assoone as God had deliuered them from one affli- ction(which was the continuall ciuill war- res of one kingdome with an other) he sent them a second calamitie farre greater per- haps, than the first, induring for other 200. yeares, which was the continuall incursions and deuastations of the Danes. Who pur- sued them not onlie for temporall respects, to gett their country from them but also for religion it self (the saide Danes beeing then Pagans) as appeareth by the cruell murders

Afflictiõ by the Danes fromthe yeare 800. dovvne= vvard.

and

and Martyrdomes as well of *Saint Edmund*
King of the Eaftangles, martyred by them
about the yeare of Chrift 885. as of holie
Elphegus Archbishop of Canterburie, fome
ages after, about the yeare 1011. and of
diuers others ouerlong heere to recount.
And yet notwithftanding, when the faid
Danes, with their *K. Canutus* fonne of *Svva-*
nus, came once by Gods holie grace to be
Chriftians (which was foone after the forfaid Martyrdome of the holie Archbifhop
Elphegus) they fubmitted themfelues with
humilitie and feruour of fpiritt to that very
fame Chriftian-faith of their enemies the
Englishmen, which they had perfecuted in
them before, taking them alfo for their in-
ftructors. Which is a token, that there was
no other Chriftian faith knowne in the
world at that day for them to imbrace, but
only that which the English profeffed, to
the embracing wherof, there is no doubt,
but the miracles wrought continually in
confirmation of the truth of that faith (as
well at the tombes of the forefaid Martyrs
S. Edmund and *Elphegus* flayne by the Danes
themfelues, as other wayes alfo) did greatly
moue and animate them.

20.   But whatfoeuer the chiefe motiues
were to moue this nation to embrace Chriftian religion, this is certaine, that foone
after this time of *S. Elphegus* his death, God
deliuered

[marginal notes:]
S. Ed-
mund &
S. Elphe-
gus mar-
tyred by
Danes.

Osbertus
in vita
S. Elph.
apud
Sur. 21.
April.
Malm.
lib. 1.
Pontif.
Angl.pa.
116.
Matth.
VVeſt-
monaſt.
an. Dom.
1011. &
1012.

deliuered the whole kingdome of England
into the Danes hands vnder the forefaid
K. *Canutus,* about the yeare of Chrift 1020.
And he reigned & held the fame peaceably
for all moft 20. yeares. In which time he
beeing now Chriftian did many notable
actes of a good religious Kinge, Went to
Rome for deuotion to vifitt the holy fepui-
chres of *S. Peter* & *S. Paul,* gaue greate Almes
there'and els where, made iuft lawes in England, loued and fauoured exceedingly the
English nation, vfed them with all confidence both at home and abroad, maried
K. *Emma* mother to K. *Edvvard* the Confeffor,
therby to vnite himfelf the more to the
nation. And finally became of a perfecutor
and conqueror, one of the beft Kinges, that
England perhaps had in many ages to gouerne her.

The good acts of K. Canutus after his conuersion.

21. *VVilliam of Malmesbury* liuing (as it hath
been faid) fome 500. yeares agone vnder
K. Henry the firft, fonne to William Conqueror, writeth many moft excellent religious actes of this King Canutus, faying
amongft other thinges thus : *Monafteria per
Angliam, &c.* He did repaire all the monafteries in England, that were ouerthrowne or
defaced by the warres of his Father *Svvanus*
or himfelfe. He did build churches in all the
places, where he had fought any battailles.
And appointed prieftes for the faid churches

Malmcf. de gestk Regum Angl. lib. 2. c. 11.
,,
,,
,,

,, ches, who ſhould pray continually to the
,, worldes end for the ſoules of them that had
,, been ſlayne in thoſe places. He was preſent
,, at the conſecration of a goodly church in a
,, place called *Aſchendum* (where he had his
,, chiefeſt victory) cauſing both the nobles of
,, the Engliſh and Daniſh nation, to offer
,, with him riche giftes to the ſaid church, &c.

22. Ouer the body of bleſſed *Saint Edmund,*
which the auncient Danes had ſlaine, he
builded a church worthy the greatneſſe of
his kingly heart, appointing their both an
Abbott and Monks, and geuing them many
poſſeſſions. In ſo much as by the greatneſſe
of his giftes, that monaſtery at this day is
aboue all the reſt in England. He tooke vp
with his owne hands the body of *Saint Elphegus* Archbiſhopp of Canterbury (ſlaine
not long before by his Danes) and cauſed
,, the ſame to be caried vnto Canterbury: re-
,, uerincing the ſame with worthy honour.
,, He gaue ſuch greate gifts & rares ieweles
,, to the church of Wincheſter, that the ſhi-
,, ning of pretious ſtones, did dazele the eyes
,, of ſuch, as did beholde them, &c. In
,, the 15. yeare of his kingdome he went to
,, Rome by land, and hauing ſtayed ſome
,, daies there, & redeming his ſinnes by almes
,, in thoſe churches, he returned by Sea to
England, &c.

23. Thus and much more doeth *VVilliam of
Malmeſ-*

The buildinge the Abbay of Edmudꝰbærie, & riche endovvꝰment therof by K. Canꝰtus.

Malmesbury write of this notable K. *Canutus* a terrible and fierce warriour before his conuersion, and much giuen to blood and impietie, wherby may easely be seene, what force Catholique religion is of, to make chaunge in a mans manners, vvhere it truly entreth. Let Protestants shew vs some such examples of Princes conuerted to their religion. But to goe forward in *Malmesbury*: he setteth downe after all this a large epistle of K. *Canutus*, which he wrote from Rome, or in the way homeward, vnto the tvvo Archbishops, *Egelnothus* & *Alfricus*, the first of Canterbury, the other of Yorke, & by them to the whole realme, giuing them accoumpt of his iourney to Rome. Where amongst other things he writeth thus: *Knutus Rex totius Angliæ, & Denmarkiæ, & Noruegiæ, & partis Suecorum, &c. notifico vobis, me nouiter iuisse Romam, oratum pro redemptione peccaminum meorum, &c.* I Canutus King of ail England, Denmarke and Norway, and parte of Swetia, &c. doe giue you to vnderstande that of late I went to Rome, to pray for the redemption » of my sinnes, and for the health of my king- » domes and people : hauing made a vow of » this iourney long agoe, but could neuer » performe it vntill now, by reason I was let- » ted by the affaires of my kingdomes. And » now I doe yelde most hearly thankes to my » allmighty God, that he hath graunted me » this

K. Canutus his letter from Rome.
Malm. ibid. fol. 14.

,, this grace to come and viſitt in my life time
,, the bleſſed Apoſtles *S. Peter* and *S. Paul* and
,, all the Sanctuary that is within & without
,, this citty: and according to my deſire to ho-
,, nour and worſhipp the ſame in my owne
,, perſon, &c.

24.   Thus he wrote. And moreouer adioyned manie other pious ordinances in the
ſame epiſtle to be obſerued in England, for
reſtitutions to be made, almes to be geuen,
and other good deedes to be done, exhor-
ting all to performe them willinglie, and
threatning them that ſhould do the cõtrary.

Hovv
K. Canu
tus per-
formed
his good
deſires
vvhen
he retur-
ned frõ
Rome.
Ibid. fol.
42.

And *VVilliam* of *Malmeſbury* ſaith, that returning after to England he cauſed the ſame to
be ſtrictlie obſerued. And gaue manie new
priuiledges to Churches. And one among
other to the Church of Canterburie, which
Malmesbury ſetteth downe at length, and in
the end hath theſe words. *Si quis verò, &c.*
Yf any man ſhall performe this my ordination with a prompt will, almighty God by
the interceſsion of the moſt bleſſed virgin
,, Mary and all his ſaints, encreaſe his portion
,, in the land of the liuing. And this donation
,, of priuiledge is written and promulgated in
,, the preſence of me *K. Canutus,* in the wodden
,, Church, in the yeare of Chriſt 1032.

23. Thus farre writeth *VVilliam* of *Malmeſbury*
of this kinges pious diſpoſition after his
comming from *Rome.* And *Iohn Stovv* addeth
out

out of *Henry* of *Huntington*, as followeth. *After* *Sto. in*
this time, *Canutus neuer bare crovvne vpon his head,* *Cbron.*
But he *fett the fame vpon the head of the Crucifix at* *pag. 116.*
V Vinchefter &c. And thus much of his piety
and other fruicts of true Chriftian faith,
which he had receyued . And it is no fmall
argument of the diuine power therof, that
yt could fo mollifie and chaunge fo fearce a
warriour & cruell a perfecutor, as this King
was before his conuerfion.

26. So as now we haue brought downe
the continuance & fuccefsion of one, & the
felf fame Chriftian religion in Englãd from
Saint Auguftine & *K. Ethelbert*, vnto *K. Canutus,*
for the fpace of 400. yeares . And that this
vvas no particular religion of England
alone , but the common generall faith not
onlie of *Rome*, but of all Chriftendome befids, at that day, And confequentlie the onlie
Catholike religion of thofe ages: appeareth
in like manner by other words of the Kings
former letter recorded by *Malmesbury*, where
he faith. *Sit autē vobis notum, &c.* Be it knowne *Ibidem*
vnto you , that in this laft folénity of Eafter, *apud*
there was a great affemblie of nobilitie here *Malm.*
in Rome, togeather with *Pope Iohn* and the *fol. 41.*
Emperour *Conrade* (to witt, all the greateft *K. Ca-*
princes from the hill *Garganus* vnto this *nutus*
other next Sea) all vvhich did receyue me *vvas*
moft honorablie , and did prefent me vvith *Catho-*
magnificent gifts, &c. Thus vvrote the *like,*

P Kinge:

Kinge: vvherby vve may eafely perceyue,
that *K. Canutus* vvas heald in all points for a
perfe&t Catholike Prince, feeing that both
Pope Iohn the xx. and the Emperour *Conrade*
the fecond, did efteeme and honour him fo
highlie.

27.　After *Canutus* fucceeded in the kingdome of England his tvvo fonnes *Herald* &
Hardicanutus, for 2. or 3. yeares. And then
K. *Edvvard the Confeffor*, for 23. yeares togeather. After vvhofe death the fecond *Herald*
fonne of Earle *Goodvvin* holding the kingdome by violence, againft both Englifh and
Danes, fcarce one yeare: *VVilliam* duke of
Normandy came in, as all men know, & conquered the lande tovvards the end of the
yeare 1066. and helde the fame all daies of
his life, and fo hath his pofteritie after kim
by male or female vnto our time, and haue
continued the fame Religion, vvhich he
found or brought into England (for all was
one) for the fpace of 500. yeares vnto *K.*
Henry the 8. his time, which may be prooued
befide other vvayes, by the fucceffion of our
Archbifhoppes of Canterburie. *Stigand* an
English man, being the 23. from *S. Auguftine*,
holding the fame, when *VVilliam* the *Conque-*
rour got the crovvne, to vvhom fucceeded
Lanfrancke, and to him *Anfelmus*, and fo fuc-
cefsiuelie one after another: none of them
euer being noted to be contrarie to his pre-
de ceffor

1043.

The fuc-
ceffion
of Ca-
tholique
religion
fince the
cóqueft.

deceſſor in Religion, vntill *Thomas Cranmer*
in K. *Henry* the 8. his time. Who applied himſelfe to the Religion, vvhich the ſtate and
Prince liked beſt to allow of in that time.
And after the Kings death, agreed to breake
his laſt vvill and teſtament, in chaunging
that Religion into Zwinglianiſme, moſt
deteſted by his Maieſtie. And after againe
conſpired to put dovvne and deſtroy all the
King his children, and to ſett vp the Duke
of Suffolks daughter. And finaliie, vvas put
to death both for hereſie and treaſon in
Queene Maries time, as after more particularlie ſhal be ſhevved. And this vvas the firſt
chaunge of Religion in anie Archbiſhop of
Canterburie, from the beginning vnto his
daies.

Thomas Cran-
mer Ar-
chbiſ. of
Canter-
bury.

28.   So as from K. *Ethelbert,* the firſt Chriſt-
ned Engliſh King, vnto K *Henry* the 8. being
the 18. from *VVilliam* the *Conquerour,* & more
than 80. from the ſaid *Ethelbert,* one and the
ſelf ſame faith endured in England, and the
ſelf ſame Church floriſhed, vnder ſo manie
different both Kings and nations, as before
hath bin ſhewed. And the like vve haue declared to haue bin for the firſt 600. yeares
vnder the Britanes, to vvitt, that they neuer
are knovvne to haue chaunged their Religion. Which being ſo, the deduction and
demonſtration is ſo cleare, as anie reaſonable man can eyther make or require for

The cõ-
cluſion
of this
dedu-
ction.

proofe;

proofe, that one and the ſelf ſame religion endured from the beginning to the ending among them.

29. Vnto vvhich kind of proofe the auncient holie father & martyr *S. Irenæus,* giueth great authoritie by a like argument. For that hauing made the like enumeration of the Bishops of *Rome,* (as vve do novv of our Archbishoppes of Canterburie) againſt the heretiques of his daies, and that from *S. Peter* dovvnvvard to *Pope Eleutherius,* that liued with him : he inferreth this concluſion:

Iren. l. 3. aduerſus hereſ. cap. 3. *Eſt pleniſsima hæc oſtenſio, vnam & eandem viuificatricem fidem eſſe, quæ in Eccleſijs ab Apoſtolis & conſeruata & tradita in vnitate,&c.* This is a moſt full proofe, that one and the ſelf ſame liuelie
" faith, hath bin cōſerued in the Church from
" the Apoſtles daies vnto our time, deliuered
" from one to another in vnitie, &c. And if that vvere a moſt full proofe & demonſtration in *S. Irenæus* iudgement againſt the heretiques of his time: the ſame is novv much more to vs, hauing ſeene the ſucceſsion of ſo manie ages ſince, and noted the manner of like proofe and argument in all other fathers after him. As namelie of S. Auguſtine

*Aug. in pſal. contra partem Donati.
Aug. ep. 165.* *Numerate ſacerdotes vel ab ipſa Petri Sede, & in ordine illo Patrum, quis cui ſucceſsit videte.* Number the preiſts that haue ſucceded the one to the other euen from the ſeat of Peter himſelf. And then further. *In hoc ordine ſucceſsionis nullus Do-*

lus Donatista Episcopus inuenitur. No one Dona-
tift Bishopp is to be found in this ranck of
fuccefsion. And yet more.

30. *Et si in illum ordinem Episcoporum quisquam* *Aug.ibid*
traditor per illa tempora subrepsisset, nihil praiudica-
ret Ecclesia. And if anie traitor in thofe daies
fhould haue crept into that order and ranke
of Roman Bishops (for of them he fpeaketh) it fhould not haue preiudicated the
Church of God.

31. Which faying of *Saint Auften* may ferue
vs, not onlie to anfwere whatfoeuer heretiks do, or may obiect true or falfe againft
the liues of anie later Roman Bishops, but
for defence alfo of the ranke and fuccefsion
of our Archbishops of *Canterbury*, notwith- | Thomas
ftanding the Apoftafie of *Thomas Cranmer*, or | Crámer
anie other his like, that for thefe later yeares | his Apo-
may haue crept in (as *Saint Auften* faith) or | ftafie
byn thruft in, and by violence occupied that | doth not
Sea and feat vnworthilie, either in refpect | preiudi-
of his life, or religio, or both, feeing that the | cate the
former fuccefsion as vvell of men as of do- | Canter-
ctrine, from *Saint Auften* to *Cranmer*, is mani- | burie.
feft and euident for the fpace of 900. yeares
vvithout interruption, as alfo that they
vvere vnited all this time in faith and doctrine, with the vniuerfall Church of Chriftendome, as members & branches of their
head and bodie; and that the firft breach and
interruption made therof in that Sea by

Cranmer

Cranmer and continued after him by fome
of his followers, was noted prefentlie and
contradicted, yea cenfured and condemned
alfo by fentence of the whole Church, and
thervpon reiected & abhorred by the principall of his owne people, both cleargy and
laity at that time.

32.   And the fame contradiction endureth
to this day, and will do euer, in thofe that
conferue their auncient faith and religion,
and do adhere to the lawfull fuccefsion
of his predecefsors againft him and his partners, vntill it pleafe almightie God to put
the faid order & lawfull fuccefsion in ioynt
againe, and reftore that cheefe and head
conduct of our countrey to his former integritie, wherby the water of true Catholike
religion vvas vvont to be deryued to the
people of our land, & vvil be againe vvhen
Gods wrath for our finnes fhalbe pacified,
and his mercy induce him to permitt (as
often otherwife he hath done) that all returne to the accuftomed auncient courfe of
Catholike faith, and religion againe, feeing
in verie deed there is none but that; for fo
much as fects and new religions are but inuentions & entertayneméts of time, whilft
God punifheth fome finnes in his feruants,
and after all returneth where it was before.

33.   And this haue vve fpoken by the way,
and by occafion of *Cranmer* that was the firft
                                        Arch-

Archbishop of *Canterbury* that euer brake
from the Roman faith, but, notwithstanding his Apostasie, Catholike religion was
not extinguished in England by that, but
remained there still all *K. Henries* time, as also
during the raignes of his three Children
King, & Queenes, *Edvvard, Mary* & *Elizabeth*
vnto these our daies, as in the next chapter
following more largelie & particularlie we
are to demonstrate.

HOW CATHOLIKE RELIGION
HATH CONTINVED AND PERSEVE-
red in England during the times and raignes of
K. Henry *the* 8. *and his three Children,* K.
Edward, Q. Mary, *and* Q. Elizabeth *not-*
vvithstanding all the troubles, changes, alterations
and tribulations that haue fallen out, and that the
same religion is like to continue to the vvorldes
end, yf our synnes hinder it not.

CHAP. XII.

THE deduction which we haue hitherto
made of Catholike religion from our
first conuersion, vnder *Saint Gregory* and *K.*
Ethelbert of *Kent*, vnto the raigne of *K. Henry*
the 8. with whome concurred in the Sea of
Rome *Leo* 10. and *Clemens* 7. and other Popes
Successors of *Saint Gregory*, hath byn for the
most part in time of peace and without any
publike discontinuance at all, but now

Anno
Domini
600.
Anno
1509.

P 4   are

are we to profecute the fame matter from
the alteration made by K. *Henry* downward
vnto our daies, and therin to fhew, that albeit in the externall face and forme of Religion, there haue byn diuers mutations, as
tempeftuous winds and ftormes for the prefent, yet hath the Catholike religion held
firme her continuance throughout all thefe
tempefts, yea fhewed her felfe more cleare,
eminent and notorious by the confefsion of
her moft conftant members, then fhee did
before in peace, which is the proper priuiledg and excellency of truth, and of the
Cath. Church (that is the pillar of truth)
aboue all fects and herefies (as *Saint Cyprian*,
Saint Auften, and other fathers do note) to
come out of perfecution, as gold out of fire
more bright, illuftrious, and eminent then
before, or as an excellent fhipp well tackled
and fkilfullie guided, breaketh thorow the
waues without hurt at all.

2.   And this hath byn proued now by the
experience of 1600. yeares, wherin this fhip
of the Cath. Church hath paffed thorow
no fewer ftormes then there are yeares and
ouercome them all; vvheras many hundred
fects and fectaries in the meane fpace haue
byn broken in peeces, perished and confumed, eyther by diuifion among themfelues,
or with a little externe perfecution or difcipline of the Church, vvherof I fhall not
need

Ann.Do-
mino
1530.

1.Tim.3.
The
Cath.
faith
grovveth
by perfe-
cution
aud affli-
ction &
herefie
is ouer-
throuen.

need to alleadg manie examples, for that
the vvorld is full of them, and all hiſtories
do teſtifie, and our former deduction hath
made it cleere, & one domeſticall example
of our owne daies there is before our eyes,
vvhich may ſerue for all the reſt, to vvitt,
that ſome ſeueritie being begone by our
State againſt two oppoſite religions in England the Catholiks and Puritans, (though
much more rigorous againſt the former
then the ſecõd)yet hath Catholike religion
increaſed therby, and puritaniſme byn broken and in manner diſſolued. The reaſon of
vvhich different ſucceſſe vve ſhall touch
afterwards. Now to the purpoſe vve haue
in hand.

3. For the firſt 20. yeares of *K. Henryes*
raigne vnto the yeare of Chriſt 1530. no
man can denie, but that the integritie of
Catholike religion, vnion&cõmunion with
the reſt of Chriſtendome, & perfect ſubordination to the Sea Apoſtolike of Rome remained in England vvhole, as the ſaid King
had receaued it from the moſt prudent, religious, and victorious Prince his father *K.*
Henry the 7.& he againe from his renowned
anceſtors, whome yet *K. Henry* the 8. as he
did excell in knowledg of learning: ſo vvas
he nothing inferior to them in zeale of defending the puritie of Cath. faith, as may
appeare by the multitude of Sectaries and

here-

heretiks as vvell *VValdenſians, Arrians, Anabaptiſts, Lolhards* and *VVickliſſians,* as *Lutherans,
Zvvinglians; Caluiniſts,* and the like, burned by
him, for diſſenting from the vniuerſall
knowne Church and Roman religion in
the firſt ſaid 20. yeares of his raigne, vvhich
Fox ſetteth downe vvith great complaint
and regreett, & vve ſhall after declare more
at large in the ſecond and third parts of this
treatiſe.

4.　And when *Luther* afterward roſe vp, in
the 8. yeare of this glorious Kings raigne,
which was the yeare of Chriſt 1517. *K. Henry*
cauſed firſt the famous learned Biſhop *Iohn
Fiſher* of *Rocheſter* to cõfute the madd fellow,
& after he vouchſafed to do the ſame himſelfe by a moſt excellẽt booke, which I haue
read, and ſeene ſubſcribed vvith his owne
hand, vvith the dedication therof, by his
Embaſſador *D. Clarke* (after Biſhop of *Bath*
and *VVells*) vnto *Pope Leo* 10. ｛Who in gratifi-
cation therof, gaue his Maieſtie and all his
poſteritie, the moſt honorable ſtyle and title
of *Defender of the faith.*

K. Henr.
booke
againſt
Luther,
dedica-
ted to
Leo 10.
an. Dom.
1523.

5.　And thus continued *K. Henry* and the
religion vnder him in England, vntill the
forſaid yeare 1530. at vvhat time there happened a moſt fatall and vnfortunate contention betweene *Clement* 7. the Pope & him,
about his diuorce from *Q. Katherine.* He began firſt to ſhew his greete and diſpleaſure
against

The be-
ginning
of the K.
breach
vvith
the Pope

againſt *Cardinall VVolſey*, & ſecondlie againſt
the whole cleargy of England, condemning
the one & the other in the forfeature of *Præ-
murire*, vvho in their ſubmiſsion and ſuppli-
cation for pardon, either of feare or flattery
called him *ſupreme head* of their Church of
England.

Steve
an. Dom.
1530.

6.   The King alſo began to ſhew openlie
his diſguſt with the Pope for not yelding to
his pretence and petition : but vvhat ? vvas
the Kings Religion changed by this? or did
he alter his iudgment in faith for this diſaf-
fection towards the Pope? no truly, as well
appeareth by his other actions ; For he frequented the maſſe no leſſe then before , he
burned heretiks more then euer , as appeareth by Fox his accoumpt, and ſo yow ſhall
ſee in all the reſidue of his life , vvhich were
16. yeares after this. And albeit at this time
being much troubled with this breach with
the Pope, he attended leſſe to repreſſe hereſy for ſome yeares, then he had done before,
yet was his iudgment no leſſe againſt them
then from the beginning, and the longer he
liued, the more grew his auerſio from them,
as may eaſily appeare to him, that will but
looke ouer the yeares that enſued after this
diſguſt & breach with the *Pope Clement* the 7.
For albeit in the next yeare after , to vvitt
1531. he proceeded to ſhew his auerſion
from that Pope, yet did not he neglect the

*K. Hen-
ry vvin-
ked for
a time
at ſome
here-
tiks.*

punish-

punishment of Lutherans, as may appeare
by the burning of *Dauid Foſter*, *Valentine
Freeſe*, *Iohn Teukesbury* the old man of *Buckin-
gham* & other which Fox doth:cōplaine of.

7. In the yeare 1532. The King proceeding
in the ſame diſcontenment with the Pope,
did certaine things rather to terrifie him,
then to make anie change of Religion, as
making *Syr Thomas Audley* Chancelour in
the place of *Syr Thomas More*, which *Audley*
was ſuſpected, to fauour Lutheraniſme: in
vſing alſo familiarlie *Thomas Cromvvell* a man
of the ſame humor or worſe. To which end
alſo he going ouer into France, conferred
with *Francis* the French King, & perſuaded
him to ſummon the Pope to a Generall
councell, but he vvould not, vvhervpon
K. Henry returning into England, not onlie
ſpake open vvords againſt Pope *Clement*, but
ſuffered one *Doctor Cutvvyne*, Deane of *Hert-
fort*, to preach publikelie againſt him in a ſermon before the K. himſelfe, in the church of
the Franciſcan friars of *Greenvvich*, who paſſed ſo farre in that veyne, as a graue religious
Father named *Elſtovv*, reprehended him publikelie out of the quire or roodloft, for
which he vvas ſent to priſon. And this was
the firſt open cōtradiction, that *K. Henry* had
within his Realme about this controuerſie
with the Pope, and yet doth Fox recount
vnto vs diuers of his martyrs moſt oppoſite
to the

Thomas
Audley.

Thomas
Crom-
vvell.

F. El-
ſtovv
contra-
dicteth
the prea-
cher in
defence
of the
Pope be-
fore the
King.

to the Pope, that were burnt by the Kings
authoritie this yeare, as namelie : *Iames Bay-
nam, Robert Debnam, Nicolas Marish, Robert King,*
and others.

8. There followed the yeare 1533. wherin *Anno*
his Maiestie was married to *Q. Anne Bullen,* & *1533.*
consequentlie this yeare passed most in
triumph about Coronation of the said
Queene, as also the birth and baptisme of
her Maiestie that now is: so as little was
done in matters of Religion any way, but
a great gate seemed to be opened to the *Protestants* and to *Luthers* fauourers by this marriage, in so much that Fox doth assigne the
ground of his ghospell principallie from
this yeare in respect both of the Kings and
Queenes inclination, as he presumeth, and The be-
of the great authoritie of *Cranmer, Cromvvell,* ginning
and some other that he calleth his ghospel- of Fox
lers, or patrons rather of his ghospell. And his gho-
yet if you behould the externall face of the Englād.
English Church at this day, all these named
and others held the Cath. faith, vse & rites,
and both K. and Queene *Cranmer* and *Cromvvell* vvent as deuoutlie to Masse as euer before, and so remained they in outward shew
(I meane the former three) euen to their
deathes; And *Cromvvell* when he was to dy,
protested on the scaffold, that he vvas a
good Cath. man, and neuer doubted of anie
of the Church sacraments then vsed , & the
like

like would *Cranmer* haue done no doubt, if he had byn brought to the ſcaffold in *K.Henries* daies, as he vvas to the fire afterwards, in *Q. Maries*, vvhich had byn a happie caſe for him.

9.   There enſued the yeare 1534. vvhich vvas the yeare indeed of open breach vvith Rome, for that an excommunication being ſett forth by *Pope Clement* the 7. againſt *K. Henry* the 8. vpon notice giuen of his marriage, and the ſaid excommunication ſett vp in *Dunkerke* & other townes in Flanders, which did import the conſent alſo and concurrance of *Charles* the Emperour, and then certaine propheſies being blowne abroad at home, as comming from *Elizabeth Barton,* ſurnamed *the holy maid of Kent,* about the Kings depriuation; he was much more exaſperated then before, and ſo calling a Parlament cauſed the Popes authoritie to be vvholie extinguiſhed & transferred to himſelfe, & made diuers Biſhops in order to preach at Paules croſſe againſt the Popes ſupremacie ouer the Cath. Church. But what? may we think that theſe Biſhops did in ſo ſmall a time chaunge their beleefe in matters of faith? The King alſo being angry with diuers friars, as namelie with *F. Elſtovv* before named, that contraried *Cutvyne* the preacher, when he inueighed againſt the Popes authoritie, did this yeare vpon the 11. of

Auguſt

August ordaine, that all the obseruant friars *Ho. pag.* 964. of *Saint Francis* ordre should be thrust out of their conuents, beginning vvith *Greenvvich* where the said contradiction was made; & to seeme somwhat to fauour the *Augustine* friars, of whose order *Luther* had byn, he commaunded them for the present to be put in their places, yet did he at the very same time cause *Iohn Frith* to be burned in Smithfield, for denying the blessed Sacrament, & this by his owne particular order: vvhich *Frith* and his *M. Tyndall* vvere the greatest enemies that friars had. The Franciscan Friars put out of their conuéts.

10.   He burned also this yeare *Henry Poyle*, *VVilliam Tracy*, and other protestants, as Fox testifieth in his calendar: so as we may see that the kings faith was as before, & though he were content to suffer some newfangled spiritts to ruffle at this time, as namely *Friar Barnes* in London, where he preached most seditiouslie, and *Hugh Latimer* in *Bristovv*, where as *Stovv* saith he stirred a notorious tumult, causing the Maior to suffer lay-men to preach, and to prohibite and imprison Priests, & other like disorders, yet what the King thought inwardlie of them, he declared afterwards by his Acts, when he burned *Barnes* and cast *Latimer* into the Tower, and kept him there with euident danger of his life so long as himselfe liued, which disposition of *K. Henry*, *Tyndale* smelling at the Heretiks burned *an.* 1534. *Stovv. an.* 1534.

same

same seaſon, vvrote from Flanders to his ſcholler *Iohn Frith* priſoner in the Tower of London in theſe words: *And novv me thinketh I ſmell a counſell to be taken, &c. But yovv muſt vnderſtãd that it is not of a pure heart & the loue of truth, but to auenge themſelues, & to eat the vvhores fleſh, and to ſucke the marrovv of her bones, &c.*

Se the letter of Tindall to Frith ſet dovvne by Fox *pag.* 987.

So wrote that honeſt man, ſignifying that K. *Henry* vvas reſolued to make an outward ſhew in fauouring the ghoſpellers, not for loue, or liking he had of them, but to reuenge himſelfe of the Pope, and to enioy the goods of Monaſteries & other ſpirituall liuings, which he, in his blaſphemous hereticall veyne, calleth *the vvhores fleſh and marrovv of her bones.*

11.   Well then, this was the beginning of their ghoſpell in England, by their owne confeſsion and interpretation, and ſo whatſoeuer vvas done from this yeare forward againſt Catholiks or Cath. Religion, vnto the 31. yeare of his raigne, vvhich vvas of Chriſt 1540. to witt for 5. whole years, was vpon theſe grounds and to the former ends of reuenge & intereſt, yf we beleeue proteſtants themſelues; in which point notwithſtanding, for that diuers godly, learned and zealous men could not be contét to follow the kings affeƈtions, as other did, & namely B. *Fisher* of *Rocheſter*, *Syr Thomas More* late Chauncelor of England, and diuers moſt

Reuerend

Reuerend and venerable Abbots, Priors, &
Doctors, and other their like, they were
content to giue their bloud in defence of
Cath. vnitie againſt this ſchiſme, as the Abbots of *Glaſtenburie*, of *VVhaley*, of *Redding*, *Doctor Forreſt* Q. Catherines Confeſſor, *Doctor
Povvell*, and the like.

12.   Some others, and amongſt them one
moſt neere to the King himſelfe both in
bloud and affection, namely *Cardinall Pole*
oppoſed himſelfe by publike writing from
Padua, as vve may ſee by thoſe 3. learned
books left by him in Latin *de vnitate Eccleſia*.
Others alſo of the ſame blood Royall as the
Marqueſſe of *Exceſter* and Counteſſe of Saliſbury, the ſaid Cardinalls mother, ſhewed
their deslike, which afterwards vvas cauſe
of their ruine; And many ſhires alſo of the
Realme at this time, not being ſo patient as
to beare theſe innouations, tooke armes &
fell into great commotions, as in Lincolne-
ſhire, Yorkeshire, Somerſettſhire and ſome
other prouinces, making all their quarrells
for matters of Religion.

13.   So as by this we ſee, that Cath. Religion
remayned ſtill in England both in Prince
and people, but that the Prince for a time
thought good for other ends to tolerate and
winke at diſorders therin, vntill the forſaid
yeare of 1540. when calling all his Realme
togeather both ſpirituall and temporall to

Q   examine

examine vvell this matter of Religion, they decreed that famous Statute both in Pariament & confiftorie Ecclefiafticall, called the

The Statute of 6. Articles an. 1540.

Statute of 6. Articles, or as Iohn Fox nameth it, *the vvhipp vvith 6. ftrings or lashes,* in which decree are condemned for deteftable herefies, all the moft fubftantiall points of Proteftants doctrine, efpecially of Zwinglians and Caluinifts, and moft feuere punishment of death appointed vnto the defenders and maynteyners therof, vvherby the Cath. iudgment & cenfure of the whole Realme in that behalfe vvas feene, and the King himfelfe made further declaration therof prefentlie for his owne part, by putting away his Germane wife *Anne of Cleeue*, by vvhich the ghofpellers had thought to haue drawne him further into league and religion vvith the proteftant German Princes; & by punishinge Cromwell the head and fountaine of moft of thefe innouations by the loffe of his head. He burned alfo immediatlie after this Statute in Smithfield vpon the promulgation therof three famous heretiks, *Barnes, Ierome,* and *Gerard*; the firft an erneft Lutheran, the other two Zwinglians.

The burning of Friar Barnes a Lutheran, vvith Gerard, and Ierome Zvvinglians.

14. All thefe demonftrations I fay K. *Henry* made this yeare of his Cath. opinion and iudgment in all points, except in matter of fupremacy which was his owne intereft.

And

And for the other fix yeares vvhich he liued afterwards he varied not from this, but rather confirmed the fame, as we may fee by his burning of *Anne Askevv*, for denying the Reall prefence in the Sacrament, not many moneths before his death, and by his owne hearing of maffe in his bedd, and receauing the bleffed Sacrament on his knees vvhen he was not able to ftand on his feete ; but efpeciallie by that which *B. Gardiner* teftified vvhile he liued, and preached the fame in a publike fermon at Paules Croffe, that the faid King not long before his dying day, when he fent him Embaffador to a *Diete* in *Germany*, gaue him fpeciall comifsion in fe-crett, to procure by the meanes of fome Cath. Princes, and of the Popes legate and *Nuntio* there, fome honorable condition for his Maiefties reconciliation with the 'Pope and Sea of Rome againe, which though God of his fecrett iudgment permitted him not to effectuate by the fhortneffe of his life: Yet appeareth it by this what his fenfe in matters of religion was.

K. Henry gaue comifsion for his Reconciliation vvith Rome.

15. So then now we haue that Catholik Church & Religion remayned in England during *K. Henries* raigne, both in Prince and people, though much turmoiled by faction, fchifmes, and herefie, wherin, notwithftanding, fhe no more loft her poffefsion & continuance, then fhee did in time of the raging

Arrians, Donatifts or other fectaries that preuayled in power for the prefent time, either
generallie, or in fome particular prouinces,
as Lutherans and Zwinglians alfo did in
K. *Henries* daies in diuers places, or do at this
day, which yet was and is fo, as they are eafily diftinguished from the other, not onlie
by the diuifions and differences among
themfelues, but alfo for that the vnion of
the Cath. Religion doth euer fhew it felfe
in fome regions adioyninge: yea commonly
alfo euen in thofe verie places, where thefe
fects do range and beare moft rule, fome
Catholiks remayne to contradict them
openlie, & to plead for their old poffefsion;
and the more the perfecution is, the greater

Catho-
liks in-
creafed
by perfe-
cution.

and more eminent is this Cath. contradi-
cting part ftyrred vp, and increafed by the
very power & vertue of the croffe of Chrift
in perfecution, as before hath byn noted.

16.   And this vvas the ftate of Cath. Religion in K. *Henries* raigne, to witt, that it was
held and defended publikelie, except onlie
the Article of Ecclefiafticall fupremacie denied to the Pope, whervnto notwithftanding manie thoufands of the Realme neuer
agreed, and confequentlie vvere trulie Catholiks. Heretiks alfo were punished, efpeciallie thofe three fects that principally ran-
ged at that time, to witt, *Lutherans, Anabaptifts,*
and *Zvvinglians* (all three taking their origen
from

from *Luther*) ſo as of all theſe 3. ſeꜩs *K. Henry*
burned manie, and albeit of the 4. ſort of
men that oppoſed themſelues againſt him,
to vvitt Catholiks, he put diuers alſo to
death vnder the name of Papiſts; yet both
this very name, as alſo the different manner
of their deathes, but aboue all the nature of
their cauſe, doth euidently diſtinguiſh them
from the other, and ſhew that their deathes
were true martyrdomes, and the others due
puniſhment for their wickedneſſe.

17. For firſt the name of *Papiſts*, that ſigni-
fieth them to hold vvith the Pope, as ſupreame head of their Church, importeth no
more hurt or offence, then if in any ſedition
moued within anie Realme, thoſe that hold
with the King ſhould be called kinglings,
or thoſe for example, that hold part vvith
the Maior of *London*, vvhen anie apprentices
would raiſe rebellion againſt him, ſhould
ſcornfullie be called *Maioriſts*, and generallie
for a man to hold with his lawfull ſuperiour
cannot be termed a faꜩion, and much leſſe
an hereſie.

18. Secondlie the verie difference & manner of puniſhmēt vſed by *K. Henry* towards
both parts, the one by fire, the others by
head and hanging, doth euidentlie ſhew
vvhat different iudgment he made of them,
the one as of heretiks, and the other as of
men offending againſt his ſtate and perſon,

The name of *Papiſts* not iuſtly puˢ niſha-ble.

The dif-ferent puniſh-ments vpon Catho-liks and prote-ſtants doth ſhevr vvhat K. Henry thought of them both.

Q 3   after

after he had made the ſupremacie Eccleſiaſticall to be a matter of his State and of his
royall dignitie, wherby alſo he ſhewed that
he was no ghoſpeller.

19. But now for the third point, which is
the moſt important of all the reſt, to ſhew
the difference in theſe mens cauſes, and that
the Catholiks ſuffered innocentlie for their
conſcience, and conſequentlie were true
Martyrs, & that the other ſorts of Sectaries
were puniſhed deſeruedlie as malefactors,
it is not hard to proue to him, that is of anie
meane conſideration or indifferēcy in matters. For firſt who will not graunt, but that
he that is an honeſt & good man when he
goeth to bed (for example) cannot eaſily be
made an euill man in his ſleep, without anie
motion of his affection or freewill at all?
And againe: he that is a good & true ſubiect
towards his Prince and countrey this day,
how can he well to morrow be iudged a
traitor (the higheſt ſyn of all other) yf in the
meane ſpace he chaunge not his mind, nor
do any act of word or deed contrary to that
he did before; and yet this was the cauſe of
the Catholiks put to death vnder K. *Henry*
for the ſupremacie.

20. As for example *S. Thomas More* vvas
priſoner in the Tower of London vpon
* In his ſome diſpleaſure in the yeare 1534. where
Epiſtles. he attending onlie to his prayers (as * him-
ſeife

selfe teltifieth) and to the writing of some
spirituall books perteyning to the contempt
of this present transitorie world, there passed in the meane space a statute in the parliament house, appointing that whosoeuer did
not beleeue the Kings Maiestie to be supreme head of the Church of England, in
causes Ecclesiasticall, should be a traitor and
suffer death for it: which seming a new and
straunge thing vnto him, & contrarie to the
bleefe of all his forefathers, he could not so
soone conforme himselfe thervnto, & consequentlie refused (vvhen he vvas demaunded) to subscribe to the statute, and to make
so great a chaungemét in his faith vpon the
chaunge of others, for which soone after he
was put to death, not for that he had attempted, altered, or innouated anie thing as you
see, but for that he would not alter & make
innouation. And this vvas the propre true
cause of all Catholiks that suffered for the
supremacie vnder K. *Henry* the 8.

The true cause of Cathol. suffering vnder K. Henry.

20. But on the contrarie side, the others
that were put to death by him as sectaries,
did wickedlie and presumptuouslie alter &
innouate of their owne heads manie things
about beleefe and doctrine, different from
that which they had receyued, and contrary
to the beleefe of all their forefathers auncient Christians for manie ages togeather,
and that with such obstinacie, as no reason,

Q 4   autho-

authoritie, diſcipline or order, no wittneſſe, humane or diuiné could preuaile vvith them; & albeit for this obſtinacie, each ſect pretended ſcriptures for themſelues, yet the vertue and ſubſtance of ſcriptures conſiſting in their true meaning and interpretation therof, it was intolerable pride and inſolency in them, to arrogate to themſelues the ſaid true interpretation and expoſition before the whole Church of God, that went before them; & hereofenſued the iuſtneſſe of their punishment, which in Catholiks can haue no place, as before hath byn ſhewed, yet one example of each ſort of theſe men ſhall we heere alleage, therby better to declare the caſe.

21.   *K. Henry* during his raigne cauſed ſundrie ſorts of men to be put to death about matter of Religion as is notorious; and firſt certaine *Anabaptiſts* and new *Arrians,* namelie in the 27. and 30. yeares of his ſaid raigne. In the former of theſe two condemnations were 19. men and 6. women, as *Stovve* and others do relate, and in the ſecond were 3. men and one woman condemned. Theſe *Anabaptiſts* denied amongſt other points, that Children ought to be baptized before they come to yeares of diſcretion, & can actually beleeue : for defence of which doctrine, they ſtood reſolutelie vpon manie cleere places of ſcriptures as to them then ſemed: to witt:

The cō-
demna-
tion of
Anabap-
tiſts and
Arrians
by K.
Henry.

to witt: *Qui crediderit & baptizatus fuerit, saluus
erit. Marc.* 16. He that shall beleeue and be
baptized shalde saued: Lo (say they) it is ne
cessarie to beleeue as well as to be baptized;
which infants being not able to do, ought
not to receyue baptisme in their infancie.
Or if they do, they must be rebaptized
againe when they come to yeares of discretion. Thus reasoned they. And besides this
text, they and their cheefe maisters do alleage almost 30. places of scriptures more
vvhich seeme most plaine and euident to
them, as by their books that are extant appeareth.

*Absurd positiós of Ana*baptists & Arriäs in King Henries time grouded vpon scriptu*res pre*tended.

22. The like places they do alleage also for
that other absurd position of theirs ; *that no
magistrate may punish by death :* as for example
those vvords of God in *Exodus: Non occides:
Exod.* 20. Thow shalt not kill. And againe
the saying of our Sauiour: *Omnes qui acceperint
gladiū, gladio peribunt. Math.* 26. All that vse the
sword shall perish by the sword. Thus said
the Anabaptists, from which by no meanes
could they be drawne, but went willinglie to the fire for testimonie of their opinions. The *Arrians* also denying the equality
of God the Sonne to his Father, alleaged no
lesse variety of plaine places, as they would
haue them to seeme, namelie that of Christ
himselfe in *Saint Iohn* his ghospell, *Pater meus
maior me est.* my Father is greater then I. And
manie

Io. 14.

manie other, which were to long heere to
recite. And this of them, who burned to geather obftinatly in one fire in England.

23.   But what fhall we fay of the *Lutherans*,
do not they alleage plaine places alfo, both
againft vs and Caluinifts as themfelues
thinke? For againft Caluinifts in defence of
the reall prefence in the Sacrament, they
vrge the plaine words of Chrift as we do:
Hoc eft corpus meum : This is my body. And
againft vs , for their groffe opinion that the
fubftance of bread and wyne remaineth to
geather with the body of Chrift , they alleage manie places of Scripture where it is
called bread , which places the Zwinglians
accepting, do turne the fame againft the Lutherans, affirming that for fo much as it is fo

The có-
demna-
tion of
Lutheras
& *Zuuin-*
glians by
K. *Hen-*
ry.

oftetimes called bread in the Scripture, it is
not the true body of Chrift at all: & this paffed betweene friar *Barnes* & the two Apoftata Priefts *Gerard* & *Ierome* , burned with
him : the firft a feruent Lutheran, the other
two earneft Zwinglians, all three cófumed
by fire at one ftake in Smithfield by K. *Héries*
appointment, in the 32. yeare of his raigne.

24.   But now was there a third or 4. fort
of Sectaryes in K. *Henries* dayes , who were
neyther *Anabaptifts* , *Arrians* , nor yet perfect *Lutherans* or *Zwinglians*, but would haue
the controuerfie of the Bl. Sacrament and
reall prefence, to be an indifferent thing to
                                                      be

be beleeued, or not beleeued, as euery man should thinke best: so held *VVilliam Tyndall,* as also his scholler *Iohn Frith*, whom Iohn Fox doth compare to *Saint Paul* and *Timothy,* Frith being burned in Smithfield by the Kings expresse commandement in the 26. yeare of his raigne, and Tyndall not long after in Flanders by the saide Kings procurement, as more largelie we shall declare in the 3. part of this Treatise, when we come to examine Iohn Fox his Calender of Martyrs. Now it shalbe sufficient for proofe of that we say to alleage Fox himselfe, who setting downe the articles of *Frith* for which he was burned, assigneth this for the first. *First* (saith he) *the matter of the Sacrament is no necessary article of faith vnder paine of damnation, &c. But may be beleeued or not beleeued as euery man shal thinke best.* And for proofe therof alleageth diuers arguments out of scripture, that the fathers forsooth of the old testament, were saued by the same faith that we are, and yet were not bound to beleeue the Reall presence, &c. And Fox seemeth to like well both of this argument and of the heresie.

25. Now then here be 4. or 5. sorts of sectaries condemned by *K. Henry,* & all defending themselues by shew of scriptures, but for that each of them doth reserue the interpretation of scripture to themselues, & therby teacheth new doctrine, contrarie to that
which

The opinion of *Tyndall* & *Frith* agreeing vvith nether Lutherans nor Zvvinglians.

Fox pag. 942.

which was receiued generally in the know-
en Church before them, to whofe iudgment & interpretation they vvill not yeld
themfelues: hereof it followed, that the in-
ditement of herefie lyeth trulie and iuftlie
againft them, & that they vvere vvorthilie
condemned and burned for this pride, felfe-
will and obitinacy. But on the contrarie fide
againft the Catholiks, that died for the Ecclefiafticall fupremacie of the Pope, none of
thefe accufations can iuftly be laid, for that
they do neither ftâd vpon their owne iudgment, nor haue inuented any thing of new,
nor do adhere to their owne interpretatiôs,
or expofition of fcriptures, but being accufed, do make their plea and defence farre
otherwife, to witt, that they found this doctrine of the Popes fupremacie in vfe & practife before they were borne, as a thing receiued from age to age by the knoune Cath.
Church time out of mind: that they fee all
Chriftian kingdomes and princes to haue
imbraced the fame, and Generall councells
to haue allowed therof: that the texts and
examples of fcripture alleaged for the
proofe of this article, and all others wheron
they ftand, are not inuétions of their owne,
but fo expounded by auncient fathers and
vniforme confent of the Cath. Church; that
all our Chriftian English Kings from our
firft conuerfion vnto *K. Henry* the 8. acknowledged

The dif-
ferent
plea or
defence
of Ca-
tholiks
from he-
retiks.

ledged this fpirituall authoritie of the *B.*
of *Rome*; and *K. Henry* himfelfe defended the
fame moft earneftly with his owne pen, not
many yeares before, againft Luther and Lutherans: that it is not a thing deuifed but deliuered, as *Tertullian* faid, of the Cath. faith; *Tertull.*
and therfore if anie point therof were to be *l. de præs*
altered, it muft be done by the fame autho- *fcript.*
ritie that it vvas deliuered to them, to vvitt *aduerfus*
by the vvhole Church, Councells, and ge- *hæref.*
nerall Paftors therof.

26.   This vvas the defence and pleading
of Catholiks vnder *K. Henry* the 8. to excufe
themfelues from Treafon, obiected againft
them, for holding the Popes Supremacie;
vvherin yow fee diuers notorious differences betweene the defence of the fectaries, &
them, for that amongft the Sectaries, euery
one held vvhat himfelfe thought beft, of
things inuented by themfelues, euery one
cited fcriptures, and interpreted them as he
lifted, vvithout authoritie, prefident or example of former ages, and confequentlie
they are iuftlie called heretiks, that is to fay
choofers. For that they chofe to themfelues
what to beleeue in euery fect, and reduced
the laft and finall refolution of all things to
their owne vvills and vvitts, which in matters of beleefe is the higheft crime that
againft God and his Church canne be committed.

27. But

27.   But on the other ſide the ſtate & condition of the Catholikes, and their cauſe is
quite oppoſite to this, for that they ſticke to
authoritie, obedience, integrity, example of
their anceſtors; they bring nothing of their
owne; they inuent or innouate nothing:
they ſtand only vpon that which they haue
found eſtabliſhed to them, not by this or
that man, or by this or that author of any
ſect, or by this or that particular congregation, fellowſhip, or faction, or by this or that
towne, citty, prouince, kingdome, or countrey, but generally by the whole vniuerſall
Church and Paſtors therof, & therfore properly and truly are called *Catholiks*, which
is to ſay *vniuerſall* and *generall.*

28.   And this ſhall ſuffice to ſhew the difference betweene the Catholike Martyrs, &
hereticall malefactors put to death in K. *Hen-*
ries time, wherof yet we ſhall treat more largely in the third part of this Treatiſe, where
we are to handle the particular ſtories of
Fox his Calendar-martyrs, & to compare &
paragon them with ours, ſhewing that yet
neuer doggs & catts, nor yet Sampſons foxes
did euer ſo diſagree in natures & conditiõs,
as theſe good Martyrs did in faction & contrariety of opinions amongſt the mſelues, &
conſequently could not be Martyrs or wittneſſes of any one faith whatſoeuer.

29.   And with this alſo will we end the
discourſe

**The diſ-
agremẽt
of Fox
his ca-
calendar
Martirs.**

difcourfe of *K. Henries* life, hauing fufficiently fhewed (as to me it feemeth) that the
Cath. Religion held her footing and continuance alfo vnder the raigne of this King,
no lefle perhaps then before, yea fhe fhewed
her felfe much more to the world; by the
perfecution which then fhe fuffered, then
before in the time of peace ; for that the famous and illuftrious Martyrdomes of fuch
excellét men as were *B. Fisher, S. Thomas More,
D. Forest* and many other fuch worthies, that
fuffered Martyrdome in thofe dayes, did
more illuftrate her, & made externe nations
to talke more of the zeale and Conftancy of
Englifh Cath., then euer they would haue
done if that perfecutió had not fallen out; &
the like fucceffe hath happened fince both
vnder *K. Edvvard* the 6. and her Maiefty that
now is, as briefely we fhall heere declare.

30.   And as for *K. Edvvards* raigne, as it was
but fhort, and the firft paffage from Cath.
Religion to open profefsion of herefie: fo
was it not fo fharp for effufion of bloud as
vnder *K. Henry* : For that the K. being verie
young, and thofe that gouerned in his name
not thorowlie fetled in their States and
affaires, troubled alfo with much diuifion
and emulation among themfelues, could
not attend to profecute matters fo exactlie
againft Catholiks, as fome of their defires
and appetites were ; yet began they meet-
lie

K. Ed-
vvard
the 6. his
raigne.

tlie vvell, as vve may ſe by the moſt vniuſt perſecutions and depriuations of two principall Biſhops, *Gardener* of *VVincheſter*, and *Bonner* of *London*, by ſuch violent calumnious manner as vvas propre to heretiks to vſe. The particulars wherof Iohn Fox doth ſett downe at large, vvherby a man may take a taſt vvhat they meant to haue done, if they had had time. For that *Cranmer* & *Ridley* that had byn Biſhops in K. *Henries* time, and followed his religion and humor while he liued, being now alſo reſolued to enioy the preferment and ſenſualitie of this time, ſo farre as anie vvay they might attaine vnto, getting authoritie into their hands by the Protector and others that were in moſt povver, began to lay luſtilie about them, and to pull downe all them both of the cleargy and others, whome they thought to be able or likelie to ſtand in their way, or reſiſt their inuentions.

The attempts of *Cranmer* and *Ridley* & others of their crevv in K. Edvvards daies.

31.   And herevpon diuers were laid hands on and impriſoned, diuers fled ouer ſeas, ſundrie moſt captious & calumnious queſtions & demaunds were deuiſed to intangle men : as namelie: *VVhether a King of one yeare old, vvere not as truly a King as at* 40. *or* 50. which if you did graunt concerning the title and right of his crowne (which is true) then preſently they inferred, that K.*Edvvard,* being but 9. yeares old, vvanting yet diſcretion

cretion might alfo be lawfull head of the
Church, & determine controuerfies of Religion, yea chaunge the faith and religion
which his father & all his aunceftors Kings
and Princes of England, all Parlaments, Synods, and Councells before his dayes had
left vnto him for the fpace of a thoufand
yeares and more. And albeit he had not fufficient iudgment to vnderftand what Religion meant, yet was he made iudge therof
by vertue of his birth and fuccefsion to the
crowne. And this point was wonderfully
vrged by the Protector *Seymer*, to all Preachers, Prelats, and Bifhops of that tyme, that
they fhould inculcate the fame to the people
in their fermons, to the end that himfelfe
taking all the faid child Kings authority
vpon him, might be head and iudge in his
place: wherynto that he might feeme the
more fitt and able for his excellent learning,
Iohn Bale the Apoftata friar that liued vnder
him, was not afhamed to publifh in print, &
place him for a learned author amongft his
illuftrious Britifh wryters, for that fome
proclimations perhaps paffed by his hands,
though otherwife he was knowne to be fo
vnlearned, as he could fkarce write or read.
32. But yet (as I faid) this doctrine or rather paradox, of the Child-kings fuperemi-
nent hability, high authority and fupreme
Ecclefiafticall power to determine, alter,

The at-
tempts
of *Sey-
mer* the
Prote-
ctor, &
Iohn
Bale in
flattery
tovvards
him.

*Bal. de
fcript.
Brit.
cent.* 5.
fol. 237.

chaunge

chaunge & diſpoſe of matters of religion at
his pleaſure, though he were but of one
yeare old, was founded in pulpitts euery
where at this tyme; wherof *Syr Iohn Cheke*
the Kings ſchoolemaiſter amongſt others
wrote a ſeuerall Treatiſe, beſides the large
meſſage ſent in the Kings name (but of his
writing) to the Catholike people of Deuonſhire, as after ſhal be ſhewed. The ſame alſo
was obiected greeuouſly againſt Biſhoppe
Gardner and *B. Bonner* by name, that they had
not in their ſermons appointed vnto them
by the Protector, ſo ſufficiently vrged this
point of the Kings Eccleſiaſticall power in
his nonage, as was required. And this eſpecially for that the people in diuers parts of
the realme, & namely thoſe of Deuonſhire,
ſeeing ſuch alteratiō to be made in religion
vnder the minority of a child, quite contrary to the lawes & Statutes left by *K. Henry*
the 8. and that all things went backward
both at home and abroad (the townes we
had in France being loſt, or vpon the point
of leeſing) they complayned firſt, and after
tooke armes for defence of their auncient
religion, in the beginning of the third yeare
of this Kings raigne, the people of *Somerſetſhire* and *Lincolnſhire* beginning firſt in the
moneth of may; and then in Iuly the people
of *Eſſex, Kent, Suffolke, Norfolke, Cornvvall,* and
Deuonſhire, and in Auguſt thoſe alſo of *Yor-
keſhire,*

See Stou
& other
Chroni-
clers in
the yeare
1549.

keshire, all crying and demaunding to haue
the Cath. Religion remayne at it was left
by *King Henry*, at leaft-wife vntill *K. Edvvard*
came to lawfull age, therby to be able to determine and iudge of matters of Religion,
which demaund did wounderfully trouble
and vex the *L. Seymer* Protector and other
new ghofpellers, who being hungry after
Catholiks goods, could abyde no delay in
making this defired innouation.

33.   And albeit before thefe infurrections
fell out, they did well fee by diuers their attempts, that the hart of the people was
wholly againft thofe their innouations in
Religion, as appeareth plainly by a fpeech
of the *L. Rich* then Chauncelor, to the She-
rifes and Iuftices of peace of all fhires, gathered togeather in London in the yeare
1548. being the fecond of *K. Edvvards* raigne,
as at large you may fee in Fox: yet fuch was
their importunity in this behalfe, as they
would needs go forward, which thing plea-
fing *Iohn Fox* well he wryteth thus: *By this
yovv may fee vvhat zealous care vvas in this young
King, and in the L. Protector his vncle, concerning
the reformation of Chrifts Church.*

*The ge-
nerall
auerfion
of En-
glifh
people
againft
the en-
trance
of here-
fie.*
*Fox pag.
1185.*

*Fox ibid,
1186.*

34.   The fame Fox alfo fetteth downe in
another place what the young King aun-
fwered to the *Devonshire* men, that defired
that the ftate of matters in Religion, might
remayne as *K. Henry* had ordeyned and left
them,

them; and in particular they required that
the Statute of 6. articles againſt heretiks
might ſtand in force vntill K. *Edvvard* came
to full age. Whervnto let vs heare his aunſwere, & cõſider therby how matters went
in thoſe dayes. To the firſt about the Statute
of 6. articles made by his father, and inuio-
lably kept all dayes of his life, the little child
aunſwered thus: *Knovv yovv vvhat yovv require?*

Fox pag. 1189.

They vvere lavves made, but quicklie repented, to
bloudy vvere they to be borne of our people: yovv knovv
they helped vs to extend rigour, & to dravv our ſvvord
very often, yea they vvere as a vvhetſtone vnto our
ſvvord; and for your cauſes haue vve left to vſe them,
and ſith our mercy mooued vs to vvryte our lavves
vvith milke, hovv be yovv blinded to aske them in
bloud, &c.

35.   And then further he ſaith: *But to leaue*
this manner of reaſoning vvith yovv, vve lett yovv
vvitt, that the ſame lavves haue byn annulled by our
Parlament vvith great reioyce of our ſubiects, and not
novv to be called by our ſubiects in queſtion. Dare any
of yovv ſtand againſt an Act of Parlament, &c. Aſſure
yovv moſt ſurely, that vve of no earthly thing make
ſuch accoumpt, as to haue our lavves obeyed, for heer-
in reſteth our honor. And ſhall any of yovv dare to
breath againſt our honour? &c. Lo how little accoumpt this little King Child was taught to
make of his old fathers lawes; and how
thunderingly to ſpeake for the maintenance
of his owne! But vvhen they came to the
ſecond

K. Hen-
ries la-
vves re-
iected
by his
ſonne
K. Ed-
vvard.

second point about his nonage, he is yet more refolute. For thus he wryteth.

35. In the end of your requeft (faith he) ,, yow would haue our fathers lawes ftand in ,, force vntill our full age. But to this we ,, thinke, yf ye knew what ye fpake, yow ,, would neuer haue vttered that motion, nor ,, euer haue giuen breath to fuch a thought. ,, For what thinke yow of our kingdome? Be ,, we of leffe authority for our age? yow muft K. Ed-firft know that as a King we haue no diffe- vvards rence of yeares nor tyme, but as a naturall reply to man and creature of God, we haue youth, the de-maund and by his fufferance fhall haue age. We are of the your rightfull King, your liege Lord, your people King annointed, your King crowned, the of De-uo͠ſhire. Soueraigne K. of England, not by our age but by Gods ordinance. We poffeffe our ,, crowne not by yeares, but by the bloud and ,, difcent from our Father K. *Henry* the 8. &c. ,,

36. All this and much more, did they make the innocent young King to talke & wryte in defence of their innouations, who had more intereft therin then he. And as for the Cath. people, albeit they denyed not, but that he was a true King in his minority of age, yet no man was fo foolish as to thinke (notwithftanding all thefe preachings to the contrary) but that it was a different thing for matters of Religion to be altered now in his name, then afterward by him-

ſelfe vvhen he ſhould come to age.

37.   But among all others, none vrged this argument ſo much, nor with ſuch authority, as the Kings eldeſt Syſter the Princeſſe *Lady Mary* heyre apparant to the crowne, who being a zealous Catholike, and yet wiſhing well alſo to the Protector, did by ſundry letters, to be ſeene in Fox, admonish both him and the reſt of the Councell, that they ſhould looke well what they did, during the Kings minority, in altering the will, lawes, and ordinances of his and her father K. *Henry;* for that afterward they were like inough to be called to accoumpt about the ſame, when the King her brother ſhould come to full yeares. Moreouer ſhe admoniſhed them, that they had no authority to make ſuch alteration in ſo great matters as they did, but ought rather to cōſerue things in the ſtate left vnto them by K. *Henry* her father, according as by ſollemne oath they had ſworne vnto him before his death that they would do, (but eſpecially about matters of religion) vntill the K. her brother came vnto lawfull age.

Queene Maryes admoniſtion vnto the Protector and theCouncell.

38.   By all which is cleerly ſeene, how the Cath. Religion remayned in England moſt ſubſtantially rooted in K. *Edvvards* dayes, and that hereſie entred only from the teeth outward, and was maintayned by violence of temporall authority, and according to that

Hereſie in K. Ed. daies entred by violēce.

was

was the fucceffe. For after many toyles and
tormoyles one killing another of thofe that
gouerned, when they had thought they had
laied a fure platforme to continue the fame,
by excluding the *Lady Mary* & *Lady Elizabeth*,
and thrufting in *Iane* the Duke of Suffolks
daughter after K. *Edvvards* death, and had fo
plotted & fortified that defignment, as they
thought it fure ; the only zeale of the common Cath. people, for recouering the vfe of
Cath. Religion againe, ouerthrew all, and
placed Q. *Mary*, as is notorious to the world.
And afterward yf we confider the end of
moft of them, which in thofe dayes being
Councelors, for ambition or other refpects
were promotors of herefie, as *Dudley, Pen-*
brooke, VVinchefter, Arundell, Shreusbury , Pagett,
and other, they all died Catholikely, and
moft of them in this Queenes dayes, when
with much fauour of the ftate, they might
haue fhewed them felues heretiks.

39.   And thus much for the raigne of K. *Ed-*
vvard: after whome Q. *Mary* fucceeding, reftored Cath. Religion to her feat and auncient poffeffion againe, which hauing endured only fiue yeares, it pleafed God to
giue another triall and probation to his feruants, by a new alteration, in the beginning
of her Maiefties raigne that now is : but yet
not fo forfaking them, nor their caufe, but
he left fufficient teftimony in our realme at

Catho-
like Re-
ligion
reftored
by Q.
Mary.

R 4   that

that time , what Religion had borne rule
vnto that day, & how & when the chaunge
began. For firſt ot all the Bishops and cheefe
Prelats of the realme not only refiſted this
mutation, but moſt of them ſuffered impri-
ſonment or banishment for the ſame, as
*London, VVincheſter, Durham, Carleele, VVorceſter,
Lichfield, Ely, Lincolne, Peterborovv, Aſſaph, Cheſter*, though ſome few other were not at firſt
put in priſon, but deteyned only in cuſtody
& depriued, as *Yorke, Exceſter, Bath and VVells.*
I will omitt other principal men, as Deanes
and Archdeacons of Churches, as *Doctor Cole*
of *London*, D. *Stevvard* of *VVincheſter*, D. *Robinſon*
of *Durham*, D. *Setland* of *VVorceſter*, D. *Rambridg*
of *Lichfield*, D. *Iohn Harpesfield* of *Norvvich*, D.
Ioliffe of *Briſtovv*, D. *Boxall* of *VVindſore*, D. *Nicolas Harpesfield* of *Canterbury*, D. *Dracott* of *Yorke*,
D. *Peter* of *Buchingam*, D. *Chedſey* of *Middleſex*,
and many others , which were ouerlong to
rehearce all. I omitt alſo D. *Fecknam* Abbot
of *VVeſtminſter*, & the 2. learned *Priors* of the
Carthuſians , *Chaſey* and *VVillſon*, and many
others religious men that left their liuings
and the realme, not to be forced to yeld to
this chaunge. Which multitude of learned
wittneſſes (not to ſpeake of infinite others of
leſſer degree) being the cheefe throughout
all ſhires of England where they dwelt, did
well ſhew by their conſtant profeſſion vnto
their dying dayes, what roote and foundation

Bishops & Archdeacons depriued and imprisoned for Cath. faith an. 1960.

tion Cath. Religion had in England at that time, & hath yet, I doubt not, as after shalbe shewed.

40.   And albeit in these 40. yeares and more, that haue endured since the beginning of this chaunge, the temporall state of our realme hath for our sinnes byn opposite & enemy to this Religion, with full intent to extirpate and extinguish the same, yet such is the euerlasting force of truth, & so faithfull is the holy prouidence of almighty God for defence therof, in times of most need & pressure; that the Cath. faith and profession therof, hath neuer byn more eminent and illustrious in England, then in this time of so greeuous affliction, there hauing byn aboue a hundred Priests (not to speake of others of other degree) that haue made profession therof at the barres and benches of most of all the Tribunalls and iudgment seats of England, and haue sealed also their confession with most willing offering of their bloud.

The constancy of English Catholiks in this time of persecution.

41.   And in deede that which is most rare & worthy noting in this affaire, is that most of them were borne and bread in England during the time of her Maiesties raigne, and were brought vp in the Religion that now is professed within the realme, diuers of them also had studied at the vniuersities of *Oxford* and *Cambridge*, where they had heard

R 5   the

the aduerſe part alleage for them ſelues
what they could, and them ſelues had read
& examined with no ſmall diligence, what
grounds the Proteſtants had for their opinions; which being done, they went ouer
the ſeas to heare and ſee the Catholike party, and ſo to reſolue them ſelues more ſubſtantially in ſuch matters, as neereſt concer-
ned their eternall ſaluation : wherin being
ſoundly ſatisfied in all their doubts, they
paſſed further and became Prieſts, and ſo returned into England againe, to impart to
others the hidden Treaſure of truth which
themſelues had found out. And albeit diuers
of them were of that kinred and parentage,
& ſo qualified alſo in them ſelues, that they
might haue liued both wealthfully and at
their eaſe, yf they would haue followed the
world and preſent courſe of times: yet made
they choiſe, rather to fall into manifold dau-
gers, impriſonments and death it ſelfe, then
to forſake the truth of Cath. Religion, or
forbeare to cōmunicate the ſame to others;
which is another manner of ground and
foundation for their conſtancy, then *Iohn Fox*
recounteth in many of his Martyrs, who
vpon toyes became proteſtants, & of meere
ignorance and obſtinacy went to the fire for
the ſame, as namely *Ioane Lashford* a married
maid (as he ſaith) of 20. yeares old, that
tooke auerſion from the maſſe when ſhe

The cō-
ſtant re-
ſolution
of diuers
Cath.
Prieſts.

Ioane
Lash-
ford.

was but a 11. yeares old, (vpon very good
grounds yow muſt imagine in thoſe yeares
of her age)as alſo *Agnes Potten* & *Ioane Trunch-*
field the wiues of a beerebrewer & ſhouma-
ker of *Ipſvvich*,reſolued to go to the fire vpon
a certaine viſion,that one *Samuell* a miniſter
told them that he had in the priſon with
them. And vpon the ſame ground it ſeemeth
another wench called *Roſe Nottingam*,imbra-
ced the ſaid Miniſter and kiſſed him in the
ſtreet as he went towards burning.

42.   *Andrevv Hevvit* in like manner an apprentice of London of 19. yeares old,deter-
mined to dy with *Iohn Frith* then in the Tower of London, for the opinions that he
would dy for, though yet he did not know
what his opinions were. *VVilliam Hunter* alſo another apprentice of London & of the
ſame age of 19. yeares, running away from
his Maiſter in London, and finding an old
Engliſh Bible lying in the Chappell of
Burntvvood,fell to reading therof,and therby
preſently became a Proteſtant in diuers
opinions, and would needs burne for the
ſame. *Ravvling VVhite* likewiſe is recounted
by Fox to haue byn an old poore Fiſher
man in Wales, and hearing of certaine new
freſh doctrine to be had out of the ſcriptures
in Engliſh, and greeued that himſelfe was
not able to read them, he put his little boy
to ſchoole to learne to read, which being

Fox pag.
1547. &
1517.
Agnes
Potten.
Ioane
Trunch-
field.

Roſe
Nottin-
gam.
Fox pag.
1547.

VVilliã
Hunter.

Fox pag.
1395.an.
Domini
1555.
Ravv-
ling
VVhite.

omwhat

ſomwhat inſtructed in that art, he cauſed
him to read ſcriptures vnto him, and profited ſo much therin with in a little time, that
the old fiſher man began to be a preacher, &
ſo leauing his occupation, went vp and
downe Wales with his boy after him bearing the Bible, out of which he tooke vpon
him to preach at euery towne and tauerne
therof, ſeeking therby to peruert ſuch as
were no wiſer then himſelfe, nor could he
be reſtrained from his willfull folly, vntill
the Biſhopp of *Cardiffe* apprehended him,
whome afterward alſo he was forced to
burne, for that he ſtood obſtinate in his
phantaſticall opinions, which were ſuch, as
ſkarce they agreed with any ſect whatſoeuer. And finally *Laurence Sanders*, a famous
ſcarlet Martyr of theirs, being a marryed
Prieſt, & ſeing a little baſtard of his, brought
to him in priſon by the woman that bare it,
he was ſo tenderly affected thervnto, as in
great vehemency of ſpiritt he ſaid to the
ſtanders by: what man of my vocation
would not die to make this little boy legiti-
mate & proue his mother to be no whore?

43. And of this I might giue infinite examples out of Iohn Fox, what ſubſtantiall
grounds and motiues many of his Martyrs
had to runne to the fire, or rather how without all ground or probable reaſon in the
world, but only willfull pride & obſtinacy,

Fox pag. 1414.

Fox pag. 1558.

moſt of them thruſt themſelues to death, no
leſſe then in old times did the *Maſſilians, Mon-*
taniſts, Circumcellians & *Martyriãs* moſt famous
heretiks vpon the like madneſſe, as after we
are to ſhew more at large in the third * part,
where I am to treate of theſe matters more
particularly, and to giue yow (yf I be not
deceiued) large matters of laughter or rather
of compaſsion in this behalfe. Now this
ſhalbe ſufficiét to ſhew both the great number and reſpeɛtiue qualitie of domeſticall
wittneſſes for the Cath. faith, and continuance therof in our countrey during the
time of this ſharp perſecution vnder her
Maieſtie, and that neuer more then in this
time, hath the Cath. Church byn perſpi-
cuous, honorable & eminent in our realme:
which is altogeather cōtrary to that which
Iohn Fox aſcribeth to his Church, whoſe
inuiſibility, obſcurity and lurking from the
eyes of men, he both graunteth & excuſeth,
by the preſence of perſecution againſt her.
Wheras we hold on the other ſide, that the
true Church (and conſequently ours) is euer
more viſible & notoriouſly knowne in time
of affliɛtion and perſecution, then in peace.

44. And ſo haue we ſhewed by example
of our English Church, eſpecially in this
preſent age, wherin not only domeſticall
ſufferings at home haue cóme by fame,
books, & writings to the knowledge of forrayne

Hereti-
call ha-
ſtines to
burne
for their
errors.
* *Cap. 1.*

rayne nations, and therby alſo the notice of ſo many & worthy conſtant Catholiks that are within the realme; but whole troopes alſo both of Engliſh men and women in exile for their conſciences, do repreſent the ſame dayly to their eyes, as it were by a liuely ſpectacle, to the wonder of the Chriſtian world. But aboue all the reſt muſt they needs be greatly moued with the ſight of whole companies, families, and communities of Engliſh of both ſexes, of tender age, and thoſe for the moſt part of very principal good birth and parentage, that haue come forth of our countrey for the loue of Religion, & liued with great edification in other nations, partly in Colledges & Seminaries, partly in religious couents & Monaſteries, yelding great admiration to ſtraungers for their rare vertues of piety, patience, contentment and deuotion. And as for Colledges & Seminaries thoſe of *S. Omers* and *Dovvay* in *Flaunders*, of *Rhemes* in *France*, of *Rome* in *Italy*, of *Valliadolid, Siuill* and *S. Lucars* in *Spayne*, and of *Lisbone* in *Portugall*, do ſufficiently teſtifie. And as for Monaſteries both of men and Women, they are not vnknowne, as that venerable company of Engliſh *Carthuſians* in *Mechlyn:* The honorable religious houſes of Engliſh noble and gentlewomen in *Bruxells, Lovan* and *Lisbone*, whoſe rare vertues doe ſingularly edifie all thoſe that know them, and

A great number of Engliſh youthes in exile for religion.

and greatly illuſtrate the name of our countrey for religious piety with forraine nations. All theſe (I ſay) do beare wittneſſe at
this day to the whole world, and to vs alſo,
that, God be thanked, the fire & feruour of
Catholike Religion, which Chriſt came to
plant vpon earth, is not extinguiſhed by ſo
long and greuous perſecution in our countrey, but rather increaſed at leaſt in inten-
ſion, as philoſophers do ſpeake, though not
in extenſion.

45. And truly when I conſider the matter
more ſeriouſly with my ſelfe, I doubt much
whether England, if it had continued Catholike, had euer enioyed ſuch excellent
education for their youthe at home', as by
occaſion of this tribulation God hath giuen
them abroad in forraine nations; certainly
the example is rare & neuer heard of in former times, & at this day the like is ſeene in
few other nations beſides vs, but in none of
thoſe that haue ſuffered for Catholike Religion, is this bleſſing found ſo abundantly as
in ours; God make vs gratefull for it: For if
our ingratitude turne not the courſe of his
merɔyes, hitherto vſed towards vs, it ſeemeth euident, that he will not ſuffer the
ſeed of Cath. Religion to be extinguiſhed
in England, hauing conſerued the ſame ſo
potently & ſtraungely vnto this day, which
is from the firſt preaching of the Apoſtles &
Apoſto-

*The cõ-
cluſion
of the
firſt part
of this
treatiſe.*

Apoftolike men to the Brittans, vnto the
time of *Pope Gregory* the firft, vnder whome
our English nation was conuerted, as hath
byn declared, & from thence againe downwards vnto vs, which is more then a thoufand yeares: And fo I doubt not but he will
to the worlds end, yf our finnes deferue not
the contrary. And this fhall ferue for this
firft part, conteyning the deduction & continuance of Cath. Religion in England
without interruption, for more then fiftene
hundred yeares togeather: Now will we
paffe to the fecod part, to examine the fame
fuccefsion in proteftants religion throughout all thefe ages, yf it may be found, making our conclufion as after yow fhall fee,
that as our Religion entred firft and hath
neuer left England vnto this houre: fo the
Religion of Iohn Fox, in the forme that he
would haue it, was neuer yet admitted into
Eugland publikely by any Prince, or poten-
tate whatfoeuer vntill this prefent day, nor
euer like to be. And this fhall ferue for the
firft part of our Treatife.

The end of the firft part.

THE

THE
SECOND
PART
OF THIS
TREATISE.

THE
SECOND PART
OF THIS
TREATISE,

CONTEYNINGE THE

SEARCH OF THE PROTE-
STANTES CHVRCH,

from the beginning of Christendome, to our dayes.

THE ARGVMENT.

A V I N G *declared in the former part of this treatise, hovv the faith of Christ vvas first preached to the Britans at tvvo seuerall times, and then to the English nation & all by Roman preachers, and that the said faith hath continued from age to age in a visible conspicuous Church vntill our dayes: there remaineth novv, that vve examine in this second part, vvhere the protestants Church vvas in all this time, and vvhether they had any at all? and if they had, of vvhat sort of men it consisted, and vvhether it vvere the same vvith the Church before described, or partly the same, partly differēt, or vvhether they could stand togeather being opposite in any one point of faith? moreouer, vvhether the one did persecute the other, or might be reconciled, or agreed togeather? And finally,*

S 2   *vvhat*

*vvhat is the ſtate of the one and the other at this day.
For examination of vvhich points, vve ſhall haue occaſion to runne ouer againe vvith more aduiſe all the
former ſixteene ages from Chriſt dovvnvvard, and
therin to ſee and conſider, vvbat Church floriſhed or
preuayled throughout euery age, eyther oures, or that
of Iohn Fox? And vvhich of them is likeſt to haue come
dovvne from the Apoſtles: as alſo, vvhether that
Church vvhich vvas viſibly founded by the Apoſtles, &
put on foote by them and theirs, could periſh or vaniſh
avvay to giue place to another. And theſe are the principall points of this ſecond part diſcuſſed in the Chapters follovving; though firſt, before vve enter into this
examination, vve haue thought good to treat certayne
generall points, that make vvay thervnto, as by the
next Chapter yovv ſhall preceiue.*

OF HOW GREAT IMPOR-
TANCE ECCLESIASTICALL SVCCES-
ſion is for triall of true Religion, and hovv ſectaries
haue ſought, to fly the force therof by ſaying, that
the Church is inuiſible. *Hovv fond a ſhift
this is, and hovv fooliſly* Iohn Fox *doth behaue himſelfe therin.*

CHAP. I.

THE ſentence of the philoſopher is
knowne to all: *that contraries being laid togeather do giue light the one to the other,* as white
and blacke propoſed in one table, do make
each colour more cleere, diſtinct and liuely
in it

in it felfe. For which refpect we hauing laid
open before in the firft part of this difcourfe
the knowne manifeft fuccefsion of Chriftian Religion in our Ile of England, firft
from the Apoftles times among the Britans
for the firft fix ages after Chrift: and then
againe among the English men for 9. ages
more fince their firft conuerfion from paganifme: we are now to examine, what manner of vifible fuccefsion *Iohn Fox* doth bring
vs forth of his Church, that is to fay, of the
proteftants of his religion (for the faid fifteene hundred yeares or fifteene ages) if any
fuch be. For that by this comparifon of the
one with the other, the nature & condition
of both Churches will be vnderftood. But
yet firft, I meane to note by the way certaine principall points to be confidered for
better vnderftanding of all that is to be handled in this Chapter, or about this whole
matter of Ecclefiafticall fuccefsion.

2. Wherof the firft may be that, which
I haue touched in the end of the former
Chapter, to witt of how great importance
this point is (I meane the fuccefsion & continuation of teachers, the one conforme to
the other in matter of beleefe and religion)
for cleere demonftration of truth in matters
of controuerfy, and for ftayng any difcreet
mans iudgment from wauering hither and
thither in his beleefe, according to that

*The princi-
pall
point to
be noted
of fuc-
cefsion.*

S 3   which

which holy *Saint Augustine* ſaid of himſelfe,
& felt in himſelfe. For that conſidering the
great diuerſity of ſects, that ſwarmed in his
time, and euery one pretending truth, antiquity, purity, and authoritie of ſcriptures
for their errors, & himſelfe alſo hauing byn
miſled by one of theſe ſects for many yeares:
was brought by God at length, to be a true
Catholike, and to feele in himſelfe the force
of this viſible ſucceſſion of the Catholike

S. Au-
guſtine
his eſti-
mation
of ſuc-
ceſſion.

Church. And therfore wryting againſt one,
that in time paſt had byn his maiſter as head
of the former ſect, wherin he had liued, to
witt *Fauſtus Manichæus,* after diuers other reaſons alleaged of his confidence & aſſurance
of truth in the Cath. Church, & of his firme
reſolution to dy and liue in the ſame, he
bringeth for his laſt and ſtrongeſt reaſon, the
perpetuall ſucceſſion of Biſhops in the ſame
Church and eſpecially in the Church of

Aug. ep.
contra
Fauſtum
Manich.
cap. 4.
tomo 6.

Rome: *Tenet me in Eccleſia* (ſaith he) *ab ipſa Pe-*
tri ſede, vſque ad præſentem epiſcopatum, ſucceſſio
ſacerdotum, &c. I am held in this Church
(againſt all yow ſectaries) by the ſucceſſion
of Prieſts & Biſhops, that haue come downe
,, euen from the firſt ſeat of *Saint Peter* the
,, Apoſtle, to the preſent Biſhop of Rome
,, (*Anaſtaſius*) that holdeth the Seate at this
,, day, &c.

3. Lo heere the force and eſtimation of
ſucceſſion with *Saint Auguſtine*. Wherynto
are

are conforme all other auncient fathers, yf
we would ſtand to alleage them. Yea they
ſtand ſo firmely vpon this point, & do make
ſo great accoumpt of it, as they do generally
note heretiks and ſectaries for the contrary
defect, to witt that they haue no ſucceſsion
or orderly continuation eyther of Biſhops,
or of faith among them, but did leap hither
and thither (as ours do at this day) chalenging to themſelues now this and now that,
without either order, intereſt, continuation
or ſucceſsion: *Ordinem* (ſaith *Saint Auguſtine*)
ab Apoſtolo Petro cœptum, & vſque ad hoc tempus per
traducem ſuccedentium Epiſcoporum ſeruatum per-
turbant, ordinem ſibi ſine origine vendicantes. Heretiques do trouble and breake the order of
ſucceeding of Biſhops begonne by *S. Peter,*
& brought downe by offspring, one Biſhop
ſucceedinge another; and ſo chaleng vnto
themſelues a certaine order without beginning.

4. To which effect alſo *Tertullian* more
then 200. yeares before *Saint Auguſtine*, chalenging heretiks to this combatt of ſucceſſion, ſaid: *Edant hæretici origines ſuarum Eccleſia-*
rum, euoluant ordinem epiſcoporum ſuorum, &c. Let
heretiks ſett forth the beginning of their
Churches, let them recout the order of their
ſucceeding Biſhops, yf they can. And then
hauing ſett downe for his part, & for proofe
of true Catholike ſucceſsion, the whole

ranke

Auguſt.
quæſt.
110. *in*
nou. &
vet .Teſt.
„
„
„
„
„

Tert.l.de
praſcrip.
aduerſ.
hæreſ.
„

ranke of the Bishops of Rome, from *Saint Peter* to *Pope Eleutherius*, that liued in his dayes. (Marke I pray yow the proofe he vſeth, though he were of the Church of *Africa.*) He glorieth as though he brought forth an invincible argument againſt all he-retiks, chalenging and prouoking them, to do the like, if they could: *Confingant* (ſaith he) *tale aliquid haretici*. Let heretiks bring forth or deuiſe any ſuch things for proofe of their Church, yf they can. And conſider heere (gentle Reader) how heretiks remayne con-founded by *Tertullians* iudgment for want of ſucceſsion.

Tert. ib.

5.   But this is not only *Tertullians* opinion. For *Saint Irenæus*, before him againe, obie-cteth the ſame to heretiks, againſt whome he wrote, ſaying: *Obedire oportet eis, qui ſucceſ-ſionem habent ab Apoſtolis, qui cum Epiſcopatus ſuc-ceſsione chariſmata veritatis acceperunt*. Yow ,, ought to obey theſe who haue their ſucceſ-,, ſion from the Apoſtles, who togeather with ,, the ſucceſsion of their Bishopriks haue re-,, ceyued from tyme to tyme the gifts or priui-,, leges of truth. And in another place : *Apud quas eſt ea, quæ eſt ab Apoſtolis ſucceſsio, hi fidem no-ſtram cuſtodiunt, & ſcripturas ſine periculo nobis ex-ponunt*; With whome the ſucceſsion of Bi-,, ſhops from the Apoſtles time downwards ,, is founde to haue remayned, theſe are they ,, who conſerue our faith and do expounde the

Iren. l. 4. aduerſus hæreſ. cap. 4.

Iren. ib. cap. 45.

the fcripture ynto vs without daunger. Beholde the vertue of fuccefsion, which this
B. Bishop and Martyr *Saint Irenæus*, eftemed
fo highly in his dayes, as he afcribed therto
both the infallible conferuation of faith, &
true expofition of fcriptures.

6. And it is to be noted, that he fpeaketh
not only of fuccefsion in beliefe, as euery
one of our Sectaries will feeme to pretende,
that they haue it amonge themfelues from
the Apoftles (which yet is ridiculous and
manifeftly falfe, as before hath bene decla-
ted, and after fhalbe more in particular:) but
he fpeaketh expresly alfo of the externall
fuccefsion and continuation of Bishops,
afcribinge to them & prouinge by them the
fuccefsion of one & the felf fame faith. And
to that end doth he number vp all the Bifhops of Rome from *Saint Peter* to his tyme,
as *Tertulliã* before alleaged did (notwithftanding the one liued in France, the other in
Africa) prouinge by that fuccefsion of Roman Bishops the true fuccefsion and continuation of one and the felf fame Cath. faith
to haue endured, not only in thefe feuerall
coũtreyes but alfo ouer al Chriftendome, &
that from Chrift to thofe times : efteminge
this to be a moft inuincible proofe and certaine demonftration, or (to vfe *S. Irenæus* his
owne woords)*plenißimã oftenfionem* a moft ful
probatiõ againft all heretiques whatfoeuer.

The force of fuccefsion vvith Irenæus and Tertullian & other fathers.

S 5

7. Ac-

7. Accordinge to which principle and sure
foundation, all other fathers also that haue
enfued fince, from age to age haue ftoode
very refolutely vpon this pointe of fucceffion, againft the heretiques of their times.

Hierome
dia. vlt.
contra
Lucif.

Breuem (faith *Saint Hierome*) *apertamáq̃ animi*
mei fententiam proferam, in illa effe Ecclefia perma-
nendum quæ ab Apoftolis fundata vfque ad diem hanc
durat. I will vtter briefly my fentence and
iudgement: We muft abide in that Church
which beinge founded by the Apoftles,
hath endured vnto this day. As if he had
faide, we muft be and abide in that Church,
which as it was vifibly founded and fpred
ouer the world by the Apoftles preachinge:
fo it hath vifibly bene continued vnder her
Bishops and teachers vnto this day. Which
fentence of his *S. Auguftine*, that liued with
him, though fomewhat younger, confir-

Aug.l.de
vtilitate
credent.
cap. 17.

meth in thefe woords. *Dubitabimus nos illius*
Ecclefiæ confidere gremio, quæ ab Apoftolica fede per
fucceffiones epifcoporum (fruftra hereticis circum-
latrantibus) culmen authoritatis obtinuit? Shall we
doubt ftill to reft in the lappe of that
Church, which hath kept continually the
height of her authority by fucceffion of Bifhops from the fea Apoftolique vnto this
day, notwithftandinge the vaine barkinge
of heretiques on euery fide of her?

8. Thus faide *Saint Auguftine*, of the vifible
Church in his dayes, which had not continued

nued much more then 400. yeares. But,
what would he say, if he liued in our dayes
after almost 12. hundred yeares succession
more, since he wrote this; when he should
heare farre greater and more spitefull barkinge of heretiques against the same, then
he heard in his dayes? though then also he
hearde much and much of that which we
heare now. But if *Saint Augustine* should liue
now againe, there is no doubt of one
thinge: Which is, that he would make this
his argument of succession farre more stron-
ger against our heretikes; and esteme it so
much the more, by how much the power
of Christ hath shewed it self more omnipo-
tent in continuinge the same since, for so
many ages more after him, amidst so many
troubles and turmoiles, chaunges and alterations of empires & kingdomes & temporall states, as before we haue noted. And if
in England we can number aboue 70. Archbishops of Canterbury, all of one religion,
the one succedinge the other, since our first
conuersion by *Saint Augustine* our Apostle
(not to speake any thinge of the British
Church before vs) as yow may see confessed
by *Cambden* and other newe hereticall wryters of our owne; and that this English
Church was the same in faith and belife
with the British (as before hath bene shewed) & both of them one with the Roman
and

Barking of heretiques against succession as Saint August. faith termeth it.

In descr. Cantij.

and generall Chucrh from the very beginninge to this ryme, what an antiquity is this? and how cleere and euident a ſucceſſion? and how would *Saint Auguſtine* vrge this argument againſt our proteſtants if he were now aliue againe.

9.   Sure I am, that if any one Baron, Earle, or Duke in England, could ſhewe but the halfe of theſe yeares for the continuançe & poſſeſsion of any temporall ſtate, Lordſhip, or lande in England : he would highly eſteeme therof, and therby make a glorious defence againſt any wranglinge companiō, that ſhould preſume to pretend the ſame & depriue him therof, if he could truly ſay and prooue (as we do in the cauſe of our Church) that his aunceſtres, for 13. hundreth yeares had continued in that poſſeſſion. But no man can preſcribe any ſuch time in temporall matters; & therefore are they well called temporall, for that they chaunge in a litle tyme. And he that will reade the foreſaide *Cambdens* ſtorie towards the end.of euery Engliſh ſtorie (where he taketh vpon him to recount the Earles or Dukes that haue had their ſtates and titles ouer that ſhire) he ſhall ſee ſuch a broken ſucceſsion in thoſe ſtates and ſignories, as it is pitifull to behold, no Dukedome or Earledome continuing lightly 3. or 4. generations together in any one name or familie,

And

A compariſon betvvene the durance of the Church & temporall ſtates.

And this is the frailty and vncertainty of humaine thinges.

10. But for matters of religion appertaininge to the foule, almighty God hath giuen another manner of force vnto fucceffion, both of men, & faith. As for example, in the lawe of nature he made the fame to endure by only tradition without writinge for more then two thoufande and fiue hundreth yeares, vnder the aunciét Patriarches before and after the flood of *Noë*. And afterward againe in the written lawe the Iewes continued the poffeffion of their religion by fucceffion of Bifhops and Ecclefiafticall gouernors, from *Mofes* vnto *Chrift*, aboue a thoufand and fiue hundreth yeares: notwithftandinge allvarieties of times and calamities.And no leffe from Chrift to our age hath he continued the fame in a much more glorious fort and manner. In which later time of Chriftian Religion (to fpeake only of this, for the prefent) fo many mutations haue bene made, both in the Roman Empire it felf, and all other realmes and kingdomes round about vs: as all men knowe,& may be feene in hiftories. And yet hath the fucceffion of the Catholike Church and Paftors therof together with the vnion of faith therin taught,bene moft miraculoufly conferued amongft all thefe toffings & turmoiles, breaches and diuifions of temporall

king-

kingdomes. Which could neuer haue bene,
but by the omnipotét hand of our Sauiour,
that hath defended it: eſpecially, conſideringe with all, the greate multitude of ſectes
and hereſies, that from time to time haue
riſen and attempted to impugne the ſame,
but could neuer preuaile. And this is ſufficient for this firſt and principall point of the
vertue & force of Eccleſiaſticall ſucceſsion.

The ſe-
cond
princi-
pall
point to
be conſi-
dered
about
the viſi-
bilitie
of the
Church.

11. The ſecond point to be conſidered is,
that when Luthers new Religion began,
and could alleage no ſucceſſors of Biſhops
or auncient teachers for it ſelf, but was
much preſſed with this other of the Catholiques: he deuiſed a certaine notorious and
ridiculous ſhifte, to ſay, that the true Church
was inuiſible to the eye of man, and only
ſeene by God: And conſequentlie, had no
neede of any viſible or externall ſucceſsion
of men. And this ſhift of his is diſcouered by

a *In de-
fenſ. lib.
de ſeruo
arbitr.*
b *lib. con,
Cathar.*
* *part. 1.*

that he writeth both againſt a *Eraſmus* and
b *Catharinus,* & in his wicked treatiſe *de abroganda miſſa priuata,* for taking away priuate
maſſes. Where hauing had conference with
the diuell (as himſelfe cófeſſeth,) He asketh
very ſtoutly, *who can ſhevv vs the Church, ſeing
ſhe is ſecrett and to be beleeũed only in ſpiritt?* To
whome if any man would oppoſe *Saint Aug.*

*Auguſt.
tract. in
ep. Ioan.*

that ſaith: *digito oſtendimus Eccleſiam,* we can
ſhew the Church with our fingar: ſhould
not Luther be well matched, thinke yow?

12. The

12. The like held for a time ★ *Brentius*, as ★ *cap. de* appeareth in his confession of *VVittenberge,* *concilijs.* & some others of that sect. But this opinion of Martyn Luther did not long please his followers. For that † *Philipp Melancthon,* his † *In locis* cheefe scholler, did soone after teach the *com. loco* contrary; to witt, that the Church was vi- *12. de* sible to the eyes of men also. And the a *Mag-* *Ecclef.* *deburgians* do hold the same, defining euery *lib. 1.* where the Church *to be a visible company of* *cap. 4.* *men.* Which going backe of the principall Lutherans in this point (it being done by a certaine consultation had therof among themselues (as b *Fredericus Staphylus* the Em- b *Apol.1.* perors Counselour, that had byn one of *parte.* 3. them, affirmeth) was some cause parhaps that *Iohn Caluyn* comminge presently after *Caluin.* them, tooke vpon him to defend the same *l. 4. Iust.* doctrine againe, saying: *Nobis inuisibilem, &c.* *cap. 1.* we are forced to beleeue the Church to be *§. 3.* inuisible, and to be seene only by the eyes of God. Lo Caluin putteth necessity in this point of beleefe.

13. The causes, that mooued the cheefe VVhy Lutherans to go backe from their first opi- Luthe- nion about the inuisibility of the Church, rans left were principally the apparent euidences & the para- demonstratiõs, which Catholiks do alleage dox of both out of Scriptures, Fathers, common fibility sense and reason, for ouerthrow of that of the most fond and ridiculous paradox. And Church. first

firſt out of holy ſcriptures both of the old &
new Teſtament, theſe men being not able
to alleage any one place, where the name of
Gods Church is applied to an inuiſible congregation; the Catholiks on the contrary
ſide preſſed them with many moſt euident
textes of ſcripture where it was, and is vſed
for a viſible company of men. As that in the
Num. 20. booke of numbers: *Cur eduxiſti Eccleſiam Domini in ſolitudinem?* why haſt thou brought
the Church of God into the deſert? And
3. Reg. 8. againe in the 3. booke of Kings: *Conuertitq́,
Rex faciem ſuam, & benedixit omni Eccleſiæ Iſraël;
omnis enim Eccleſia Iſraël ſtabat, &c.* The King
turning his face about did bleſſe all the
Churche of Iſraël for that all the Church of
Iſraël was preſent, &c. Which places & many the like cannot poſſiblie be vnderſtood
of an Inuiſible, but of a viſible company.

14.   And much more yf we conſider the
ſpeeches of Chriſt and his Apoſtles in the
new Teſtament, as theſe words of Chriſt:
Mat. 18. Dic Eccleſiæ, ſi Eccleſiam non audierit, &c. Tell the
Church, and yf he heare not the Church,
lett him be vnto thee as an heathen or pu-
blican. But yf the Church were inuiſible,
neyther could a man complaine to the
Church, nor heare the Church. Moreouer
S. *Paul* exhorteth the cheefe paſtors of the
Epheſians to attend diligently to their charge,
*Act. 20. in quo vos ſpiritus ſanctus poſuit epiſcopos regere Ec-
cleſiam*

clefiam Dei. In which the holy Ghoſt hath „
placed yow as Biſhopps to gouerne the „
Church of God. But how could they being „
viſible men gouerne a company that was „
inuiſible and not to be ſeene? „

15.   And yet further when *Saint Paul* and
Saint Barnabas went vp from Antioche to Ieruſalem, the ſcripture ſaith : *Deducti ſunt ab
Eccleſia, &c.* They were brought on their
way by the Church of Antioche: and when
they came to Ieruſalem, *ſuſcepti ſunt ab Eccleſia.* They were receyued by the Church.
And yet further, *aſcendit Paulus & ſalutauit
Eccleſiam.* Paul went and ſaluted the Church,
&c. All which places cannot agree poſſibly
to an inuiſible Church. And yet that this
was the true primitiue Church of Chriſt,
no man can deny.

16.   And finally, when *S. Paul* doth teache
Timothy, his ſcholler, *quomodo oporteat conuerſari
in Domo Dei, qua eſt Eccleſia, &c.* How he ſhould
conuerſe and gouerne the houſe of God,
which is his Church, *columna & firmamentum
veritatis,* the pillar & firmament of all truth.
All this (I ſay) had byn ſpoken to no purpoſe, yf the true Church of Chriſt were inuiſible. For how can a man conuerſe in a
congregatiõ, which he cannot ſee or know?
or how can the Church be a pillar and ſure
firmament of truth, to reſolue all doubts or
queſtions, that may fall out about ſcriptures,

*Act. 15.
& 18.*
Euident
ſcriptu-
res for
the viſi-
bility of
the
Church.

1. Tim. 3.

Ibid.

T   articles

articles of beleefe, and miſteries of Chriſts
Religion: yf it be an inuiſible congregation,
that no man ſeeth, diſcerneth, or knoweth
where or how to repayre vnto it, nor who
are the parſons therin conteyned?

Euident
reaſons
that the
true
Church
muſt be
viſible
contey-
ninge
both
good &
bad.

a *Marc.*
vlt.
*Ephes.*4.
1.*Pet.*3.
b *Rom.*
10. *Luc.*
11.
1.*Tim.*6.
c *Mat.*5.
Luc. 11.
*Ioan.*15.
d *Math.*
28.
1.*Cor.*12.
1.*Tim.*3.
& 5.

17. And laſtly, not to ſtand longer vpon
this matter, that is ſo euident in it ſelfe and
plaine to common ſenſe and reaſon; yf the
true Church of Chriſt, be a ſociety not of
Angells, ſpirits or ſoules departed; but of
men and women in this life, that muſt be
gouerned or gouerne therin: how can they
be inuiſible? And yf they muſt haue communion togeather in externall Sacraments
and namely in a baptiſme, and participation
of the body of Chriſt; yf they muſt b profeſſe the name and doctrine of Chriſt exter-
nally to the world, as alſo to be c perſecuted
& put to death for the ſame; yf all men muſt
repayre vnto them; and thoſe that be out of
the Church, to enter and be receiued therin;
and thoſe that be in her, to be reſolued of
their doubts; to lay downe their complaints;
to be gouerned and directed by her; and finally to obey her vnder payne of damnation: how can all this be performed, if ſhe
be inuiſible to mans eyes, and only ſeene by
the eyes of God?

18. To alleage Fathers and Doctors in this
behalfe were both endleſſe, and needleſſe.
For that all of them euery where almoſt are
occupied

occupied in settinge forth, not only the visibility, but the splendor also and greatnesse, yea the multitude and externall Maiestie of Christs Church thoroughout the world in their dayes. And only *S. Augustine* may serue for all, who dilateth himselfe euery where in this argument, shewinge how the litle stone prophesied by Daniel, was growne to be a huge mountayne, and terrible to the whole world. And that the Tabernacle of Christ *(vvhich is his Church)* was placed by him in the sunne to be seene of all. And that it was a Citty vpon a mountayne which none could be ignorant of. And other like discourses, founded on euident scriptures, wherby is refuted not only the first shifte of Luther & Caluin makinge the true Church of Christ inuisible: but also the second of these later Lutherans, who, (though ouercome with the former proofes) do graunt the Church to be a visible companie, yet do they deny it to be that externall conspicuous succession of Bishops & Councells, which haue byn most eminét in the knowne Christian Church from the Apostles downward: but rather to be some few obscure and contemptible people (which they call the elect) that haue liued or lurked from time to time in shaddowes and darknes, and knowen to few or none.

S. Augustines discourses about the visibility of the Church. See S. August. in psalm. 44. & 47. & l. 2. con. Petil. c. 32. & 104. l. 2. contra Cresco. c. 36. & l. 4. c. 58. tract. 1. & 2. in ep. Ioan. & c. 4. collat. 3. diei in Breuici

16.   But this second deuise is more fond A secōd

then

fond de-
uife of
Luthe-
rans
about an
obfcure
Church.

then the former. For where fhall a man
feeke out thefe hidden fellowes to treat
with them, or to receyue Sacraméts at their
hands? how fhall they be knowne? how
may they be trufted? whence haue they their
authoritie? what fuccefsion brings they
downe by impofition of hands from the
Apoftles time? may not euery fect of heretikes make them felues Chrifts Church by
this deuife? wherfore of this fecond point
there neede to be faid no more.

The 3.
point of
Iohn
Foxes
opinion
about
the true
Church.

20. There remaineth then a third point
to be confidered by the reader, before we
come to fett downe the fuccefsion of Iohn
Fox his Church. Who hauinge confidered
with himfelfe, that both *Luther* and *Caluin*
did hould it to be inuifible; and on the other
fide, that diuers cheefe Lutherans had
chaunged their opinions therin, and held it
to be vifible (efpecially *Flaccus Illyricus*, & the
reft of the *Magdeburgians*, who were to write
a whole ftory of their owne vifible Church
in their *Centuryes*, & *Fox* to follow them ftep
by ftep therin in his Englifh Acts & Monuments) the poore man was brought to a very
greate perplexity: for fo much as on the one
fide to leaue Luther (but efpecially Caluin)
feemed very harde vnto him. And on the
other fide, not to fticke to the *Magdeburgians*,
that are his maifters in his ftory, feemed
hard alfo. But efpecially & aboue all was he
troubled

troubled (as it seemeth) with the reason and
necesitie of the 'matter it selfe : for if the
Church of Chrift be inuifible, how can *Fox*
or the *Magdeburgians* write fo greate & large
ftories therof? to which effect *Illyricus* wrytinge, vpon the'genealogie fett downe by
Saint Mathevves Ghofpell, of the true Church
from the beginninge, faith thus: *Oftendit ifta
feries Ecclefiam & religionem veram habere certas
hiftorias fuæ originis & progreffus.* This genealogie proueth, that the true Church and religion haue affured hiftories of their beginninge and progreffe.

A greate perplex-ity of Iohn Fox.

Illyricus gloff. in Math. cap. 1.

21. Thus faid *Illyricus*, for that he and his
fellowes were then in hand (as hath byn
faid) with their Ecclefiafticall hiftories named *Centuries*. Which they could not well
haue written, houldinge the Church to be
inuifible: neither yet Iohn Fox could begin
fo greate a volume with that opinion.
Wherfore after much breakinge his braines
about this matter (as it feemeth:) he cōmeth
forth with a new opinion neuer heard of
perhaps before : affirming that the true
Church of Chrift is both vifible and inuifible, to witt, vifible to fome, and inuifible
to others; vifible to them that are in her,&
inuifible to them that are out of her. Yow
fhall heare his wordes.

Fox his nevv opi nion ma king the Church both vi= fible and inuifible

22. *Although* (faith he) *the right Church of God
be not fo inuifible in the vvorld, that none can fee it:yet*

Fox in his pro-

neither

neither is it ſo viſible againe , that euery vvorldly eye may preceyue it. For like as is the nature of truth,ſo is the proper conditiō of the true Church,that commonly none ſeeth it, but ſuch only as be members & partakers therof:& therfore they vvhich require that Gods holy Church ſhould be euident & viſible to the vvhole vvorld; ſeeme to define the great Synagoge of the vvorld,rather then the true ſpirituall Church of God.

23.   Thus ſaith he. Wherin yow ſee, that he maketh the true Church viſible but only to ſuch , as are in her and members therof. A deuiſe (I thinke) neuer heard of before,& fit for the braines of Iohn Fox, which were knowne to be out of tune, for many yeares before he died:for if he do not trifle & equiuocate, (meaning one where internall viſibility by faith, and an otherwhere externall viſibility to the eye)but doth meane indeed, as he ſhould do , and as the controuerſie is meant of externall viſibility to mans eye, then is it moſt ridiculous , that none can ſee the true Church in this world, but he that is a member of her. For ſhe is to be ſeene as well to her enemies & aduerſaries, as to her frends and children : the one to impugne & fight againſt her, the other to acknowledge & obey her. And I would (for exáples ſake) demaund of Iohn Fox, whether Herod and Nero that perſecuted the true viſible Church of Chriſt, were of that Church or noe? For if they were not , then by his ſentence they
could

could not fee her and confequentiy not perfecute her.

24. His comparifon alfo betweene truth
& the true Church, doth not hold. For that
truthe is a fpirituall thinge, to be feene only by the eye of our vnderftandinge: but the
true Churche, confiftinge of vifible men &
womé, may be feene by mans eye. Though
the truthe therof (to witt, whether this or
that vifible congregatió be the true Church
ofChrifte) is a matter of vnderftandinge &
beleefe, confirmed vnto vs by fuch argumêts
as before we haue recyted and others. So as
albeit the forefaide perfecutors *Herod* and
Nero (for example) did not fee the truthe of
that Church, which they perfecuted, in refpecte of their doctrine (for then perhaps
they would not haue done it) yet did they
both fee & knowe, that this was *Chriftes* vifible Church. to witt, a congregation pro-
fefsinge his name and Doctrine. Yea they
might knowe further, that it was his true
Churche: feing it was begon vifibly and
euidently by him and his Apoftles in theire
daies, and fo continued on without interruption. And if they had further knowne &
beleeued (as we doe) that he had promiffed
to maintaine and defende this Church vnto
the worlds end: then muft they eyther haue
doubted of his fidelity or power to performe it, or elfe muft haue beleeued alfo

Howe
enemyes
& perfe-
cutors
do fee
the true
Church.

T 4　　　　that

that this Church ¡coulde not faile, wherof proteſtantes doubting muſt needs doubt alſo, of the one or the other: to witt, of the fidelity and of the ability of our Saueour to performe his promiſſe. And this is the force of ſucceſſion, euen with enemies and infidells.

25.   But nowe let vs paſſe to the principall matter intended in this chapter, which is the ſucceſſion or deduction of the proteſtants Churche, promiſed by Iohn Fox *in his* *Fox in* *acts and monuments. VVherin* (ſaith he) *is ſett forth* *the title.* *at large, the vvhole race and courſe of the Church* *from the primitiue to theſe latter tymes of ours, &c.* Thus he promiſeth in the title: but how he doth performe it in his whole booke, wee ſhall ſee afterward in this declaration. Though in parte wee may perceyue his drift, by that he proteſteth to the Church of England before his entraunce into his ſtory in theſe words.

The pur-   *I haue taken in hand* (ſaith he) *this hiſtory, that* *poſe of* *as other ſtory vvritters heertofore haue imployed ther* *Iohn* *trauaile to magnifie the Church of Rome; ſo in this* *Fox in* *hiſtory might appeare the image of both Churches, but* *his Pro-* *eſpecially of the poore, oppreſſed & perſecuted Churche* *teſt. p. 3. of Chriſt. VVhich though it hath beene ſo long trodden* *vnder foote by enemyes, neglected in the vvorld, not* *regarded in hiſtories, and almoſt ſcarce viſible, and* *knovven to vvorldly eyes: yet hath yt beene the true* *Church only of God. VVherin he hath mightely* *vvrought*

vvrought hitherto in preseruinge the same in all ex-
treeme distresses; continually sturringe vppe from time
to time faithfull ministers, by vvhome allvvayes hath
byn kept some sparks of this true doctrine & religion.
And for so much as the true Church of God goeth not
lightly alone, but is accompanied vvith some other
Churche or Chappell of the diuell, to deface and ma-
ligne the same; necessarie it is, that the difference be-
tvvene them bothe be seene, and the discent of
the right Church to be described from the Apostles
tyme, &c.

26.   Heere we see all Iohn Fox his drifte
laid downe. Firſt he meaneth to contra-
dicte all former writers, that haue magni-
fied the Church of Rome, & the greatneſſe
and glory therof, which he calleth the diuells Chappell. And in this he muſt contra-
dicte all the auncient Fathers and writers
for diuerſe hundred yeares after Chriſte, as
Irenaus, Tertullian, Augustine, Optatus, and other
*vvriters,*that bringe downe the diſcent of rhe
true Churche of Chriſt, by the ſucceſsion of
the Biſhops & Churche of Rome, as before
yow haue heard. And ſecondly Fox meaneth to ſett out another Chriſtian Church,
trodden vnder foote before, neglected in the vvorld,
not regarded in histories, and allmost scarce visible or
knovvne. And yet vvas and is, for sooth, the only true
Church of Christ keepinge some sparck of his true do-
ctrine and religion (he doth not ſay that all was
true which ſhe held, nor that all Chriſts
doctrine

doctrine was taught in her ; but only some sparks or scrappes of true doctrine.) And further he promiseth, that the will describe *the difcent of this Church from the Apostles time.*

27.   This is Iohn Fox his promise, and we accepte therof. And though it be scarce worth the performance, to shewe vs a hidden, obscure and troden downe Churche in euery age, that keepeth some sparks of true doctrine and religion (for that euery secte and heresy, not denying Christ and his doctrine wholy, doth so:) Yet shall we accept and exacte the same (being neuer so miserable and beggarly) as we goe ouer the whole course of times and ages from Christ downeward, following therin the distribution it selfe, that Iohn Fox hath appointed to be obserued in his story. To witt , from Christ to Constantine 300. yeares: from Constantine to *Saint Gregorie* as much: From *Saint Gregorie* and *Saint Augustine* our Apostles to the conquest 400. and odd yeares : from the conquest to Wickliffe other 300. yeares: from Wickliffe to Luther about 240. from Luthers tyme to ours somwhat lesse then a hundred. In all which variety of tymes we shall examine briefly, whether Iohn Fox his Church were on foote or no? what continuance or succession it may be said to haue had ? where, when , and by what men it **was** begon, continued, and acknowledged? what

Vvhat is to be handled about Iohn Fox his Church.

what doctrine it held, and whence, & with what vnion or confirmity with it felfe, or with the Catholike Romayne Churche? Which Catholike Church being fhewed & declared in the firft part of this booke, to haue bene founded by the Apoftles, & conferued vifibily from that time hither by fuccefsion of Bifhops and Prelats, gouernors and profeffors therof: will eafely alfo bring in the notice and certificate of Iohn Fox his oppofite Church, wherof now we take in hand to intreate.

THE PARTICVLAR EXAMI-
NATION OF THE DISCENT OR
fucceßion of Iohn Fox his Churche in England or els vvhere for the firfte 300. yeares after Chrift: to vvit, vnto the tyme of Conftantine the Emperor. And vvhether any fuch Church vvas extant then in the vvorld or no, and in vvhome.

CHAP. II.

H E that will confider the proportion of Iohn Fox his booke of *acts & monuments* in the later edition, he fhall find it the greateft perhaps in volume that euer was put forth in our Englifh toungue: and the falfeft in fubftance, without perhaps, that euer was publifhed in any toungue. The volume confifteth of aboue a thoufand leaues of the largeft paper that lightly hath beene feene, **and**

and euery leafe conteyneth 4. greate co-

lumnes: and yet, yf yow conſider how many
leaues of thoſe thouſand he hath ſpent in
deduction of the whole Church eyther his
or ours, and the whole Eccleſiaſticall ſtory
therof, for the firſt thouſand yeares after
Chriſt; they are by his owne accoumpte, but
threſcore & foure. To witt, ſcarce the thir-
teth parte of that he beſtoweth in the laſt
fiue hundred yeares.

2.   And further, yf this his thouſand yeares
ſtory, conteining three ſcore & foure leaues,
be ſifted and examined what it conteyneth:
not foure of them do appertaine to that

The di-
uiſion of
1060.
yeares
in to 4.
princi-
pal parts
1.

which he ſhould handle (which is the viſible
deduction of his Church) as we ſhall endeauour briefly to ſhewe, diuidinge the whole
thouſand & threſcore yeares from Chriſt to
VVilliam the Conquerour into 4. diſtinct tymes
or ſtations, appointed out by Iohn Fox himſelfe in his booke. To witt, the firſt from
Chriſte to *Conſtantine*, conteyninge 300.

2.

yeares: the ſecond, from Conſtantine to
K. *Ethelbert* his conuerſion by Saint Auguſtine,

3.

conteyninge other 300. yeares: the third,
from K. *Ethelbert* and other ſix K. of England
raigning ioyntly with him vnto K. *Egbert* the
firſt Monarch of the Engliſh nation, which
ſpace is ſomewhat more then other two

4.

hundred yeares: and the fourth from *King
Egbert* to William the Conquerour conteyninge

ninge the fame or fome fewe more yeares.
3. Let vs now follow (I'fay) Iohn Fox,
throughout all thefe ages and different fta-
tions of tymes, and fee out of what holes or
dennes he will drawe his *little, hidden, trodden
dovvne Churche, different from the Romane vifible
Churche,* & yet endued notwithftanding *from
tyme to tyme vvith fome little fparks of truth:* which
he promifeth to bring doune from the Apoftles to our tyme. In the firft. 300. yeares
then from Chrift to *Conftantine*, wheras all
other Ecclefiafticall writers and *Saint Luke*
amongft the reft in his acts of the Apoftles,
do fett downe the vifible beginninge of
Chriftes Church by his Apoftles and difciples; their ftrengtheninge & confirmation
by the comminge of the holy Ghoft ; theire
preachinge and conuertinge of others; their
great and many miracles ; and therby, the
eftablishing & wounderfull encreafe of the
faid Church throughout the world , and
continuance of the fame downeward by
fuccefsion of Bishopps (but namely and
fpecially of the *Bishops* of *Rome*, as before hath
beene declared, and is to be feene in the writinges of *Dionyfius Areopagita* , *Iofephus, Iuftinus,
Egefippus, Clemens , Irenaeus , Tertullian, Origenes,
Iulius Africanus, Cyprian, Eufebius* , and others
of thefe ages:) Iohn Fox followeth no fuch
order at all , nor euer fo much as mentioneth any difcent of Bishops of his Church
or ours;

The firft
300. yea
res from
Chrift
to' Con∗
ftantine.
*Act.*2.3.
4. *&c.*
Eufeb. l.
I. *& 2.*
hiftor.
*Eccl. per
totum.*

*Sup. c.*8.
&. 9.

The im-
pertinēt
courſe
taken by
Iohn
Fox.
or ours; but only (to ſpend tyme and fill vp
paper) taketh vpon him to tranſlate out of
Euſebius and other autors the Martyrdomes
of ſuch as ſuffered for Chriſtian Religion in
the ten generall perſecutions of theſe firſt
300. yeares. Settinge the ſame forth alſo in
painted pictures, for no other purpoſe (as it
ſeemeth) but only to entertaine his reader
with ſome ſtrange and delightful ſpectacle:
And afterward ſo to ioyne his proteſtant
burned martyrs to thoſe of the primitiue
Church, as the paintinge being ſomwhat
like, the ſimple reader might therby be induced to thinke, that there was no greate
difference eyther in there perſons or cauſe of

Reaſons
to proo-
ue that
the old
martyrs
vvere of
our
Church
& not of
Foxes.
★Niſi in-
tegram
inuiola-
tamque
ſeruaue-
rit abſq̣
dubio in
æternum
peribit.
ſuffering.

4.   But I would aske Iohn Fox to what
purpoſe of his was the bringinge in of all
theſe martyrs of the primitiue Churche
throughout the world? were they his or our
martyrs, trow yow? for to both of vs they
cannot be martyrs that is to ſay wittneſſes:
we being of a different beleeſe. For that we
for our part do hold reſolutely the ſaying of
Saint ★ *Athanaſius* in his creed; *that vvhoſoeuer
doth not hold all and euery pointe of the Catholike
faith intyrely, ſhall periſh eternally.* Yf therfore
he will ſay, they were his martyrs, he muſt
prooue that they were in all & euery pointe
of his religion and not of ours. And to examine this pointe (to witt, of what religion
they

they were, whether more of ours or of his) diuers considerations may be brought in. As first, who of vs do more honour them? we keepe ther dayes and feasts, as all men knowe; we put them in our Ecclesiasticall calendar and martyrologe; we keepe their reliques; we honour their tombes ; we call vpon them in heauen to pray for vs, as ray-ninge in most high glory with Christ. All which protestants do mislike. Yea, Iohn Fox by name hath put the most of them (I meane of the martyrs of these first 300. yeares) quite out of his Ecclesiasticall calen-dar, to giue place to *Iohn VVickliffe, Iohn Husse, Martin Luther*, and other like compagnions: as may be seene in the very first pages of his booke. Which is a signe, that we esteeme, and honour them more, then they. Which we would not do, yf we did not persuade our selues that they were of our religion, & not of protestants, in any point of contro-uersy betweene vs.

5. Moreouer the Christian visible Church of that tyme (to witt, of those first 300. yeares, wherin these martyrs suffered and were put to death) would neuer haue re-gistred them for saints, nor admitted them into the number of true martyrs, yf in all points they had not bene of her faith and communion. No more then shee did those of diuers sects, namely of the *Marcionists* and
Montanists,

VVho do more honor the aun-cient martyrs.

See Foxes calendar in the begin-ninge of his vo-lume.

The se-cond reason.

Montanifts, who were very many; & bragged of martyrdome , and of Gods afsiftance therin , no leffe, but much more , then true Catholiks. As *Apollinaris* a moft auncient Bi-

Cap. 25. fhop (related by *Eufebius* in his fifth booke of Ecclefiafticall hiftory) doth teftifie at large. Yea,thefe heretiks(efpecially the later fort) were fo forward in martyrdome , as they held it was not lawfull to flee in tyme

Tertull. l. de fuga in perfecut. of perfecution.As may appeare by *Tertullian,* who defended the fame alfo, after he was fallen into that herefy himfelfe. *Saint Cyprian*

Epiph.in panar. hæref.80. doth inueigh often againft the martyrs of the *Nouatians,* & *Saint Epiphanius* againft thofe of the *Euphemits,* furnamed (for the multitude of their falfe martyrs) *Martyrians.* And

Auguft. contra litteras Petiliani l.2.c.83. & contra 2.ep. Gaudentij l. 2 c. 26. & alibi. Of hereticall martyrs. *Saint Auguftine,* no leffe earneftly doth deteft thofe martyrs of the *Donatifts,* who, rather then they would lacke martyrs, were ready to murder themfelues. All which martyrs notwithftandinge were reiected by the Cath. Church (though in fhew they died for Chrift) for that they agreed not with her in all points of faith and beleefe . And confequently we may inferre for moft certayne, that feeing the Cath. Church of that tyme (and of all tymes fince)hath held thefe martyrs before mentioned of the firft ten perfecutions, for true Saints and martyrs indeed,and haue continued their honorable remembrance both by hiftories and celebra-

ting.

ting their annuall feasts and memoryes: sure
it is, that they agreed fully with the said
knowne Cath. Church of those ages. Wherof we inferre againe, that seeing the faith of
those first 300. yeares was continued (as
*before we haue proued) in the second 300.
yeares, and so consequently downeward &
deliuered to vs ; and for so much as the
Church of Rome was held still for head of
all this Church: yt cannot be, that these
martyrs were of Iohn Fox his religion. And
consequently are to no purpose brought in
by him, but only for that he had nothing els
to talke of, or to make a shew of handlinge
some pious matter in his booke.

6. a Moreouer if we would take vpon vs to
reflect vpon all that is extant of the sayings
and dooings of these martyrs recorded in
their historyes, we might soone discerne of
what religion they were, and whether they
were Iohn Fox his martyrs or ours. As for
example in that aunswere of *Saint* b *Andrevv*
the Apostle & hollie martyr which he made
to *Aegeas* the proconsull, that exhorted him
to sacrifice to Idolls, *Ego* c (saith he) *omnipo-*
potenti Deo (qui vnus & verus est), immolo quoti-
die, &c. I do sacrifice daylie to almighty God
(that is one and true) not the flesh of bulles,
or bloud of goats, but the immaculate lamb
vpon the aultar, whose flesh after that all
the faithfull people haue eaten, the same

V   lamb

* *Supra*
cap. 5. 6.
a The
third
Reason.
b S. An-
drevv.
c Se the
story of
his pas-
siō vvri-
tē by the
Church
of *A-*
chaia in
those
dayes &
cited by
Remi-
gius in
psal. 21.
and by
Lāfrāke,
l. contra
Berēgar,
& by *S.*
Bernard
serm' de
S. An-
drea, &
many
others.

lamb that is facrificed, remayneth whole and aliue as before. This man, as yow fee, fpoke not as a proteftant martyr.

S. Lau-
rence.

7. The fpeech alfo of *Saint Laurence* martyr, that fuffered in Rome vnder the Emperour *Valerianus* (the fame yeare that *Saint Cyprian* did in Carthage) his fpeech (I fay) to Pope *Sixtus* B. of Rome, whofe deacon he was,& who was carried to martyrdome 3. dayes before him, doth not fhew, that he was a proteftant,but rather a plaine papift:as both *Saint Ambrofe*, *Saint Auguftine* and other later authors do relate the fame. *Cùm videret Lau-*

Ambrof.
lib. 1.
Officior.
cap. 41.
& lib. 2.
cap. 28.
Auguft.
tract.27.
in Ioan.
& ferm.
de fan-
ctis.

rentius (faith *Saint Ambrofe*) *Syxtum epifcopum suum ad martyrium duci, flere cœpit, &c.* When Laurence the deacon faw his Bifhop Sixtus to be carried away to martyrdome, he be-gan to weep,not for the others fuffering,but for his owne remaining behind him.Wher-fore he cryed vnto him in thefe words: whether do you go (o Father) without your fonne? and whether do yow haften (o holy

» Prieft) without your deacon? *Yovv vvere neuer*
» *vvont to offer facrifice vvithout a minifter*. What
» then hath difpleafed yow in me, that yow
» leaue me behind you? haue yow proued me
» parhaps to be a coward? make triall I pray
» you, whether yow haue chofen vnto your
» felfe a fitt minifter, to whome yow haue
» committed *the difpenfing of our Lords bloud*: And
» then feing you haue not denied vnto me the

fellow-

fellowſhip of adminiſtringe ſacraments, do „ not deny me the fellowſhipp of ſheadinge „ my bloud alſo with yow.

8. Thus talked *S. Laurence* of his deacons office in diſpenſinge the bloud of Chriſt from the aultar, and in miniſtring to his Biſhopp while he offered ſacrifice. Which is a phraſe farre different from Proteſtants manner of ſpeech. But yf we conſider the ſpeech of the heathen Emperour to *Saint Laurence*, ſett downe by *Aurelius Prudentius* aboue a 1200. yeares paſt, obiectinge to Chriſtian Prieſts, their ſacrificinge in gould & diſpenſinge the bloud of our Sauiour in ſiluer cuppes, and the like: we ſhall eaſily ſee, of what religion this martyr was.

S. Laurence ſpeaketh like a flatt Papiſt.

Hunc eſſe veſtris Orgijs
Morémque & artem proditum eſt;
Hanc diſciplinam fæderis;
Libent vt auro Antiſtites.
Argenteis ſcyphis ferunt
Fumare ſacrum ſanguinem,
Auróque nocturnis ſacris,
Aſtare fixos cæreos, &c.

Prudent. in hymn. de Sācto Laurentio.

We heare (ſaith the perſecutor) this to be the faſhion and deuiſe of your feaſtes, and diſcipline of your confederation, that your Biſhops muſt ſacrifice in gould, & diſpence bloud in ſiluer cuppes, & that in your night vigils youe haue waxen torches in golden candleſticks, &c. And thus much of *S. Laurence,*

rence: whoſe perſecutor ſpeaketh like a perfect proteſtant, which is an argument that
himſelfe was none.

Pont.
Diac. in
vit. Cy-
prian.
See alſo
the 28.
epiſtle
of S. Cy-
priä him
ſelfe.
Supra
p. 1. c. 6.
* Cent. 3.
cap. 4.

9. Now as for the other glorious martyr
& Biſhop *Saint Cyprian,* who ſuffered vnder
the ſame Emperour, and in the ſame yeare
that Pope *Sixtus* & *S. Laurence* did, (as appeareth by *Pontius* his deacon, that liued with
him) we haue ſhewed before, that the * *Magdeburgians* do reprehend him ſharply (I
meane *S. Cyprian)* for this very point about
offeringe ſacrifice. For that he ſaith: *Sacer-
dotem vice Chriſti fungi,* & *Deo Patri ſacrificium
offerre lib.* 2. *ep.* 3. That the Prieſt doth performe the office of Chriſt, and offereth ſacrifice, to God the Father. So as now we

Ould
martyrs
maſsing
Prieſts.

haue heere three maſsinge or ſacrificinge
Prieſts (which is the higheſt crime obiected
to Prieſts now in England) and a maſsinge
Deacon that helpeth to maſse, and all 4.
moſt glorious martyrs, within theſe firſt
300. yeares to witt, *S. Andrevv* the Apoſtle
by his owne confeſsion; *Saint Sixtus* B. of
Rome, by the teſtimony of *Saint Laurence:
Saint Cyprian* B. of *Carthage,* by the accuſation
of the *Magdeburgians;* and *Saint Laurence* the
Deacon by teſtimony of *Prudētius, S. Ambroſe,*
and others. And it were ouerlonge to paſſe
any further in this examination (for that
the examples would be infinite) this being
ſufficient to ſhew how little it maketh for

Iohn

Iohn Fox his purpofe, to haue brought in this fo large and particular a ſtory of all the martyrs of the firſt ten perſecutions: they being fo oppoſite to his late proteſtant martyrs, as they are.

10. Well then, this is fufficient for theſe martyrs. But vvhat ſhall vve ſay to the whole intent and drift of *Iohn Fox*, which ſhould haue byn (as you know) to lay before vs the continuall diſcent (throughout theſe firſt 3. ages) of his *poore oppreſſed and perſecuted (& yet the only true) Church of Chriſt, almoſt ſcarce viſible or knovvne to vvorldly eyes, &c*. This, I ſay, he ſhould haue ſhewed, & laid open to vs: for that we finde no other Chriſtian Church knowne in the world in theſe firſt 300. yeares, but only one. Which though it were much perſecuted, yet was it neyther obſcure, nor hidden from the eyes, eyther of good or badd; but moſt viſible & apparant, to all the world. And in the end of theſe 300. yeares (to witt, vnder *Conſtantine* the Emperour, and *Silueſter* the Pope of Rome) the ſame came to be ſo magnificent & glorious, as all the world remayned aſtoniſhed therat. Which appeareth partly by that which *Euſebius* and all other Eccleſiaſticall wryters do recount in the life of the ſaid *Conſtantine*, eſpecially *Euſebius* that wrote fower whole books, of the ſaid *Conſtantines* life and actions: (who was a moſt excellent

The glorious ſtate of the cath. Church vnder Conſtantine. Euſeb. lib. 4. de vita Conſtantini.

V 3 Chri-

Fovver
Churches in
Rome
builded
by Con-
ſtantin.

Christian Emperour.) And amongſt other points of his moſt pious deuotion, it is recorded that he builded 4. goodlie Churches vvithin the citty of Rome, caryinge earth to the firſt foundation of them with his owne hands, & adorninge them with holy images, endovvinge the ſame vvith riche poſſeſsions, furniture, and Eccleſiaſticall ornaments, and conſecrated pretious veſſells for diuine ſeruice. Dedicatinge the one of them (which was his owne pallace of Lateran) vnto our *Sauiour* & *Saint Iohn Baptiſt*: the other to *Saint Peter*, the third to *Saint Paul*, & the fourth to *Saint Laurence*. All which do remayne to this day. And the very manner of building therof with their aultars, fonts, pictures, 'and other ſuch like antiquityes do well ſhew vvithout books, what manner of religion was then in vſe.

11.   This was the knowne viſible Church then of Chriſtians in thoſe dayes, as glorious & renowned as can be imagined. Of which Church one wrote at that tyme to *Conſtan-tine* himſelfe, thus. ⋆ *Quis locus in terra eſt, &c.* What place is there in the whole earth, which hath not receaued the faith of Chriſt, eyther where the ſonne riſeth, or where it falleth: where the north pole is eleuated, or where the ſouthe; all is filled with the maieſtie of this God. The ſame writeth *Opta-tus: concedite Deo, &c.* Yeld this vnto Chriſt, who

⋆ *Iulius
Firmi-
cus l. ad
Imp. de
abol.
Idol.*

*Optatus
lib. 2.
contra
Parmen.*

who is God, that his garden ſpread it ſelfe ,,
ouer all the world. Can yow deny vnto ,,
him now, but that Chriſtians do poſſeſſe ,,
both Eaſt, Weſt, North, and Southe: as alſo ,,
the prouinces of innumerable Ilandes? And ,,
the ſame hath *Saint Baſil* in his 72. and 75. ,,
epiſtle: & the like *S. Hilarie lib. 6. de Trinitate.*
This then was the greatnes of this vniuerſall Catholike Churche at that day. And of
this Church were coumpted the head Biſhops (for all theſe 300. yeares,) the Popes
and Bishops of Rome, as appeareth by the
deductions made by ✶ *Irenæus, Tertullian,* and ✶ *Supra*
other before mentioned, & in this Churche *c.4. & 5.*
was held to be all Catholike truth, & none
out of it. Which beinge ſo, I would gladly
know, what *poore, obſcure, troden dovvne Churche,*
neglected in the vvorld, not regarded in hiſtoryes, and
almoſt ſcarce viſible or knovvne (which yet he
ſaith to be the only true Churche of God)
can Iohn Fox find vs out in theſe firſt 300.
yeares? eſpecially ſeeing he ſaith alſo, that it
muſt be differēt from the Church of Rome,
as from the diuels chappell: and that it muſt
come downe from the Apoſtles tyme, & alwayes hould ſome ſparkles of true doctrine. The ob-
12. For example or proofe wherof not- ſcure
withſtandinge, he mentioneth no one man, mathe-
woman, or childe, that was of that Churche maticall
in all theſe 300. yeares. And conſequently he of Iohn
driueth vs to imagine or ſeeke out, who Fox.
  V 4   they

they are that made vp this *obſcure Churche* of his, different and oppoſitt to the Romane. And I can find none, except the knowne heretiks of theſe firſt 3. ages: to whom the deſcription of his Church may eaſily agree. For firſt, none will deny, but that albeit they were many in number, as *Simon Magus* and his followers, the *Nicolaits, Cerynthians, Ebionites, Menandrians, Saturnians,* in the firſt age: *Baſilidians, Gnoſticks, Cerdoniſts, Marcioniſts, Valentinians, Encratites, Montaniſts,* and other, in the ſecond age. As alſo, *Helcheſits, Nouatians, Sabellians, Manichees,* and many more, in the third age; And that in diuers contreyes & prouinces they had their followers, their Churches, their aſſemblies, vnder the name of reformed Chriſtians, elect people, and men of more perfection, then the reſt: Yet in reſpect of the glorious Catholik Church, that ſhined throughout the world, they were iuſt as *Iohn Fox* deſcribeth his people heer. To witt, *a poore oppreſſed and perſecuted Church, &c.* Oppreſſed by force of truth, and perſecuted by the famous vvrytinges of Cath. Doctours againſt them. As (after the Apoſtles themſelues) *Saint Ignatius, Iuſtinus Martyr, Saint Dionyſe of Corinth, Saint Polycarpe, Irenæus, Clem. Alexandrinus, Tertullian, Origen, Cyprian, Amonius, Pamphilus, Arnobius,* & others. They were perſecuted alſo by the excommunications and ſpirituall cenſures of all Cath.

The cheefe heretikes of the firſt 300. yeares.

Hovv ould heretikes vvere perſecuted.

Cath. Bishoppes throughout the world:but
especially by the Popes of Rome, from
Saint Peter to *Pope Siluester,* which were 33. in
number,all martyrs, and euery one of them
condemned the heretikes of his tyme.

13. This accursed new Church also of heretikes had the other qualitie ascribed in
like manner by Iohn Fox to his Church.
To witt, that they were *neglected in the Christian vvorld and not regarded in storyes;* but only
to recount them to their shame and damnation. Finally the last commendation also
was not wantinge to them, that they were
almost scarse visible or knovvne, in respect of the
florishinge Catholike Church. And lastlie,
these congregations & swarmes of heretiks
(though neuer so much diuyded amonge
themselues) continued indeed from the
Apostles by a kind of broken succession of
tymes, the one rysing and the other falling.
And they had the last point also specified by
Iohn Fox, *of keepinge some sparks of true doctrine
in relligion.* For that (as *Saint Augustine* writeth)
*Nulla falsa doctrina est, quæ aliqua vera non inter-
misceat;* There is no doctrine so false which
doth not enterlace some true thinges. And
this is proper to heresies. For that otherwayes if they had no pointes of true doctrine, they should be rather Apostats, then
properly heretikes. For that Apostats are
those,that deny all Christs doctrine:but he-

Hovv ould heretickes agree to Iohn Fox his Church

Aug.l.2. quæst. Euang. cap. 40.

V 5   retikes

retikes do graunt fome partes, and denie
others.

A pointe
much to
be no-
ted.
14. About which point of ould heretikes
and their affinity with the proteftantes of
this age, it is woorth the noting, that whatfoeuer fome of our late English wryters
(efpecially the minifter *O. E.* or *Mathevv Sut-
cliffe*) do prattle to the contrary: yet fhall
yow neuer find any one article of thofe, that
are in controuerfy and held by vs at this day
againft the proteftantes, to haue byn held
fingularly by any one ould heretike in that
fenfe, as we do hould the fame. And much
leffe condemned for herefy in him or them,
by the Church in thes dayes or by any one
Father therof. And on the other fyde yow
fhall find diuers doctrines held by them,
and condemned in them by the Church for
herefies (I meane the heretikes of the firft
300. yeares) which the proteftátes do hould
at this day properly, and in the fame fenfe,
that thofe heretikes did. And we do condemne the fame for herefies in them, as the
primitiue Church did in the other. As for
example, that of the *Pfeudoapoftoli* heretikes
called *falfe Apoftles*, who did thinke *only faith
to be fufficient to faluation vvithout vvorkes.* Againft
which herefie *S. Auguftine* faith were written
the epiftles of *Saint Iames, Saint Iude*, S. *Peter*,
and *Saint Iohn*.

*Aug. lib.
de fide
& oper.
c. 14. &
de vnico
bap.c.10.*

15. That other point alfo, which S. *Ignatius*
repor-

reporteth of certayne heretikes in his tyme;
qui non confitebantur Euchariftiam effe carnem fal-
uatoris noftri Iefu Chrifti, qua pro peccatis noftris
paß.i eft. Who did not confeffe that the Eu-
charift was the flesh of our Sauiour Iefu
Chrift that fuffered for vs. That other doctrine in like manner, that *Theodoretus* wryteth of the *Nouatians: His, qui ab ipfis tinguntur,*
facrum chrifma non præbent: quocirca eos, qui ex hac
hærefi corpori Ecclefiæ coniunguntur, benedicti patres
vngi iufferunt. To thofe that are baptized by
them (the Nouatians) they do not giue holy
chrifme, for which caufe, whofoeuer retur-
ninge from that herefie are to be adioyned
to the body of the Cath. Church, the holy
Fathers commaunded that they fhould be
annointed with the faid chrifme.

16. *Cornelius* alfo, B. of Rome, complaineth
that the faid *Nouatus*, and *Nouatians* did not
receyue the facrament of Confirmation. For
talkinge of *Nouatus* he faith : *Qui figillo Domini*
ab Epifcopo non fignatus fuit: quomodo (quæfo) fan-
ctum Spiritum adeptus eft? He that was not fi-
gned with the feale of our Lord by the Bifhopp: how could he (thinke you) obteyne
the holy Ghoft? The fame heretickes alfo
denyed the power of abfoluinge from finne
in Priefts, as alfo confeffion & fatisfaction.
Accordinge as the fame holy B. and Pope Cor-
nelius obiecteth vnto them, by the teftimony
of *Saint Cyprian.*

Apud Theod. dial. 3.

Theod. l. 3. *hæret. fabulat. cap.* 35.

Ovvld herefies held for-mally againe by pro-teftates.

Cornel. Papa apud Eufeb. lib. 6. *hiftor. cap.* 35.

Cypr. l. 4. *epift.* 2.

And

And finally to go no further within theſe
firſt 300. yeares, *Saint Hierome* obiecteth for
an hereſie to the *Manichees* the denyinge of
mans free will ſaying, *Manichæorum dogma eſt*
hominum damnare naturam, & liberum auſerre ar-
bitrium. It is the doctrine of the *Manichees* to
condemne mans nature, and to take away
free will. So ſaith *Saint Hierome,* and *S. Chry-*
ſoſtome & *S. Auguſtine,* do alſo teſtifie the ſame
of the *Manichees* expreſſely. And though perhaps the *Manichees* held that doctrine vpon
other grounds, then the proteſtants do: yet
in the hereſie it ſelfe they do plainlie ſimbolize and agree.

Hier. in
prœm.
dialog.
contra
Pelag.
Chriſoſt.
hom. 43.
in Ioan.
Aug. lib.
contra
Manich.
& epi-
ſtola 28.

17. Theſe are matters then moſt euident
and cleere, nor can they be denyed, but that
theſe opiniôs are held by Proteſtants at this
day, in the very ſame wordes, ſenſe, & meaninge, as they were by the fornamed ould
heretickes; wherin alſo they were anathematized and condemned by the knowne
Cath. Church of theſe auncient ages.

Old he-
reſies
fraudu-
lently
obiected
to Ca-
tholiks.

18. But now, when on the contrary ſide
ſome ſectaries of our tyme (to cure or couer
this wound of theirs) will needs like apes
obiect to vs againe, that we hold ſome old
condemned errors and hereſies alſo (or rather ſome ſhaddow or ſimilitude therof:)
yow ſhall euer find one of theſe two frauds
or falſhoods in their obiection; to witt, that
eyther they obiect vnto vs that, which we
indeed

indeed hold not at all, or at least not in the
sense which they object it, or that the thing
in truth is noe error in it selfe, nor euer
was held or condemned for such in the
sense and meaninge in which we hold yt,
though it may haue some little externall similitude with that which was an error. As
for example, O. E. obiecteth vnto vs, that
we do simbolize and participate with two
old heresies, the one of the *Angelici. qui Angelos
adorabant*, that did adore Angells, as *Saint Augustine* saith : The other of the *Collyridians* (so
called of the greeke word *Collyra* signifyinge
a little triangle cake or bunne, that those
heretikes, being women, did offer in sacrifice to our B. lady.) But in both these examples, we vtterly deny, that we agree in doctrine or practise with those heretiks. Seing
that we neyther adore nor worshipp with
diuine honour angells or other Saints, nor
do offer sacrifice to the Mother of God, but
only to God himselfe alone : though in the
honour and memory also of his Mother &
other Saints glorified by him. Which doctrine of ours is extant in all our books. So
as here is manifestly found the first fraud of
our aduersaries : which is, to obiect to vs,
that which we hold not indeed.

19. And the other falshood also cannot be
denyed, wherby they affirme, the doctrine,
which we truly hold and practise in this behalfe

The first fraude.

Aug. ha- res. 39.

D. Thom. 2. 2. q. 85. art. 2.

The se- cond fraude.

halfe about honouring of Saints, to haue bin
at any tyme held for error, or condemned
by the auncient Cath. Church or teachers
therof for such. Truth it is, that the *Magde-*
burgians are not ashamed to note this for an
error in *Origen*: *Inuocandos Angelos Origenes pu-*
tauit. homil. 1. *in Ezech. Origen* thought Angells to be inuoked. And then againe: *hanc*
formulam inuocandi angelos proponit: Veni Angele,
& suscipe conuersum ab errore pristino, &c. and he
setteth downe this forme of praying to Angells; Come Angell receyue him that is conuerted from his former errors, &c.

Cent. 3. cap. 4. &.§. de angelis.

20.   But I would haue the *Magdeburgians* or
any of their parteners, shew me, when, or
where this sentence of *Origen* was euer noted or condemned by antiquity for error or
heresie, as some other doctrines of his were.
Certaine it is, they can not. Which is a singular argument against them. For that those
watchmen of the Church, that noted and
condemned those other errors of his, would
haue noted also this, if it had ben taken for
an error in those dayes. And further I say to
the *Magdeburgians*, lett them tell vs, whether
other holy fathers (yea the chiefest of Gods
Church) after *Origen* did not hould the very
same doctrine? Sure I am that the *Magdebur-*
gians themselues in the very next century
after, do condemne by name *Saint Ephrem*, &
Saint Hilary for this doctrine of inuocation
of An-

About honoringe & inuoca-tion of Angells.

of Angells in the same sense, that *Origen* did hold yt. And then againe, in the same third century they do reprehend by name for in-uocation of other Saints (which is the same controuersie) the graueft Doctors of the Church: to witt, *Saint Athanasius, Saint Basill, S. Gregory Nazianzen, S. Ambrose, S. Epiphanius Ephrem* and *Prudentius*, cytinge their plaine words, and condemninge their doctrine in this behalfe. So as yf this were an heresie,all these fathers were heretiks. Which were a blasphemous cogitation to thinke: & much more to speake or vtter: & thus much of the first obiection about honouringe Angells & other saints, wherin Proteftants do only calumniate our doings, as yow see.

Cent. 3. *cap.* 4.

21. As for the *Collyridians*, he that will read Saint *Epiphanius*, who wryteth of that madd foud fantafticall error of certayne women in *Thracia* (for so he tearmeth them) that would needs make our B. lady a goddeffe, and offer sacrifice vnto her: he shall find this father to handle two things at large. First, that notwithftandinge our B. lady for the priuilege of bearinge the Sauiour of the world, be highly to be honoured : yet not *vltra decorum* (as his words be) that is , not more then is decent or beyond the limits of a creature . Seing she is not God, though the mother of God. And confequently, these *Thraciane* women did foolishlie and

Epiph. lib. 3. *tom.* 2. *haref.*78, & 79.

About the he-refie of the Col-lyridias.

wicked-

wickedly, in deuifinge this publike facrifice
vnto her.

22. Secondly, that albeit this their facrifice
had byn offered by them to God himfelfe:
yet was it vnlawfully done by women. For
that neyther in the old nor new teftament
(faith he) was it appointed, that women
fhould do the function of facrifice, but men
only, and thofe Priefts.

<table>
<tr><td>Marck
this dif-
courfe
of Epi-
phanius
about
facrifi-
cinge in
the nevv
lavve.</td><td>And this argument *Saint Epiphanius* profe-
cuteth very largely. Prouinge that in the
new teftament and Chriftian Church the
Apoftles only, and other Priefts fucceedinge
by impofition of hands, had authority to fa-
crifice:but noe women, noe not the mother
of Chrift her felf. Who fhould haue had that
priuilege aboue all other women, yf any of
her fex might haue byn admitted. And after
our B. lady he addeth thefe that followeth:</td></tr>
</table>

Epiph.
ibid.

Fuerunt (faith he) *quatuor filiæ Philippo Euange-*
*liftæ prophetantes, fed non facrificantes, &c.*Philipp
the Euangelift had 4. daughters, that prophefied, but not that facrificed. And againe.

Ibid. ha-
ref. 79.

Et miniftrarum quidem Diaconiffarum appellatarum
ordo eft in Ecclefia : fed non ad facrificandum, &c.
Diaconißis indiguit Ecclefiafticus ordo, nufquam au-
tem eas presbyteras aut facrificulas conftituit, &c.
Vnde igitur hic rurfus mulierum faftus & infania
muliebris? There is (faith he) in the Chriftian
Church an order of them that are called
diaconiffes, but not to facrifice. The Eccle-
faafticall

fiasticall order had need of thefe diaconiffes (at the beginninge) but yet neuer ordeyned them as Priefts or Sacrificers. And whence then is now come againe, this pryde of women, or womanish madneffe, as to take vpon them to facrifice in the Church?

23. By all which difcourfe, you may eafily fee, what was the true herefie condemned in thefe *Collyridians*: to witt, *colere Sanctos vltra modum & decorum*, as the words of holy *Epiphanius* are, that is to worfhip Saints beyond meafure and decency, and aboue the nature, and condition of creatures. Which is forbidden by Gods Church, but not to honour them as feruants of his, and him in them. Yow will fee alfo, what opinion and vfe of Chriftian Sacrifice there was in *Epiphanius* his dayes, & how it was denyed to women, & practifed by Priefts only. Which yet the fectaries of thefe dayes cannot abyde to heare of. And heere now will we make an end of thefe firft 300. yeares after Chrift, wherin, as yow fee, Iohn Fox hath putt downe no fuccefsion of his Church at all, eyther in men or doctrine. For as for men (to witt, Bishops, Paftors, and teachers, fucceedinge one to the other from the Apoftles downward) they were all of the Roman vifible Church. And fo were all other that bere the name of Chriftians (except the heretiks before named) and of the faid

Christiã facrifice.

The vifible fuccefsion of the Church in the firft 300. yeares.

X   Romane

Romane and Cath. Church the chiefe leaders were, from *Saint Peter* vnto *Siluefter*, 33.
Popes (as before hath byn mencioned) all
martyrs, and wittneſſes of the ſame faith.
And in other principall Patriarchall ſeats,
wherin the Apoſtles had held the firſt
chaires, (as *Antioche, Hieruſalem, Alexandria,* &
the like)there had ſucceeded other holy Biſhops : as alſo in infinite other places throughout the world. So as in the Emperour
Conſtantines time, who liued in the end of
theſe firſt 300. yeares, & was the firſt Chriſtian Emperour, that publikelie profeſſed
Chriſtian Religiõ,the ſaid Chriſtiã Church
was ſo glorious, as in the firſt Councell of
Nice there were 318.principall Biſhops ioyned togeather,the moſt of them of *Aſia* only.
Wherby we ſee, how illuſtrious and eminent the ſaid Catholike Church and Religion was in that tyme.

24.   By which we do moſt euidently in-
The
ſumme
of that
vvhich
hath bin
ſaid hi-
therto.
ferre,that eyther Iohn Fox *his obſcure and trodden dovvne Church ſcarſe viſible* (as he ſaith) *to
the vvorld,*was not at all in thoſe dayes: or els
it lurked only in ſome of the forenamed heretiks. For yf he ſay, that the great perſpi-
cuous Roman Church was his at that time:
then how doth he define his Church *to be
obſcure and ſcarſe viſible to the vvorld ?* And mo-
★*Part* 1.
*e.*5 & 6. reouer we haue ſhewed ★ before, that the
Biſhops, Doctors, teachers, martyrs, and
cheeſe

cheefe members, or guiders of this great illuftrious Church, were oppofite to him and
his Church both in faith and doctrine. And
this by the confefsion of his owne Doctors
& writers the *Magdeburgiās* & others, that reprehend & cōdemne the fathers of the 2. &
3. ages for holdinge diuers principall points
of doctrine, now alfo in cōtrouerfie againft
them, and for vs. And we haue fhewed alfo
that this great vniuerfall and Cath. Church
had all truth in it, that was reuealed by
Chrift, *and not fome fparks only*, as Fox requireth in his Church. And that it had continuall fuccefsion of multitudes of true teachers without interruption, and not *one ftar-*
ting vp in one age, and another in another, wherwith Fox feemeth to be contented for the
continuation of his Church.

25.   And finally if Fox comming at length
to be afhamed of his former definition of
an obfcure and troden dovvne Church, and of the
fparkled doctrine of truth therin taught, fhould
leaue the fame, & offer to lay hands on the
great illuftrious and vifible Church of thefe
firft 300. yeares, fayinge that this was his
(which yet yow haue feene by many arguments demonftrated that it cannot be) I
fhalbe content to admit fo ridiculous a pretence for a time, with cōdition that he will
ftand to yt & go forward with this Church
in the fequent ages, and not to difclayme

The con-
clufion
of this
chapter
vvith an
offer to
Fox.

X 2   from

from her to his *hidden Church* againe. Which yf he yeld vnto, then haue we now a viſible and eminent true Church on foote (by confeſsion of both partyes) which we muſt follow to the worlds end. For that ſhe cannot perish againe, as before we haue declared. For which cauſe I am to proſecute the ſame from age to age in this treatiſe, from this tyme downwards to our daies in the Chapters that do enſue. Where we ſhall ſee, who ſticketh to her, and who flyeth from her: who followeth her conſtantly, or who giueth the ſlipp. For that ſhee being now once ſo potent, notorious, and illuſtrious, as both parts do confeſſe (yf he will ſtand to yt in earneſt, that ſhe is his Church alſo) it is not poſſible, that ſhe ſhould be loſt, ſhrinke or fade away agayne: But that all the world muſt ſee it, how, where, when, and by whome ſo great an accident ſhould fall out: neyther can Fox and his people being now once in her and of her (by his owne pretence) be found out of her afterward: but only by Apoſtaſie or hereſie and runninge away. This then let vs examine in the ages followinge.

THE

THE PROSECVTION OF THE

SAME MATTER, TO VVITT, OF THE *defcent of the* Catholike *and* Proteftant *Church for other three hundred yeares, that is from* Pope Sylueſter *and* Conſtantine , *to* Pope Gregorie, & Mauritius *the Emperour. And vvhere* Iohn Fox *his Church lay hidd in this tyme.*

CHAP. III.

AND thus (hauinge runne ouer the firſt three ages after Chriſt) we muſt now paſſe to the ſecond ſtation, which is for other 300. yeares. Beginninge from *Conſtantine* the Emperour downward vnto the tyme of *Saint Gregorie,* vnder whom *Saint Auguſtine* came into England. In which ſpace of tyme, the Catholike Chriſtian Church ſpread ouer all the world (as before yow haue heard) did growe, and confirme it ſelfe powerfully (eſpecially after perſecution did ceaſe, as by all ſtories appeareth) hauing had 32. Popes, betweene *Syluefter* , and *Gregorie,* wherof 30. were holden for great Sainčts, and 3. or 4. were martyrs.

2. The Fathers, and Doctors alſo of theſe three ages were moſt excellent men both Grecians and Latyns. And it ſeemeth, that, what wanted in theſe 3. ages from the former thrce in glorie of martyrdome , it was ſupplyed by the excellency of learninge. As

for

for example, in the fourth age after Chrift, (which is the firft of the fecond three) did

The Fa-thers Doctors & coun-cells of the fe-côd 300. yeares after Chrift.

florish *Eufebius, Lactantius, Rheticius, Iuuencus, Athanafius, Hilarius, Optatus, Climacus, Bafill, Nazianfen, Ambrofe, Prudentius, Hierome, Chryfo-ftome, Epiphanius, Cyril,* and diuers others. In the 5. age *Saint Auguftine, Poßidonius, Sulpitius, Orofius, Caßianus, Profper, Vincentius Lyrinenfis, Fulgentius,* and many more. And in the fixte age *Caßiodorus, Emifenus, Procopius, Fortunatus Venantius, Euagrius, Gregorius Turonenfis, and Gregory the great.* Ali which filled the world with their excellét books both Greeke & Latyn. Befids many Generall, Nationall, and Pro-uinciall Counceils. Wherof fiue were vni-uerfall, the firft of *Nice,* the fecond of *Conftan-tinople,* the third of *Ephefus,* the fourth of *Chal-cedon* (wherin there were 630. Bifhops) and the fifth was of *Conftantinople* the fecond time. But of Prouinciall, and Nationall Councels there are receaued to the number of almoft 70. to haue byn held in his time.

Iohn Fox fin-deth not a hole for his poore Church in thofe 300. yeares.

3. By all which concurfe of teftimonies the force & vnitie of Catholike faith is fhe-wed: to witt, that thefe *Fathers, Doctors, Popes,* and *Councells* agreeinge togeather all throu-ghout the world in one and the felfe fame faith and Religion, & continuinge the fame from age to age, with fo great Authority of refpect, and Maieftie, as not only all Eccle-fiafticall perfons of what nations foeuer &

other

other Chriſtian people, but all temporall Princes Kings & Emperours in like manner (except ſuch as were noted with any particular hereſy, as ſome Emperours of the Eaſt) did wholy ſubmitt themſelues with one conſent of mind. Wherby this viſible illuſtrious Roman Church was made ſo great, and vniuerſall, notorious and knowne, embracinge all Chriſtendome, at it is wholy impoſsible for Iohn Fox to find out any creeping hidden Church, bearing the name of Chriſtian in theſe three ages, and yet different from this viſible & ſplendent Church of Rome, which he calleth the diuels Chappell. And much more harde will it be for him, to find out this, in theſe later 300. yeares, then in the former. For that the externall glorie of this Church was increaſed much more in theſe three ages, then in the firſt three before treated of, which paſſed all in perſecution.

4. The hereſies alſo and ſects of this tyme (beinge aboue 50. in number) were beaten downe more ſtrongly by the foreſaid *Fathers, Biſhops,* and *Councells,* then before. By reaſon they had more time & leyſure from perſecution to attend vnto them, then had the former 3. ages. The principall hereſies of this fourth age were *Melitians, Donatiſts, Arrians, Nouatians, Macedonians, Luciferians, Aërians, Eunomians, Apollinarians, Aetians,* Priſcillianiſts,

The heretiks of the ſecōd 300. yeares after Chriſt.

X 4

lianiſts, *Iouinians*, *Vigilantians*, *Collyridians*, *Heluidians*, *Antimarians*, and other the like. And in
the fifth age were *Pelagians*, *Neſtorians*, *Eutychians*, and other ſuch rabble. And in the ſixt
age, *Seuerians*, *Monothelites*, *Chryſtolytes*, *Agnoites*,
Sadduces, *Theopaſchites*, and the like. Out of
which *Synagoges*, & Congregations of wranglinge ſpirits, which ſucceeded one an other
in diuers times, places and countryes, and
oppoſed themſelues maliciouſly out of their
obſcure corners againſt the ſhininge light of
the foreſaid Cath. Church; if Iohn Fox will
frame his poore & beggarly Church (which
yet he holdeth for the only true Church
of God) oppreſſed, and troden downe (as
he ſaith) *and almoſt ſcarce viſible to vvorldly eyes*,
he may do it which great probability. For
that theſe fellowes, were neglected, and
troden downe in deed, by the other oppoſite Roman Church. And yet did they (as
Iohn Fox requireth for the ſucceſſion of his
Church) continue and riſe vp from tyme to
tyme (though by no orderly ſucceſſion of
Biſhops or doctrine, as hath byn ſaid) yea
they had that other quality alſo proper to
Iohn Fox his Church, that they alwayes
kept ſome ſparks of true doctrine and religion togeather with their hereſies.

So as in this reſpect of obſcuritie, & contemptibility, Iohn Fox may eaſely ioyne his
Church with them: as alſo in hauinge ſome
ſparkles

In his
prote-
ſtation
to the
English
Church
pag. 9.

sparkles of true doctrine, but not the whole
body of true doctrine among them.

5. He may ioyne also in diuers particular
doctrines, which these men held, as peculiar
heresies to themselues, & were condemned
by the Church for such in those dayes, and
are held also in these dayes by Iohn Fox his
Church in the very selfe same words, sense,
and meaninge, as they were held by those
heretiks. As namely, he may ioyne with the
Donatists, who said *that they were the only
Church, and called the Succession of Bishops in the
Church of Rome* (as Sectaries do at this day)
the Chaire of pestilence. And moreouer, that the
whole Church besids themselues had erred,
&c. Which is the comon songe also of our
moderne Protestants. And further if yow
will see how neere of kynne these *Donatists*,
and our *Protestants* be both in manners, conditions, doctrine and beliefe : do yow read
Saint Augustine, *Optatus*, and other writers,
that obiected against them, these things followinge. To witt, *That they had cast the blessed
Sacrament of the Aultar to dogges: ouer threw Aultars, broke Chalices and sold them, cast a bottle of
holy Chrisme out of the Church windowv, shaued
Priests heads to take avvay their Vnction, turned
Nunnes out of their Monasteries to the vvorld, pollu-
ted all Church stuffe,* and the like. And whether
Iohn Fox & his fellowes do not ioyne also
in these points, lett the reader iudge.

Commu
nication
of do-
ctrine
betvvee
ne pro-
testants,
& here-
riks of
the se-
côd 300.
yeares
after
Christ.

Aug.lib.
de haref.
her. 69.
Optatus
l.2. idem
lib. 6.

X 5 6. They

6. They may ioyne in like manner with the *Eunomians* for their only faith, who affir-

Auguſt. hareſ.54. med (as *Saint Auguſtine* ſaith) *quòd nihil cuiquam obeſſet quorumlibet perpetratio ac perſeuerantia peccatorum, ſi huius, quæ ab illis docebatur, fidei particeps eſſet.* That the committinge and perſeue-

„ rance in neuer ſo great ſinnes, could not
„ hurt him that was partaker of their faith.

Pacian. ep. 1. & 3. ad Simpron. Auguſt. har. 53. They may ioyne alſo with the *Nouatians* of that tyme in *denying the Churches povver in forgiuinge ſinnes.* They may ioyne with the *Aërians*, who taught (as *Saint Auguſtine* ſaith) *non oportere orare, vel oblationem offerre pro mortuis*; that we ought not to pray or offer oblations for them that be dead. And further: *That ſolemne feaſts are not to be appointed by the Church: but euery one to faſt vvhen he vvould, leaſt he ſhould ſeeme to be vnder the lavv, &c.*

Auguſt. har. 82. Hierom li. contra Iouiniã. 7. Thus teſtifieth *S. Auguſtine* of him. And of *Iouinian*, that followed him, both the ſaid Father, and *Saint Hierom* (that wrote againſt him) do accuſe him to haue held: *That all ſinnes vvere equall before God*, that faſting from certaine meats vvas not profitable; that chaſte marriage was equall in honour, and meritt to profeſſed Virginity in Nunnes, and that he had byn cauſe that ſome Nunnes had married in Rome, and finally that the reward in heauen was equall to all men. And is not this good currant proteſtant doctrine and practiſe at this day? but let vs goe forward.

They

They may ioyne also with the *Heluidians,* or *Antidicomarians* in impugning our B. Lady, & equalling marriage with Virginity. And much more with *Vigilantius* in impugninge the continent sole life of cleargy men, worship of martyrs at their tombes, vse of candles and torches in the Church by day time, Inuocation of Sainds, vowes of pouerty, and the like.

Hierom. li.contra Vigilan-tium.

8.   I will go no further. For that this is sufficient, for to see, what communion Iohn Fox his Church did hold in thefe three ages, eyther with the common knowne Cath. Church of Chrift, or with thefe lurking affemblies of heretiques purfued and perfecuted by the faid Church. And for that Iohn Fox is guilty to himfelfe in this behalfe, he hath proceeded accordingly in his ads and monuments. For wheras he promifeth a feuerall booke of thefe fecond 300. yeares vnder this title. *The fecond Booke conteyning the next* 300. *yeares after Chrift, &c.* He not findinge any fufficient matter for his purpofe to patch vp this fecond booke with all, as he did the former, with recountinge the martyrs of thofe tymes: what fhifte, deuifeth he (thinke yow) to bleare his readers eyes withall, and to feeme to fay fomwhat in the continuation of his ftorie? yow fhall heare briefly. And by this one tricke yow may learne to know the man and his meaninge

The poore fhift of Ihon Fox.

Fox pag. 95.

meaninge for the tyme to come.

9. Firſt he writeth but fiue leaues in all for the continuatiõ of the ſtorie of theſe ſecond 300. yeares. A ſhort volume, yow will ſay, for ſo great, and copious an argument. And yet further yow muſt know, that of theſe fiue leaues he paſſeth two, in telling tales of matters, that fell vnder *Pope Eleutherius*, and K. *Lucius* more then a hundred yeares before. And conſequently it ſhould haue byn told in his former booke by order of tyme and ſtorie. And then the other three leaues he ſpendeth in ſettinge downe the entrance of the *Saxons* into England, about the yeare of Chriſt 449. and the ſucceſsion of their pagan Kings vnto S. *Auguſtine* his comming. As of all the foreſaid glorious Chriſtian Church for 300. yeares togeather, (to witt, from *Pope Sylueſter*, and *Conſtantine* vnto *Pope Gregorie* and *Mauritius* the Emperour, wherin ſhe floriſhed more then in any other three ages) we find only fiue leaues deſigned, but ſcarce three lines performed. Wherby yow may perceyue how litle part Iohn Fox perſwadeth himſelfe to haue in theſe three ages, for his hidden Church. Yow may conſider alſo, what an honeſt bargainer he is, & how well he performeth his promiſe made in the firſt page of his whole worke: wherin he ſaith, that he will ſett *foorth at large the vvhole race and courſe of the Church, from the primi-*

tiue

Iohn Fox his ſhifte to fill vp this ſecond booke.

An. 180.

tiue age to these later tymes of ours, &c. Wherof
yow see he hath performed nothinge at all
hitherto, eyther largely, or briefly. I meane
of this race or course of any Church generall or particular, domesticall or forrayne,
good or badd, true or false, his or ours. For
of the first 300. yeares, he wrote only the
ten persecutions, as yow haue seene: and of
the second 300. yeares he writeth nothing
at all.

10. Which (if yow consider well) is a
straunge confession, of his owne weaknes,
and pouertie. Seing that these three ages (to
witt, the 4. 5. and 6.) are the most aboundant of matter, that are to be found in the
Church of Christ from the beginning. And
so might he see by the Centuries of his Maisters the *Magdeburgians.* Who do enlarge
themselues much more in these three ages,
then in the former. Enforced thervnto by
the multitude of matter : though all against
themselues, as before hath bene noted and
here will also appeare. Which Iohn Fox
well perceauinge, thought best by sleight
of silence to auoide that inconuenience of
treatinge a history, so apparantly against
himself. Which sleight notwithstandinge
(or rather flight) euery man of meane vnderstandinge doth easely see. Consideringe,
that (accordinge to the argument of his
booke, and particular promise made before)
he

he ſhould haue declared to vs, that the Religion of *Britanie* in theſe 300. yeares next before the entrance of *Saint Auguſtine*, was for him, and his Church; and not for ours: yea, different from the *Roman Religion* brought in by *Augnſtin*, as often yow haue heard him proteſt. And heere had byn the proper place to haue proued it, if it had byn proueable. And wheras in the ſame proteſtation of his, prefixed before his whole volume, he auouched (as yow haue heard) that the chiefe Britiſh preachers & teachers of theſe times, before *Saint Auſtens* comminge (as *Faſtidius, Ninianuſ, Patricius, Dubritius, Congellus, Dauid, Aſſaphus, Gildas,* and others before mentioned) were true teachers, & taught the Ghoſpell rightly, accordinge to the proteſtant faith, & conſequētly were of his Religion: he ought heere to haue proued the ſame by their wrytings, liues, acts and monuments, as I haue ſhewed the contrary by all theſe kind of arguments and proofes before. But the Fox knowinge the difficulty and perill of this combate, would not enter into the ſame, nor take vpon him to defend or iuſtify any thing at all: though neuer ſo much promiſſed or proteſted in his prefaces, and preambles at the beginninge. Wherof the reaſons are theſe that enſue.

In his proteſtation to the Engliſh Church *pag.* 10.

VVhat Fox ſhould haue treated in his 2. booke, & ſecōd 300. yeares after Chriſt. *Sup. part* 1. *cap.* 5.

11. Firſt, for that touchinge the Britiſh Church duringe theſe three ages, he had nothinge

nothinge at all to wryte or relate in very deed, but that would be manifestly against himselfe, if he had wrytten or related it and descended to particulars. For (accordinge to that yow haue heard before in diuers parts of this treatise) that as the first faith of the Britans came from *Rome*, and therby they were made members of the *Roman* Church from the beginning: so remayned they vnited with the same in all pointes of faith and religion (except some fewe abuses crept in, amonge parte of them, towards the later end of these three ages) vntill the conuersion of the English by *Saint Augustine* to the same *Roman* faith. Which point is proued so euidently by so many signes, arguments, & demonstrations, as little comforte might Iohn Fox haue to enter into this discourse or examination. And consequently, though he had promised in the beginninge to treat this subiect of the British Church: yet comminge to the place, & tyme, when he should haue performed his promise, he thought better to withdraw him selfe sleightly by vtter silence, then to put himselfe in bryars by makinge, any mention at all therof. And thus much for his silence concerninge the Christian Church of Britanie in these three ages.

VVhy Fox vvriteth nothinge of the Church of Britanie in these 3. ages.

12. But for the generall Catholike Church of Christendome, though these tymes yeald

aboun-

aboundant matter(as hath byn said:)yet the whole ftreame, and current therof running quite againft him, he thought beft in like manner to decline craftelie the medlinge or wreftlinge therwith. And fo much the more, for that he had feene the pittifull pleight wherin his Maifters the *Magdeburgiãs* had caft themfelues in their 4.5.and 6.Centuries, by ouer large relatinge the acts and gefts of thefe three ages againft themfelues and their owne Religion. Beinge forced to fpend a great parte of their labours, not fo much in relating what the Fathers of thofe ages write or held, as to anfwere and refute the fame, & fhewe that it was not true, nor the faid Doctors, & Fathers to be beleeued therin. Which trouble Iohn Fox (like a ioylie Fox in deed) thought beft to auoid by art of filence. I will in this place for example fake only, and to giue yow a taft of the faid *Magdeburgians* dealinge throughout their whole worke (from which Iohn Fox taketh the principall parts of his) lett yow fee fome points taken out of their fourth centurie dedicated to her Maieftie of England, with a fharpe inuectiue (as before hath byn fhewed) vfed by them againft the Caluinifts therin. Which centurie conteyneth the fourth hundred yeare after Chrift, & the firft of the three which now we haue in hand, from *Conftantine* downward.

Enc. 2.
cap. 5.&
Sup. p. 1.
cap. 6.

Wherin

Wherin they fpend aboue 400. leaues in folio, and more then twice as much in the other two centuries that enfue : Iohn Fox not hauinge beftowed foure leaues vpon all three ages, as yow haue heard.

13. And that yow may perceyue how this one centurie of the *Magdeburgians* commeth to make fo great a volume, yow muft note, that it is deuided into certayne large Chapters or heads of different matters. As for example, firft of the propagation of Chriftian Religion in that age, and the ftate therof throughout all Countreyes, kingdomes and nations. Which is a large matter, as yow fee, comprehendinge the ftories of all Ecclefiafticall writers. Secondly of perfecutions, troubles & iarres, that haue paffed; as alfo of peace & tranquillitie. Then, of doctrine, good or badd : then of herefies; then of rites, and ceremonies, then of Ecclefiafticall gouernment, then of Schifmes, then of Synods and Councels : then of Bishops, Doctors and teachers, their liues, works, and actions at large : then of heretiks their beginnings', and endings: then of Martyrs: then of miracles, then of Pagan common wealthes alfo, and other fuch points capable, as you fee of longe difcourfes. Which I thought good once to note, to th'end, that thofe, which haue not read the centuries, may know in generall what matters they

The fubftance, and methode of of the Magdeburgians Centuries.

Y   handle,

handle, & what methode they vſe therin.

14.   Secondly it is to be noted about the ſame affaire , that in all theſe heads and chapters there be diuers things , which are not in controuerſie among vs : I meane betweene Cath. and Proteſtants, but are common to vs both , at leaſt in ſome degrees. Other points there are, that they affirme, & we deny; or we affirme and they deny. There is a third kind alſo of points, wherin, though we & Proteſtāts do not agree fully, eyther in the doctrine or in the practiſe: yet one ſecte of them differeth more or leſſe from vs, then th'other. And in all theſe three points yow ſhall ſee ſome breefe examples of the *Magdeburgians* manner of proceedinge in this fourth age. Notinge to yow firſt by the way their owne teſtimony of the excellent learninge of the Doctors and teachers

Cent. 4. therof in theſe wordes. *Habuit hæc ætas , ſi quæ* *cap.* 4. *vnquam alia, plurimos præſtantes & illuſtres Docto-* *pag.* 159. *res, vt Arnobium , Lactantium, &c.* This age (if The ever any other) had very many moſt excel- praiſe of the Do- lent, and famous Doctors, as *Arnobius, Lactan-* ctors & *tius, Euſebius, Athanaſius, Hilarius, Victorinus, Ba-* Fathers *ſilius, Nazianſenus, Ambroſius, Prudentius, Epipha-* of the 4. *nius, Theophilus, Hieronymus , Fauſtinus, Didymus,* age by *Ephræm, Optatus*, and others: out of which we the *Mag* ſhall ſhewe and declare what was the forme *deburs* of Chriſtian doctrine vſed in this age. *gians*.

15.   Lo theere the teſtimony of the *Magde-* *burgians*

burgians of the famous Doctors, teachers, and leaders of Chrifts Church in this age. And beinge fuch as they fay, fo excellently learned, and indewed with Chrifts fpirite for guydinge of his Church : is it probable (thinke yow) that thefe foure *German Magdeburgians, Illyricus, VVigandus, Iudex* and *Faber,* fhall come to prefume afterward to condemne them all of ignorance and lacke of fpirite , when they fpeake againft them? Trulie they cannot do it with any fhamefaftnes or modeftie at all: or be beleeued by any difcreete man, if they do it. Well then, lett vs examine this point a little.

16. In their Chapter of Doctrine , when they talke of thefe points of God, and the B. Trinitie, of three diftinct parfons, of the natures, and wills of Chrift, and other fuch matter, (wherin they and we do not differ) they alleage thefe Fathers aboundantly. And no maruaile. For as longe as they teach Catholike Doctrine, they haue all the Fathers works and volumes for them. But when they touch any point, wherin there is controuerfie betweene vs : there they fall out prefentlie with the faid Fathers for holdinge againft them. As for example, in one paragraph of this Chapter and Doctrine, (which paragraph is, *De lib. Arbitrio*) they beginne it thus. *De lib. Arbitrio quæ commodè & tollerabiliter a Doctoribus huius ætatis tradita videntur, fic*

About freevvil. Cent. 4. pag. 211.

tur, *fic habent*. Thofe things which feeme
vnto vs to haue byn commodiouslief, and
tollerably deliuered by the Doctors of this
age about Free will, are thefe that follow.
Wherin they cenfure firft (as yow fee) all
Doctors of this age, fo greatly extolled by
them before: as though they hadd deliuered
many things incommodious,& intollerable
about Free will. As indeed afterwards in an
other Chapter intituled *the declininge of true*
doctrine, (conteyninge the incommodious opinions, &
errors of thefe Doctors) they fpeake more plainly thus: *Patres omnes ferè huius ætatis de lib. Arbi-*
trio confusè loquuntur, & contra manifefta fcripturæ
fanctæ teftimonia. Almoft all the Fathers of this
age do fpeake confufedly of free will, and
againft the manifeft teftimonyes of hollie
Scripture. And for proofe of this, they name
in particular *Lactantius, Athanafius, Bafil, Na-*
zianzen, Epiphanius, Hieronymus, and *Gregorius*
Niffenus. Condemninge them all, for not denyinge altogether Free will in man after
his fall.

17. Againe in the fame Chapter of Doctryne, and paragraph *De Pænitentia,* they begin thus: *Doctrinam de Pænitentia, vt grauis per*
fefe, & magni eft momenti, ita fatis tenuiter & fri-
gidè (quantum quidem ex fcriptis eius videre eft)
quemadmodum & in fuperioribus faculis tractatam
videas ab hac ætate : Nos igitur ea, quæ de hac parte
mediocriter & rectè, & vtiliter dicta effe videntur
recitabi-;

Ib. pag. 287. & 291.

Ccut. 4. pag.231.

recitabimus. The doctrine of pennance as it is
a graue matter in it selfe, & of great impor- "
tance, so do we see it handled by this age, "
(as also by the former ages) very sleightly, "
and coldly, as we may see by their writings "
extant. Wherfore we shall recite heere "
those things only of this matter, which "
seeme vnto vs to haue byn spoken, by the "
said Fathers with some mediocrity, recti- "
tude, and vtilitie, &c. See now their iudg- "
ment & censure of all the Fathers, not only
of this age : but of all the former ages also
since Christ: As hauing writté both sleightly, and coldlie. And yet further in an other
chapter of declyninge doctrine, they say,
*Pænitentiam hæc ætas (vt ferè & superiores) neque
rectè definijt, neque partes eius satis explicauit : imò
nec de fide (necessaria Pænitentiæ parte) propemodùm
aliquid habet.* This fourth age, as neyther the ,,
other three before, haue eyther giuen the ,,
true definition of pennance, nor sufficiently ,,
declared the parts therof, nay they speake ,,
nothinge almost of faith, which yet is a ne- ,,
cessarie parte of penance.

Cent. 4.
cap. 4.

18. Thus they pronounce boldly of all the
ages since Christ, not exceptinge that of the
Apostles themselues. And who can suffer so
wicked a slaúder? as though they had made
no mencion of faith at all, or as though
when they prescribe fastinge, prayer, sor-
row, and teares to pennance, they excluded

faith?

faith? where as it is euident, euen vnto children, that no man can performe theſe things
except he haue firſt faith, and do beleeue in
him, whom he ſeeketh to pleaſe and pacifie.
I ſay nothinge heere, of the intollerable iniuries, and falſe calumniations, which they
do inferre vpon the holly Fathers, without
all cauſe, if their words were examined. As
for example, in this very place, they condemne *Saint Ephrem* for deprauing pennance
and excludinge faith from the ſame, for that
he ſaith : *Per lachrymas huius breuiſſimi temporis
peccata (Deus) dimittit, &c. Et, cùm ſanauerit,
mercedem conferet lachrymarum.* God (ſaith this
Sainct) doth pardon our ſinnes by our
,, teares ſhedd in this ſhort tyme of our life: &
,, when he hath healed vs, he will geue vs a
,, reward alſo for our teares. Who ſeeth not,
but that this holly Father ſuppoſeth faith
in him, that doth weepe: and conſequently
is not ſubiect to the wicked ſlaunder of the
Magdeburgians, affirminge him to exclude
faith? yet thus they vſe both him and all
Fathers lightly, when they cite them, to refute their ſentencs : alleaginge them commonly with ſome falſe calumniation. But
lett vs go forward.

19. When they come to ſpeake of the doctrine of the B. *Sacrament and reall preſence* (for
that in this they hold with vs againſt the
Sacramentaries, & Caluiniſts) they do cyte
the

*Cent. 4.
pag. 294.
Ephr. l. 2.
de com-
punctio-
ne cordis
cap. 3.*

The bleſ-
ſed Sa-
cramēt.

the Fathers aboundantly. As that of *S. Am-*
brose : Didicisti, quia quod accipis corpus Christi est.
Thou hast learned, that the thinge which
thou receyuest, is the body of Christ. And
againe: *Bibi sanguinem è Christo, idque in veritate,*
non in vmbra aut similitudine. I haue dronke the
bloud of Christ,& that in truth not in a sha-
dow or similitude. And then out of *S. Hilla-*
rie: Si verè verbum caro factum est, & nos verè ver-
bum carnem cibo dominico sumimus. If the word
of God be truly made flesh,then do we truly receyue that flesh in the Lords Supper.
And further they alleage *Saint Hierom, Arno-*
*bius, Iuuencus,*and others of this age, that haue
the like testimonies, and cleare speaches for
proofe of this veritie. Which do seeme to
them so strong & manifest demonstrations
against the Zwinglian, and Caluinian doctrine,auowinge to the contrarie: that they
hold them for obstinatly blynd, that deny
or resist the same. And this, for that the doctrine pleaseth them. But if we steppe a
foote further to the doctriné of this *B. Sacra-*
ment made also *a Sacrifice,* and so testified by
the same Fathers, that affirmed the reall
phesence: then our good *Magdeburgians,* that
comméded them so highly before, do flatly
leaue both them and vs, and do place their
sayings in their other Chapter of incommodious speaches. Accoumptinge them for
strawe,and stubble,and erroneous doctrine.

Cent. 4.
*Pag.*242.
Ambr.
lib. 4. *de*
Sacr.c. 4.

Hil. l. 8.
de Tri-
nitate.
»

Incom-

Incommode dictum eſt ; (ſay they) *quòd citatur ex*
" *Athanaſy libello, &c.* It was ſpoken incommo-
" diouſly by *Athanaſius* in his booke of the
" Image of Chriſt, where he denyeth expreſ-
" ly that there is any thinge remayninge in
" this world of the fleſh and bloud of Chriſt,
" but only that which is daily made ſpiritual-
" ly by the hands of Prieſts vpon the Aultar.

Nazian- It is a new phraſe alſo of *Nazianzen*, when
zen orat. he ſaith, *Mox incruenti Sacrificij oblatione manus*
1. in Iu-
liam. *commaculat*, preſently he did ſteyne his hands
with the oblation of the vnblouddy Sacri-
Ambr. fice. Againe they accuſe *S. Ambroſe* for vſinge
lib. 5. theſe words, *Miſſam facere, Offerre, Offerre Sa-*
ep. 33. *crificium, &c.* To ſay Maſſe, to offer, to offer
Niſſen vp Sacrifice, &c. They reprehend *Gregorie*
Orat. Ca *Niſſen*, for teaching of tranſmutation, or
techiſti- tranſubſtantiation : *Dei verbo ſanctificatum pa-*
ca. *nem , in Dei verbi corpus credimus immutari.* We
" do beleeue that the bread which is ſancti-
" fied by the word of God, is by the ſame
" word of God chaunged into the body of the
" ſonne of God.

20. It would be ouerlonge to treat of all
Cent. 4. the points in cōtrouerſy for which the *Mag-*
pag. 292. *deburgians* do reprehend and condemne the
Fathers of this age, which ſo highly they
commended a litle before. For about Iuſti-
fication by only faith, they condemne by
Hier. in name *Lactantius, Nilus, Chromatius, Ephraëm*, &
cap. 3. ad *Saint Hierom.* And why ? for that he ſaith,
Galat.
non

non sufficit murum habere fidei, nisi ipsa fidesbonis operibus confirmetur , It is not ynough to haue the wall of faith, except faith be confirmed with good works. Which yet yow haue heard approued by the sentence of Syr Fr. Hastings before. *Enc. 2. cap. 16.*

21. They condemne the same *Lactantius* together with *Saint Gregory Nissen, Saint Hillarie, Saint Nazianzen, Saint Ambrose, Saint Ephraëm,* and *Theophilus Alexandrinus,* for attributing too much to good works; but especially to those that are voluntary. *Inter omnia opera* (say they) *Electitijs plurimum hæc ætas tribuit* . *Sic enim ait Theophilus, hi qui ieiunia,id est,Angelicam conuersationem in terris imitantur,per continentiam breui & paruo labore, magna sibi & æterna cōciliant præmia.* But among all other works (say the *Magdeburgians)* this age doth attribute most vnto voluntarie works or such as are chosen by a mans selfe,for so saith *Theophilus* Archbishop of *Alexandria,* those that do follow fastinge that is to say an Angelicall conuersation vpon earth , do gayne vnto themselues by this short, and small labour of abstinence great, and eternall rewards. *Cent. 4. pag.293.* *Theoph. Alexād. lib.3. de Pascha-te.* „ „ „ „ „ „ „ „ „ „

22. About *satisfaction* they reprehend greatlie, and put it for an errour in great *Hillarius,* for that he writeth vpon these words of the psalme , *My eyes haue brought foorth fountayes of vvaters,&c. Hæc pænitentia vox est,lachrymis orare, lachrymis ingemiscere* , this is the voice of true *Cent. 4. pag.294. Hilar.in psal.118.*

pen-

„ pennance to pray with teares, and ſigh with
„ teares. And againe: *Hæc venia peccati eſt, fontem
fletus flere , & largo lachrymarum imbre madeſieri,*
„ this is the forgiuenes of ſinne , to weepe a
„ whole fountayne of teares; & to waſh our
„ ſelues with a large ſhowre of weepinge, &c.
This did greatly diſcontent our goodfel-
low *Germans*, but *Saint Hillarius* was of an
other opinion.

The fa-
thers
condem
ned for
diuers
doctri-
nes held
againſt
prote-
ſtants.

23. What ſhould I recyte heere other controuerſies: ſeinge it would but weary the
Reader? for about, *Inuocation*, *and prayer to
Saincts* they condemne by name *S. Athanaſius
lib. de Incarnatione*, for prayinge to our lady:
Saint Baſil oratióne in 40. *Martyres,* for prayinge
to the ſaid 40. Martyrs: *S. Gregorie Nazianzen
oratione in Baſilium,* for prayinge to *Saint Baſil,*
after he was dead. Alſo for prayinge to *Saint
Cyprian* after he was martyred, *Orat. in Cyprianum.* They condemne alſo *Saint Ambroſe lib. de
viduis*, for prayinge to *S. Peter*, and *S. Andrevv*,
and *our Lady.* They condemne *Prudentius* for
prayinge to *Saint Laurence*; and in an other
place to *Saint Vincentius,* and *Caſſianus Martyrs,
Hym. in Laur. Vincent,* and *Caſſianum.* They
condemne *Epiphanius* for ſaying, that prayers
of the liuinge do helpe the dead. *Hæreſ.* 75.
They condemne *S. Ephrem* for ſayinge, that
the Saincts in Paradiſe did pray for them,
that are aliue *lib.* 1. *de compunctine cordis cap.* 13.

Cent. 4.
pag. 299.

24. As for *vnvvritten Tradition*, they condemne

demne all the Fathers of this age one by
one : recytinge their sentences, & reiecting
them. They condemne by name *Lactantius*,
Prudentius, and *Hieronymus*, for holdinge *Pur-*
gatorie : they condemne *Saint Epiphanius*, for
affirminge that the Church admitteth no
man to marry after he is Priest. *Et hæc certe*
sancta Dei Ecclesia cum sinceritate obseruat, and
truly the holy Church of God (saith *Epipha-*
nius) doth obserue this custome, with all sincerity. And this much be spoken only about
one Chapter (to witt, of doctrine) hauinge
ouerskipped many other things for breuitie
sake in the same Chapter.

Epiph.
tem. 1.
lib. 2.
Cent. 4.
pag.303.

25.   But if I would passe to other Chapters
(especially that *of rites and ceremonies*, which
is their sixt (in order) there would be no
end. For first in the very first paragraph
about rytes, or ceremonyes belonginge to
Churches seruice, and publike meetinge,
(which is but one of almost 20. large para-
graphes conteyned in this Chapter) they
sett downe these rytes followinge which
do easely shewe, that our Religion, and not
theirs was in practise in this 4. age. As for
example, the building of Churches in honour of Saincts by *Costantine* & others at the
beginninge of this age: & dedicatinge them
to the same Saincts, out of *Eusebius* and other
Authors *pag.* 407. *nu.* 50. Dedications also
and consecrations of the same temples, or
                                                   Churches,

Cent. 4.
cap. 6.
pag.407.
num. 50.
54.
Euseb.

Churches, and the dayes of the ſaid conſecration kept holy and feſtiuall with great

Athan.   ſolemnitie out of *Athanaſius* and others, *ibid.*
Seruice at midnight vſed in the Churches

S. Baſil. at that tyme: out of *Saint Baſil*, & others. *ibid.*
Socrat. Aultar builded in Churches for Chriſtian
l. 5. c. 22. Sacrifice, by the teſtimony of *Socrates, Sozo-*
Theod. *menus, Theodoretus,* and others, *ibid.* The inter-
l. 5. c. 18.
Opt. l. 6. pretation alſo, what an Aultar meaneth, ſet
downe by *Optatus: Quid eſt Altare, niſi ſedes cor-*
Zozim. *poris, & ſanguinis Chriſti?* What is an Aultar
li. 6. c. 6. but the ſeate of the body & bloud of Chriſt?
Euſ. l. 4. Images alſo ſet vp and painted in Churches
de vita in this age out of *Sozomenus, Euſebius, Optatus*
Conſtan- and others. *pag. 409. Cæreas candelas, & lam-*
tini.
Opt. l. 1. *pades,* torches wax candels, and burninge
contra lamps, ſett vp in the Church by *Conſtantine*
Parmen. himſelfe: out of *Euſebius lib. 4. de vita Conſtant.*
pag. 410. Of vigils and watches kept in

Baſil. Church feaſts: out of *Baſil, Theodorete,* and
others, *ibid.* The vſe of *Litanies* in thoſe

Baſil. ep. dayes they ſhewe out of *Baſil, Theodorete:* and
63. others, *ibid.*
Zozim.
l. 4. c. 16. 26. I leaue many more rites and Catholike
Ceremonies ſet downe by them in this firſt
paragragh which is of publique meetings,
Churches, &c. But if I would paſſe from
this vnto many other heads handled by
them, as about the vſe of baptiſme, and adminiſtration of other Sacraments and Sacrifice, about feaſts, faſts, mariage, burying,
honoringe

honoringe martyrs tombes, pilgrymages,
consecratinge of Monks and Nunnes, and
other such points(which these *Magdeburgians*
do handle heere at large out of the Fathers
of this age and practise of that Church, to
the number of 19. or 20. all against themselues) it were sufficient to make a seuerall
booke a parte. As for example, about baptisme they teach vs, that those, who are to
be baptised, must first be confessed of their
sinnes; that they must say *abrenuntio tibi Sa-*
thana, & omnibus operibus tuis: that they must be
prepared by exorcismes, and after baptisme
be annoynted with holy Chrisme, that they
must fast a certayne number of dayes before
their baptisme; that they must thrise be di-
ued in the water, that they must haue lamps
lightened at their baptisme. And for the
blessed Sacrament of the Aultar they shewe
vs, how it was wont to be administred, and
sent, (when occasion was offred) from one
place to another: how often it should be receyued, and with what reuerence, and with
what vigils and prayers before. And how it
was wont to be caryed to them, that lay on
their death bedd, & how they were bound
to confesse it openly to be the true body &
blood of Christ, before they receyued it.
And what great myracles fell out for proofe
& confirmation of the truth about this reall
presence. These, and almost infinite other
points

Cent. 4.
pag. 118.
119.
120.

pa. 431.
432.
433.
points like vnto thefe, the *Magdeburgians* do proue at length to haue byn in vfe through out this 4. age by the teftimonyes and wri-tings of the principall Doctors therof.

27. Wherfore I will leaue to the reader to confider, what manner of people thefe Lu-theran writers are, who do record fo many important teftimonies againft themfelues. And hauinge alleaged them, then they re-fute all againe prefently, with this bare fhifte, that they are eyther Iewifh or Pagan ceremonies brought in by the Fathers vpon fuperftition: and fo not to be regarded. And this they thinke to be fufficient to refute them all. As for example, talkinge of the ce-remony of faftinge in thofe dayes, what meats they did eate, & how rigorously they abftayned, and how longe, thefe good fel-lowes do write this ; *Ieiunia obferuaffe religio-fius quidem feu fuperftitiofius, quàm fuperioribus fe-culis huius atatis Chriftianos hiftoriæ teftantur.* Hi-
,, ftories do teftifie vnto vs that the Chriftians
,, of this age did obferue faftinge dayes more
,, religiously, or rather more fuperftitiously,
,, then any age before, for that humayne Tra-
,, ditions beganne now to be more multi-
,, plyed. And *Epiphanius* doth fay, that the faft
., of wednefdayes and frydayes was obferued
,, at this time, as a *tradition of the Apoftles*. But we find no fuch thinge in their works. Thus faid thefe *Germanes*, that neuer parhaps fafted

da y

The an-
ciet ob-
feruatio
of fa-
ftes.

day in their life, nor euer abstayned for de-
uotiō sake from any good morsell of meate,
that their lipps could reach vnto. And so
much of these men. For they are not worth
the spendinge of tyme to refute them.

Well then, by these fewe examples taken
out of two Chapters only of the *Magdeburgians* about this 4. age, we see what may be
gathered, if we would go ouer all the three
centuries for these three ages (from *Constantine* to *Saint Gregorie.*) And therby also we see
the reason, why Fox wrote so litle of these
three ages, beinge wholy against them.

28. But now parhaps the reader will aske,
how it falleth out, that Iohn Fox hauinge
dedicated a speciall booke (to witt his second of acts and monuments) vnto these
three ages after *Constantine* (for so is his title)
how (I say) he could make vp a distinct
booke, and yet say nothinge of the Ecclesiasticall affaires therin conteyned? whervnto
I aunswere, that this is an other Foxly fetch
of his, to promise and not performe, and to
do one thinge for an other. For that dispay-
ringe to haue matter to his purpose out of
the former three ages (as hath byn shewed)
he slideth away sleightly to another argument, which he had not promised in his
title. To wit, of some things fallen out in
our English Church in the next two hundred yeares after, from the time of *S. Augustin,*
and

Fox pag.
95.
Hovv
Fox fil-
leth vp
his se-
cond
booke
vvith
matter
not to
his pur-
pose.

and *K. Ethelbert* , vnto the tyme of *K. Egbert,*
firſt monarch of the Engliſh about the yeare
of Chriſt 800. But for that theſe two ages,
(to witt, the ſeauenth, and eyght) do conteyne the times of our Primitiue Engliſh
Church, I thinke beſt to treat ſeuerally therof in the next Chapter following, this being
ſufficient to ſhewe that in theſe ſecond 300.
yeares, Iohn Fox had as litle Rome for his
Church, as in the former.

HOW MATTERS PASSED IN
THE CHRISTIAN CHVRCH BOTH
abroad and at home in England duringe the third
ſtation of time from Pope Gregory *and* King
Ethelbert *of Kent* , *vnto* K. Egbert *our firſt*
monarch, conteyninge the ſpace of 200. *yeares.*

CHAP. IV.

The 3.
ſtation
of times
from *K.*
Ethel-
bert an.
600. to
K. Eg-
bert an.
800.

THERE followeth in orde: the third diſtinction or ſtation of tymes, appointed
by Ihon Fox in the beginninge of his hiſtory, and promiſed by him to be handled
diſtinctly in the proſecution of his worke.
And ſo in deed this ſtation ought to haue
byn aboue the reſt. For that it conteyneth the tyme of our Engliſh primitiue
Church, to witt, the two firſt hundred
yeares therof from *S. Auguſtine* downward.
But (as yow haue heard before) he findinge
ſcarce any thinge in theſe two ages, which
delighted

delighted his hereticall humour, no not our
very conuersion it selfe from Paganisme to
Christian Religion, he shuffleth the same
ouer in the end of his forsaid second booke
togeather with the second 300. yeares after
Christ, from *Constantine* to *Pope Gregory* (as before hath bin shewed.) So as he included the
acts of 500. yeares of the most famous and
glorious tymes, that euer were in the
Church of God, (whether we respect the
generall & vniuersal Church, or the Church
of England in particular) in a little booke of
a dozen leaues only; of which dozen leaues
the least part doth concerne this time:
wheras, when he cōmeth downe to handle
the acts and gests of *Iohn VVickliffe, Iohn Husse,
Hierome of Prage,* and other such paltry heretiks, not worth the talkinge of, he writeth
whole volumes, & many hundred leaues togeather, but of these 200. yeares of our first
conuersion and primitiue Church, Fathers,
Doctors & Saincts therof, he writeth both
very little & most contemptuously. And yet
wanted he not authors to giue him matter
in this behalfe, seinge that *S. Bede* (that liued
in the first of these 200. yeares) hath left 5.
whole bookes of the acts and gestes therof,
besides other that haue ensued, as *Gosselinus,
Malmesbury, VVestmonasteriensis,* and others.

2. But the truth is, that Iohn Fox seinge
these tymes to be wholy against him, and

*Why
Iohn
Fox shif-
ted ouer
these
200. yea-
res so
sleight-
ly.*

Z   that

The con
temptu-
ous vvri-
tinge of
Iohn
Fox in
this ſta-
tion of
200. yea
res.

that they lay downe more cleerly before vs
(if it may be) then the reſt, (eſpecially to
Engliſhmen) the truth and euidency of the
Cath. Roman faith: he had no hart nor co-
rage to deale much therwith, but ſought to
ſhuffle ouer in ſilence, ſo much as he might
conueniently, and the reſt to diſcreditt by
ſcoffes, taunts, corruption and falſification,
as after yow ſhall ſee. For I haue thought
good to make a diſtinct Chapter of theſe
two ages, and therby ſomwhat to lett yow
ſee and behould what paſſed therin (though
very breeifly) and how Iohn Fox doth behaue himſelfe in relatinge the ſame.

Popes
and Em-
perors
of theſe
200.
years.

3. Firſt then, yf we conſider the vniuerſall Church of Chriſtendome in theſe 200.
yeares (which are the 700. & 800. of Chriſt)
there are recounted to haue ſitten in the
Roman Sea 33. Popes, from *Gregory* the firſt
to *Leo* the third: and in the eaſt Empire (the
weſt beinge decayed before) ſome 19. or 20.
Emperors raigned, one after another, from
Mauritius to *Conſtantine* the 6. & *Irene* his mother. In whoſe tyme *Charles* the great of
France was made Emperor of the weſt, by
the forſaid *Pope Leo* the third. And duringe

The
cheefe
doctors
from
an. 600.
to 800.

this race of time, the ſaid vniuerſall Church
floriſhed greatly by learned men and holy
Biſhops. Wherof the principall were *Saint
Iſidorus* Archb. of *Siuill*, *Sophronius*, *Leontius*,
Theodorus, Archb. of *Canterbury*, *Venerable Bede*,

Ioannes

Ioannes Damaſcenus , Paulus Diaconus , Alcuinus
our Countreyman, *Vſuardus*, and others.

4. This time had many learned councells Councel
alſo : wherof two were generall , the one general.
beinge the 3. of *Conſtantinople* the other the
ſecond of *Nice*. Wherby were beatē downe
all the heretiks of thoſe dayes:the principall
wherof beinge the *Iacobites* , the *Armenians* Heretiks
Monothelites, Neophonites, Lampetians, Agnychites, of this
*Iconomachians,*or *Image-breakers,*and other the time.
like. Beſides all this, there was added to the
greatnes of this Church , the new conuerſion of many countreyes from paganiſme to
Chriſtian Religion . Amongſt which may Conuer-
principally be recoūted our Engliſh Saxons, ſion of
as alſo by their means diuers prouinces Englād.
afterward of high and low Germany. And
this for the continuance and going forward
of the Chriſtian Cath. Church in generall,
planted by Chriſt , and brought downe by
ſucceſsion from the Apoſtles tyme.

5. But if yow will talke of our new Engliſh Church , planted in this meane ſpace,
and inſerted or vnited to that generall
Cath.Church,as a branch or member to the
whole body , and as a new daughter ſubor-
dinate to her mother : we ſhall ſee her progreſſe to be conforme thervnto . To witt,
that ſhe multiplyed mightely in theſe 200.
yeares, both in number, doctrine, and great
piety of life. Which Iohn Fox himſelfe is
Z 2   forced

forced to confeſſe, in that he hauinge told vs of the conuerſion of ſeauen Engliſh Saxon kingdomes within the compaſſe of this tyme: he ſetteth downe diuers tables in the end of all, wherof one is, of 17. Archbiſhops of *Canterbury* from *Auguſtine* to *Celnothus,* that liued with K. *Egbert:* and another table of 30. Cathedrall Churches, abbyes, and nunryes builded, & aboundantly endowed by Chriſtian Engliſh Kings, Queens and Biſhopps of that tyme: and a third table of 9. ſeuerall Kings beſides many more of cheefe nobility both men and women, who leauinge the world & their temporall ſtates, entred into religious life, the more ſtrictly to ſerue almighty God. All which Iohn Fox is forced to recount againſt himſelfe, and ſindeth no one in all this tyme of 200. yeares (& much leſſe any company) on whome he dareth lay hands to build vp his hidden Church in England withall.

6.   And it is to be noted by the Reader, and by vs to be repeated againe for better memoryes ſake (that which before we admoniſhed) to witt, that Fox ſindeth theſe 200. yeaas of our firſt Engliſh primitiue Church ſo barren of matter for his purpoſe, as in the whole ſtory therof, he ſpendeth only eight leaues of paper, and theſe rather in deriding and ſcoffinge the ſame and principall pillars therof, then wryting any Eccleſiaſticall hiſtory.

ſtory. For which cauſe, yow ſhall find theſe notes & titles commonly wrytten ouer the heads of his leaues and pages, *Auguſtines arriuall in Kent : Gregory the baſeſt Pope, but the beſt: proud Auguſtine ; liynge miracles: ſhauen crovvnes; Beda his birth,* and the like. Of which learned holy mans ſtory (I meane *Saint Bede*) he maketh ſo little accounte, as in the ſame place, recytinge a letter out of him written by a holy man (*Ceolfride* Abbot of *Shiruyn* in Northumberland to *Naitonus* K. of the Picts) he ſaith thus. *The copy of vvhich letter, as it is in Bede, I haue annexed. Not for any great reaſon therin conteyned; but only to delight the Reader vvith ſome paſtime in ſeinge the fond ignorance of that monkiſh age, &c.* Wherby we may ſee the drift of this pleaſant Fox in theſe his Acts and monuments. Which is, to diſcreditt that whole tyme, and all our primitiue Church.

Fox his ſcoffing ſtory of the Engliſh primitiue Church. *pag.*107. 113. *&c. Bed. l.*1. *hiſt.c.*21. *Fox pag.* 113.

7. But yet to the end, that the ſayinge of Chriſt may be fulfilled in him: *Ex ore tuo te iudico ſerue nequam*; I do iudg thee out of thy owne mouth thow wicked ſeruant : I ſhall heere ſett downe two nationall Synods gathered in England in theſe two ages by two famous Archbiſhops of Canterbury the one *Theodorus* in the yeare of Chriſt 680. and related by *Beda*; and the other *Saint Cuthbert* in the yeare 747 .related by *VVilliam* of *Malmeſbury* after *Bedes* death. And both of them ſett downe by Fox. And by vewing the decrees

*Mat.*18.

*Beda l.*4. *hiſt. c.* 5. *Malm. de geſt. Pont. Angl. lib.* 10.

Z 3 of

of theſe two ſynods, yow will ſee, whether thoſe ages were ſo fond in ignorance, as Fox maketh them. Out of the firſt Synod holden at *Thetford* Fox gathereth ten decrees in theſe words.

Fox pag.
112.
col. 2.
n. 63.
Decrees
of an En
gliſh ſy-
nod *ann.*
Domini
680. out
of Fox.

8.   Firſt, (that Eaſter day ſhould be vniformally kept and obſerued throughout the whole Realme vpon a certayne day, *Videlicet prima* 14. *luna menſis primi.*

Secondly, that no Biſhopp ſhould intermedle within the dioceſſe of another.

Thirdly, that monaſteries conſecrated vnto God, ſhould be exempt and free from the iuriſdiction of the Biſhops.

,,   Fourthly, that the monks ſhould not ſtray
,, from one place (that is, from one monaſtery
,, to another without the licence of their Ab-
,, bot. Alſo to keep the ſame obedience, which
,, they promiſed at their firſt entringe.

,,   Fifthly, that no cleargy man ſhould for-
,, ſake his owne Biſhopp, and be receyued in
,, any other place, without letters commen-
,, datory of his owne Biſhopp.

,,   Sixtly, that forren Biſhopps and cleargy
,, men cominge into the Realme, ſhould be
,, content only with the benefitt of ſuch ho-
,, ſpitality, as ſhould be offered them. Neyther
,, ſhould they intermeddle any further within
,, the precinct of any Biſhopp, without his
,, ſpeciall permiſſion.

,,   Seauently, that Synods prouinciall ſhould
                                            be kept

be kept within the realme, at leaſt once a »
yeare. »

Eightly, that no Biſhopp ſhould preferre »
himſelfe before another, but muſt obſerue »
the tyme and order of his conſecration. »

Ninthly, that the number of Biſhopps »
ſhould be augmented, as the number of »
people increaſed. »

Tenthly, that no marriage ſhould be ad- »
mitted, but that which was lawfull: no in- »
ceſt to be ſuffered; Neyther any man to putt »
away his wife for any cauſe, except only for »
fornication, after the rule of the Ghoſpell. »
And theſe be the principall chapters of that »
Synode, &c.

9. Out of the ſecond Synod holden by a
place called Clonisho, Fox gathereth 31. decrees as followeth.

1. Firſt that Biſhopps ſhould be more dili- *Fox pag.*
gent in ſeinge to their office, and in admo- *115. col.*
niſhinge the people of their faults. *1. n. 84.*

2. That they ſhould liue in a peaceable *The de-*
mind togeather, notwithſtandinge they *crees of*
were in place diſſeuered aſunder. *a ſecond*
ſynod
3. That euery Biſhop once a yeare ſhould *out of*
goe about all the pariſhes of his dioceſſe. *Fox an.*
Domini
4. That the ſaid Biſhops euery one in his *747.*
dioceſſe ſhould moniſh their Abbots and »
monks to liue regularly: and that prelats .,
ſhould not oppreſſe their inferiors, but »
loue them.

5. That

,, 5.   That they ſhould teach the monaſte-
,, ryes', which the ſecular men had inuaded,
,, and could not then be taken from them, to
,, liue regularly.

,, 6.   That none ſhould be admitted to or-
,, ders, before his life ſhould be examined.

,, 7.   That in monaſteries the readinge of
,, holy ſcripture ſhould be more frequented.

,, 8.   That prieſts ſhould be no diſpoſers of
,, ſecular buſyneſſe.

,, 9.   That they ſhould take no money for
,, baptizinge infants.

,, 10.   That they ſhould both learne & teach
,, the lords prayer and the creed in Engliſh.

,, 11.   That all ſhould ioyne togeather in
,, their miniſtery after one vniforme rite and
,, manner.

,, 12.   That in a modeſt voyce they ſhould
,, ſinge in the Church.

,, 13.   That all holy and feſtiuall dayes ſhould
,, be celebrated at one tyme togeather.

,, 14.   That the ſabaoth day be reuerendly
,, obſerued and kept.

,, 15.   That the ſeauen houres canonicall
,, euery day be obſerued.

,, 16.   That the rogation dayes both the
,, greater and leſſer ſhould not be omitted.

,, 17.   That the feaſt of *S. Gregory* and *S. Augu-*
,, *ſtine* our patron ſhould be obſerued.

,, 18.   That the faſt of the foure times ſhould
,, be kept and obſerued.

19. That

19. That monks and nunnes ſhould go re- „
gularly apparayled. „

20. That Biſhops ſhould ſee theſe decrees „
not neglected. „

21. That the Church men ſhould not giue „
themſelues vnto dronkenneſſe. „

22. That the communion ſhould not be „
neglected of the Church-men. „

23. Item, that the ſame alſo ſhould be ob- „
ſerued of the laymen, as tyme required. „

24. That laymen firſt ſhould be well tryed, „
before they entred into Religious order. „

25. That almes ſhould not be neglected. „

26. That Biſhops ſhould ſee theſe decrees „
to be notifyed to the people. „

27. They diſputed of the profitt of almes. „

28. They diſputed of the profitt of ſin- „
ginge pſalmes. „

29. That the congregation ſhould be con- „
ſtituted after the hability of their goods. „

30. That monks ſhould not diuell among „
laymen. „

31. That publike prayer ſhould be made „
for kinges and princes. „

Theſe decrees & ordinances beinge thus „
amonge the Biſhops concluded: *Cutbert* the „
Archbiſhop ſendeth the copy therof to *Boni-* „
face, which *Boniface*, (otherwayes named „
VVenfride an Engliſhman borne) was then „
Archbiſhop of *Mentz*, and after made a mar- „
tyr, as the popiſh ſtoryes terme him. „

10. Thus

10.   Thus farre I thought good to ſett downe the decrees of theſe two Synods of the firſt two ages of our primitiue Church in the words themſelues of Iohn Fox. Wherby yow might ſee, or at leaſtwiſe make ſome gheſſe of the learninge and vertue of theſe tymes, which Fox endeauoreth by all meanes to bring in contempt. Which point, (I meane of their learning, piety and godly ſolicitude for gouerninge our new founded Church of England) would more euidently haue appeared by theſe two Synods, yf this lyinge hiſtoriographer had not vſed heere alſo his too Fox-like tricks of falſifyinge and fraudulent omiſsion of other things, which he ſhould haue related. For better vnderſtandinge of theſe which he hath heere ſett downe, I ſhall ſpeake a word or two of them breifely. For it were infinite to follow him in all theſe traces, turnings, and wyndings of his.

Deceyt-full turnings & wyndings of Iohn Fox.

11.   Firſt then, touchinge the former councell or Synod holden by *Theodorus* Archb. of *Canterbury*, and related by *Saint Bede* (for of this only will I treat for breuityes ſake, to ſhowe an example therby, how yow may truſt Iohn Fox in the reſt which he writeth) theſe points may be noted. Firſt, that wheras he ſaith, that this Synod was held in the yeare of Chriſt 680. and quoteth *Bede* for the ſame in his marget: he falſifieth him plainly.

For

For that Beds words are thefe, fett downe
at length.

Facta eft hæc fynodus ab incarnatione Domini fex- *Bed.l.4.*
centefimo feptuagefimo tertio: quo anno Rex Cantua- *cap. 5.*
riorum Egbertus, menfe Iulio obierat,&c. This Sy- "
nod was made in the yeare after the Incar- "
nation of Chrift 673. in which yeare *Egbert* "
K. of Kent was dead in the moneth of Iuly "
before. The fame teftifieth *S. Bede* in other
words in the very fame chapter, fayinge
thus: *That this Synod vvas gathered the 24. of* *Bed.ibid.*
September in the third yeare of the raigne of K. Eg-
fride of Northumberland; who began his raigne
accordinge to *Stovv* in the yeare of Chrift
670. All which Fox hauinge feene, yet fet- *Vvillfull*
teth downe, as out of *Bede*, that it was in the *errors*
yeare of Chrift. 680. *of Iohn Fox.*

12. Secondly Fox writeth thus of the place:
In the tyme of this Theodorus a prouinciall Synod
vvas holden at Thetford mentioned in the Story of
Bede. But he, that will read *Saint Bede* himfelfe, fhall find thefe words *in loco qui dicitur*
Herudfrod, in a place called *Herudfrod,* that is *Bed. l.4.*
Hartford, as *VVilliam Cambden* doth teftifie in *cap. 5.*
his defcription of *Hartfordshire* cytinge alfo *Cambd.*
this very Councell out of *Bede* held at *Herud-* *in de-*
frod. So as I maruayle, how dotinge Fox did *fcript.*
fall vpon *Thetford.* *Britan.*
Com.
13. But thirdly, there follow more mali- *Hartf.*
tious changings and falfifications in cytinge *pag.302.*
the Articles themfelues of this Synod.

Wherof

Wherof he fcarfe relateth any one without
fome alteration : as each man may fee, that
will compare them with the originall of
Saint Bede himfelfe. I fhall touch for example
the firft and the laft of the ten, for that they
haue more expreffe malice in them, then the
reft, which I do lett paffe.

14. The firft decree of this Synod was (faith
Fox) *That Eafter day fhould be vniformally kept &*
Fox pag.
112.
obferued throughout the whole Realme, vpon one cer-
tayne day, videlicet 1. 14. luna menfis primi. That
is to fay vpon the firft 14. moone or day of
the moone of the firft moneth, to witt, of
March : which is iuft as the Iewes do obferue it, againft the vfe and cuftome of the
Church of Rome. And is an old condemned
error and herefie, as before yow haue heard
difcuffed at large in the fecond third, and
fourth Chapters of this treatyfe. And yow
muft note, that Fox maketh this decree to
fay, that this fourteenth moone, or 14. day of
the firft moone of March (for this is the
phrafe of Ecclefiafticall calculation, to fay,
luna prima, luna 2. luna 3. for the firft, fecond
or third day of the moone) muft be *certayne*
or certaynly obferued, fo as it may not be altered, nor Eafter obferued vpon any other
day. Wherin ftandeth the formality of the
former error, as hath byn declared; for that
it putteth a necefsity of obferuinge the old
Iewifh law, and therby dothe euacuate the
force

force of Chriſt his grace & ghoſpell, as yow
haue heard before diſcuſſed. Which beinge
ſoe, will yow eaſily beleeue, that the whole
Church of England could be brought to
decree ſuch an error in a publike councell,
and that *Saint Bede* in particular would euer
relate the ſame with his approbation, ſeinge
he miſliked the ſame ſo greatly in ſome of
the Britans, as in the former chapters of this
treatyſe we haue declared?

Sup. cap. 2. 3, & 4.

15. Well then, lett vs ſee what the words
of *Saint Bede* himſelfe are in this Synodicall
decree corrupted by Fox. *Primum Capitulum,*
(ſaith he relatinge it out of the words of the
canons themſelues) *vt ſanctum diem Paſcha in
communi omnes ſeruemus, Dominica poſt 14. lunam
primi menſis.* The firſt Article of our decrees
(ſaith the councell) is, that we do all in
common obſerue the holy day of Eaſter
vpon the Sunday next after the fourtenth
moone of the firſt moneth.

Bed. l. 4. hiſtor. cap. 5.

,,
,,
,,
,,

16. Thus ſaith the decree, truly related by
Saint Bede: quite contrary to that which Fox
related before, he puttinge out & puttinge
in of his owne, with out ſhame or conſcience, what he thought beſt in this little
ſentence, to make thoſe Fathers ſeeme to
ſay (as he would haue them) in fauour of a
condemned hereſie. To which effect he
putteth out (as yow haue ſeene) the word,
Dominica, which maketh or marreth all the
matter,

The vvic ked fal-ſifyinge of Saint Bede by Iohn Fox.

matter, and then for *poſt* 14. *lunam*, written at large in *Saint Bede*, he putteth in *prima* 14. *luna*, ſhort in numbers only, to make it more obſcure, addinge *prima* of his owne: and puttinge out *poſt*, from the words of the Councell: therby to make the ſenſe more cleere in fauour of the hereſie. For that *prima* 14. *luna menſis primi* (which are his) words do ſignifie, the fourthtenth day of the firſt moone of March expreſſely. And moreouer, he addeth of his owne theſe words, *vpon one certayne day*, which the decree hath not. Meaninge therby that this 14. day muſt be obſerued with ſuch *certainty*, as it may not be altered or differred, to any Sunday: But muſt be obſerued, as an immoueable feaſt. Which out of *Luther* we haue ſhowed before alſo to be his meaninge. And thus much of the firſt decree.

Fox is taken in his malitious dealing, about the decree of obſeruation of Eaſter.

Sup. c. 3.

17.   The laſt and 10. decree hath no leſſe fraud & malice vſed againſt yt by Fox, then this firſt. For the malitious ſhameleſſe fellow would make thoſe fathers of that Synod, to fauour the doctrine and practiſe of the proteſtants in putting away their wiues for fornication, and marrying another. For to this effect he citeth the cannon. *Tenthly, that no man may putt avvay his vvife for any cauſe, except only for fornication, after the rule of the ghoſpell.* And there breaketh of, as though the councell had ſaid no more, nor added any further

Fox 111.

further caution or explication of their meaninge. Wherof it would enſue (as proteſtants do inferre)that ſeinge a man may putt
away one wife for fornication, and is not
bound to liue vnmarryed, yf he haue not
the gift of continency, he may lawfully take
another wife. As the practiſe of proteſtants
is at this day in England. But the Reader
muſt know, that immediatly after the former words by him recyted, there follow in
the cannon other, that marre all his markett. For thus they ly togeather.

About marryinge a ſecond vvife the firſt beinge aliue.

18. *Nullus coniugem propriam, niſi (vt ſanctum
Euangelium docet) fornicationis cauſa relinquat.
Quòd ſi quiſquam propriam expulerit coniugem legi-
timo ſibi matrimonio coniunctam, ſi Chriſtianus eſſe
rectè voluerit nulli alteri copuletur: ſed ita perma-
neat, aut propriæ reconcilietur coniugi.* Let no
man leaue his owne wife, but only, as the
holy ghoſpell teacheth vs, for the cauſe of
fornication, and if any man ſhould put away
his wife, that is ioyned vnto him by lawfull marriage, yf he wilbe a true Chriſtian
lett him not marry another, but eyther remayne ſo in continency, or be reconciled to
his owne wife againe.

Bed. l.4. cap. 5. pag. 227.

,,
,,
,,
,,
,,
,,
,,
,,

19. Lo heere the fidelity of Iohn Fox in relatinge matters. This cannon determineth
two things yow ſee. Firſt that a man may
not leaue the company or cohabitation of
his wife, but only for the ſin of fornication
committed

committed by her. The second, that beinge
so separated, he may not marry another for
any cause: but eyther must remayne continent, or be reconcyled to his former wife
againe. And this was the doctrine of the
Catholike Church then, and is now. Which
our Fox would faine haue concealed from
his reader, and haue made him beleeue, that
the old primitiue English Church, had byn
for them and their practice at this day. But
the poore Raynart is taken at euery wyndinge, when he is followed. Which were
impossible to do in all his false doublings.
And so these two examples only shall suffice
to show his tricks in this first point of falsification. Lett vs passe to the second of willfull omission.

Guilfull
omissiōs
of Iohn
Fox.

20.   There remayneth to say a word or
two of his omissions, wherby he leaueth
out of purpose from his story those things
which might giue creditt or reputation to
our English Church in these aunciét times:
which he seeketh by all means to make ridiculous and contemptible. As for example,
the number and quality of the Prelats and
learned men, that then florished and were
present in these Synods, the Reasons and
arguments, and other like circumstances
partly sett downe by *Saint Bede* and other
authors vpon diuers occasions, and partly
regiftred in the very prefaces of the Synods
them-

themselues. As for example, in this first Synod heere cyted they begiue thus:

21.   *In nomine Domini Dei, & Saluatoris Iesu* Bed. *l. 4.*
Christi, &c. In the name of our Lord God & *cap.* 5.
Sauiour *Iesus Christ* raygninge for euer, and „
goueringe his Church, yt pleased him that „
we should meet togeather, accordinge to „
the custome of the venerable Cannons of „
the Church to handle necessary busynes of „
our English Church. Wherfore we mett A Sinod
togeather vpon the 24. day of the moneth holden
of September, in the first indiction in a place at *He-*
called *Herudfrod,* I *Theodorus* (though vnwor- *ʳᵘᵈfʳᵒᵈ*
thy) appointed by the Sea Apostolike B. of „ *an. 673.*
the Church of *Canterbury,* and our fellow „
Bishop and brother, the most reuerend *Bisy* „
B. of the Eastangles, and our brother and „
fellow Priest *VVilfrid* B. of the nation of *Nor-* „
thumbers was present by his proper legats. „
There were present also our brethren and „
fellow-Priests *Putta* B. of the Castle of *Kent,* „
commonly called *Rhofessester, Eleutherius* also „
B. of the West-saxons, and *VVinfride* B. of „
the Mercians. And when we were all come „
togeather and euery man sett accordinge to „
his order and degree, I said vnto them.   „

Most deare brethren I beseech yow for „
the feare and loue of our Sauiour, that we „
may handle heere in common the things „
that belonge vnto our faith, to the end that „
these things, which haue byn decreed and „

defined

,, defined by the holy auncient Fathers about
,, the ſame, may be kept vncorrupt by vs
,, all, &c.

22. This is part of the Preface to the firſt
Synod: out of which the former decrees related and corrupted by Fox (as yow haue
heard) were taken. And by the very words
of this entrance or preface there is more ſerious grauity ſignified, then Fox would
ſeeme to acknowledge at this day in England. But 7. yeare after this againe the ſaid
Theodorus made another Synod, paſſed ouer
in ſylence by Fox but *Saint Bede* relateth the
ſame in theſe words.

23. *His temporibus audiens Theodorus, &c.* At
this time *Theodorus* the Archbishop, hearinge
that the Church of *Conſtantinople* was greatly
troubled by the hereſie of *Eutyches* (that denied two natures to be in Chriſt or that his
flesh was like ours) and deſyringe greatly
that the Churches of England, ouer which
he had iuriſdiction, ſhould contynue free
from ſuch infection, he gathered togeather
a Synod of very many venerable prieſts and
learned Bishops, and fyndinge them, after
diligent inquiry made, to agree all togeather in one Cath. faith, he thought good to
ſett the ſame downe by Synodicall letters
for inſtruction and memory of poſterity:
which began thus: In the name of our Lord
Ieſus Chriſt our Sauiour in the raigne of our
most

Bed. l.4. cap. 17.

Leo PP. epiſt. 10. ad Flauian. Theod. dial. 2. Euagr. l.2. c. 4.
A ſecond councell of Arch-bishop *Theodorus.*

moſt pious princes and lords *Egfrid* K. of the
Northumbers anno 10. vpon the 15. day before
the calends of October, the 8. indiction, &
Etheldred raigning ouer the Mercians the ſixt
yeare of his raigne, and *Aldulphus* being king
of the Eaſtangles the 17. yeare of his raigne,
and *Lodtharius* beinge K. of Kent, in the 7.
yeare of his raigne, & *Theodorus* by the grace
of God Archbishop of the Ile of Britany &
of the citty of *Canterbury,* beinge preſident of
the Synod, togeather with the reſt of the
Biſhops of the ſame Iland, venerable men
ſittinge with him in Councell, and the holy
ſacred ghoſpell beinge laid downe before
them in aplace called in the Saxon tongue
Hedtfield, after treaty had, they expounded
the right Cath. faith in this manner.

24. *Sicut Dominus noſter Ieſus,&c.* As our Lord
Ieſus, takinge our fleſh vpon him, did deliuer vnto his diſciples that ſaw him in perſon, and heard his ſpeeches, and as the Sym-
bolum or creed of the holy Fathers haue deliuered vnto vs, and as generally all whole
and vniuerſall Synods and all the company
of holy fathers & doctors of the holy Cath.
Church haue taught vs, ſo do we following
their ſteppes both piously and Catholikely
accordinge to their doctrine (inſpired to
them from heauen) profeſſe and beleeue, &
conſtantly confeſſe accordinge to the ſaid
holy Fathers beleefe, that the father the „

The mā-
ner of
decree-
inge in
old ſy-
nods &
national
councels
accor-
dinge to
their an-
ceſtors.

,, ſonne and the holy Ghoſt are properly and
,, truly a conſubſtantiall Trinity in vnity and
,, vnity in Trinity, &c. We receyue alſo the
,, holy and vniuerſall fiue Synods that haue
,, byn held before our tyme by the bleſſed
,, Chriſtian fathers our aunceſtors, to witt,
,, thoſe 318. holy Bishops in the firſt Councell

a *Anno* 315.

of ᵃ *Nice*, againſt *Arrius* and his wicked doctrine: and of the 150. other fathers and Bi-

b *Anno* 380.

ſhops in the firſt Councell of ᵇ *Conſtantinople*
againſt the hereſie of *Macedonius*: and of the
,, 200. Godly Bishops of the Councell of

c *Anno* 428.

ᶜ *Epheſus* againſt *Neſtorius* and his errors: and
of the 230. Bishops in the Councell of ᵈ *Cal-*

d *Anno* 457.

cedon againſt *Eutyches* and his doctrine: and of
the other 165. Fathers gathered togeather in

e *Anno* 532.

the ſecond generall Councell of e *Conſtanti-*
nople againſt diuers heretiks & hereſies, &c.
,, We do receiue all theſe Councells, and we
,, do glorifie our Lord *Ieſus Chriſt*, as they glo-
,, rified him, adding nothing nor taking any
,, thing away. We do anathematize and ac-
,, curſe alſo, both by hart and mouth, all
,, thoſe, whome theſe fathers did anathema-
,, tize and accurſe: and we do receyue them,
,, whome they receyued, &c.

25.   Behould heere the maner and forme of
Catholike Councels of old tyme. Who laid
downe firſt the Ghoſpell in the middeſt, &
then after due examination of ſcriptures,
conſidered that antiquity of Fathers and
councells

councells had determined in Gods Church before them, euen from Chrift and his Apoftles downeward: and therin infifted, agreing all in one, and reiecting and accurfing all new contrary or different doctrines and Doctors. And by his means and by the afsiftance of the holy Ghoft promifed by Chrift vnto his Church, hath fhee continued now for fixtene hundred yeares one and the felfe fame. Wheras fectaries lacking this humility, wifdome, and fubordination, but efpecially Gods grace, are deuided and confunied among themfelues.

26.   But I will paffe no further in this point. This which I haue faid being fufficient to fhew that there were more learned men in England in thefe times of our primitiue Church, then phantafticall Fox would haue men beleeue. Which is greatly confirmed by that, which *Malmesbury* writeth (and Fox alfo confeffeth the fame) that, a generall councell beinge gathered foone after this, which we haue mentioned, in *Conftantinople* both of the Eaft and weft Church againft the *Monothelites* (that denyed *tvvo diftinct vvills in Chrift*) our Archb. *Theodorus*, with fome other learned men of our English Cleargy, was called for by Pope *Agatho* to be one of his legats in the faid councell, where there were 331. Bishops gathered togeather by order of the faid *Agatho*. B. of

Fox pag. 113.

Anno Domini 682. The cou̅fell of Conftantinople in Trullo.

Rome,

A a 3

Rome, againſt the patriarches of *Antioch,* *Alexandria* and *Conſtantinople* (which thinge ſheweth the great power and authority of the Biſhop of Rome, euen in Greece it ſelfe at that day) the Emperour *Conſtantine* the fourth being preſent himſelfe.

27. And to this councell (as is ſaid) was the forſaid *Theodorus* Archb. of Canterbury with diuers other Biſhops called by name by Pope *Agatho*, as we may ſee in his letter to the ſaid councell cyted by *Malmesbury* in theſe words: *Sperabamus de Britannia Theodorum, &c.* We did hope to haue had from Britany *Theodore* my brother and fellow Biſhop and Archbiſhop of that great Iland, and a philoſopher, togeather with others which hitherto do remayne there: And then to ,, haue ioyned them to our humility. And for ,, this cauſe we haue hitherto differred the councell. *Vides quanti eum fecerit* (ſaith *Malmeſbury*) *vt eius expectatione, vniuerſale Concilium differret.* Yow ſee of what accoumpt this ,, Archbishop was with Pope *Agatho* that he ,, would differre a generall councell for his ,, expectation. Thus writeth he wherby euery indifferent man will eaſely ſee, that this tyme of our primitiue English Church (which Fox by contempt ſo often calleth ignorant and monkish) was not deuoid of rare learned men : and ſo hath continued vntill our dayes, *fruſtra circumlatrantibus hæreticis,*

Plat. in
vita
Agathi
PP.
Paul.
Diac.l.1.
hiſt.
Malm.
lib. 1. *de*
geſt. Pōt.
Angl.
*pag.*112.

Malm.
ibid.

ticis, (to vſe *Saint Auguſtines* words) heretiks
in vayne barkinge on euery ſide againſt it.
With whom Iohn Fox thought good to
beare a barking parte alſo, & not being able
to find out any one hole or corner for his
Church in thoſe ages, except only among
the heretiks before named: he thought good
at leaſt to rayle and ſpitt at them, as he paſſeth by, and ſo will he do more, and more
the lower he goeth : vntill at length he fall
to plaine Apoſtaſie, and forſakinge them
openly will ioyne with the knowne condemned heretiks & enimies of this Church.
Which Church hitherto notwithſtandinge
he will ſeeme in ſome ſort to follow,
though lazely and dragginge behind, and as
it were werye of her companie, & looking
about him, which way he may giue the ſlip
and betake himſelfe to his heeles. As will
better appeare by that, which enſeweth.

Auguſt. lib. de vtilitate credendi cap. 17.

THE FOVRTH STATION
OR DIVISION OF TIMES FROM
K. Egbert *vnto* William Conqueror *con-*
teyninge the ſpace of ſome 260. *yeares: and hovv*
Iohn Fox *his Church paſſed in theſe dayes, and*
vvhether there vvere any Pope Ioane *or noe?*

CHAP. V.

Y ov v haue heard before how Ihon Fox
in his ſecond booke promiſing to handle

The 4. ſtation from *an. Domini* 800. to 1066.

Aa 4   but

but 300. yeares, touched in the acts of 500. in leſſe then a dozen leaues, ſhewinge the ſmall ſtore of matter he had for his Church in thoſe ages. Now his next booke is intitu-*Fox pag. 121.* led thus: *The third booke conteyning the next 300. yeares from the raigne of Egbert vnto the tyme of VVilliam Conqueror.* So is his title. And yet, yf yow count the yeares from the beginninge of K. *Egbert* his raigne *(Anno Domini* 802. accordinge to Stow, or 800. accordinge to others, vnto the entrance of the conqueror *anno* 1066.) yow ſhall find but, only 264. yeares, and from K. *Egbert* his death but 234. So as Fox is in no one thinge exact or punctuall. And theſe 264. yeares may be counted the fourth ſtation or parcell of tyme from Chriſt downward. Which now we are breefely to examine and run ouer, as we haue done the former ſtations or limitations appointed.

2.   Firſt then, concerninge the generall Roman Church, it continued in theſe ages, as in the former by continuall ſucceſſion of her Biſhops & gouernors; altering nothing in beleefe and doctrine from her aunceſtors. And breefly to repeat the ſumme of all, there ruled in the Sea of Rome in theſe two ages and a halfe, (as ſupreme knowen and acknowledged paſtors of this great viſible Church ſome 60. Popes from *Leo* the third, that crowned *Charles* the *great* (and therby reſtored

restored the Westerne Empire) vnto the
time of *Alexander* the second, vnder whome
duke *VVilliam* of *Normandy* conquered England. And in the Westerne Empire there
raigned some 18. Emperors in this space
from *Charles* the *Greate* to *Henry* the 4. and
in the Easterne Empire some 25. from *Nicephorus* the first to *Constantine* the tenth. All
which Popes, Emperors and Princes, were
of one religion, faith and beleefe in those
dayes. And albeit soone after the Sea of
Constantinople and Greeke Church, by
occasion of emulation against the Roman
Empire, did begin to detract their due obedience from the Roman Church, & therby
fell by little and little into diuers errors of
doctrine also, and finally were deliuered
ouer as all the world seeth) in to the subiection & seruitude of the Turks: yet in these
ages there was vnion and due subordination betweene both Churches. Which may
appeare by that one only Generall Coun- The 8.
cell beinge held in Constantinople (euen generall
against *Phocius*, that was patriarch of the said counsell.
citty) beinge gathered by order of Pope
Adrian the 2. and *Basilius* the Grecian Emperor concurringe therin. This councell was *Anno*
of 300. Bishops, and confirmed by the said *Domini*
Pope *Adrian*, beinge the 8. generall councell 870.
in order, and the fourth of those, that were
held in *Constantinople*. Wherby it cometh also

to be noted, that all the generall councells held hitherto in the Chriſtian Church (for the ſpace of 900. yeares) being 8. in number, as hath byn ſaid, from the firſt Councell of *Nice* vnto this, and from this to the firſt generall Councell of *Laterane*, holden in the yeare of Chriſt 1115. vnder Pope *Innocentius* the 3. were all held in *Greece*, but yet by order of the Biſhops of Rome, ſending thither their legats and confirminge the ſame afterward by themſelues. Without which confirmation they were neuer held for lawfull in the Chriſtian world. Which is no ſmall argument of the greatneſſe and authority of the Church of Rome from tyme to tyme.

3. It ſhall not be needfull to ſpeake of the particular hereſies of theſe 2. or 3. ages, which in effect were none of any name: but only two the *Iconoclaſts* or Image-breakers, & the *Berengarians* or Sacramētaryes both of them agreeinge in their particular hereſies with the Caluiniſts of our times: though in many other things different, as it is wont to be. The firſt of them was begon before theſe tymes by *Leo* the 3. Emperor of *Conſtantinople* ſurnamed *Iſaurus*, about the yeare of Chriſt 750. as before hath byn noted and renewed againe by *Claudius Taurinenſis*. The ſecond was begone 300. yeare after by *Berengarius*, about the yeare of Chriſt 1050. and abiured by him againe, as hereafter ſhalbe ſhewed.

The he-
reſies of
theſe
ages.

The

The cheefe Doctors and fathers that defended true religion in thefe ages were *Turpinus*, *Eginhardus*, *Haymo*, *Rabanus*, *Frecolphus*, *Hincmarus*, *Io. Diaconus*, *Remigius*, *Theophylactus*, and others in the 9. age. And then in the other, *Odo*, *Ado*, *Rhegino*, *Luitprandus*, *Rhatbodus*, *Abbo Floriacenfis* & others. And th'other halfe of the 11. age, *Bruchardus*, *Petrus Damianus*, *Lancfrancus* and many others.

The Fathers & Doctors of thefe tymes.

4. And this was the ftate of the vniuerfall Chriftian Church in thefe ages. Whervnto in all refpects was conforme the particular Church of England, as the daughter to her mother. Which may be demonftrated partly by the continuall difcent of; Archbifhops in England, which were to the number of 16. from *Celnothus* that liued with K. *Egbert* vnto *Stigand* that poffeffed the Sea of Canterbury, whom William conqueror came in though afterward he caufed him to be depofed by a comifsion from Rome, in the yeare of Chrift 1070 as *Iohn Stovv* and others do note.

The Archb. of Canterbury in thefe ages.

5. I do pretermitt the fuccefsion of other Bifhopriks in England for breuities fake. The kings alfo of England that poffeffed that crowne from *Egbert* to *VVilliam* the conquerour were fome 20. in number, (if we count *Canutus* the Dane, & his two children amonge the reft.) All which kings, of what nation or ftate foeuer, agreed fully in faith and

Kings of England in this tyme.

and beleefe with the said Archbishops and Bishops of our land, and they againe with the whole vniuersall Roman Church, as appeareth by their acts and monuments, and Iohn Fox also confesseth.

6.   Which beinge so, it is hard to say or imagine, where Iohn Fox in these ages will picke out a different Christian Church (though it be neuer so *poore* and *creapinge*) for him and his, eyther in England or out of England, during this time. And much more hard it is to thinke, how he can deuise any visible continuation of the said obscure, and troden downe Church (as he promised to do) euen from the Apostles time to our age. His only refuge must be (as before we haue often noted) to runne to the condemned heretiks of these tymes, yf he find any for his purpose. Which yet he dareth not openly to do, as yow haue seene throughout all the former ages. But afterward, when he commeth neere home, to witt, after Pope *Innocentius* the 3. & *Iohn VVickliffe* he taketh more hart: affirminge our Church to haue vtterly perished, and a new visible offspringe of his Church to haue started vp. To witt, all the sectaries and heretiks cast out and condemned of our Church, as yow shall see more particularly, when we come to that place.

7.   For the present ages, that we are now in, he doth not so much as lay hands vpon

the

Fox in protest. ad Eccl. Angl. pag. 10.

the *Iconoclasts* or *Berengarians* nor doth seeme
to count them for his brethren. Though in
the principall points of their heresies they
agree with him, as is notorious. And *Iohn
Fox* to haue some visible members of his
Church in these ages ought to haue shaken
hands with them, but the poore fellow was
ashamed to build his Church openly of so
auncient heretiks. Though afterward, when
he beginneth to build indeed and to gather
stones togeather, he calleth for the *Berengarians* againe, which now he casteth away, as
after yow shall see.

8. But now perhaps yow will aske me, yf
Iohn Fox do sett downe noe succession in
these ages (as nether in the former of his
Church or ours:) what doth the simple fellow in all this third booke of his ? Wherto
I answere first, that albeit he promiseth in
the title, that this third booke, *shall conteyne
the Acts and monuments of* 300. *yeares togeather
with the whole race and course of the Church, &c.*
Yet hath the whole booke but 17. leaues in
all. Which is little more, then one leafe to
euery 20. yeares race & course of the whole
Church. And surely, he that so courseth
ouer an Ecclesiasticall history, may be called
rather a courser indeed, then an historio-
grapher.

9. Nay further he is so enuious to the famous acts of our English Church in these
dayes

VVhat Fox han-dleth in these 300. yeares.

dayes (efpecially with forrayne nations) as
he eyther concealeth vtterly the fame, or

Martyr-
log.Rom.
5. Iunij.
VVilleb.
in eius
vita Vi-
celius in
hagiolog.
Epitome
operum
Beda an.
754.
maketh reprochfull mention therof. As for
example, when he fpeaketh of the moft famous and renowned Saint of our English
nation *Saint VVenfride* (called afterward *Bo-*
nifacius) and accounted by all authors the
Apoftle of Germany, for that he began principally their conuerfion, and was afterward
moft glorioufly martyred by the pagans for
preachinge Chrifts Ghofpell, with aboue
fifty fellowes, the moft of them Englishmen. Of this man (I fay) how fpeaketh Fox?
yow fhall heare prefently. But firft fhall yow
fee the words of a German wryter in his

Adam
Bremēs.
hift.
Ecc. c.4.
„
„
„
praife *Primus omnium* (faith he) *qui Auftrales*
Germaniæ partes, &c. The firft of all, that
brought the foutherne parts of Germany
to the knowledg of Chriftian religion from
Idolatry, was *VVenfride* an Englifhman by
nation, a true philofopher of our Sauiour,

S. Boni-
face an
English-
man an
Apoftle
of Ger-
many
an. 750.
and after for his vertue called *Boniface*, and
Archbifhop of *Moguntia*. And albeit fome authors do name fome others that preached
in fundry places before him: yet this man
(as another Paul the Apoftle) did go before
all in labour of preachinge, &c.

10.   So wryteth *Adam Bremenfis* a Saxon, &
Cannon of the firft and head Church, that
was builded in Saxony after their conuerfion by the preaching of Englifhmen. For
so he

so he sheweth in particular, that Englishmen were their conuerters: but especially
foure most famous learned preachers and
feruent zealators of multiplyinge the Christian faith: to witt, *VVillebrordus VVillebaldus,*
VVillericus & *VVillehadus.* All which were renowned Apostolicall Bishops in Germany.
a *VVillebrord* was sent ouer out of England
with a leuen companions towards the conuersion of Germany by the holy Abbott S.
Egbert, as both *S. Bede,* & other authors after
him do testify. And by *Pope Sergius* the second
was made Bishopp of *Vltraiectum* in *Frisia,* &
was the Apostle of that countrey, as also a
principall conuerter of the kingdome of
Denmarck.

11. b *VVillebaldus* was Bishop of *Aystte* in *Saxony*
where he conuerted many thousands to
Christian faith, and was canonized with
vniuersall ioy of all that countrey by Pope
Leo the 7. in the yeare of Christ 1004. as
authors do recount.

12. Saint c *VVillehad* and *S. VVillerike* were
both Bishops of *Breme* in Saxony: *Post passio-*
nem Sancti Bonifacy (saith our forsaid German
author) *VVillehadus* d *& ipse Angligena feruens*
amore martyrij properauit in Frisiam, &c. After
the passion of *Saint Boniface, Saint VVillehad* an
Englishman also, burninge with the loue of
martyrdome made hast also to come into
Frisia, where the other was martyred, &c.
And 11. 12.

a *S.VVil-*
lebrord
an. 730.
B. of
vtright.
Bed. *l.* 3.
*hist.c.*27.
& lib. 5.
cap. 23.
Tritem.
de viris
*illust.l.*3.
*cap.*137.
b *S.VVil-*
lebaldus
an. 760.
B. of
Aystte
Demo-
crit.
lib. 2. *de*
missa in
Catalog.
episcop.
de Aystte.
Marcell.
in vit. S,
Suneber-
ti cap. 6.
& 14.
c *S.VVil-*
lehad Bi
shop of
Breme
an. 780.
d *Adam*
Bremēs.
cap. 9.

And then ſheweth he, how this bleſſed
man after the côuerſion of many thouſands
was ſent by the Emperor *Charles* the *Great*
to preach to the northerne parts of Saxony.
Which he did with great feruour, till *VVin-*
dekind, a pagan Tyrant of that countrey, mo-
uinge warre againſt *Charles,* droue him out.
Vpon which occaſion he retyred himſelfe
to contemplatiue life for two yeares toga-
ther in France, vntill after he was called out
againe by the ſaid Charles to be B. of *Breme.*
In which charge he both liued and died
moſt holily.

S. VVille-
ricus B.
of Bre-
me an.
790.
Brem. in
hiſt. c.12.
Erpold.
Lindenb.
in hiſt.
Archiep.
Brem. in
VVilleri-
cum.

13.   And next to him ſucceeded one of his
diſciples *VVillericus,* and lead an Apoſtolicall
life in the ſame charge for the ſpace of 50.
yeares togeather, as *Adam Bremenſis, Erpoldus*
Lindenbrughenſis and others do teſtifie.

These mens acts then, and other ſuch
like had byn fitt matter for Iohn Fox to
haue handled in his Eccleſiaſticall hiſtory of
theſe ages : eſpecially if he could haue ſhewed, that any one of theſe, that wrought ſo
infinite miracles both aliue and dead (as the
former authors do teſtifie)had byn of his religion. But Fox doth paſſe ouer all with ſilence. (I meane both them & their actions)
but only that he taketh occaſion to ſpeake
contemptuouſly of the firſt and father of the
reſt, *Saint Boniface:* for hauinge ſpoken of the
later Synod of thoſe two, which we haue
mentioned

mentioned in the former chapter to haue
byn held in England by *Theodorus* and *Saint
Cuthbert* Archbishops of *Canterbury:* he wry- *Fox pag.*
teth thus: *Cuthbert the Archbishop of Canterbury* 115.
*sent the copy of the Synod to Boniface, othervvayes
named VVinfride an Englishman, then Archbishop of
Mentz and after made a martyr, as the Popish Storyes terme him.*

14. Behould Iohn Fox scarce counteth
him a martyr, though he were put to death
by pagans for preachinge Christian faith.
And a little after, meaninge to put downe a
certayne godly epistle of the said *Boniface* or
VVenfride wrytten to *Ethelbald* K. of the *Mer-*
cians, reprehendinge him for his licentious
life; Fox wryteth thus: I *Thought this epistle not* *Ibid col.*
vnvvorthy heere to be inserted: not so much for the *2. n.78.*
authors sake, as for that some good matter peraduen-
ture may be picked therout, for other Princes to be-
hould and consider, &c.

15. Heere now yow see the estimation and *Fox*
affection of Iohn Fox to *Boniface*, of whome *goeth*
the Christian world of those tymes, both *discredit*
thought and spoke of so reuerently for so *S. Boni-*
many ages. But let vs heere, what *Iohn Bale* *face.*
will say. For he beinge an Apostata wilbe
more contumelious I trow: *VVinifridus Boni-*
facius (saith he) *claro Anglorum sanguine Londini*
natus, &c. VVinifrid (called also *Boniface*) was *Bal. cent.*
borne at London of noble English bloud, & *1. script.*
afterward went to Rome, where Pope *Gre-* *Brit. fol.*
B b *gory* *54.*

,, *gory* the fecond hauinge tryed the mans faith
,, and feene his magnificence of mind, or ra-
,, ther his fhamelefle pride:thought him a fel-
,, low fitt for his affayrs, and fo fent him with
,, full authority into Germany to a wild
,, people (as then they were called) to force
,, them to his faith. Neyther hath there byn
,, any man fince the birth of Chrift, that, hath
,, more properly exprefled the fecond beaft

The
vvicked
fpeechof
Iohn
Bale
againft
S. Boni-
face.

in the *Apocalips* with two hornes then he.
For that the Pope beinge the great Anti-
Chrift, he was the fecond, &c. He did figne
with the Popes character a hundred thoufand men in *Bauaria* only, adioyninge them
to the kingdome of Anti-Chrift, rather by
feare, then by pious doctrine,&c. He built
,, the monaftery of *Fulda*, where no woman
,, might enter, &c.

16.　Still yow fee one quarrelle of *Iohn Bale*
againft monks, is, for fhuttinge out women
from their monafteryes. Which as it was
holily inftituted and obferued by auncient
monks: fo if it had byn well kept in his monaftery of *Norvvich*, it may be, he had continued a monke,as he began, and neuer come
acquaynted with *Dorothy*, that drew him out

★ *Bal.*
cent. 5.
fol. 245.

from thence, as himfelfe ★ confeffeth. But
is there any wicked tongue in the world,
that can fpeake more impioufly, then this
fellow doth of fo rare an Apoftolike man, &
of his actions: yea of the conuerfion of infidels

dels to Chriſtian faith and their holy baptiſme, callinge it ; *ſigninge vvith the character of
the beaſt?* Who but a beaſt indeed , or a man
of a beaſtly mind , would ſpeake ſo ? Yf I
ſhould alleage the teſtimonies of all ancient
authors ſince his time in praiſe and admiration of ſo zelous and holy martyr : I ſhould
oppreſſe both *Fox* and *Bale* with their very
names and authority.

17.   But to returne to Fox againe , yow
haue heard what he omitteth of the Church
of England, which he might haue well diſcourſed of, in handlinge theſe tymes, ſeinge
he paſſeth ouer our particular Church ſo
ſleightly. Yow will demand perchange,
what he wryteth or ſetteth downe of the
vniuerſall Roman Church? Truly in effect
he handleth nothinge of moment nor coherence. Though to bringe in a certayne
impertinent tale , wherof he deſireth to
ſpeake , to witt of *Pope Ioane ;* he ſetteth vs
downe a ſhort ranke of ſome few Popes,
but namely of *Pope Leo* the fourth , vnto
whome he adioyneth *Pope Iohn* the eight, &
after him *Benedict* the third, & then *Pope Nicolas* the firſt. And this *Pope Iohn* the eight,
(which entred betweene *Leo* and *Benedict*)
he will needs haue to haue byn a woman,
whome he calleth *Pope Ioane.* And albeit
Iohn Fox his words be as fooliſh and blaſphemous, as they are wont in ſuch caſes: yet

About
the fable
of *Pope
Ioane.*

B b 2   will

will I recyte them heere, to the end yow
may ſee what truth or probability, this ſo
much blazed & canuaſed hereticall fiction
hath in yt.

Fox pag.
124.

18.   *And heere next* (ſaith he) *follovveth novv,
and commeth in the vvhore of Babylon rightly in her
true colors, by the permiſſion of God, and manifeſtly
vvithout all tergiuerſation to appeare to the vvorld.*

Fox his
feigned
fable of
Pope
Ioane
blaſphe-
mouſly
related.

*And that not only after the ſpirituall ſenſe, but after
the very letter & the right forme of an vvhore indeed.
For after this Leo aboue mentioned, the Cardinalls
proceeding to their ordinary election after a ſollemne
maſſe of the holy Ghoſt: to the perpetuall ſhame of
them, and of that Sea, in ſteed of a man Pope elected
a vvhore indeed, called by the name of Iohn the 8.
vvho ſate tvvo yeares & ſix monethes,&c. The vvo-
mans proper name vvas Gilberta, &c.*

19.   Behould Iohn Fox deſcribeth ſo particularly this woman and her election, as if
he had byn preſent and ſeene all paſſe. But
ſuppoſe all this were true, which he hath
wrytten (as we ſhall proue it preſently to be
altogeather falſe) ſuppoſe, I ſay, that by error ſuch a woman had byn choſen : what
had enſued of that? or what had this preiudicated the Church of Chriſt? *Saint Auguſtine*
asketh the very ſame queſtion in a like caſe,
when hauinge recyted vp the Popes of
Rome from Chriſt to his dayes, (to witt,
from *Saint Peter* to *Pope Anaſtaſius*) he maketh
this demaund: what if any Iudas or traytor
had

had entred amonge thefe, or byn chofen by
error of men ? *Si quifquam traditor* (faith he)
per illa tempora fubrepfiffet? yf any traytor in
thofe dayes, had crept in, what had enfued
therof ? And then he maketh the anfwere
prefently: *Nihil praiudicaret Ecclefia & innocen-*
tibus Chriftianis. And the very like do I anfwere in this cafe . For I would aske Iohn
Fox, yf Immediatly after the Apoftles time,
(whiles yet he confeffeth, the Church of
Rome to haue byn in good ftate & the true
Church of Chrift) any woman or *Herma-*
phroditus, or any that had not byn baptized,
or yf a layman and not Prieft, (and confequently not capable of that place and dignity) had by error of men crept into the office
of cheefe Bifhopp (which as it may happen
by humayne frayltie, fo yet we affure our
felues that the prouidéce of God will neuer
permitt it, in fo high & fupreeme a dignitie
of his Church) but if it fhould haue happened out, had this preiudicated that Apoftolike Church ? or made yt the *vvhore* of *Baby-*
lon, as Fox inferreth of this later Church?
Truly I thinke he dareth not fay fo. For that
it is euident ; it were a plaine cauill . The
only inconuenience of that cafe beinge (if it
fhould fall out) that the Church fhould
lacke a ttue head for the tyme : as fhe doth,
when any Pope dyeth vntill another be
chofen. And whatfoeuer inconuenience

Aug. ep.
165. ad
litteras
cuiufdã
Donati-
fta.

Yf Pope
Ioane
had byn
fhe had
not pre-
iudica-
ted the
Church.

can

can be imagined in this caſe, is more againſt
the proteſtants, then vs. For that their
Church admitteth for laufull and ſupreame
head therof eyther man or woman: Which
our Church doth not. Heere then is ſeene
Iohn Fox his folly in vrginge this point,

20.   Againe, I would aske the ſimple fellow, that repeateth ſo often the word *vvhore*
in this place, as though he were delighted
therwith: whether that word vſed by *Saint
Iohn* in the Apocalips, to witt *Meretrix Babylon*) were meant of a particular perſon, as he
applyeth it: or rather of a citty or multitude?
yf he will anſwere any thinge at all, he muſt
needs graunt the ſecond. For that the viſion
deſcribeth plainly the citty of Rome ſitua-
ted vpon ſeauen hilles, that ſlew the martyrs of Chriſt, & infected the whole world
with the variety and confuſion of her Ido-
latryes. Which ſentences beinge not ap-
pliable to the Church or congregation of
Chriſtians in thoſe dayes, (that was holy, as
Fox will confeſſe) but rather to the ſtate &
preſent condition of Rome vnder thoſe pagan perſecutinge Emperors, that afflicted
Chriſtians and forced men to Idolatry
(which ſtate was propheſied that it ſhould
fall, and be ouerthrowne ſoone after by
Chriſts power, as we haue ſeene it fulfilled:) all this, I ſay, beinge put togeather &
conſidered, it is a moſt ridiculous thinge, to
                                                    apply

The
vvhore
of *Baby-
lon* vvas
the per-
ſecuting
citty of
Rome
vnder
the pa-
gan Em-
perors.

apply this prophefie of the whore of Babylon (as Fox doth) to any particular Pope
Iohn, Ioane, or *Iill*, yf any fuch had byn.

21.   But the very truth is, that this whole
ftory of Pope *Ioane* is a meere fable, and fo
knowen to the learneder fort of Proteftants
themfelues : but,that they will not leaue of
to delude the world with it, for lacke of
other matter.   Yf yow aske me, how it be-
gane, and hath continued in mens mouthes
fo longe? I anfwere,eyther vpon fimplicity,
or malice, or both. Vpon fimplicity it feemeth it was begone by the firft author and
relater therof *Martinus Polonus*, that liued
about 300. yeares gone: & aboue 400. after
the thinge is faid, to haue fallen out. Who
was a very fimple man, as appeareth by many otherfabulous relations, which he maketh. And yet doth not he auer it, but only
with this limitation *(vt afferitur) as it is faid.*
Wherby he fheweth,to haue receyued it by
only vulgar rumor, without any certayne
author or ground. And we fhall after fhew
the occafion of the forfaid falfe rumor.

22.   But the matter beinge once on foote,it
was continued partly by curiofity of later
wryters, that tooke it out of *Polonus*, as *Platina*, and ✶ others relatinge yt with the fame
reftri&ion *(vt aiunt,* as men fay:) and partly
by malice and emulation of them, that fauoured the German Empire againft the

The be-
ginning
of the
fable of
Pope
Ioane.

*Mart.
Polon. in
vit. im-
perat. &
Pontif.
Papa*
109. *an.
Chrifti*
855.
✶ *Se a
larg re-
futation
of this
fable by
Onu-
phrius
in his ad
dition to
Platina.*

Pope & were glad to haue such a matter of some dishonour to obiect against the Sea of Rome. Which humor our later sectaryes also haue thought best to continew.

23. But if we go to more auncient writers, such (I meane) as liued in the very tyme or soone after the matter is prerended to haue fallen out, (that is to say with *Leo* 4. that held the Sea 8. yeare, 6. monethes and 3. dayes from the yeare of Christ 847. to 855. & with *Pope Benedictus* 3. that immediatly followed him after some few dayes of vacancy, to witt from the yeare 855. to 858. these authors, I say, do shew euidently, that these two Popes, beinge both Romans, succeded immediatly one after the other, without any *Iohn* or *Ioane* comminge in betweene them. As for example *Anastasius Bibliothecarius,* a man of great reputatiõ, that liued in both these Popes tymes, and was present at both their elections and wrote the particulars therof sheweth amongst other points : *that* Leo the 4. *died the* 16. *day before the calends of Au-*

*Anastas.
iu vita
Leon.* 4.

guft , *and that all the cleargie of Rome gathered togeather* (he doth not say the Cardinalls as foolish Iohn Fox doth, for that, that kind of election was not then in vse) *vvith one consent did choose Benedict the* 3. *&c.*

24. Thus writeth *Anastasius*; and with him do agree the historiographers that followed next after him, as *Audomarus* , *Luitprandus, Rhegino,*

Rhegino, Hermanus Contractus, Lambertus Schafna-
bergensis, Otho Frisengensis, Conradus, Abbas Vrsper-
gens. and others longe before *Martinus Polonus.*
Who in their chronologies do place *Benedi-*
ctus 3. immediatly after *Leo* 4. without ad-
mitting any other man or woman betwene
them. And the very same also doth write *Ado*
Bishop of *Vienna* that liued at the same time.
Leone obeunte , *Benedictus in sede Apostolica consti-*
tuitur, Leo the fourth being dead *Benedict* was
placed for him in the Apostolicall Sea. And
as for *Ioannes* 8. they do place him foure
Popes after *Leo* 4. to witt next to *Adrianus* 2.
and say he was a Romane and raigned ten
yeares distinctly . So as if they should misse
in this count of Popes and yeares , the error
must needs be manifest in chronologie. Yea
not only latyn writers, but euen the greeke
historiographers *Zonaras, Cedrenus, Curopalatas,*
and others, that wrote before *Martinus Polonus*
of matters concerning the Latyn Church in
those dayes, & were no frends to the same,
and would haue byn content of such an aduantage to obiect against yt: yet wryte they
nothinge ther of at all . Which is an euident
proofe that there was no such matter.

25.   But besides these authorityes of externall authors, I haue one argument also of no
small moment (as it seemeth to me) taken
from our aunciet English historyes wrytten
in the Latyn tongue: to witt *VVilliam* of Mal-

Ancient
Authors
that do
exclu-
ded pope
Ioane.

*Ado in
chron.
an. Domi
ni* 855.

An argu
mēt out
of En-
glish hi-
storio-
graphers
for ouer-
thro-
vvig the
fable of
Pope
Ioane.

mesbury,

mesbury , Henry Huntington, Roger Houeden, Florentius Vigornienfis, and Mathevv of VVeſtminſter.
Wherof the firſt foure liued fiue hundred
yeares gone and are elder then Polonus. And
the lateſt of them 300. yeares, & was equall
with him. And no one of them all maketh
any mention of this Pope Ioane. Which yet in
reaſon they ſhould haue done aboue others.
For that they do all agree , that in the tyme
of Pope Leo the fourth towards the end of his
raigne about the yeare of Chriſt 853. K. Ethelvvolfe before mentioned, ſonne to K. Egbert,
(hauinge put his kingdome of England in
the beſt order he could , and left the gouernment therof for his abſence to his eldeſt
ſonne Aethelbald aſsiſted with the helpes of
his ſecond and third brothers, Athelbricke and
Athelred) tooke his iorney to Rome leadinge
with him his fourth ſonne Alured or Alfred
(who afterward alſo was King) which he-
loued moſt tenderly aboue the reſt of his
children. And comminge to Rome he deliuered the ſame Alfred beinge yet of very
young age , accordinge to the accoumpt of
Mathevv VVeſtminſter, into the hands of the
ſaid Pope Leo 4. to be inſtructed and brought
vp by him (as Iohn Fox alſo relateth. And
that the ſaid Pope receaued him with great
kindnes, and was his Godfather in the Sacrament of Confirmation , detayninge him
there with him. But how long this Prince
ſtayed

The
going of
K. Ethel-
vvolfe
& prince
Alfred
to Rome.

ftayed in Rome after his fathers returne,
though it be not fett downe in particular:
yet, that it was fome number of yeares, feemeth euident; both for that he returned
more learned and otherwife better qualified, then any Saxon king had byn before
him, and for that we find no mention of his
acts in England, vntill in the reygne of his
third brother *Athebred* (for all three raygned
in order after *Ethelvvolfe* their father) vpon
the yeare 871. at the famous battell of *Rea-*
ding in Barkefhire, fought againft the Danes.
Where he beinge prefent and lieftennant to
his brother the King, though he were but
22. yeares old (accordinge to the account of
Florentius and of *Mathevv VVeftminfter*;) yet
feinge the enemyes armie to preffe vpon
him, and his brother to ftay ouerlonge at
maffe, he gaue them battle in very vnequall
place: but with fuch valour, as he obteyned
a notable victory, &c. But to our purpofe
of *Pope Ioane.*

26.   It is very like by that which I haue
faid, that this Prince *Alfred* liuinge in Rome
when *Pope Leo* the 4. died, and when *Pope Be-*
nedict the 3. was chofen: muft needs haue
knowne alfo *Pope Ioane*, yf any fuch had entred and liued two yeares and a halfe, betwene them, (as Fox would haue yt.) And
further that fome of our auncient hiftoriographers wrytinge of thofe tymes fo particularly,

Sto. an.
871.
Math.
VVeft.
849.
Florent.
in chron.
eodē an.

VVhy
English
vvryters
fhould
haue vv-
ritten of
Pope
Ioane
more
then
others,
if any
fuch had
euer byn.

cularly, as they do, would haue made ſome
mention therof eſpecially if this ſhee Pope
were an Engliſh woman or called *Ioannes Anglus* (as *Polonus* ſaith, or *Anglicus* as *Platina* relateth, or if ſhe were borne, brought vp, or had ſtuddied in England, as the *Magdebugians* and others of their ſect deuiſe, or if ſhe went vp and downe the world in the company of an Engliſh monke of the monaſtery of *Fulda*, as Iohn Fox doth fable) it is like (I ſay) that if any of theſe things had byn true, Prince *Afred* or ſome of his trayne reſidinge then in Rome, would haue knowne her or byn acquainted with her, or with the monke that lead her about, or at leaſt wayes haue receyued ſome ſpeciall help at her hand, when ſhee came to be Pope, which would haue deſerued ſome memory in our hiſtoryes. But our forſaid wryters do not only not make any mention of her, or of any *Iohn* or *Ioane* Engliſh Pope, that came betwene *Leo* 4. and *Benedict* the third: but do expreſſely exclude the ſame by placinge the one immediatly after the other, & aſſigning them their diſtinct number of yeares before mentioned, to witt 8. and 3. monethes to *Leo*, and two yeares and ſix monethes immediatly followinge to *Benedictus* 3. For ſo doth a *Malmesbury* in his chronologie, & b *Florentius*, in his chronicon, and c *Mathevv* of Weſtminſter in his hiſtory, whoſe words
are

*Mart.
Polon.
lib.4. de
Pont.
an. 855.
Plat. in
Ioan. 8.*

*a Malm.
in faſt.
reg. &
epiſcop.
Angl.
an. 847.
& 855.
b Florent
Vigorn.
in chron.
an. 853.
& 858.
c Math.
VVeſtm.
in chron.*

are thefe: *Anno gratiæ* 855. *Leone Papa defuncto, succeßit ei Benedictus annis duobus, mensibus sex, & diebus decem.* In the yeare of grace 855. *Pope* „ *Leo* the fourth beinge dead *Benedict* the 3.did „ fucceed him, and fate two yeares fix mo- „ nethes and ten dayes, &c. Which agreeth with all the other auncient externe authors before mentioned. So as heere is neyther place nor time left for *Ioannes Anglicus* to haue come betwene them.

27. And all thefe authors did write (as hath byn noted)eyther before,or with *Martinus Polonus*, who is taken to haue byn the firft relator of this fable. And though in fome printed copies of the chronicles of *Marianus Scotus,*and *Sigebertus* (fomwhat elder then *Martinus Polonus)* there be mention in a word or two of this tale, with this ground (*vt ferunt*) as men fay : yet in more auncient handwrytten originalls found in ★ *Flanders,* and other places,noe fuch thing is feene but rather to the contrary. With diuers euident fignes & coniectures, that thofe few words now found in the printed copyes, were added by others afterward in *Germany* where the worke lay for many yeares duringe the contention of German Emperors againft the Sea of Rome.

28. But befides all this, there enfueth another argumét more euident in my opinion, then any of the reft hitherto alleaged , for

ouerthrow

★ *There is extant the originall of Sigeber-tus in* Monaft. Iemla-cenfi *in* Flâders, *& of the corrup-tion of* Maria-nus Sco-tus *in this be-halfe read him that fet-teth forth* Metrop. Alberti Cranzij *anno* 1574.

ouerthrow of this fable. Which is, that about a hundred and seuenty yeares after this deuised election of *Pope Ioane* (to witt, vpon the yeare of Christ 1020.) the Church and patriarches of Constantinople, beinge in some contention with Rome, *Pope Leo* the 9. wrote a long letter to *Michell* patriarch of *Constantinople*, reprehendinge certayne abuses of that Church, and amonge other, that they were said to haue promoted Eunuches to Priesthood, and therby also a greater inconuenience fallen out, which was that a woman had crept in to be patriarch. Which yet he saith, that for the horror of the fact he would not beleeue. *Absit* (saith he) *vt velimus credere quod publica fama non dubitat asserere, &c.* God forbidd we should beleeue, that which publike fame doubteth not to affirme, which is that the Church of *Constantinople* by promotinge Eunuches to Priesthood against the cannon of the councell of *Nice*)promoted once a woman to the Bishops Sea, which is so abhominable a thing, as the horror therof doth not permitt vs to beleeue it, &c.

29.   Thus wrote he. Which no doubt he would neuer haue durst to do yf the Patriarch of *Constantinople* might haue returned the matter backe vpon him againe and said; this was but a slaunderons report falsely raised against the Church of *Constantinople*, but

A most euident argumét against the fable of Pope Ioane.

Epistola Leon. 9. cap. 5. & 23.

but that a woman indeed had byn promoted in the Roman Church. How cold *Pope
Leo* haue anſwered this reply? Wherfore
moſt certayne it ſeemeth, that at this tyme
there was not ſo much as any rumor or
mention of any woman Pope that euer had
byn in the Roman Church, this beinge 250.
yeares before *Martinus Polonus* wrote. For
which cauſe alſo it is thought very probably
that this rumor of the Church of *Coſtantinople*
might be the occaſion of the tale raiſed after
againſt Rome. For that *Martinus Polonus* being
a very ſimple man, & liuinge ſo longe after
(as hath byn ſaid) & hearinge an vncertayne
fame of a woman promoted to cheefe
Prieſthood, might aſcribe that to Rome,
which belonged to *Conſtantinople*. Which
being once wrytten by him paſſed to others
after him, and ſo came to our heretiks.

*A pro-
bable
cōiectu-
re of the
firſt ori-
gine of
this fa-
ble of
Pope
Ioane.*

30. Finally, howſoeuer this bee of the firſt
occaſion or inuention of the fable, certayne
it is, that moſt euidently it is a fable: & that
if other arguments fayled, yet there be ſo
many incongruityes, ſimplicityes, abſurdityes, varietyes and contrarietyes in the very
narratiō it ſelfe, as it diſcouereth the whole
matter to be a meere fable & fiction indeed
and a rumor of vulgar people without
ground. For *Martinus Polonus* beginneth his
narration thus: *Poſt leonem ſedit Ioannes Anglus
natione Margantinus*; After *Leo* the third ſate

*Mart.
Pol. in
vit. Imp.
& Pont.
an. 855.*

Iohn

Iohn Engliſh by nation a Margantine, but
where this countrey of Margantia is, no
man can tell. And it followeth, *quæ alibi legi-
tur fuiſſe Benedictus 3.* which otherwhere is
read to be *Benedictus* the 3. So as this man ſeemeth to confound him with *Benedict*, and
conſequently aſcribeth to him the ſame
tyme of his raigne, that is aſſigned to *Benedictus* (to witt, two yeares and fiue months.
And yet preſently after, he ſaith, that *Benedictus* was a Roman ſonne to *Pratolus*, &c.

31.   *Platina*, that tooke it out of this man,
to make the tale ſomwhat more probable
beginneth thus: *Ioannes Anglicus ex Maguntiaco
oriundus, &c.* Iohn of England borne at Maguntiacum, &c. Then how could he be
Iohn or Iohne of England yf he were borne
at Maguntiacum? and where is this *Maguntiacum*? and how doth it agree with Margantinus vſed by *Polonus*? But then come in
the * *Magdeburgians* and ſay contrary: That
he was *Moguntinus, oriundus ex Anglia:* of * *Moguntia* in Germany borne in England. And
contrary to this *Bibliander* (another German
ſectary) contradicteth that againe, ſaying
in his chronicles: *that he was not borne in England, but brought vp and ſtuddied there.* And ſo
yow ſee their contradiction about the place
both of birth and contrey.

32.   But beſides this, there are infinite
other diſagreements, and diſconueniences
in this

*Platt. in
vit.
Ioan. 8.*

*✶Cent.9.
cap. 20.
✶Mentz.*

*Bibliad.
in tabu-
lis Chro-
nic.*

in this ſtory. For that ſome do feigne him to
be *Ioannes* 8. ſome 9. Iohn Fox ſaith, that ſhe
was called *Gilberta* before, & that ſhe went *Fox pag.*
with an Engliſh monke out of the Abbey of *124.*
Fulda in *Germany* to *Athens*, *and there ſtuddied in
mans apparell*. Wheras it is knowne, that
⋆ Athens at that time had no ſcoole in it at all: *⋆ This is
nor in many yeares before. If ſhe were bread *euident*
alſo or brought vp in England or went in *by Cedre-
nius*, and
an Engliſh monks company (as Fox ſaith) *Zonaras*
and if ſhe were an Engliſh Prieſts daughter *in vit.*
(as the *Magdeburgians* deuiſe) it is like that *Michael.
& Theod.*
Prince *Alfred* or ſome of his trayne reſi- *Imp. an.*
dinge then in Rome (as before hath byn *Chriſti*
ſaid) would haue heard or knowne of the *856.*
matter.

33. But Iohn Fox goeth further and telleth *Fox ibid.*
vs out of his fingars ends, *that the Cardinalls*
(forſooth) *mett ſollemly after the death of* Leo
4. *ſaid their Maſſe of the holy Ghoſt, and ſo proceeded to their ordinary election and brought forth Gilberta, &c.* But this is all ſcoffinge folery. For
that Cardinalls had not the election of
Popes at that tyme. And he that will read
the forſaid *Anaſtaſius Bibliothecarius*, (that was *Aunciēt
circum-*
preſent at the election of *Pope Benedictus* and *ſpection*
deſcribeth the particularityes therof) ſhall *in choo-*
ſee another manner of election in vſe at that *ſing Po-*
day by the whole cleargie. Moreouer he *pes.*
ſhall ſe, that the cuſtome was not to chooſe
at that tyme any, but ſuch as were knowne
C c   and

and tried men, and fuch as had liued for the
moſt part of their life in Rome it felfe, and
had giuen great fatisfactiō in their manners
and behaued themfelues well in other inferior Eccleſiaſticall charges laid vpon them.
34. All which beinge fo, lett any man of
reafon tell me, how it is pofsible to imma-
gine, that men of thoſe tymes were fo fond
and abfurd, as to chooſe to fo high a dignity
among them an vnknowne man or wo-
man, whofe parents and countrey were not
knowen, nor proofe had of their conuerſa-
tiō, & much more that they would chooſe,
fuch a perfon as this is reported to be : hauinge wandred the world vp and downe
with a monke, as Fox affirmeth. How
could all this ly hidden ? was there none,
that eyther by countenance, voyce, or other
actions of hers, could fufpect this fraud?
how happened her owne louers had not
difcouered her, or her incontinent life? how
could fhe paffe through prieſthood, and
other Eccleſiaſticall orders? how by fo many vnder offices and degrees, as they muſt,
before they come to be Popes, without
defcryinge?
35. And finally (not to ſtand vpon more
improbabilityes) eyther this *Pope Ione* was
young, or old, when ſhe was choſen. Yf ſhe
were young, that was againſt the cuſtome
to chooſe young Popes, as may appeare by
the

the great number of Popes, that liued in that
dignity aboue the number of Emperors,
that succeded often in their youthe. Besides
it is a most vnlikely thinge, that the whole
Roman clergy would choose a Pope without a beard, especially a straunger. But if
she were old, when she was chosen, then
how did she beare a child publikely in procession, as our heretiks affirme? how did
they not discerne her to be a woman or an
Eunuch, seeinge she had no beard in her
old age?

36. Againe how could she be nyne moneths with child in that place without
beinge discouered or suspected by some?
how durst she go forth in publike procefsion, when she knew her selfe so neere her
tyme? how is she said to haue gone from the
palace of *Saint Peter* to *S. Iohn Lateran*, wheras
the Popes lay not then in the *Vatican* at *Saint
Peters:* but at *Saint Iohn Lateran* it selfe? finally
there are so many fond improbabilities and
morall impofsibilityes in this tale (especially being ioyned with the graue testimonies
of so many auncient authors and historiographers as before we haue recited to the
contrary as no man of any meane iudgemēt,
discretion or comon sence, will giue credit therto: But will easely see the vanity of
so ridiculous a fiction. Wherfore this shall
suffice for the confutation of this hereticall
fable.

fable. Though as before hath byn ſhewed,)
yf it were or had byn true: yet no preiudice
could come to vs therby, that hold, no
woman good or badd can be head of our
Church.

THE NARRATION OF EN-
GLISH ECCLESIASTICAL AFFAIRES,
during this fourth ſtation or diſtinction of time is
continued, and the abſurdities of Iohn Fox are
diſcouered.

CHAP. VI.

WHERFORE now we ſhall returne to
follow the threed of IohnFox his ſtory againe. And wheras you asked me before
what indeed the poore fellow performeth
in this his third booke: I now will aunſwere, as then I began to ſay, that in very
truth, he meerly trifleth out the time: handlinge nothinge of that he ſhould haue done
of the orderly deſcent, race or courſe of the
Church; but tellinge vs impertinent and tri-
uiall matters, and for the moſt part not Eccleſiaſticall but temporall to be found in
euery chronicler? To witt, certayne ſcrapps
of the liues of our Engliſh kings from *K. Eg-*
bert, Ethelvvolſe, Ethelbald, Ethelread, Alured and
the reſt, vnto *K. Edvvard* the Conſeſſor, and
ſo to *VVilliam Conqueror*, cenſuringe euery
Prince (when he talketh of ſpirituall matters)

VVhy
Fox fal-
leth out
vvith
the auñ-
cient
Chriſtiã
Engliſh
Kings &
Queeñes.

Se Fox
from
pag.130.
131. &c.

ters) for their beleefe, actions and doings in
religion. As for example reprehendinge
them, for that they builded fo many monafteryes: and much more, for that fo many of
them & their children entred to be monks
and nunnes: that they gaue fo much lands,
liuings and priuiledges to abbeyes, and
Churches: and for that they went on pilgrimages, offered almes for their finnes, ordeyned maffes to be faid for them, when they
were dead: that they beleeued fo eafily miracles, went to fhrift, humbled themfelues
to Priefts, and other fuch like religious
actions, which do greatly difpleafe Fox.

Fox pag.
110.

2.   And to fhew yow fome few examples,
he beginneth firft with *Ethelvvolfe* foonne to
K. *Egbert* mislikinge a certayne donation of
lands which he gaue to the Church in his
tyme for almes, to pacifie, (as he faith) Gods
wrath, therby the fooner, for diuertinge the
cruell perfecution and inundation of the
Danes, which had begon in his fathers K.
Egbert his tyme, & endured ftill to the vtter
defolation of the land. His wo·ds are thefe:
Poft multiplices tribulationes ad affligendum vfque
ad internecionem Ego Ethelvvolfus Rex. &c. After
many tribulations afflictinge vs euen to
death, I K. *Ethelvvolfe* togeather with the
councell of my Bifhops and Princes haue
taken this holfome & agreeable refolution
to giue fome portion of the land of my in-

The do-
nation
of Kinge
Ethel-
vvolfe
an. 844.
Fox pag.
110.
Malm.
lib. 2. de
geftis
Angl.
Reg.

heritance

„ heritance vnto God and the Bl. Virgin
„ Mary, and to all the reſt of his Saints, to be
„ poſſeſſed by them for euer, &c. To the end
„ that they may powre out prayers for vs to
„ God ſo much the more diligently, &c.

3.   Thus farre Iohn Fox. Though *VVilliam*
of *Malmesbury* doth relate the ſame farre dif-
ferently, and much more largly. tellinge,
what Biſhops were preſent at the makinge
of this chart: to witt, *Alſtane* Biſhop of *Shyr-
borne* (afterward tranſlated to *Saliſbury*) and
Svvithine B. of *VVincheſter*. And what pſalmes
and maſſes were appointed by the ſaid Biſhops for the K. in reſpect of theſe almes &
the like. All which do greatly diſpleaſe
Iohn Fox, but help him nothinge at all : but
diſgraceth rather his new Church, this hap-
peninge in the yeare of Chriſt 844.

Fox ibid.   4.   The like donation doth Fox recyte out
The do-   of *VVilliam* of *Malmesbury* made by K. *Ethel-*
nation   *bald* K. of the Mercians ſome yeares before
of *Kingt*   (to witt about the yeare of Chriſt 740.)
Ethel-   where he ſaith : *Ego Ethelbaldus Merciorum rex*
bald.   *pro amore cæleſtis Patriæ, &c.* I *Ethelbald* K. of the
Malm.   Mercians for the loue I haue to my heauen-
lib. 1. *de*   ly countrey, and for the health of my ſoule
geſt. reg.   haue thought good to ſtudy how by good
Angl.   works I may free the ſame from the chaines
„ of ſinne. Wherfore ſeinge almighty God for
„ his mercy and clemency, without any pre-
„ cedent meritt of myne, hath giuen me my
                                                    crowne

crowne of this gouernment I do willingly ,,
out of that, which he hath giuen me, reſtore ,,
to him againe by way of almes this that fol- ,,
lowweth, &c.

5 Thus farre that good king. Which greatly alſo misliketh Iohn Fox. And he ſaith in
particular, that two things do much offend
him, in theſe donations to Churches and
monaſteries: the firſt, *That they ſhould' erect* **Fox pag.**
theſe nonaſteries of monks and nunnes (ſaith he) **120.**
to liue ſolely and ſingly by themſelues, out of the holy
ſtate of matrimony. And ſecondly : *that vnto this*
their zeale & deuotion vvas not ioyned the knovvledg
of Chriſts Ghoſpell, ſpecially in the Article of our free
Iuſtificaton by the faith of Ieſu Chriſt.

6. Lo heere what two quarrells our Fox
hath pickt out against theſe auncient Chriſtians. The firſt, that ſo many did profeſſe
the holy ſtate of virginity, and continency;
the other, that by doinge ſo many good
works, they lacked the knowledge of the
proteſtants Ghoſpell, which iuſtifieth by
only faith without good works. But they
might anſwere with *Saint Iames.* Thou haſt **Iam. ☞**
faith and I haue vvorks, ſhevv me thy faith vvithout
vvorks, and I vvill ſhevv thee my faith by vvorks.
And that theſe good works did proceed of
faith contrary to the cauill of Iohn Fox is
euident by thoſe pious words of the King
where he ſaith: *Seing 'almighty God of his mercy*
and clemency vvithout any precedent meritt of myne

hath

hath giuen me my crovvne I do vvillingly reſtore to him againe, &c.

7.   But Fox goeth forward in ieſtinge at the ſaid K. Ethelvvolfe, ſayinge: *that he that hal byn once nuzeled vp (in his youth) amonge Prieſts, he vvas alvvayes good and deuout to holy Church, &c.*

Fox pagi 123.

„ And then paſſeth he on to ſhew , how after
„ the eſtabliſhinge of matters in his owne
„ kingdome he went to Rome , and carried
„ with him his little ſonne *Alured* or *Alfre* co-
„ mittinge him to the bringinge vp of *Pope Leo*
„ the fourth , as before hath byn ſaid , where
„ alſo he redified the Engliſh ſchoole founded
„ by K. *Offa*, & deſtroyed by fire a little before

The al-mes and pious deeds of K.Ethel-vvolfe.

vnder K. *Egbert* Moreouer he gaue (ſaith Fox) Yerely to be paid in Rome 300.marks to be diſtributed in this manner 100. marks to mayntaine the lights of *S. Peters* Church
„ and another hundred marks to mayntaine
„ the lights of *Saint Pauls* Church, and the
„ third hundred to be diſpoſed in good works
„ at the Popes appointment. At all which Fox
„ ieſteth alſo merely,buildinge his Church by
„ theſe mocks and mewes.

8.   And to like effect he recyteth a miracle regiſtred by *VVilliam Malmesbury*, and by the charter of K. *Ethelſtonne* ſonne and heire to K. *Edvvard* the elder, which kinge hauinge eſcaped a great danger at *VVincheſter,* where one of his ſubiects named Duke *Alphred,*and other of his nobles conſpiringe to geather preſently

Fox pag. 133.

prefently after his fathers death, would haue
put out his eyes, but he efcaping that danger
tooke the faid *Alphred* prifoner , and for that
he denyed that he had any fuch intention,
the good king, thought there was no better
triall then to fend him to Rome to *Pope Iohn*
the 11. to be tried by a follemne religious
oath before him. The Pope made him
fweare before *Saint Peters* aultar , who for-
fwearinge the faid confpiracy fell downe
prefently before the faid altar in the fight of
all the people, and was carried thence in the
armes of his feruants to the forfaid fchoole
of Englifhmen , where he died the third
night after , wherwith the Pope and all
Rome remayned aftonifhed , and the Pope
fent prefently into England, to know of the
King, whether he would pardon him, and
fuffer his body to be buried in Chriftian fe-
pulcher , which K. *Athelftane* after confulta-
tion had with the reft of his nobility, and by
the earneft intercefsion of *Duke Alfred* his
frends was content that he fhould be fo buried, but yet by fentéce of the whole realme
the poffefsions of the faid *Alphred* were adiudged to the Kings vfe, who beftowed
them all vpon Churches and monafteryes
to the honor of God and *S. Peter* which had
giuen this iudgment in the controuerfie.

9. All this is teftified by the faid Kings
Charter recorded by *VVilliam* of *Malmesbury*

A mira-
cle in
Rome
vpon an
Englifh
Duke
an. 933.

Cc 5   and

and recited by Fox, and the ſaid Charter towards the end hath theſe words : *Et ſic iudi-*

Malm.
lib. 2. de
geſt. reg.
Angl.
fol. 28.

cata eſt mihi tota poſſeſſio eius in magnis & modicis,
quam Deo & Sancto Petro dedi, nec iuſtiùs noui quàm
Deo & Sancto Petro hanc poſſeſſionem dare, qui emu-
lum meum in conſpectu omnium cadere fecerunt , &
mihi proſperitatem regni largiti ſunt. And by this

,, meanes the whole poſſeſsion both great &
,, ſmall (of *Duke Alphred*) was adiudged vnto
,, me, which I gaue to God and to *Saint Peter,*
,, nor do I know to whome I ſhould more
,, iuſtly giue the ſame, then to God & to *Saint*
,, *Peter,* who made my aduerſary to falldowne
,, in the ſight of all men and gaue vnto me the
,, proſperity of my kingdome. Thus wrote he
about the yeare of Chriſt 933. as Iohn Fox
counteth ; and I maruaile he would relate
this ſtory beinge ſo much againſt himſelfe
and his religion, & in confirmation of ours
as it is , for that it ſheweth that God and

Miracles
vvrougt
in Rome
in confir
mation
of Cath.
religiō.
an. 933.

Saint Peter in thoſe dayes wrought miracles
in Rome, when Fox ſaith that the faith and
religiō of Rome was farre out of order from
the true Ghoſpell; but this is the miſery and
calamity of this poore fellow and his cauſe,
as often before I haue noted , that eyther he
muſt wryte nothinge at all of theſe tymes
and ages or els he muſt wryte teſtimonyes
againſt himſelfe.

Fox pag.
116.

10.   I will giue yow one ſhort example
more, where he alleageth vs a narration of a
very

very old wryter which he faith he had in *Ex vetu-*
wrytten hand lent him by one named *VVil-* *ſto exem*
liam Carre, and thervpon he citeth it ſtill by *plari*
the name of *Hiſtoria Cariana*, this ſtory being *riana.*
wrytten as it ſeemeth in thoſe ages, and of
the miſeryes happened to England by the
incurſiōs of Danes & other infidels ſeeketh
out the cauſes of Gods wrath in this behalfe, ſayinge thus: *In Anglorum quidem Eccleſia*
primitiua, Religio clariſsimè ſplenduit, &c. In the
primitiue Church of England religion did »
moſt cleerly ſhyne, in ſo much the ˉ Kings, »
Queenes, Princes, Dukes, Conſulls, Barons »
and rulers of Churches incenſed with the »
deſire of the kingdome of heauen, laboured »
and ſtyrred (as it were) amongſt themſelues ».
to enter into monaſticall life, and into vo- »
luntary exile and ſolytarines, forſakinge all »
to follow their Lord wher in proceſſe of »
tyme all vertue ſo much decayed amonge »
them, that in fraud and treachery none ſee- »
med like vnto them neyther was to them »
any thinge odious or hatefull but piety and »
iuſtice, nor any thing in price and honour »
but ciuill warre and ſheadinge bloud, wher- »
fore almighty God ſent vpon them pagan »
and cruell nations like ſwarmes of bees.

11. This relateth Fox out of his *Carian* ſto- *Fox rela-*
ry, and i know not to what end he ſhould *teth mat-*
ters
relate yt, but only to ſhew, that while En- *againſt*
gliſhmen liued godly accordinge to the fa- *himſelfe*
ſhion

ſhion or their primitiue Church, they eſteemed and honoured highely religious and
monaſticall life, and many leauinge the
world, with the pleaſures and poſſeſſions
therof entred into that religious courſe, in-
deauoring to follow and imitate their Lord
and maiſter therin, and that ſo long was
England happy & bleſſed by God, to which
effect if Iohn Fox do alleage the ſame, then
is it euident what a good concluſion he doth
make againſt himſelfe & his religion at this
day, that are ſuch profeſſed enemyes to that
kind of life ſo highely heere comended, and
conſequently the relator therof doth ſhew
himſelfe to be aſwell Iohn Foole as Iohn
Fox not conſideringe what maketh for him
or againſt him.

12.   But to the end that we ſhould not
thinke, that he hath made peace or freend-
ſhip with monks for all this, or that he liketh their life or profeſſion any thing the
better for ſo many praiſes giuen them by
auncient authors, he ſcoldeth at them euery
where & vpon euery occaſion writing ouer
the pages & titles of his booke theſe ſuper-
ſcriptions, *Monks, ſuperſtitious monks, monks mar-*
ried, monks meere laymen in old times and the like.
And if I ſhould number vp the manifeſt lyes
which the miſerable and poore ſpitefull fellow inuenteth againſt them for ſome ſhow
of proofe yow would táke pitty of him, and
                                            not

not of the monks. Yow shall heare one short
discourse of his about them, and therby you
may iudg of the rest.

13. *Monks* (saith he) *vvere nothing els in old* Fox pag.
tyme, but laymen leading a more stricter trade of life, 138.
as may sufficiently appeare by Augustine lib. de mori-
bus Ecclesiæ cap. 13. *Item lib. de oper. Monachorum* Alyinge
Item ep. ad Aurelium. Also by Hierome and Helio- discour-
dorus vvrytinge these vvords: Alia monachorum est se of Fox
causa, alia Clericorum: Clerici pascunt oues, ego about
pascor. One thing perteyneth to monks another thing monks.
to them of the cleargie. They of the Cleargy feede the
flocke, I am fedd, &c. By all vvhich is euident that
monks vvere no other in former ages of the Church
but only lay-men differing from Priests, &c.

14.   Thus writeth Fox. Which alone were
sufficient to shew his peeuish fraud & folly
in all his writings. For Albeit *Saint Augustine*
in the places by him quoted, had wrytten
any such thing as he affirmeth (which is
quite false, and so shall the Reader find, that
will examine the places:) yet the very
words of *Saint Hierome* by Fox himselfe adioyned, do cleerly interprett both his owne
and *Saint Augustine* his meaninge, and conuince Fox for a meere maleuolous cauiller.
For that *Saint Hierome* doth not deny, that
monks are cleargy men or Priests. For then
he should deny himselfe to haue byn Priest
or of the cleargy, seinge he confesseth himselfe to be a monke. But his meaninge is to
shew

shew the different end and office of some
cleargy men, (to witt secular Prieſts & Biſhops that haue care of ſoules) from monks.
For that the one do attend principally to
action, the other to contemplation: the one
to preachinge, the other to praying: the one
to feed others, the others to be fedd. In
which later number *Saint Hierome* for humility putteth alſo himſelfe. Whome yet I
thinke Iohn Fox will not affirme to haue
byn a meere layman, and not Prieſt and
cleargy man. And ſo is this cauill of his
againſt monks *(that in old time they vvere laymen)*
ſhewed to be moſt vayne and malitious. For
what will he ſay of *Saint Baſill, Saint Nazianzen, Saint Auguſtine, Saint Gregory*? were they
not monks, Prieſts, and Biſhops alſo? how
then were monks meerely lay-men in old
tyme?

15.   The like notorious folly conioyned
with falſhood he vſeth to prooue marryed
monks: alleadging *Saint Athanaſius* his words
*epiſt. ad Diacont. qui ait ſe nouiſſe & monachos
& epiſcopos coniuges & liberorum patres*. Who
ſaith, that he knew both monks & Biſhops
married men, and fathers of children. But
what proueth this? do not we ſe euery day
euen now in our Church both Biſhops,
Prieſts and religious men, that haue once
byn married and ſome of them alſo to haue
had children, and after the death of their

wyues

VVhe-
ther
monks
vvere
meere
laymen
in old
time, or
no?

wyues to haue entred into Ecclesiasticall &
religious orders? what fond deludinge of his
reader is this ? he should haue proued, that
they had marryed after they had byn Priests
or monks: and then had he said somwhat.
but this he could not do, and so thought best
to make a fond florish of the other.

16. Nay in the very Greeke Church at this
day, where Priests are permitted, that were
marryed before, though their wyues be liuinge: yet yf their said wyues dy, they are
not permitted to marry againe. And as for
monks (out of which order only Bishops are
made in that Church) they were neuer permitted to marry after their profession of religion. Nay *S. Epiphanius* (a cheefe pillar of
that Church, when it was perfectly Catholike aboue 1200. yeares gone) saith plainely,
as the *Magdeburgians* also alleage him: That
the holy Church of God admitted not in
his dayes any man to Priesthood, or episco-
pall dignity, that eyther marryed the second
tyme, or did not absteyne from conuersation with his first wife, yf she liued, after he
was admitted to Priesthood: *Reuera* (saith
he) *non suscipit sancta dei prædicatio post Christi
aduentum eos, qui à nuptijs, mortua ipsorum vxore,
secundis nuptijs coniuncti sunt: propter excellentem
Sacerdotij honorem & dignitatem. Et hæc certè Sancta Dei Ecclesia cum sinceritate obseruat, &c.* In
very truth the holy preachinge of God after
the

*Epiph. l.
2. tom. 1.*

*Magdeb.
cent. 4.
cap. 4.
pag. 303.*

the comminge of Chriſt doth not admitt
thoſe to be Prieſts, who after their firſt marriage and their wife dead do ioyne themſelues againe in ſecond marriage . And this
doth the holy Church of God obſerue with
ſincerity in reſpect of the excellent honour
and dignity of Prieſthood, &c. So ſaith *Epi-*
phanius: and addeth preſently: *Sed adhuc viuen-*

Epiph.
ibid.

tem & liberos gignentem, &c. But further then
this, the ſaid holy Church of Chriſt doth
,, not admit to Prieſthood a man of one wife,
,, if he liue and gett children as before. But
,, only ſhe admitteth him to be a Deacon,
,, Prieſt, Biſhopp, or Subdeacon (eſpecially
,, where the cleargie is ſincere) who is con-
,, tent to conteyne from his wife, that he vſed
,, before, or to liue in widdowhood, yf his
,, wife be dead.

A cleer
teſtimo-
ny of S.
Epipha-
nius for
the con-
tinency
of mon-
kes and
Prieſtes
in his
dayes.

17. Thus wryteth this holy Doctor, not
only of his owne iudgment, but of the
whole conſent of the vniuerſall Catholike
Church in his dayes : not only of monks,
that make a more ſtrait profeſſion of chaſtity, but of all cleargy men alſo, that liued
within holy orders to witt, Subdeacons
Deacons, Prieſts, and Biſhops . Of whome
thus much be ſpoken by occaſion of Iohn
Fox his notorious ly, *that monks vvere only lay*
men and married in old tyme. And by this we
may ſee his affection towards them & their
profeſſion. And there were noe end, yf
I ſhould

I fhould profecute all his peeuifh picking of
quarrells againft them, vpon euery occafion,
or without occafion, therby to fhew his he-
reticail ftomake in that behalfe. One only
example I will fhew yow more, & fo make
an end.

18. There is a ftory recorded by *VVilliam* of
Malmesbury, and other auncient authenticall
authors, (as Fox himfelfe confeffeth) touching our famous forfaid Englifh King *Alfred* fourth fonne to the forenamed K. *Ethelvvolfe* and nephew to K. *Egbert*, brought vp
in *Rome* by *Pope Leo* the 4. (as hath byn faid,)
who being driuen into great extremytes by
the Conqueft of the Danes againft him, was
releeued and comforted, by the appearinge
of *Saint Cuthbert*, miraculously fortellinge
him, what fhould fucceed in thofe warres,
and confirming the fame with other predictions alfo ; which afterwards were fulfilled. Which ftory though it be one of the
moft rareft, that be to be read in our Englifh
hiftoryes, and with moft comfort alfo by
him that will confider it with attention &
indifferency, and teftified alfo vnto vs, as
authentically as any ftory may be in this
kind, (not only by the faid *Malmesbury* aboue
500. yeares gone, but by diuers others in
like manner, and of like creditt, as Fox himfelfe is forced to confeffe:) yet, for that *Saint
Cuthbert* principall actor therin, was an vn-

*A nota-
ble ftory
of K. Al-
fred
hovv he
receaued
comfort
in his ta-
bulation
by Saint
Cutbert.*

D d   maried

maried monke, he cannot abide the ftory,
but calleth it *a dreaminge fable*, and fo doth
pretermitt the fame in foure words. I fhall
recount it as breefly as I may out of *Malmef-*
bury: Solebat ipfe (faith he meaninge K. *Alfred*)
in tempora poftea fæliciora reductus, cafus fuos iu-
cunda, hilariáq̃ comitate familiaribus exponere,qua-
literáq̃ per B. Cuthberti meritum eos euaferit, &c.

Malm.
lib.2. de
reg.
Angl.
fol. 23.

,, 19.   K. *Alfred* was wont afterward, when
,, he was brought from his mifery to more
,, happy tymes,to recount pleafantly & cour-
,, teously to his familiar frends the chaunces
,, and calamityes, which he had paffed : and
,, how he had efcaped them by the meritt and
,, benefitt of Bl. *S. Cuthbert*,&c. So beginneth
,, *Malmesbury* his Narration. The fumme
,, wherof is this.

20.   K. *Alfred* and his aunceftors hauinge
loft vnto the Danes all the North, Eaft,and
Weft parts of England : he had only three
fhires to hide himfelfe in vpon the South
fea, to witt *Somerfettshire, Hampshire* & *VVilt-*
fhire whether alfo the Danes followed him
with a great army vnder their captaine *Gor-*
mond. And the poore K.being deftitute of all
humayne helpe, wanting both money, vi-
ctualls and men (for all forfooke him vpon
feare) he had no other refuge for fauing his
life, then with a few trufty feruants of his
and his mother (the Dolefull Queene)to fly
into a little Iland in Somerfettshire, called
then

then *Adaling* (wholy befett with waters and
myre in the middeft of marifhe ground, & a
litle wood ioyned thervnto) to hide themfelues in where himfelf & his mother being
lodged in a certayne Swineheards cottage,
the reft made fhift for themfelues, as they
might lying on the ground. But two things
for the prefent preffed them moft. The firft,
honger for want of victualles; the fecond,
feare of *Gormonds* campe, that lay fo neare
them. Wherfore fendinge forth his men to
feeke fome fish by night (for that they durft
not fhew themfelues by day) the K. and his
mother with wofull harts repofed a litle
their weary bodyes and minds in the faid
Swineheards howfe: And beinge entred in
to a litle flumber, behold (faith the ftory)
there appeared to the K. *Saint Cuthbert*, telling him both his name, & that he was fent
to him by God to comfort him, and to tell
him, that albeit his iuftice had hitherto
chaftned Englifhmen for their finnes by
the fworde of the Danes: yet that he would
not extinguish them in refpect of fo many
Sainets that had byn of that Nation; and
from this day foreward would fett them vp
againe, *Modo tandem Deus indigenarum, Sanctorum meritis fuper eam mifericordiæ oculo refpicit.*
Now at leangth God for the meritts of Inglish Sainets doth looke vpon England
with the eye of mercy. He tould him fur-

*The pi-
tifull
cafe of
K. Al-
phreed
preffed
by the
Danes
an. 879.*

*Malm.
ibid.*

ther, that himſelfe from this ſtate of ex-
treame miſery ſhould be reſtored very
ſhortly to a floriſhing ſtate of his kingdome.
For which he gaue him preſently a ſigne or
token; ſaying, that albeit that night was a
very contrary tyme to Fiſhers, both for that
all ryuers were frozen, and a litle rayne
being fallen vpon the ſame, had made it vn-
fitt for men to trauayle in that arte: yet his
men ſhould come home all loden with incredible abundance of fiſh. Thus he tould
him, perſuadinge him, that when he ſhould
ſee all theſe things performed, he ſhould remember to be thankfull to God, and his
ſeruants for their fauour towards him, and
ſo departed.

The ap-
pearinge
of *Saint
Cutbert*
to *K. Al-
phred* &
his mo-
ther.

21.   The K. being wonderfully comforted
with this viſion, awaked for ioye, and calling vpon his mother, the Q. who lay neere
him, and had enioyed the ſelf ſame viſion:
they recounted togeather all particulars,
expecting with greedineſſe, when their ſeruants ſhould returne from fiſhinge to confirme the ſame, which ſoone after enſued,
Et tantam piſcium copiam exhibuere (ſaith Malmeſbury) *vt cuiuſuis magni exercitus ingluuiem,
exaturare poſſe videretur*. And they brought
with them to the K. ſo great ſtore of fiſh, as
it might ſeeme to be ſufficient to ſatisfie the
hunger of neuer ſo great an army, wherwith *K. Alfred* being encouraged, he aduen-
tured

tured a ſtraunge attempt, which was to goe in to the Danes campe with one ſeruant only, fayninge themſelues *Muſicians.* Where with ſinginge of ſonges & ſoundinge their inſtruments, they paſſed through the whole campe diſcouering their diſorders, & where & when they weare more weake. And ſo retyring themſelues to their cōpany againe, and arming ſuch men, as he could ; ſecretly ſet vpon them with ſuch fierceneſſe, as they killed many and put the reſt to flight, and conſtrayned the Danes with their ſaid K. *Gormond*, to demaund peace & offer hoſtages for the ſame. Which were accepted vpon two conditions : the firſt, that all of them ſhould retyre out of England, except ſuch as would be Chriſtians: the ſecond, that theſe Chriſtian Danes ſhould be content only with the kingdome of the Eaſt Angles, to witt *Norfolk* and *Suffolk.* All which was admitted, & K. *Gormond* himſelfe made a Chriſtian and Godſonne to K. *Alphred,* accepting the ſaid kingdome of the Eaſt Angles as tributary vnto him, & from this day foreward K. *Alphred* went gaigninge more and more puttinge his enemies to flight, vntill he had recouered all his whole kingdome againe. And this both he & his mother were wont to recount all dayes of their life after, & the euents themſelues did euidently declare the truth of the miracle, recorded as hath byn

A ſtraunge attēpt & victory of K. *Alphred* vpon the viſion of S. *Cuthbert.*

ſaid

ſaid by our beſt hiſtoriographers. All which
notwithſtandinge Iohn Fox wryteth thus.

Fox pag.
128.

*Lett vs paſſe ouer theſe dreaminge fables though they
be teſtified by diuerſe authors as VVilliam Malmesb.
Polychronicon: Roger Houedon, Iornalenſis, and others
more, &c.* Wherby yow may ſee, what a
faithleſſe Eccleſiaſtical Chronicler this Fox
is, that paſſeth ouer things of purpoſe, that
are left wrytten by ſo many and graue authors. And then how perfidious he ſheweth
himſelfe in cenſuringe for *dreaminge fables* ſo
important miracles, ſhewed by God for te-
ſtification of his loue and prouidence towards our countrey and the ſauinge and re-
ſtoringe therof.

The
great im
pudency
of Iohn
Fox in
reie-
cting all
our aun-
cient hi-
ſtorio-
gra-
phers.

22. For which infidelity this miſerable fellow hath noe other argument (exceptinge
only his foreſaid hatred to *Saint Cuthbert* and
other monks) but only for that the viſion
was in tyme of ſleepe or ſlumbringe, and for
that cauſe he calleth yt a *dreaminge fable.*

Howv
God
doth ap-
peare &
reueale
matters
often ti-
mes in
ſleepe.

Which kind of argument yf we ſhould admitt, we muſt euacuatt alſo and bringe in
doubt and contempt, moſt of the principall
miſteries and miracles of the old and new
teſtament. Where commonly things were
reuealed to Gods ſeruants in viſions by
ſleepe as *Geneſis* 28. *Vidit Iacob in ſomnis ſcalam
ſtantem.* Iacob did ſee a ladder in his ſleep.
And againe in the ſame booke. *cap. 31. dixit
Angelus dei ad me in ſomnis.* The Angell of God
ſaid

said vnto me in my sleepe. *Ioseph* also had all his affaires reuealed vnto him not only in sleepe, but also *per somnia* by dreames indeed. *Genesis* 37. 40. 41.

23. The like is related of *Saul* 3. *Reg.* 3. and of *Daniell, Dan.* 7. And finally God promiseth by *Ioell* of *Saincts* of the new testament, *Senes vestri somnia somniabant. Ioel.* 2. which *S.* Peter in the Acts of the Apostles *(cap.* 2. *vers.* 17.) interpreteth of true visions sent from God by the holly Ghost, saying, *This is the meaning of that vvhich is said by the Prophett Ioel. VVhich shall come to passe in the latter dayes, I shall povvre ovvt of my spiritt vpon all flesh and your sonnes shall prophetize, and youer daughters, and younge men shall see visions, and your elder people shall dreame dreames, &c.* And finally if we consider the story of our Sauiours Infancy recounted by *Saint Mathevves* Gospell, we shall find the most part of his misteries reuealed to our Bl. Lady and *Saint Ioseph* in sleep, as *Math.* 1. *vers.* 20. *Gabriel apparuit Ioseph in somnis.* The Angell *Gabriell* appeared to *Saint Ioseph* in his sleep and told him that he should not put away his wife. And then in the 2. chapter talkinge of the *Magi,* he saith: *Et responso accepto in somnis,* they receyuinge an answere from God in their sleep, that they should not returne to *Herod,* they returned by another way. Who beinge gone, the Euangelist saith againe. *Ecce Angelus Domini*   *Math.*2.

apparuit in somnis Ioseph. Behould the Angell of God appeared to *Ioseph* againe in his sleep & warned him to fly into Egipt. And then, when he should come out of Egipt againe, he being in doubt whether to go; *Admonitus in somnis secessit in partes Galilea.* He being warned in his sleep what to do, went & carried Christ into the parts of Galiley, &c.

24.   Lo heere a very frequent custome of almighty God, to warne men of his will in time of sleep. And albeit all kind of dreames or representations in tyme of sleep be not easily to be credited, as the * scripture in other places doth admonish vs: yet God saith also; *Si quis fuerit inter vos propheta Domini in visione apparebo ei, & per somnu loquar ad illum.* Yf there be any amonge yow, that is a prophet of God (to whome I meane to reueyle „ my secrets) to him I will appeare in vision, „ and to him will I speake in sleep. And this is sufficient to shew that all are not dreaminge fables, which are vttered in sleep, as the incredulous & infidelle humor of Iohn Fox and of moderne heretiks would haue it seeme, when it is against them.

25.   But in their owne sectaries, they do admire and extoll any thing neuer so phantasticall : yea though it be a vision or reuelation from the diuell himselfe. For so *Luther* in his booke about the Abrogatinge of the Masse doth recount of himselfe, how the diuell

2. Paral. 33. Leuit 19. Deut.18. Psal. 72. Num. 12. vers. 6.

Luth. l. de abroganda missa.

diuell did appeare vnto him by night and
reasoned with him against the said masse.
And in another booke wrytten to the Senators of the cittyes of Germany, and talkinge
of other sectaryes , that did brag of visions,
voyces and apparitions of spiritts (to witt
the *Svvinkfeldians* & *Anabaptists*) he saith thus
of himselfe. *Ego quoque fui in spiritu, atque etiam* Luth. *l.*
vidi spiritus (si omnino de proprijs gloriandum est) Teutoni-
forte plus quàm ipsi adhuc intra annum videbunt. co ad se-
I my selfe was also in spiritt (which he spea-
keth to the imitation of *Saint Iohn* the Euangelist in his reuelations) And haue seene also *Apoc.* 1.
spiritts (yf I must needs glory of my owne *vers.* 10.
gifts)and perhaps I haue seene more spirits, ,,
then they which bragg so much of seinge ,,
spiritts, will se with in one yeare. This said ,,
Luther of himselfe : and hence we must ,,
imagine , that he so often said of himselfe, ,,
certum se esse, doctrinam suam è cælo esse petitam. Luth.
That he was certayne his doctrine came cont·Reg.
from heauen. And *Sleydane* euery where in Angl.
his story doth compare him and his visions
and reuelations with those of the ould prophetts.

26.   *Carolstadius* also a cheefe beginner of
the Sacramentary doctrine , braggeth (as
Kemnitius a cheefe Lutheran reporteth) that Kemnit.
it was reueyled vnto him from heauen, *in repet.*
how he should vnderstand those words *de Eu-*
Hoc est corpus meum, by different pointinge of *art.* 31.
  D d 5   the

the ſentence, from that which it was wont

Svvingl.
in ſubſid
de Euch.
to be. And *Svvinglius* affirmeth of himſelfe, that he had a voyce by night from heauen (which yet *Luther* ſaith was from the diuell) tellinge him how he ſhould expound thoſe

Mat.16.
words *(Hoc eſt corpus meum)*contrary to all antiquity, by the example of thoſe words of

Exod.12.
verſ. 11.
* Infra
cap. 8.
part 2.
Exodus phaſe, id eſt, tranſitus Domini, &c. And we are a little after to ſhew more at larg in this * treatiſe, how *Iohn Fox* alſo had a voyce and reuelation from heauen on a ſunday morning, as he lay in his bedd, about vnderſtandinge of the myſticall numbers in the

Apoc.13.
verſ. 5.
Apocalips of 42. monethes aſſigned by the Angell to the raigne of Anti-Chriſt.

The viſions of Iohn Fox his martyrs.
27.   But yf we ſhould recount all the viſions and reuelations which Iohn Fox doth attribute to his ragged martyrs, that he ſetteth downe in his calendar, & how highly he would haue them eſteemed, there would be no end. Let any man read, what he wryteth of the viſions and voyces, that *Samuell* a miniſter of *Ipſvvich* had in his ſleep, when

Fox pag.
1547.
col. 1.
num. 46.
he was in priſon: *He fell into a ſleep*(ſaith Fox) *at vvhich tyme one clad in vvhite ſeemed to ſtand before him, comfortinge him in theſe vvords: Samuell, Samuell, be of good cheere, &c.   No leſſe memorable is it* (ſaith Fox) *and vvorthy to be noted touchinge the three ladders, vvhich the ſaid Samuell ſavve in his ſleep ſett vp tovvards heauen, vvherof one vvas greater and longer then the other at the beginninge, but*
after

after all three made equall. Which vision Fox
doth expound thus: that *Samuell* beinge in
prison with two women of his sect, *Agnes
Potten* a beerbruers wife, & *Ioane Trunchfield* a
showmakers wife of the same towne: *Agnes
& Ioane* were persuaded by *Samuell* to burne
with him as after they did, *and consequently*
(saith Fox) *though Samuell* was the greater
ladder at the beginning, & higher towards
heauen (as beinge a minister or preacher)
and the other two lesser ladders signified by
the brewers and shomakers wyues; yet at
length, were they all three made equall by
the glory of martyrdome.

28. Thus reasoneth Fox. And then comminge to talke of the same two women a
part, he sheweth that *Agnes Potten* the Bre-
wers wife had visions also. *Pottens vvife* (saith   *Fox pag.*
he) *in a night a little before her death being asleep in*   *1398.*
her bedd, savv a bright burning fire right vp as a pole;
By which vision he showeth that the sho-
makers wife, who was fearfull to dy and
would haue drawne backe, *vvas encoraged by*
the other to go also to the fire. And do yow not   Ridicu-
see here the spiritt of the *Circumcellians* and   culous
Massilians to run willfully to death? From   dreames
this Fox passeth to recout another straunge   & visiõs
propheticall dreame of one *VVilliam Hunter,*   allovved
an apprentice of *London* of 19. yeares old,   by Iohn
who would needs be burned also and no-   Fox in
thinge cold keep him from yt: much enco-   his mar-
raged   tyrs.

raged as it ſeemeth by his dreame.

29.   And from this againe he runneth to other more ſollemne dreames & viſions of *Iohn Rough,* a Scottiſh miniſter, director of a certayne ſecrett Proteſtant Congregation in London in Q. Maryes dayes : and of one *Cuthbert Simpſon* the Deacon or clarke of that congregation. Which two had dreames and viſions, the one concerninge the other of them. Which Fox thinketh worthy of ſo great conſideration, as he wryteth thus in his margent : *The viſions ſent to Gods Saints concerninge their afflictions.* Now then touchinge the firſt *Saint Rough,* yow muſt know that he had byn a Dominican friar in *Scotland,* (as Fox confeſſeth,) and from thence runninge away into England gatt himſelfe a mate, or (as he calleth her) a *Kate.* With whome lying in bedd, he had a viſion of his fellow *Simpſon* vvhich Fox recounteth in theſe words: The friday at night before maſter *Rongh* was taken, being in his bedd he dreamed that he ſaw two of the guard leadinge *Cuthbert Simpſon* deacon of his congregation to priſon, and that he had the booke about him wherin were wrytten the names of all

» them that were of that congregation.
» Whervpon being ſore troubled he awaked
» and called his wife, *Kate* ſtrike light, for I am
» much troubled with my brother *Cuthbert*
» this night. And when ſhe had ſo done he

gaue

The ſcottish Apoſtatas friars dreame and his *Kate. Fox pag.* 1843. *col.* 1. *num* 44.

gaue himfelfe to read on his booke a while, „
and then feeling fleep to come vpon him he „
put out the candle, and fo gaue himfelfe to „
reit againe. And beinge a fleep he dreamed „
the like dreame, and a waking therwith he „
faid. O *Kate*, my brother *Cuthbert* is gone. „
So they lighted a candle againe and rofe. „
This is the vifion of the fcottifh friar, which
caufed his Kate twice to ftrike fiar, and light
the candle, as yow fee.

30.   The other vifion of his *Clarke Simpfon*
(that kept the bedrole of the names of his
fecrett congregation, and was afterward
burned with him in Smithfield) Fox defcribeth in this manner. *Before Simpfons burninge*
(faith he) *beinge in the Bishops Colehoufe in the*
ftocks, he had a very ftraunge vifion or apparition,
vvhich he himfelfe vvith his ovvue mouth declared,to
the godly learned man Maifter Auften,& to his ovvne
vvife, &c. Thus beginneth Fox to relate the
vifion. Noting firft (as you fe) that he fpoke
it with his owne mouth, as though it were
a great matter:and then he entreth to make
a long Apology againft the papifts in defence of thefe vifions, though theirs be not
to be beleeued.

31.   *They vvill aske me* (faith he) *vvhy fhould* Fox pag.
I more require thefe to be credited of them, then 1844.
theirs of vs? This is the demaund which he
frameth in behalfe of the papifts. And I
thinke, no man will fay, butthat it is reafonable.

nable. Let vs heare his anſwere. *Firſt* (ſaith he) *I vvryte not this , bynding any man preciſely to beleeue the ſame , as they do theirs.* Lo heere is a foolery with a manifeſt ly : the foolery is in tellinge vs ſo preciſe beleeuinge all viſions and dreames , which no wiſe man euer thought or ſpake. The ly is in that he affirmeth vs to teach that ſuch preciſe beleeſe is neceſſary in viſions amonge vs. But lett is heare him further in his anſwere to the for-

Ibidem. mer demaund. *It is no good argument* (ſaith he) *to reaſon thus: viſions be not true in ſome. Ergo they be true in none.* This part we graunt. But what is this to his purpoſe or proofe: his meaning is, that ours be not true viſions and his be. But

Hovv farre Catholike do giue credit to viſions & hovv they examine the ſame. who ſhalbe iudges? He and his would be. But this is no reaſon; and we on the contrary ſide do ſay much more equally *Nec mihi nec tibi,* neyther he or we, as particular men, ought to iudge of theſe things : but the Catholike Church, which by her Biſhops and Paſtors do examine the proofes weight and moment of euery one of theſe things that fall out : and accordinge to the quality meritt, and condition of them, to whome they happen ; as alſo of the witneſſes and teſtimonyes, wherby they are prooued, ſhe doth iugde of the truth or probability of euery thinge. And to her therfore we ſtand , and not to the phantaſticall broken braines of Iohn Fox: that maketh miracles & viſions,

where

where he listeth: and authorizeth or discrediteth them, when yt pleaseth him againe.

32.   And thus much by occasion of *S. Cuthberts* apparition to *K. Alfred.* The holynesse of which Saint how highly it was esteemed in the dayes of this King about the yeare of Christ 878. yow herby see, himselfe liuinge some 200. yeares before. For that he died vpon the yeare 687.the 20.of March,which day hath euer since byn celebrated with perpetuall memory,not only by the Church of England, but also by the vniuersall : and that most worthyly , as may appeare by his life written largly by *Saint Bede.* Howsoeuer Iohn Fox do speake contemptuously of him heere, and his fellow *Iohn Bale* doth reuile him. But for what thinke you? you shall heare his complaints. *Omnia ad amuβim monachus didicit quæ ad monachismum spectare nouit, nulla penitus de Euangelio facta mentione.* He being a monke learned exactly all things, that appertayned to the life of monks : but neuer made mentiõ of the Ghospel. And is this likely or probable,trow you,that he neuer so much as mentioned the Ghospell:seing that monks profession,and forme of life is taken out of the Ghospell ? But what more ensueth? Harken & yow shall heare the Apostata vtter his spiritt. *Fæmineum genus* (saith he) *exosum ei erat, &c.* Women-kind was hatefull vnto him, &c. This is the same accusation

Hereticall hatred against *S. Cuthbert.*

Bed. l.4. hist.cap. 27. 28. 29. vid. Præfat. Bal.cent. 1.script. Brit. in Cuthb.

Mat. 19.

Bal.ibid.

cuſation that the *Magdeburgians* laid to S. **Cy-**

✶ *Supra*
part. 1.
cap. 6.
prian (yf ✶ yow remember) for that he prayſed virginity. But how doth Bale gather this
hatred of S. *Cuthbert* againſt woman-kind?

Ibid.
yt followeth. *Decretum fecit contra mulieres, ne
eius ingrederentur monaſteria.* He made a decree
againſt women, that they ſhould not enter
in to his Monaſteryes. This decree friar
Bale, that loued woman-kind, liked not.

Ibid.
But he addeth a further accuſation. *That in
the 2. yeare of his Biſhopricke Saint Cuthbert left the
ſame & no leſſe hypocritically, then idlely made himſelfe an anchorete, leadinge for the reſt of his dayes a
ſolitary retyred life:* Se what matters they picke
out to obiect vnto Gods Saints, which
themſelues cannot or will not immitate.

33.   Finally to end this Chapter, and therwith this fourth ſtation or tyme, Iohn Fox,
after much triflying heere and there, ſetteth
downe in the laſt words of this his third
booke a very breefe Catalogue of the Archbiſhops of Canterbury of theſe ages with
this title : *The names and order of the Archbiſhops
of Canterbury from the time of* K. *Egbert to* VVilliam

The
Archb.
of Can-
terbury
of this
tyme
ſcoffed
at by
Fox.
Conquerour, &c. Which he beginneth with
Etheldrenus that was the 18. in order, and endeth with *Lanfrancus* who was the 34. making certayne notes or rather ſcoffes & ieſts
vpon them all. Eſpecially vpon thoſe, that
were moſt renowned for their holyneſſe &
multitude of miracles recorded by old writers:

ters: as namely *Saint Dunstan,* of whome *Mal-*
mesbury and others hauinge left written, that
among other miracles happened vnto him,
one was, that his harp (wherwith he was
wont in his youth to praise God after the
imitation of *K. Dauid)* hanginge vp by his
bed side on a pynne vpon the wall, he heard
one night a voyce of Angells singe in his
Church this verse *Gaudent in cælis animæ san-*
ctorum, at what tyme his said harp also gaue
a sound of it selfe moued eyther by the said
Angells or otherwise by miracle from God.
Wherat Iohn Fox in his hereticall veyne
maketh much pastime, though (as already
you haue heard, & shall do more in the third
part of this booke) he esteemeth highly certayne deuised miracles of his miserable
martyrs. And so much of this.

34. But now as touchinge the principall
point of all this discourse (which ought to
haue bin the visible deductiō of his Church
from *K. Egbert* to *VVilliam Conquerour)* there is
not so much as one word spoken. For all,
that he wryteth, is of our Church & this in
lyes, fables, scoffes, and tants (as yow see)
but of his owne Church nothing, no not so
much as of any one person, that in all agreed
with him, or his Church in these daies concerning Religion. Nay let him shew vs any
one man, woman or Child, heretike or
Catholike in all this tyme, who was fully of

E e   the

the religion now held in England, and that
theſe beleeued no more nor leſſe, then Fox
and his fellowes do at this day, and we will
yeld, that he hath brought vs forth ſome viſible Church and ſucceſsion therof, though
it be but of three or foure perſons.

35. Lo with how little we are content.
And ſeing Iohn Fox will not dare, nor any
man for him (in my opinion) to take vpon
him this enterpriſe, (to witt, to ſhew the
ſucceſsion of any three or foure perſons
throughout the ſpace of this firſt 1000.
yeares after Chriſt, who did in all things
beleeue and profeſſe the faith and religion,
that now is held in England, wherunto alſo Iohn Fox himſelfe agreed fully while he
liued, as may appeare by the puritanicall
points in his ſtory, which he commendeth
and defendeth in the liues of *Rogers, Hooper,*
and other their firſt Engliſh parents, as after
ſhalbe ⋆ ſhewed:) for ſo much (I ſay) as this
is ſo, and that neuer any three perſons of
what condition, Religion, ſex, or ſect
ſoeuer, can be ſhewed to haue agreed fully
in the proteſtants religion, that now in England is profeſſed, not only for the tyme of
theſe firſt 1000. yeares of Chriſtianity, but
neyther for the other 500. next following,
nor that our Engliſh proteſtants of theſe
dayes will bind themſelues in all and euery
point of doctrine, faith and beleefe, to ſtand
to any

Heretiks
ſeeke to
pull do⁺
vvne &
not to
build vp.
⋆*Part* 3.

to any one vifible congregation Church,
Conuenticle, Society or number of men
whatfoeuer,profefsinge the name of Chrift
that haue byn knowne to lyue vpon earth,
from the Apoftles time downward,but that
they do vary from them in one article of
beleefe or other.

36. Yf all this (I fay)be true and moft certayne and made euident by this our deduction, & that we offer to ioyne any further
iffue, that fhalbe demaunded,with any proteftant liuinge, vpon this point, that fhall
haue any thinge to fay or reply in this matter, this beinge fo ; then is it euident, what
a fuccefsion of the proteftants Church Iohn
Fox bringeth or is able to bring downe, or
any man for him, notwithftandinge his
vayne bragg and florifh in the firft title of
his booke, *that he vvould fett dovvne the vvhole race and courfe of the Church, &c.* The folly and falfhood of which florifh fhall better alfo appeare by that which enfueth from the conqueft downward. Fox in the title of his Acts and Monuments.

THE

THE FIFTH STATION OF

TIME, CONTEYNING OTHER 300. *yeares frōm* William Conqueror, *vnto the tyme of* Iohn Wickliffe, *vvherin is examined, vvhether the* Cath. Roman *Church did periſh in this tyme, as* Fox *affirmeth. Here is treated alſo of* Pope Hildebrande, *and of the marriage of* Prieſtes.

CHAP. VII.

The 5. ſtation from *an.* Domini 1066. vn to 1370. Fox in the title.

YOVV haue ſeene, good reader, by our former treatiſe how briefe and barren Iohn Fox hath bene hetherto in relatinge vnto vs Eccleſiaſticall matters, for more then a 1000. years. For though he promiſed in the firſt title of his booke (as before yow haue heard) *thathe vvould ſett forth at large, the vvhole race and courſe of the Church from the primi-tiue age vnto theſe later tymes of ours, &c.* And

Fox p. 1.

againe in another title, *that he vvas to lay before vs the acts and monuments of Chriſtian martyrs, and matters Eccleſiaſticall paſſed in the Church of Chriſt, from the primitiue beginninge to theſe our dayes, as vvell in other, countreyes, as namely in the Realmes of England, & alſo of Scotland diſcourſed at large, &c.*

The breuity and barren-ueſſe of Iohn Fox in performing his promiſe.

Yet this large diſcourſe for more then a thouſand years, is concluded by him in leſſe then ſeauenty leaues of paper, wherof al-moſt fifty are of impertinent matter: to wit, of certayne differences, which he would

picke

picke out betwene the old Romane Church
and that which is now : and in the relation
of the firſt ten perſecutions vnder heathen
Emperors which before we haue declared,
how little they appertayne to his argumēt;
or ſubiect taken in hand, which was to
ſet dovvne the race and courſe of the vvhole Church.
And this being ſo, yow may conſider, what
ſtore of Eccleſiaſticall matters he findeth to
his purpoſe in theſe firſt 1000. yeares, ſeing
he ſcarſe ſpendeth 30. whole leaues therin:
wherof alſo the far greater parte (I meane
of that, he wryteth in theſe few leaues) is
meere temporall or impertinent, as in part,
Yow haue heard. And how then doth he
tell vs of Eccleſiaſticall matters diſcourſed at large,
and ſo forth? *And of the vvhole race and courſe of
the Church ſet forth largely by him, &c.* Do yow
ſe how theſe men do face, & lye to deceaue
their readers?

2. But let vs not complaine (I pray yow)
of breuity or barrenneſſe in Iohn Fox, nor
of lacke of volume, ſeinge he hath ſet forth
the greateſt perhaps, that euer was in our
Engliſh tongue. And if he haue bene ouer
ſhorte for the thouſand years paſt, vnto the
tyme of *VVilliam Conqueror :* he will as much
exceede in length now for the other 500.
years, that are to enſue from the *Conqueror* to
Q. Eliſabeth. Vpon which time he beſtoweth
aboue nine hundred leaues. And the reaſon

of this

VVhy Fox vvriteth ſo little of the former ages, .& ſo largely of the ſequent.

of this ſo notable difference or inequality is that, which we haue touched before : to witt, that he findinge the whole courſe of theſe former tymes & ages of the Chriſtian Church to be againſt him, nor darıng openly to reieẛ that Church nor manifeſtly to ioyne with her enemyes adiudged by her for heretiks : he choſe to ſpeake as little of thoſe tymes, & affairs, as he could. But now hath he taken another reſolutiō much more deſperate in hand : which is, to deny our Church to be any longer a Church, and to ſett vp another of his in her place. By which means he wil come to haue matter inough. For that this beinge ſuppoſed, and he preſuminge that all the Aẛs & Monuments of this Church (I meane the generall Romane Church) receaued hither vnto throughout the world for Chriſts Church, are wicked and rebellious vnto God, and Aẛs of the Diuelles Synagogue, from the tyme that Iohn Fox aſsigneth of her fall and apoſtaſie : and that on the contrary ſide, all the wrytings, aẛions and geſts of all ſorts of Heretiks againſt this Church from that tyme, are the Aẛs & Monuments of the true Church of Chriſt ; ſuppoſinge all this, I ſay, (as Fox doth) there can not want matter, either on the one ſide or the other, to fill vp volumes. And the lower he paſſeth downward, the more matter he findeth . For that ſeẛs and

Hovv Fox cō-meth to encreaſe his later bookes.

ſeẛa-

fectaries encreafinge dayly(whom he rege-
ftreth for Saints and pillars of his Church)
the volume of his booke muft needs growe
greatly. And fo is it feene by this fourth
booke, wherin from the conqueft to the
later end of *K. Edvvard* the third his raigne,
when *VVickliffe* began (conteyninge 300.
years: to wit,from *anno Domini* 1066.to 1370.
there are fpent aboue a hundred leaues of
paper. Which is much more, then was in
the former 1066. years. But in the fifth
booke from *Iohn VVick.* his tyme to *K. Henry*
the eighth (which are but 140. years) are
conteyned vpon the point of 200. leaues.
And then againe from the beginninge of *K.
Henryes* raigne to the entraunce of *Q. Elifa-
beth* (beinge but fifty years) he fpendeth
aboue 600. leaues. And by this yow may
iudge both of the fubiect and fubftance of
Iohn Fox his huge volume. Though we are
to looke into the fame fome what more
particularly alfo, as we paffe it ouer in this
and the enfuinge Chapters.

3. Well then, this beinge his deuife and
refolution for the prefent,to haue no longer
patience with our Church, but wholy to
deny the fame: his greateft difficulty feemeth to be about the tyme and caufes. To
witt, where, or when, or how, or vpon
what occafion, fhe perifhed or vanifh:d
away. For that feing fhe hath continued by

his

his confession also for so many yeares and ages, & come downe vnto our dayes, vnder the selfe same succession of Bishops, Pastors, and teachers, as before : and consequently also, with the selfe same doctrine and religion and with the same externall power & maiestie. Which it was wont : it seemeth a very harde thinge vpon the sodayne either to annihilate so great and mighty a kingdome, or (that with is much more difficulte) to make so strange a metamorphosis and mutation in her, as that she hauing bene hetherto the Church of Christ, his spouse, his kingdome, his deárest beloued, & beawtifyed with his graces, directed by his spirit, enriched with his most pretious giftes and indowments, & so acknowledged also by Fox himselfe in former ages ; that now she should become Christs enemy, and aduersary vpon the sodaine, & the kingdome of Satan, his eternall foe, and yet to retaine still the name place estimation, and externall dignity, which she had before, professinge with no lesse shew of duty her obedience, and lóue to Christ, then in former tymes she was wont. This chaunge & metamorphosis, (I say) is most wonderfull, & incredible to all those, that beleeue Christ to be God, & to haue bene able to performe his promise, that hell gats should neuer preuaile against this Church. Wherfore we are to exa-

Marginal notes:

An impossible deuise to annihilate this vniuersall visible Church.

A strang & incredible mutation.

to examine fomewhat more diligently in
this chapter, how this matter could fall out,
and when, and by what occafion come to
paffe. For that fo great and rare a mutation,
as this is, neuer fell out yet in the world before. Though temporall ftats and kingdoms
haue had their changes. Nay, all temporall
mutations of Empyres kingdomes, ftats and
monarchyes haue bene made principally to
fhew the contrary ftability and immutable
continuation of Chrifts Church once plan- *Sup. cap.*
ted in the world. As in part we haue declared before, fhewinge how that in all tymes
and feafone in all variety and variations of
ftats, poeple, countreyes, and dominions,
(as well in England, as elfwhere) the Chriftian Cath. Religion remayned one and the
felfe fame among them all. To which effect
alfo is that notable prophefy of *Daniel*, when
(fortelling firft the breaking & ouerthrow,
of all foure monarchyes by him mentioned)
he addeth, as a notorious oppofition to the
fame, the ftability & immortality of Chrifts *Dan.* 2.
Church and kingdome once fet on foote, in *verf.* 44.
thefe words. *In the dayes of thefe kingdomes, God* The pro-
of heauen fhall rayfe vp a kingdome that fhall neuer phefie
be diffipated neather fhall this kingdome be geuen to of *Da-*
another people. This kingdome fhall confume and niel
vveare out all the other kingdomes, but it felfe fhall about
ftande for euer. bility of
Chrifts
4.   Thus faith *Daniel* and the moft of thefe Church.

points we haue ſene verifyed and fulfilled already. For God of heauen hath rayſed this kingdome, & viſible Church of Chriſt, which then ſeemed a ſtrāge matter:he hath encreaſed & continued the ſame for a thouſand years and more, as Fox will confeſſe (which is a longer tyme,then any temporall monarchy lightly hath continued, without change.) he hath ouerthrowne in this tyme and conſumed the other kingdomes and monarchyes mentioned by him. Now remayne the other two clauſes to be fulfilled in like manner: to wit, that it ſhall ſtand for euer (or as Chriſt expoundeth it, *vſque ad conſummationem ſæculi,*to the worlds end) and then, *quod alteri populo non tradetur*, that this kingdome ſhall not be deliuered ouer to another people from that,which poſſeſſed it from the beginninge. The quite contrary wherof teacheth here Iohn Fox,affirminge this Church (that hath bene accoumpted the true Church and kingdome of Chriſt for a 1000. yeares paſt) is now no more his Church,or kingdome.Nor theſe Popes, Biſhops and Paſtors (that are found in her to haue come downe by continual ſucceſsion) are now no more the true and lawfull guydes or gouernors therof. But that it apperteyneth to others,and conſequently this kingdome of Chriſt is taken from them and deliuered to another people : to wit , to the

Beren-

Berengarians, to the *VValdenses,* to the *Albanen-
ses* to the *VVickliffians, Lutherans, Svvinglians,* &
other like people of later ages.

5. This is Iohn Fox his madde assertion;
where in yow see, he should proue two
points. First, that our Church is lost and
fallen, and our men rightly dispossessed of
the interest therof. And then, that his men
(to witt, these new sectaries) haue entered
in to iust possession of that name and title
of the trew Church: both which points
we deny. Yow shall se, how he beginneth
to proue the first : that is to say, the fall and
ouerthrow of the vniuersall visible Church
surnamed the Romane.

And thus hetherto (faith he) *stood the condition* In his
of the Church of Christ (meaninge the next protesta-
 tiö to the
ages before the conquest) *albeit not vvithout* Church
some repugnance and difficulty : yet in some meane of En-
state of the truth and verity, till the tyme of Pope gland.
*Hildebrand, called Gregory the 7. vvhich vvas
near about the yeare* 1080. *and of Pope Innocentius* 3. *in the yeare* 1215. *by vvhome all vvas turned
vpside dovvne, all order broken, true doctryne defaced, Christian faith extinguished, &c.*

6. Here yow see Iohn Fox to assigne
two tymes and two Popes, when and by
whome not only the true Church was
ouerthrowne, but Christian faith also vtterly extinguished (to witt *Gregory* the 7. and
Innocētius the 3. two of the most renowmed
men,

men, both for vertues and learninge, that
haue poſſeſſed that Sea ſince the time of our
conqueſt, or in many ages before, if we will
beleeue all the auncient Authors that haue
written of them) wherin I dare Ioine iſſue
with Iohn Fox, or any of his cubbes whatſoeuer, that will defend him in this notorious ſlaunder againſt theſe two worthy
men. For as for *Innocentius* 3. he is affirmed
to haue bene one of the moſt excellent
Popes for good life and rare learninge, that
Pope In- for theſe 1000. years held that See. Of
nocent 3. whome *Blondus* amongſt other authors wri-
Blond. teth thus, *Suauiſſimus erat in Gallijs famæ odor,*
decad. 2. *grauitatis, ſanctitatis, ac reru̅ geſtarum eius pontifi-*
lib. 7. *cijs, &c.* The fame and ſent of this Popes gra-
pag. 297. uity, holynes of life, and greatnes of his
actions was moſt ſweete throughout all
Fraunce, &c. And for his learning the ſame
Geneb. Author ſaith, *libros doctrina plenos ſcripſit.* He
in chron. wrote moſt learned bookes. In which Kind
an 1198. diuers Authors do report that he wrote
Cicarell. more then moſt of the other Popes of Rome
in vita before his tyme put togeather.
Inocentij
3. *Platin.* 7. And as for *Gregory* the 7. albeit he had
ibid. many enemyes ſtyrred vp againſt him by
the Emperor *Henry* the 4. and other, whome
he ſought to puniſh and reforme for their
misbehaueour: yet yf we will beleeue the
cheefe authors of that age and thoſe that liued either with him or next vnto him,
(as

(as *Anselmus* Archbishop of Canterbury, *Ma-*
rianus Scotus, *Otho Frisingensis*, *Aeneas Syluius*,
Lambertus Schafnaburgensis, *Vincentius Gallus*,
Abbas Vrspergensis, *Auentinus*, *Sigebertus*, *Tritemius*
and many others) he was not only very
learned wise, anda man of great courage in
resisting the forsaid most dissolut Emperor,
that liued scandalously and oppressed the
Church : but also he was reputed of a most
holy life , in so much as God wrought diuers miracles by him.

8. The very forme of his election recorded by *Platina*, *Sabellicus*, & others, doth shew
what he was , when they say : *Elegimus hodie*
21. Maij anno Domini 1072. *in verum Christi Vica-*
rium, Hildebrandum Archidiaconum, virum multa
doctrina, magna pietatis, prudentia, iustitia, constan-
tia, religionis, &c. We haue chosed this day
the 21 of May 1072. for true Vicar of Christ
a man of much learninge , great piety, prudence , iustice, constancy and religion, &c.
This was the testimony of the whole cleargie of Rome , that knew him better , then
Iohn Fox, & his fellowes. Against whome
Lambertus Schafnabergensis talkinge of his
whole life afterwards, saith : *Signa & pro-*
digia, qua per orationes Gregorij Papa frequentiùs
fiebant, & zelus eius feruentißimus pro Deo & Ec-
clesiasticis legibus satis eum contra venenatas detra-
ctorum linguas communiebant. The signes and
miracles, which oftentymes were done by
the

Anselm.
epist. ad
Abbat.
Hyrsarg.
Marian.
Scotus
Lamb.
Scafna-
burg.
Vincent.
Gallus,
Sigebert.
Auent.
& omnes
in chro-
nicis an.
1075.
1076.
&c.
”
”
”
”
About
PopeHil-
debrand
alias
Gregory
the 7.
”

,, the prayers of *Pope Gregory* the 7. & his moſt
,, feruent zeale for the honour of God and
,, defence of Eccleſiaſticall lawes, did ſuffi-
,, ciently defend him againſt the venemous
,, tongues of detractors.

9. *Vincentius* alſo *Gallus* in his hiſtory relateth out of a more auncient hiſtoriographer
then himſelfe, named *Gulielmus Hiſtoricus; Hil-*
debrandum dono prophetiæ præditum fuiſſe. That
Hildebrand the Pope was indued with the
gift of propheſie. Which he ſhoweth by diuers particular examples of euents fortold
by him. And this of *Gregory* the ſeauenth.

The vi- 10. But what do the ſame authors, yea
ces of Germanes themſelues, wryte of their Em-
the Em- peror his enemy *Henry* the fourth? Surely it
perour is ſhamefull to report his adulteryes, Symo-
Henry niacall ſellinge of benefices, robberyes and
the 4. ſpoyling of poore particular men, thruſting
in wycked people into places of prelates &
Anno the like. *Principes regni rogat,* (ſaith *Lambertus*)
Domini *vt patiantur ipſum vxorem repudiare, &c.* He did
1069. requeſt the princes of the Empire, that they
,, would ſuffer him to put away his wife.
,, Telling them, what the Pope by his legate
,, had oppoſed to the contrary. Which beinge
,, heard by them, they were of the Popes opinion; *Principes aiebant æquè cenſere Rom. Pontifi-*
cem; ita fractus magis, quàm inflexus Rex ab incepto
abſtinuit. The princes affirmed that the B. of
Rome had reaſon to determyne as he did,
and

and so the K. rather forced, then chaunged
in mynde, absteyned from his purposed
deuorce.

11. Lo heere the first beginninge of falling
out betwixt the Emperour and the Pope.
Which was encreased, for that two yeare
after, the Pope depriued (as the same author
saith) one *Charles* for symmony and theft: to
whome the Emperour had sold for money
the Bishopricke of Constance. And this he
did by a Councell of Princes and Prelats
held in Germany it selfe, the Emperour
being present. *Cùm etiam* (saith he) *rex in iu-*
dicio assideret, causamꝗ Caroli, quoad posset, tuere-
tur. Bishop Charles was deposed, notwithstandinge that the King was present in that
iudgment, & defended him and his cause, as
much as he could. And this was an encrease
of falling out betwene them: *But the constan-*
cy (saith the same author) *and inuincible mynd*
of Hildebrand against couetousnes, did exclude all ar-
guments of humayne deceyts and subtiltyes.

12. *Vrspergensis* in like manner, that liued in
the same tyme, reckoneth vp many particulars of the Emperors wicked behauiour
in these words: *Cœpit Principes despicere, nobiles*
opprimere. He began to despise the Princes,
oppresse the nobles and nobility, and giue
himselfe to incontinency. Which *Auentinus*
(an author not misliked by the protestants)
vttereth more particularly in these words:

Henricum

Lamb.
Schafn.
an. Domi-
ni 1071.
,,
,,
,,
Lamb.
ibid.

Vrsp. an.
Domini
1068.

lib. 4.
Annaliŭ
Boiorŭ.

Henricum ſtupris, amoribus, impudicitiæ, & adulterij flægraſſe infamia, nec amici quidem negant. The very frends of *Henry* the Emperor do not deny but that he was infamous for his wicked life in lechery fornication, & adultery.

13.   And finally not to name any more, *Marianus Scotus* that liued in thos dayes wryteth thus of the whole cõtrouerſie betwene them. *Gregory the 7.* (ſaith he) *beinge ſtyrred vp by the iuſt clamors of Catholike men, and hearinge the immanity of Henry the Emperor his vvickednes, cryed out againſt by them: did excommunicate him for the ſame, but eſpecially for the ſinne of ſimmony, in buyinge and ſellinge biſhoprickes. VVhich fact of the Pope did like very vvell all good Cath. men: but diſpleaſed ſuch, as vvould buy and ſell benefices and vvere fauourers of the ſaid Emperor.*

Marian.
Scot. in
chron.
an.1075.

14.   And thus much be ſpoken of the learning, liues, and vertue of theſe two particular Popes, *Gregory* the 7. and *Innocentius* the third, whome Iohn Fox would needs haue vs beleeue, that they had ouerturned Gods Church and extinguiſhed Chriſtian Religion vtterly in the world. But eſpecially he rageth euery where and with greateſt acerbitye againſt *Gregory* the 7. dilating himſelfe in many large diſcourſes of that argument, and telling ſo many & apparant lyes of him and his actes and endes, as were a matter incredible to him, that hath not examined them. Neither may I ſtand to recount them

all

all or the more parte (for yt would require
a volume) but by one or two yow ſhall be
able to iudge of the reſt.

   I read and find (ſaith Fox) *that in a councell hol-* Fox pag.
den at Rome by Pope Hildebrand and other Biſhops 158. c.2.
*they did enact three things. Firſt, that no Prieſts
hereafter ſhould marry vviues. Secondly, that all
ſuche, as vvere maried ſhould be diuorced. Thirdly,
that none hereafter ſhould be admitted to the order
of Prieſthood, but ſhould ſvvere perpetuall chaſtitye.*
15. Truly it is a ſtraunge thinge to ſee and
conſider the wilfull obſtinacie & precipita-
tion of heretiks. Fox hathe gathered out
three points decreed in this councell, which
councell yet he citeth not nor any author
for yt. And ſo with more ſaftie he playeth
the Dauus. He leaueth out a fourth point,
which was the principall or rather only
point touching Prieſts mariage handled in
that councell. To witt, that what Prieſt ſo
euer ſhould be knowen to keepe a concu-
bine vnder pretenſe of his wife, or ſhould
be knowen to haue bought his benefice by
Symonie, and would not repent or amend,
they were forbidden to enter the Churche
and ſay Maſſe, & other men were forbidden
to heare their Maſſe. With which decree
many licentious Prieſts, that would not be
reſtrayned from their looſe life, beinge offended; and many more laymen, that de-
pended of the ſaid Emperor, takinge their
          F f   part

A great part cried out againſt this good Pope, for contra-that he went about to reforme theſe two diction ſcandalous abuſes, Symonie & Fornication againſt in the worſer ſort of Prieſts. And two no-*Pope Hil-*table calumniations among other they rai-*debrand*ſed againſt him. The firſt, that he did not for his hold the Maſſe to be good or auaylable Chriſtiã which was ſaid by a Symoniacall or adulte-zeale. rous Prieſt. Which he neuer ſaid or ment: The firſt but only that for a puniſhment and in dete-calum-ſtation of thoſe ſynnes, he wold haue men niation. to forbeare the hearinge of ſuche Prieſtes Maſſes: ſeinge there wanted not other good Prieſts to ſupply their places and funċtions. Neyther was he the firſt Pope that made like decree for puniſhinge of concubinary Prieſts, by forbyddinge other men to heare *Diſtinċt.* their Maſſes. For that both *Pope Alexander* 32. cap. the 2. and *Nicholas* the ſecond, his Predeceſ-*Præter §.* ſors, made the ſame decree, as appeareth in *verũ &* their canons yet extant. *c. nullus.*

The 2. 16. The other calumnation againſt this calum-Pope was this, which Fox and the *Magde-* niation. *burgians* do heere ſett downe, that he was *Fox vbi* the firſt that began to forbydd mariage of Prieſts in *ſupra.* the VVeſtchurche. For ſo are the words of the *Cent.*11. *Magdeburgians.* And herevpon hath Iohn Fox *cap.* 7. framed out of the councell the three points afore mentioned, as handled and decreed then, (which is falſe) and paſſeth ouer the fourth with ſylence, wherein the only con-trouerſie

trouerfie confifteth. And this appeareth in
the lines that do imediatly followe in Fox
where he putteth downe the copie in In-
glifh of *Pope Gregories* Bull about this matter,
wherein he faith thus. *If there be any Priefts*   *Fox pag.*
Deacons or fubdeacons, that vvill ftill remayne in the   *1 58. col.*
fynne of fornication: vve forbydd them the Churches   *2. n. 80.*
entrance, till they amend and repent. But if they per-
feuere in their fynne, vve charge that none prefume
to heare their feruice.

17. By which woords we fee, that *Pope*   *Many*
Gregory did not treat heere as Fox faith, that   *falfities*
no Priefts hereafter fhould marry wiues (as   *and im-*
though it had byn in vfe or lawfull before)   *poftures*
or that fuch as were married fhould be de-   *of Fox.*
uorced by this new decree. And much leffe
was it decreed now, as Fox deuifeth, that
none hereafter fhould be admitted to the
order of Priefthood, but fhould fweare perpetuall chaftity. All thefe points (I fay) are
either fayned or fraudulently fett downe by
our Fox: as though thefe things had byn in
lawfull vfe before, & that now by *Pope Gre-*
gory began this prohibition. But yow haue
heard by *Pope Gregories* owne woords, that
he prefumeth that all Priefts, that after
Priefthood haue carnall conuerfation with
women, do liue in fornication: accordinge
to the doctrine cuftome and practife of the
auncient Catholik Church of Chrift. And
therfore where Fox vfeth the woords of

mariage

mariage and lawfull wiues, *Pope Gregory* calleth it fornication, & concubinarie uſe. And

Diſtinct.
32. c.
Prater §
verum.
apud An
ton. tit.
16.
Tritem.
in chron.
anno
1075.

ſo yt is in the canon ; *Officium Symoniacorum,*
& in fornicatione iacentium, ſcienter nullo modo re-
cipiatis. Do yow not wittingly admytt the
office or ſeruice of ſuch Prieſts, as lyue in
Symonie or Fornication. And *Tritemius* relateth the matter thus. *Laicis interdixit, ne*
Miſſas ſacerdotum concubinas habentium audire pra-
ſumant. Pope *Gregory* forbad laymen to heare
the Maſſe of ſuche Prieſts, as were knowen
to haue concubines.

The true
ſtate of
the con-
trouerſy

18.   This then was the controuerſie, whether Prieſts, that lyued with women (contrary to the auncient Canons of the Catholike Churche) were rightly puniſhed by
Pope *Gregorie,* Pope *Alexander,* Pope *Nicholas* and
ſome other Popes, by debarringe them to
ſay Maſſe publikely or other men to heare
their Maſſes: the controuerſie was not,
whether it was lawfull for them to marry
or noe ? or whether they ſhould promiſe
chaſtity at their entringe into Prieſthood?
For this Pope *Gregory* tooke as a thing determyned from all antiquytie before him: eſpecially in the Latin Churche. And ſo teſtifieth *Marianus Scotus,* that liued in his tyme.

Marian.
Scot. in
Chron.
an.1096.
& Tom.
4. Conc.
pag. 79.

Iſte Papa (ſaith he) *Synodo facta, ex decreto S. Petri*
Apoſtoli & Sancti Clementis, aliorumq; Sanctorum
Patrum vetuit & interdixit clericis (maxime diuino
miniſterio conſecratis) vxores habere, vel cum mu-
lieribus

lierihus habitare nisi quas Nicena Synodus vel aly Canones exceperunt. This *Pope* (*Gregory* the 7.) hauinge made a Synod, did accordinge to the decree of *Saint Peter* the Apoftle & *Saint Clement* his fucceffor, and of other holie fathers, forbyd vnto Cleargie men (efpecially to fuch as were confecrated to Gods feruice) to haue wiues, or to dwell with women; excepting fuch only, as the firft councell of Nice and other Ecclefiafticall canons did except or permitt.

The cou̅cell of Nice for bidding vviues to priefts and Bifhops.

19. This teftifieth *Marianus* of the Popes intention, and that he made his decree according to the decrees, canons meaninge & practife of all holy Fathers his predeceffors from *Saint Peter* downeward in the Latin Churche. And yf we goe to the councell of Nice for the exception heere mencioned; what women were allowed to dwell in howfe with Priefts in thofe dayes: we fhall find all women to be forbidden to liue with Bifhops, Priefts or deacons, *præter matrem, fororem vel amitam*, the mother, fifter or the Awnte. But noe mencion at all of the wife, which fhould haue byn the firft, that fhould haue byn excepted by the councell, yf any fuche thing had byn lawfull or permitted in thofe dayes. For albeit in the Greeke Churche, where this councell was held, fome were made Priefts, that were maried before: yet were they neuer permitted to

Conc. Nic. Can. 3.

Ff 3   marry,

The
vvhole
ſtreme
of aun-
cient
Greeke
Fathers
againſt
the ma-
riage of
Prieſts
Origen
hom. 23.
in lib.
Num.

marry, after they were Prieſts, nor are not at
this day. And if we conſider the whole
ſtreame of Greeke Fathers in this behalfe:
we ſhall ſee them no leſſe by their writings,
then by their doings and examples, ioyne
with the Latyn Churche, in this point
about the contynency of Prieſts & Biſhops,
euen from the beginning. *Illius ſolius eſt oſſerre
ſacrificium* (ſaith *Origen* aboue 1400. yeares
agoe) *qui perpetuæ ſe deuouerit caſtitati.* To him
only belongeth to offer Sacrifice, who hath
vowed himſelfe to perpetuall chaſtity.

20.   Behold ſacrifice and vowinge of chaſtitie in Prieſts of the Greeke Churche
aboue 700. yeare before the tyme, that Fox
ſaith it was decreed firſt of all by *Pope Gregorie* the 7. that they ſhould not marry. And
Euſebius in the next age after beinge one of
them, that were of the councell of Nice,

Euſeb.
lib. 1. De-
moſtrat.
Euang.
cap. 9.

ſaith: *Eos, qui ſacrati ſunt, & in Dei miniſterio cul-
túque occupati, continere deinceps ſeipſos a commer-
cio vxoris decet.* Yt becommeth them that are
conſecrated and occupied in the ſeruice of
God, to conteyne themſelues for the time to
come from all dealinge with wiues. There
follow in the ſame age with *Euſebius* diuers
other fathers: as *Saint Cyrill, S. Gregory Nyſſen,
Saint Chryſoſtome, S. Epiphany,* all which writinge of this matter are of the ſame opinion.

Cyrill.
Cat. 12.

*Qui apud Ieſum bene fungitur ſacerdotio, abſtinet a
muliere* ſaith *Saint Cyrill.* He that performeth
                                          the

the office of a Priest well in the sight of
Iesus (that is to say is a good Christian Priest)
doth absteine from all wome. To like sense
do wryte *Saint Gregory Nyssen*, *lib. de virginit.* *Sup. c. 3.*
cap. vlt. and *Saint Chrisostome*, *hom. 2. de patien.* *cap. vlt.*
Iob. And as for *Saint Epiphany*, we haue alleagged *Cent. 4.*
ged him before, as reprehended by the *Mag-* *pag. 303.*
deburgians, for affirminge this rule of Priests *Epiph.*
continency from mariage to haue ben ob- *tom. 1.*
serued in his tyme throughout the whole *lib. 2.*
Church, *vvith great sincerity vvheresoeuer good* *Item hab*
cleargie men vvere. *res. 59.*

21. It were in vayne to alleage the Latyn
Fathers. For that our enemyes confesse
them to be all of the contrary iudgment to
them. But when noe other argument were,
the very example of so great a multitude of
famous learned and holy Bishops, Doctors
teachers & preachers of those first ages after
Christ, that liued contynent and were not
married (as *Saint Ignatius*, *Saint Polycarpe*, *Cle-*
mens Alexandrinus, *Saint Athanasius*, *Saint Basill*,
Saint Gregory Nazianzen, *Saint Chrysostome Saint*
Epiphanius, *Saint Cyrill*, and many other of the
Greeke Churche : as also *Saint Cyprian*, *Saint*
Hillary, *Saint Ambrose*, *Saint Hierome*, *Saint Au-*
gustine, and aboue 50. Popes of Rome held
all for Saintes, and the most of them Martyrs in the Latyn Churche) these mens example (I say) is a sufficient argument to
shew, what was the spirit of Christ in those
dayes,

dayes, to him that hathe any feeling therof.

22.   But to ſay noe more of this and to returne to make an end of our ſpeache of *Pope
Gregory* the 7. (whome our proteſtants for
his ſingular vertue and conſtancy in Gods
cauſe can not abyde) Fox concludeth thus
of this deathe. *Antoninus vvriteth that Hildebrand as he lay a dyinge, deſired one of his Cardinalls
to goe to the Emperour and deſire him forgiuenes, abſoluinge both him and his partners from excommunication, &c.* And true it is that *Saint Antoninus*
Archbiſhop of Florence relateth ſome ſuche
thinge vpon other mens ſpeeches, ſayinge
*Quod miſit Cardinalem ad Imperatorem & ad to-
tam Eccleſiam, vt optaret ei indulgentiam.* That he
ſent the Cardinall to the Emperour and to
all the Churche, to wiſhe him indulgence.
And what maruaill (yf yt had byn ſo) that a
man lyinge at deathes doare, would gladly
be at peace with all the world? But why
had not Fox ſett downe the other woords
of *Antoninus* preſently followinge? *Quæ tamen
vera eſſe non credo, multis de cauſis.* Which yet for
many cauſes I do not beleue to be true.
Here yow may ſee that Fox is ſtill a Fox.

23.   *Nauclerus* reporteth that his laſt woords
lyinge on his deathe bead in *Salerno*, were
thoſe of the pſalme. *Dilexi iuſtitiam & odui
iniquitatem, propterea morior in exilio. &c.* I haue
loued Iuſtice and hated iniquity, & for this
doe I dy in baniſhment, being driuen a way
from

Fox pag.
164.

Anton.
part. 2.
tit. 16.
cap. 1. §.
21.

Naucl.
generat.
37.

from my Sea by the violence of the Emperor. Thus wrote *Nauclerus* of him, though
a Germane, adding thefe woords: *Vir fuit* The de-
Gregorius timens Deum, iuftitia & æquitatis ama- ath of
tor, in aduerfis conftans. Pope *Gregorie* was a man *Gregory*
that feared God, a great louer of Iuftice & the 7.
equytie, conftant in aduerfitie . And *Platina* *Plat. in*
that flattereth not Popes, as our Proteftants *vita Gre*
do confeffe, wrytinge of him faith: *Vir certe* *gorÿ 7.*
Deo gratus, &c. Truly he was a man gratefull
to God, prudent, iuft, clement and a Pa-
trone of all poore : but efpecially of pupills
& wydowes. *Cranzius* alfo a German faith:
Henricus Gregorium 7. virum fanctum infectatus eft.
Henry the Emperor perfecuted *Pope Gregory*
the 7. beinge a holy man.

24. But to omytt this and to fpeake noe
more of Popes liues or learninge , fpecially
of thefe two (*Gregory* and *Innocentius*) fo well
knowen, but only to confider their faith &
belief (for that principally indeede concerneth our purpofe, feeinge that albeit they
fhould be wicked or vnlearned yet might A ridicu
they be true Popes:) I would aske Iohn lous de-
Fox, what one article of beliefe any one of uife of
thefe two Popes liuinge more then 100. Fox
yeares the one after the other, did they howv 2.
differ in, from their predeceffors? or were Popes
noted by their fucceffors for the fame? And ouer-
if no fuch article can be brought forth (as the threvv
moft certainly there can not) how then Church.

could

could thefe two Popes either iointly or fe-
uerally ouerthrow fo greate a Church di-
fperfed ouer all the world , (as was at that
time the Roman) and much more extinguish the whole Chriftian faith , as Iohn
Fox affirmeth?

25.   Is not this plaine madnes , to affirme
that any one or two Popes could ouer-
throwe a whole Church or extinguish
Chriftian faith: efpecially liuing 100. yeares
one from the other, as hath bene faid ? For
if the firft had donne it , then what needed
the helpe of the fecond ? or if the fame
Church perfeuered in Chriftian faith for
100. yeares togeather after the firft: then did
not he ouerthrow the fame . And yet doth
Iohn Fox delight himfelfe fo much in this
fancy, as in diuerfe places of his booke he
foundeth his whole difcourfes theron, as
we fhall fee in the chapter followinge.

THERE

THERE FOLLOWETH A DREA-

MING IMAGINATION OF IOHN FOX, *contrary to it selfe, about the fall of the Roman Church and rising of Antichrist:vvith the rest that remaineth of our Ecclesiasticall history from the conquest to* Wicklif.

CHAP. VIII.

IOHN Fox taking vpon him in his veyne of fancy to distinguish times, and to de-termine, when the Church of Rome fell sick and died, when Antichrist was borne, and other like vayne imaginations:prouing also the same by certaine reuelations made vnto himselfe, as he lay on his bedde vpon a sonday in the morninge: He setteth downe for a grounde this distinction of tymes in the very beginninge of his actes and monu-mentes in these woords, *First* (saith he) *I vvill treate of the sufferinge time of the Church, vvhich continued from the Apostles age about* 300. *yeares. Secondly of the florishinge tyme of the Church, vvhich lasted other* 300. *yeares. Thirdly of the declininge tyme of the Church, vvhich comprehendeth also other* 300. *yeares, vntill the loosinge out of Sathan vvhich vvas* 1000. *yeares after the ceasinge of the persecu-tion. Fourthly follovveth the tyme of Antichrist or loosinge of Sathan or desolation of the Church, &c.*

2. Lo here Iohn Fox maketh a different accoumpt from the former, as though the

time

time of Antichriſt and looſing of Sathan for ouerthrowinge the true Church, had begonne much ſooner then vnder *Pope Gregory* and *Innocentius*; to witt, from the yeare of Chriſt 900. which was almoſt 200. yeares before *Gregory* the 7. was borne. And yet doth he alſo contradict himſelfe in this, if yow marke him. For that he ſaith, this looſinge of Sathan was about the thouſande yeare after the ceaſinge of perſecution. Which ceaſinge beinge counted by Fox himſelfe from the time of *Conſtantine* the greate (when he ſaith Sathan was bound vp for 1000. yeares) the endinge therof muſt fall not vpon the yeare of Chriſt 900. as in this his accoumpt : but rather vpon the yeare of Chriſt 1300. at which time he was lett forth againe (if we beleeue Iohn Fox) and had power giuen him, not only to impugne, but to ouerthrow the Church. Contrary to that which Chriſt had promiſed *Mat. 16.* *that hell gates ſhould not preuaile againſt her.*

3. But let vs ſee a thirde place, where Iohn Fox handleth this miſterie different from both theſe now alleaged: to witt, in the beginninge of his fifth booke, from Wicklif downeward, where he maketh another accoumpt yet of byndinge & looſinge of Sathan and ouerthrowinge the true Church. And this forſooth, out of the 20. chapter of the *Apocalips* by a large text. Which hauinge recited,

recited, he faith thus. *By thefe vvoords of the Re-* Fox di-
uelation three fpeciall thinges are to be noted. Firft uerfe ty-
the beinge abroade of Sathan. Secondly his byndinge mes con
vp. And thirdly the loofinge out of him againe after a tradi-
thoufande yeares confummate, &c. cting
4.   Thus he hath there. And then a litle about
after he maketh his accoumpt thus. *The byn-* bynding
dinge vp of Sathan after peace giuen to the Church and loo-
(countinge from the 30. *yeare of Chrift) vvas anno* Sathan.
Domini 294. *vvhich lafted for* 1000. *yeares vntill*
anno 1294. *about vvhich yeare Pope Boniface the* 8.
vvas made Pope, and made the 6. *booke of the decre-*
talles, confirmed the order of Fryars and priuileged
them vvith great freedomes.

So writeth Fox and confirmeth his fentence by certaine old verfes written by a
Monke (as he faith) which affirme that.

Cùm fuerint anni completi mille ducenti
Et decies feni poft partum virginis almæ.
Tunc Antichriftus nafcetur Dæmone plenus.

That is: When a thoufande two hundreth „
& threefcore yeares after the virgins child- „
birth fhall be ended : then fhall Antichrift „
be borne replenifhed with the fpiritt of Sa- „
than. Which Fox will needes haue to be
meant by the forfaide *Bonifacius* the 8. as
though he aboue others had ouerthrowne
the Church,and had byn the firft Antichrift
among Popes. Which if it were true, then
can it not fall either vpon *Gregory* the 7. or
Innocentius 3. no nor vpon Boniface himfelfe,
named

named by him. For that he was not made
Pope 34. yeares after this deuiſed prophecie
did appoint Antichriſt to be borne, to witt
1260. ſeeinge he was made Pope (as Fox alſo confeſſeth) *anno* 1294.

5.   But the beſt paſtime is, to heare what
immediately followeth in Fox, which are
theſe woords: Theſe verſes (ſaith he) were
written (as appeareth by the ſaid Author)
anno Domini 1285. Well Syr Iohn, & what of
this? doth not this ouerthrow all the credit
of your prophecy? ſeeinge it ſheweth that
theſe verſes were writen 25. yeares after the
day appointed by the prophecy was paſt?

6.   So we ſee, that this man hauing toyled
ſo much to drawe all that is ſpoken in the
Apocalips or booke of Reuelation concerning Antichriſt and the bynding & looſing
of Sathan to fall vpon the Popes & Roman
Church: he can not tell, where to lay it, but
playeth notoriously the foole, and is contrary to himſelfe, as by the examination of
the three places alleaged may appeare. For
in the firſt, he affirmeth Chriſtian faith to

*In proteſ-
ſtation
pag. 9.*

haue byn extinguiſhed either by *Pope Gregory*
the 7. (in the yeare of Chriſt 1080.) or by
Innocentius 3. in the yeare 1215. and heere he
will haue it to haue byn vnder *Bonifacius* 8.
which was almoſt another hundred yeares
after *Innocentius*.

7.   In the ſecond place he will haue the
looſing

looſing of Sathan, & conſequently alſo the
fall of the Church, to haue byn almoſt 200.
yeares before *Gregory* the 7. (that is to ſay in
the yeare of Chriſt 900.) and all the reſt
downward to haue byn vnder Antichriſt,
which he calleth *the tyme of deſolation & raigne
of Sathan ouer the Church,* & he confirmeth the
ſame againe in the beginninge of another
treatiſe foilowinge , where repeatinge the
diuiſion of his whole worke , he ſaith : *that
his intention is firſt to declare the ſuffering time of the
Church for 300. yeares: ſecondly the floriſhing tyme
for other 300. thirdly the declyninge tyme, for other
300. yeares. Fourthly the time of Antichriſt raigning
and raging ſince the looſing of Sathan for other 400.
yeares. Fiftthly the reforming time of Chriſts Church
in theſe later 300. yeares ſince Iohn Vvickliffe be-
gann, and after Luther and other like people.*

8. Thus ſaith Fox: wherin he agreeth ſomwhat (as yow ſee) with his laſt former accoumpt, that Sathan was lett looſe to ouerthrow the Church about the yeare of
Chriſt 900. which yet is quite contrary to
that, which he writeth in his firſt place before alleaged , that the forſaid Church was
ouerthrowen by *Pope Gregory* the 7. and *Innocentius* 3. ſome hundred of yeares after that
tyme. But much more contrary it is to that,
which he wryteth laſtly out of the Apocalips in his fourth place alleaged : to witt,
that Sathan vvas bound vp for a thouſand yeares,

Which

*Acts and
monu-
ments
pag. 1.*

*Fox pag.
27. c. 1.*

Which number of yeares after the firſt ten
perſecutions, he ſaith, muſt begin from the
yeare of Chriſt 294. which he endeauou-
reth (though fondly) to prooue out of the
13. chapter of the Apocalips, where it is ſaid;
Apoc. 13. *that povver vvas giuen by the dragon to the beaſt* (to
verſ. 5. wit to Antichriſt) *to ſpeake blaſphemy and to do
vvhat liſted him for* 42. *monethes*, which make
(as all men know) 3. yeares & a halfe. Which
is the tyme allotted by *Saint Iohn*, (according
to all auncient fathers interpretations) to
the raigne of Antichriſt in the end of the
world. And it is ſo expounded in other
places of this reuelation it ſelfe : to witt, by
Apoc. 12. theſe words, *a tyme, tymes, and halfe a tyme*: and
Apoc. 11. in another place by 1260. *dayes*; and then
verſ. 11. againe by 42. *monethes*. All which numbers
being examined, do make vp iuſt the forſaid
3. yeares and a halfe, propheſied and expreſ-
Dan. 11. ſed in like manner by *Daniell* the prophet.

9.   And in this there is no doubt or queſtion among Catholiks or auncient writers,
but that Antichriſt (a particular perſon deſigned for that end from the beginninge of
the world) ſhall appeare and haue power
giuen him from the diuell to tormoyle and
afflict the Church of Chriſt for the ſpace of
3. yeares and a halfe before the day of iudgment. Only the hereticks of our tyme to di-
uert theſe propheſies from the true Antichriſt and apply them to certayne Biſhops
of Rome,

of Rome, do beat their heads, how to deuife
out fome new expofitions of thefe numbers
neuer heard or thought of before. And
namely Iohn Fox more fondly then the reft
wlll haue the number of 42. monethes to
import 294. yeares, that is euery moneth to
fignifie 7. yeares, or (as fantaftically he calleth it) *a fabboth of yeares.* For proofe wherof
he hauinge neither authority nor any one
example of fcripture, he confirmeth it by a
reuelation of his owne, as after yow fhall
heare.

10.   His deuife therfore is, that the 1000.
yeares wherin Sathan, is faid in the Apocalips to be tyed vp, muft beginne, as yow fee,
after the faid 294. yeares of heathen perfecution were ended. So that the loofing out
of Sathan againft the Church againe, muft
fall in the yeare of Chrift 1294. when *Bonifacius* the 8. was chofen Pope, or as the monks
prophefie was, vpon the yeare 1260. when
Antichrift was borne. Which is both contrary to that he faid before, that he was loofed about the yeare 900. as alfo that the
Popes *Gregory* the 7. and *Innocentius* the 3. (by
Sathans help no doubt) ouerthrew the
Church about the yeare of Chrift 1080. or
1215. for yf Sathan was bound & not loofed
vntill the yeare of Chrift 1294. how could
he ouerthrow the Church before?

11.   Wherfore all thefe new interpretations

of the words of the Apocalips, are but
phantaſticall deuiſes of wrangling heretiks:
ſeeing the auncient fathers do interpret all
theſe things farre otherwayes. And firſt
they put the byndinge vp of Sathan for a
thouſand yeares there mentioned before
the other number of 42. monethes giuen to
Antichriſt to worke his will: and do ſay,
that the ſaid looſinge of Sathan began from
the very death and paſſion of Chriſt, when
the power of Sathan was bound, according
to the ſaying of Chriſt himſelfe in *Saint Iohns*
Goſpell drawing neere to his paſſion. *Novv
the Prince of this vvorld ſhalbe caſt forth.* And ſecondly they do interpret theſe thouſand
yeares not to ſignifie any certayne time, but
generally to ſignifie all the whole courſe of
tyme betwene the death of Chriſt vnto the
comming of Antichriſt 3. yeares and a halfe
before the day of iudgmēt; according to the
ordinary phraſe of ſcripture: as for example.
quod mandauit Deus in mille generationes, God
hath commaunded his precept to be kept
for a thouſand generations, that is to ſay, to
the worlds end: and not for any certayne
tyme. And againe in *Iob: yf a iuſt man ſhould
contend vvith God, he cannot anſvvere him one for a
thouſand.*

12. This then is the auncient interpretation
of holy Doctors, quite contrary to theſe
new fancies of Iohn Fox, whoſe expoſitiōs
are

*Aug. lib.
10. de
Ciuit.
cap. 6. 7.
8. 9.
Primaſ.
19. &
Beda in
10. Apoc.
Greg. l.
9. mor.
c. 1. &
lib. 35.
cap. 10.
Apoc. 20.
Ioan. 12.*

*Pſalm.
140.*

Iob. 9.

are both contrary to himfelfe, (as in part yow haue feene) and oppofite to the words and fenfe of fcripture it felfe. For wheras firft thefe 42. monethes (importinge by his account 294. yeares) were giuen to Sathan to worke his will againft the Saints of God: the fcripture faith, *they vvere giuen to the beaft* (that is to fay to Antichrift) *by the Dragon,* and not to the Dragon himfelfe: And fecondly, whereas he would needs haue the 42. mo-nethes to fignifie 294. yeares, the fcriptures do expound them by 1260. dayes, which make iuft 3. yeares and a halfe, as hath byn faid.

Apoc. 13. verf. 4. 5. 6.

13.   Thirdly Fox fhall neuer find any place or example in fcripture, where the word *moneth* either in Greeke or Latyn doth fig-nifie, *feauen dayes, vveeks or yeares,* as in *Daniell* the Greeke word *Hebdomada* doth, and may, by his proper fignification. And yet is Iohn Fox fo fond and refolute in his deuife as all other profes and probabilityes fayling him, he will needs confirme yt by a reuelation from God, which he recounteth in thefe words following.

14.   *Becaufe the matter* (faith he) *being of no fmall importance, greatly appertayneth vnto the publike vtility of the Church, and leaft any fhould mifdoubt me heerin, to follovv any priuate interpretations of my ovvne: I thought good to communicate to the Reader, that vvhich hath byn imparted vnto me, in the*

Act. and mon. pag. 90. A reue-lation impar-ted to Iohn Fox.

Gg 2   *opening*

openıng of theſe myſticall numbers ın the foreſaid
booke of reuelation, conteyned by occaſion as follovveth, &c.

15.   As I vvas in hand vvith theſe hiſtoryes, &c.
Being vexod and turmoyled ın ſpiritt about the rec-
koning of theſe numbers and yeares, it ſo happened
vpon a ſunday in the morninge lyinge in my bedd and
muſing about theſe numbers, ſuddenly it vvas anſvvered to my mind, as vvith a maieſty thus invvardly
ſaying vvithin me, thou foole, count theſe monethes by ſabbotts as the vveeks of Danieii are counted
by ſabbotts. The Lord I take to vvittneſſe, thus it vvas.
VVhervpon thus being admoniſhed, I began to reckon
the 42. monethes by ſabbotts, firſt of the monethes, &
that vvould not ſerue: and then by ſabbotts of yeares,
and then I began to feele ſome probable vnderſtandinge, yet not ſatiſfied heervvith eftſoones I repayred
to certaine marchants of my acquaintance, (of
vvhome one is departed, a true and faithfull ſeruant
of the Lord, the othor tvvo yet aliue and vvittneſſes
heerof)to vvhome the number of theſe forſaid monethes being propounded and examined by ſabboits of
yeares, the vvhole ſomme vvas found to ſurmount to
294. yeares, conteyning the full and iuſt tyme of the
forſaid perſecutions, neyther more nor leſſe, &c.

16.   And thus you haue the reuelation made
to Iohn Fox. Which he ſaith, that he relateth vnto vs, for that we ſhall not miſdoubt
the truth therof, nor think that he followeth any priuate interpretation of his owne,
but that it came from God immediately.
                                                        And

And this is the first dreame of Iohn Fox in
his bed. And the second ridiculous point is,
that he went to 3. marchants to conferre
this reuelation, and that they approued the
same. The third point is open folly, where
he saith that this number of 294. conteyneth the full and iust tyme of the first persecutions of Christians vnder Pagan Emperors, neither more nor lesse, which before
hath byn refuted, and is euident in it selfe.
Seeing that from Christ to the victory of
Constantine against *Maxentius*, there are assi-
gned by *Eusebius* 318. yeares and yet did not
this persecution of Christians cease then
neither. But continued vnder *Licinius* and
other tirants for diuers years after. See then,
how iust these numbers fall out, *neyther more
nor lesse.* All which being considered, I find
no one thinge so true or credible in all this
reuelation, as those words of the spirit vnto
him saying, *thou foole.* For that this maketh
him a foole indeed by reuelation. And so
much of him and of this whole matter of
bynding and loosinge Sathan and reigne of
Antichrist. Now lett vs returne to the continuation of our conference with Iohn Fox
about his Church.

17.   The deduction of the Cath. Roman
Church from *VVilliam Conquerer* downward
vnto *Iohn VVicklifes* tyme is no lesse easy and
cleare: but rather more, then the former de-

duction

duction from Chriſt to the *conqueſt*. For that
the Church was now more ſpread and eſtabliſhed ouer the world, then in any other
former ages. And to come vnto the particulars, there ſate in the Sea of Rome, as high
Biſhops of the vniuerſall Church, from
Pope Alexander the ſecond, that ſent a banner
bleſſed vnto *VVilliam Conqueror* at his entrance into England (and was the hundred
ſixty two Pope from *S. Peter* to our time)vn-
to *Pope Gregory* the eleuenth (vnder whome
VVicklif began his doctrine) 45. Popes. And
in the Roman Empyre, from *Henry* the 4.
vnto *Charles* the fowerth ſucceeded 19. Emperors. And in the crowne of England ten
or eleuen Kings from the *Conqueror* to *K. Edvvard* the 3. vnder which Kings there ſucceeded by election in the Metropolitan Sea
of Canterbury from *Stigand* and *Lanfranke*
vnto *Thomas Arundel*, twentie Archbiſhops.
All which both Popes, and Emperors of the
vniuerſall Church, as alſo the Kings and
Archbiſhops of our Iland, agreed vniformally in faith and religion, without any
difference at all. And ſo it continued in our
Iland. For albeit towards the end of this
tyme *Iohn VVickliffe* with his followers and
ſome other Sectaryes (eſpecially the Lollards) roſe vp in our country and cauſed
many troubles both in England and other
places: yet neither the ſtate of England nor
any

The ſuc-
ceſſion
of the
vniuer-
ſall
Church,
as alſo of
England
from the
yeare
1066.
dovvn-
vvard.

any of our princes (and much leſſe any Bi-
ſhoppes or Archbiſhops)euer ſuffered themſelues to be infected therwith. So as for the
manifeſt continuation both of men and doctrine in theſe ages, we haue no leſſe viſible
ſucceſsion both of Biſhops, Doctors, and
faith, than before we haue ſhewed in the
former ages;the ſucceſsion of Biſhops being
euident in euery countrey and Church by
their particular ſtories and recordes, as alſo
of teachers and doctrine, as now we ſhall
ſhew.

18.   The principall learned men alſo and
Doctors of this tyme from the conqueſt to
VVickliffe are knowne. As for example, *Bur-*
chardus, Petrus Damianus, Lanfranke, Anſelmus,
Oecumenius,Marianus Scotus,Iuo Carnotenſis,Lam-
bertus Schafnaburgenſis,Rupertus Abbas,Euthymius,
Saint Bernard, Peter Lombard, Gratianus,Albertus
Magnus., Saint Thomas of Aquin, Nicephorus Ca-
*lixtus,*and many other downward. In which
tyme there are accoumpted ſome ten or
eleuen Synods and councells to haue been
held in diuers countreyes, for ſuppreſsing of
hereſies & ſects,that did from tyme to tyme
peepe vp:and reforming of abuſes in former
tymes. And two of them to haue been generall: to witt,that of *Lateran* & of *Conſtance,*
wherin Wicklif was condemned.

19.   The moſt notorious ſects alſo of this
time which againſt theſe Doctors, councells,

The princi-
pall lear-
ned men
of this
time.

The ſects
& ſecta-
ries of
this
time.

Gg 4

cells, and Synods did ſtriue, were the *Bogo-*
milians, the *Petrobuſians*, the *Arnardiſtes*, the
VValdenſes or poore men of *Lions*, the *Albigen-*
ſes of *Tholoſa*, the *Cathari* or Puritans, the *Fla-*
gellantes or Whippers, the *Begardians*, the *Be-*
guiſnes and *Fraticelli* or little brethren, the
Lollardes and *VVicklifiſts*, and the reſt that enſued. Againſt all which the Church proceeded in all this tyme by cenſures of councells and Biſhops: as in all other tymes before againſt ſuch men, and muſt do to the
worldes end.

20.   And now this being ſo, tell me (good
Reader) whether it be not true, which *Saint*

Aug.l.1.
quaſt.
euangel.
q. 38. &
tract. 2.
in epiſt.
Ioan.

Auguſtine ſaith *that it is as eaſy in all ages to ſee,*
vvhere the true viſible Church goeth, as to ſee the
ſunne at noone tyme, vvhen it ſhineth cleereſt. And
where will Iohn Fox goe now to ſeeke
himſelfe a priuate hidden Church amonge
Chriſtians. Except he patch it vp of thoſe
heretiks by me named and other like, as he
doth. And therin dealeth, as yf one hauinge
ſhewed the diſcent and continuance of the
moſt noble and moſt auncient houſe of England by their armes and actions: would
condemne them all preſently to haue dege-
nerated, and bring in a company of Beggars
or brothers, that haue runne out of that
houſe or were beaten from thence: affirminge theſe only to be of the auncient race

A fitt
compa-

of that family. Or as yf a man would ſay of
the

the citty of London, that for thefe thoufand
yeares and more all thofe men or women,
that haue been punifhed by the fame citty
for malefactors, were the true Citizens in
deed: and the others, that punifhed them,
only intruders.

21. In which examples notwithftandinge
though they be ridiculous: yet is there much
more reafon or probability, than in the
other. For that any temporall houfe or family what foeuer, may degenerate, and be
wholy peruerted. And any citty whatfoeuer may erre, alter or be turned vpfide
downe by diforder: but the Cath. Church
cannot, except we deny both the promife
power and Godhead of Chrift himfelfe, as
our heretiks in effect doe (though not in
wordes) whileft they make to themfelues
a nevv fcarfe vifible Church of elect people, to
witt of their owne election and therby are
forced to fay, that the greate vifible Church
begonne by Chrift and continued for many
ages togeather did at length (about the time
appointed by Fox though they cannot
agree at what time) wholy forfake Chrift
and fall to Apoftafie, becomming the Synagoge of Sathan an enemy to Chrift in fteed
of his family, kingdome and dearly beloued
Spoufe: which is fo foule, and foolifh yea
ignominious and monftrous an abfurdity
that it doth not only contradict the whole

Gg 5 courfe

courſe of Scriptures which did prophecy &
foretel the viſible durance and continuance
of this Church vntill the worlds end, but
that it ſhould alſo be the pillar and firmament of trueth, and ſo aſsiſted by Chriſt and
his holy ſpiritt, that it ſhould neuer erre nor
bringe into errour, and much leſſe fade
away or periſh.

Pſalm.
47. 88.
Eſay. 61.
Dan. 2.
Mat. 16.
1. Tim. 3.
Ioan. 16.
Mat. 18.

22. The moſt learned Father *Saint Augu-*
ſtine doth handle this matter euery where
againſt the *Donatiſts,* who like our proteſtāts
would needes haue the vniuerſall viſible
Church in their time to haue erred & fallen
from Chriſt, and they only as elect veſſells
make the true Church, though ſcarſe viſible
to the eyes of the world, as Fox ſaith of his
Church gathered vp of lurkinge heretiks
heere & there as after you ſhall ſee declared.
Againſt which abſurdity *Saint Auguſtine* diſputed moſt learnedly, ſoluinge firſt the arguments which they alleadg of ſome euill
men or Popes, that may haue been in the
Church, yf all were true as they ſay: *Nullius*
hominis quamuis ſceleratum & immane peccatū &c.
That no mans ſinne, beinge neuer ſo heynous can preiudicate the promiſes of God
,, (for the viſible continuance of the Church,
,, to the worlds end) neyther can any impiety
,, of any men whatſoeuer within the Church,
,, bring to paſſe that the faith of God which
,, was conteyned in the promiſes made to
the

S. Augu-
ſtine
impug-
neth the
former
abſurdi-
tie.

Aug. l. 1.
c. 1. con-
tra epiſt.
Parmen.

the auncient Fathers cōcerning the Church ,,
of Chriſt to come, and to be ſpread ouer the ,,
world & now fullfilled in our daies, ſhould ,,
be made voyd, &c.

23. And againe. *Albeit this Church be ſom-* *Ibid. ep:*
tymes obſcured and ſhaddovved by multitude of *48. ad*
ſcandalls, yea euen then doth ſhee ſhine, and is emi- *Vincent.*
nent in her moſt firme members, &c. And yet further: *Sed illa Eccleſia quæ fuit omnium gentium non* *Aug. in*
eſt; perijt; hoc dicunt qui in illa non ſunt: O impuden- *pſalm.*
tem vocem! illa non eſt, quia in illa tu non es? But *conc. 2.*
perhaps yow will ſay (ſaith he to *Donatiſts*) ,,
that, that Church which was gathered to- ,,
geather of all nations from the beginninge, ,,
is not now, it hath periſhed, (or fallen from ,,
Chriſt) Thus ſay they which are not in her: ,,
O impudent ſpeeche! is not ſhe no longer a ,,
Church for that thou art not in her?

24. Heere (I trow) Fox wil be aſhamed,
or his fellowes for him, ſeeinge this is their
ordinary ſpeech, that this great viſible
Church began by Chriſt and his Apoſtles,
held on well for a time, but at length fell to
Apoſtaſy as *Saint Auguſtine* ſaith of his heretiks in the ſame place: *Dicunt, impletæ ſunt ſcri-* *Aug. ib:*
ptura, crediderunt omnes gentes, ſed apoſtatauit &
perijt Eccleſia. Theſe heretiks ſay that the ,,
ſcriptures were fulfilled, that all nations be- ,,
leeued and entred into this Church, but that ,,
after a tyme it fell to Apoſtaſy and periſhed. ,,
But what anſwereth *Saint Auguſtine* to this ,,
impudent

impudent obiectió? he oppoſetn the words

Mat. 28. of Chriſt himſelfe: *Ecce ego vobiſcum ſum vſque ad conſummationem ſaculi.* Behould I am with you to the end of the world: as who would ſay, by this doctrine they make Chriſt a lyar and a deceyuer, that promiſed more then he could performe, nay in very deed they deny heerby his whole deity, & do euacuate all the miſteryes of his whole incarnation, life, paſsion, reſurrection, aſſenſion, and ſending of the holy Ghoſt, &c.

Abſurdi- **25.** For to what end, was all this done,
tyes and but to gather togeather, found, ſtabliſh, and
impie- to conſerue this Church vnto the end of the
tyes en- world? For what was Chriſt incarnate and
ſuinge God made man, but to be head of this
vpon Church? why did he preach, gather his
the for- Apoſtles & diſciples, inſtruct them, prayed
mer do- for them, and their continuance, left ſacra-
ctrine. ments among them, but that they ſhould viſibly begin this Church? why did Chriſt ſend the holy Ghoſt, but to direct and con-firme the ſame, not for one age or two, but to the worlds end? how did Chriſt com-maund men vnder paine of damnation to ¤nter into this Church and abſolutely to heare and obey the ſame, yf only it were to endure for certayne ages, and then to periſh? How could *pagans, infidells, Ievves, turks, mores,* or other like people (if by Gods inſpiration they ſhould haue a deſire to be Chriſtians) know

know what to do, or whether to go, or
where to be truly instructed, yf they came
after the tyme appointed by Fox, when the
visible Roman Church had perished? to
witt, after the tyme of *Pope Gregory* the 7.
when Fox saith, *that Christian faith vvas novv*
extinguished in the vniuersall visible Church
aboue 500. yeares gone; & yet on the other
side, this new Church of *VVickliffians, Hußits*
and others of that sect, (which he putteth
to be the true Church) was not yet borne
by two or three hundred yeares: so as then
he must needs confesse, that either there was
no Christian Church at all for some ages, or
that he must place it in some other obscure
heretiks and sectaryes of that tyme named
by me before, yet he doth not agree at all, in
their articles of religion.

26. Well then this shalbe sufficient to shew
the absurdity of Iohn Fox his deuise for
ouerthrow of our Church and setting vp of
his owne, patchinge it vp of the heretiks of
these later ages. And yet yow must note,
that for the first 300. yeares next after the
Conquest to this time of the rising of *VVickliffe*
(which conteyne the whole substance of
his fourth booke & therin a hundred leaues
of paper) he scarse findeth any heretiks
whome he dareth to chalenge for members
of his Church fully, though some liking he
sheweth to the forsaid *VValdenses* and *Albi-*
genses:

The pat-
ching vp
of Fox
his
Church
in these
ages.

genses: fo as all the fubftantiall building of his Church beginneth only from *VVickliffe* downward, of whome we fhall talke more particularly in the chapter followinge.

27.   But perhaps then yow wil! aske me, how doth he fill vp thefe hundred leaues of paper in this his fourth booke, if heere alfo he alleage fo little for his *vifible Church*? I fhall tell yow breefly. He goeth from King to King, and from Archbifhop to Archbifhop fhewing what ftrifes or difagreeméts, futes or controuerfies fell out betwene our two Archbifhops of *Canterbury* & *Torke*, betwene our Kings, Archbifhops, religious orders & fecular Priefts, Cannons and their Bifhops, and other fuch quarrels in thofe tymes, making fcornfull notes vpon euery point, and then he putteth downe a bedrole of all the particular orders of religious men in England, entituling the fame: *The rabblement of religious orders.* Then cometh he in with a complaint of the nobles of England againft the exactions and couetoufnes of Popes in thofe dayes, and many letters, and wrytings about the fame, but citeth commonly no author for any thing. Then bringeth he in what variance at diuers tymes there paffed betwene the Popes and the cittyzens of Rome, what ftriues betwene fome Popes and Emperors: betwixt Kings of France & Kings of Englad; & much like other matter little

The fubftance of Fox his fourth booke conteyninge 300. yeares from the conqueft to VVickliffe.

Fox pag. 236.

Ibidem pag. 241.

Ibidem pag. 255.

little to the purpose he tooke in hand,
which was to sett downe *the race and course* of
his Church.

28. But the greatest part of this booke doth
take vp the particular lying treatise againſt
Pope Gregory the 7. againſt *Lanfranke*, *Anſelme* and *Thomas Beckett* Archbiſhops of *Canterbury*, the counterfett deuiſed poyſoninge
of K. *Iohn* by a monke or friar; the ſtory or
perſecution (as he calleth it) of the heretiks,
named *VValdenſes* or *poore men of Lions*, and *Albigenſes* of *Tholoſa* and the like; we ſhall ſay a
word or two of eych point.

29. As for *Pope Gregory* called before *Hildebrand* he ſo rayleth vpon him, as if he had
byn the wickedeſt man that euer liued, and
the Emperor the beſt, & yet haue yow hard
the graue teſtimonyes before of the principall auncient authors to the contrary in
them both. But do yow heare Fox himſelfe
ſpeake. *Novv let vs proceed* (ſaith he) *to the contentions betvvene vvicked Hildebrand and the godly
Emperor, &c.* Lo how he ſanctifieth the Emperor, for hatred to the Pope.

30. Of Archbiſhop *Lanfranke*, ſo highly
commended by all writers for his vertue &
rare learning, wherby he confuted moſt excellently the new riſen hereſie of *Berengariu*
Fox writeth thus : *I thinke, that vnleſſe Lanfranke had brought vvith him leſſe ſuperſtition and
more ſincere ſcience into Chriſt his Church, he might*
have

*Pope Cre-
gory* the
7.

Fox pag.
159. col.
2. n. 10.

*Of Lan-
franck.*

Fox pag.
167.

Of Saint
Anſelme
See Ed-
uerus in
vit. S.
Anſel.
apud
ſur. tom.
2. Ed-
mund.
Câtuar.
in vit.
Henr. de
viris il-
luſtribus
cap. 7.
Trit. de
viris il-
luſt. l. 1.
cap. 101.
& l. 3.
cap. 329.
Fox pag.
175.
Of Saint
Tho. Bec-
kett.
★ En-
count. 2.
cap. 10.
11. 16.

Fox pag.
209.

haue kept him ſtill in his countrey and haue confuted
Berengarius at home. Do yow ſe how wiſe a
confutation this is?

31. Saint *Anſelme* followed after *Lanfranck*
in the Archbiſhopricke of Canterbury, and
was baniſhed by *VVilliam Rufus*, and died
vpon the 22. of Aprill in the yeare 1109. and
is held for a Saint by all poſterity, & his ſaid
day kept feſtiuall throughout Chriſtendome: And yet ſo wryteth Fox his ſtory as
though K. *Rufus* (whoſe manners yet all Engliſh hiſtoriagraphers both heretiks & Catholiks do greatly blame) had had the right
and *Anſelmus* had offered the wrong, in ſo
much as in one place Fox maketh this mar-
ginall note againſt this holy man: *The proud
ſtoutneſſe of a prelate in a vvrong cauſe.*

32. How large a treatiſe Fox maketh of
Saint *Thomas Beckett* and his contention with
K. *Henry* the ſecond, and how ſhamfully he
doth bely and reuile him euery where, hath
byn ſhewed ſufficiently ★ before in my Anſwere to *S. Fr. Haſtings*, as alſo of the fable of
the poyſoning of *King Iohn*. And as for the
hiſtories of the *VValdenſes* and *Albigenſes,*
whome he meaneth to lay for the firſt foun-
dations of his *viſible Church* vpon earth, he
handleth matters ſo falſely and partially,
contrary to the teſtimony of all antiquity,
as a man may eaſily ſee that the whole con-
texture of his ſtory is nothing els, but a perpetuall

petuall woué thred of willfull & malitious
falſhoods, and for that I ſhall haue occaſion
to ſpeake againe of theſe heretiks in the
next chapter, wherin we haue to handle the
ſucceſsion of Iohn Fox his viſible proteſtant Church from *VVickliffe* downward , I
ſhall ſay no more therof heere, but remitt
me to that which enſueth.

OF THE TIME FROM IOHN
VVICKLIFFE VNTO THE BEGIN-
ning of the Raigne of K. Henry *the* 8. *conteyninge about* 140. *yeares : and hovv the Roman
Church and Iohn Fox his Church paſſed in theſe
tymes.*

CHAP. IX.

BY that which hath byn ſaid before from
age to age, of the apparant and manifeſt
deſcent , progreſſe and continuation of the
Cath. Roman Church, and of her State and
condition, as well in England , as in other
parts of the Chriſtian world (at the ryſing
of *Iohn VVickliffe* an Engliſhman about the
yeare of Chriſt 1371.) it is not hard to make
the like deduction of the ſame Church from
that tyme vnto the yeare of Chriſt 1560.
when her maieſtie that now is had a little
before begone her raigne , and eſtabliſhed
the forme of religion that now is held in
England . For as for the Popes and cheefe
H h   Eccle-

Eccleſiaſticall gouernors of the Roman Church in this tyme, they are publikely knowen: their names, number, and ſucceſſion one to another from *Innocentius* the 6. *Vrbanus* the 5. and *Gregory* the 11. (who firſt condemned wicklifes doctrine) vnto *Pope Pius* 5. that entred the Roman Sea at the beginninge of her maieſties raigne: beinge in number about 30. and all of one faith and religion the one with the other.

2. The Emperors alſo both of the Weſt, and Eaſt Empire (ſo long as it laſted) are knowne to haue byn of the ſelfe ſame Religion, excepting ſome diſobedience & ſchiſmaticall opinions in ſome of the Greeke Emperors againſt the Church of Rome. For which it may be thought that God of his iuſtice gaue them ouer at length, togeather with their Empire into Infidells hands about the yeare of Chriſt 1450. *Conſtantinus* the 12. of that name, ſurnamed *Paleologus,* being the laſt of that race.

3. The maner alſo of proceeding in Eccleſiaſticall matters by this Church in this tyme, was like vnto the former: to witt by conſeruing & continuing the faith of their aunceſtors and precedent times. Defending the ſame with like diligence againſt innouations of heretiks, partly by the wrytings of Cath. learned men, Doctors & preachers which in theſe ages were: as *Gregorius Ariminenſis,*

nenſis Laurentius Iuſtinianus, Thomas de Kempis, The prin
Bartholomeus Vrbinas, Thomas VValdenſis, Ioannes cipall
Gerſon, Alphonſus Toſtatus, Sanctus Vincentius, San- learned
ctus Antoninus, Sanctus Bernardinus Senenſis, Nico- men of
laus Cuſanus, Io. Tritemius, Io. *Nauclerus, Alber-* this age.
tus Pius, Eckius, Empſerus, Clicthoueus, and many
other learned Cath. writers. By whoſe diligence, the heretiks in theſe ages were euery where refuted. But eſpecially were they
repreſſed by the authority of Synods and
councells, as well prouinciall and nationall,
as generall alſo. To which effect were their
later Generall councells, the firſt of *Florence* Generall
vnder *Pope Eugenius* 4. againſt the heretiks & councell
ſchiſmatiks of thoſe tymes about the yeare of Floof Chriſt 1432. the ſecond of *Lateran* vnder rence.
Iulius the 2. and *Leo decimus* about the yeare Generall
of Chriſt 1513. and the third of *Trent* againſt councell
Lutherans, Zvvinglians, Caluiniſts, Anabaptiſts and ran.
other ſuch freſher heretiks of our dayes, vnder *Pope Paulus* 4. *Pius* 4. and *Pius Quintus.* Coũcell
Which councell was begone about the of Trent
yeare 1445.

4. And albeit in this tyme (as in former
ages)there wanted not troubleſome ſpiritts
& new fangling heads to impugne & exerciſe this Church, as the *VVickliffians, Huſſits,
Pickards, Adamits, Thaborites, Orebites* and other
ſuch ſectaryes going before *Lutherans, Zvvinglians, Caluiniſts, Anabaptiſts, Trinitarians,* and
other like new dogmatiſts of our dayes: yet

were

were they alwayes diſcouered, reſiſted, vanquiſhed, and condemned by the ſame ordinary proceſſe of Eccleſiaſtical cenſures, & iudgment: excommunicated, anathematized, and deliuered ouer to Sathan by the authority of this Church, as all other heretiks were in former ages. And conſequently are like to haue the ſelfe ſame finall end, howſoeuer they ruffle or reſiſt for a tyme.

Cōdemnation of hereſies.

5. And this being now the demonſtration of our Cath. Church moſt cleare & euident to all them, that haue eyes of vnderſtanding to ſee, and grace to conſider the truth: lett vs paſſe ouer to the vew of Iohn Fox his Church, which hauing byn hitherto inuiſible from Chriſt downward, and only imaginary or mathematicall, as yow haue ſeene (for that he hath ſcarſe named any to haue byn of that Church:) yet now from this tyme forward he will beginne to exhibite vnto vs a reall viſible Church on his part, that is to ſay, a ſucceſsion or rather repreſentation of diuers profeſſors of his religion, or of ſome points therof at leaſt wiſe, wherin they differ from the Romane. For he doth not thinke it needfull for thoſe of his Church to agree in all articles, nor doth he bind himſelfe to the rule of *S. Auguſtine: Eccleſia vniuerſaliter perfecta eſt & in nullo claudicat.* The true Church is vniuerſally perfect, and doth halt in no one point of beleefe.

Aug. de geneſ. ad litteram cap. 1.

But

But he thinketh it fufficient for his men to
agree in fome things againft the Roman
Church and to haue *fome fparkles of truth in it,*
as before he ★ affirmed : albeit therwithall ★ *In his*
they fhould haue fome blemifhes and errors *proteft.*
alfo, as a little after we will declare. *pag. 9.*

6. The catalogue of thefe proteftant profeffors, wherof Fox would make vp his
Church, we fhall handle in the chapter following. Now we are only to tell yow, that
from this tyme of *VVickliffe* downwards, he
meaneth to lay downe the vifible fucceffion of his Church. And to that effect he
ftoreth vp all thofe, that held the articles of
the forfaid *V Vickliffe* or *Huffe,* for Ghofpellers
of his Church, whatfoeuer they held otherwife againft him, or different among themfelues. And yf any of them or others were
punifhed for their opinions, by our Church:
then doth he regifter them for martyrs or
confeffors of the fame Church. Which yet
he neuer durft do before this tyme, albeit
there were diuers other fectaryes in former
ages, that fimbolized with him in diuers articles, as hath byn fhewed.

7. Yea in this matter we may fee Iohn Fox
alfo play the Fox, & fetch many wyndings
& turnings to deceaue the Reader, for that
at the very entrance of his prolix & tedious A *ftar-*
treatife of *Iohn VVickliffe,* whome he propo- *ting hole*
feth *as a chofen man raifed vp by God for lightening* Fox.

H h 3 *the*

the vvorld, *and impugning the Church of Rome* he leaueth to himſelfe a ſtartinge hole for all neceſſityes, when he ſhalbe preſſed: telling vs, *that albeit in Iohn VVickliffes opinions & aſſer-tions ſome blemiſhes perhaps may be noted : yet ſuch blemiſhes they be , vvhich rather declare him to be a man , that might erre, then vvhich directly did fight againſt Chriſt our Sauiour, &c.*

8.   Conſider, I pray yow, what a defence this is. *Perhappes* (ſaith he) *ſome blemiſhes may be noted,* as though the matter were in doubt, whether he had any blemiſhes in his do-ctrine or noe. Which yet after the Fox is forced to cofeſſe & to diſclaime them open-ly. And further he addeth full wiſely: *that yf he haue blemiſhes or errors in doctrine they are ſuch, as do rather proue that he vvas a man, & might erre: then that he did fight directly againſt Chriſt.* Marke the manner of his defence : his errors do prooue oniy , *that he vvas a man and might erre.* And ſo I ſay alſo of the worſt heretiks, that their errors and blemiſhes in doctrine do proue that they were men and erring men. Yea wicked men alſo, in that they obſtina-tely defended their owne errors. And ſo I ſay of *VVickliffe* in like manner. But marke that, which followeth : *rather then that he did fight directly againſt Chriſt.* Which is as much to ſay, that it importeth not much, though he impugned Chriſt indirectly , if directly he did not fight againſt him . And may not any

Fox pag. 390. col. 2. n. 33.

any heretiks, that euer liued, be defended in this fort? no heretiks do openly and directly impugne Chrift: but rather pretend to honor him aboue others. Bearinge euer the names not only of Chriftians: but alfo of the beft and moft reformed Chriftians. And confequently they neuer fought directly againft Chrift, but indirectly: pretending one thing, and doing another.

9. After Iohn Fox hath greatly inftified *VVickliffe* by diuers leaues of paper togeather: he cometh to fett downe 23. of his firft articles condemned by the Church of England at that day. And that (as Fox confeffeth) by fpeciall chofen iudges gathered togeather, to witt 8. Bifhops, 15. religious learned men of diuers orders, 14. Doctors, & 6. bachlers of diuinity. All which Fox doth name and contemne, and yet thefe articles though in diuers points they concurre with *Luther, Zvvinglius* and *Caluyn* his doctrine in thefe dayes: yet in others they do greatly difagree. And Fox I thinke will not defend them. As for example, the fourth article is:

Fox pag. 400. col. 2. Speciall Iudges appointed to examine VVicklifs doctrine.

That if a Bishop or Priest should giue holy orders, or confecrate the Sacrament of the aultar, or minifter baptifme, vvhiles he is in mortall fyn: it vvere nothing auayleable.

10. Will Fox yeld to this article, thinke yow? for if he do, we may call in doubt whether euer he were well baptifed, and

H h 4   confe-

confequently whether he were a Chriftian: feeinge it may be doubted, whether the Prieft, that baptized him were in mortall fyn or no, when he did it. And againe the 9. article is:

That it is againft fcripture, for any ecclefiaficall minifters to haue any temporall poffefsions at all.

This article if Fox will graunt: yet his fellow minifters and his Lords the Bifnops I prefume will hardly yeld thervnto; but will pretend fcriptures to the contrary againft Wickliffe. Let vs fee the reft.

VVic-kliffes heretical articles. Fox pag. 400.

The 10. article is: *that no prelate ought to ex-communicate any perfon: except he knovv him firft to be excommunicated by God.*

The 15. is: *That fo long as a man is in deadly fyn: he is nether Bifhop nor Prelate.*

The 16. is: *That temporall Lords may according to their ovvne vvills and difcretion, take avvay the temporall goods from any Church-men, vvhenfoeuer they offend.*

The 17. is: *That tythes are meere almes, and may be detayned by the parifhioners, and beftovved vvhere they vvill at their pleafure.*

11. Thefe were fome of Wickliffes firft arti-cles condemned at Oxford about the yeare of Chrift 1380. but after he publifhed many worfe. And I would here know of Iohn Fox, whether he and his fellow minifters will allow of thefe articles or noe? & if not, but that they will haue them acccompted

for

for his *blemishes or errors*(as Fox calleth them)
then may we alſo with better reaſon accout
for blemiſhes and errors his other propoſi-
tions : wherin he agreeth with the proteſtants againſt vs. As I doubt not, but that
Iohn Fox will accoumpt thoſe alſo,wherin
he agreeth with vs againſt him, which are
many,& farre more then the former,wher-
in he ioyneth with him againſt vs , as may
be gathered by theſe few articles alleaged
heere by. Fox himſelfe . Wherby (though
mingled with much other erroneous doctrine as you ſee) it is euident that *VVickliffe*
held diuers points alſo of Cath. Religion, as
holy orders, conſecration , excommunication,diſtinction of veniall & mortall ſinnes
& other like. For which cauſe I maruayle,
why Iohn Fox would alleage theſe articles:
but only to confound himſelfe, & to ſhew,
that his holy patriarke *VVickliffe*, is ſo full of
blemiſhes,as ſcarce any vnſpotted thing can
be found in his doctrine.

12. But this is the beggery of this new
Church , that it cannot be made vp but by
ſuch dunghill clouts gathered togeather
from vnder the feet of their aduerſaries.For
albeit, *VVickliffe, Huſſe* and other like ſectaryes did hold many more articles with vs
againſt the proteſtants , then with them
againſt vs : yet ſuch is the integrity, purity,
ſeuerity , yea maieſtie of our Church, that

*Fox his
Church
made vp
of our
dunghill
clouts.*

for fo much as that they agreed not in all &
euery point of beleefe; we (accordinge to
the creed of *Athanafiu*) reiect them, and as
fpotted and blemifhed ragges do caft them
out to the dunghill. Whome poore Fox gathereth vp againe with great diligence, putting them into his calendar, for Saints and
cheife pillars of his new Church, & fo confequently maketh his Church of our fhue-
clouts. Which how honorable a thing it
may be efteemed, lett euery man iudge: for
if thefe heretiks did agree with him in all
points of his doctrine, though by ioyning
with them he fhould fhew himfelfe an heretike: yet they not agreeinge but in fome
points only, and impugning him in the reft,
it fheweth a maruelous bafe mynd & lacke
of common fenfe, to make them pillars of
his Church, as he doth.

13.   But there is yet another point worfe
then this. Which is, that he doth not only
allow of the religion of thefe men, but defendeth alfo, and iuftifieth their life and
actions in what caufe foeuer, and though
neuer fo orderly and lawfully condemned
by the Church or ftate of thofe dayes, yea
though they were conuinced to haue con-
fpired the Kings murder and ruyne to
the ftate, or had broken forth into open
warre and hoftility againft the fame.
As did *Syr Iohn Old caftle* (by his wife called
L. *Cobham*)

L. *Kobham*) *Syr Roger Acton* and many other their followers, in the first yeare of *K. Henry* the 5.which story you may read in *Iohn Stovv* truly related out of *Thomas VValsingham* and other auncient wryters.

*Sto. & VValsingham an.*1414.

14. He setteth downe also without blushinge (I meane Fox) as well the records of the chauncery, as the act of parliament it selfe , wherby they were condemned of open treason and confessed rebellion ; For which 69. were condemned in one day by publike sentence; and yet doth the madd fellow take vpon him to excuse and defend them all by a long discourse of many leaues togeather. Scoffing and iesting, as well at their arraigment and sentence giuen, as also at the act of parliament holden at *Leicester anno* 2. ' *Henr.* 5. *cap.* 7. and in 'the yeare of Christ 1415. And after all he setteth forth in contempt of this publike iudgment, a great painted pagent or picture of those , that were hanged for that fact of open rebellion in *S. Giles* field in London , as of true Saints and martyrs. Namely of *Syr Roger Acton* and others, *pag.* 540. And some leaues after that againe, he setteth out another particular pagent of the seuerall execution of *Syr Iohn Oldcastle* with this tittle: *The description of the cruell martyrdome of Syr Iohn Oldcastle L. Cobham.* And more then this, he appointeth vnto them their seuerall festiuall dayes in redd letters

*Fox from pag.*530, *to* 540.

Fox pag. 592.

letters (which were the dayes of their hanginge) as vnto ſolemne martyrs, the firſt
vpon the 6. of Ianuary with this title: *Syr*
Roger Acton Knight martyr, And the other vpon
the fifth of February with this inſcription
in his calendar: *Syr Iohn Oldcaſtle L. Cobham*
martyr. Wherby we may ſee, that theſe men
do not meaſure things, as they are in them
ſelues: but as they ſerue to maintaine their
faction.

15.   And it is further to be noted, that albeit theſe two rebellious knights *(Acton* and
Oldcaſtle) beſides all other their conuicted
crimes ; did make pub'ike profeſsion of a
farre different faith from Iohn Fox (as may
be ſeene by the confeſsions & proteſtations
ſett downe by Fox himſelfe)yea & the later
of them alſo, did openly recant all the errors
and hereſies, that he had held before : yet
notwithſtandinge will not Fox ſo let them
goe, but perforce will haue them to be of
his Church whether they will or noe. It
would be ouerlonge to rehearſe many examples, ſome few ſhall yow haue for a taſt.

16.   Page 512. Fox ſetteth downe the proteſtation of *Syr Iohn Old caſtle* with this title:
The Chriſtian beleefe of the Lord Cobham . By
which title yow ſee that he liketh well of
his beleefe, and holdeth it for truly Chriſtian. Well, marke what followeth. When
after other articles about the bleſſed trinity
and

For ma-
keth ad-
uerſary
heretiks,
of his
Church
vvhe-
ther they
vvill or
noe.

& Chrifts deity, *Syr Iohn Oldcaftle* commeth
to treat of the Sacrament of the aultar he
protefteth thus : *And for as much as I am falfely*
accufed of a misbeleefe in the Sacrament of the
aultar: I fignify heere to all men, that this is my faith
concerning that : I beleeue in that Sacrament to be
conteyned very Chrifts body and bloud, vnder the fi-
militudes of vvyne and bread, yea the fame body that
vvas conceaued of the holy Ghoft, borne of the Virgin
Mary, donne on the croffe, died and vvas buryed, and
arofe the third day from the death, and novv is glori-
fied in heauen. This was his confefsion & is related heere by Fox, & wil Fox agree to this,
thinke yow? It may be he will, for that he
faith nothing againft yt at all in this place.
17. But fome leaues after, repeating another teftimonial of the faid *Oldcaftles* beleefe
witneffed by his owne frends, concerninge
this article, he wryteth thus : *Furthermore he*
beleeueth that the bleffed facrament of the aultar is
verily and truly Chriftes body in forme of bread.
Vpon which words Fox maketh this commentary in the margent: *In forme of bread but*
notvvithout bread, he meaneth. Yea, Iohn, is that
his meaning? how then ftandeth this, with
his former words, *vnder the fimilitudes of bread*
and vvyne? Is the fimilitude of bread, true
bread? who feeth not this filly fhift of a
poore bayted Fox, that cannot tell whether
to turne his head? But marke yet a farre
worfe fhift.

18. *Syr*

18.   *Syr Iohn Oldcaſtle* ſhewinge his beleefe about 3. ſorts of men, the one of Saints now in heauen, the ſecond in purgatory, the third

Fox pag. 314.

here militant vpon earth, ſaith thus: *The holy Church I beleeue to be diuided into three ſorts or companyes, vvherof the firſt are novv in heauen, &c. the ſecond ſort are in purgatory abiding the mercy of God and a full deliuerance of payne. The third vpon earth, &c.* To this ſpeech of purgatory, Fox

Fox his perfidious dealinge.

thought beſt, (leaſt it might diſgrace his new martyr) to add this parentheſis of his owne (*if any ſuch place be in the ſcriptures, &c.*) and by this you may perceyue, how he proceedeth in all the reſt: to witt, moſt perfidiouſly like a Fox in all.

19.   Furthermore he ſetteth downe at length a very ample and earneſt recantation of the ſaid *Syr Iohn Oldcaſtle* taken out of the records, as authentically made as can be de-

Fox pag. 519.

uiſed. Wherin he thus proteſted. *In nomine Dei, amen, I Iohn Oldcaſtle denounced, detected and conuicted of and vpon diuers articles ſauouring hereſy and error, &c. I being euill ſeduced by diuers ſeditious preachers, haue greuouſly erred, heretically perſiſted, blaſphemouſly anſvvered, and obſtinately rebelled, &c.* And hauing recounted at length all his former condemned and hereticall

The abiuration of Syr Iohn Old caſtle.

opinions, he endeth thus: *Ouer and beſides all this, I Iohn Oldcaſtle vtterly forſaking and renouncing all the aforeſaid errors and hereſies and all other like vnto them, lay my hand heere vpon this booke & euangell*

euangell of God, and svveare, that I shall neuer more
from henceforth hold these aforesaid heresies, nor yet
any other like vnto them vvittingly, &c. All which
recantation and abiuration being related at
large by Iohn Fox; he saith nothinge at all
against it: but only that it was deuised *by the*
Bishops vvithout his consent. Alleaginge no one
author, wittnes, wrytinge, record, reason,
or probable coniecture for proofe therof,
but folloveth the fond shift before touched
by me against the *Magdeburgenses* of him, that
being accused of heynous crimes bringeth
in first the best wittnesses of all the citty to
proue the same against himselfe, and then
answereth all with only sayinge, that they
are lyars and know not what they say. In
which kind I cannot omitt to alleage an
example or two more for your better satisfaction in this behalfe.

Supra
part. 1.
cap. 5.

20 This Fox in his protestation to the
Church of England, wherin he pretendeth
to put the very summe of all his whole volume, being desirous to proue the antiquity
of this his visible Church, not only by these
wittnesses, (the *VVicklifsians, Hussits, Lollards*
and other sectaries of that tyme aboue 200.
yeares gone) but also by the testimonyes of
diuers statutes and acts of parlaments made
against them in England at the same tyme:
he cyteth sundry statutes and acts of Parlament for that purpose, and presently discrediteth

diteth the ſame againe tellinge yow, that
yow muſt not beleeue them, but rather him
and his words againſt them all. yow ſhall
heare him in his owne words.

Fox in
his prot.
pag. 10.
21.   Let any man (ſaith he) peruſe the acts
and ſtatutes of Parlaments, paſſed in this
Realme of auncient tymes, & therin conſi-
,, der the courſe of tymes, where he may find
,, and read *Anno 5. Reg. Richardi 2.* in the yeare
,, of our Lord 1380. of a great number, that
,, there be called euill perſons goinge about
,, from towne to towne in freeſe gownes,
,, preachinge vnto the people, &c. Which

Fox his
facility
in reie-
ctinge
parla-
ments.
preachers though the words of the ſtatute
do tearme them to be diſſembling perſons,
preaching diuers ſermons conteyning hereſies and notorious errors, to the emble-
miſhment of Chriſtian faith, &c. Yet not-
,, withſtandinge may euery true Chriſtian
,, Reader conceaue of thoſe preachers to haue
,, taught no other Doctrine, then now they
,, heare their owne preachers in pulpitts
,, preach, &c.

22.   Marke heere 3. points (good Reader.)
Firſt, that if all this were true, that the VVickliffians had preached no other doctrine, then
the proteſtants do now : yet nothing followeth of this, but that proteſtants doctrine
was condemned for hereſie not only by the
Church lawes, but alſo by diuers acts of Engliſh parlaments aboue 200. yeares paſt.
                                        Which

Which thinge what help or creditt it can bring to Fox his religion, which ſtandeth cheeſly in England by authority of farre later acts of parlament, I do not ſee. For that herof only may be inferred two cōcluſions, yf his premiſes be true. The firſt, that proteſtants were condemned for heretiks by acts of parlament 200. yeares gone. The ſecond, if thoſe auncient acts of parlaments were of little force in matters of religion: then later acts, that haue eſtabliſhed a different religion, may alſo be called in queſtion, and that with much more reaſon and probability.

23. Secondly I ſay, that this aſſertion of Fox is moſt apparantly falſe (to witt, that the Wickliffian preachers taught no other doctrine, then now do teach the proteſtant preachers) if the articles before alleaged out of himſelfe, be truly written by him. For neither do the proteſtant preachers in England at this day teach the *reall preſence* in the bleſſed ſacrament of the altar, or the *doctrine of purgatory* (as yow haue heard *Syr Iohn Oldcaſtle* a cheefe *VVickliffian* profeſſe a little before) nor yet do proteſtants hold thoſe articles of *Iohn VVickliffe* himſelfe, (which in this chapter we haue mētioned) as held nether by them nor vs. And much leſſe do they hold any other Cath. opinions, which the *VVickliffians* did, togeather with

I i   their

their heresies. So as this is a notorious vn-
truth and cannot be dissembled or denied.

24. Thirdly, we may consider of the particular point which before I noted, that
Iohn Fox is not ashamed to cite a whole
parlament, against himselfe: and then in a
word to reiect the same, as of no creditt in
the world, in respect of him and his deniall
or reiection. *The parlament* (saith he) *calleth
those freese govvne preachers (the VVickliffians) dissembling persons: but yovv must thinke notvvithstan-
ding, they vvere very honest men.* The parlament
saith, that they preached heresies and notorious errors: but Iohn Fox saith, it was true
Christian doctrine. Whome shall we heere
beleue, either the whole parlament, who
liued with them and examined both their
doctrine and doings, or Iohn Fox, that cometh more then 200. yeares after them, and
will needs make himselfe their brother
whether they will or noe: and iudge also of
the parlament? But lett vs heare him yet
further.

Fox pag.
10. *in
protest.*
Another
parla-
mét re-
iected
by Fox.
25. *Furthermore* (saith he) *yovv shall find like-
vvise in statuto anno* 2. *Henr.*4.*cap.*15. *in the yeare
of our Lord* 1402. *another like company of godly
preachers and faithfull defenders of true doctrine.
VVhome albeit the vvords of the statute there,
through corruption of tyme, do falsely tearme to be
false & peruerse preachers vnder dissembled holynes,
teachinge in those dayes openly and priuily nevv do-*
ctrine

ctrine and hereticall opinions, &c. Yet notvvithstan-
dinge vvhosoeuer readeth historyes, and the orderly
descent of tymes, shall vnderstand these to be no false
teachers, but faithfull vvitnesses of the truth, &c.

26. Lo heere the teitimony of another
parlament of our countrey held 22. yeares
after the former, which Iohn Fox reiecteth,
with the same facility, that he did the other.
For wheras the parlament, that had examined the matter, protesteth, that they had
found them false, peruerse and dissembling
people teaching new doctrine & hereticall
opinions: Fox auerreth the contrary, *that*
they vvere good preachers, and faithfull defenders of
true doctrine, and holy vvittnesses of Gods truth. And
for proofe heerof, he saith, *that vvhosoeuer rea-*
deth historyes, and conferreth the order and descent of
tymes shall vnderstand thus much to be true. But
how & by what meanes a man shall gather
this vnderstanding, he telleth vs not. And
by the historicall discourses and conference
of tymes, which we haue hitherto made in
this booke, we vnderstand the contrary.
Findinge in deed by descent and order of
tymes, that these opinions of *VVickliffe, Husse*
and *Lollards* and the like, were new hereticall opinions in deed, and taken and iudged
so by all Christendome at their vprising; &
appearance in the world. Wherfore this is
playne impudency in Fox, to say that by
readinge histories and notinge descent of

tymes, theſe men are by him iuſtified from
being ſectaryes.

Fox ib.   27.   It followeth in Fox: *Of the like number*
pag. 10.   *alſo (ſaith he) of like true faithfull fauourers and*
followers of Gods holy word, we find in the yeare of
our Lord 1422. ſpecified in a letter ſent from Henry
Chicheſley Archbishop of Canterbury to Pope Martyn
the 5. of many infected heere in England (as he ſaid)
by the hereſies of Vuickliffe and Huſſe, &c. Who
though they be tearmed for heretiks & ſchiſmatikes:
yet ſerued they the liuinge Lord, within the arke of
his true ſpirituall and viſible Church. And where is
then the friuolous bragg of the papiſtes, which make
ſo much of their painted ſheaths, &c.

28.   Do yow ſee in what ioylity of mynd
Iohn Fox is put by findinge out this ſucceſſion of his new viſible Church for aboue
200. yeares downward? Do yow heare
how he vaunteth of antiquity & long continuance? albeit indeed he nameth not con-
Yf Vuick- tinuance, nor can he. Fot that (I thinke) he
kliffian   will not graunt, that the *Vuickliffian* Church
prea-   doth endure vnto this day, or that if a num-
chers   ber of thoſe *Vuickliffian* holy teachers and
were   faithfull wittneſſes of the truth, ſo much
now   prayſed heere by him, ſhould come into
aliue the *England* at this day, or *Scotland*, or into *Germa-*
prote-   *ny* or *Geneua*, or among any other ſect or ſort
ſtants   of proteſtants whatſoeuer, & ſhould preach
would   that doctrine, which they preached then,
not ad-   (to witt, againſt the Church of Rome in
mitt   many
them.

many points, but yet defendinge that number of sacraments which they did, the *Reall presence, sacrifice of the masse*; togeather with those extrauagant articles also before mentioned, to witt, *that it is against the scriptures that Bishops or true ministers should haue any temporall lands and liuings; and that tythes are not due, & that both princes and Prelats, do leefe their off.ces, authorityes, and dignityes, vvhensoeuer they fall into mortall sinne, &c.*) Yf these men, (I say) that were so true preachers and principall guiders of the arke of Iohn Fox his true visible and spirituall Church in those dayes, should reuiue and preach againe in these dayes: would his brethren the protestants in England or out of England receyue them, thinke yow? and if it be certayne, that they would not: how were they true preachers then, and not now? or how can these and they be true brethren of one faith, religion, or Church? Doth not euery simple man or woman see this folly and absurd contradiction?

29. But to returne to the matter in hand about reiectinge Parlaments and other publike testimonyes, we see that Iohn Fox with the same facility both reciteth and reiecteth the letter of the Archbishop of Canterbury wrytten to the Pope, about those *VVickliffians* of his tyme 20. yeares after the former Patlament was holden. But yet

in con-

conformity of that which the ſaid Parlamēt vnder K.*Henry* the fourth, & the other before vnder K.*Richard* the 2. did teſtifie : as well of the ſaid ſectaryes hypocriſy and diſſimulation; as of their wicked errors & hereſies. All which Fox cōtemninge, ſaith to the cōtrary, *that they ſerued faithfully the liuing Lord vvithin the arke of his true ſpirituall and viſible Church, &c.*

30.   And it is to be noted, that ſcarſe euer throughout this whole volume of acts, and monuments from Chriſt downward (for the ſpace of 1400. yeares) doth Fox talke of any viſible Church on his ſide, but only now, when he commeth to theſe *VVickliſfians* and other like ſectaryes. And yet, to ſpeake warily alſo, he adioyneth vnto it the word *ſpirituall* to haue ſome ſtarting hole to runne out, when he ſhalbe preſſed about the true nature of viſible ſucceſſion. Which we meane to do in the next chapter following. But in the meane ſpace, it is a matter worth good laughter to heare him ſay, *that papiſts do bragg of their paynted ſheath, concerning their Churches antiquity and ſucceſſion: and that he hath ſufficiently proued before by the continuall deſcent of his Church after the doctrine that novv is reformed, that it hath ſtood and byn continued from the beginninge* (for ſo are his words) yea and that *viſibly* as now he addeth. Wherat (I know) no man can chuſe but laughe, that hath read this our Treatiſe. Wherin we
haue

Hovv Fox hath found out a viſible Church & from vvhēce.

Hovv the mēbers of I. Fox his viſible Church do hang togeather.

haue shewed all the contrary, to witt the visible discent of the Roman Church by orderly succession from th'Apostles tyme, and that Iohn Fox hath not so much as named any different succession, or discent of his Church distinct from the other, vntill the time of *Innocentius* 3. 1200. yeares after Christ. And what maner of deductiō or collection of heretiks & sectaryes he bringeth downe from thence, and how well they agree and hang togeather, eyther in tyme, place, function or faith, we shall examine a little after. 31. But now before we end this chapter, we are to aduertise the Reader, that besides the sects before named of the *Petrobusiãs, Henricians, VValdensians* or poore men of *Lions,* the *Albigensians,* & *VVicklissians:* there was another sect in England called *Lollards* more famous then the rest, in respect of *Lollards Tovver* somwhat renowned in *London* for the imprisonmēts of those Sectaryes in that place. But when and how this sect of heretiks began, is not so cleere. For that some (as *Prateolus* and others) seeme to affirme that it tooke his origin in England as a brood of the *VVicklisists,* for that they were more famous there, then in other places. And therfore he saith *Lollardi ex Anglia & ex VViclississtarum secta originem duxerunt.* The *Lollards* had their beginning from England, & from the sect of the *VVickliffians.* And he addeth, that

Of Lollards & their beginning in England. *Prat.lib.* 10. *heres.* *pag.* 157.

I i 4   it was

it was about the yeare 1360. Which cannot
ſtand. For that we haue ſhewed before, how
VVickliffe began to publiſh his doctrine after
this: to witt, about the yeare 1370. Wherfore the Abbot *Tritemius*, a German Chronicler, declareth the matter more particu-

Trit. in larly and truly, ſayinge : *That there vvas a cer-*
chron. *tayne heretike in Germany called Gualter Lolhard,*
an. Do- *vvho about the yeare of Chriſt* 1315. takinge cer-
mini tayne doctrine from the *Albigenſes* and *VVal-*
1315. *denſes*, that went before him, and adding (as
the faſhion is of ſectaryes) diuers new opinions of his owne, made a particular ſect,
who were called *Lolhards*. Wherby it appeareth, that this ſect began in Germany aboue
50. yeares before the ſect of *VVickliffe* in England, and heerby enſued, that *VVickliffians*
taking afterwards diuers opinions from the
ſaid *Lolhards* were comonly alſo called *Lol-*
hards. And Iohn Fox himſelfe recytinge the
ſentence of Condemnation of B. *Treſnant* of
Herford againſt one *VVilliam Svvynderby*, an
Apoſtata Prieſt, for *VVickliffian* hereſies, (in
the yeare of Chriſt 1391. the 24. of Iune) he
ſetteth downe theſe words of the ſaid Bi-

Fox pag. ſhopp: We being excited through the infor-
429. col. mation of many credible & faithfull Chri-
1. n. 15. ſtians of our *Dioceſſe* to roote out peſtiferous
„ plantes, as ſheep diſeaſed with an incurable
„ ſickneſſe, going about to infect the whole
„ and ſound flocke, that is to ſay certayne
preachers,

preachers, or more truly execrable offen- *VVicklif-*
ders, of the new sect, vulgarly called *Lol-* *fians* vve
hards, &c. re called
Lollards.

32. Lo heere *VVickliffians* at this tyme (for
such a one was this *Svvindery*) were commonly called *Lohards* 20. yeates and more
after *VVickliffe* had begunne his doctrine. So
as rather *VVickliffians* are to be said to haue
come forth of *Lolhards*, then *Lolhards* of *VVic-*
kliffians.

33. And albeit these two sects beginning,
(as yow haue heard) the one in Germany,
and the other in England, with the distance
of some 50. yeares of their offspring, had many opinions common to them both (especially against the Roman Church, against
inuocation of Saints, fastings, prayers and
the sacraments of pennance, matrimony,
extreme vnction and the like:) yet had they
their peculiar opinions also, wherby they
were made a seuerall sect. As for example,
the *Lolhards* impugned not only the forsaid The pe-
3. sacraments of *pennance*, *Matrimony and ex-* culiar
treme vnction (as some *VVickliffians* did:) but opiniōs
Baptisme, and the *Euchariste*, in like manner. *Lollards.*
They held also for their peculiar opinions, *Trit ib.*
(as *Tritemius* saith) that *Lucifer* with the rest
of his Angells were iniuriously thrust out of 1.
heauen by *Michaëll* and his Angells, and consequently to be restored againe at the day of
iudgment. And that *Michaëll* & his Angells,
I i 5 are to

are to be damned for the forſaid iniury and to be deliuered ouer to euerlaſtinge puniſhment, from the day of iudgment forward.

2.   That our lady: could not beare Chriſt and remayne a virgin, for that ſo he ſhould haue

3.   byn an Angell, and not a man. That God hauinge giuen the earth to the vſe of man, accordinge to the ſayinge of the pſalme *Ter-*

*Pſal.*113 *ram autem dedit filijs hominum,* God hath giuen the earth to the children of men : he doth conſequently puniſh ſuch wickednes, as is done vpon earth. But if any thinge be done vnder ground, it is not puniſhable. And therfore in caues and cellers vnder ground, they were accuſtomed to exerciſe all abhomination.And of this he relateth a certayne ſtory happened in Germany, which was that one *Giſla* (a yong woman of their ſect) cominge to be burned for hereſie, ſhe was asked whether ſhe were a virgin or noe: whervnto ſhe anſwered,that aboue ground ſhe was, but vnder ground not.

Flagel- 34.   There followed many other hereſies
lantes or alſo from this time downward vnto *K.Hen-*
vvhip- *ry* the 8. dis dayes,which preuayled diuersly
ping he in diuers countreyes, as the *Flagellants* or
retiks whippers, which made a new baptiſme of
an. Dom. bloud, & held diuers articles of the *Lolhards*
1350. in Germany and Hungary about the yeare
Trit. in of Chriſt 1350.as *Tritemius* ſaith. The *Huſſites*
chron. alſo in *Bohemia*, who had their doctrine of
*an.*1350   *Iohn*

Iohn Husse scholer of *Iohn Vuickliffe* (but yet in
diuers articles differinge from him) about
the yeare of Chrift 1415. as *Aeneas Syluius* declareth at large. And vpon this mans teachinge, and the doctrine of *Hierome* of *Prage*
(that liued at the fame tyme) there fpronge
vp diuers different fects in *Bohemia*, as the
*Orebites, Adamites, Drecentians, Gallecians, Roche-
zanites, Iacobites, Thaborites* and others. Wherof *Aeneas Syluius, Bonfinius*, and other authors
do treate. And *Bonfinius* writeth, that *Mathias*
K. of Hungary was wont to fay in his daies,
that the fects and fectaryes of *Bohemia* were
fo diuers and contrary one to the other, as if
no other argument were againft them, this
were fufficient to ouerthrow them all. And
the fame confufion remayneth there vnto
this day.

*Aeneas
Sylu. hir
ftor. Bo-
hem. cai
35.*

The di-
uerfity
of fects
amongft
the Huf-
fits.
*Bon. De-
cad. 4.
lib. 2.*

35. And this fhall fuffice for the herefies of
this fifth Station of time: efpecially fuch as
preuayled moft in England from *Vuickliffe*
vnto K. *Henry* the 8. in whofe dayes *Luther*
rofe vp and made a new fect. For albeit in
many points he fymbolized & had concurrance with moft of thefe fects, but efpecially with the *Lolhards* and *Vuickliffians* (vnder
whofe names all fectaries comonly couered
themfelues in our countrey:) yet had *Luther*
diuers points alfo peculiar to him, and his,
which made them properly a diftinct and
feuerall fect. Which himfelfe confeffeth in
like

like manner difclayminge by name from *Huſſe* and *Huſſits*, in theſe wor ds: *Non recte faciunt, qui me Huſſitam vocant: non enim mecum ille ſenſit.* They do not well that call me a *Huſſite.* For he doth not agree with me in doctrine. And as for *VVickliffe* we may ſee the ſame iudgment of *Luther* by the teſtimony of *Philipp Melancthon,* that faith of him: *nec intellexit nec tenuit fidei iuſtitiam*, he neither vnderſtood nor held the iuſtice of faith, which is the very foundation of Luthers Ghoſpell and doctrine.

Luth. in reſponſ. ad Roſſenſem art. 30.

Melant. epiſt. ad Freder Mechonium.

36.   And againe in the ſame place, he obiecteth diuers other erroneous doctrines vnto him, *as that he doth take avvay all ciuill and politike gouernment : that he holdeth for vnlavvfull to Prieſts to poſſeſſe any thing proper, that no tithes are to be paid*, and the like. Which doctrines of *VVickliffe* notwithſtandinge our *Iohn Fox* defendeth, commending highely the teachers and profeſſors therof in all his tract of tyme from *K. Edvvard* the 3. to *K. Henry* the 8. canonizinge them for Saints that were any way puniſhed or called in queſtion for any of theſe doctrines, vnder the raignes of the *K. Richard* the ſecond or *K. Henry* the 4. fifth, ſixt, or ſeauenth, and other Kings of that tyme. And in this argument is ſpent the whole ſumme of his fifth and ſixt books, in which books the very titles of the pages may ſufficiently teſtifie, what is handled therin.

therin. As for example page 406. vnder the
raigne of K. *Richard* the second, is this title:
The first lavv for burninge the professors of the Gho-
spell. Wherby yow see, that he calleth all
these men, whether they be *VVickliffians,*
Hussits, or *Lolhards,* professors of Christs Ghospell, and consequently must he needs hold
for euangelicall truth all, which they did
hold. And so in effect de doth, in handlinge
their causes throughout these two bookes
against the Bishopps and Princes, that
punished them: though in cleere words
and Categoricall propositions he dare not
do yt.

Anno
Domini
1382.

37. And this is the stuttering and stamme-
ringe, turninge and wyndinge 'of this our
Fox, as you neuer can know where to haue
him. For that now he affirmeth, now he
denieth, now he leaueth the matter doubtfull, now he moueth a question, but solueth
it not: now he gainsaieth and contradicteth
himselfe. Now he saith one thing in words,
and prosecuteth another in deed. As for example, he confesseth before in words, as
yow haue heard, that *VVickliffe had diuers ble-*
mishes in doctrine (that is to say, errors and heresies) & so it may appeare, as well by that,
which we haue sett downe therof, as also
by the iudgment of *Melancthon*: and yet in
prosecution of his worke, Iohn Fox will
not sticke to commend the worst of those

Hovv
Fox be-
haueth
himselfe
in defen-
dinge
VVicklif-
sians and
their do-
ctrine.

doctrines,

doctrines , as we may fee by the vety titles of the pages fett ouer thefe books.

38.   As for example, page 420. he putteth this title ouer the faid page: *Temporalities may be taken from the Cleargy,&c.* And then yet further in the fame page , he putteth this head or beginning to a long difcourfe about this matter in thefe words: *The fecond difputation in the vniuerfity of Prage , vpon the* 17. *Article of Iohn VVickliffe moft fruitfull to be read, prouing by* 24. *reafons out of the fcriptures, that temporall Lords and Princes, may take avvay tēporalityes from the cleargy, &c.* This is the title of this fruitfull difcourfe for takinge away all temporall fruits from the cleargy. But how fruitfull foeuer this difputation may feeme to Iohn Fox againft cleargy temporalityes, that perhaps could gett none for himfelfe ; yet to others of his cleargy, that poffeffe temporalityes, I doubt much whether it will feeme fo fruitfull, or be fo well liked of as by Iohn Fox, who for his 24. reafons alleaged for the fame , may chance be related into fome rank of the 24. orders, fitt for a man of his degree and meritts.

39.   Moreouer page 426. he hath this title: *Tythes proued to be pure almes.* Which title I thinke alfo will not greatly contēt the moft of his fellow minifters, yf their parifhioners fhould ftand vpon this doctrine with them, to witt ; *that their tythes are pure almes* accor-
                                          dinge

dinge to the Ghospell of *Iohn VVickliffe* and
Iohn Fox: And consequently they may deny,
or deteyne them when they list, or giue so
much therof vnto Ministers as they list and
no more, which oftentimes perhaps would
be very little. But what would these ministers, thinke you, (but especially their wiues
& children say of this doctrine) if once they
felt hunger come vpon them therby? yet
Fox prosecuteth the same title ouer other
pages. As for example page 446. he hath
these words: *Tythes not expressely commaunded a*
nevv by Christ; and then hath he this other
note: Yf Tythes be claymed by force of the
old law, then Priests by the same law are
bound to haue no temporalityes. And this
matter Fox doth prosecute at large, as one
Article among other, of one *VValter Brute* a
lay-man of the sect of *VVickliffe*. In whome
saith Fox, *the mighty operation of Gods spiritt did*
effectuate such constancy, as in this and other Articles
he resisted openly the B. of Herford *in his time, &c.*
Lo heere the approbation of *Brute* his spirit,
whose 4. Article was, as Fox himselfe setteth downe: *That no man is bound to giue Tythes:*
And yf any man vvill needs giue, he may giue to
vvhome he vvill, excludinge therby their curates.
Another article also was of the said *Brute:*
That a Priest receyuinge by bargaine any thinge of
yearly annuity, is therby a schismatike and excom-
municate. Which if it be true, then are his

marginal notes:
Fox al-
loweth
taking
avvay of
tithes &
tempo-
ralities
from the
clergy.

Fox pag.
348.

                                    ministers

miniſters in a hard caſe at this day in England, who do bargine for their ſeruice, and wages due thervnto.

40.　And ſo goeth Fox on from point to point to ratify *Iohn VVickliffes* doctrine, or at leaſt the profeſſors therof. Not conſideringe (ſimple fellow) how much they differ from him or make againſt him, ſo they be contrary to the Pope of Rome, or condemned by him. For further proofe of which folly and blind ignorance, we ſhall paſſe now to treat in a ſeuerall chapter, what manner of continuance and ſucceſsion of his Church he deuiſeth, throughout the rabble of theſe oppoſite ſects, from the tyme of *Pope Innocentius* the 3. to the raigne of K. *Henry* the 8. wherby I doubt not, but the reader will remayne ſufficiently inſtructed of theſe mens madneſſe, that of ſo contrary and repugnant ſpirits will needs frame to themſelues the vnity of a true Chriſtian Church.

THE

THE MOST ABSVRD AND

RIDICVLOVS SVCCESSION OF *Sectaryes* appointed by *Iohn Fox* for the continuance of his Church from *Pope* Innocentius 3.
dovvnvvards: vvhere alfo by this occafion,is declared the true nature and conditions of lavvfull Ecclefiaficall fucceßion.

CHAP. X.

HAVING now followed Iohn Fox throu
ghout all this treatife from Chrifts time
to ours, to fee what vifible courfe and race
he would fett downe,afwell of his Church,
as oures (accordinge to his promife made in
the beginninge of his acts and monuments)
we haue found him hitherto to haue talked
only in a manner of our Church , that is to
fay of the vniuerfall Roman Church per-
fpicuously come downe by fuccefsion of
yeares and ages from th' Apoftles to vs,nei-
ther did *Iohn Fox* for twelue hundred yeares
togeather fo much as name vnto vs any
other congregatiõ of men or women, fmall
or great, good or badd (that in this tyme
bare the name of a Chriftian Church) befides the other. Nor did he pretend any fuccefsion , fearinge perhaps thofe words of
Tertullian ✱ before recited : *Confingant tale ali-*
quid hæretici, &c. Let heretiks prefume to
feigne or deuife any fuch fucce{sion of Bi-

✱ *Supra*
cap. 10.
Tertull.
l. de præ-
fcript.

K k   fhops

ſhops teachers & Paſtors for their Church, as we haue alleaged for ours if they dare.

2.   But now from *Pope Innocentius* tyme downwards, Iohn Fox preſuminge that all the other Church was fallen from God (a great preſumption indeed, as before hath byn ſhewed) he bringeth vs forth in place therof another company of men, which he ſaith in thoſe dayes made the true Church, (for that they were condemned by the other Church which he holdeth for the falſe.) And theſe were a certayne rablement of Sectaryes different in opinions, & profeſsions not only from vs, but alſo from Iohn Fox & his crewe, & moſt of all among themſelues, being of diuers cotreyes, ſectes, times, ages, offices & functions, and cohering togeather in noe other forme at all of ſucceſsion, but that one roſe or ſpronge vp after the other. For which cauſe Fox himſelfe in his acts & monuments doth not handle their affayres as of any congregation, that euer met togeather, or ſaw perhaps one another, or had conference, order, ſubordination or ſucceſsion among themſelues, but only tieth them togeather in a certayne liſt or catalogue as Sampſons foxes were by the tayles. Which liſt or catalogue he ſetteth downe in his forſaid proteſtation to the Church of England. Tellinge vs firſt, that duringe the tyme of the laſt 400. yeares from *Pope Innocentius* down-

Iudic. 15.

downwards, *the true Church of Christ durst not*   *Fox in*
openly appeare in the face of the vvorld, being oppres- *protest.*
sed by tiranny. But yet that it remayned from tyme to *ad Eccl.*
tyme visibly in certayne chosen members,that not only *Angl.*
bare secret good affection to sincere doctrine, but stood
also in the defence of truth against the Church of
Rome.

3. This is his affertion, which he proueth
by a large lift or catalogue (as I haue faid) of
fundry that were in this tyme cenfured and
condemned in fome part of doctrine by the
faid Roman Church. *In vvhich catalogue* (faith *Fox ib.*
he) *firft to pretermit Bertramus, and Beringarius,* *pag. 10.*
vvhich vvere before Pope Innocentius the third a
* *learned multitude of fufficient vvittneffes heere* * *VVhat*
might he produced, vvhose names neyther are obscure *learning*
nor doctrine vnknovvne, as Ioachim Abbot of Cala- *they*
bria, Almaricus a learned Bishopp that vvas iudged *vvere of*
an heretike for holding against Images : besides the *you shall*
martyrs of Alfatia of vvhome vve read a hundred to *see after-*
be burned by Pope Innocentius in one day. Adde like- *vvards.*
vvyse (faith he) *to these the VValdenses, and Al-*
bigenses , Marsilius Patauinus, Gulielmus de Sancto
Amore , Symon Tornacensis, Arnoldus de noua villa,
Ioannes Semica , besides diuers others preachers in
Sueuia ftanding against the Pope, anno 1240. *&c.*

4. Thus beginneth Fox his catalogue,and
then goeth he forward with *Ioannes Anglicus*
a maifter of *Paris, Petrus Ioannis* a mynorite, *Marke*
burned after his death, *Robert Groshead Bishop* *vvhat*
of Lincolne, called *Malleus Romanorum, &c.* *men les*
        Kk 2   And *doth*

And further he addeth *Ioannes de Ganduno,
Eudo Duke of Burgundy*, that counceled the
French King to receaue the Popes *Extraua-
gants Dantes* an Italian poet that wrote
againſt Popes, monks and friars, together
with Petrarcha & them *Conradus Hagaz*, impriſoned for preachinge againſt the maſſe
anno 1339. *&c.* And to theſe againe he coope-
leth *Franciſcus de Arcaterra* and others burned
for new opinions, *Gregorius Ariminenſis, Armachanus, Occham*, and others as though theſe
had byn all of the ſame opiniõs. And finally
he falleth vpon the *Lollards, VVickliffians, Huſ-
ſets,* and their followers in *England* & *Bohemia,*
ſuccedinge one after another now in this
contrey, now in that, now vpon one occaſion, & now vpon another; vntill the raigne
of *K. Henry* the 8. when *Martyn Luther* began
his profeſſion, who did agree and ſimbolize
in diuers points with the ſaid former ſects
of *VValdenſes* & *Albigenſes, Lollards, VVickliffians*
and *Huſſites* and differed in others as before
hath b/n declared and after the Lutherans
did follow agayne other partely agreinge,
& pertely diſagreinge, as *Svvinglius, Caluinus,
Beza, Oecolampadius,* & others vnto our dayes
and euery one affirminge his opinions to be
the new Ghoſpell.

5. And this is the viſible ſucceſſion (forſooth) which Iohn Fox hath deuiſed to ſett
downe for the proofe of his new Church,

and

and the antiquity therof for 400.yeares paſt.
And it is like, as yf a man in England to diſgrace the citty of London, ſhould ſeeke out
the records of all thoſe , that haue byn hanged at Tyborne for theft or murders for
400. yeares : and hauinge found them out,
ſhould produce them for wittneſſes of the
truth and for honeſt men & good cittizeus.
Condemninge both the iudges and Iurers,
and whole contrey, that gaue ſentence and
verdict againſt them. And yet if yow will
ſee how Iohn Fox playeth the foole indeed
& braggeth of this ſucceſsiō of his Church:
do yow harken what he wryteth preſently
vpon the enumeration of theſe forſaid pillars of his Church.

6.   *VVherfore yf any be ſo beguyled in his opinion*
(ſaith he   *as to thinke that the doctrine of the*
Church of Rome (as novv it ſtandeth,) be of ſuch an-
tiquity, and that the ſame vvas neuer impugned be-
fore the tyme o/ Luther and Zvvinglius novv of late:
lett him read theſe hiſtoryes , and peruſe the acts of
Parlaments paſſed in this Realme of auncient tyme,
as anno 5. *Regis Richardi* 2. 1380. *&c.* Did yow
euer heare a man in his witts reaſon in this
ſort? how doth this catalogue (I pray yow)
of condemned heretiks (for theſe laſt 400.
yeares) impugne the antiquity of the Roman Church or doctrine before that tyme?
And againe who doth deny, but that the
ſame Roman Church, and doctrine was

impugned by old heretiks long before *Lu-ther* and *Zvvinglius*? yea and before *VVickliffe*, *VValdenſes*, *Albigenſes*, and *Berengarius* were borne? as by our former deduction hath appeared, that ſhe was impugned by heretiks of euery age? And moreouer to what purpoſe doth Fox will vs to read theſe hiſtoryes, & the acts of parlaments paſſed againſt *VVickliffians* in the tyme of *K. Richard* the 2.? To what purpoſe (I ſay) doth this ſimple fellow talke & wryte this againſt himſelfe? ſeinge that by theſe hiſtoryes and ſtatutes we learne nothinge (as before we haue noted) but only that his elder brethren the *Lollards* & *VVickliffians* were condemned for heretiks by publike authority of our realme, aboue 200. yeares gone. Which we graunt vnto him without further proofe.

Fondrea ſoninge of Iohn Fox.

7. Wherfore to leaue this childiſh babling, that is without ſenſe, conſequence or reaſon, and to returne to ſome more ſerious argument:we ſhall handle heere two points for better diſcuſſion of this ſucceſsion of ſectaryes alleaged by Iohn Fox. Firſt, what are the conditions neceſſarily required to a good Eccleſiaſtical ſucceſsion,for demonſtrating a Church. And then, what manner of men theſe were indeed, which Fox doth heere aſsigne for repreſentation of his Church. And all ſhalbe done with as much breuity as may be.

Tvvo pointes to be handled in this chapter.

8. The

8. The first condition is, that this succession of men that make the Church, be vniuerfall both in place and time. That is to fay
(to vſe *S. Auguſtine* his words) *non quæ hoc loco
eſt, ſed quæ hoc loco, & per totum orbem terrarū: nec
illa quæ hoc tempore, ſed ab ipſo Abel, vſque in finem,
&c.* That it be not in this or that particular
place only, but in this place & throughout
the whole world, and that it be not only in
this or that time, but that it be from *Abell* to
the end of the worlde. By which words
of *S. Auguſtine* we ſee, that the viſibie ſucceſſion of the true Church muſt be vniuerſall,
firſt in place, and that it muſt be a viſible
company profeſsing Chriſt vnder one faith
and doctrine, not in this or that particular
contrey, prouince or place only, but ouer all
the world, where Chriſtians are. And ſo we
ſee it verified in the ſucceſsion of the Roman Church in our former deductions.

9. Secondly it muſt be vniuerſall in tyme,
for that it muſt not beginne from *Iohn VVickliffe* only, *Bertramus*, or *Berengarius* (as Iohn
Fox doth appoint the viſibility of his
Church) but it muſt come downe from the
Apoſtles, and endure viſibly to the end of
the world, yea from *Abell* himſelfe (as *S. Auguſtine* ſaith) for that euen from him Chriſt
inſtituted a viſible Church, and continued
the ſame by ſucceſſiō, vnder all three lawes
both of *Nature*, of *Moyſes*, and of *Grace*, as

The con-
ditions
of Eccl.
ſucceſ-
ſion.
*Aug. in
pſal.* 90.
Conc. 1.
& eadē
ferè in
pſal.* 56.
,,

True
ſucceſſiō
of the
Church
muſt be
vniuer-
ſall both
in place.
& time.

Saint

Saint Auguſtine in his books *de Ciuitate Dei* doth declare at large and in our dayes *Doctor Sanders* moſt learnedly in his excellēt worke *De viſibili Monarchia* doth proue the ſame.

10.   So as this collection of Sectaryes al-leaged heere by Iohn Fox, beinge neyther vniuerſall in place, nor agreeinge in faith with the vniuerſall knowne Church of Chriſtendome, but with particular aſſem-blies, (one in one place, & another in ano-ther) nor yet hauing vniuerſality of tyme, as not comming downe from th' Apoſtles age but only for ſome 400. yeares, as Fox him-ſelfe confeſſeth: theſe men (I ſay) cannot make a true Church though they haue ſome ſparks of true doctrine among them as Fox braggeth, ſeinge it is true which *S. Auguſtine* affirmeth: *Quicunque credunt, quòd Chriſtus Ieſus in carne venerit, & quòd ſit filius Dei, &c. Et tamen ab eius corpore, quod eſt Eccleſia ita diſſentiunt, vt eo-rum communio non ſit cum toto quacunque diffundi-tur, ſed in aliqua parte ſeparata inueniatur, mani-feſtum eſt eos non eſſe in Catholica Eccleſia.* Who-
,, ſoeuer doth beleeue that Chriſt Ieſus came
,, in fleſh, and that he is the ſonne of God, &c.
,, And that they do ſo diſcent from his body,
,, that is the Church, as they do not commu-
,, nicate with the whole ſpread ouer all parts,
,, but only with ſome ſeparate part, it is ma-
,, nifeſt that theſe men are not of the Cath.
,, Church: and thus much of the firſt cōdition.

Aug. l.
de vnit.
Eccleſia
cap. 4.

11. The

11. The second point to be considered is, when the auncient fathers do stand vpon visible succession of men, as a note of the true Church: they meane it specially by Bishops, that come downe by continuall succession from th'Apostles time to ours: *Ecclesia* (saith *Saint Augustine*) *ab Apostolorum temporibus per Episcoporum successiones certissimas vsque ad nostrum, & deinceps tempora, perseuerat.* The true Church doth perseuer from th'Apostles tyme vnto ours, and after vs againe, to the worlds end by most certayne succession of Bishops, &c. *Saint Irenæus* also, *Tertullian*, *Optatus*, and *Saint Augustine* before alleaged, do eych of them as yow haue heard deduce the visible succession of the Church from the Apostles to their dayes by the visible succession of the Roman Bishops.

12. And finally, the sentence of the said holy Father *Saint Augustine* is notoriously knowne in many parts of his works concerninge the importance of this succession: *Tenet me* (saith he) *in Ecclesia Catholica ab ipsa sede Petri ad præsentem Episcopatum successio sacerdotum.* The succession of Priests (he meaneth Bishops) from the Seat of *S. Peter* vnto the present B. of Rome holdeth me in the Cath. Church. And againe against his ould maister *Faustus* the Manichy: *Vides in hac re, quid Ecclesia Catholicæ valeat authoritas, quæ ab ipsis fundatissimis sedibus Apostolorum vsq3 ad hodiernū diem, succedentium*

Succession is vnderstood principally of Bishops.

Aug. l. 1. contra aduers. leg. & prophe. cap. 20.

Iren. l. 3. cap. 3. Tertull. de præscript. Opt. l. 2. contra Donat. Aug. ep. 165.

August. cont. ep. fundam. cap. 4.

Aug. l. 2. contra Faust. cap. 2.

>> *cedentium ſibimet Epiſcoporū ſerie,& tot populorum*
>> *conſenſione firmatur.* Doſt thou not ſee of what
>> force the authority of the Cath. Church is,
>> which being eſtabliſhed, by the moſt firme
>> foundations of the Apoſtolike Sea, doth en-
>> dure vnto this day by the race of Biſhops,
>> ſucceedinge one th' other, & by the conſent
>> of ſo many nations vnder their gouernmēt?

Foure points required in true ſucceſſiō of the Cath. Church.

13.   Behould heere 4. things eſpecially required by *S. Auguſtine* in ſucceſſion of men,
that muſt demonſtrate a true Church. Firſt,
that the cheefe heads therof muſt be Biſhops. Secondly, they muſt ſucceed orderly
one to another. Thirdly, they muſt come
downe from the very Apoſtles, as before
hath byn ſhewed. Fourthly, Chriſtian nations muſt agree in the ſame faith vnder
them. All which foure points are to be
found in the ſucceſsion of the vniuerſall
Roman Church, as yow haue ſeene: but no
one of them (and much leſſe all) are to be
found in this rabblement of hereſies and
ſectaryes, ſcraped togeather by Iohn Fox in
his former catalogue. For neither were they
Biſhopps at all, but priuate men, as after
ſhalbe ſhewed (though Fox moſt falſely
doth affirme one of them to haue bin a learned Biſhopp.) Nor did they ſucceed, in office, function, charge or Iuriſdiction the
one to the other, or concurred in one tyme,
countrey or place: but one in one corner and
another

another in another: one ftept vp in *Germany,* another in *France,* another in *Italy,* and another in *England.* The one a Prieft, another a friar another a marchant, & th' other a fouldiar or craftefman, of different ftates, profefsions, and conditions. Yea of different faith and religion alfo, as prefently fhalbe fhewed. Neither had they any relation one to the other, more then *Botley* to *Bilingfgate* or *Canterbury* to *Conftantinople.* And as for antiquity, and comming downe by fuccefsion from th' Apoftles, they are farre from yt, as Fox himfelfe confefseth, in that he beginneth his catalogue only from *Pope Innocentius* twelue hundred yeares after Chrift as yow haue heard. So as yf Chrift had any vifible Church before this tyme, it muft needs be oures, by Fox his owne confefsion.

The fuccefsiue pillars of Fox his Church haue no connexion or coherence the one vvith the other.

14. And finally, the laft point mentioned heere, & fo highely efteemed by *S. Auguftine* of the confent of people and nations, *tot populorum confenfione firmatur,* wherofhe maketh fuch accoumpt in another place, as he faith: *Anathema erit quifquis annunciauerit Ecclefiam præter communicationem omnium gentium:* He fhalbe accurfed, whofoeuer fhall fay the Church to be any other, but the communication of all nations. This quality, I fay, he that fhal confider & examine in thefe poore fellowes alleaged by Fox (who were but a few outcafts of euery countrey, where they fpronge)

Aug. ep. 48. ad Vincent. Rogatiã.

ſpronge) ſhall find it ſo ridiculous and contemptible a thinge in reſpect of the mayne
conſent of nations vnder the Roman
Church, as without laughter it cannot be
ſpoken of.

15. Finally of this ridiculous ſucceſsion of
heretiks the ſame holy father writeth fitly
in theſe words: *Videtis certè multos præciſos a*
radice Chriſtianæ ſocietatis, quæ per ſedes Apoſtolo-
rum & ſucceſsiones Epiſcoporum certa per orbem pro-
pagatione diffunditur, de ſola figura originis ſub
Chriſtiano nomine quaſi areſcentia ſarmenta glo-
riari, quas hæreſes & ſchiſmata nominamus. Truly
,, yow ſe many cutt of from the roote of this
,, Chriſtian ſociety *(the Church)* which ſocie-
,, ty is ſpread ouer all the world by the ſeats of
,, th' Apoſtles, and ſucceſsion of Biſhops as it
,, were by a moſt certayne propagation or ge-
,, neration, and theſe fellowes do bragg of a
,, certayne figure or ſimilitude of a beginning
or ſucceſsion vnder the name of Chriſtians,
but are indeed withered branches cutt of
from the vyne, and theſe we call heretiks
and ſchiſmatiks. Thus ſaith *Saint Auguſtine.*
And could any man deſcribe better, the
apiſh imitation of Iohn Fox endeauou-
ring to bring in his ſucceſsion of a few condemned heretiks *de ſola figura originis ſub Chri-*
ſtiano nomine gloriantes, bragging only of a certayne ſimilitude of beginning & ſucceſsion,
vnder the name of reformed Chriſtians: but
indeed

Aug. ep.
42. ad
Man-
drenſ. &
tract. 2.
in epiſt.
Ioan.

A nota-
ble ſay-
inge of
S. *Aug.*
tou-
chinge
Fox his
Church.

indeed cast out and condemned by the vniuersall Church?

16. This then is the second point to be noted about the quality of Ecclesiasticall succession. But another ther is of no lesse mo- *The 3.*
ment, but rather more. And this is, that *point re-*
those who succeed one another in the selfe *quired*
same Church, be also of one faith & beleefe *in suc-*
in all articles of religion. For if they differ, *Vnity of*
though it were but in any one substantiall *faith.*
point, they cannot be of one Church, nor of
one communion, nor be saued togeather.
For that, as there is but one God, one
Christ, one Church, and one baptisme (as
the Apostle testifieth:) so is there but one
only faith in the same Church to be saued
by. Which all men musthold vnitedly,
wholy & inuiolately: or else (as in the creed
of *Saint Athanasius* is affirmed) *absque dubio in* *Athan-*
æternum peribit without doubt he shall perish *in Symb.*
eternally that disagreeth or dissenteth.

17. It were a long matter to stand heere
vpon the proofe of this point: to witt, how † *Dom.*
exact and seuere the Cath. Church is, and *Thom*
euer hath byn in defendinge this strict sim- *22. q. 5.*
plicity, vnion and conformity of faith, in all *art. 3.&*
Caët. in
those, that wilbe her children. *Saint† Thomas* *eundem*
handleth the matter at large and very sub- *& Greg.*
stantially, and so do other schoolemen after *de valës.*
him, shewing: that whosoeuer erreth in any *ead. 4.*
d.sp. 1.
one article of Catholike faith obstinately, *punct. 3.*
leeseth

„ leeſeth his whole faith in all the reſt, which
„ he ſeemeth to beleeue. And yeldeth moſt
euident reaſons for the ſame. And of the
ſame ſeuerity were the auncient fathers in
this behalfe. As *Saint Cyprian,* who applying
to this purpoſe thoſe words of Chriſt; *qui
non eſt mecum, aduerſum me eſt :* he that is not
with me is againſt me, ſaith it was ment by
Chriſt of all ſorts of heretiks whatſoeuer.
Gregory Nazianzen alſo wryteth: *qui vno verbo,
tanquam veneni gutta inſiciunt, &c.* They who
by any one word, as with a dropp of poyſon
„ do infect the ſimple faith of Chriſt, are to be
„ caſt out of the Church as heretiks, &c. And
*Saint Hierome : propter vnum etiam verbum , aut
duo, &c.* For one word or two contrary to
the Cath. faith many hereſies haue byn caſt
out of the Church. And finally *Saint Auguſtine*
hauing reckoned vp eighty particular hereſies in his booke, to *Quod-valt-deus ,* he ſaith:
„ that there may chaunce to lurke many
„ other petty hereſies vnknowne to him; *qua-
rum aliquam quiſquis tenuerit, Chriſtianus Catholicus non erit* : of which hereſies whoſoeuer
ſhall hold any one he ſhall not be a Catho-
„ like Chriſtian, and conſequently cannot be
„ ſaued.

18.   Marke the ſeuerity of this holy man,
affirming that whoſoeuer holdeth any leaſt
hidden hereſy whatſoeuer cannot be ſaued.
A dreadfull ſentence (no doubt) for many of
⟨ our

Marginal notes:
*Cyp. l. 1.
ep. 6. ad
Magnū.
Luc. 11.*

*Nazia.
tract. de
fide.*

*Hier. l. 3.
Apol.
contra
Ruffin.*

*Aug. l. de
hereſ. in
fine.*

A dread-
full cen-

our contreymen at this day (if well they thought of their owne cafe) who thinke it lawfull, or at leaftwife not much dangerous to hould priuate opinions at their owne pleafure. Yea many of them thinking as the old *Donatifts* did, which *Saint Auguftine* relateth, and greatly condemneth : *nihil intereffe credentes, in qua, quifque parte Chriftianus fit,* beleeuing that it is not of great importance in what part (*fect or faction*) foeuer a man be a Chriftian , fo he beleue in Chrift. Thus thought the *Donatifts,* and are much reprehended by *Saint Auguftine* for yt. And this no doubt is the opinion of many Englishmen at this day, who being toffed hither and thither with variety of controuerfies, and not knowinge what to refolue, or beinge wearied with the labour to feeke the truth, do enclyne eafily to this abfurd error , that a man beleeuing piously in Iefus Chrift *crucified* (or as *Syr Francis Haftings* and *O. E.* before faid , *in Chrift crucified*) may be faued and be held for a brother, fo he be againft the Pope and Church of Rome.

19. And the fame fheweth Iohn Fox, that he beleeueth alfo , in that he citeth heere fo many different fects and fectaryes for his brethren & fathers, and cheefe pillars of his obfcure and troden downe Church : notwithftandinge they differed neuer fo much from him in diuers articles of their beleefe,

as fhall

fure of the fathers againft thofe that be infected vvith herefie.
Aug. ep. 48. *ad Vincent.*

Enc. 1.

as ſhall appeare by the particular examination that enſueth. For albeit it would be
ouerlonge to examine the whole catalogue
before ſett downe: yet the principall members therof we ſhall runne ouer, and therby
let yow ſee what truth or ſubſtance there is
in it, or wiſdome in the alleager. Firſt then
he beginneth his catalogue thus.

The ca-
talogue
of Iohn
Fox his
Church
men.

20. *To pretermitt* (ſaith he) *Bertramus and Be-*
rengarius (vvhich vvere before Pope Innocentius) a
learned multitude of ſufficient vvittneſſes might be
produced, &c. It was well he pretermitted
theſe two which were both againſt him
flatly. For as for *Bertramus* he was wholy of
the Roman religion and ſo liued and died.
Nor euer taught he any one point of proteſtant doctrine in his life, as may appeare by
Tritemius, and other that wryte of him, he
being a monke & ſo continued to his dying
day, which was aboue 800. yeares gone.
though after his death, when *Berengarius* had
begon his hereſie, ſome of his followers did
forge a little pamphlet in his name, as fauo-
ringe the *Berengarian* hereſie againſt the *Reall*
preſence of Chriſts body in the Sacrament.
But the fraud was preſently diſcouered and
reiected. So as this man could not be of
Fox his communion holdinge all points of
religion againſt him, and with vs. And this
is the firſt folly and falſhood of our Fox in
the firſt man by him alleaged.

Bertra-
mus no
prote-
ſtant.
Trit. in
verbo.
Bertra-
mus
Sand. de
viſib. mo
narch.
har.133.

21. Now

21. Now as for *Berengarius* Archdeacon of
Tovvars in France, though he once held the
error againſt the *Reall preſence* in the ſacrament: yet did he oftentymes recant the
ſame, as appeareth by his * abiurations,
(which Fox himſelfe confeſſeth.) And in all
othet points was a perfeƈt Catholike. So
that we may more iuſtly make him of our
Church, then Fox of his, yf we would take
any ſuch broken wares, as Fox doth. But
wee reieƈt all, that are not complete.
Though (if it be true, that *Gerſon* and
many others do wryte) that *Berengarius*
*died very penitent for his former error,*he was and
is of our Church. And whether he did, or
not: he cannot be of Foxes by any reaſon.
Both for that euen in this error, while he
held it, he was farre differēt both from *Cal-*
uyn or *Luther:* and in all the reſt of his beliefe
an aduerſary, as hath byn ſaid. To which
effeƈt the words of the *Magdeburgians* are to
be noted which are theſe: *Leo the* 9. (ſay
they) *deſerued in this one thinge no ſmall praiſe*
aboue his predeceſſors, that preſently at the beginning,
he condemned the hereſie of berengarius, togeather
vvith the author in a Synod at Rome. So ſay Fox
his maiſters. Whervnto I maruayle what he
will aunſwere, ſeinge they caſt away that
which he ſo earneſtly and carefully gathereth vp.

22. But now lett vs ſee the reſt of his ranke

Beren-
garius
no pro-
teſtant.

* *De cō-*
ſecrat.
diſt. 2.*c.*
Ego Be-
renga-
rius.
Fox pag.
146.
Gerſon
lib.cōtra
Romant.

*Cent.*11.
*cap.*10.
*pa.*527.

L l   *Ioachim*

Ioachim Abbot (faith he) of *Calabria*, *Almaricus a learned Bishopp*, &c. As for *Ioachim* Fox doth not tell vs what he held of his opinions to make him of his Church. Nor any other author, that I haue read : but only that he, being an old man and half out of his witts, was cenfured by the Pope for certayne fond prophecies, and fome errors alfo, about the bleffed Trinity. As appeareth by the decree extant in the Canon law againft him, & by other authors that haue written of him. So as he being a Cath. man in all the reft, and neuer dreaming aperhaps of any proteftant propofition in his life: Fox hath no other reafon to make him of his Church, but only for that he was cenfured in fome thing by the Pope. Which how good reafon it is, euery man doth fee. For fo much as euery malefactor condemned by the Pope, fhould by this reafon be iuftified.

23.   As for *Almaricus* the learned Bifhopp *iudged for an heretike* (faith Fox) *for holdinge againft images in the time of Pope Innocentius 3.* Firft you muft know that he was neuer Bifhop, either learned or vnlearned, but only of Fox his makinge. For that his higheft degree, that euer he was knowne to haue, was a Doctorfhippe in *Paris*, he beinge borne in the towne of *Charlers*, as teftifieth *Cafarius*, that liued with him. Secondly, if he held againft Images (as Fox their faith) he was

not

Marginal notes:

Abbot
Ioachim
no pro-
teftant.

Extrau.
de Tri-
nit.
Guido
Carmel.
Bernar.
Luxem.
in cata-
log. hare-
ticorum.

Almari-
cus vvas
no Bi-
fhop,
nor con-
demned
only for
images.

Cæfar.
lib. dial.
d. 5.

not iudged, an heretike only by *Innocentius*
for that herefie, but he and all other of that
opinion were côdemned aboue 400.yeares
before that tyme, by the fecond generall
councell of *Nice.* Thirdly, the truth is, that
this man was condemned firft by the vniuerfity of *Paris*, and then by *Innocentius*, and
by a Synode in Rome, for many more deteftable herefies, then for holdinge againft
Images. And fome fo foule, as Fox himfelfe
will be afhamed to defend them, though he
make him a Saint of his Church. And therfore like a Fox he left them out. As for example, the forefaid *Cæfarius* wryteth thus,
Almaricus magifter prauitatis hæc afferuit, Almericus
a maifter of error taught thefe propofitions
followinge.

24. *That there is no refurrection of bodies at all.*

That there is no paradife, nor hell.

That the body of Chrift, is no more in the
Sacrament after the words of confecration,
then in a ftone or horfe.

That God fpake as much in *Ouid*, as in
Auguftine. And other fuch abfurd propofitions to the number of 20. for which he was
burned openly in *Paris*, in the yeare of Chrift
1208. *Cum alijs quibufdam hæreticis blafphemis in*
perfonas S. Trinitatis, faith *Gagninus*, with certayne other blafphemous heretiks againft
the perfons of the bleffed Trinity.

25. This doth relate not only the faid

Margin notes:
Concil. Nican. C. 6.

Gagnin, li. 6. hift. Franc.

Gerſon tract. 3.
in Matt.
Paul. Æ-mil. lib.
6. *hiſtor.*
Gallia.
Genebr.
in chron.
an. 1208

Gagninus , but *Cæſarius* alſo , as before I haue cited. *Gerſon* alſo chancellour of the ſame vniuerſity , *Paulus Aemilius* and *Genebrordus* two learned and reuerend Biſhopps . And now let the reader conſider, what a *S. Iohn Fox* hath choſen , as the ſecond piller of his Church after *Pope Innocentius*. And how falſe a companion he is, in that he telleth vs, that he was a learned Biſhopp, and condemned only for holdinge againſt images. And thuſmuch of *Abbot Ioachim* & *Almaricus*: euill choſen by Iohn Fox, for the firſt founders of his hierarchie, ſeeinge that neither of them agreed with him, or his, in faith and beliefe. There followeth in Fox: *The Martyrs of Alſatia, of vvhome vve reade* (ſaith he) *a hundred to be burned in one day by the ſaid Innocentius, &c.* To ſhew Fox, to be a Fox in all things, and to deale ſincerely in nothinge, I ſhall alleage the words of the authors, that write of this matter. *Certayne heretiks* (ſay they) *to the number of* 80. *vvere burned in Argentina in Svvitzerland, for that they denied fornication to be any ſinne at all, for that it is a naturall act : and that it vvas as lavvfull to eate fleſh in Lent, as at any other tyme, &c.*

Naucler.
in hiſt.
Tritem.
in chron.
Monaſt.
Hirſang.
Genebr.
in chron.
an. 1215.

26. Behold, what holy martyrs theſe were, and whether it be likely they were burned by *Pope Innocentius* , ſeinge they were burned in *Argentina*. Conſider alſo that of 80. he maketh there a hūdred, by the art of exaggeration and multiplication. *Adde likevviſe to theſe* (ſaith he)

(faith he) *VValdenſes or Albigenſes, vvith a greater number more, to vvhich number belonged Raymundus Earle of Tholoſe, Marſilius Patauinus, Gulielmus de Sancto amore, Symon Tornacenſis, &c.* Here if Iohn Fox do take the *VValdenſes* & *Albigenſes* to be all one ſect (as it ſeemeth he doth for that he vſeth the word (or) and adioyneth the earle of *Tholoſe* as belonginge to them both) then is it both falſe and greate ignorance alſo in him. For that the *VValdenſes* otherwiſe called *the poore men of Lions*, began about the yeare of Chriſt 1160. or 1180. as other men write, before *Innocentius* 3. came to be Pope. Their beginninge was by one *VValdo* a rich citizen of the towne, who geuinge all his wealth to a certayne community or brotherhood of men (whom he called the poore men of Lions) made a ſociety of them with certayne rules, after the forme of a religious confraternity (as *Aeneas Syluius* deſcribeth) pretending holines at the beginninge, and with that pretence went afterward to Rome, and demaunded an approbation of that ſociety from *Pope Lucius,* (as teſtifieth alſo *Vrſpergenſis*) who was then preſent in Rome and ſaw them. But the Pope ſeeing certayne ſuperſtitions amonge them, refuſed the ſame. Wherwith they being offended, began to cry out againſt the Pope, & therwith to defend diuers errors, & moſt abſurd hereſies. Wherof as ſome are held at

The VValdenſes or poore men of Lions.

Æn. Sil. lib. 4. de orig. Bohemor. cap. 35. Vrſperg. in chron. an. 1212. Guido Carm. in hæreſ. VValdeſ. Anton. p. 3. ſum. ti. 11. c. 7.

this

this day by the proteſtats, ſo diuers are not: nor will Iohn Fox I preſume defend them. As for example, theſe that follow, noted generally by all authors, that write of them.

,, 27. 1. That all carnall concupiſcence, and ,, coniunction is lawfull, when luſt doth ,, burne vs.

,, 2. That all oathes are vnlawfull vnto Chriſtians, for any cauſe whatſoeuer in this world, becauſe it is written, *Nolite iurare* do nott ſweare. *Mat.* 5. *Iac.* 5.

,, 3. That no Iudgment of life and death ,, is permitted to Chriſtians in this life. For ,, that it is written, *Nolite iudicare. Mat.*7.*Luc.*6.

,, 4. That the *Creed* of the Apoſtles, is to be ,, contemned, and no accompt at all, to be ,, made of yt.

,, 5. That no other prayer is to be vſed by ,, Chriſtians, but only the *Pater noſter* ſett ,, downe in Scripture.

,, 6. That the power of conſecratinge the ,, body of Chriſt, and of hearinge confeſsions, ,, was left by Chriſt not only to prieſts, but ,, alſo to lay men, yf they be iuſt.

,, 7. That no Prieſts muſt haue any liuings at all: but muſt liue on almes, and that no Biſhops, or other dignity is to be admitted in the cleargie, but that all muſt be equall.

,, 8. That Maſſe is to be ſaid once only ,, euery yeare: to witt, vpon Maundy thurſ-,, day, when the Sacrament was inſtituted

and

and the Apo.tles made Priefts . For that „
Chrift fajd, *do this in my remembrance* , to witt *Luc.* 22.
(fay they) that which he did at that time. 1.*Cor.*11

9. Item, that the words of confecration »
muft be no other , but only the *Pater nofter*, »
feauen tymes faid ouer the bread, &c. »

10. By all which , and other articles to
the number of 33. condemned by the Church,
(which *Prateolus* and others do recount) a
man may fee , that as thefe heretiks agreed
with Proteftants in fome points : fo did
they diffent in many more . Yea, heald
diuers points of Catholike religion againft
Proteftats togeather with thefe errors. And
confequently , I fee no reafon why thefe
men fhould be gathered vp by Iohn Fox, as
chofen members of that proteftant Church :
but for that they haue no other , & yet will
needs feeme to haue fome . And thus much
for the *VValdenfes.*

28. The *Albigenfes* were another fect of heretiks ryfing fome 30. or 40. years after the
VValdenfes, vnder *Innocentius* 3. *an.Domini* 1216.
and their beginninge was at a towne called
Albigium. in the prouince of *Tholofa.* Who albeit in fome points they agreed with the
faid *VValdenfes*: yet (as all Sects are wont to
do,) they differed greatly in many other articles; and grew fo faft , in number as *Cefa-*
rius faith, that in a little tyme they infected a
thoufand cityes, and great townes round

The Al-
bigenfes
& their
blafphe-
mous o-
pinions
& actios

Cefar.
Ciftert.
5.*d,dial.*

L l 4   about

Anton.
p.3. tit.
19.ca. 1.
Vincent.
in ſpec.
l. 3.

about, and had an army of 70000. fighting
men to defend their hereſie. For which
cauſe alſo they called helpe from the Mores
in Barbary, but yet were ouercome by the
Cath. army that was aboue 8000. (as hiſtoriographers do write) the captayne wherof
was the moſt Chriſtian Prince *Symon* of
Momfort. And after this battaile geuen, the
moſt part of thoſe heretiks were conuerted
by *Saint Dominiks* preachinge.

Ceſar. 5.
diſt. dia-
log.
Luxem.
hæreſi
Albig.
Prateol.
& Sand.
ibidem.

29. The points that theſe men held, beſide
the deniall of the Popes ſupremacy, purgatory, prayer for the dead, and ſome other
ſuch articles wherin they agreed with the
Proteſtants of our dayes: they held alſo many other articles, wherin they diſagreed
both from the Proteſtants and vs. As for
example.

,, 1. They held with the Manichyes, that
,, there were two Gods: one good, and an
,, other euill: and that as the good God crea-
,, ted the ſoule, ſo the euell created the body.

Abſurd
articles
of the
Albigen-
ſes, &
their he-
reſies.

2. They denied all reſurrection of the
body. And that it was in vaine for Chriſtians to vſe any kind of prayer at all, or to
haue Churches for that purpoſe. Seinge it
profiteth nothinge, all things beinge irreuo-
cably determined by Gods prouidence.

,, 3. That externall baptiſme was an Idle
,, ceremony, & to be reiected as ſuperfluous.

,, 4. That mens ſoules did paſſe from one
to ano-

to another: yea thorough beaſts & ſerpents. „
And that God created no new ſouls from „
the beginninge of the world: but changeth „
them only from body to body, &c.

30.   Theſe & many other ſuch like beaſtly
abſurdities of theirs, are recorded by the
writers of thoſe times, and namely by thoſe
here quoted. And more then this, their foule
wicked behauiour, is related to haue bene
ſo adhominable, as Chriſtian modeſty doth
ſcarſe permit to be repeated: as for example,
of doing their eaſement vpon the Altar, and makinge
themſelues cleane vvith the palle and corporalls
there of.

Their abuſing the body of a ſtrompet vpon „
a high Altar, in deſpight of a crucifix that „
ſtood there whoſe ears, noſe, & armes they „
cut of, and then tyinge a haltar about his „
necke, they drew him moſt ſcornfully about „
the ſtreets of *Tholoſa*, &c. and other like. And
theſe are the Sainꞓts gathered vp by Iohn
Fox to frame his new Church.

31.   And for that all the reſt, that do enſue
in his catalogue, of particular men of his religion, from thoſe downward, to *Iohn VVic-*
kliffe were commonly infeꞓted with ſome
points of theſe two generall ſeꞓts, the *VVal-*
denſes or *Albigenſes:* it ſhall not be needfull to
ſtand vpon the examination, of euery one of
them, ſeing that their opinions are knowne
to be ſuch, as they could not poſsibly be of

one Church with Fox and his companye.
Yet muſt we note this by the way alſo, that
Fox doth committ infinite confuſion, falſe-
hood, and coſenage, in all this his enumeration, accoumpting ſome for diſciples of the
Albigenſes, that liued a 100. years before them.
As *Marſilius Patauinus,* who liued vnder *Pope
Paſchaſius* 2. about the yeare 1110. which is
more then an 100. yeares before *Pope Inno-
tius* 3. (as both *Aluarus* and *Alphonſus de Caſtro*
do teſtifie) and neuer held any points of the
formar hereſies, but only ſome propoſitiōs,
againſt the degrees, and liuinge of Eccleſiaſticall perſons. And the like falſhood is to be
vnderſtood of *Gulielmus de Sancto Amore,* who
liuinge about the yeare 1250. was a Cath.
man in all points, and only had ſome quare-
lings with religious orders. As in like ſorte
Armachanus, Archbiſhop of *Armach* in Ireland alſo had. For which cauſe only Fox
maketh him of his Church; though in matters of religion, he held no one article of the
proteſtant faith with him, different from
the Cath. And conſequently Fox doth ex-
treamely abuſe them, by conioyninge them
here with diuerſe heretiques burned for the
foreſaid blaſphemous opinions.

32. The like may be ſaid of *VViliam Occam*
and *Gregorius Arminenſis* (two Cath. ſchoole-
men, & euery day alleadged for ſuch in our
ſchooles) *Robert Groſſead* alſo, our learned
Biſhop

Bifhop of *Lincolne*, is in the fame predicamét:
as in like manner *Dantes* & *Petrarcha* (Italian
poets) that neuer held any iote of proteftant **Catho-**
religion in the world. And yet are brought **like men**
in here by Iohn Fox, as men of his Church **abufed**
and beleefe, with the greateft falſhood and **by Fox.**
foolery in the world. And this forſooth, for
that in ſome place of their works, they reprehend the manners of Rome, or liues of
ſome Popes in thoſe daies.Which is as good
an argument, as ifa man would proue, that
Saint Paule was not of the faith,or religion of
the *Corinthians*,for that he reprehended them
ſharpely, for fornication vſed among them. **1.*Cor.*5.**
33. Wherfore to leaue the rable that followeth of this people (as namely 36. citizens
of *Moguntia* burned *an.Dom.*1390. & an other
company of like people to witt, 140. putt in
the fire throughout the prouince of *Narbone*,
and 24. more putt to death in *Paris*, in the
yeare 1210. and other particular Saints of
his Church recounted and canonized by
Fox:) To leaue theſe (I ſay) and to come
downe to our *Lolhards*, and *VVickliffians*, and
there followers in England ; we haue treated of their doctrine ſufficiently before in
the precedent chapter, ſhewinge how farre
different it was,from that of Fox & his fellowes. But now for their actions, we are
to conſider,that the *Lolhards* began from the
yeare of Chriſt 1320. ortherabout and *VVic-*
kliffe

kliffe from the yeare 1370. & therwith raiſed
infinite troubles, garboyles, and tumults in
our coútrey. As may appeare by the lamen-
table ſtory ſet downe by *Thomas VValſingam*,
of the whole people put in commotió in *K.
Richard* the 2. his time againſt the nobility, &
cleargy, by theſe kind of people, vnder their
ſeditious Captaynes *Iack Strauv, vvat Tiler* &
the reſt. And ſo againe, vnderſome other
kings, whilſt this hereſie laſted. And namely
againſt the two valiant, & moſt, Catholike
Princes *K. Henry* the 4. and *K. Henry* the 5. his
ſonne. In the firſt yeare of whoſe raigne, (to
witt, *K. Henry* the 5.) ʃ*Iohn Stovv* writeth thus.

The firſt publike tumults of Lol-lards & Vvicklif-fians in England an. Dom. 1381. Sto. anno Domini. 1414.

34.   *The fauorers of VVicklifes doctrine did nayle
vp ſhedules vpon the Church dores of London, conteyninge that there vvere an hundred thouſand ready, to
riſe againſt all ſuch as could not avvay vvith their
ſect, &c.*   And heron followed the open re-

Sup. c. 9.   bellió of *Syr Iohn Oldcaſtle* & *Syr Roger Acton* &
others in *S. Giles* field by *Holborne,* which before we haue touched. And yet was the
prouidence of God ſuch, as this ſect could
neuer preuaile in England, neyther then or
after (ſo Catholike were our Princes) vntill
ſome points therof beinge renewed by *Luther* and *Zvvinglius,* the later was admitted in
K. Edvvards dayes, I meane the ſect of *Zvvinglius* as all men know. Beinge the firſt ſect
that euer was admitted publikely in England , eyther by Brittans or Engliſhmen
from

from to that daye. For as for *K. Henry* the
8. though in the matter of the Popes fupremacy he admitted the opinion of *Luther:*
yet in other things (as ∗ before we haue fhewed at large) he held in all articles, the ∗*Part.*1.
Cath. Roman faith, with fingular hatred *cap.* 12.
againft both *Lollards*, *VVickliffians*, and *Luthe-*
rans, but much more againft *Zvvinglians*, and
other fuch Sacramentary fectaryes. As by
his lawes made for their punifhment and re-
prefsion, doth fufficiently appeare.

35. And albeit his maieftie hauing yelded
once, in that one point of Ecclefiafticall fupremacy, and fubordination , (which held
before all the reft in ioynt) it was no maruayle, though fects and fectaryes did grow
vpon him fo faft, as withall his feuere lawes   The gre
he could hardly repreffe them in his owne   at incó-
daves , yet much more were the iudgments   uenáces
of God feene after his death, in that prefent-   enfieng.:
ly all was turned vpfidedowne in the mino-   vpon *K.*
rity of his fonne: Notwithftandinge his la-   *Henry*
wes, teftament, and ordinances to the con-   the 8.
trary. And that by thofe , whome he moft   yelding
trufted in that behalfe, and who in his dayes   in one
had fhewed themfelues, moft earneft againft   point
Zvvinglians, and their doctrine of the Sacra-   only to
ment, as a thinge moft abhorred by the old   heretti.
King their maifter. I meane, *Cranmer, Ridley,*   ques.
Seymer and *Dudley* the cheefe changers of all
in *K. Edvvards* dayes.

36. But

36.   But this is the common euent, where princes be not carefull at the beginninge (as *VValfingam* doth well note about the rifinge of *VVickliffes* herefie in the end of K. *Edvvard* the 3. his tyme) when that old King was now impotent, and wholy gouerned by women, leauinge the care of his kingdome, in the hands of his fonne the *Duke* of *Lancafter*, and others that followed him, who hauinge partly emulation, and iarres with the Bifhops of *Canterbury, VVinchefter, London*, and fome other principall men of the cleargy, & partly defiringe to inuade Church liuings, which *VVickliffe* preached to be lawfull, they were content to winke at him, yea and to vfe him, and his doctrine openly, againft the faid Bifhops, and Cleargy, as alfo againft monks, and Abbotts in the beginninge of K. *Richard* the 2. his tyme, as appeareth both in the faid *VValfingham* and *Stovv*, who relate the callinge of *VVickliffe* to London for this effect, where he was publikely and fcandaloufly borne out by the faid *Duke*, and *Syr Henry Percy*, & others of that faction, againft the faid Bifhops, monks, & Abbotts, which here we fhall fett downe, in *Stovves* owne words, taken by bim out of *VValfingham* and other writers, which do conteyne the very fumme of all the doings, and meanings of both partyes in thofe dayes.

37.   In the meane tyme (faith he) the *Duke* of *Lan-*

Herefies to be ftopped at the beginning.

*Sto. an.
Domini
1377.
pag.425.*

of *Lancaster* ceased not (with his fellowes) to imagine how he might bringe to passe, that which he had longe continued in his mind (to wit for encroaching vpon Church liuings, and reuenginge himselfe against some Bishops, and the citty of London that stood with them) for he saw that it would be hard for him to obtayne his purpose, the Church standinge in her full state, and very daungerous to attempt publikely, the lawes and customes of London beinge in force, wherfore he laboured, first to ouerthrow as well the liberties of the Church, as of the citty, for which cause he called vnto him a certayne deuine, who many yeares before, in all his acts in the schooles, had inueighed against the Church, for that he had byn depriued by the Archbishop of *Canterbury* from a certaine benefice, that he vniustly, as was said, was incombent vpon within the citty of *Oxford:* his name was *Iohn VVickliffe,* who with his disciples, were of the common people called *Lollards,* they went barefooted, and basely clothed: to witt, in course russett garments downe to the heeles; they preached especially against monks, and other Religious men that had possessions, &c. 38. They affirmed, that temporall Lords if they had need, might lawfully take the goods of such religious persons to releeue their necessityes, &c. And when he had

,,
,,
,,
,,
,,
,,
,,
,,
,,
,,
Vpon
vvhat
cause &
motiues
VVickliff
began
his do-
ctrine.
The ha-
bitt of
the first
*VVicklif-
fians.*

taught

taught theſe, & many others ſuch doctrines,
not only in the ſchooles in *Oxford*, but alſo
had preached them publikely in *London*, that
he might therby gett the fauour of the ſaid
Duke, and others, whome he found prone
" to heare his opinions; the *Duke* and *Syr Henry*
" *Percy* commended highly his ſaid opinions,
" and endeauored to extoll his learninge and
" honeſty of life aboue all other. Who ther-
" fore being thus ſett forth with their fauour,
" feared not to ſpread his doctrine much more
" then before, going from Church to Church,
" and preachinge his opinions, wheruppon at
" length, the Biſhops awakened their Archb.
" whoſent for this Iohn to come, & anſwere
" to thoſe things which were ſpoken of him.
" And the *Duke* hearinge therof ſent for 4.
" Doctors of diuinity of euery order of beg-
" ging friars one (for vnto them *VVickliffe* ad-
" ioyned himſelfe approuinge their pouerty,
" & extollinge their perfection, againſt other
" religious orders that had poſſeſſiós) whome
" the *Duke* aduertiſed, that with a naturall and
" old hate he purſued the religious perſons,
" that had poſſeſſions, neyther was it diffi-
" culte, to compell the willinge friars, to aide
" him in this point.
" 39.   Hitherto are the words of *Iohn Stovv.*
Wherby yow may preceyue the true cauſes
of this new Ghoſpell of *Iohn VVickliffe,* ſo
highly comended by *Iohn Fox* who affirmeth
his

his doctrine *to haue proceed from the strong opera-* The first
tion of Chrifts spiritt, &c. Firſt yow ſee that motiue
Iohn VVickliffe had for his motion the deſire of *Iohn*
of reuenge againſt the Biſhops and cleargy, *VVickliff*
for that he was depriued of a benefice in *fauou-*
Oxford, which he had poſſeſſed vniuſtly. Se- *rers.*
condly was he moued with enuy againſt
monks, togeather with ambition of gayning
the *Duke* of *Lancaſter,* and his followers by
teaching them, that it was lawfull to inuade
Church liuings at their pleaſure. Thirdly,
the very ſame motiues of ambition, coue-
tuouſnes, & emulation againſt the Biſhops,
ſtyrred vp the *Duke* and his adherents, and
fourthly both parts, as well the heretiks, as
their fauourers, were content to vſe & abuſe
the infirmity of ſome emulation, betwene
friars & monks about matters of perfection,
pouerty, and poſſeſsions. Which pious motyues we do read comonly to haue byn the
cauſes of all other ancient hereſies from
tyme to tyme. As comminge from one, and
the ſelfe ſame ſpiritt of him that is the proper
author of all ſedition, ſchiſme, and hereſie, &
profeſſed enemy to the vnion of Gods only
ſpouſe and Cath. Church *Lucifer* himſelfe.

40. Furrthermore *VValſingham* doth ſhew,
how that by this fauour, and out bearing of
the *Duke* of Lancaſter, and his partners, both
the vniuerſity of *Oxford* where *VVickliffe* began, was brought to be cold in reſiſting him,
M m and

and the Prince himſelfe in puniſhinge him.
And this appeared by two Apoſtolicall
Breues wrytten by *Pope Gregory* the 11. in the
yeare of Chriſt 1378. regiſtred by *VValſingam.*
The one to the *vniuerſity of Oxford,* reprehen-
ding them for their ſaid coldnes & ſlackneſſe
in reſiſtinge the ſaid hereſies. And the other
to the *Archbiſhop of Canterbury* and B. *of London,*
to deale with the King & Queene, & other
nobility to putt them in mind, as well of
their duty, as alſo of their negligence hitherto vſed in this behalfe. But what followed
of this? I meane of this negligence in reſiſtinge this ſect of *VVickliffe* at the beginning?
Truly there followed or rather flowed ſuch
ſeas of calamities, as were neuer ſeene in our
coûtrey before, nor ſcarſe heard of in others.

41.   For wheras K. *Edvvard* the 3. had byn
a moſt glorious king, his end was pittifull:
his heyre K. *Richard* after infinite ſedition,
contention, and bloudſhed of the nobility,
and others was depoſed, and made away.
The bloudy diuiſion of the houſe of *Lancaſter* and *Yorke* came in, & endured for almoſt
an hundred yeares, with the ruine not only
of the royall line of *Lancaſter,* by whome ſpecially *VVickliffe* was fauoured at the beginning (as yow haue heard) but with the ouerthrow alſo of many other noble princes,
and familyes, and moſt pernicious warres &
garboyles continued, both at home and
abroad

Tvvo
Apoſto-
licall
Breues
vvritten
into En-
gland
againſt
VVicklif-
fians.
VValſing
ın vıt.
Rich. 2.
an.1378.

Th: cala
mityes
in Eng-
land by
VVickliff
his do-
ctrine.

abroad with the losses of all our goodly *States, Prouinces* & *Countreyes* in France. Vnto all which, the diuision of harts, mynds and iudgments brought in by *VVickliffes* doctrine did help not a little, and the calamityes so continued vntill the tyme of the most wise, Christian, and Cath. K. *Henry* the 7. Who as he extinguished the reliques of this wicked *VVickliffian* seed (as may appeare by Iohn Fox, who setteth out in print and paintinge 12. seuerall pageants of the Popes highest greatnesse, honour and supreme power in the end of *K. Henry* the 7. his life:) so did he happily also extinguish all temporall diuision, about the succession of our Imperiall crowne. And had not our sinnes deserued that his sonne had opened, the gapp againe (though not perhaps meaninge yt) to other sects and diuisions of *Lutherans* & *Zvvinglians,* (no lesse malitious and pernitious then the former) England had byn a happy state at this day.

42. Well then, of these men, whome not only the whole vniuersall Church did condemne as heretiks, for their wicked opiniōs, but English †parlaments also (that hadd best cause to know their liues) did sentence by their publike acts, *for hypocrits, seditious, and pernicious people in manners* as ★ Fox himselfe among others confesseth : of these (I say) he maketh vp his Church vntill he come

Fox pag. 716. 717. & dein-ceps.

The praise of K. Henry the 7.

† *Stat. an. 5. Ricardi 2. an. Chriſti 1390. & an. 2. Henr. 4. an. Chriſti 1402.*
★ *Fox in his proteſt. pag. 10.*

downe

downe to *Lutherans, Zwinglians* & other ſuch freſher ſectaryes vnder *K. Henry* the 8. and his children. Which ſectaryes Fox will needs coople togeather in one catalogue & calendar of Saints appointinge *Wickliffe* his feaſt vpon the ſecond of *Ianuary*, with the title of *Preacher and Martyr* (though he died quietly in his bedd) as after ſhalbe ſhewed. And that of *Luther* vpon the 17. of *February* with the title only of *Confeſſor* (but both of them in read letters.) Notwithſtanding that the authors of theſe three ſects do diſclayme one from another, as in the former chapter yow haue heard. So as this forcible drawing of oppoſite ſectaries into one catalogue, and calendar of Saints; is like to that of *Cacui*, who drew bulles backewards by the tayles into his caue. And this ſhall ſuffice for the contemplation of this ſtrange compoſition, and combination of Fox his Church, from *Wickliffes* tyme downe to *K. Henry* the 8. of whoſe raigne and matters conteyned therin, we ſhall now ſucceſſiuely beginne our ſpeech.

T H E

THE SEARCH OF IOHN FOX

HIS CHVRCHE IS CONTINVED
vnder the gouernment and raigne of K. Henry
the 8. *& his children: And it is discussed vvhat
manner of Church,* Iohn Fox *then had, or may be
imagined to haue hadd.*

CHAP. XI.

HAVING made our former search or
pursute for the finding of Iohn Fox his
Church throughout the precedent yeares,
and ages of the Christian world, from the
Apostles time vnto the raigne of K. *Henry* the
eight, and declared most euidently (as to vs
it seemeth) that the said Church, was neuer
yet to be found in any of those tymes and
ages, except perhaps in some such broken
and contemptible heretiks, and so opposite
and contrary the one of them to another,
as cannot possibly be thought to make a
Church, that requireth vnity and conformity of faith: there remaineth now, that we
proceed to examine, what may be found for
Iohn Fox his purpose, vnder the raigne of
K. *Henry* the 8. downwards to our tyme. For
that, (as often hath byn noted) of this tyme
doth Iohn Fox bragg & glory in his booke,
as of the florishinge tyme of his Ghospell.
Which appeareth not only by that he imployeth the halfe of his whole volume, in

Mm 3 these

theſe only 30. yeares that paſſed betweene
the breach of *K. Henry* with the Pope vnto
the entrance of *Q. Elizabeth* : but alſo by a
braue triumphant picture ſet in the firſt page
of *K. Henryes* rayne, with his feet vpon the
backe of *Pope Clement* the 7. and other circumſtances of hereticall inſolency, which
preſently we ſhall declare.

A falſe flatte-ringe picture ſet out by Fox of K. Henry the 8.

2.   But firſt of all you muſt vnderſtand, that
in the 12. laſt pages of *K. Henry* the 7. life, yt
pleaſed Iohn Fox to ſett downe pleaſantly
12. larg printed and painted pageants of the
Popes greatneſſe in thoſe dayes, togeather
with his papall caſes reſerued to himſelfe,
his dominion both ſpirituall and temporall,
his great riches, the *vniuerſall* obedience both
of temporall & ſpirituall Princes vnto him,
and other ſuch like points. All which being
but a melancholy meditation and ſpectacle
for proteſtants, Iohn Fox in the next page
ſetteth downe a meryer contemplation : to
witt K. *Henry* the 8. placed by him in a high
throne with *Clement* the 7. vnder his feete
grouelinge on the ground with his croſſe-
keyes and triple crowne in the duſt. Wherat
many friars are painted ſtaringe and gazinge
and wepinge round about, and *B. Fiſher* and
Syr Thomas More pitifully alſo weepinge, and
ſtoopinge downe to help him vpp againe.
And on the other ſide, *K. Henry* is painted
with the Ghoſpell in his lapp, and his ſword
in his

Fox pag. 732.

in his right hand, lifted vp to defence therof.
Which ghospell is also holpen to be held
vp by *Cramner* & *Cromvvell*, that on his said
right hand do afsift the king with great có-
tentment of the new minifters. Who are
paynted heere to ftand very grauely con-
templating of the matter with a singular
comfort:& all other Bishopps, Abbotts, Ec-
clesiafticall and temporall men, bewayling
and mourning.

3. And this is Iohn Fox his pleasant (or rather peeuish) inuention, to entertayne the
eyes of the simple readers and lookers on, &
to make paftime for fooles, wherof himfelfe
was a follemne father, while he liued. And
I would aske the feely fellow heere, how
K. *Henry*, though he brake with *Pope Clement*,
vpon fome matters of difpleafure (as is notorious) and refufed to yeld him fpirituall
obedience in England (as he and his ance-
ftors had done euer before:) yet how could
he iuftly, or truly be faid to haue caft him
downe with his crowne, & crofse, as heere
in painted? Seinge that *Pope Clement* his au- Fox his
thority, power, and fpirituall iurifdiction, pageáts
throughout the Chriftian world was no exami-
leffe after *K. Henryes* breach, then before. And ned.
albeit the realme of England withdrew her
fpirituall obedience from him : yet the encreafe of new Churches in the *Indyes*, was of
much more authority, and iurifdiction vnto

him,

him and his fucceffors in that kind, then he or they loft in England, Germany or other parts, that retyred themfelues from his and their obedience.

4. Further, I would aske this *Iohn Deuifer*, that deuifed this wife reprefentation: how could K. *Henryes* fword be faid to be in defence of the Proteftants Ghofpell, when, by their owne affirmation, he was the greateft perfecutor of their brethren that euer was K. of England, from the beginninge of that monarchy to his dayes? For fo fheweth Fox himfelf, in that he in his Calendar of Saints, fetteth downe more martyrs of his fect, made by K. *Henry* only, then by all the other former Kings and Queens of England, from the firft entrance of Chriftian faith to his tyme. As we are to fhew more largely in the 3. parte of this treatife, when we come to examine his faid Calendar. But yet in the meane fpace, yf yow will haue fome taft, how fauourable K. *Henry* of his owne inclination was to thefe new Ghofpellers: yow may read, what Fox fetteth downe in the fecond part of his Acts and Monuments of this matter. Where among other complaints of this Kings raigne, yow fhall find in one place, no leffe then fourteene whole pages of names (by way of Table or Catalogue) of godly men and women, (as he calleth them) apprehended, perfecuted and imprifoned

for the

See frō *pag.663.* vnto 751. That K. *Henryes* fvvord vvas not for the nevv Gho-fpell, but againft yt.

for the Ghospells sake by the B. of *Lincolne*
in one yeare? The king himselfe beinge the
cheefe author, & incytor to the persecution,
as appeareth by a lettere of the said kings,
writen to the said B. of *Lincolne* vpon the 20.
of Octobre 1521.& the 13. yeare of his raigne
which lettere Fox doth register vnder this
title: *The copy of the kings letter for the aid of Iohn* *Fox pag.*
Longland Bishop of Lincolne against the seruants of *764.*
Chrift, falsely then called heretiks, &c.

5. Lo heere K.*Henry* proued to be an ayder,
and incyter of persecution against Ghospellers,tearmed the seruâts of God by Fox, but
heretiks by the king. And if so many of these
good fellowes, were persecuted by him in
one yeare, vnder one Bishopp only, within
one diocesse: what may be imagined throughout the whole realme? Truly [yow may *See frō*
read in Fox himselfe, very large and lamen- *pag.887.*
table complaints, of this kings reigne, and *to 912.*
diuers copious lists, of these persecuted *& agai-*
Saints of his Church, sett downe by him: *pag.949.*
especially from the forsaid yeare of Chrift *to 957.*
1521. vnto 1531. which was the last ten
yeares, before the breach with the Pope.

6. But what did he from his breach forward? did he spare the new Ghospellers
any thinge more for his breach with the
Pope? Truly it cannot be denied, but that
for some yeares he winked at their doings
somwhat more then before: considering the

new

new difficultyes wherin he had caſt himſelfe, by his new diſvnion, and breach, as before we haue noted in the end of the former
part. But aſſoone as he had put his domeſticall affayres in ſome quiett, and ſecurity, he
returned againe to his former courſe & cuſtome, of reſtrayning theſe new vnruly ſpiritts, by callinge them to accompt for their
innouations: & proceeded iuridically againſt
them, according to Church canons, and according to his former iudgment, in matters
of Religion. Which as I might ſhew by diuers wayes of profes, as well of acts of parlaments, as proclamations, iniunctions, and
other declarations of his will and opinion
in this behalfe: ſo will we alleag only 2. or 3.
examples in the firſt kind, beſids thoſe
which we haue ſett downe in the ★ former part.

That K-
Henry
afrer his
breach
vvith
Rome
vvas ſtil
an ene-
my to
prote-
ſtants
religion.

★ cap. 12.

7.   In the 31. yeare of his raigne, which
was 7. or 8. yeares after his breach, With the
Pope there was an act made for aboliſhinge
of diuerſity of opinions about Chriſtian faith,
which beginneth thus : *VVhere the Kings moſt
excellent Maieſtie is by Gods lavv ſupreme head immediatly vnder him, of the vvhole Church of England, &c. Intendinge the conſeruation of the ſame
Church, in a true, ſincere, and vniforme doctrine of
Chriſts religion, &c.* Thus beginneth his preface. And then he determineth togeather
with the parlament: *That vvhoſoeuer ſhall deny
the reall*

See Sta-
tut 31.
Henr. 8.
cap. 14.

the reall presence in the Sacrament of the aulter, or affirme that the communion, is necessary vnder both kinds, or that Priests may by Gods lavv take vvyues after Priesthood, or that vovves of chastity are not to be obserued, or that priuate masses are not to be said, or that sacramentall and auricular confession is not necessary, &c. All these he condemneth as heretiks, and for such *to be apprehended, arraigned, condemned and burned,* as at large is to be seene in the Statute.

Statutes in religion made by K. Henry against protestants.

8.   And the very next yeare after, perceauinge that, notwithstanding his former statute against protestant opinions, the same did grow & was spread abroad in England: he ordeyned another statute, which beginneth thus. *VVhere the Kings Royall Maiestie of his blessed and gratious disposition, &c. VVell vveighing that out of sundry outvvard parts, & places there haue sprong, byn sovvven, and sett forth diuers hereticall, erroneous and dangerous opinions, and doctrines in the Religion of Christ, vvherby his graces liege people may be induced to vnfaithfulnesse, misbeleefe, miscreancy, and contempt of God, to the vtter confusion and damnation of soules, &c. For this cause his Maiestie according to the very Ghospell and lavv of God, meaneth to haue matters determined and declared, &c.*

Statut. an. 32. regni Henr. 8. cap. 26.

Thus he wryteth in the Statute remittinge himselfe to his further declaration. Which is wholy against protestants, whose faith and religion yow see here called by the King *vnfaithfulnesse, misbeleefe, miscreancy,* contempt of God,

The very ghospell against our nevv ghospellers by K. Henry iudgment.

God, hereticall, erroneous and dangerous doctrine,
tending to vtter confusion & damnation of soules,&c.
And this prooued by the pure word of God
and the very Ghospell it selfe, as his Maiestie
affirmeth.

9.   And will yow haue more cleere testimony of his setled iudgement against protestáts, then this? But yet heare further. For
that the same king diuers yeares after this
againe, towards the end of his dayes, hauing had good experiéce of the falshood of
protestants, in corrupting the very scriptures themselues by their crafty translations,
notes, and commentaries: he was forced
to forbidd vnder greeuous punishments, the
reading of the forsaid scriptures in English,
which before he had permitted, as appeareth by a peculiar Statute made for that
purpose, & for inhibiting protestáts books,
sermons, and preachings, in the 34. and 35.
yeares of his raigne: this Statute being intituled: *An act for the aduauncement of true reli-*
gion: sayinge therin as followeth. *VVhere the*
K. most royall Maiestie surpreme head of the Church
of England, and also of Ireland perceaueth, that, not-
vvithstanding such holy doctrines and documents, as
his maiestie hath hitherto caused to be sett forth, be-
sides the great liberty granted vnto them, in hauing
the nevv and old testament amonge them, vvhich not-
vvithstanding many seditious, arrogant, and igno-
rant parsons, pretending to be learned, haue the per-
fect and

K. *Henry*
foibid-
deth the
prote-
stants
transla-
tion of
the scri-
ptures.

Stat. *an.*
regni
Hen. 8.
34.&35.
cap. 1.

fect and true knovvledg,vnderstanding, & iugdment
of sacred scriptures, &c. Intending to subuert the
very, true and perfect exposition therof, after their
peruerse fantasyes, haue taken vpon them not only to
preach, theache, declare, &c. But also by printed
books, ballads, playes, rymes,songs, and other fanta-
syes subtily to beguile his maiesties liege subiects,&c.

10.   Behould K. Henry his description of
protestants,their witt,nature, condition,&
doctrine. But now followeth the remedy.
VVherfore to ordeyne and establish a certayne forme
of pure and sincere teaching, agreable to Gods vvorde
& true doctrine of the Cath.and Apostolicall Church,
&c. Be it enacted, that all manner of books of the
ould and nevv testament in English, beinge of the
crafty, false,and vntrue Translation of VVilliam
Tyndall, and all other books and vvrytings in the En-
glish tounge, teachinge, or composinge any matter of
Christian Religion,contrary to that doctrine, vvhich
since the yeare of our Lord God 1540. *is, hath, or*
shalbe sett forth by his maiestie is clearly and vtterly
abolished,&c. This ordeyned *K. Henry* of the
protestants books and doctrine. And this
censure he gaue of *VVilliam Tyndalls,* truth,
and honesty in translatinge the scriptures,
whome Fox calleth, *not only the true seruant*
and martyr of God, but the Apostle also of England
in his our later age.

11.   Wherfore I do nott see. how Fox,can
with any reason make K. Henry to be a
Ghospeller of his religion or so earnest a
defender

The very true and perfect exposition of scriptures prescribed by K.Henry against the protestants.

VVilliam Tyndalls Translation of the scriptures condemned together vvith the protestants books. Fox pag. 981.

defender of the fame : or wy he fhould
paint him out with the bible in his hand,
holden vp by *Cranmer* and *Cromvvell*, as before hath byn faid, & feene in his paynting.
feing he contemned euer their doctrine, &
burned the profeffors therof, as notorious
heretiks vnto his dying day. Which is euident by many exemples, but moft cleere &
notorious by that of *Iohn Lambert* a famous
Zuinglian , with whome in folemne publike audience he difputed, in prefence of
all his cleargy, and nobylity of the realme,
and caufed Cramner to do the like , and in
the end made Cromwell as his Vicar generall , to giue the fentence of death againft
him, and burne him in Smithfield. And this
not two yeares before *Cromvvells* owne condemnation by parlament for like herefie,
by the kings owne purfute: as may appeare
by the act of his condemnation yet extant.
And the fame (no doubt would he haue
done with *Cramner*, which was the other
vpholder of his arme to maintayne the new
ghofpel, according to Fox his picture) yf he
had knowne or fufpected him , not only for
an vpholder of that herefie, but that he had
fo much as fecretly and inwardly fauoured
the fame. And for this very caufe, did King
Henry vfe that folemne and fharpe iudgment , vpon *Lambert* and made *Cramner* to
difpute fo earneftly againft him, for the reall
prefence,

The fo-
lemne
iudgmẽt
and con-
demna-
tion of
Lambert
by the
King.
Anno 32.
Renr. 8.

prefence, (wherof afterward he made alfo
the faid *Cramner* wryte and print a booke
for more euident attestation therin.) And
to the fame end he made Cromwell to
pronounce the fetence, that all men might
fee and know (but especially his fauourits)
that whomfoeuer he found faulty in that
behalfe, fhould expe&t no fauour at his
hand. Whervpon when he had fpoken to
Lambert, asking him what he had to fay
more for himfelfe, why he fhould not dy,
and the other falling downe on his knees,
remitted himfelfe to his princely mercy: the
King anfwered with a loud voyce in thefe
words, as Fox relateth them. *If yovv remitt*
your felfe to my iudgment, yovy muft dy. for I vvilbe
no patron of heretiks. And by and by turning himfelfe
to Cromvvell, he faid : Cromvvell reade the fentence
of condemnation againft him. (vvhich Cromvvell
(addeth Fox) *vvas a that tyme, the cheefe frend*
of the ghofpellers.) vvho taking the fchedele of con-
demnation in his hand, read the fame, &c.

Fox pag.
1026.
col. 1.
num. 78r

12.   Thus writeth Fox, and putteth in the
margent this note. *The King condemneth the*
martyr of Chrift Iohn Lambert. And againe in
another place : *Thus vvas Iohn Lambert in this*
bloudy feffion, by the King iudged and condemned to
death, &c. And then fpeaketh he very disho-
norably of K. Henry about this matter, cy-
ting him to the laft day of iudgment, to receyue his fentence for this fentence. So as

Fox and
K. Henry
fallen
out.

how-

howfoeuer they flatter the memory of this King for glofing with her Maieftie in out-ward words: yet is it cleere enough, what they thinke of him in their harts, & fpeake of him in corners. And howfoeuer Fox paint him out with their ghofpell in his lap, & fword in his hand to defended yt, calling him euery where ghofpeller: yet can they not deny, but that the fharpeft edg of the fword fell vpon them.

13. And here I cannot omitt to let yow heare Fox his complaint, of euill lucke, and misfortune in this behalfe, that the king with *Crammer* and *Cromvvell* & fome others of his ghofpell, and ghofpellers fhould fo vnluckily concurre to the condemninge, & burning of this feruét brother of their gho-fpell, *Lambert*. Heere (faith Fox) *it is much to be maruailed at, to fee hovv vnfortunately it came to paffe in this matter, that through the peftiferous and crafty Counfell of Gardener Bishopp of VVinchefter, fathan did heere performe the condemnation of this Lambert, by no other minifters, then ghofpellers them-felues.* This is Fox his complaint, laying all the fault (as yow fee) vpon *B. Gardener,* as though he had byn able to haue induced all thefe ghofpellers, and among others the king, himfelfe, and his ghofpelling Coun-felors, to haué concurred to the burning of their owne brother *Lambert:* if they had byn then of his Ghofpell! But the truth is, that

farre

none of them at that tyme were come so
farre forward, as to be Zwinglians. For as
for the king himselfe, he hated them deadly, both then and vnto his dying day: as also
the Lutherans, though he bare somwhat
more with them, then with the other in respect of their holdinge the reall presence in
the Sacrament, wherunto he was most de-
uont. And as for *Cramner* and *Cromvvell,* yt
may be that in those dayes they weare a
little touched with Lutheranisme. The
former, to enioy his woman which he kept
secretly, by whome he was also made a
Zwinglian in K. Edwards dayes. The second, for his gayne and aduauncement. Yet
the said Cromwell, comminge soone after
this, to be beheaded, on the scaffold said
these words among others, as Fox relateth
them: *And novv I pray yovv, that be heere, to beare
me record, that I dy in the Cath. faith: not doubting
of any article of my my faith ; no nor doubtinge
in any sacrament of the Church. Many haue slande-
red me, and reported, that I haue byn a bearer out of
such as haue maynteyned euill opinions: vvhich is vntrue, &c.* And then a little after, he addeth
agayne. *The deuill is ready to seduce vs, and I haue
byn seduced. But beare me vvittnesse, that I dy in the
Cath. faith of the vvhole Church.*

Fox pag.
1086.
The pro
testatiō
of Crō-
vvell at
his de-
ath, that
he vvas
a Cathe
like.

14.   Thus relateth Fox of his last confession, and putteth in his margent this note:
A true Christian confession of the L. Cromvvell at his

death.

death. Which if Iohn Fox meane truly indeed, and that *Cromvvell* himſelfe meant it
alſo truly and ſincerely as he ſpake, and was
vnderſtood of the people : then died he a
Cath. in all points, and beleeued all ſacraments of that Church, which then in England was held for Catholike, and oppoſite
to the new ghoſpellers at that tyme. By
whome he confeſſed he had byn ſomwhat
ſeduced: & yet denyeth, that he euer was a
bearer out of them, as you ſee. And if all this
be true indeed, how then can this confeſſion of the *L. Cromvvell be called a true Chriſtian
confeſſion* with Iohn Fox? Seing it is a Cath.
confeſſion, and renounceth Fox his religion vtterly. And yſit were a falſe, feigned,
and diſſembled confeſſion of Cromwell, &
meant contrary to the ſound of his words,
at the houre of his death : how was he a
true Chriſtian man in ſo diſſemblinge, and
lyinge, and this at his very going out of the
world? And here I would haue Iohn Fox
to ſolue me this *dilemma,* both for his owne
and Cromwells creditt. Whome notwithſtandinge all this, Fox will needs enforce
to be of his ghoſpell, whether he will or
noe. Wryting of him thus in another place:
*In this vvorthy and noble perſon, beſides diuers other
eminēt vertues, three things eſpecially are to be conſidered: his floriſhing authority, his excelling vviſdome,
and his feruent zeale to Chriſt, & to his ghoſpell. &c.*

And

Iohn
Fox is
ſore preſ
ſed', a-
bout the
L. Crom-
vvell.

Fox pag.
1084.

And so much of him & his fellow *Cranmer*, the two cheefe pillars and vnder proppers of Iohn Fox his ghospell with *K. Henry.*

15. And herby we may in part contemplate the first beginninge, fountayne, origen and offspring of I. Fox his ghospell in England. Wherof we haue spoken somwhat before, in the last chapter of the former part of this Treatise, where we alleaged the words of *VVilliam Tyndall*, write to *Iohn Fryth* his scholer, at the very beginninge, when *K. Henry* first seemed to fauour the ghospell. Wherin *Tyndall* saith, that he had smelled a certayne counsell taken against papists. But that *Frith* must vnderstand, that it was not for God, but for reueng & to enioy the spoyle of the Church: these were the first motyues, yf we beleefe *Tyndall*, whome Iohn Fox holdeth and calleth *an Apostle of England*. So as this testimony comminge from him, must needs be also Apostolike, yf not Euangelicall.

16. But what was the progresse of this ghospell so begun in England? I haue shewed before, that not long after this beginninge, (to wit, in the yeare of Christ 1536.) *K. Henry* beinge disposed vpon former motyues, to make some certayne alterations, did not take councell nor direction from the new ghospellers to do it: but rather sett forth a booke of his owne, intituled thus: *Articles deuised by the Kings highnesse.* So do testi-

fie both

Tyndals iudgmēt and testimony of the first moe tiues tovvards protestancy in *K. Henry.*
Fox *pag.* 977.

ſie both *Hall*, *Holinshed*, and *Stovv*. And then *Hall*, who liued in thoſe dayes, addeth further: *In this booke are eſpecially mentioned but 3. Sacraments, vvith the vvhich the Lincolnshiremen vvere offended.* And then againe afterwards, he writeth *This booke eſpecially treated of no more, then three ſacraments. VVhere alvvayes before the people had byn taught 7. Sacraments, &c. VVhich articles being deliuered to the people, the inhabitants of the North parts being very ignorant, and rude, & not knovving vvhat true religion meant, &c. Said: novv yovv ſee, Frends, that 4. Sacraments of ſeauen are taken from vs, and ſhortly yovv ſhall leeſe the other three alſo, except yovv looke about yovv, &c.* Thus wryteth *Hall* of the beginninge of the inſurrection of *Lincolne, Yorke,* and other ſhires, by occaſion of theſe new deuiſed articles in religion. Wherby notwithſtanding we ſee, that *K. Henry* thinking beſt to make ſome alteratiō, though he ment not indeed to take away any ſacrament (as afterwards appeared:) yet diſdained he to take his platforme from the proteſtāts, or goſpellers of thoſe dayes. But deuiſed of himſelfe the innouation, which for the preſent he meant to make. Wherof I haue heard of a certaine ſtory not vnpleaſant, nor from the purpoſe, which therfore here I will ſett downe.

17. A certayne Courteour at that day (ſome ſay it was *Syr Francis Bryan*) talkinge with a lady that was ſomwhat forward in the new

Hall. in chronic. an, regn. Henr. 8. 28. fol. 228.
The firſt booke of alte= ratiō of Religiō in Eu= gland de uiſed by K. Hen= ry.

A cer= taine cō ference

the new ghospell, about this booke of the
kings, then lately come forth, she seemed
to mislike greatly the title therof; to witt,
Articles deuised by the Kings Highnesse, &c. Saying
that it semed not a fitt title to authorize
matters in Religion, to ascribe them to a
mortall knigs deuise. Whervnto the Courteour answered: Truly (madame) I will tell
you my conceyt plainely. Yf we must needs
haue deuises in Religion, I had rather haue
them from a King, then from a knaue, as
your deuises are. I meane that knaue, *Friar
Martyn:* who not yet 20, yeares agone was
deuiser of your new Religion, and behaued
himselfe so lewdly in answeringe his Maiestie, with scorne, and contempt, as I must
needs call him a knaue. Though otherwise
I do not hate altogeather the profession of
friars, as your ladishipp knoweth. Moreouer
(said he) it is not vnknowne neither to your
ladyshipp, nor vs: that he deuised these
new tricks of Religion, which yow now
so much esteeme, and reuerence, Not for
God, or deuotion, or to do pennance, but
for ambition, and to reuenge himselfe vpon
the Dominican Friars, that had gotte from
him the preachinge of the Popes bulles. As
also to gett himselfe the vse of a wench, and
that a nunne also, which now he holdeth.
And soone after him againe three other
married Priests his schollers (to witt, *Oeco-*

betvve-
ne a
Cour-
teour &
a lady a-
bout de-
uising
nouel-
tyes in
religion

*Cocl. in
vit. Lu-
theri, &
Sur. ann.
Domini*
1516.
& 1517.

lampa-

lampadius, Carolſtadius, and *Zvvinglius*) deuiſed another Religion of the Sacramentaryes, againſt their ſaid maiſter. And ſince theſe againe, we heare euery day of other freſh vpſtarts, that deuiſe vs new doctrines. And there is no end of deuiſing or deuiſers. And I would rather for my part, ſticke to the de-uiſinge of a King, that hath maieſtie in him, and a counſell to aſsiſt him, (eſpecially ſuch a King as ours is) then to a thouſand of theſe companions putt together.

The re-ply of the lady vvith the Courte-ours an-ſvvere.

18. It is true (ſaid the lady) when they are deuiſes indeed of men, but whē they bring ſcriptures with thē to proue their ſayings: then are they not mens deuiſes, but Gods eternall truth and word. And will yow ſay ſo, madame (quoth he:) and do yow not remember, what adoe we had the laſt yeare about this tyme, with certaine *Hollanders* heere in England? Whome our Biſhopps & Doctors could not ouercome by ſcriptures, not withſtanding they held moſt horrible hereſies, which make my heares to ſtand vpright to thinke of them, againſt the man-hood and fleſh of Chriſt our Sauiour, and againſt the virginity of his bleſſed mother, and againſt the baptiſme of infants, and the like wicked blaſphemyes. I was my ſelfe preſent, at the condemnatiō of 14. of them in Paules Church in one day, & heard them diſpute & alleage ſcriptures ſo faſt for their

✳ Of theſe Hollan-ders ſee Holin-ſhed an. 27. Henr. 8. menſe maiō. 1535.

here-

herefies, as I was amazed thereat. And after, I faw fome of thefe knaues burned in
Smithfield, & they went fo merely to their
death, finging, and chaunting fcriptures, as
I began to thinke with my felfe, whether
their deuife was not of fome valew or noe:
vntill afterward thinking better of the
matter, I blefled my felfe from them, and fo
lett them goe.

19. Oh (faid the lady) but thefe were
knaues indeed, that deuifed new doctrines,
of their owne heads: and were very heretiks not worthy to be beleeued. But how
fhal I know (quoth the courteoure) that
your deuifers haue not done the like, feing
thefe alleaged fcriptures no lefle, then they?
And did one thing more, which is, that
they went to the fiar, and burned for their
doctrine, when they might haue liued,
which your friar, and his fchollers before
named, haue not hitherto done. And finally
(madame) I fay as at the beginninge I faid:
yf we muft needs follow deuifinge, we
Courtiars had much rather follow a King,
then a friar in fuch a matter. For how many yeares (madame) haue friars fhorne their
heads, and no Courtier hath euer followed
them hitherto therin? but now his maieftie
hauing begone this laft May, (as you know)
to poll * his head, and comaunded others to
do the like: yow cannot find any vnfhorne

Nn 4   head

* See
*Holin-
fhed* and
Stovv of
this po-
ling *an.*
1535.

head in the court among vs men, though
yow women be exempted. And ſo I conclude that the deuiſe of a King is of more
creditt, then the deuiſe of a friar. And with
this the Lady laughed. And ſo the conference was ended.

20.   And thus much for the firſt deuiſinge
or ſettinge vp of new religion in England.
Now, for the going forward therof, lett vs
heare a larg teſtimony of Iohn Fox himſelfe, and therby iudg how Apoſtolike the
maner was of promoting the ſame. *To many,*
vvhich be yet aliue (ſaith Fox) *and can teſtifie*
theſe things, it is not vnknovvne, hovv variable the
ſtate of Religion ſtood in thoſe dayes. Hovv hardly &
vvith vvhat difficulty it came forth: vvhat chances
and changes it ſuffered: euen as the King vvas ruled
and gaue eare ſome tyme to one, and ſomtyme to ano-
ther, ſo one vvhile it vvent forvvard, & another ſeaſon
it vvent as much backvvard againe. And ſome tyme
clean altered and changed for a ſeaſon, according as
they could preuaile, vvhich vvere about the King, &c.

21.   Heere now yow ſee both the beginninge and progreſſe of Fox his ghoſpell.
Wherof in the margent he maketh this
note. *The courſe of the ghoſpell interrupted by mali-*
tious enemyes. Heere yow do heare him ſay,
that the birth of his ghoſpell came forth
hardly and vvith great difficulty and ſtrayning. And
then, that it grew or went backeward, as
the K. was ruled by others, and gaue creditt
                                    to this

The gro
vving &
goiny
forvvard
of the
nevv
ghoſpell
vnder K.
Henry.
Fox pag.
1036.

to this or that man or woman. For so he
commeth in presently with his examples of
Q. Anne, and Cromvvell. So long (saith he) *as Q.* *Fox ib.*
Anne liued, the ghospell had indifferent succeß. But
after that shee by sinister instigation, of some about
the King, vvas made avvay, the course of the ghospell
began againe to enclyne: but that the Lord then styr-
red vp the L. Cromvvell, opportunely to help in that
behalfe. VVho did much auayle for the increase of
Gods true Religion. And much more had brought it to
perfection, yf the pestilent aduersaryes, maligning the
prosperous glory of the ghospell, had not by contrary
practising, vndermyned him, and supplanted his ver-
tuous proceedings.

22. Behould heere a wise discourse of Iohn
Fox. Wherby, if nothinge els were, yow
might perceyue, how iustly, and truly that
spiritt of maiestie that spake to him in his
bedd vpon a sunday in the morning (yf yow
remember, called him * *Thou foole.* For that *See be-*
no man, but a very foole indeed, would *fore*
haue brought forth these examples to haue *cap. 7.*
proued his purpose: Being both impertinēt
and cleerly false in themselues.

23. And first, they are impertinent or rather against himselfe. For that they shew,
that his ghospell had noe other beginning
in England, but vpon affection of men and
women. False also are the examples, yf we
consider the tymes themselues. For that the
forsaid new booke *of deuised Articles*, (men-

tioned

tioned by *Hall* and *Holinshed*) as the first publike alteration in points of Religion, difcouered in K. *Henry*, was made & sett forth
after the death of *Q. Anne Bullen*, to wit vpon
the 8. of Inne 1536. wheras the Q. died vpon
the 19. of May before. And Fox himselfe,
hauing related the said Articles, and booke,
as set forth after the death of *Q. Anne*, he saith

Fox pag. thus. *This booke treated especially but of 3. Sacra-*
991. col. *ments Baptisme, Penance & the Supper of the Lord.*
2. n. 30. *For which the Lincolneshire men tooke armes, &c.*
And then he addeth this note in the mar-
gent: *Alteration of Religion a little beginneth.* And
after againe presently this other note: *Com-*

K. Hen- *motion in Lincolneshire.* Wherby is euident out
ryes be- of his owne words, that the first beginning
ginning of any alteration, in points of Religion to-
of alte- wards his ghospell, was after the death of
ration *Q. Anne Bullen.* And consequently, it is a ridi-
after the
death of culous foolery, which he wryteth before:
Q. Anne *that so long as Q. Anne liued, the ghospell had indif-*
Bullen. *rent successe, &c.*

24.   The other example also of *Cromvell*,
is no lesse apparantly false. For that besids
the particulars, which yow haue heard before, of his assistinge to punithe, and burne
protestants, and his sentence of death giuen
against *Lambert*, with the protestation he
made at his owne death of his beinge Catholike, and neuer doubtinge of any one
point of Cath. Religion: besides all this

(I say)

(I fay) it is notorious, that when the feuere
Statute of fix Articles, was made againft all
forts of Proteſtants, in the 31. yeare of *King*
Henryes raigne, (which was in the moneth
of Aprill, 1540. as appeareth both by the
booke of *Statutes* it felfe, and *Hall, Holinshed,*
& other Chroniclers) Cromwell was then
in his higheſt authority, & fauour with the
King, as is euident. For that in tyme of the
very fame Parlament, befides all his other
great offices before receyued, (as of *Baron,*
Councelour, knight of Gartar, maiſter of the Ievvels,
Vicar generall in fpirituall affayres, and otherlike titles)he was created alſo *Earle of Eſſex &*
high Chamberlayne of England. Which *Holin-*
shed fetteth downe in thefe wordes: *The* 18.
of Aprill at VVeſtminſter, vvas L. Thomas Cromvvell
created Earle of Eſſex, & ordayned great Chamber-
layne of England. VVhich office the Earles of Oxford
vvere vvont euer to enioy. Alſo Gregory his fonne
vvas made Lord Cromvvell, &c. Thus wryteth
he. And yf in Cromwells moſt floriſhinge
tyme, this Act of 6. Articles came out for
puniſhment of Proteſtants, the moſt feue-
reſt that can be imagined: how fond and
childiſh a babling was that, before vſed by
Fox, when he telleth vs, that as long as he
good *L. Cromvvell* was in credit, or bare rule
with the King, their ghoſpell went profpe-
rouſly? &c.

25. Well then, by all this we may fee, how
poore,

poore, and trodden downe a ftate *Iohn Fox*
his Church & religion held, vnder K. *Henry*,
notwithftanding all his braggs, and flatte-
ring of him in his pictures. Which yet, that
yow may not thinke, we meane only of the
temporall or externall condition, or contemptibility of his Church, (for of that perhapps he would bragg, feing he defines his
Church by the words *obfcure and trodden
dovvne*) I would haue yow here confider
breifly but two things, only for the end of
this chapter. Which directly do appertayne
to the true fpirituall mifery of Fox his
Church, and Religion, in thofe dayes vnder
K. *Kenry*: yf a confufion of phantafticall opinions, errors, and herefies may be called a
Religion.

26.   The firft is, that in K. *Henryes* dayes (at
least wayes for a great part therof) the proteftants fects, were not yet fully diftinguifhed into their Claffes or orders: but were a
great confufed heape of new opinions. All
going vnder the name of ghofpellers or pro
teftats, as well *Lutherans, Oecolampadiãs, Zvvinglians* and other facramentaryes, as *VValden-
fians, V Vickliffiãs, Anabaptifts, Libertynes* & other
such like. So as in this firft heap, & maffe of
ghofpellers, were conteined all the feuerall
fects, that fince haue byn diftinguifhed. As
the 4. elements and particular parts therof
were conteyned (accordinge to the poetts
fiction)

The firft
point of
fpiritual
mifery
of the
ghofpel-
lers
church
vnder
K. Hen-
ry.
*Confu-
fion.*

fiction) in that great confused *Chaos* of the
world, before it was diſtinguiſhed. Or to
ſpeake more properly, they were as the
beares whelpes, when firſt they are borne,
& new fallen from their mothers wombe:
to witt, certayne difforme, groſſe, confuſed
things, which by often lickinge of their parents are poliſhed at laſt, and brought to
ſome faſhion of handſome creatures, ſuch as
yow know beares whelpes to be.

27.   And euen ſo was it in thoſe daies with
proteſtants religion. For that euery man,
that would hold a new opinion of what
ſect ſoeuer, or would ſpeake againſt the
Cath. Church or doctrine then vſed, was
admitted preſently for a brother of the new
ghoſpell, and for a ſincere ſeruant of God,
and holy ghoſpeller (as Iohn Fox euery
where calleth them without diſtinction)
whether he were a *Lutheran, Zvvinglian, Ana-
baptiſt*, *VValdenſian*, *VVickleſiſt*, *Lolhard* or
whatſoeuer els. But ſince that tyme, this
Chaos hath byn ſomwhat more diſtinguiſhed, and poliſhed, and euery ſort of ſectaryes deuided into their Claſſes. Which Luther himſelfe began firſt to do: noting 9. diſtinct ſects to haue riſen in few yeares after
him out of his doctrine, and theſe only of
ſacramentaries. Whervnto his cheefe ſcholler *Melacthon*, a little before his death, in his
iudgmet written to the Palſgraue or Prince
Electer.

*Luth. in
parua
Confeſſ.
de Cœna
Domini.*

Melan-
chon. li.
de ſuo iu-
dicio ad
Elect.
Rhen. an.
Domini
1560.
Freder.
Staphil.
l. de Con-
cord.
Luth.
Lyndan.
in dubi-
tant.
Prat.
initio li.
de vit.
& ſectis
haret.

Elector Of *Rhene*, added ſix more to be amonge the Lutherans themſelues. But others that haue gathered them more exa-ctly, and diſtinctly (as *Staphilus*, a moſt lear-ned man, and Councelor to the Emperour: Biſhopp *Lyndan*, Doctor *Gabriel Prateolus*, and others) do deuide them into a farre greater number. Diſtributinge firſt the ghoſpellers of our time, that haue proceeded of Luther, and by occaſion of his doctrine, ſince the yeare of Chriſt 1517. into 3. or 4. claſſes. Wherof the firſt is of plaine Lutherans, de-uided among themſelues into eleuen ſects: And theſe againe beinge ſubdeuided, into other 3. Claſſes of *ſoft, riged*, and *extrauagant Lutherans*, do make aboue 30. other diuiſions and ſects.

28.   The ſecond generall claſſis is of *Semi-lutherani*, halfelutherans, that do partly agree with Luther, and partly diſagree, but yet with an eleuen differences. Which beinge obſtinately, held by their authors, and pro-

The dif-
ferent
claſſes &
ſorts of
ſectaries
ſpronge
from
Luther,
ſince the
yeare
1517.

feſſors, do make eleuen different ſects. The third vniuerſall Claſsis or order of new ghoſpellers are of *Anti-lutherani*, thoſe that are quite oppoſite to Luther, as Sacramen-taryes, and the like. Wherof are ſett downe 56. diſtinct ſects, and the firſt of theſe is of Sacramentaryes, beinge ſubdeuided into 9. ſects, yow may imagine to what number the ſumme will riſe.

29. The

29. The fourth generall classis of new
gholpellers of our tyme, are the Anabaptifts, begon by *Bernard Rotman,* an vnlearned fellow of the laity, but a fcholler and
fonne of Luther, about the yeare of Chrift
1524. that is 7. yeare after Luther began.
And this fort of men are deuided againe in-
13. fects, as in the forfaid authors may be
read. All which deduction, and diftinction
was not made, nor knowne in Englad (except very confufedly) in K. *Henryes* tyme.
But all were accoumpted good gholpellers,
& of one Church & faction, and fo would
Iohn Fox haue them accoumpted alfo now.
For prooffe werof, wherfoeuer they were
contradicted, reftrained, punished or burned for what opinion foeuer, Iohn Fox
putteth them downe exprefsly for Confeffors and Martyrs of his Church. Excepting only the Anabaptifts, which openly
he doth not admitt. For that now alfo they
are burned in England by the proteftant
Magiftrate. But yet nether doth he reiect
them by name: but holdeth himfelfe filent
in their affayre, though he doth fett downe
fundry for martyrs in his Calendar, which
held of their opinions, as in the next part of
this Treatife we are to fhew by many examples. And thus much of the firft point
concetning the confufion, obfcurity, impu-
rity and imperfections of Ionh Fox his
Church

Howv Iohn Fox coo pleth all fectaries in his Church.

Church vnder K. *Henry* which was not yet
ſtrayned from her ſuds, yᵗ Fox at that tyme
may be ſaid to haue had any Church at all.

30.   There followeth the other point of
Antipathy, contradiction, and expoſition
among themſelues, that were holden by
Fox, to haue byn the cheefe pillars of his
Church in thoſe daies. And as for the kinge,
Q. Anne, Cramner, ond *Cromvvell:* we haue ſpoken of already. The other (yf we beleeue
himſelfe) were *Thomas Bilney, Iohn Frith, VVilliam Tyndall:* all three rubricated martyrs in
his Calendar. And then in blacke lettres
(but of the ſame order of martyrdome) *Robert
Barnes, VVilliam Ierome, Thomas Gerard, Iohn Lā-
bert, Peter German, Andrevv Hevvitt, Iohn Colyns,
VVilliam Covvbridg,* and diuers others, that
not only profeſſed his ghoſpell as he ſaith:
but willingly alſo gaue their blood, in a holy, and liuely ſacriſice for teſtimony therof.
And to theſe he addeth diuers holy Confeſſors of the ſame confeſſion: to witt, *Eraſmus Roterodamus, Picus Mirandola, Philipp Melan-
ćthon, K. Edovvard the 6.* and the like.

31.   But now, yf I ſhould goe about, to
draw all theſe martyrs and confeſſors of
his Church, into any one forme of faith, and
beleefe, good or badd, (which is neceſſary,
yow know, to make a Church) it would
proue a farre harder enterpriſe, then to
coople all the catts of any great Citty, by
the

The 1.
ſpiritu-
all miſe-
ry of Io.
Fox his
Church
contra-
diction
among
themſel-
ues in
their be-
leefe.

the heads togeather, & to make them stand
so for an houre of their owne will, lookinge
one vpon the other, without turning their
heads a side. For as for *Bilney,* yow shall perceaue by my Treatise in the next part, that
he neuer held, but very few of the protestants opinions, & very many against them
with vs. And abiured those few of the protestants, at two seuerall tymes, and died in
that abiuration. *Frith* also and *Tyndall,* were
most opposite to Fox in many points of beleefe. I meane opposite both to *Luther,* and
Zvvinglius in the Controuersy of the Sacrament. Holding the *Reall presence* to be a thing
indifferét, & to be beleeued or not beleeued,
as euery man thinketh good, with other
notable particular heresies of their owne, as
in due * place we are to shew. *Robert Barnes*
was an earnest Lutheran; as *Tyndall* testifieth
to *Frith:* and as for *Gerard, Hierome,* & *Lambert,*
though they were Zwinglians: yet not after
Fox his fashion, but different from him in
many points of doctrine. As we shall declare, when we come to handle of them seuerally: as also of *Ridley, Hooper, Rogers, Latymer,* in the next part of this Treatise. Shewinge that vnder *K. Henry* they were only
Lutherans, yf so farre forward at that time.
32. And as for *Andrevv Hevvitt* he was of
no religion in particular, when he died: but
said only, that he would dy for the religion

See part 3. of Bilney die 10. Martij an.1531.

Thomas Bilney
Io. Frith
VVilliã Tyndal.

Part 3. die 2. Ian. & die 6. Octob.

Friar Barnes
Gerard,
Ierome & Lambert.
Ridley,
Hooper
Rogers,
Laty-
mer.
Andrevv
Hevvit.

that

that *Iohn Frith* held, whatſoeuer it were,
as ✶ before we haue noted *Peter German* in-
clyned indeed to Zwinglianiſme : but togeather with that (as when we come vnto
his ✶ holyday, we ſhall ſhew) he denyed
Chriſt to haue taken flew of the Virgin
Mary, and other like holy aſſertions. As for
Colyns, and *Coubridge*, burned alſo for hereſy
vnder K. Henry, and aſsigned for Calendar
martyrs by Fox, vpon the 10. and 11. dayes
of October : himſelfe confeſſeth afterward
vpon better conſideratiō, *that he thinketh them
not vvorthy of the number of Gods profeſſed martyrs.*
but yet holdeth (as he ſaith) *that they are belonging to the holy company of Chriſts ſaints.* The
firſt of theſe two, held vp a dogg, ro be wor-
ſhipped of the people, inſtead of the bleſſed
Sacrament. The ſecond denied the name of
Chriſt flattly. Which Fox not denying, excuſeth the matter thus, ſaying: that the one,
and the other of them were madd, and di-
ſtracted of their witt s, as more largly we
ſhall ſhew afterwards in diſcuſsion of the
Calendar. And thus much of his Martyrs.

33. Now for his Confeſſors, *Eraſmus Rote-
radamus, Picus Mirandula, Friar Bucer, Philipp Melancthon, K. Edvvard* the 6. and others, (which
he ſetteth downe for Saints in the end of
his Calendar, and moneth of December)
they do agree in Religion, as iuſt as Germans lippes (to vſe the vulgar prouerbe)
eyther

✶ *Part* 1.
cap. 12.
Peter
German,
✶ *See his
day part*
3. *&* 13.
Octob.
Colyns
& Cou-
bridg
made
martyrs.
Fox pag.
1033.

Fox his
Confeſ-
ſors vn-
der K.
Henry.

eyther with Fox, or among themselues. For
as for *Erasmus*, whome euery where Fox
maketh (as it were) the father, & firſt maiſter
of new ghoſpellinge in England; yow ſhall
ſo heare him defend himſelfe by his owne
words in the next part of this * Treatiſe, as
you will ſay, they abuſe him egregiouſly, to
hold him for any proteſtant at all, hauinge
written ſo ſharpely againſt their firſt Captaine Luther as he did: repeatinge often
tymes theſe words: *Chriſtum agnoſco, Lutherum
non agnoſco, Eccleſiam Romanam agnoſco.* I acknowledg Chriſt, I do not acknowledg Luther, I acknowledg the Romā Church, &c.
34.   And the like iniury they offer to *Picus*
Earle of *Mirandula,* who neuer held any one
Proteſtant opinion in his life. As we ſhall
ſhew, when we come to his place in the
Calendar. And as for *Bucer,* and *Melanĉthon,*
they were Lutherans in deed, & open enemyes for many yeares againſt *Zvvinglius,* and
Zwinglians, that are the flower of Iohn
Fox his Church. And though *Friar Bucer*
afterward (to haue the free vſe of his woman in England) diſſembled egregiouſly in
ſome things, to pleaſe the Proteĉtor for a
tyme, and ſeemed to beare with the Sacramentaryes: yet told he the *L. Dudley* then
Duke of *Northumberland,* being asked confi-
dently his opinion of the Sacrament by the
ſaid Duke, in the preſence of the *L. Pagett,*
O o 2   then

*Erasmus
Rottera-
damus.*

* *die 26.
Decemb.*

*Erasm.
lib. 16.
ep. 11.*

*Picus
Miran-
dula.*

*Bucer
Melan-
ĉthon.*

Friar Bucers anſvvere to the Duke of Northū berland. then a proteſtant, (who teſtifie the ſame publikely afterward:) that for the *Reall preſence* yt cold not be denyed, yf we beleeue all that the Euangeliſts do wryte. But whether all be to be beleeued or noe he ſaid merely, that was a matter of more diſputation.

Of *K. Edvvard.* the 6. 35. And laſtly concerning *K. Edvvard* the 6. ſet downe alſo by Fox in read letters, for a ſollemne Confeſſor of his Religion: yf we talke of *K. Henryes* tyme, he was a very yong Confeſſor. For that he was ſcarſe 9. yeares old, when his father died. And it is very probable, that the religion, which he at that age coulde receiue, was rather ſuch as his father had cauſed him to be taught during his life: then ſuch as it pleaſed Fox to aſſigne vnto him afterwards. But yf Fox meane, that he was a confeſſor of their Religion after his fathers death: albeit it be hard to ſay of what Religion the Child would haue byn if he had liued ; yet do I thinke him rather worthy to be accompted a martyr of Fox his Church, then a Confeſſor. Seinge it is probable, that the bringinge in of that Religion and change of ſtate left by his father, was the cauſe of his immature death. For that if matters had remayned, as his father left them, and no protector choſen (as he appointed) nor *VVriotheſly* the Chauncelour putt out of his office, nor other Cath. Councelors (moſt faithfull to the conſeruation

tion of the kings bloud,) had byn difgraced
& difplaced by that vnlucky change : like it
is, that the good yong king might haue liued many fayre yeares more, and his two
filters neuer haue fallen into thofe imminēt
dangers of prefent deftruction, which they
once faw themfelues in, by the ambition of
new ghofpelling faction. But enoughe of
this, and of all the raigne of *K. Henry* the 8.
Now fhall we paffe breefly ouer the reft,
that remayneth.

WHETHER FOX HIS CHVRCH
HATH HAD ANY PLACE VNDER
K. Edward, Queene Mary, *and her maieftie*
that novv raigneth : and hovv farre it hath byn
admitted, or is admitted at this day.

Chap. XII.

ALBEYT Iohn Fox did paint out *K.*
Henry the 8. in the the firft page of his
life, fittinge with his feet vpon the Popes
backe, and the ghofpell in his lapp, with his
fword lifted vp in his right hand, to defend
the fame (as before yow haue heard:) yet
did he paint *Cromvvell* and *Cramner* ftayinge
vp the faid fword, leaft yt fhould fall vpon
the proteftants themfelues, as we haue fhewed that in effect yt did. But now in the
firft page of *K. Edvvards* raigne, Fox hath a
much more ample and triumphant pageant

Two
fond pa-
geants
of K.
Henry
& K. Ed-
vvard.

O o 3   for

for the child aboue his father. Who though
he were but nyne yeares old, yet seemeth
Fox to make him a fuller head of the
Church, then his father. Placing him in a
high throne of maiestie, and his stretched
out sword in the right hand, and with the
other, (which is the left) he deliuereth the
ghospell vnto the people, and prelates, that
stand round about him. Where Fox wryteth in the margent this note: *K. Edvvard deli-*
uering the Bible to the prelats, &c. As though the
Bible had taken authority from the Childs
deliueringe. Who beinge so tender of age as
he was, (and of likelyhood scarce able to
read the same, and much lesse to vnderstand
yt) as well he might haue deliuered them
the poeme of *Chaucer*, or the story of *Guy* of
VVervvicke, or of Beuis of Southampton (yf
yt had byn put into his hand to deliuer) as
this was by his vncle the protector; that
knew full neere as little of the contents, as
the child himselfe.

2.   But besides this Maiesticall representation of deliuering the ghospell, there be two
or three other pageants in the same page.
Other
Ridicu-
lous
payn-
tings of
Fox.
The first is of pullinge downe Images, with
great diligence euery where, and burninge
them, with this sentence wrytten vnder:
The temple vvell purged. And then is there a
great shipp, paynted with men, women, &
Children, carrying their Church stuffe into
that

that fhipp: to witt bells, books, images, and
candles: and amongſt other things alſo, the
bleſſed Sacrament. And ouer the fhipp is
written thus: *The fhipp of the Romiſh Church.*
And on the ſide this ſentence: *Shipp ouer your*
trinketts, and be packing, yovv papiſts. And thus is
Iohn Fox his pleaſant head delighted with
theſe fancyes. But who ſeeth not, how
childiſh this folly is. Seinge ſcarſe ſix yeares
after this triumph, when Q. *Mary* came in,
a man might haue ſaid to him agayne, & his
fellowes: *Shipp ouer your trinketts, and be packing*
yovv proteſtants.

3.   But yf we conſider in deed, the different wares, and trinketts, which this Cath.
Roman fhipp carryed away from England
at that tyme, and thoſe which the new proteſtants fhipp brought in ſoone after from
Germany, Geneua, Svvizerland and other places:
we ſhall eaſily diſcouer, whether the loſſe
were greater for our nation, by the departure of the one, or by the comming in of the
other. For that in the Roman fhipp was carryed away, not only the bleſſed ſacrament,
as Fox ſaith, and payneth it out (which yet
is the higheſt & moſt pretious treaſure, that
Chriſt hath left to Chriſtians vpon earth:)
but with that alſo all kind of vertue, & honeſty for the moſt part. For that all modeſty, grauity, learning, piety, deuotion, peace,
concord, vnity & charity was carried away.

And in the new ghoſpellinge ſhipp, came in all the contrary vices : namely of ſedition, diuiſion, pride, temerity, curioſity, nouel-tyes, ſenſuality, impiety, and Atheiſme. And in place of many ſober, honeſt, and graue men, that retyred themſelues, vpon this change, there came running into England a mayne number of wanton Apoſtata prieſts, and friars, ech one with his mate and dame at his ſide, hungry and turbulent people) as *Friar Bale*, *Friar Bucer*, *Friar Couerdale*, *Friar Martyr*, and otherlike. Who ioyninge with other of their owne ſect in England, in ſuch a veyne of innouations, as quickly brought all vpon their owne heads. And ſo though after all theſe forſaid 3. pictures and *repreſentations* (to witt, *the bible diſtributed*, *the Churches ſpoyled: and the Cath. Roman ſhipp ſent avvay*) 1o. Fox doth make a fourth fayre pageant, of the proteſtants kind and confortable meting togeather, at their communion table, and their peaceable breaking of bread. Yet yf yow conſider what preſently enſued in their actions, (I meane of their changinge, choppinge, pullinge downe, and ſettinge vp in thoſe few yeares, that it endured) yow wil eaſily ſee the frutes of that new goſpell. 4. For firſt all begunne with manifeſt perfidiouſneſſe againſt the old king, that was dead. For wheras he had two things in abhomination aboue the reſt; firſt that his

sonne

VVhat the Romanſhip carryed avvay & vvhat the proteſtants ſhipp brought into England.

A picture of the proteſtants agreement.

fonne fhould haue a protector (confidering the fatall euents therof in former tymes) for which caufe he appointed fixteene *Tutors*, to gouerne with equall authority, duringe the minority of his fonne;the other that herefie (but efpecially Zwinglianifme) fhould enter into his Realme : both thefe things were determined contrary to the faid kings will, and ordination, within three dayes after his death,and aboue a dozen before he was buryed. For that the young Child being proclaymed King vpon the 28. of Ianuary, & his father not buried vntill the 14. of February: his vncle the Earle of *Hartford,* was made protector both of the King, and whole Realme, vpon the firft of the faid moneth of February following: and this by the priuate authority of the more part of the executors only, without expecting any parlament, or confent of the Realme, for fo great a change,and charge,as that was.

5.　And albeit for obteyning the confents of the greater parts of executors to this mutation, great aduancements and dignityes were promifed, and fome of them alfo performed (for that the *Lord Dudley* was made Earle of *VVarvvicke,* the *Lo. Parre* Marqueffe of *Northampton*,the Lord Chancelour *VVriothefley* was created Earle of *Southampton*, *Syr Thomas Seymer* was made *Lo.Sudley,* and high Admirall of England, and other the like,

Promotions made by the protector in the beginning of K.Edward dayes.

O o 5　　　　and

and this with in 15. dayes after the Protectors aduancement) and though hope alſo
was giuen to thoſe, that were Catholikely
inclyned (as the moſt of them were, yf they
had followed their conſciences) that no
great alteration of religion ſhould be made
for the preſent: yet 20. dayes had ſcarſe paſſed, after this aduauncement, but that the
protectors fingars did ſo eagerly itche to be
doing, and tamperinge about innouation in
Religion, as vpon the 6. of March next followinge, he ſent away comiſſioners into all
parts of the realme, to pull downe Images,
and other Eccleſiaſticall ornaments, throughout all the Churches of the realme, & to
make other innouations by his authority,
which now in all things he would haue to
be the kings. And for that the chauncelour
VVriotheſley reſiſted the ſame, & would haue
had it ſtayed vntill a parlamēt might be called: his office was taken from him, therby to
terrify others from ſpeaking in like caſes. Biſhop *Tonſtall* alſo was putt beſide the councell for like offence, though he were one of
the 16. executors appointed by K. *Henry*. So
as now the protector would needs haue all
things abſolutely in his owne hand, both
without law, and before law, yea expreſſely
againſt the lawes of K. *Henry* yet in force.

6.   And for that both he and his followers
did eaſily ſee, the affection of the Realme
to be

Holin-
ſhed,
Stovv &
others
an. Dom.
1547.

to be wholy againſt theſe mutations,(as before we haue, ſhewed in the end of our former part:)he deuiſed with the Lo. Dudley, who ſoothed him in all at that tyme, the iourney into *Scotland* of muſſelborough field which all men know,vnder pretéce to gayne the young Queene by force,to Marry with the King. But yet euery man of iudgment,& diſcourſe, did eaſily ſee, that not to be a thing likely, to gett ſuch a princeſſe by way of armes frō her ſubiects. Neither was K. *Edvv.* of ſuch age, as they needed to haue haſtened ſo much, to gett him a wife ſo ſoone (he being but 9. yeres olde) but that the matter might haue byn treated peaceably,with the Scotts,to haue concurred willingly, for their owne intereſt, to that coniunctiō of both Realmes by that Marriage, accordinge as they had done in K. *Henryes* tyme. And ſo wrote *B. Gardener* to the protector, preſently vpon the firſt ſermon he heard the B.of *Saint Dauids in VVales,* make in London, about that matter, I meane, to exhort the people to the enterpriſe of Scotland. For that now all preachers, were ſet a worke by the ſaid protector, and Earle of *VVarvvicke* to ſhew the great glory, and vtilityes of that attempt.

The iorney into Scotland vvhy it vvas deuiſed in K.Edvv. tyme.

7. But the true cauſe of this enterpriſe was indeed, to haue therby a iuſt pretence, and occaſion to rayſe an army within the land,

and

and to call in forrayne forces (as they did both Germans & Italians vnder *Petro Gamboa* that had ferued *K. Henry* at *Bologne*, and other leaders) who they thought would be alwayes more fure ynto them, then Englifh fouldiars in occafions of Religion. And fo it fell out indeed. For the very next yeare after, thefe forraine fouldiars, did ftand the protector in very good fteed, when diuers fhires of the Realme tooke armes for defence of their Religion, in the third yeare of *K. Edvvards* raigne, as after yow fhall heare. 8. This then was the firft fommers worke after *K. Edvvards* coronation: to witt, that the protector made his voyage towards Scotland, hauinge firft fent comifsioners, and preachers (as you haue heard) into all fhires, to preach againft Images, procefsion, litanyes, pilgrimages, maffe, praying to Saints. And this of his owne authority, without, and againft law. For that no parlament had yet difanulled the Religion left by *K. Henry*. Which thing fo much greeued the common Cath. people, as they began to exclaime euery where againft the faid comifsioners. And one of them called *Body* was flayne in Cornwall. For which diuers men were executed, in fundry places of that fhire. And a Prieft fent vp to be hanged, drawne, and quartered in Smithfield, for the terror of others, for that he was faid by fome to haue

byn

byn acceſſary to the ſaid *Bodyes* deathe.

9. And this was the beginninge of plan-tinge new Religion in England, by autho-rity of the protector, vnder a child King. Which protector notwithſtanding, for that he miſtruſted his home doctors, (as well as his home ſouldiars) to be ſufficient for ſo great a worke, as the planting of a new Re-ligion: he ſent ouer into Germany for di-uers ſtrange Sectaryes, of what Religion ſoeuer, ſo they were not Catholike. But eſpecially he deſired to haue Apoſtata friars, that had tyed themſelues to ſiſters. Aſſuring himſelfe, that they would be moſt plyable to his purpoſe. And ſo their came into En-gland *Martyn Bucer* a Dominican Friar, who vnto that day had byn an earneſt Lutheran: and *Peter Martyr* a channon regular that in-clyned to Zwinglianiſme: but yet came with great indifferency to preach, & teach, what he ſhould be appoynted. *Bernardinus Ochinus* was the third, who had byn a Fran-ciſcan friar : and by takinge a woman had loſt all Religion. Writing a booke *de Polyga-mia*, for hauinge many wyues at once and died after a Iew.

10. Theſe three were diſtributed into 3. principall fountaynes of the land, *London, Oxford,* and *Cambridg.* And with theſe ioyned other of the ſame coate, and profeſſion, as *Couerdall* an Auguſtine friar, *Bale* a Carme-lite,

The ruſhing in of Apoſtatas into En-gland.

Bernard ochinus vid Sander. l. de viſib. Mo-narch. pag. 627.

lite,and other like Inglifhmen,as before we
haue fhewed. All which beginninge to
preach in diuers parts of the land , filled
mens heads with noueltyes , and contentions. But had not the gift of the old Apo-
ftolicall preachers , to preach the felfe fame
faith,& doctrine euery where.But fo many
men , fo many opinions were fett abroach,
euery man following his owne fancy.Only
they agreed in impugninge the Catholike
Church, rytes, doctrine , and feruice : but
among themfelues they could not agree.

11.   Which thing being fignified to the
Protector, both before his departure , and
whyle he was in the Scottifh iourney : it
greeued him excedingly , and wrote backe
to *Cramner, Ridley*, and the reft, that they
fhould feeke fome meanes of agreement,&
conformity , and that they fhould make haft
to end the common feruice booke,or booke
of common prayer, doctrine,& rites,which
they had begunne! to treat of,before his departure out of London. But this was not fo
easy to do, for that new factions , and diuifions were growne now among them,efpe-
cially vpon the arriuall of the forfaid new
preachers , as well Englifh , as ftrangers
from beyond the feas . For albeit the ftrangers coulde not much help, in making this
Englifh communion booke , or rather new
maffe booke : yet did they hurt and hinder
                                          the

The cau
fes of
iarres be
tveeen:
the nevv
prote-
ftant
prea-
chers.

the fame much by the variety of opinions,
which they brought with them in matter
of doctrine. Some of them comming from
Saxony , and others from Zwitzerland.
Where there were different new fects, and
doctrines held, & taught. And for fo much,
as in this booke not only the rites, and ceremonies of feruice , & adminiftration of Sacraments : but the doctrine alfo of their
number and natures , and other articles of
beleefe were to be expreffed , or at leaft
wayes infinuated; herof arofe a great warre.
For that *Bucer* would haue one thing, *Peter
Martyr* another , *Ochinus* a third. And then
ftepped in *Iohn Bale*, & *Milo Couerdall*, frefhely
come with their new doctrine, & wanton
women from beyond feas, and would haue
roome amongft the reft.

12.   But aboue all others did trouble the
markett at this tym e, two heady marryed
priefts , come alfo from beyoud the feas: to
wit *Iohn Hooper*, and *Iohn Rogers*, the one from
VVittenberg with a German wife ; the other
from *Argentine* with a Burgundian Syfter
(as Fox teftifieth.) who diffentinge wholy from the courfe begon, by *Cramner*, and
Ridley , and bearinge fpeciall emulation
againft them , as accompting themfelues
more learned, and zealous, and more reformed then they, (as in their liues we fhall
fhew , when we come to their places in the
Calendar.)

Calendar.) they being potent in ſpeech, and faction, and had in eſtimation of the people in reſpect of their former baniſhment, they made this agreement at the firſt beginning much more difficult. Eſpecially for that one *Hugh Latimer*, more turbulent then any of them all, and of more regard with the common people, for that he had byn Biſhopp in K. Henryes dayes; ioyned with *Hooper* and *Rogers*, againſt *Cramner*, and *Ridley*. For that they were not inclyned to reſtore him his Biſhopricke of Worceſter, wherof he had byn depriued by K. *Henry* the 8.

Stovv
æn. 1539.

13.   Whervpon the Protector, when he returned to London from the Scottiſh voyage, in the end of the ſommer, he was greatly troubled to ſee theſe diuiſions. But eſpecially, for that he found nothing ready, as he had hope for the new cōmunion booke: but only that the old religion was impugned, and the new not yet framed, and infinite ſtrife was raiſed both about the one & the other. Yet a Parlament being called togeather vpon the 4. of Nouemb., *an. Domini* 1547. & the firſt of K. Edw.: they thought to giue an attempt to ſee, what might be done; to haue ſome alteration eſtabliſhed. But yt would hardly be: notwithſtanding all art, power, and perſuaſion was vſed by the Protector, and his people, to obteyne the ſame. For that in this Parlament
they

they gatt only two things of moment to be
determined about Religion. The firſt was,
that all former penall ſtatutes made againſt
any heretike or ſectary whatſoeuer, from
K. Edward the third downward (to witt,
for the ſpace almoſt of 200. yeares) ſhould
be reuoked. But namely the ſtatutes made
againſt *Lolhards, VVickliffians, Huſſits, Anabaptiſts*
and the reſt, in the firſt yeare of *K. Richard*
the ſecond, and in the 2. yeare of *K. Henry*
the 5. and in the 25. 31. 33. 34. and 35. yeares
of *K. Henry* the 8. againſt what hereſies heretiks or ſectaryes ſoeuer. All theſe lawes
and ſtatutes (I ſay) were recalled, annulled,
and taken away, togeather with their puniſhments, prohibitions, or other reſtraints
whatſoeuer. So as now euery man might
thinke, ſay, preach, or teach what he
thought beſt. And this iudgeth Fox to be a
goodly ſweet liberty of the ghoſpell, where
no man is bound nor forced to any thinge.
And this determyned a child of 9. yeares
ould, againſt the decrees of all his prudent
anceſtors for 200. yeares vpward.

14. But yet in all this free liberty of ſectaryes, to ſay, wryte, and teach, what they
liſt, the puniſhment of death was reſerued
vnto Catholiks, that ſhould ſpeake in defence of the doctrine of the Popes Supremacy, or in derogation of the ſupreme Eccleſiaſticall headſhipp of this young King.

And

Margin notes:

Statut. an. Domini 1547. Edou. 6. an. 1.

Liberty and im-punity grauted to all he-retiks.

And this was the firſt and principall beginning of the ghoſpell in K. *Edvvards* tyme, to
giue euery man liberty to do and beleeue
what he would, ſo he were not a Cath.
Which is much like the opening of priſons
and common gayles in the beginninge of a
Rebellion, when all malefactors are made
free from feare of lawes, ſo they will ioyne
in faction with the Rebellious. And vpon
the openinge of this gate, no maruayle
though all ſectaryes ruſted in, and among
others diuers Arrians, Anabaptiſts, Trinitarians, and like heretiks began to preach preſently their doctrines, with ſuch publicity,
as *Cranmer* and his fellowes for repreſſinge
therof, were enforced to ſitt in publike
iudgment and condemne diuers of them to
death. Albeit I do not ſee, by what law;
hauinge now reuoked & anulled all former
ſtatutes, made againſt heretiks for their puniſhment, as hath byn ſaid. And namely he

condemned *Ioane* of *Kent* (alias *Ioane Knell,*)
that had byn a handmayd of *Anne Askevv*,
burned before in the laſt yeare of K. *Henry*
the 8. for denyinge the *Reall preſence.* And
Ioane had profited ſo much vnder Annes
doctrine, as now ſhe denyed Chriſt to haue
taken fleſh of the Bl. Virgine. Who was ſo
reſolute with her ſcriptures againſt *Cranmer*
and his aſſiſtants ſittinge vpon her, and her
fellowes in our Ladyes chappell of *S. Paules*
Church

Ioane
knell
condem
ned and
burned
by *Cran-
mer.*
Sto. in
Chron.
*an.*1549.

Church in London vpon the 27. of Aprill,
when he gaue sentence of death against her:
that she reproached him greatly for his in-
constancy in Religion, telling him that he
condemned not long before *Anne Askeuv* for
a peece of bread, and now condemned her
for a peece of flesh. And that as he was come
now to beleeue the first, which then he had
condemned: so would he come in tyme, to
beleeue the second, &c.

15. And for that O. E. in his defence of
Syr Francis Hastings, would not seeme to
thinke this matter to be true: I do assure the
Reader in all sincerity, that I haue it by relation, and asseueration of a worshipfull, &
honorable ★ knight, that afterward was of   ★ *Syr*
Q. Maryes priuy councell: and was either   *Francis*
present, when these things were spoken by   *Ingle-*
Ioane of *Kent*, or heard yt from them, that   *field.*
were present. From whome also I receiued
diuers other particularityes, which in this
chapter and the former are touched by me.
Knowinge the man to be of such wysdome
and entyre creditt, as I can hardly follow a
better author in things of his tyme.

16. Well then, this is the first point obteyned in this first parlament of K. *Edvvard*: that
all sects had impunity. Wherof Fox glorieth much in these words: *These meeke and*
gentle tymes of K. Edvvard, vnder the gouerment of
this noble protector, haue this one commendation pro-

per to them, that during the vvhole tyme of the 6.
yeares of this kings much tranquillity, and as it vvere
a breathing time vvas graunted to the vvhole Church
Fox pag.
1180. col.
2. n. 40. *of England, &c.* Neither in Smithfield *nor any other*
quarter of this Realme, any vvas heard to ſuffer for
any matter of Religion, eyther papiſt or proteſtant,
Fox his
imperti-
nēt brag
of impu-
nity vn-
der K.
Edvv. *eyther for one opinion or other. except only tvvo ; one*
an Englishvvoman called Ioane *of* Kent, *the other*
a Duchman nomed Georg Paris, *vvho died for cer-*
tayne Articles not much neceſſary here to be rehear-
ſed. Behould heere Fox vnwillinge to rehearſe the Articles of theſe two new ghoſpellers. Which were no other, but the de-
nyall of Chriſt himſelfe. And for that he
ſaith no man ſuffered for Religion it ſelfe
(eyther Catholike or proteſtant) in all K.
Edvvards dayes : I would aske him, what he
would ſay to ſo many hundreds, as were
ſlayne, and put to death in Somerſetſhire, Deuonſhire, Cornvvall, Lincolnſhire, Norfolke, Torke-
The ſuf-
feringe
of Ca-
tholiks
vnder
K. Edvv. *ſhire* and other places in the 3. yeare of K.
Edvvards Raigue, that were forced to take
armes for defence of their Religion, violently wreſted from them, againſt all truth,
reaſon, law, and order? Was not this ſuffe-
ringe alſo for Religion ? But lett vs heare
Iohn Fox himſelfe confeſſe vnto vs, the
manner of entrance of his ghoſpell, into
England.

Fox pag.
1180.
n. 14. 17.   *After ſofter beginnings* (ſaith he) *by little &*
little, greater things follovved in the reformation of
the

the Churches, and a nevv face of things began novv to appeare, as it vvere on a stage, nevv players comming in, and the other thrust out. For the most part the Bishopps of Churches, and diocefes vvere changed, &c. Bonner Bishop of London vvas comitted to the Marshallfea, and depriued: Gardener B. of VVinchefter and Tonftall B. of Durham vvere caft into the tovver &c. Lo heere by Fox his owne confefsion, what *peace, and meeknesse* there was vfed, *in thefe gentle tymes of* K. *Edvvard, vnder the gouernment of this noble protector*: though they were but 6. yeares in all: And let the Reader confefle,that Fox hath a fpeciall gift to contradict himfelfe: though it be in the felfe fame page. But now to the fecond point concluded in this Parlament about matters of Religion.

18. The fecond point was about the Bl. Sacrament of the Aultar, and vfe therof. Which as it was a very important, & principall point for thefe new ghofpellers of K. *Edvvards* dayes to declare their opinions, whether they would be Lutherans, ac Sacramentaryes:fo they being wholy deuided among themfelues in this point, (fome of them comming from *VVittenberg,* and other places of Saxony, which followed Luther, fome other from *Stfasburg, Bafill,* and other townes among the Zwitzers, where the doctrine of *Zvvinglius* bare rule, others that were home proteftants, and defired to paffe

The fecond point handled in the firft parlament about the blefed Sacramet.

Pp 3 no furno further in neither of theſe two particular ſects & factiõs, but only ſo farre as was needfull for holding their womē they had taken, as *Cranmer* & his fellowes) they could in no caſe come to any accord, or agreemēt in this matter, but only to publiſh an Act or ſtatute like a ſhipmās hoſe, that determined neither the one, nor the other. The title wherof was this. *An Act againſt ſuch perſons as ſhall vn-reuerently ſpeake against the Sacrament of the body & bloud of Chriſt, (commonly called the Sacrament of the Aultar) & for the receyuing therof vnder both kinds.* And then beginneth the Statute thus.

Stat.an.
1. Edvv.
6. cap. 1.

19. The Kings moſt excellēt maieſtie mea-
„ ning the gouernāce of his moſt louing ſub-
„ iects, to be in moſt perfect vnity, & concord
„ in all things, & in eſpecially in the true faith
„ & Religion of God, & wiſhing the ſame to
„ be brought to paſſe, withall Clemency on
his part, as his moſt princely ſerenity and maieſtie hath already declared, &c. This is the preface, & after comming to the matter, they ſay: In the moſt confortable Sacramēt of the body, and bloud of our Sauiour Ieſus
„ Chriſt, (commonly called the Sacrament of
„ the Aultar, &c.) Which Sacrament was in-
„ ſtituted by no leſſe author, then our Sauiour
„ both God and man, when at his laſt ſupper

*The ſta-
tute
about
the Bl.
Sacra-
ment.*

Mat. 26.
Luc. 22.
1. Cor. 11.

he did take the bread into his holy hands, & did ſay: *Take yovv, and eate, this is my body, vvhich is geuen and broken for yovv, &c.* Which words
ſpoken

spoken of yt, being of eternall, infallible and vndoubted truth, yet the said Sacrament all this notwithstanding, hath byn of late maruelously abused, by such manner of men before rehearsed, who of wickednesse, or els of ignorance, & want of learning, for certayne abuses hertofore committed of some, in misusing therof, haue condened in their harts, & speach the whole thing, & contemptuously deproued, despised, or reuyled, the same most holy, & blessed Sacrament, & not only disputed or reasoned vnreuerently, and vngodly of that high mistery, but also in their sermons, preachings, readings, talks, tunes, songs, playes, or iests, do name, and call yt by such vile, and vnseemely words, as Christian eares do abhorre to heare rehearsed: For reformation wherof, be yt enacted, &c.

20. This is their narration, and according thervnto, they do sett downe remedy and punishment for them, that shall speake any contemptuous words, to depraue, despise, or reuile this Sacrament. But what the words or sense therof are in particular, or what they meane by this despising, or deprauinge, they do not sett downe, as they ought to haue done, yf they had meant playnly. Though by the words of their said narration it may appeare, this Statute was made principally against Sacramentaryes, that deny the *Reall presence* of the body, and

bloud of our Sauiour, *and do diſpute, and reaſon vnreuerently and vngodly therof* : this beinge the higheſt iniury, contempt or deprauatió that can be done to yt. But it pleaſed not the makers of this ſtatute to be vnderſtood, or to deale cleerly for the preſent in this behalfe: but rather to ſpeake obſcurely and doubtfully, to the end they might afterward haue a ſtartinge hole to go out at, and become Zwinglians or Caluiniſts, when they would. The other clauſe of adminiſtringe the Sacrament vnder both kinds, to all ſorts of people, they put downe more cleerly with this exceptió only: *except neceßity otherwiſe require.* By which words they allow alſo the vſe vnder one kind, in tyme of neceſsity. Which is farre from that, which ſince that tyme they haue taught.

Deceytfull dealinge in this ſtatute.

21. Theſe were the two things of moſt moment determined about religion in this firſt Parlament. Two other things were attempted by the ghoſpellers, with moſt earneſt endeauour, but they could not be obtayned. The firſt was to haue a booke of common prayer paſſe, which they had compoſed in haſt, out of the maſſe booke for alteringe the ſeruice, & maſſe into Engliſh, or rather for aboliſhinge of the maſſe, & bringinge in the new cómunion in place therof. And this booke was compoſed by certaine appointed by the protector, & *Cranmer.* But

when

when it came to the parlament to paſſe, it was miſliked, and contradicted, not only by Catholiks, but by many proteſtants alſo. Eſpecially thoſe that were the moſt forward, as *Hooper, Rogers,* and ſome other. Who according to Fox, were Puritans in thoſe dayes, & would neither take the oath of ſupremacy to the yong K., (as we ſhall ſhew more largely when we come to treat of them ſeuerally in the next part of this Treatiſe) nor yet weare Typpett, capp, or Surpleſſe. And misliked moreouer the whole gouernment Eccleſiaſticall in that tyme, neyther agreed with the opinions of doctrine ſett downe by that booke. And ſo yt was reiected with no ſmall greefe, both of the Duke protector and Archb. *Cranmer.*

The firſt communion booke in English reiected.

22. The other point propoſed, & reiected alſo, was about allowance of Prieſts and friars marriages, and legitimation of their children. Wherin great force was made by them, that had taken women firſt, & ſought approbation afterwards, but could not gett yt for the preſent. Though in the next parlament about a yeare after, they obteyned a certayne mittigation therin, as yow ſhall heare.

The allovvāce of Prieſt & friars mariages reiected in this parlament.

23. Now then this Parlament being thus paſt, and ended vpon the 20. day of December, and the protector much greeued, that noe more could be obtayned therin, to the

The reſolute proceedinge of the L. Protector.

fauour

fauour of the new ghoſpellers; he thought
good for the time to come, to vſe his kingly
authority vnder the name of the young
child for the altering of diuers points in religion, vſing *Cranmer* and ſome other alſo of
the counſell for his inſtruments. And firſt

Fox pag.
1183.

they began with B. *Bonner* as may appeare
by a letter from the ſaide *Bonner* wryten to
B. *Gardiner* of *VVincheſter* the 28. of *Ianuary*
1548. wherin the writeth thus : *My very good
Lord, theſe be to aduertiſe your Lordſhipp, that my
L. of Canterburyes grace this preſent 28.of Ianuary,
ſent me his letters miſſiue conteyninge this in effect.
That my L. Protectors grace, vvith aduiſe of other
the K.Maieſties moſt honorable counſell, for certayne
conſiderations them mouing, are fully reſolued, that*

Candles
aſhes,
an i pal-
mes for-
bidden
by the
Prote-
ctor.

*no candles ſhalbe borne vpon Candlemaſſe day, nor
from henceforth aſhes, nor palmes vſed any longer.
requiring me to cauſe admonition therof to be geuen
vnto your Lordſhipp and other Biſhopps vvith celeri-
ty, &c.* Thus much there.

24.   And after this againe vpon the 11. of
the next moneth of February, the ſaid protector with ſome others of the counſell, at
his appointment, wrote to *Cranmer,* and by
him to all Biſhopps of the Realme, com-
maunding them to pull downe all Images,
in theſe words, amongſt others : *VVe haue
thought good* (ſaith he) *to ſignifie vnto yovv that his
highneſſe pleaſure, vvith the aduiſe and conſent of vs
the Lord Protector and the reſt of the counſell is, that*
                                        immediatly

Fox ib.
col. 2.

immediatly vpon the fight hereof, vvith as conuenient diligence, as you may, you giue order that all Images, remayning in any Church, or Chappell, &c. Be remoued and taken avvay. And in the execution hereof vve requyre both yovv, and the reft of the Bishopps, to vfe fuch forefight, as the fame may be quietly done, vvith as good fatisfaction of the people as may be, &c. From Somerfett place the 11. of February. 1548. Your louing frends: Edwarde fomerfett, Henr. Arundell, Anthony Wingfield, Iohn Ruffell, Thomas Seymer, William Paget.

Images taken avvay by the protectors letter before the parlament.

25   And now candells, ashes, and Images beinge gone (as yow fee) there followed in the next moneth after, (to witt, of March,) that the protector defiringe ftill to go forward with his defigment of alteration, fent abroad a proclamation in the kings name, with a certayne communion booke in Englifh, to be vfed for adminiftration of Sacraments, in fteed of the maffe booke. But whether it was the very fame, that was reiected a little before in the parlament, or an other patched vp afterward, or the fame mended or altered, is not fo cleare. But great care there was had by the protector, & his adherents, that this booke should be admitted, and put in practife prefently, euen before it was allowed in parlament. To which effect Fox fetteth downe a large letter of the councell to all the Bifhops, exhortinge and commanding them, in the kings name,

A nevv communion booke thruft vpon Catholiks by the protectors only authority.

to ad-to admitt, and putt in practife this booke.

Fox pag.
1184.
col. 1.

VVe haue thought good (fay they) *to pray and require* yow Lordfhipps, and neuerthelesse in
the K. Maiefties our moft dread Lords
» name to commaund you, to haue a diligent,
» earneft, and carefull refpect to caufe thefe
» books to be deliuered to euery parfon, vicar,
» and curate within your diocesse, with fuch
» diligence as they may haue fufficient tyme
» well to inftruct, and aduife themfelues, for
» the diftribution of the moft holy commu-
» nion, accordinge to the order of this booke
» before this Eafter tyme, &c. Prayinge yow
» to confider, that this order is fett forth, to
» the entent there fhould be in all parts of the
» Realme, one vniforme manner, quiettly
» vfed. To the execution wherof we do eft-
» fones require you to haue a diligent refpect,
» as yow tender the kings maiefties pleafure,
» & will anfwere to the contrary, &c. From
» Weftminfter the 13. of March 1548.

26.   By all which, and by much more that
might be alleaged, it is euident; that all, that
was hitherto done againft Cath. Religion
for thefe firft two yeares, vntill the fecond
parlament, was done by priuate authority
of the Protector and his adherents, before

The con
fufion
that in-
fued in
England law and againft law. And now what a Ba-
bylonicall confufion enfued in England
vpon thefe Innouations, in all Churches,
parifhes & Bifhoppriks commonly, is won-
derfull

derfull to recount. For some Priests said the
Latyn masse, some the English communiõ,
some both, some neyther: some said halfe of
the one, & halfe of the other. And this was
very ordinary: to witt, to say the *Introitus* &
Confiteor in English : and then the collects,
& some other parts in Latyn. And after that
againe the Epistles & ghospells in English,
and then the Canon of the Masse in Latyn,
& lastly the Benediction, & last ghospell in
English. And this mingle-mangle did euery
man make at his pleasure , as he thought it
would be most gratefull to the people.

vpon the first Innoua-tion.

27.   But that which was of more importance,& impiety;some did consecrate bread
& wyne, others did not, but would tell the
people before hand plainly, they would not
consecrate: but restore them their bread and
wine backe againe, as they receyued it from
them.   Only adding to yt the Church benediction. And these that did consecrate , did
consecrate in diuers formes, some aloud,
some in secret, some in one forme of words,
and others in an other. And after consecra-
tion some did hould vp the host to be ado-
red after the ould fashion, and some did not;
And of those that were present , some did
kneele downe and adore , others did shutte
their eyes, others turned their faces aside,
others ran out of the Church, blaspheming,
and crying Idolatry.

28. And

28. And as this confusion was in spirituall matters, during these first two yeares of K. *Edvvards* raigne : so no lesse was it in temporall affaires, especially in the citty of *London*, where a great mortality and pestilence was among the people, as *Stovv* saith. And no lesse amazement, to see three cheefe Bishops sent to prison, *Gardiner* of *VVinchester*, *Bonner* of *London*, and *Tonstall* of *Duresme*. But the greatest banding was betwixt the protector, & his brother the Admirall, & betwene their wyues, *Queene Catheryne Parre* and the Duchesse of Somersett. In which contention diuers cheefe ministers and Apostata friars were sticklers; but especially *Hugh Latymer*, that inueighed in his sermons against the Admirall in fauour of the Protector. On the other side Friar Bale was wholy addicted to *Q. Catherine* and her praises, hauing printed and sett her forth, in those very dayes for a famous writer, and one of the miracles of womankind in his booke *De scriptoribus Britannicis*. For so he saith: *Ingenij viribus, litteratum peritia, verborum elegantia, & animi generositate fœmineas dotes exuperat, &c*. She doth exceed the gifts of womankind in the force of her witt, in the skill of her learninge, in the elegancy of her words, and generosity of mynd. And againe. *Magnarum virtutum, ac vnicum hoc saculo pietatis exemplar, &c*. She is the only example of greate vertues and piety in this

The troubles and garboyles in temporall affayres, ensuinge vpon Ecclesiasticall confusion.

Bal. de script. Britan. fol. 238.

this our age. With which excessiue prayses
the Duchesse of Somersett, that thought her
selfe as wise and learned as the other, was so
offended, as friar Bale could gett no preferment, while her husband was in authority.

29.   But now came on the second parlament, which was vpon the 4. day of No-
uember 1548. and second yeare of K. Edw.
raigne. And the protector, and his ghospellers had made all the preparation possible
to gett voyce therin, for establissing of that,
which they desired in religion. As yt is no
maruayle, yf yt were not heard to do, seing
the cheefe Bishopps were now restrayned,
terrified, or put in prison, some other of the
layty also disgraced, as the Earle of *Southam-*
pton, Arundell, and others. The Lord Protector and Dudley armed with the remayn-
der of their forces made for Scotland. And
the displeasure of the said Protector being
held now for so dreadfull a matter to any
that resisted his designes, as it was expected
dayly, that his owne brother the Admirall
should be made away by him vpon like displeasure.

30.   But to speake of this Parlament begon now (as we haue saide) two things (as
yow remember) were excluded in the last
parlamet, that could not passe, though neuer
so much desyred, and vrged by the Protector and his frends. To witt, the new communion

The se-
cõd par-
lamet of
K. Edvv.
an. 1548.
4. Nouëb.

munion booke, and the allowance of prieſts and friars marriages. but now both of them paſſed : albeit the ſecond with a greater limitation, as yow will ſee, for the title of the Statute is only this . *An Act to take avvay all poſitiue lavves of man made againſt the marriage of prieſts.* Wherby yow ſee, that the Parlament being importuned by prieſts, and friars, that had gotten them women, to haue them allowed by Parlament: they only obtayned to be free from teporall puniſhment appointed for the ſame leauinge them to god for the reſt, whether after their vowes made of chaſtity, they were bound to obſerue the ſame, or no. Nay in the very act it ſelfe, they do highly comend chaſtity in prieſts ſaying: *that it vvere not only better for prieſts* and miniſters of the Church to liue chaſt, ſole, and ſeparate from the company of women: &c. but that it were moſt to be wiſhed, that they would willingly, and of themſelues endeauour to keep a perpetuall chaſtity, and abſtinence from the vſe of women. Yet for as much as the contrary hath byn ſeene, &c. Be yt enacted that all lawes poſityue, Canons, or conſtitutions hertofore made by authority of man only (which doth prohibite or forbidd marriage to any Eccleſiaſticall perſon) &c. Shalbe vtterly voyd & of none effect, togeather with the paines, penalties, crimes, actiōs therunto annexed, &c.

Statut. ānno 2. Edou. 6. cap. 21 anno Domini 1548. The ſtatute of impunity for Prieſts & friars to marry

　　　　　　　　　　31. Thus

31. Thus goeth the Statute. Wherin yow see there is nothing, but impunity geuen to incontinent Priests, & friars to vse women without feare of punishment in this world. And therby yow may consider, that the first and cheefe endeauors of these new ghospellers tended principally to breake downe hedges, and to dissolue Cath. discipline, and to take away punishmēts appointed aswell to heretiks and heresie in generall (as by the former parlament yow haue seene) as also to loose & incontinēt cleargy men for their dissolute life. And thus much of the first point. Lett vs come to the second, about the new communion booke.

32. This booke, though it were made new againe by great diligence, both of the composers, which the protectors and his followers had chosen out for that purpose, as also by the vew of *Cranmer*, *Ridley* and others of cheefe authority in the cleargy: yet had it maruelous difficulty to passe, as may appeare by the very Act of Parlament it selfe. For that it was not only contradicted by Catholiks, but also by many protestants themselues. Mislikinge not only the rytes & ceremonyes therin appointed, but the very articles of doctrine also. And in this were most vehemēt the forsaid faction of *Hooper*, *Rogers*, *Latymer* and some others, being at that tyme Puritans, as before we haue noted.

The second contention about their new cōmunion booke.

Q q   33. But

330.   But the chiefest, and whotest contention of all (whereof the principall point of
their new Religion seemed to depend) was,
whether they should be Lutheras, or Zwinglians, concerninge the blessed Sacrament.
Seing they coulde not wel longer dissemble
the same, as they had donne in the former
parliament: though otherwise (as I haue
faid) it was fome what hard to determine.
For that to the Lutherans enclined not only *Cranmer, Ridley,* and other in Ecclesiasticall
authority, that had liued, and borne rule
vnder *K. Henry* the 8. before. But many of
the noble men also, & counselors, that were
halfe Catholiks and halfe protestants. Protestants, for liberty of eatinge of flesh on
forbidden daies, possessing Church liuings,
disobligation of confession, and restitution,
and other such motyues: But yet for other
matters were rather Catholike in iudgmēt,
& with these concurred such, as were come
out of Saxony, and had studied vnder Luther, as *Bucer, Bale, Couerdall,* and others. All
which seemed to stand for the reall presence at that tyme. But against these were
the Sacramentaries, whose profession being
of the fresher frame, more pleased the protector, and some other ytching eares. And
therby did ouerbeare the other side, at
length by the number of some few voyces
in parlament, but yet with great difficulty.
Wher-

The Zvvin-glian faction did ouer beare the Lutherā in *K. Ed-vvards* dayes.

Whervpon the said Parlamēt was cōtinued
in disputation, and contention, especially
about this matter for the space of 4. monethes and a halfe: to witt, from the 4. of No-
uember, vnto the 14. of March, and in the
meane space, all was in suspence, of what
religion England should be. For as on the
one side many that knew or suspected the
protectors inclination, did thinke and lay
wagers, that Zwinglianisme would pre-
uayle:so others hearing that the Archbishop
*Cranmer,*and his part stood resolutely on the
other side,and had punished diuers for speaking against the Masse, & *Reall presence* in the
Sacrament a little before, to witt, one *Tho-*
mas Dobbe a maister of art in Cambridg (as
Fox telleth vs) cast into the counter by
Cranmer, and held there till he died, and *Iohn*
Hume, imprisoned for the same cause by the
said Archbishop. This (I say) made many
to expect & bett on the other side. But especially this doubt, and expectation was notorious in the vniuersities of *Oxford,* & *Cam-*
*bridge,*where *Peter Martyr,*and *Bucer,*had read
now for the space of a yeare and more, and
were oftentymes vrged and pressed much
by their schollers, (wherof the farre greater
parts in those daies were Catholiks,) to declare themselues cleerly, of what opinion
they weare, touching the Sacrament of the
Aultar, and the reall presence. To witt,

Q q 2   whether

Tvvo men cast into pri-son by Crämer for spea-kinge against the Sa-crament of the Aultar. Fox pag. 1180. & 1181.

whether they were Lutherans or Zwinglians. But they kept themfelues a loofe, &
indifferent or rather doubtfull, fo farre as
they could, vntill the determination of the
parlament fhould come. Yet was Peter
Martyr putt into a great ftrayt therby. For
that hauinge taken vpon him to read, and
expound to the fchollers of *Oxford* the firft
Epiftle to the *Corinthians* (wherin the
Apoftle in the eleuenth chapter handleth
the inftitution of the Bl. Sacrament) he had
thought to haue come to that place iuft at
the very tyme, when the Parlament fhould
haue determyned this controuerfie.

The pers
plexity
of Peter
Martyr
in Ox-
ford
about ex
pouding
*Hoc eft
corpus
meum.*

34.   But the contention enduringe longer
by fome monethes, then he expected: he
was come to the eleuenth chapter long before they could end in London. Whervpon
many pofts went to and froe betwene him
& *Cranmer*, to requyre a fpeedy refolution.
Alleaginge that he could not deteyne himfelfe any longer, but that being come to the
words *Hoc eft corpus meum,* he muft.needs declare himfelfe a Lutheran, or a Zwinglian.
But he was willed to ftay, and entertayne
himfelfe in other matter, vntill the determination might come. And fo the poore friar
did with admiration and laughter of all his
fchollers: ftandinge vpon thofe precedent
words; *accepit panem, &c, Et gratias agens, &c.
Fregit,&c.Et dixit,&c. accipite & manducate,&c.*
                                                        difcour-

difcourfinge largely of euery one of thefe points and bearinge of from the other that enfued. But when at length the poft came, that Zwinglianifme muft be defended:then ftepped vp *Peter Martyr* boldly the next day, and faid,*Hoc eft corpus meum.* This is my body, interpreting yt, this is the figne of my body. Adding moreouer , that he wondered how any man coulde be of any other opinion, feing this expofition was fo cleere! Wheras yf the poft had brought other newes , him-felfe alfo would haue taught the contrary opinion. And this ftory did teftifie whiles they liued , *Doctor Sanders, Doctor Allen, Doctor Stapleton,* & others,that were prefent at this trifling and tergiuerfation of this Apoftata friar. And thus began our Zwinglian gho-fpell in England vnder K. *Edvvard* the 6.

Diffem-bling & tergiuer fation of Peter Martyr.

35. Now lett vs heare a word or two out of the ftatute it felfe about this communion booke , and profefsion of Zwinglianifme, eftablifhed in Englåd after two yeares ftrife among the proteftåts. *VVhere of long time*(faith the Act) there hath byn, in this Realme of England, diuers formes of common prayer, commonly called the feruice of the Church, afwell concerninge Mattins & euenfong,as alfo the holy communion called the Maffe, &c. And where the K.Maieftie with th'ad-uife of his moft entyrely beloued vncle the L. Protector , and others of his Highneffe

Statut. anno 2. Edvv. 6. cap. 1.
,,
,,
,,
,,
,,
,,
,,

councell,

,, councell, hath heretofore diuers tymes aſ-
,, ſaied to ſtay Innouations,or new rytes,con-
,, cerning the premiſſes:yet the ſame hath not
,, had ſuch good ſucceſſe, as his highneſſe re-
,, quired in that behalfe. Wherupon his hi-
,, ghneſſe by the moſt prudent aduiſe afore-
,, ſaid, being pleaſed to beare with the frailty
,, & weakneſſe of his ſubiects in that behalfe,
,, of his great clemency, hath not bene only
,, content to abſtayne from puniſhment in

The nevv cō̃munion booke made vpon the frailty, & vveakneſſe of ſubiects.

,, that behalfe : but alſo, to the entent that an
vniforme, quiett,and godly order ſhould be
had,concerning the premiſſes, hath appointed the Archbiſhop of Canterbury, & certayne of the moſt learned, and diſcreet Biſhops, to conſider, & ponder the premiſſes:
& therupō hauing as well eye & reſpect, to
the *moſt ſincere, and pure Chriſtian Religion, taught*
,, by the ſcriptures, as to the vſages of of the
,, primitiue Church, ſhould draw and make
,, one cōuenient & meet order,rite,& faſhion,
,, of common prayer & adminiſtration of Sa-
,, craments,to be vſed in England,wales, &c.
,, The which at this tyme by the aid of the
,, holy Ghoſt, with vniforme agreement, is
,, of them concluded,ſet forth, & deliuered to
:, his highneſſe great comfort,& quietneſſe of
:, mind, in a booke entituled. *The booke of com-*
,, *mon prayer and adminiſtration of Sacraments, &c.*

36.   This is the preface to that act of parlament. Wherby yow may ſee, that this
commu-

communion booke, was deuised first for hearinge with the frailty of them, that sought Innouations: And then, that it was preformed by vniforme consent, & aid of the holy Ghost, according to the *most sincere and pure Christian Religion taught in the scriptures.* And thirdly, that the young child prince, receiued *great cofort, & quietnesse of mind therby.* All which is ridiculous, yf yow consider what a multitude of errors, and grosse absurdityes, the later protestants (especially the preciser sort of them) haue gathered out against this booke. Yea after it was twise more renewed, altered and amended, (accordinge to the pure word of God, (as was pretended once in K. *Edwards* dayes it selfe) & then againe in the beginning of her maiesties raigne: wherof though I haue spoken sufficiently, in my defence of the first Encounter against *Syr Francis* hastings, yet cannot I omitt to admonish the Reader in this place, to reade the 9. chapter of the second booke intituled *Daungerous Positions, &c.* sett forth by publike permission, and printed in London *anno* 1593. In which chapter yow shall see put togeather, the words of diuers new ghospellers, conceringe this communion booke, affirmed here in the Statute to be accordinge *to the most sincere, and pure Christian Religion, taught by the scriptures.* But they say the contrary: to witt, *that it is full of corruption,*

The sud gement & speeches of the purer sort of protestants against the forsaid communion booke.

ruption, and that many of the contents therof are against the vvord of God, The Sacraments vvickedley mangled, and prophaned therin, the Lords ſupper not eaten, but made a pageant and ſtage play. That their publike baptiſme is full of childiſh ſuperſtitious toyes.

37.   And finally, not to ſtand any longer vpon this proofe, how the later ghoſpellers according to their *pure vvord of God*, do reiect and contemne the *very pure vvord of God* of *Cranmer*, and *Ridleyes tyme*, (alleaginge for reaſon among other things, as the *Suruey of pretended diſcipline* ſaith *cap.* 28. *That the ſunne of the ghoſpell ſhineth more cleere in theſe daies then in thoſe:*) not to ſtand (I ſay) vpon this, Fox himſelfe doth ſufficiently ſhew, that this *pure communion booke* and order therin ſett downe, was misliked, and reiected by the moſt zealous ſort of proteſtants, euen in thoſe dayes. As may appeare by that which the ſaid Iohn Fox telleth vs, when he talketh of the propheticall ſpiritt of *Iohn Rogers* the miniſter, that was burned in Q. Maryes dayes: how he ſent word to the brethren by a certayne booke-bynder, that except the ghoſpellers, when they returned into England againe (for ſo ſaith Fox he propheſied they ſhould) did follow the forme and plott ſett downe by him and *Hooper* (different from this of *Cranmer* and others) they ſhould haue as badd an end, as he and his followes

Fox pag. 1355.

fellowes had, that were bnrned vnder
Q. Mary.

38. But yet for the prefent, this was the
pure vvord of God, and the *vvorke of the holy Ghoft*
and no man might mislike or reproue it
without daunger and great punifhment,
efpecially yf he were a Catholike, for
aboue all others they were to be punifhed;
(efpecially the Cath. Bifhopps in prifon for
refifting the former booke obtruded in the
firft parlament) which yet was pardoned to
others. For fo faith the Statute immediatly
after the former words: *That all and fingular*
perfon and perfons, that haue offended concerning the
promifes, (other then fuch as novv be and remayne in
vvard in the tovver of London or in the fleet) may be
pardoned therof.

Catholi-
ques ex-
cepted
from
pardon
in the
ftatute.

39. But to returne to our ftory, and firft
plantinge of the ghofpell vnder K. *Edvvard*,
yow muft note, that togeather with this
comedy of the new booke of feruice difputed & paffed in this Parlament, wherin the
proteÐor was a cheefe part and AÐor: fo
was there a bloudy Tragedy handled in like
manner, wherof he was both head and in-
ftigator. For that about the midft of the parlament (to witt, vpon the 16. of Ianuary)
he caufed his brother L.† *Thomas Seymer* high
Admirall of England to be fuddainly arre-
fted and fent prifoner to the tower, beinge
in mourninge apparrell at that tyme for the

† The
apprehē-
fion and
condem-
natiõ &
death of
the L.
Tho. Sey-
mer by
his bro-
ther and
other
nevv go
fpellers.

late

late death of his wife *Quene Katherine Parre.*
And not ſuffering the ſaid brother of his, to
be heard or come to his tryall, he cauſed a
condemnation to paſſe againſt him in the
ſaid parlament , which beginneth thus:
VVhere Syr Thomas Seymer, knight, Lord Seymer of
Sudley, high admirall of England, not hauing God be-
fore his eyes, &c. Thus beginneth the acte.
And then followeth, a long narration of
his offences, (as that he deſired to haue the
cuſtody of the King, was ambitious, and
marryed *Q. Katherine Parre* ſecretly before he
told the King or his brother of yt, and after
helped to make her away againe, with ſecret intentio to Marry the Lady Elizabeth,
if he cold get her, was vngratefull, for many
benefits both of the King, and his ſaid bro-

Stat. an.
2. Edou.
*6 ſap.*18.
an.Domi
ni 1548. ther the L. Protector, perſuaded the yong
King to take the gouernmét into his owne
hands, and therby to exclude the ſaid protector from his dignity, and gouernment)
it was inferred, that the ſaid L. Admirall
aſpired to the crowne it ſelfe, and to the de-
ſtructio of the Kings perſon, lands, realme,
Church and common wealth, &c.

40.   All theſe things (I ſay) & many other,
are related in this Act of Parlament of At-
taynder againſt the *L. Seymer*, *Syr VVilliam*
Sharington, & other his frends, & followers,
but not proued at all by any thing extant in
the narration. But yet ſuch was the force of
his

his brother, and other cheefe ghofpellers againft him (a dolefull beginninge of the new ghofpell for him) as he was condemned to be hanged, drawne, and quartered, & vpon fauour was beheaded vpon the 20. of March followinge. And prefently the protector, as triumphing both ouer his mother, and brother (as one faid in thofe dayes, for that the Church was as well his mother, as the admirall his brother) he made a proclamation vpon the 6. of Aprill, to putt downe the maffe throughout the whole Realme. Whervpon there enfued fuch reuell prefently in London & in other places of the Realme, as was ftrange & pittifull, the bleffed Sacrament being thruft out in haft of euery Church, and altars pulled downe. And vpon the tenth of Aprill (beinge but foure dayes after) the whole Cloyfter of S. Paules Church in London, was throwne downe, and togeather with that a goodly worke of Antiquity cunningly wrought called *the Daunce of Paules*, inuironing the faid cloifter was beaten downe, and defaced alfo. Another goodly monumēt in like manner of antiquity belonginge to the fame Church, called the charnell houfe of Paules, (where the tombes, bones and memoryes of dead men were) was all beaten downe by the fury of this tyme, the dead mens bones caft out to the fields: as

both

The Reuell that infued prefently vpon this parlament of 4. of Nouēber 1548.

both Holinſhed, Stow and other Chroniclers do relate.

Holinſh.
Stovv
an. Do-
mini
1549.
41.   And for that the protector had deſigned to raiſe a famous pallace, worthy of his greatneſſe and renowne, for his habitation & perpetuall memory, called *Somerſett place:* he firſt cauſed the pariſh Church of the *ſtrond* without *temple barre*, togeather with *ſtrond Inne* & *ſtrond-bridg* to be pulled downe to giue place to that pallace. And to the end he might haue ſtone for the ſame more neare at hand, and with leſſe charges: he cauſed the fayre goodly Church of *S. Iohn* of *Ieruſalem* neere *Smithfield* (belonginge in former tyme to the knights of the *Rhods*) to be vndermyned & with gunnpowder to be ouerthrowen, and the ſtone therof to be applyed to the buildinge of his ſaid houſe and pallace.

42.   And this was the forme of the firſt plantinge of the new ghoſpell in London by gunpowder, tearinge and rentinge of auncient monuments & ouerthrowing of Churches: farre vnlike to the firſt planting of Chriſtian faith in England by S. Auſten, and his fellowes before in part by vs deſcribed. And yf this Reuell was in London in the ſight of the Prince, and councell, and where moſt order & law ought to be kept, we may eaſily imagine what was practiſed throughout all the other parts of the realme

where

where leſſe reſpect was borne to the publike magiſtrate, by no leſſe vnruly ſpiritts
then were in London. Wherypon the
poore afflicted Cath. people were forced
to take armes, for their defence. And heere
hence began the commotions and inſurre-
ctions aboue mentioned of diuers ſhires for
retayning their Religion. But being ouercome and oppreſſed by martiall law and by
the troupes of Engliſh and forrayne ſoldiars
made for the Scottiſh voyage not long before: there enſued infinite miſery, murder,
maſſacre, and mortality in the Realme. All
which the Earle of *VVarvvicke*, with the help
of others of the nobiłıty, laying afterwards
to the protectors charge in the end of the
very next yeare, (to witt the third of K. *Edvvards* raigne) they caſt him into the Tower,
depriued him of his protector-ſhipp, & had
cutt of his head alſo at that tyme, had not
the Ducheſſe of Somerſett prudently pacified the Earle of Warwicke, by preſentinge
a riche casket of Iewells vnto the counteſſe
his wife. (Wheryhto my Author was priuy,) and moreouer ſhe offred a new com-
plott of affinity betwene the ſaid Earle and
Duke, which afterward was effectuated;
to witt, the marriage betwene the ſonne
of the Earle and daughter of the Duke. All
which, togeather with a moſt humble,
lowly and baſe ſubmiſſion made by the ſaid
Protector,

The pro
tector
caſt into
the To-
vver the
4. of
October
*an.*1549.

Protector, (which is extant in our Croni-
cles) moued the Earle to pardon him for
the prefent, and to reftore him a kind of liberty at his owne houfe, & after that againe
to the councell, and kings prefence (for of
all he was depriued) but neuer to the pro-
tectorfhip. Nay foone after he caft him into
prifon againe, & cutt of his head, as all men
know. And had thervnto the help of many
cheefe ghofpellers, who not long after this,
laid other complotts (conforme to the turbulent humour and fruits of this ghofpell)
and made other new allyances betwene the
houfe of *Suffolke*, that was moft forward of
all others in ghofpelling, and the faid Earle
of Warwicke, now Duke of Northumberland. Which allyances are fuppofed to haue
fhortened the yonge vnfortunate kings life,
and knowne to haue ment the fubuerfion
of the whole courfe of the Royall lyne, and
fucceffion appointed by K. *Henry* the 8. (cut-
ting of his two daughters Mary and Elizabeth that remayned after K. *Edvvard*) if God
had not ftraungly defended them, by cut-
ting of thefe Euangelicall complotts.

43.   Wherfore to be no longer in this matter, which is cleare ynough of yt felfe: we
do fee, how the firft publike introduction,
of proteftant religion that euer was admitted in England, from Chrift to that tyme,
came in both vnder K. *Henry* & much more
vnder

vnder K. *Edvvard* his fonne. To witt, how
and vpon what occafions, by whome, and
what men the fame was both preached, &
fauoured: & what effects, by what meanes,
and in what forme, and fafhion yt was performed. For as for the occafion: they haue
byn declared before. But vnder K. *Edvvard* it
is euident, that they were the child hood &
infancy of a tender young Prince, togeather
with the ambition, couetuoufnes, pride, &
defire of fole comaundry in his vncle the
protector. Which motiues made him
breake the will and teftament, lawes and
ordinances of his old dread Lord K. *Henry*
before almoft his bloud was cold after his
death. And the like inductions of promotions, drew after him others, that did fecond
his actions, fo long as they were profitable
vnto them.

The con
clufion
concer-
ning the
occafiõs
meanes,
men,
euents
& fruits
of the
nevv
ghofpel.

44. As for the men that firft and principally broached thefe doctrines; they were
for the moft part married friars, & Apoftata
Priefts. That liuinge in concupifcence of
women, and other fenfuality, defired to
maintayne & continew the fame by the liberty of this new ghofpell. The promotors
and fauourers of thefe men, were fuch efpecially of the layity, and cleargy, as had more
intereft by the change for their owne pro-
motion, & aduancement, then confcience,
or perfuafion of iudgment, for the truthe of
their

their Religion. As would appeare yf we
ſhould name them one by one, that then
were of the councell and cheefe authority.
The effects and ſpirituall fruits of this firſt
change were (as yow haue ſeene & heard)
the moſt notorious vices of ambition, diſſimulation, hatred, deceyt, tyranny and ſub-
uerſion one of another, togeather with diuiſion, diſſention, garboiles and deſolation
of the Realme: yea playne Atheiſme, irreli-
gioſity and contempt of all religion, that
euer was knowne to haue riſen vp in any
kingdome of the world, within the compaſſe of ſo few yeares. And (that which is
moſt markable) there followed preſently
the ouerthrow of all the principall Actors
and authors of theſe innouations by Gods
owne wonderfull hand. And this more in
theſe ſix yeares, then in & ſixty or ſixſcore,
or perhaps 600. hath ben ſeene to haue fallen out in England in other tymes. And no
doubt, but yt is of ſingular conſideration,
A conſi- that wheras true Chriſtian Religion (but
deration eſpecially any chaunge or reformation to
of much the better part is admitted) there preſently
impor- do enſue by vſuall conſequéce great effects
tance. of piety, deuotion, charity & vertuous life,
yf the reformation be ſincere, & come from
God in deed: here on the contrary ſide the
prouidence of God did ſhew a notorious
document to the whole world, of the falſhood

fhood & wickedneffe of this new ghofpell
in that the firft profeffors and promotors
therof in our land, fell to more open wickedneffe in thefe fiue yeares, then in fo many fiftyes before as hath byn faid.

45. And the cheefe Captayne and ringlea-
der of all this dance of Innouations after
the protector himfelfe, (to witt, the Duke
of Northumberland) comming foone after
to calamity, fell into the accompt & recko-
ning of this matter, and made alonge vehement declaration therof in the Chappell of
the tower, before diuers of the counfell, the
day before he was putt to death, to witt
vpon the 21. of Auguft 1553. Shewinge that
he had found true by good experience, that
this new ghofpell (which he had followed
hitherto) teded to nothing, but to Atheifme
in Religion, diffolution of life, and pertur-
bation of the common-wealth, which he
repeated againe at his death, and the fame
was prefently put in print, and fo yt remay-
ned. Though *Holinshed*, *Hooker* and *Harifon* *Holinſh.*
(like falfe companions as they be) do leaue *an.Domi*
yt out wholy of their large Chronicle: tel- *ni* 1553.
linge only, that he and the Duke of Somer- *pa.*1089.
fett were buryed one by the other in the
Tower. But *Stovv* proceedeth more hand-
fomely. For though he omitt the larger re-
hearfall of the matter, & do fpeake of other
things leffe odious : yet doth he fo fett
R r   downe

downe the thing, as the truth may eaſily be
ſeene therby: which the other companions
do holde from vs of purpoſe, for thus he
wryteth.

Stovv in
chron.
an.1553.

46.   *The reſt of the Dukes ſpeach almoſt in euery*
point, vvas as he had ſaid in the Chappell of the To-
vver. Sauing that vvhen he had made confeſſion of
his beleeſe (Stow dare not tell what beleeſe,
for that it was wholy Catholike with many
vehement proteſtations againſt the hereſies
of that tyme) *he had theſe vvords. Heere I do pro-*

The
Duke of
Northū-
berland
his con-
feſſion
of his
faith at
his de-
ath.

teſt vnto yovv good people moſt earneſtly, euen from
the bottome of my hart, that this vvhich I haue ſpo-
ken, is of my ſelfe, not beinge required nor moued
thervnto by any man, for any flattery or hope of life.
I take vvittneſſe of my Lord of VVorceſter here, my
ould frend and ghoſtly father, that he found me in
this mynd & opinion vvhen he came to me. But I haue
declared this only vpon my ovvne mind and affection,
and for the zeale and loue, that I beare to my natu-
rall countrey. And I could (good people) rehearſe
much more euen by experience that I haue of this
euill, that is happened to this Realme by theſe occa-
ſions. But novv (yovv knovv) I haue another thing to
do, vvhervnto I muſt prepare me, &c. And hauing
thus ſpoken he kneeled dovvne, ſayinge to them that
vvere about: I beſeech yovv all to beare me vvittneſſe,
that I dy in the true Cath. faith, and then ſaid he the
Pſalmes of Miſerere and De profundis, his Pater
noſter, &c.

47.   This is *Stovv* his narration. Wherby
yow

yow fe firſt the diſhoneſty and falſhood of
the other Chroniclers, that leaue yt quite
out: and the coſenage of Iohn Fox, that
only ſaith it in two or three lynes and lyeth
moſt ſhamefully, *affirminge that he hauinge pro-*
miſe made vnto him, that though his head vvere vpon
the blocke he ſhould haue his pardon, yf he vvould re-
cant, he conſented thervnto. Which yet yow ſee
the Duke proteſteth the contrary vpon his
death, that it was not for *flattery or hope of life*
or vpon any mans inductiō, but only vpon
conſcience, firſt to ſaue his owne ſoule, and
then for deſire to deliuer his naturall countrey from the infection of hereſie and calamityes theron inſuinge.

48.　And thus much of thoſe men & their
fruits, who firſt planted this ghoſpell. But
now as for the meanes wherby theſe things
were wrought, yow haue heard them before, that they were all comonly by pulling
downe, thruſtinge out, diſſoluinge of diſcipline, geuing immunity from puniſhments
to all ſorts of hereriks, and of wiuinge to
looſe Prieſts and Apoſtata friars, and other
like licentious libertyes farre different from
the purity, ſeuerity, & ſtraytnes of life vſed
by the firſt planters of Chriſts ghoſpell. And
as for the forme and faſhion of this new religion ſet vp vnder this child King, yt was,
as yow haue heard both their owne men &
oures teſtiſie, compounded and patched vp

Fox pag. 120.

The forme & faſhion of Fox his nevv Church an I Re-ligion.

Rr 2　　　　of

of all diuerſity of ſects and religions as it
pleaſed the compoſers, many things they
tooke and retayned of oures, as well in doctrine, as in rites, and ceremonyes. Some
things of the Lutherans; ſome others of the
Zwinglians; ſome of the reliques of K. *Henryes* mutation, as that of the ſupreme head
of the Church, (a ſingular point of doctrine
proper to England aboue all other nations)
but moſt of this compoſition was of their
owne inuentiõs, which yet neither the proteſtants, that remained in ſecret vnder Q.
Mary, did wholy allow, as appeareth by
that which I haue cited before of *Iohn Rogers*
prophecy, nor the other, that began againe
vnder her Maieſtie that now is, did wholy
readmitt the forme and faſhion, but made a
new of their owne, as by their communion
booke is euident, nor do the purer ſort of
Caluiniſts in theſe dayes any way like or
approue the one or the other, as before we
haue ſhewed.

49.   Whervpon I may conclude as well
this Chapter, as alſo this whole ſecond
part, that neyther vnder K. *Henry* the 8. nor
K. *Edvvard* the ſixt, nor Q. *Mary,* had Iohn
Fox any diſtinct Church extant or knowen
to the world. Eſpecially yf his Church be
the puritan congregation, as he will ſeeme
to ſignifie in many places of his Acts and
Monuments. But whether he haue any
ſuch

ſuch Church now viſible vnder her Maieſtie at this day in England, and in what ſtate
and condition it ſtandeth, I will not ſtand
to enquyre or diſcuſſe: but do leaue yt to my
Lords of *Lambert* and *London* whome moſt it
concerneth, being ſufficient for me to haue
ſhewed throughout all former Chriſtian
ages, that Iohn Fox hath had no Church of
any Antiquity, and conſequently, if he haue
any now, yt muſt be a very young Church,
and of ſo tender age, as he may marry her to
what ſect or ſectary he liſteth for her
youth, and that with hope of brood and
iſſue. And ſo much of all this matter.

THE CONCLVSION OF BOTH
THESE FORMER PARTES, TOGEA-
ther vvith a particular diſcourſe of the notorious
different proceedinge of Catholikes and Prote-
ſtantes, in ſearchinge out the truth of matters in
Controuerſie.

CHAP. XIII.

B Y all that hitherto hath byn wrytten
and diſcourſed (good Chriſtian Reader)
about the former ſubiect of diſcerning true
Religion, and the way wherby to know &
find the ſame, I do not doubt, but that of thy
prudence thow haſt obſerued a farre different courſe holden by vs that are Catholiks,
and our aduerſaryes in this behalfe, we ſeeking

king to make matters playne, euident, eafy,
perfpicuous & demonftrable (fo farr as may
be) euen to the eye yt felfe, wheras our aduerfaryes and namely Iohn Fox, according
to that which by reading this Treatife yow
haue feene, doth all togeather the contrary,
intanglinge himfelfe and his reader with
fuch obfcurityes, difficultyes and contradictions, both about tymes, matter, & men, as
he findeth not wheie to begin, nor where
to end, nor yet how to go forward or backward, in that he had taken in hand, which
I fuppofe to haue byn aboundantly fhewed
by that which hitherto hath byn wrytten;
For wheras we, for our partes, begin cleerly
with the very firft corpes or body of religion, inftituted by Chrift himfelfe, and the
firft profeffors therof that made a Church or
Chriftian congregation, and do neuer after
leaue the fame, but do deduce it vifibly and
without interruption from that tyme to
this, and therby do fhew the beginning and
continuance of one and the felfe fame religion from their daies to ours: I. Fox on the
other fide knoweth not well eyther where
to begin, where to infift, or where to end, as
fufficiently yow haue feene tryed. For albeit in the title of his booke he tell vs, that
he will bring downe his Church from the
Apoftles tyme to ours, and then after in his
pag. 8. proteftation to the Chriftian Reader he
                                            doth

doth tell vs further, that his true Church is different from the great visible Roman Church: yet in the prosecution of his worke he setteth forth, and describeth only the Roman Church as before we haue declared, and doth not so much as name any distinct visible Church of his owne or other, except only of such heretiks, as himself also condemneth for such, different from the said Roman Church for the space of almost 1200. yeares: and then falleth he into such a strange extrauagant humour of building a new Church for himselfe and his, out of all sorts and sects of later heretiks, as being not able in all points for very shame to allow their opinions, (which in many pointes are most absurd and contradictory both to him & vs, as also among themselues) he findeth himselfe extreemely intangled, nor cannot tell which way to wynd (though he be a Fox) nor yet which way to turne his head, but is forced to double hither and thither, to go forth and backe, say and vnsay, and to cast a hundred shaddowes of wranglinge gloses vpon the whole matter, therby to obscure the same to the eyes and eares of his Reader.

The sleights & shifts of Iohn Fox in his wri-tings.

2. And finally it seemeth to me that the difference betwene vs and him, and his, to witt betwene Catholiks and protestants in this behalfe, is not much vnlike to that of

R r 4   two

two cloth ſellers of London, the one a Royall marchant, which layeth open his wares cleerely, geueth into your hands the whole peece of cloth at midday, willeth yow to view and behold yt in the ſunne, remoueth all veyles, pentices and other ſtoppings of light that may giue obſcurity, or impediment to the manifeſt beholdinge, handlinge and diſcerninge therof. Wheras contrariwiſe the other, being a crafty broker or poore pedler, hauinge noe ſubſtantiall wares indeed to ſell, but ſuch as is falſe made and deceytfully wrought, and taken vp alſo for the moſt part of the others leauings, ſeeketh by all meanes poſſible to ſel in corners, and to ſhut out the ſunne that it be not well ſeene, or to giue yow a ſight therof by falſe lights only, neyther will he deliuer yow the whole peece into your hand to be examined thorowly by your ſelfe, but ſheweth yow one end therof only, different from the reſt which he ſuppreſſeth. And this manner of proceedinge ſhall yow find verified on their ſide throughout this whole Treatiſe, & we haue done already, I doubt not, if you haue read it ouer with attention, yet meane I in this place to diſcouer the ſame ſomwhat more in particular, for an vpſhot and concluſion of theſe firſt two parts of my Treatiſe.

3. Three ſpeciall differences then I do find
betwene

A comparison expreſſing the differét dealinge of Catholiks and proteſtants about ſeekinge the true Church and religion.

betwene our aduersaryes & vs concerninge
the affaire of this Treatise, about the finding
out of true Religion by the true Church, &
by the beginninge, progresse, and continuance therof. The first is the estimation of
the thing in it selfe; the second the assigning
out or descriptiō therof; the third the marks
and proprieties, wherby to know and discerne the same, of euery one wherof I shall
speake a word or two in order.

3. Diffe-
rences.

4. For estimation of the great importance
& singular moment of this matter, the difference is euident betwene vs, for that we
affirme the findinge out and holdinge this
Church, to be of such weight, as that all
lyeth therin for certainty & security of beleefe, and for determinge of all doubts
and controuersies, in all tymes and places,
and in all matters of religion whatsoeuer,
euen from Christ to the worlds end. For
we say with S. Austen when any difficulty
falleth out: *Quisquis falli metuit huius obscuritate
quæstionis, Ecclesiam de illa consulat.* Whosoeuer
doth feare to be deceyued by the obscurity
of this question in controuersie, lett him go
to the Church for his resolution, and he
shalbe secure: we say also with *Lactantius Fir-
mianus* before S. Austen, who was Maister
and Tutor to *Crispus* sonne to Constantine
the great: *Sola Catholica Ecclesia est, quæ verum
Dei cultum retinet, hic autem est fons veritatis, hoc*

1.
The dif-
ferēt esti
mation
of the
Church
& lineall
discent
therof,
betwe-
ne Ca-
tholiks
and pro-
testants.
*Aug.l.1.
contr.
Crescon.
cap.* 33.
"
*Lactant.
lib.* 4.
*diuin.
Instit.
cap.vlt.*

Rr 5

domi-

domicilium fidei, hoc templum Dei, quo ſi quis non intrauerit, vel à quo ſi quis exierit, à ſpe vitæ, ac ſalutis æterna alienus eſt. The only Cath. Church

„ is that which hath the true worſhipp of al-
„ mighty God in yt, and this is the fountayne
„ of all truth, this is the houſe or habitation of
„ faith, this is the temple of God, into which
„ whoſoeuer doth not enter, or out of which
„ whoſoeuer doth depart, he is deuoyd of all
„ hope of life and euerlaſting ſaluation.

5.   Thus wrote *Lactantius* therteene hundred yeares gone, & addeth preſently theſe words following, wherby he weil ſheweth the conformity of ſpiritt of thoſe old hereſide-margin: *Lactant. ibid.* tiks, with ours at this day. *Sed tamen ſinguli quique cætus hæreticorum ſe potiſſimum Chriſtianos, & ſuam eſſe Catholicam Eccleſiam putant.* But yet

side-margin: All heretiques do chalenge to be the true Church.

euery congregation of heretiks do thinke themſelues cheefely and principally to be Chriſtians, and their Church to be the Catholike Church. And do not ours ſo in like manner at this day ? But lett vs go forward to ſpeake a word or two more, of the different eſtimation we make of this matter.

6.   *Saint Cyprian* that liued more then 60. yeares before *Lactantius*, maketh the very ſame account with him, and vs, that all is loſt, yf we leeſe or miſſe this Church : side-margin: *Cyp. l. de ſimpl. Prælat.* *Ardeant* (ſaith he) *licet flammis, &c.* Albeit ſuch Chriſtians as are not in this Church ſhould liue neuer ſo well, yea ſhould be ſo forward
and

and feruerous in defence of Christian Reli- „
gion, as they should burne in flames for the „
same, or be deuoured by beasts, yet this „
should be to them *non corona fidei. sed pœna per-* „
fidiæ: not a crowne of faith but a punishment „
for their persidiousnesse. Which doctrine „
of *Saint Cyprian, Saint Augustine* as a deuout „
scholler of his doth often repeat: *Foris ab Ec-* *Aug. ep.*
clesia constitutus (saith he to a donatist) *æterno* 204. *ad*
supplicio punieris, etiamsi pro Christi nomine viuus *Donatũ.*
incendereris. Thow being out of the Catho- *presbyt.*
like Church, thow shalt be punished with *tist.* *Donas*
eternall torment, albeit thow wert burned „
aliue for the name of Christ.

7. And finally not to go from the fornamed holy man *Saint Cyprian* in this behalfe,
who died for the defence of Christs faith, &
the true Cath. Church, and is a most blessed No man
martyr and Doctor to vs all, he after a long can be
discourse made, touching a Christian man saued
that misseth in this point of finding out and out of
following the true Cath. Church, and yet the true
in other things endeauoreth to liue well & Church.
sheweth great zeale in Gods cause, and desireth in his mynd euen to dy for the same, of
this man he pronounceth this sentence.
Nunquam perueniet ad Christi præmia, &c. Alie- *Cyprian*
nus est, prophanus est, hostis est, habere non potest *tract. de*
Deum Patrem, qui Ecclesiam non habet matrem. *clesia.* *vnit. Ec-*
This man, notwithstandinge all his other „
good works & endeauors, shall neuer come „
to enioy

„ to enioy the rewards of Chriſt in heauen,
„ he is an alien, he is prophane, he is an ene-
„ my, he cannot haue God for his father
„ which hath not the Church for his mother.

8.   Thus ſaid *Saint Cyprian,* as alſo all auncient holy fathers after him, wherof I might
alleage many authorityes yf yt were not
ouer long, and the ſame ſay we that are Catholiks, and do hold the ſame faith and
Church with them at this day. We do hold
(I ſay) that the firſt and principall point of
all other for a Chriſtian man, that meaneth
his owne ſaluation, is to ſeeke out the true
Cath. Church, and to conſider whether he
be of yt, or in yt, or no? For yf he be not,
then all other diligence and labour is voyd
and in vayne, except yt be to ſeeke out this,
and yf he be in yt, then is he in the right
way of Saluation, not for that all be ſaued,
who are within her (as in the ſecond point
ſhalbe ſhewed) but for that all thoſe, who
are out of her ſhalbe certainly damned, as
now yow haue heard out of the cheefeſt fathers of the auncient Cath. Church. And
this is the firſt point of ſingular moment,
for which we eſteeme this Church ſo highely, for that no ſaluation can be had
without her.

9.   But ſecondly we eſteeme alſo the importance of this matter by the great and excellent helpes, which in this Church aboue

all

Howv
much it
impor-
teth
eache
man to
cóſider,
vvhe-
ther he
be in the
true
Church
or no?

all other congregations., Christian men
haue to procure their saluation, though all
do not vse the same to their best benefitt, &
therby do miscarry. For to come to some
particulars, we say,that in this Church,and
no where els is the truth of faith and certainty therof,and this by the perpetuall assi-
stance of the holy Ghost promised thervnto
by the founder God himselfe. In this
Church, is the infallible iudgment both
about the books of scripture and their interpretation, as all other doubts and controuersies, accordinge to that yow haue
heard before out of *Saint Augustine*. In this
Church alone & no where els is there true
priesthood by lawfull succession, vnction,
and imposition of hands, and consequently
remission also of sinnes by the authority
they haue from Christ to that effect. In this
Church is the true number, vse, and force
of holy Sacraments, and grace giuen by
them. In this Church is vnity of faith and
doctrine; communion of Saints,and of meritts and prayers, which no where els is to
be found. And finally in this Church alone
is there warrant and security from error,as-
surance from ouerthrow,fayling, or fading,
which security is established by the promise
of Christ himselfe, as our God creator and
redeemer,& to endure vnto the worlds end.
10. All these vtilityes and most singular
                            benefitts

The be-
nefitts
by being
in the
Church.

*Marc.
vltim.*

*Mat.*18.

*Ioan.*20.

†The cō
tempti
bility of
of the
prote-
ſtants
Church
euen
amonge
the m-
ſelues.
★*See Lu-
ther ep.
ad Alb.
March.
pruſſæ &
ep. ad
Iacob.
Brem.
Aurif.
tit. har.
VVeſtph.
l. cont.
Caluin.
Stanch.
l. de Trin.
& Mes
diat.
Heſhuſ.
in deſeſ.
con. Cal.
uinum.
Cali. ad:
monit.
contra
VVeſtph.
Kemnit.
ep. ad*

benefitts do we beleeue to be in this Cath.
Church, aboue all other congregations in
the world. In reſpect wherof, we hold this
Church to be our ſhip, our rocke, our caſtle,
our fortreſſe, our miſtreſſe, our mother, our
ſkilfull pilote throughout all ſtorms of hereſies, our pillar and firmament of truth
againſt falſhood, our houſe of refuge againſt
tribulation, our protection, our direction,
our help, aid, and ſecurity in all points; and
yf any man periſh in her, it is by his owne
default, but out of her, none can but periſh.
And this is our eſtimation of this affayre.

11.   But now how different an accompt,
proteſtants do make both of this, or their
owne Church, is eaſily ſeene by their owne
words & doings: for † as they contemne &
impugne our Church, which we hold for
the only true, ſo do they ſeldome ſpeake of
their owne. For when ſhall yow heare a
miniſter or proteſtāt writer, alleage the authority of his Church againſt vs, or againſt
his owne fellowes, when they fall out (as
often they do) or yf he ſhould, how lightly
is it eſteemed euen by themſelues? yow
may ★ read the egre contentions of the proteſtant Churches of Saxony which are Lutherans, againſt thoſe of *Heidelberg*, & other
townes of the *Palſgraues* countrey, that are
of a different ſect; & of theſe againe, againſt
other conſorts of other prouinces, both of
Zwitzer-

Zwitzerland and other parts of Germany, yea betweene the soft and seuere Lutherans themselues, as betweene the Caluinian Churches of England and Scotland; And in England it selfe betweene the Protestants, Puritans and Brownysts at this day, (who are nothinge els but soft and seuere Caluinists). In all which sharp contentions, yf any part do but name the authority of their seuerall Church (which is very seldome,) the other presently falleth into laughter, holding the authority therof so ridiculous, as it is not worth the naminge: so as the argument taken from the authority of the Church, (which with vs is of so high esteeme, as we say with *Saint Austen*, *that vve vvould not beleeue the Ghospell, yf the authority of the Church, did not mooue vs thervnto*) with these fellowes is most base and contemptible.

12. Moreouer when they talke of their owne Churches, though euery sect and sectary for honors sake would be content to haue them accompted Catholike (as *Lactantius* before testified of the heretiks of his tyme) yet do they speake yt so coldly, & do vse the word Catholike so sparingly, as they will shew, that in their consciences they do not beleeue yt: and a man might answere them as Saint Austen answered *Gaudentius* the Donatist, whose sect being a particular company of heretiks in Africa,

presumed

Elector. Brandi- burg. Con sess. Tigur. tract. 3. &c.
See also the tvvo Inglish books, the one called dange- rous po- sitions, theother A suruey of disci- plinary doctrine &c.
† *Aug. cont ep- fund. cap. 5.*
Lactan. l. 4. c. vlt.
VVhat Church S. Cy- prian & S. Augu- stine do call Ca- tholike.

preſumed by little and little firſt in ieſt and
then in earneſt, to call themſelues Catholiks
and their Church the Cath. Church (as proteſtants do at this day), and being reprehended for yt by S. Auſten and others,
would needs proue the ſame by the definition of Catholike taken out of S. Cyprian.

Aug. l. 3.
contra
Gaudēt.
Donat.
cap. 1.
S. Auſten (I ſay) after a longe refutation
therof out of S. Cyprian his words to the
contrary, concludeth thus: *Quid igitur, & vos*
ipſos, &c. Why then do yow go about both
„ to deceyue your ſelues and other men with
„ impudent lyes againſt *Saint Cypprian*, yf your
„ Church be the Cath. Church by the teſti-
„ mony of this martyr, ſhew vs that your
„ Church doth ſtrech her beames and bowes
„ throughout the whole Chriſtian world, as
Cyp. l. de
vnit.
Eccl.
ours doth, for this *Saint Cyprian* called Catholike, &c. So as by S. Auſtens argument,
yf the proteſtants cannot ſhew that their
Church hath her beames and bowes ſpread
throughout all the Chriſtian world, & that
her faith is the generall faith receyued
amongſt all Chriſtians and not only of particular prouinces, then cannot they call her
or eſteeme her for Catholike, as in deed
they do not, but for faſhion ſake, and from
the teeth outward, as hath byn ſhewed.

13.   For when they come to ſett her out in
her beſt coulors, they make her but a very
obſcure baſe and contemptible thing, firſt
in our-

in outward shew, calling her, *the poore, op-pressed, and persecuted Church* (as Fox his words are) *troden vnder feet, neglected in the vvorld, not regarded in historyes, and almost scarse visible, &c.* So as where all the auncient fathers do triumph and vaunt against both heretiks and heathens (as we do at this day against protestants) that the Cath. Church is more eminent and splendent then the sunne yt selfe, and more famously knowen then any other temporall kingdome or monarchie that euer was in the world; Fox of his Church confesseth, that she is scarse visible, neglected in the world, not regarded in historyes, &c.

Fox in his pro-test. pag. 8. The ba-senes & obscuri-ty of the prote-stant Church by their ovvne confes-sion.

14. And then againe he playeth fast and loose, makinge her visible and inuisible. *Although* (saith he) *the right Church be not so inui-sible in the vvorld as none can see it, yet nether is yt so vsible againe that euery vvorldly eye may perceyue it.* So saith he. But how contrary to this was *Saint Chrisostome*, who would not yeld that the right Cath. Church could be asmuch as obscured, by any force or meanes whatsoe-uer, and therof vauntinge against infidells saith: yt may be perhaps that some heathen heere will despise my arrogancy (about the Maiestie of our Church) but lett him haue patience to expect vntill I come forth with my profes, and then shall he learne the force of truth, and how yt is easier for the sunne

Fox in protest. ibid. See S. Austen of this very point tract. 1. in ep. Ioan. & lib.cont. ep. Petil. c. 14. & in psalm. 30.conc. 2. & ali-bi.

yt selfe

Chriſoſt.
hom. 4.
de verbis
Iſaia.
vidit.
Domi-
nũ, &c.

yt ſelfe to be wholy extinguiſhed then for the Church to be ſo much as darkened or obſcured. Thus ſaid *Saint Chriſoſtome*. And marke (good Reader) the difference of ſpiritts: *Saint Chriſoſt.* vaunteth of the outward ſplendor and Maieſtie of his Church, and Iohn Fox contrarywiſe doth bragg of the obſcurity and contemptibility of their Church, and ſo againe wheras we do hold and highly eſteeme that our Church hath all truth of Chriſts doctrine and religion in yt, Fox wryteth of his Church, as before

Fox ib.

we haue recorded: *that by Gods mighty prouidence there hath alvvayes byn kept in her ſome ſparks of Chriſts true doctrine and religion.*

15. Againe wheras we glory, that in our Church there is power to abſolue from ſinnes, ſecurity from error, and the like: Fox denyeth theſe priuiledges to be in his Church, obiectinge vnto vs for an error,

Fox in
the dif-
ference,
&c. Be-
tvvixt
the old
Romane
Church
and the
nevv
pag. 26.
Acts &
Monu-
ments
pa.1560.

againſt the firſt, in a certayne Treatiſe of his before his acts and monuments, *that vve in our Church haue confeßion and abſolution at the prieſts hands, &c.* And againſt the ſecond he bringeth in a large conference of *Ridley* and *Latimer* agreeing togeather, that the greater part of the vniuerſall Cath. Church may erre, but yet fearfully, as yow ſhall ſee more largely in the third part of this treatiſe, when we ſhall come to treat of theſe Foxian Saints & their feſtiuall dayes, Acts and

and monuments. The fame Patriarks alfo
do cenfure *Saint Auguftines* fpeach before by
me alleaged, *for an exceßiue vehemency* (for fo
are their words)where he faith:*that he vvould
not beleeue the ghoßell, yf th' authority of the Cath.
Church did not moue him thervnto* ; fignifyinge
therby , as before hath byn noted, that he
could not know fcriptures to be fcriptures,
nor the ghofpell to be ghofpel, neither their
fenfe and meaning to be fuch as they were
taken for, but by th' authority of the vniuerfall Cath. Church, that had conferued
them from time to time and deliuered them
to him, and to the reft of the world for fuch
to be beleued.

Fox pag.
1561, col.
2. n. 74.
Auguft.
contr. ep.
Fũdam.
cap. 5.

16. Wherfore to conclude this matter,
feing that Iohn Fox doth allow fo well
this doctrine of his patriarks *Ridley* and *Latimer*, and therby doth take from the true
Church (and confequently in his meaninge
from his owne) all this excellent authority
which *Saint Auften* and other fathers do
afcribe to the Cath. Church, to witt the
foueraignty of approuing or reiecting true
or falfe fcriptures, of difcerninge betwene
books and books, and iudging of their true
interpretations; and feing further he taketh
away from his Church both confeffion and
abfolution of finnes, and all Efficacy of Sacraments, leauing them only to bare fignes,
that do fignify & not worke, feing he taketh

VVhat
Iohn
Fox ta-
keth
from his
Church.

S s 2   away

away from her all infallibility of doctrine,
confeſſing that ſhe may erre, & contenteth
himſelfe that ſhe retayne euer ſome ſparkies
only of true doctrine and religion, as before
hath byn ſhewed out of his owne words; &
conſidering moreouer, that he maketh her
ſoo poore a thing as now yow haue ſeene,
and furniſheth her with ſuch ragges, to witt
with ſuch variety of ſectaryes as is ridiculous to name, they diſagreeinge amonge
themſelues, and the one moſt oppoſite to
the other in doctrine and beleefe, ſhe being
such a Church (I ſay) ſo poore & miſerable,
ſo obſcure and ragged, ſo doubtfull and vncertayne, no maruayle though they make
little accompt of her, or giue ſmall creditt
vnto her, which in very deed is no greater,
then is giuen to the worſt man, or moſt di-
ſhoneſt woman liuing, which is to beleeue
her ſo farre, as ſhe can proue by others what
ſhe ſaith to be true, to witt by ſcriptures,
without which witneſſe none of her owne
children or houſhould will creditt or beleeue her, which is a markable point, for
that with the ſame condition they will beleeue the diuell himſelfe, and muſt do, yf he
alleage ſcriptures in the true ſenſe and
meaninge.

The proteſtants beleeue the diuell as much as their owne Church.

17.   And this is th' eſtimation which proteſtants do hold of their new Church. Now
lett vs paſſe to ſpeake a word only about
the

the second point which concerneth th' assigninge out or description of this Church. Cleere yt is, and cannot be denied, that Catholiks do assigne such a Church as may be seene and knowne by all men, begun visibly by Christ himselfe in Iury, when he gathered his Apostles and disciples togeather, and continued afterward with infinite increase, of nations and people, contreyes and kingdomes, that in tract of time adioyned themselues thervnto, & that this most manifest, notorious and knowne Church hath endured euer since vnder the name of the Christian Cath. Church, for the space of sixteene hundred yeares, as we haue shewed before both largly and particularly in the former two parts of this Treatise, which is playne dealinge, clere and manifest ; wheras on th' other side the Protestants of our dayes followinge herin the steppes of old heretiks their ancestors, do seeke to assigne such a Church, as no man can tell where to find it ; for that it is rather imaginary, mathematicall, or metaphysicall, then sensible to mans eyes, consistinge (as they teach) of iust and predestinate men only, whome, where, or how to find, yow see how vncertayne and difficult a thing it is, in this mortall life.

18. Wherfore as th' ancient fathers condemned wholy the heretiks of their tymes, for this fond and pernicious deuise & wrote

eagerly

*Cyp. l. 4.
epiſt.* 2.
*Epiph. in
hær. Ca-
thar.
Aug. l. de
hær. c. 69.
& 88. &
l. 3. cont.
Parmen.
cap.* 2.
eagerly againſt the ſame, as *S. Cyprian* againſt
the *Nouatians, Saint Epiphanius*, and *Saint Auſten*
againſt the *Donatiſts* & *Pelagians:* For that vnder this couer & colour, they would make
themſelues to be the only true Church, to
witt euery ſect their owne ſectaryes and
congregation, ſayinge that they only are
predeſtinate, iuſt, holy and Gods choſen
people, and conſequently alſo his only true
Church: ſo do wee at this day ſtand in the
very ſame controuerſie with proteſtants
that ſeeke the ſame euaſion and refuge.

19. And he that hath but ſo much leaſure,
as to read ouer the conference of the third
day, had betwene *S. Auſten*, and other Cath.
Biſhops on the one ſide, and the Biſhops
The con-
ference
at Car-
thage be-
tvvene
Catho-
liks and
Dona-
tiſts.
of the Donatiſts on th' other ſide at *Carthage*
by th' Emperors permiſſion and appointment, euen vpon this very queſtion of aſ-
ſiginge the Church, he ſhall ſee the matter
moſt cleerly handled; & that the Catholiks
of this tyme do vrge nothing in this point,
but that *Saint Auſten* and his fellow Cath.
Biſhops did vrge in that conference againſt
the Donatiſts, & that the proteſtants of our
tyme do take no other courſe of ſhifting and
defending themſelues therin, then the Donatiſts did in thoſe dayes. For that after infinite delayes and tergiuerſations vſed before they could be brought to this conference, which *Saint Auſten* ſetteth downe in
the

the collation of the first and second day:
when at length in the third dayes meeting
they came to ioyne vpon the controuersie
in hand, they began first about the word
Catholike it selfe, which the Catholiques
vrged againft the Donatistes, as we do now
againft the sectaryes of this age; and the
Donatistes fought to auoide the same by the
very same sleights which ours do; as appeareth by *Saint Augustines* words.

20. *Donatistæ* (faith *Saint Austen*) *refponderunt,*
Catholicum nomen non ex vniuersitate gentium , sed
ex plenitudine Sacramétorum institutum, & petiue-
runt, vt probarent Catholici, &c. The Donatists
did answere that the name Catholike did
not import the vniuersality of nations,
(professinge our Christian faith) but the
fulnes rather of Sacraments (which they
held to be in their Church)and further they
required , that the Catholiks should proue
that all nations did communicate with
them and their Church: which thing when
the Catholiks most willingly admitted and
desired of the iudges , that they might be
suffered to proue yt , the Donatists presently ran to another question , flippinge from
this cause of the Church that was in hand.
21. Thus wryteth *Saint Austen* of this matter, wherby yow see, that the Catholiks in
those dayes as we in these , did vrge those
heretiks with the force of this name Catho-

*Aug. in Breuicu-
lo Collat.
3. cap. 3.*

"
"
"
"
"
"
"
"
"
"
"
"
"
"
"
"
The first
point
difcuf-
fed be-
tvveene
S. Auft

Ss 4   like

and the
Dona-
tiſts
about
the na,
me Ca-
tholike.

lique and with the ſignification and poſſeſſion therof on their ſide, importing (as they
inferred) the vniuerſality of all nations profeſſing the faith of Chriſt, ſo as they in thoſe
dayes aſsigned the great vniuerſall, viſible
and knowne Church for the trew, which
Church had byn gathered by the cőuerſion
of all nations, wheras the Donatiſts to fly
this argument, were forced to ſay, that the
name Catholike ſignified only the vniuerſality or fulnes of Sacraments, and conſequently in what particular congregation
ſoeuer, this fulnes was found, (as in theirs
for ſooth they pretended yt was) there was
th' only true Cath. Church, which was a
playne ſhift as yow ſee. And is not this the
ſelfe ſame manner of proceedinge of all our
ſectaryes at this day? Doth not euery one
of them bragg, that their Church only hath
the fulneſſe and right vſe of Sacraments, &
the true preaching of Gods word? do not
the *Lutherans* ſay this? Do not the *Zvvinglians,
Caluiniſts, Brovvniſts* and *Puritans* preach the
like? And do not the *Anabaptiſts* and *Trinitarians* affirme the very ſame? Chis then was
a very ſhift in the Donatiſts, and ſo yt is in
our proteſtants.

The ſe-
cond
point be
tvvene
the Do-
natiſts
and Ca-
tholiks.

22. After this firſt running from the cauſe,
Saint Auſten ſheweth that the Donatiſts full
ſoare againſt their wills were brought vnto
yt againe by *Marcellinus* the Tribune appointed

ted by the Emperor to afsist in that conference. And wheras rhe Catholiks had giuen
vp some dayes before a large wrytinge, shewinge by infinite testimonyes of holy scriptures, that the Church of Christ fortold by
his prophetts, and instituted by himselfe,
could not be any particular Church or conuenticle in Africa, or out of Africa, but an
vniuersall, visible and illustrious Church
spread ouer all nations, and with which all
nations conuerted to Christ should communicate in one; The Donatists (saith S.
Austen) after a longe conference & councell „
held amonge themselues, did answere this „
wrytinge of the Catholiks, by another large „
impertinent writing of theirs, but quite „
from the purpose, not answeringe so much „
as one text alleaged by the Catholiks for „
this vniuersality of the Church. *Non solum* *Angust.*
(saith S. Austin) *pertractare, sed omnino nec attin-* *Coll. 3.*
gere voluerunt. The Donatists not only would *cap. 8.*
not handle fully, or answere these testimo- „
nyes alleaged by the Catholiks, for the vni- „
uersality & externe Maiestie of the Church „
but not so much as touch any one of them.
23. And then saith he further: *Nec aliquod*
testimonium in tam prolixa epistola sua, proferre ausi
sunt, de scripturis sanctis, quo assererent, Ecclesiam
partis Donati esse prædictam & prænunciatam; sicut
tam multa Catholici protulerunt, pro Ecclesia, cui
communicant, quæ incipiens ab Hierusalem toto orbe

diffun-

›› *diffunditur, &c.* Neither durſt the Donatiſts
›› in ſo large an epiſtle of theirs (which they
›› gaue vp) bringe forth any one teſtimony
›› of holy ſcripture , wherby they might
›› proue that the particular Church of the
›› part or faction of *Donatus*, was propheſied
›› or fortold by the ſaid ſcriptures, wheras the
›› Catholiks on the other ſide brought forth
›› many ſcriptures for proofe of that vniuer-
›› ſall Church , with which they communi-
›› cate , which Church beginning from Hie-
›› ruſalem, was ſpread ouer all the world. And
thus wryteth S. Auſten of their dealinge in
in that point.

The 3. point diſcuſſed betvveene the Catholiks and the Donatiſts at Carthage.

24. And preſently after this he ſheweth
that they fell to the diſcuſſion of a third
point, to witt, whether the true Catholike
Church of Chriſt , to whome he promiſed
thoſe ſingular graces and priuiledges which
the ſcripture ſetteth downe , ſhould conſiſt
of good men only, as the Donatiſts held; or
of the mixture of good and euill in this life,
as the Cath. taught ; wherin the Donatiſts
thought themſelues to haue a great aduantage : firſt, for that it might ſeeme to the
ſimple people there preſent , to be a more
pious opinion to hold, that only good men
were Gods flocke , and of his true Church:
Secondly, for that they had many places of
ſcripture that might ſeeme to fauour the
ſame (for ſo ſaith S. Auſten) *Illud oſtendere*
tentaue-

Collat.3. cap. 8.

tenfauerunt, prolatis multis teftimonijs diuinarum fcripturarum, quod Ecclefia Dei, non cum malorum hominum commixtione futura prædicta fit. They endeauored to fhew by many teftimonyes alleaged out of holy fcriptures, that it was not fortold or prophefied of the Church, that fhe fhould confift of the mixture of good and euill men, &c. Behold here how old heretiks abounded alfo in alleaginge fcriptures, as well as oures, at this day; but all from the purpofe, for whatfoeuer the Donatifts alleaged out of the fcriptures, for the fanctity and purity of Gods Church, yt was eyther to be vnderftood of the triumphant Church in the next life, or of the better part of the Church in this life, to witt fuch as are not only of th'externall body of the Church, but alfo of the foule, as this holy father fpeaketh; that is to fay endewed and adorned with all neceffary vertues.

25. But on the contrary fide when S. Auften and his fellowe Bifhops, to proue that Chrifts Church in this world confifted both of goood and badd, alleaged thofe euident parables of our Sauiour vfed about this matter; as that of the nett caft into the Sea, that comprehended all kind of fifh both good and badd, fome to be caft away, and fome to be vfed: that alfo of the barne floare which had in yt both chaffe and corne, the one to be burned, the other to be laid vp in

Gods

A contention about the para-bles of Chrift concerning the Church.
Mat.13. Mat. 3. Luc. 3.

Gods eternall granary: The other alſo of corne and cockle permitted to grow in one field to the day of iudgment; & of the ſheep & goats that liue in Gods flocke vnder the ſelfe ſame ſheppards in this world, but yet the one to be conſumed with euerlaſtinge fire in the end therof; and the other to be taken into eternall ioy: when theſe parables (I ſay) with many other teſtimonies of ſcriptures had byn alleaged by the Catholiks againſt the Donatiſts hereſie; it was a world to ſee, what ſhifts, deceyts, and tergiuerſations they vſed to auoyd the ſame, denyinge ſome, as inuented by the Catholiks, other, they ſought to auoyd by falſe and crafty expoſitions, and other ſuch ſhifts, which yow may read at large in *Saint Auguſtine.*

26.   And for that this may be ſufficient for a taſt, to ſhew the different manner of proceedinge betwene Catholiks and heretiks, both old and new, about this point of aſſigninge out the true Church, where, and in whome yt is, and how to be found; I ſhall paſſe no further in this matter, but only add a word or two of the third point, which is the difference betweene vs in layinge forth the proprietyes and notes, wherby this Church may be knowne and diſtinguiſhed from all others; which point, though yt may ſufficiently be ſeene and gathered by that which already we haue ſaid, yet, for pro-
ſmiſe

*Marc: 3.
& 13.
Mat. 29.*

*Collat. 3.
cap. 9.
10. & 11.*

The third principall difference about the proprietyes & marks of the true Church.

mise sake, must somwhat also be spoken
heere, which in effect shalbe nothinge but
this; that the difference betwene vs and the
protestants in deliuering these proprietyes,
is not farre vnlike to that of two gentle-
men, that should send forth two seruants
into the markett place, where many men
are to seeke out some learned phisition (for
examples sake) geuing them certayne notes
to find him by, but fare different; for that
the one deliuereth eyther generall notes
only, that are common to all, or most men;
as that he hath a head, beard, two eyes, two
armes, and the like, or els certayne inward
inuisible proprietyes: as that he is learned,
wise, meeke, chast, &c. That he is a good
phisition, cureth excellently well, and followeth therin exactly the precepts of *Hyp-
pocrates* and *Galen*, and finally hath all things
necessary, or needfull for that effect: which
marks beinge little to the purpose, as yow
see for knowinge or discerninge out the
said phisition from any other, the messenger
might weary himselfe, before he found that
which he seeked for.

*A com-
parison
of diffe-
rent ge-
uinge of
notes to
find a
thinge
by.*

27. But the other that sendeth forth his
messenger, consideringe, that marks and
signes must be more knowne then the thing
yt selfe, wherof they are marks, and not
common to many, but proper and peculiar
to that which is sought for; telleth his seruant,

uant, what fpeciall name the phifition is
called by, what age, what countenance,and
what ftature he is of,what apparell he wea-
reth, what gefture and manner of going he
vfeth,what found of voyce he hath in fpea-
king,and aboue all where he dweileth,how
his houfe may be found, knowne & difcer-
ned from all others: All which fignes being
geuen, we muft needs fay, that the fearcher
is a very fimple or negligent fellow yf he
miffe him.

28.   And this very difference is to be noted
betweene the proteftants and vs in deliuering proprietyes to know the Church by,
for that the Catholiks geue found and fure
notes, proper and peculiar to one only
Church, which is the true Cath. Church,
& thefe notes not inuented by themfelues,
but founded in Scriptures, and deliuered by
the tradition of Chrift and his Apoftles, and
vfed by the ancient Fathers and Doctors
of the Church, to this very purpofe of di-
ftinguifhinge her therby from all congregations and conuenticles of heretiks whatfoeuer: Of which notes and proprietyes
yow haue heard fome before,mentioned in
the conference betweene *Saint Auguftine* and
the Donatifts, as the name Catholike and
the auncient poffefsion therof; vniuerfality
ouer all Chriftendome, and multitude of
nations and gentils conuerted to one Chriftian

stian Church and faith, participatinge, and
holdinge the communion of one, and the
selfe same number of Sacraméts: wherunto
are added by other Fathers, and the selfe
same Doctor in other places, diuers other
proprietyes alfo, as antiquity with continuation and fuccesfion from age to age; vi-
fibility with moft perfpicuous, & illuftrious
progreffe, apparant and admirable to the
whole world; vnity and conformity in doctrine by one rule of faith throughout all
ages: Notorious fanctity in many members
of this Church teftified by infinite miracles,
and fupernaturall operations; the conuerfion of infinite pagans and gentils, with
ouerthrow, and extirpation of their Idolatrie, which was a thinge prophefied to be
fulfilled by the true Church only.

Proprie-
tyes and
marks
of the
true
Church
giuen
by the
Catho-
liks.

29.   Thefe notes (I fay) and diuers others
are fet downe by holy Fathers, as both proper and peculiar to the only true Catholike
Church of Chrift, and agreeing to no hereticall congregation whatfoeuer; as alfo manifeft, and notorious, and moft eafy to be
iudged of by all people. For thefe two conditions ought to haue true marks (as before
hath byn mentioned) the firft, that they be
peculiar and not common; the fecond, that
they be more notoriously knowne, and
more eafily found out, then the thinge yt
felfe, which they do demonftrate: wherof
yow

yow may read in particular ın *Saint* **Cyprian** againſt the *Nouatians* ; *Saint Hierome* againſt the *Luciſerians* ; *Saint Auguſtine* againſt the *Donatiſts* and *Pelagians Optatus*, againſt the ſame *Donatiſts*;and *Vincentius Lyrineȵſis* againſt all ſorts of heretiks; and this ıs the reall and ſubſtantiall dealing of Catholiks.

30.   But the proteſtants on the contrary ſide do geue ſuch marks and notes as are eyther generall and common, or els more obſcure & harder to be found out & iudged of,then the matter in controuerſie as before we haue ſignified, by the compariſons of ſeekinge out the phiſition ; as for example, Martyn Luther, father of our proteſtants, hauinge lefte the communion of the true Church of God, and made a new conuenticle to himſelfe, would needs make it the true Church of God, and proue the ſame by certayne marks and proprietyes deuiſed by himſelfe, which he ſetteth downe to the number of 7. wherof the firſt was, the true preaching of the ghoſpell; the ſecond, the right adminiſtration of baptiſme; the third, the lawfull vſe of the Euchariſt; the fourth the due exerciſe of the Eccleſiaſticall keyes in abſoluinge and retayninge ſinnes ; the fifth , the lawfull election of miniſters; the ſixth , publike prayer, and ſinginge of pſalmes in a knowne tongue; the ſeauenth, the miſterie of the croſſe in bearing tribulations:

Luth.lıb. de conc. parte vlȥ tıma.

The markes of the Church fondly ſett doȥ vvne by heretikes.

tions: Thefe were Luthers notes, which other proteftants after him, and namely the *Magdeburgians*, and Iohn Caluin do abridge, to the number of two only, to witt, the true preaching of the ghofpell; and the fincere vfe of Sacraments.

*Magdeb.
cent.1.
lib.2.c.4.
Calu.l.4.
Inftit.
cap.1.*

31. But now what manner of notes thefe be, which euery fect may & do chalenge as proper to themfelues (which they cannot do with any probability, with the marks & notes of the Catholike Church before fet downe) is eafie to iudge; for what fect will not fay,& fweare alfo, if need be, that they only preach the word of God truly, & that they only adminifter the Sacraméts rightly, and that they vfe the Ecclefiafticall keyes duely, and that the election of minifters is lawfully made among them, and that they haue publike prayer, & finging of pfalmes, bearing the croffe,and the like?and it is harder to conuince them in any one of thefe notes,then in the principall point it felfe,to witt, that they are not the Cath. Chriftian Church of Chrift; fo as thefe marks being common,and not proper, and leffe manifeft then the thinge it felfe,wherof they are put for marks; it followeth, that they are fond, vaine and ridiculous, and that the inuentors therof did rather feeke to obfcure, and hyde the Church, then to declare, and manifeft the fame by fuch proprietyes.

T t   32. And

32. And heere will we make an end of all
this difcourfe referuing the reft vnto the
third parte, which is to be printed feueral-
ly, for that the bulke of thefe two hath
growne to a fufficient bigneffe for one
tome or volume; only I might note to the
reader in this laft paragrafe, that as our aduerfaryes do imitate the Donatifts in the
point before mencioned, out of their con-
 *Proteftât ference with *Saint Auguftine* and other Ca-
minifters tholike Bifhops: fo haue they done it al-
do fly so hitherto, in flying all equall and lawfull
publique conference with vs, as the Donatifts did
confe- with thofe old Catholiks, fo much as lay
rence as in their power, vntill it was impofed vpon
the Do- them, by commandement of the Empe-
natifts rour at the petition of *S.Auguftine*, & the Ca-
did.* tholike party, as the said Father doth relate
in his forenamed booke writen of that conference, telling vs two points in particular
of their dealing in that affayre, which he
Aug. in expreffeth in thefe words, *Qui caufam bonam*
Breuic. *non fe habere sciebant, id egerunt primum, ne collatio*
Præfat. *fieret, aut caufa ipfa ageretur, sed quia hoc obtinere*
ad coll.1. *minimè poterant, id effecerunt multiplicitate gefto-*
diei. *rum, vt quod actum eft, non facilè legeretur.* The
,, Donatifts knowing they had an euill caufe,
,, endeauored firft to bringe to paffe that the
,, conferéce fhould not be made, nor the caufe
,, it felfe be handled at all; but when they
,, could not obtayne this, then went they
about:

about to put downe so many things in writing as they might not easely be read.

33. Thus writeth *Saint Augustine*; and for
this cause thought he good to sett downe a
summe of all that passed callinge it *Breuicu-*
lum Collationum, shewinge perspicuously the
infinite Cauillations, frauds, and shiftes of
these heretiks to auoyd all due tryall; for
when after all other delayes, both partyes
were now mett together, *instare cæperunt* Coll. 1.
(saith he) *vt prius agæretur de tempore, de manda-* cap. 8.
to, de persona; de causa, tunc ad negotij merita vè-
niretur. The Donatists began to make new
instance (after all other Cauillations, and
exceptions taken before) that first it might
be treated about the tyme, that this conference should endure, and about the Emperors commaundement or edict, and clauses
therof and about the person as well of the
iudge, and assistants, as the disputers of
both parts, and finally of the whole cause of
differéce, what had passed therin betweene
them hitherto, and then after all this (forsooth) they should come to examyne the
merits of the principall businesse or controuersie in hand, which in effect would neuer
be, for that about euery one of these points
the Donatists had many quarrels as *Saint*
Augustine sheweth, and by eache one therof
they sought delayes; and particularly wheras order had byn taken that 18. Bishops of

The ter-
giuersa-
tion of
the Do-
natists to
fly pu-
blik try-
all.
„
„
„
„
„
„
„
„
„
„

ech ſide ſhould ſuffice, they would needs
haue all their ſide to be admitted, and ſo for

Coll. 1.
c. 11. 12.
13. & 14.
oſtentatiōs ſake they entered (ſaith *S. Auguſtine*) with great pompe into Carthage to the
number of 279. Biſhops of that ſect of Donatus (a pittifull ſight for Catholiks) together with all their trayne. Other ſhiftes, delayes, & tergiuerſations of theirs I leaue for
breuityes ſake to be read in *S. Aug.* himſelfe.
34.   But how well our Engliſh aduerſaries
haue imitated this manner of proceeding of
the Donatiſts, for ſhifting of all publike conference and tryall for theſe 44. yeares of
her Maieſties raigne, being ſo often and earneſtly demaunded at their hands; is ſufficiently knowne and nedeth not to be pro-

Hovv
Engliſh
miniſters
haue fled
publike
confe-
rence hi-
therto.
ued or repeated here. But if it would pleaſe
almighty God to inſpire her Maieſtie to
force them thervnto, as he did the Emperour to compell the Donatiſts to a publike
tryall, I do not doubt, but the like yſſue
would enſue, and the like ſentence be giuen in that cauſe, by any indifferēt iudge, as
was giuen by *Marcellinus* in the former con-

Coll. 3.
cap. 25.
trouerſie, to witt, (as *S. Auguſtines* words are)
*Confutatos a Catholicis Donatiſtas, omnium docu-
mentorum manifeſtatione pronunciauit.* Marcel-
„ linus did pronounce by his definitiue ſen-
„ tence, that the Catholiks had confuted the
„ Donatiſts, with manifeſtation of all kind of
„ learninge. And ſo much for this matter.

A TABLE

A TABLE

of the particular matters con-
teined in this booke.

A.

Tt 3   *Aristobulus*

He

The

likes profeſſinge the Roman faith, part. 1. cap. 10.
num. 10. 11. till the end of the Chapter.

C.

Cere-

Communion.

His

King

Eleutherius

The

The

Ghospell

He

Henry

Liberty

I.

S. *Ireneus*

Late

Late *Lutheraus* opinion confessinge the Church to be visible, but consistinge only of the elect, is but a fond deuise, part.2.cap. 1. num. 18.19.

Lutheran faction in K. Edward the 6. his dayes ouerborne by the Zvvinglian, part. 2. cap. 12. num. 33.

M.

MAgdeburgians theire sentence about the conuersion of Britanie, part. 1. cap. 2. num. 7.

Theire false dealinge about the same examined, ibid. num. 9.10.11.

They falslie make Geffrey of Monmouth a Cardinall, ibid. num. 11.

Theire falsifying of tymes, ibid. num. 12.

Theire absurd kind of reasoning, ibid. num.14.

Innocentius the 1. Pope impudently slaundered by them, ibid. num. 16.

Theire historie, part. 1. cap. 6. num. 4.

Theire proud title against the vvritings of auncient fathers, ibid.

They abuse S. Cyprian, ibid. num. 11. 12.

Theire ridiculous manner of proceeding, ibid. nu.14.

Theire fraudulent shifts in alleaging and discrediting the fathers, part. 1. cap. 7. num. 1.

Theire iudgment of the fathers and Doctors of the second age, ibid. num. 3.

Theire quippes against the fathers, ibid. num. 5.

All Doctors in Eleutherius his tyme said by them to be in darknes about freevvill, ibid. num. 6.

They accuse S. Cyprian to hate vvoomen, ibid. nu.13.

The Magdeburgians pittifull plight, part. 2. cap.3. num. 12.

The pith and substance of theire Centuries, num. 13.

Theire praise touching the fathers and Doctors of the fourth age, ibid. num.14.

They fall out vvith them about Freevvill, about Penance, the Blessed Sacrament, Iustification, Good vvoorks, Satisfaction, Praying to Sainćts, vvritten Traditions, Rites and Ceremonies, and about many other matters, ibid. a num. 15. ad 27.

Queene

They

Q.

R.

Catho-

T.

VVhere

Z.

FINIS.